Baptism and the New Life

Søren Agersnap

Baptism
and the New Life

A Study of Romans 6.1-14

AARHUS UNIVERSITY PRESS

AARHUS UNIVERSITY PRESS
Langelandsgade 177
DK-8200 Aarhus N
Fax (+ 45) 8942 5380

73 Lime Walk
Headington, Oxford OX3 7AD
Fax (+ 44) 1865 750 079

Box 511
Oakville, Conn. 06779
Fax (+ 1) 860 945 9468

Denne afhandling er af Det teologiske Fakultet ved Aarhus Universitet
antaget til forsvar for den teologiske doktorgrad.
Århus, 3. februar 1997
Peter Widmann
h.a. decanus

Forsvaret finder sted fredag den 27. august 1999 kl. 13 prc.
i Juridisk Auditorium, bygning 343, Aarhus Universitet.

Preface

Producing a thesis like this in order to obtain the Danish title of *dr.theol.*, demands many years of study and hard work, and as a result one feels indebted to many.

I want to thank the Faculties of Theology at the Universities of Copenhagen and Aarhus and the Danish Research Council for the Humanities for granting research scholarships to me.

Thanks also to colleagues and friends from my time at the Universities. I particularly want to thank Professor dr.theol. Niels Peter Lemche, chief consultant dr.theol. Mogens Stiller Kjärgaard and lecturer Frands Ole Overgaard for encouragement and many pleasant hours; Mrs Tut Amnéus, secretary for the Institute of New Testament, Aarhus University, for invaluable practical help, and Professor dr.theol. Søren Giversen for support in the last phase.

I am also grateful that it was possible to continue my work on the thesis after I had become parish priest in Linå, Voel and Sejs-Svejbæk. A special thanks to my Bishop at that time, Herluf Eriksen, who gave me three months' leave in 1991 to enable me to resume my work on this thesis.

Furthermore, I am grateful to the Theological Faculty, Aarhus University, for accepting the thesis and giving me much practical help, to the Danish Research Council for the Humanities for funding the translation and giving financial support for the publication of the book, to the translators for their patient work and to my British colleague here in Luxemburg, Rev. Clifford Poole, who advised me during proof-reading.

Most of all, I want to thank my family, my wife and children, who shared life with me during the long period of working on the thesis, never complaining that I neglected them — and never making me feel that they had cause for complaint.

The Danish Vicarage in Luxemburg, June 1999   *Søren Agersnap*

Contents

Introduction

Part One:
Preparatory studies of the historical background

Part two:
Review of the text

Contents 11

Introduction

I

Theses and points of discussion
relative to Rom 6.1-14

1. Basic point of view: Baptism gives certainty about the new life

The interpretation of Rom 6.1-14 that I wish to assert and submit can for the
time being be presented in five points, which are mutually dependent on one
another:

1. *The enthusiastic intention in Rom 6.1-11.* The basic viewpoint is that Paul
expresses the limitless excitement about salvation that is the mainstay of his
entire letter.[1] Paul's only significant aim is to emphasise how this absolute
certainty of salvation after baptism must prevail in the Christians' life. This
is evident from the rendering of the thought process in the verses:

The leading questions in verses 1-2 establish that the Christians are dead
to sin, and cannot go on living in it.

Verse 3 refers to the awareness that baptism into Christ is a baptism
giving a connection with his death, and it is concluded from this in verse 4
that this 'burial with Christ' will be followed by *a new life*, corresponding to
his life and based upon the same power as that which manifested itself in
Christ's resurrection. Verse 5 elaborates on this: if the Christians have been
connected with something similar to the death of Christ, so must they also
be connected with something similar to his resurrection.

The reasoning continues in verses 6-8: there is a reference (in verse 6) to
the awareness that the Christians are 'crucified with Christ', so that the sinful
body and the slavery under sin of the old existence should disappear (since
he who is dead is free of sin, as it reads in verse 7). But if the Christians now
are 'dead with Christ' they must also (according to verse 8) believe that they
will *live with him*.

This is supported by verses 9-11. There is again (in verses 9-10) a reference to a knowledge which can presuppose that after death Christ is
beyond the power of sin, since he had died to sin as a once-and-for-all event

---

1. Cf. my presentation of this — Søren Agersnap, Gudsforståelsen hos Paulus [Paul's understanding of God], in: Sigfred Pedersen (ed.), *Gudsbegrebet* [The concept of God],
Copenhagen 1985, pp. 95-114.

and is living his life to God. Similarly (according to verse 11), the Christians, with the connection they have with Christ, must consider themselves as dead to sin and *alive to God*.

2. *The paraenetic consequence*. Rom 6.12-14 asserts, especially at the end of the section of text, that the direct and evident consequence of the fact that those baptised have received the new righteous life is that this life must necessarily be lived according to its purpose. It is no longer relevant as in the past to be under the power of sin and lust and to fight on that side (verses 12-13a). The only possibility for those no longer under law and sin but under grace is to take part in God's fight for righteousness (verses 13b-14).

3. *Conceptual background and origin of the text*. I wish to assert that Paul clearly bases himself on a perception that baptism gives a connection with the death of Christ. This, in its origin also, is a genuine Christian concept: from the very beginning and fundamentally, Christ's act of redemption, his death being the pivotal point, has been linked to the total turnabout that consequently occurred in the life of the Christians, and this turnabout is manifested in the baptism itself. From this starting point, Paul guides the thought process in the direction of God's death-defeating power, which broke through in Christ's resurrection. This same power is the basis of the life of the baptised; it is a life in the conviction that God will in the same way allow it to proceed according to his will. Thereby, in the course of the text, Paul approaches another widespread concept concerning Christ's precursive act.

4. *The presupposed concept of baptism*. Baptism is looked back upon as God's action: an effect occurred of the salvation events which took place at the end of Jesus' life on earth. This was decisive for the baptised, who were released from the old life's bonding with sin and death and were placed in a new righteous life. It is not said how baptism achieved these effects. The emphasis is on the subsequent and sustained significance of God's intervention: it created a certain belief in God's continued support.

5. *The fundamental Christology*. It is important that there is in Rom 6.1-14 a complex coherence between Jesus' act of redemption and his precursive act. Jesus' death on the Cross has a redemptive effect: the baptised are released from the power of sin. But Jesus' precursive act is also given substantial emphasis; his life, its content and strength and the progress through death to resurrection become a pattern for the life of the Christians; and what is crucial here is the resurrection, whereby the power of sin and death is finally overcome. This means that the Christology behind the text cannot be re-

duced to a single, tangible and inexhaustible motif; the Christological statements in the text make sense as references to a longer sequence of events.

The main purpose of this work is to defend and amplify these theses. But in
so doing its possible significance ought not to be exhausted. Three further
points must be included in the picture.

First, the theses involve a confrontation with other points of view. My
theses may in themselves appear unremarkable and quite apparent, but
viewed against the background of this century's Pauline research they are distinguished very sharply indeed from dominant opinions. As will be seen
from the research survey in the next section, there has been a tendency to interpret Rom 6.1-14 on the basis of religio-historical and traditio-historical
theories. To regard the text as an offshoot of mythological, mystery-religious
or mystical concepts will involve tensions, reservations and dialectics; the intention may look entirely different, and one is given a different view of the
concept of baptism and Christology. These viewpoints are under debate, and
there is an increasing tendency to confront them. But for this very reason
discussion of them still plays a large part in the interpretation of the text and
many of its details, and this must therefore also apply in the present study
of the text. So as not to lose sight of the actual content of the text by reason
of this confrontation, I have formulated my theses positively and have indicated in the title of the thesis that Paul uses the reference to baptism to imprint the joy of the new life.

The second point that should be mentioned is that my theses all concern
Rom 6.1-14 as a whole; moreover, a large number of detailed questions arise
that must be discussed, and here I advance new or overlooked interpretations of certain passages. I wish to stress from the outset that my overall understanding of Rom 6.1-14 does not depend upon and rely upon these
alternative interpretations of the details; rather the contrary: when prevalent
understandings of the section of text have been confronted, an opening can
be made for new and simpler interpretations.

Finally, it must be established that in the first place the theses apply only
to Rom 6.1-14. But since this text is central to Paul's theology and discussion
of it, the views presented may also be of significance to other Pauline texts
and Pauline theology. This can be considered later.

2. Rom 6.1-14 in this century's research

2.1. Rom 6.1-14 as Christian mysticism and mystery religiousness

Since this section is to concern itself only with the main lines in the history
of research, I find it reasonable to begin at around the turn of the century. At

that time, several of the subjects for discussion emerged which still characterise interpretation of the text. What is particularly striking is the great interest
in the text's religio-historical background. In Rom 6, many commentators
find a sacrament mysticism which is believed to have been influenced by the
initiation rites of the Hellenic mystery religions.[2] Or it is seen as a distinct
Pauline mysticism, more marked by his Judeo-Christian background.[3]

But before I come to this discussion I would like to draw attention to
one point which is fundamental to everyone's understanding. There is a consensus about *the Pauline intention* in the text: Paul consistently expresses himself with enthusiasm about the certainty of final redemption, about the total
turnabout from the old sinful existence to the new righteous life.[4] This was
the general basis of discussion at this point in time, and it is this that leads
the thought towards mysticism and the strangeness of Paul's conception.

This conception of the text then gives rise to two sets of questions. First,
how can the definitive promise of salvation and righteousness in Rom 6.3-11
harmonise with the fact that Paul immediately afterwards, in Rom 6.12-13,
also demands righteousness? This should be superfluous — a tension between soteriological and paraenetic formulations, the so-called indicative-
imperative problem. Secondly, the question of the origin of Paul's line of
thought is also raised, and the answer is the theory of a religio-historical dependence on Hellenic mystery religion. This theory, in turn, becomes of
significance to understanding the text's view of baptism and Christology.

The two problem areas will be dealt with in greater detail.

2. Thus in particular 'Die religionsgeschichtliche Schule' (The religio-historical school), see
Albrecht Dieterich, *Eine Mithrasliturgie*, Leipzig 1903, pp. 162-78, Herman Gunkel, *Zum
religionsgeschichtlichen Verständnis des Neuen Testaments* (FRLANT 1), Göttingen 1903, p.
83ff., Wilhelm Bousset, *Die Religion des Judentums im neutestamentlichen Zeitalter*, Tübingen
1903, p. 182, *Kyrios Christos* (FRLANT 21), Göttingen 1921, p. 107ff., W. Heitmüller, *Taufe
und Abendmahl bei Paulus*, Tübingen 1903, p. 9ff., *Taufe und Abendmahl im Urchristentum*,
Tübingen 1911, p. 21ff., Hans Windisch, *Taufe und Sünde im ältesten Christentum bis auf
Origenes*, Tübingen 1908, p. 167ff., R. Reitzenstein, *Die hellenistischen Mysterienreligionen*[3],
Leipzig 1927 (originally 1910), Martin Dibelius, Die Isisweihe bei Apulejus und verwandte Initiationsriten, (originally 1917) in: *Botschaft und Geschichte* II, Tübingen 1956, pp.
30-79; p. 71f., cf. note 12 below.
3. Thus Adolf Deissmann, *Paulus*, Tübingen 1925, p. 143, Albert Schweitzer, *Die Mystik des
Apostels Paulus*, Tübingen 1930, pp. 18-20, 222ff., cf. note 21 below.
4. Besides the above, this is also strongly emphasised in Paul Wernle, *Der Christ und die
Sünde bei Paulus*, Freiburg 1897, p. 100ff., William Sanday and Arthur C. Headlam, *The
Epistle to the Romans (ICC)*[5], Edinburgh 1898, p. 153ff., William Wrede, *Paulus*, Halle 1904,
p. 61ff. This perception corresponds to some degree to my first thesis, although the conclusions this draws are, as will be shown, different.

The tension between the promise of salvation and paraenesis. The indicative-imperative problem has been basically described in Paul Wernle's monograph of 1897: *'Der Christ und die Sünde bei Paulus'*, which links up in particular with Gal 5.25 and Rom 6.[5] Since the basic point is that Paul expresses himself with ardent enthusiasm, the indicatives in Rom 6.3-11 must be crucial, the unconditional promise of salvation. Salvation must accordingly consist of a possession of the spirit which made the Christian free from sin and made of him an entirely new creation with new abilities. It thus becomes superfluous and directly self-contradictory that immediately afterwards in Rom 6.12-13 imperatives follow and a demand is made, for the Christian should be able to do all this for himself with his new gifts.[6]

If scholars are to seek to resolve the problem in this period, they characteristically concentrates on *explaining* how this antinomy, this self-contradiction, has arisen — psychologically or historically. The indicative may be seen as an expression of 'pure doctrinairism', 'heaven-defying idealism', the theoretical attitude; the imperative then expresses a realism, and takes into account the necessary practice within the Christian communities.[7] The contradiction may also be explained in that the indicative and imperative have roots in various Christian traditions (baptismal sacramentalism and baptismal paraenesis) which Paul wished at the same time to uphold.[8] This sets the stage for the religio-historical explanation that the enthusiasm and the sacramentalism have been adopted from the mysteries (whereas the paraenesis is a remainder from Paul's Jewish past).

In the second place, it is also possible to find attempts to *understand* the substantial connection between indicative and imperative terms. And then we encounter concepts which still characterise the discussion: the formulation 'Werde, was du bist!';[9] the idea that righteousness bestowed, which is God's hidden righteousness, must be manifested or realised in the Christians' existence;[10] and the concept that there is a dialectic between the

---

5. See in particular Wernle, *Christ*, p. 89, p. 100ff. Other passages discussed are 1 Thess 4.3-8; 1 Cor 5.7; 6.9-11; Rom 8.12-13; Phil 2.12-13.
6. See Wernle, *Christ*, p. 89, p. 103ff., cf. p. 165ff., Windisch, *Taufe*, p. 167ff., Hans Windisch, Das Problem des paulinischen Imperatives, ZNW 23 (1924), pp. 265-81.
7. Thus Wernle, *Christ*, p. 105 (Wernle considers, however, that the imperative is of little weight and that the tension is therefore very limited in Paul — in contrast to what applies to the reformers — p. 106), Holtzmann, *Lehrbuch* II, p. 164, Hans Lietzmann, *An die Römer* (HNT 8)⁵, Tübingen 1971, p. 66f. Cf. also the critical review by Rudolf Bultmann, Das Problem der Ethik bei Paulus, ZNW 23 (1924), pp. 123-40.
8. See Windisch, Problem, p. 267ff.
9. Thus Otto Pfleiderer, *Das Urchristentum I*², Berlin 1902, p. 291, Holtzmann, *Lehrbuch II*², p. 169.
10. Thus Windisch, Problem, p. 271, which quite consciously formulates a synergism as Paul's attitude.

aspect of salvation which has already been realised and that which comes only with parousia.[11]

The mystery-religious background. At the end of the last century, exegetes orientated towards the history of religion began to connect Pauline enthusiasm with the Hellenistic mystery religions, gradually extending this to the assumption that in Rom 6 Paul depends directly upon concepts adopted from the Hellenistic mysteries.[12]

As concerns the mystery religions, these exegetes fasten on the point that the emphasis in the central rites was on the death and resurrection of the vegetation deities. On initiation into the mysteries, the mystes is said to follow ritually the deity's destiny and re-live the god's death and resurrection. By virtue of the ritual alone, the initiate is beyond death, made divine, fused together with the deity. This is the interpretation of, in particular, the Demeter cult in Eleusis, the Isis-Osiris mysteries of Egypt and the Attic cult of Asia Minor. Another variation of this concept is said to be found in a gnostic development of the mysteries which has its centre in an incorporation into a cosmic redeemer figure.[13]

Rom 6.3-11 is read in the same way. The submersion of baptism is said to have been perceived as a symbolic burial with Christ and the emergence from the water as a resurrection with him, so that the Christian is located within Christ.[14] The question in verse 3: 'Do you not know ...' refers to known sacramentalist traditions.[15] Through the submersion of baptism one moves 'into Christ'. One has 'grown together with Christ by virtue of an imitation', and 'together with him' one is crucified, buried and resurrected to a new life. And finally it is directly expressed that one is incorporated 'in

---

11. See Wrede, *Paulus*, p. 62f.
12. See the survey of the origin of the viewpoint in H. Holtzmann, Sakramentliches im Neuen Testament, *ARW* 7 (1904), pp. 60-69, and the survey of the later development in Günter Wagner, *Das religionsgeschichtliche Problem von Römer 6,1-11* (AThANT 39), Zürich 1962, p. 15ff. According to these, the viewpoint is said to have been introduced by Gustav Anrich, *Das antike Mysterienwesen in seinem Einfluss auf das Christentum*, Göttingen 1894, which, however, only indicated an analogy between the mysteries (p. 111), as was suggested earlier by Otto Pfleiderer, *Das Urchristentum*, Berlin 1887, p. 259 n. But soon after a widespread viewpoint was that Paul was dependent upon the mystery religions. Cf. in addition to the interpreters referred to in note 2 above Holtzmann, *Lehrbuch*, p. 178ff., Lietzmann, *Römer*, p. 65ff., Alfred Loisy, *Les mystères païens et le mystère chrétien*, Paris 1919, p. 270ff., Johannes Leipoldt, *Die urchristliche Taufe im Lichte der Religionsgeschichte*, Leipzig 1928, p. 38ff. See also note 25 below.
13. The material is presented below in Chapter II.
14. See Heitmüller, *Taufe*, 1911, p. 18ff., Lietzmann, *Römer*, p. 65, Bousset, *Kyrios*, p. 107.
15. Thus Lietzmann, *Römer*, p. 67, Windisch, *Taufe*, p. 171.

Christ'.[16] Attempts have been made, especially by Wilhelm Heitmüller, to use similar sacramentalist concepts in other passages of the Pauline corpus as evidence that Paul employs the Hellenistic-Christian communities' baptismal concepts, so that, by way of these traditions, there is a connection back to the Hellenistic mystery religion.[17]

It will have significant theological consequence if Paul is understood on the basis of a dependence upon the mystery religions.

Paul's view of baptism will seem magical and sacramentalist. Against this background, despite an aversion in principle to such a concept of baptism, Heitmüller felt compelled to assert that according to Paul baptism operated quite automatically 'ex opere operato (im eigentlich katholischen Sinne)'.[18] This view has met with sympathy from Catholic theologians.[19]

16. This literal interpretation of εἰς Χριστὸν... ἐβαπτίσθημεν in Rom 6.3, of σύμφυτοι γεγόνα-μεν τῷ ὁμοιώματι in Rom 6.5, of σὺν Χριστῷ in Rom 6,4-8, of ἐν Χριστῷ in Rom 6.11 is to be found in Heitmüller, *Taufe*, 1903, p. 20, *Taufe*, 1911, p. 16, 22f., Lietzmann, *Römer*, p. 64ff., Bousset, *Kyrios*, p. 107, 110f.
17. See Wilhelm Heitmüller, Zum Problem Paulus und Jesus, ZNW 13 (1912), pp. 320-37, which emphasises that Paul takes his theological viewpoints from Hellenistic Christianity (not from Jesus or primitive Christianity), and the viewpoint has become wide-spread, thus Bousset, *Kyrios*, p. 75, Dibelius, *Botschaft* II, p. 72; see also Rudolf Bultmann, *Theologie des Neuen Testaments*[6], Tübingen 1968, p. 66f., where this theory becomes crucially important to the description of Paul's entire theology; cf. also note 45 below. Through Heitmüller's theory, possible traditions behind other Pauline texts become of significance to the theory of a mysterious background to Rom 6. In particular 1 Cor 15.29; Gal 3.27; 1 Cor 12.13; Col 2.11-3.4 are taken into consideration.
18. See Heitmüller, *Taufe*, 1903, p. 14, cf. also Bousset, *Kyrios*, p. 139, where the sacramentalist automatic is expressed very radically: 'Man schliesse den Kontakt, und der elektrische Strom flutet.'
19. Very clearly in the theory that baptism is a Christian cult mystery, cf. in particular Odo Casel, *Das christliche Kultmysterium*[4], Regensburg 1960, has dealt with Rom 6 in *Jahrbuch für Liturgiewissenschaft* 14 (1934; published 1938) in various reviews (p. 212f., pp. 243-47 and pp. 371-73), where Paul's connection with the mystery religions' concepts is emphasised, stressing however that Paul's cult mystery is of a higher nature (this position is incidentally particularly characterised by a distinctive interpretation of Rom 6.5, cf. the exegesis below in Chapter VII, section 3). Also, Catholic researchers who oppose the theory of a cult mystery can give a certain weight to the mystery religions in order to underline the sacramental in baptism, thus Otto Kuss, Zur paulinischen und nach-paulinischen Tauflehre im Neuen Testament, in: *Auslegung und Verkündigung* I, Regensburg 1957, pp. 121-50; p. 133ff., *Der Römerbrief*, Regensburg 1957ff., p. 331f., p. 371, p. 376. Also in Rudolf Schnackenburg, *Das Heilsgeschehen bei der Taufe nach dem Apostel Paulus* (MThSt I/1), Munich 1950, p. 186, the contribution of the religio-historical school is assessed as positive on this point, although the theory of mystery-religious dependence is sharply rejected. Similarly, M.-J. Lagrange, *Saint Paul — Épitre aux Romains*, Paris 1950, p. 149, where there is a certain amount of agreement with the religio-historical school of the sacramental in the text (but a criticism of the lack of distinction between the sacramental and the magical).

As concerns *Christology*, it becomes a matter of Christ-mysticism.[20] The crucial point becomes Christ's mystical presence in the rite, as experienced by the Christians, giving power and strength, and this is the basis of the strong enthusiasm Rom 6 is meant to express. Arriving at this view results from the ruthlessly radical open-mindedness with which historical criticism approached the texts at the time of the religio-historical school. The concept is not immediately compatible with a traditional Protestant understanding of Paul's theology, to which justification by faith alone is crucial.

2.2. Criticism of the mystery interpretation

The interpretation model has also met with opposition, both as regards the theory of the religio-historical background in the mysteries and the concept that in Rom 6 there is tension between an enthusiastic promise of salvation and a more down-to-earth demand.

Criticism of the mystery-religious interpretation is to be found in various forms. In some cases merely the religio-historical derivation is denied. Here the text is still meant to concern death and resurrection with Christ, and the content is still seen as a Christ-mysticism, but a special Pauline mysticism; it is only disputed that Paul adopted it from Hellenistic religion.[21]

It is more important in this context that a more radical confrontation with the interpretation is to be found, which also rejects that the content of Rom 6 is mysticism of the kind to be found in Hellenistic surroundings. The confrontation thus also involves a different understanding of Christology and of the view of baptism. The confrontation has been advanced most effectively in Günter Wagner's monograph on the religio-historical problem in Rom 6, in which almost all the arguments that in the course of time have been advanced against the religio-historical interpretation are assembled.[22]

---

20. See Bousset, *Kyrios*, p. 104ff., Heitmüller, *Taufe*, 1911, p. 22, Martin Dibelius, Glaube und Mystik bei Paulus, in: *Botschaft und Geschichte* II, Tübingen 1956, pp. 94-116.
21. Thus Deissmann, *Paulus*, p. 143; the position has been elaborated in Johannes Schneider, *Die Passionsmystik des Paulus* (UNT 15), Leipzig 1929. See also Schweitzer, *Mystik*, pp. 18-20, 222ff., Wilhelm Traugott Hahn, *Der Mitsterben und Mitauferstehen mit Christus*, Gütersloh 1937, p. 90ff., Victor Warnach, Taufe und Christusgeschehen nach Römer 6, *ALW* 3 (1954), pp. 284-366, Die Tauflehre des Römerbriefes in der neueren theologischen Diskussion, *ALW* 5 (1958), pp. 274-332, where Casel's opinion of Rom 6 (cf. note 19 above) has been elaborated exegetically, but without taking account of dependence on the mystery religions.
22. See the survey of earlier works with the same objective in Wagner, *Problem*, p. 15ff. Cf. also Arthur Darby Nock, Early Gentile Christianity and its Hellenistic Background, in: *Essays on Religion and the Ancient World* I-II, Oxford 1972, pp. 49-133, Hellenistic Mysteries and Christian Sacraments, loc. cit., pp. 791-820, Paul Althaus, *Der Brief an die Römer* (NTD 6)[13], Göttingen 1978, pp. 65-67, Stig Hanson, *The Unity of the Church in the New Testament*,

The main emphasis is on the treatment of the religio-historical material which has been introduced as parallel texts. Wagner contests that the concepts which should count as parallels to Rom 6 existed at all in Hellenistic and Oriental mystery religions.[23]

In interpreting Rom 6, he can indicate a series of observations which show that all the features said to be offshoots of the mysteries' sacramentalism and mysticism can be interpreted differently, i.e. as an expression of binding to and dependency upon Christ.[24]

It can now be established that the religio-historical interpretation of Rom 6.1-11 is outmoded, at least in the radical form which envisages that Paul depends directly and positively on the mysteries.[25] But nevertheless the do-

---

Uppsala 1946, pp. 82-84, Schnackenburg, *Heilsgeschehen*, pp. 132-39, Todes- und Lebensgemeinschaft mit Christus. Neue Studien zu Röm 6,1-11, *MüThZ* 6 (1955), pp. 32-53, Anders Nygren, *Pauli brev til romarna*, Lund 1944, p. 243, Markus Barth, *Die Taufe — ein Sakrament?* Zollikon 1951, p. 186ff., Ernest Best, *One Body in Christ*, London 1955, p. 45ff., Edvin Larsson, *Christus als Vorbild* (ASNU 23), Uppsala 1962, p. 20ff., Mathis Rissi, *Die Taufe für die Toten* (AThANT 42), Zürich 1962, p. 69ff., Gerhard Delling, *Die Taufe im Neuen Testament*, Berlin 1963, p. 126f., Hans-Wilhelm Schmidt, *Der Brief des Paulus an die Römer* (ThHkNT 6), Berlin 1963, p. 107, Wilhelm Thüsing, *Per Christum in Deum* (NTA. NF 1), Münster 1963, p. 62f., Herman Ridderbos, *Paulus*, Wuppertal 1970, p. 286f., C.E.B. Cranfield, *The Epistle to the Romans* I (ICC), Edinburgh 1975, p. 302f., Joseph A. Fitzmyer, *Romans* (AncB 33), New York 1993, p. 431.

23. See Wagner, *Problem*, pp. 69-280, where the specific text material included in the course of time to support the mystery theory is thoroughly and critically examined, cf. also Chapter II below.

24. See Wagner, *Problem*, p. 289ff., which has assembled the most important arguments on this point also; the religio-historical interpretation of the features in Rom 6.3ff., referred to above in connection with notes 15-16, is contradicted. Wagner emphasises: that 'Do you not know ...' in Rom 6.3 may refer to something other than a tradition already known (pp. 290-92), and that the reference includes v. 3 only and not the continuation (p. 292f., 297); that εἰς Χριστόν in v. 3, like σὺν Χριστῷ in Rom 6.4-8 and ἐν Χριστῷ in Rom 6.11, express the close association (p. 299f., 303-6); that the burial-resurrection symbolism is not found in Rom 6.4ff. and is contradicted by the lack of interest in emergence and by the future-tense forms in Rom 6.5b,8b., whereby the Christians' resurrection is expressly described as something in the future (pp. 294-96); that Rom 6.5 relates to the Christians' connection with the form of Christ's death, and not with a cultic imitation as a means of growing together with Christ (p. 293f.).

25. The position has only rarely been asserted since the 1950s: Carl Schneider, *Geistesgeschichte des antiken Christentums* I, Munich 1954, p. 121ff., *Geistesgeschichte des antiken Christentums* II, Munich 1954, p. 201ff., *Die antiken Mysterien in ihrer Einheit und Vielfalt*, Hamburg 1979, p. 6ff., Johannes Leipoldt, Die altchristliche Taufe religionsgeschichtlich betrachtet, *WZ(L)* 3 (1953-54), pp. 63-74, S.G.F. Brandon, *Man and his Destiny in the Great Religions*, Manchester 1962, p. 215, Ritual Technique of Salvation, in: S.G.F. Brandon (ed.), *The Saviour God*, Manchester 1963, pp. 17-36; p. 31ff., *History, Time and Deity*, Manchester 1965, pp. 26-29, 162. There is also however a significant reversion to similar viewpoints in Gerhard Sellin, *Der Streit um die Auferstehung der Toten* (FRLANT 138), Göttingen 1986, especially p. 215f., 254, 283f., and Hans Dieter Betz, Transferring a Ritual: Paul's In-

minant viewpoint of research was not that the text must be interpreted without regard to theories about Hellenistic mystery religions. Instead, another main tendency was first to characterise the interpretation of Rom 6 to mean that Paul uses Hellenistic mystery-religious baptism concepts but does so critically, so that the sacramentalist and magical aspects are brushed aside. This interpretation model is gaining ground, probably because it is associated with a different criticism of the mystical interpretations.

The solution of the indicative-imperative problem is also discussed, since it becomes clear that the problem is treated unsatisfactorily if, like Wernle and the religio-historical school, it is assumed that Paul expresses himself with boundless enthusiasm and mysteriousness in the salvation indicative, subsequently to contradict himself in the paraenetic imperatives.

Rudolph Bultmann in particular presented new views in the 1924 article 'Das Problem der Ethik bei Paulus'. This was a confrontation with the tendency of research up to that time to assume that a self-contradiction in Paul was simply an aporime or an antinomy which one then sought to explain, historically or psychologically, with no attempt whatsoever to try to understand the connection between the two sets of statements.[26] A crucial argument is the important observation that Paul himself links the two aspects together in several characteristic passages, in that the imperative emanates from and is substantiated in the indicative. Paul has thus seen a connection. This intensifies the problem. It becomes a direct paradox. A freedom from sin is asserted, and at the same time a continued struggle against sin is demanded. One must then try to understand this paradox. What Paul wishes to express by the concepts then becomes more important than the religio-historical background in the mysteries, which Bultmann recognises.[27] Bultmann understands Paul to mean that he wishes to express a paradoxical reality. The breach which has occurred with the world up to that time does not involve, as in the mysteries, the possession of new abilities and powers.[28] What has happened through justification cannot be recognised in empirical man. This depends on God's judgement alone, and can only be believed.

Men are sinners even if justified, and are therefore still subject to the demand.[29] According to this interpretation, there is a dialectic in the Chris-

terpretation of Baptism in Romans 6, in: Troels Engberg-Pedersen (ed.), *Paul in His Hellenistic Context*, Minneapolis 1995, pp. 84-118, cf. note 70 below.

26. Bultmann, Problem, p. 123ff.
27. Bultmann, Problem, p. 131ff.
28. Bultmann, Problem, p. 136f.
29. Bultmann, Problem, p. 135ff.

tian existence between the righteousness bestowed and man's fundamental sinfulness.[30]

What breaks new ground in Bultmann's treatment of the problem-complex is the claim that one must *understand* (not merely explain) the linking together of indicative and imperative in Paul.

A simple and intriguing interpretation gradually emerged as the interpretation of Rom 6.1-14 as Paul's corrective modification of mystery-religious traditions was elaborated.

2.3. Rom 6.1-14 as a Pauline modification of Hellenistic baptism mysticism

This brings us to the second main tendency in the interpretation which began to prevail in the 1930s. Since then, the dominant opinion of research has for many years been that Rom 6.1-14 is to be perceived as Paul's independent and critical adaptation of mysterious concepts of baptism taken from the Hellenistic communities. Paul can make use of these concepts, since they are concerned with baptism as the absolutely vital act of salvation in which all that matters is God's power; this can be used as a genuine expression of the fact that what happens at baptism rests upon God's action — it is God's definitive promise of salvation. But at the same time Paul modifies the tradition, since he must distance himself from any idea that salvation was automatically guaranteed by way of a magical rite of which one is definitively in possession, such as a new divine nature or the like. For Paul, final salvation is still in the future. This interpretation model is thus characterised by dialectic. There is a dialectic between those sections of the Hellenistic Christian tradition with which Paul can associate and those parts he can contradict. And Paul's interpretation of salvation is dialectic, in the sense that essential aspects of salvation have already arrived, while final salvation is not yet a reality.[31]

---

30. In Bultmann's interpretation of 1924, which has in many points been maintained in Bultmann, *Theologie*, p. 332ff., the emphasis in on the paradox, and the coincidence between righteousness and sinfulness is due to the radical distance between God and man, which has the result that man is *always* a sinner as far as God is concerned. Difficulties have arisen in comprehending this paradoxical interpretation, as asserted from the outset by Windisch, Problem, p. 275 n. 1. Bultmann has indeed also made use in other contexts of the simpler conceptual model in which the dialectic is conditioned by time: righteousness is *already* bestowed, but the final salvation has not yet occurred, cf. note 55 below.

31. To avoid misunderstanding, I wish to stress that when I speak of 'a dialectic interpretation' of the text this is merely a formal characteristic of the interpretation in which I draw attention to the important features referred to. Thus I do not insist that this interpretation is especially linked to 'dialectic theology' (or dialectic materialism, or philosophical dialectics). As will be seen, there are significant 'dialectic theologians' among the

Bultmann may be seen as a pioneer in regard to this type of interpretation. There was certainly in the past an awareness of the differences between the supposedly mysterious concepts and the Pauline use of them; the more sublime form given to concepts by Paul has frequently been pointed out.[32] But if, with Bultmann, it is emphasised that the text is to be understood — that it is not enough merely to explain its religio-historical background — a marked shift in emphasis occurs. Interest in the interplay between tradition and use intensifies. The emphasis comes to be on the Pauline subject-matter of the text. Bultmann has also described the relationship between the early Christian preaching and contemporary religious currents such as 'Anknüpfung und Widerspruch' (connection and contradiction).[33] To be understood, the early Christian preachers, including Paul, must use the religious language and prevalent ideas of the time as a starting point, and then demonstrate that the novelty they were conveying breached all expectations. Rom 6 is understood in this way.[34] The Pauline modification of the adopted tradition thus indeed becomes an important point, paving the way for the dialectic interpretation.

The interpretation model is to be found in an elaborated form in Günther Bornkamm, Niklaus Gäumann and Ernst Käsemann.[35] In addition, a large number of significant interpreters base themselves on such an interpretation, particularly in German Protestant exegesis. And this still contin-

opponents of the interpretation, in the same way as opponents of 'dialectic theology' also can go along with this.

32. See Otto Pfleiderer, *Das Urchristentum* I², Berlin 1902, p. 333, Gunkel, *Verständnis*, p. 85, Lietzmann, *Römer*, p. 65f., Bousset, *Kyrios*, especially p. 140, where it is emphasised that Paul breaks through all belief in mysteries and mysterious speculation and allows the gospel to speak. Even in Heitmüller, *Taufe*, 1911, p. 26 and other passages, the importance of belief in the case of Paul is stressed.

33. Especially in the 1946 article with this heading, now in Rudolf Bultmann, *Glauben und Verstehen* II³, Tübingen 1961, pp. 117-32.

34. Not only in Bultmann, *Glauben* II, p. 127ff., but also in Kirche und Lehre im Neuen Testament (originally 1929), in: *Glauben und Verstehen* I⁴, Tübingen 1961, pp. 153-87; p. 167, and *Theologie*, p. 143f., 312. Bultmann's interpretation is also apparent from brief notes; Neues Testament und Mythologie, in: Hans-Werner Bartsch (ed.), *Kerygma und Mythos*⁴, Hamburg-Bergstedt 1960, pp. 15-48; p. 30, 45, Der Mensch zwischen den Zeiten nach dem Neuen Testament, in: *Glauben und Verstehen* III², Tübingen 1962, pp. 35-54; p. 53f., Geschichte und Eschatologie im Neuen Testament, loc. cit. pp. 91-106; p. 103f. Cf. also Hans von Soden, Sakrament und Ethik bei Paulus (originally 1931), in: *Urchristentum und Geschichte*, Tübingen 1951, pp. 239-75; p. 271.

35. Günther Bornkamm, Taufe und neues Leben bei Paulus (originally 1939), in: *Das Ende des Gesetzes. Paulusstudien. Gesammelte Aufsätze* I (BEvTh 16)⁵, Munich 1966, pp. 34-50. Niklaus Gäumann, *Taufe und Ethik. Studien zu Römer 6* (BEvTh 47), Munich 1967. Ernst Käsemann, *An die Römer* (HNT 8a)³, Tübingen 1974, p. 164ff.

ues.[36] Such an interpretation is often taken as a matter of course by brief references to Rom 6.[37]

36. See Erich Dinkler, Zum Problem der Ethik bei Paulus. Rechtsname und Rechtsverzicht (originally 1952), in: *Signum crucis*, Tübingen 1967, pp. 204-40; p. 231ff., Die Taufaussagen des Neuen Testaments, in: Fritz Viering (ed.), *Zu Karl Barths Lehre von der Taufe*, Gütersloh 1971, pp. 60-153; p. 71ff., Römer 6,1-14 und das Verhältnis von Taufe und Rechtfertigung bei Paulus, in: Lorenzo De Lorenzi (ed.), *Battesimo e Giustizia in Rom 6 e 8*, Rome 1974, pp. 83-126; p. 87, 110, Herbert Braun, Das 'Stirb und Werde' in der Antike und im Neuen Testament, in: *Gesammelte Studien zum Neuen Testament und seiner Umwelt²*, Tübingen 1961, pp. 136-58; p. 152ff., Ernst Käsemann, Zum Thema der urchristlichen Apokalyptik, in: *Exegetische Versuche und Besinnungen II³*, Göttingen 1968, pp. 105-31; p. 120f., 126, 130, Eduard Lohse, Taufe und Rechtfertigung bei Paulus, *KuD* 11 (1965), pp. 308-24; p. 314ff., *Umwelt des Neuen Testaments (NTD* Erg. 1), Göttingen 1971, p. 173ff., Robert C. Tannehill, *Dying and Rising with Christ. A Study in Pauline Theology (BZNW* 32), Berlin 1967, p. 7ff., Hans Conzelmann, *Grundriss der Theologie des Neuen Testaments²*, Munich 1968, p. 66f., 296-300, Egon Brandenburger, Die Auferstehung des Glaubenden als historisches und theologisches Problem, *WuD* NF 9 (1967), pp. 16-33, Otto Merk, *Handeln aus Glauben (MThSt* 5), Marburg 1968, p. 23ff., Günther Bornkamm, *Paulus (UB* 119), Stuttgart 1968, p. 197f., Werner Georg Kümmel, *Die Theologie des Neuen Testaments nach seinen Hauptzeugen (NTD* Erg. 3), Göttingen 1969, p. 189ff., Hartwig Thyen, *Studien zur Sündevergebung (FRLANT* 96), Göttingen 1970, p. 196ff., Karl-Adolf Bauer, *Leiblichkeit das Ende aller Werke Gottes (StNT* 4), Gütersloh 1971, pp. 152-58, Peter von der Osten-Sacken, *Römer 8 als Beispiel paulinischer Soteriologie (FRLANT* 112), Göttingen 1975, p. 177ff., Jürgen Becker, *Auferstehung der Toten im Urchristentum (SBS* 82), Stuttgart 1975, p. 58ff., Gerhard Barth, *Die Taufe in frühchristlicher Zeit (BThSt* 4), Neukirchen-Vluyn 1981, pp. 80-106, Udo Schnelle, *Gerechtigkeit und Christusgegenwart (GTA* 24), Göttingen 1983, p. 75ff., Jost Eckert, Die Taufe und das neue Leben. Röm 6,1-11 im Kontext der paulinischen Theologie, *MüThZ* 38 (1987), pp. 203-222, Walter Schmithals, *Der Römerbrief. Ein Kommentar*, Gütersloh 1988, p. 186ff. This group includes interpreters who envisage a different background but yet adopt a Pauline modification of similar concepts, thus Eduard Schweizer, Die 'Mystik' des Sterbens und Auferstehens mit Christus bei Paulus, *EvTh* 26 (1966), pp. 239-57; p. 246ff., Dying and Rising with Christ, *NTS* 14 (1968), pp. 1-14; p. 8, Peter Siber, *Mit Christus leben (AThANT* 61), Zürich 1971, especially p. 205, Andreas Davidsen, *Paulus*, Copenhagen 1986, p. 66. Cf. also notes 37, 79 and 81 below.

37. See Jacob Jervell, *Imago Dei (FRLANT* 58), Göttingen 1960, p. 257, Harald Hegermann, *Die Vorstellung vom Schöpfungsmittler im hellenistischen Judentum und Urchristentum (TU* 82), Berlin 1961, p. 121f., 143f., James M. Robinson, Kerygma und Geschichte im Neuen Testament, *ZThK* 62 (1962), pp. 294-337; p. 302ff., Hans Dieter Betz, *Nachfolge und Nachahmung Jesu Christi im Neuen Testament (BHTh* 37), Tübingen 1967, p. 174, *Galatians (Hermeneia)*, Philadelphia 1979, p. 186f., Kurt Niederwimmer, Das Problem der Ethik bei Paulus, *ThZ* 24 (1968), pp. 81-92; p. 85ff., Günter Kegel, *Auferstehung Jesu — Auferstehung der Toten*, Gütersloh 1971, p. 51f., Robert Jewett, *Paul's Anthropological Terms (AGJU* 10), Leiden 1971, p. 293f., Klaus Wengst, *Christologische Formeln und Lieder des Urchristentums (StNT* 7), Gütersloh 1972, p. 47, 187, Gottfried Schille, *Osterglaube*, Stuttgart 1973, p. 35, James D.G. Dunn, *Jesus and the Spirit*, London 1975, p. 268, Andreas Lindemann, *Die Aufhebung der Zeit (StNT* 12), Gütersloh 1975, p. 30f., Paul Hoffmann, Auferstehung I/3. Auferstehung der Toten. Neues Testament, *TRE* 4 (1979), pp. 450-67; p. 457, Auferstehung II/1. Auferstehung Jesu Christi. Neues Testament, *TRE* 4 (1979), pp. 478-513; p. 483, Hans-Josef Klauck, *Herrenmahl und hellenistischer Kult (NA* NF 15), Münster 1982, p. 283, 319, Walter

This indeed gives an exciting and intriguing idea of the text. This should be apparent from the following outline of the basis for the interpretation and its consequences for the important theological matters discussed in the context of Rom 6.1-14.

The basis for this interpretation of Rom 6.1-14 is again theories about an *historical background in Hellenistic mystery religions*. But this is a more subtle concept of the genesis of the passage than at the time of the religio-historical school.

Those who follow this interpretation may adopt many of the objections which have arisen against theories that Paul used pagan, mysterious ideas; there are marked difference between the mysteries and Paul's baptismal concepts in Rom 6. But this does not mean that they must completely reject the idea that Paul uses mystery-religious concepts; the difference must indeed be interpreted as Paul's correction of the Hellenistic baptismal concepts he adopts; there is no reason therefore to reject that Paul employs a manner of thought which in the final analysis originates from the Hellenistic mystery religions. They can in this way take into consideration the arguments from both sides of the discussion.

It is possible to make much of criticism of the original religio-historical interpretation — particularly so in regard to Gäumann, who gave the most comprehensive account. He largely contradicts all aspects of the religio-historical school's interpretation of Rom 6.3-11: only in Rom 6.3 is Paul said to refer directly to a known tradition. It is denied that there is submersion-emersion symbolism in Rom 6.3-4; it is a baptism 'into Christ'. Also, in the terms 'with Christ' in Rom 6.4,6,8 and 'in Christ' in Rom 6.11, one should not think of a unio mystica. Rom 6.5 is not meant to relate to a ritual imitation.[38] Finally, it is stressed that the mode of thought is not worded as one might expect against a mystery-religious background; Rom 6.4 is not

Klaiber, *Rechtfertigung und Gemeinde* (FRLANT 127), Göttingen 1982, p. 120, Pheme Perkins, *Resurrection*, Garden City New York 1984, p. 273, C. Clifton Black II, Pauline Perspectives on Death in Romans 5-8, *JBL* 103 (1984), pp. 413-33; p. 422f., Nikolaus Walter, 'Hellenistische Eschatologie' im Neuen Testament, in: Erich Grässer and Otto Merk (ed.), *Glaube und Eschatologie*, Tübingen 1985, pp. 335-56; p. 345, Georg Strecker, Indicative and Imperative according to Paul, *Austr.Bib.Rev.* 25 (1987), pp. 60-72; p. 64.

38. See Gäumann, *Taufe*, particularly pp. 55-61, 73ff. Note that he follows Wagner's criticism of the religio-historical interpretation in as good as all respects, cf. notes 15-16 and 24 above. The same applies to Käsemann, *Römer*, p. 157ff., who has, however, the local interpretation of ἐβαπτίσθημεν εἰς Χριστόν. Cf. also Bornkamm, *Ende*, p. 42f., which turns in particular towards the interpretation of σύμφυτοι τῷ ὁμοιώματι in Rom 6.5 which makes it into a ritual fusion with Christ.

concerned with a burial *and* resurrection with Christ, and in Rom 6.5,8 the link to Christ's resurrection and the new life is futuristic.[39]

Nevertheless, this does not lead to a rejection of the link with the Hellenistic mystery religions but to an identification of tensions in the text, which are indeed said to have arisen because Paul modifies the mysterious concepts. It is thought that Wagner has gone too far in his scepticism.[40] It cannot be excluded that Paul is more indirectly (and to some extent negatively) dependent upon Hellenistic traditions. It is still possible to imagine that in Rom 6 Paul bases himself on concepts influenced by a mystery-religious mode of thought. The background may be either that baptism is seen as an initiation ritual with a magical-sacramentalist effect in which Christ's death and resurrection are timeless events with an immediate effect by virtue of the ritual repetition for those baptised,[41] or Paul may base himself on a more gnosticising further development of mystery thought: by baptism, one is incorporated in the cosmic redeemers's body, and because Christ, as the supra-individual, has been through degradation to exaltation this also applies to those who have merged together with him.[42] Paul's use of such ideas in Rom 6 is supported by several arguments.

It is concluded that some (relatively few) texts are still to be found which — not as a whole but in individual instances — may count as religio-historical parallels to Rom 6.1-11.[43] But this is assumed to be sufficient,

39. Here, the difference between Paul and the mysteries is emphasised even more strongly, because it is interpreted as a dissociation. See Gäumann, *Taufe*, p. 75f., 79, 84. Cf. Bornkamm, *Ende*, p. 38, 43, Tannehill, *Dying*, p. 11f., Käsemann, *Römer*, p. 158f., 161.

40. Thus Gäumann, *Taufe*, p. 39ff., Käsemann, *Römer*, p. 152f. Note in this connection the harsh treatment of Wagner's work, especially at the beginning: Hans Conzelmann (rec.), Günther Wagner, Das religionsgeschichtliche Problem von Röm 6,1-11, *EvTh* 24 (1964), pp. 171-72, Tannehill, *Dying*, p. 2, Betz, *Nachfolge*, p. 174 n. 7, cf. p. 67 n. 5 (which concerns 'apologetische Schein-Skepsis'), Thyen, *Studien*, p. 197.

41. See Gäumann, *Taufe*, p. 37ff., Bornkamm, *Paulus*, p. 197, Conzelmann, *Grundriss*, p. 66f.

42. Thus Bultmann, *Theologie*, p. 298f., Tannehill, *Dying*, p. 29f., 39, Thyen, *Studien*, p. 203f. Although there is a great difference between the mystery-religious sacramental magic and the gnostic concept of an incorporation into a super-individual being, it is almost never registered that two different interpretation models are concerned, and they are often mixed up. Thus Käsemann, *Römer*, p. 154, where there is an abrupt reference to baptism, partly as an initiation rite giving participation in the Christ fate and partly as an incorporation into the Christ body. Differently in Bultmann, *Theologie*, p. 297ff., where he is clearly working with a connection and a gradual transition between the two concepts.

43. See thus the survey of the texts in Gäumann, *Taufe*, pp. 40-44, where only Apuleius, Metam. 11, Firmicus Maternus, De err. 22,1-2, the 'Mithras liturgy' and the Themistios fragment are true parallels. Cf. also Käsemann, *Römer*, p. 153, where only one text is mentioned: Apuleius, Metam. 11.11ff.,23-24.

since all texts may be seen as reflecting one train of thought which is common to the syncretistic environment of the whole period.[44]

Further, Heitmüller's opinion, that the Christian concepts came to Paul via the Hellenistic communities, is seen as important. Paul is thus dependent upon the Hellenistic way of thinking which is also to be detected behind other Pauline texts.[45] This 'detour' can be used to explain inconsistencies between the religio-historical material and Rom 6.[46]

In addition, this viewpoint is defended by the assertion that the concepts we encounter in Rom 6.1-11 cannot be explained on the basis of other assumptions — nor on the basis of judeo-christian traditions.[47]

Finally, it is asserted that Rom 6 itself is a religio-historical source, and should be used in the reconstruction of mystery thought.[48] The tensions found in the text become an argument for the assumed background. In the text, Paul avoids speaking of an immediate resurrection with Christ in Rom 6.4, and uses the future tense in Rom 6.5,8 when speaking of the final salvation, because he distances himself from the concepts he uses about baptism as a cult mystery.[49] This also emerges in Rom 6.10 in the expression 'once for all', which emphasises that Jesus' death is an historic event and not a timeless myth which can be repeated ritually.[50]

This understanding of the background and genesis of the text results in a different opinion in regard to the other points of discussion.

This concerns the understanding of *the intention in Rom 6.1-11*.

The assumption that Paul wishes simultaneously to take over the Hellenistic communities' perception of baptism and to adopt a critical attitude towards the tradition taken over can easily lead to the conclusion that the text has a dual intent.

In the first place it is indeed stressed that the main subject-matter of Rom 6.1-11 is the enthusiastic certainty of salvation, which is common to

---

44. Thus Conzelmann (rec.), Wagner, p. 171f., Gäumann, *Taufe*, p. 39f., cf. p. 45f., Thyen, *Studien*, p. 197, Käsemann, *Römer*, p. 153.
45. See in particular Gäumann, *Taufe*, p. 38f., p. 46ff., which gives great weight to the observation that Heitmüller introduced in 1912, cf. note 17 above. Reference is made to the traditio-historical treatment of a number of Pauline texts and more generally to the Corinthian enthusiasm, cf. Chapter III below.
46. See Gäumann, *Taufe*, p. 39f.
47. Thus Gäumann, *Taufe*, p. 37f., Kümmel, *Theologie*, p. 190, Käsemann, *Römer*, p. 153, cf. Lietzmann, *Römer*, p. 67.
48. Thus Conzelmann (rec.), Wagner, p. 172.
49. Thus Bultmann, *Theologie*, p. 143f., Gäumann, *Taufe*, p. 75f., 79, 83f., Käsemann, *Römer*, p. 153, G. Barth, *Taufe*, p. 96, cf. Bornkamm, *Ende*, p. 38, 43. See note 39 above.
50. See Bornkamm, *Ende*, p. 40, cf. Gäumann, *Taufe*, p. 48f., 128f., Käsemann, *Römer*, p. 162.

Paul and the source. Paul can indeed use the traditional concepts because they express the fact that God's decisive act of salvation falls to the share of the Christians and opens new opportunities without contribution on their part. The Pauline reservations are then merely listed without emphasising that this is an important point in the text.[51]

But later, particularly in the context of the interpretation of Rom 6.12-14, it is assumed that in Rom 6.1-11 Paul will tell the Romans two things: that the old life is past, but also that the new life has not arrived in its final, glorious form.[52] Many shorter interpretations of Rom 6.1-11 draw direct attention to a dialectic in the Pauline intentions between the already-given and the still-absent salvation.[53] The brief, sympathetic references to the text may even make the confrontation with the enthusiastic Hellenistic concept of baptism appear as the only crucial point.[54]

This interpretation of the intention in Rom 6.1-11 sets the stage for a simple resolution of the problems associated with *indicative-imperative tension in Rom 6*. This can be linked to the tension to be seen in the section of text between the tradition applied — which sets the scene for the salvation indicative — and the Pauline reservations relative to the tradition — which makes the imperative possible. It becomes a dual eschatology where the Christians come to live in an interval in time in which deliverance from the power of sin and renewal of the God-relationship has occurred, whereas the

---

51. Thus Bornkamm, *Ende*, p. 43f., where in the interpretation itself of Rom 6.1-11 great reticence is displayed in understanding these reservations as a true point. The same applies to the detail-exegesis of Rom 6.4,5,8 in Gäumann, *Taufe* p. 76f., 79, 83f. Already before this, however, (p. 48f.), Gäumann has directly asserted that the Pauline intention in elucidations of baptism in Rom 6 is to be found in the modifications in vv. 4, 5 and 8, whereby Paul adopts a critical attitude towards the Hellenistic-Christian gnostically inspired concept of baptism, that the resurrection has already taken place. The reservations are stressed most strongly in Käsemann, *Römer*, p. 158ff., and here the modification appears to be highly emphasised (especially top of p. 159).

52. Thus Bornkamm, *Ende*, p. 46f., Gäumann, *Taufe*, p. 88ff., p. 128ff., Käsemann, *Römer*, p. 169.

53. See Dinkler, *Signum*, p. 232, Lohse, *Taufe*, p. 317, Bornkamm, *Paulus*, p. 197. Also in Schweizer, 'Mystik', p. 249, there is a clearly dialectic interpretation (although Schweizer rejects dependence on the mysteries and merely assumes that an enthusiastic community-tradition with a different origin is modified). Hans Hübner, Kreuz und Auferstehung im Neuen Testament, ThR 54 (1989), pp. 262-306; p. 271 refers to the eschatological reservation as the point in Rom 6 as entirely self-evident.

54. See Käsemann, *Versuche* II, p. 120f., 126f., Herbert Braun, Der Sinn der neutestamentlichen Christologie, in: *Gesammelte Studien zum Neuen Testament und seiner Umwelt*[2], Tübingen 1961, pp. 243-82; p. 267, Jewett, *Terms*, p. 215, 293f., Gäumann, *Taufe*, p. 48, Hans Conzelmann, Die Schule des Paulus, in: Carl Andresen and Günter Klein (ed.), *Theologia crucis — signum crucis. Festschrift für Erich Dinkler zum 70. Geburtstag*, Tübingen 1979, pp. 85-96; p. 91, 95.

final defeat of death and sin is lacking. In this interregnum between 'already' and 'not yet' there is a need for a demand.[55]

The starting point is the original formulation of the indicative-imperative problem-complex: if Paul promises the final salvation, this would presumably mean a freedom from sin and an all-encompassing renewal of human possibilities and capacities, which would make every demand superfluous.[56] At the same time, Bultmann's recognition is maintained that the imperative is derived from and substantiated by the indicative — so that the contradiction cannot be explained away as something Paul 'arrives at'; by the imperative formulations in Rom 6.12-13, Paul is to raise demands for precisely that which has already been given the Christians according to the indicatives in verses 1-11.[57]

The solution is the eschatological reservation. This is to be found in Paul's modifications of the Hellenistic baptismal traditions in Rom 6.3-11. It is also to be seen in the context of Rom 6.12, which reads: 'Therefore, do not let sin exercise dominion in your mortal bodies, to make you obey their passions.' The crucial point is meant to be that the Christians still have a mortal body, which is threatened by sin. It is thus emphasised that salvation has not occurred in the final sense.[58] By pointing out the deficiencies, the over-enthusiastic consequences of the Hellenistic view of baptism is averted — and this applies not only to this chapter but also to Rom 8.[59] Salvation is

---

55. This interpretation, which rests upon a time-conditioned dialectic, is also to be found in Bultmann — despite his original interpretation, cf. note 30 above. See in particular Bultmann, Mythologie, p. 30, where the Christian's situation is defined as 'ein ständiges Unterwegssein zwischen dem "noch nicht" und dem "doch schon".' The addition of the imperative to the indicative means: 'die Glaubensentscheidung ist nicht ein für allemal vollzogen, sondern sie ist jeweils in der konkreten Situation zu bewähren.' Bultmann expresses himself similarly elsewhere: Glauben II, p. 55f., cf. p. 129, Glauben III, p. 53f. Also Bornkamm, Ende, p. 44ff. (where the hiddenness of the new existence is emphasised as a background to the demand), Käsemann, Versuche II, p. 130, Römer, p. 164ff., cf. p. 215f., 222ff., 231, Gäumann, Taufe, p. 48, 128ff., Dinkler, Signum, p. 231ff., Lohse, Taufe, p. 317f., Tannehill, Dying, p. 77ff., Merk, Handeln, p. 34ff., Conzelmann, Grundriss, p. 311f., Kümmel, Theologie, pp. 199-203, Schmithals, Römerbrief, p. 188.

56. Se Tannehill, Dying, p. 78, Kümmel, Theologie, p. 200, Jewett, Terms, p. 293 (who considers that the position is completely new), Peter Tachau, 'Einst' und 'Jetzt' im Neuen Testament (FRLANT 105), Göttingen 1972, p. 118, cf. above in connection with note 6.

57. See Bornkamm, Ende, p. 34, 47, Tannehill, Dying, p. 78, 80, Kümmel, Theologie, p. 199f. Cf. notes 29-32 above.

58. See Bornkamm, Ende, p. 46, Dinkler, Signum, p. 231f., Merk, Handeln, p. 29, Lohse, Taufe, p. 317f., Tannehill, Dying, p. 77f., Gäumann, Taufe, p. 88, Kümmel, Theologie, p. 172, Käsemann, Römer, p. 168f.

59. See Tannehill, Dying, p. 78, Kümmel, Theologie, pp. 199-203, and especially Käsemann, Versuche II, p. 130, Römer, p. 164ff., 215f., 222ff., 231.

thus still 'extra nos', so that man continues to stand before God, who is the supreme power of existence.

The demand which is then given space comes to be concerned with the dedication of salvation. The imperative must stress that in the period leading up to the final salvation one must *safeguard* and *uphold* the righteousness bestowed, or it becomes an emphasising that in the continued existence one is wholly dependent upon the baptismal grace bestowed, on which one must constantly *make a decision*.[60]

As regards the question of the *understanding of baptism* and *Christology* in the Rom 6.1-14 section of the text, the modification interpretation also takes on substantial significance.

Paul's understanding of these matters is particularly established antithetically. By emphasising the distance between Paul's perception and the traditions he employs, those who hold this view can underline what Paul in any event does *not* think of baptism and Christ. They can thus distance themselves from the (especially from a Protestant viewpoint) unfortunate consequences of the mysterious interpretation of the religio-historical school: Rom 6 is not perceived as mysticism, and by baptism there is no magical or mystical incorporation in Christ. Also, baptism is not a Hellenistic rite in which the deity is followed through death and resurrection to certain immortality.[61]

It may then be pointed out that Paul's own understanding of baptism and Christology moves in a different direction. In contrast to the traditional mysticism and magic of baptism, Paul's perception of baptism is characterised more by personal decision and faith. Bultmann stresses that baptism becomes the basis of new ethical conduct,[62] that it is an act of confession,[63] and that radicalisation of the line of thought occurs, so that man (with Christ) is delivered over to death and becomes new with a new will.[64] Gäumann emphasises that in Rom 6.3-11 Paul uses the same basic Christian concept as is quoted in 1 Cor 15.3-5 concerning Christ's death, burial and re-

---

60. Thus Bultmann, Mythologie, p. 30, Bornkamm, *Ende*, p. 47ff., Käsemann, *Römer*, p. 168. Gäumann, *Taufe*, p. 129, speaks plainly of realising the new existence.

61. Thus Bultmann, *Glauben* I, p. 167, *Glauben* II, p. 129, *Glauben* III, p. 53, *Theologie*, p. 313, Conzelmann, *Grundriss*, p. 297, Kümmel, *Theologie*, p. 190, Gäumann, *Taufe*, p. 126ff., Käsemann, *Römer*, p. 158f.

62. Bultmann, *Theologie*, p. 312f., cf. *Glauben* I, p. 167f., *Glauben* III, p. 53, Conzelmann, *Grundriss*, p. 299f.

63. Bultmann, *Theologie*, p. 313, *Glauben* I, p. 167f., cf. Kümmel, *Theologie*, p. 190, which points out that in baptism the same affiliation to Christ is established as in belief.

64. Bultmann, *Glauben* II, p. 129, cf. Käsemann, *Römer*, p. 157.

surrection;[65] this is to be Paul's counterbalance to Hellenistic sacramental-ism, and because it is in the form of a 'credo' Gäumann concludes that Paul emphasises the faith in the context of baptism.[66] Käsemann notes that the 'vicariousness idea' dominates the context.[67] In Christology terms, this means that Hellenistic exaltation theology is supplanted by Paul's theology of the Cross.

2.4. Criticism of the modification interpretation

Only late in the history of research was there a direct turning away from this modification interpretation and the special traditio-historical working method.

But it is clear that the attacks of Wagner and others on the religio-historical base also affects this method of interpretation.[68] This is reflected in the almost angry reactions to Wagner's work, and the subsequent very de-fensive argument that it is still possible to assume Pauline dependence upon the mysteries.[69] But one cannot get around the fact that there must have been a minimum of agreement between Paul and the religious concepts which in the final analysis are assumed to be his source; and there is a fundamental burden of proof.

Only in the most recent accounts, especially in A.J.M. Wedderburn's monograph of 1987, are theories about Rom 6 as a critical and modified adoption of the Hellenistic mysterious traditions tackled.[70] It is asked

---

65. Gäumann, *Taufe*, p. 61f. This reference also explains why Paul speaks of burial with Christ in Rom 6.4.
66. Gäumann, *Taufe*, p. 126ff.
67. Käsemann, *Römer*, p. 157.
68. Cf. section 2.2 above and especially note 22.
69. See section 2.3 above, especially in the context of notes 40-49.
70. See in particular A.J.M. Wedderburn, *Baptism and Resurrection* (*WUNT* 44), Tübingen 1987. The consistent attitude has been prepared in a number of his works: Hellenistic Christian Traditions in Romans 6? *NTS* 29 (1983), pp. 337-55, Paul and the Hellenistic Cults. On Posing the right Questions, in: Ugo Bianchi and Maarten J. Vermaseren, *La soteriologia dei culti orientali nell' impero romano* (*EPRO* 92), Leiden 1982, pp. 817-33, The Soteriology of the Mysteries and Pauline Baptismal Theology, *Nov.Tes.* 29 (1987), pp. 53-72. Cf. Hubert Frankemölle, *Das Taufverständnis des Paulus* (*SBS* 47), Stuttgart 1970, p. 106f. with n. 44, Gerhard Sellin, 'Die Auferstehung ist schon geschehen', *Nov.Test.* 25 (1983), pp. 221-37, James D.G. Dunn, *Romans 1-8* (*WBC* 38a), Dallas 1988, p. 308ff., John Ziesler, *Paul's Letter to the Romans*, London 1989, p. 154f., Peter Stuhlmacher, *Der Brief an die Römer* (*NTD* 6)[14], Göttingen 1989, p. 84ff. Especially interesting is Betz, Transferring, the most recent contribution to the debate on Rom 6 which it has been possible to incorporate into this thesis; he is the first to adopt a really critical attitude towards Wedderburn, *Baptism*. Betz describes it (p. 99 n. 66) as a purely negative hypothesis that he rejects the connection between Paul and the mystery religions. His own hypothesis (pp. 84-86, 107ff.) is that in

critically *whether* there really are the tensions and corrections in the text that are assumed — why Paul does not reject incorrect views more clearly — and why this special and difficult documentable tradition is assumed as the background and not other possibilities.[71] I have myself in the past confronted this interpretation model in connection with other texts, and also suggested a confrontation in respect of Rom 6. I have opposed scholars who wish to find in Rom 6,12 an 'eschatological reservation' against the certainty of salvation and to use this as a key to an understanding of the indicative-imperative problem; this is contradicted by the text's structure and by the points it makes.[72]

Traugott Holz objects in principle to this form of traditio-historical work on the texts, including Rom 6.[73] The method leads to the isolation of various lines of tradition, so that it presents a picture of the situation in which all important New Testament statements can be perceived only as revisions and as polemics against other statements. This is followed by a criticism of central theories about the development of early Christianity; in continuation of Martin Hengel, it is questionable whether there is sufficient time for the 'pre-Pauline' Hellenistic Christianity which is the precondition for this tra-

Rom 6 Paul takes the common Christian concepts of baptism and so transforms them that he arrives at an interpretation of the baptism ritual analogous to a mystery ritual. He is thus ultimately in agreement with Wedderburn and the other interpreters referred to on the critical point: that basically Paul is not dependent upon a mystery religiousness which he modifies. Betz has indeed also left the 'modification interpretation', as is clearly stated on p. 110 n. 92 (it is rather an 'inverted modification theory' in which Paul is to modify the Christians' baptism concept in the direction of the mystery rituals). Similarly, in Sellin, *Streit*, p. 27 n. 46, p. 63 n. 92, there is a sharp rejection of the modification interpretation and Pauline dependence on the coherent pre-Pauline Gentile-Christian Christology; but this is combined with the assumption that Paul gradually came closer to a mysterious way of thought (p. 215, 254, 283), cf. also Oepke, βάπτω, βαπτίζω, *ThWNT* I (1930), pp. 527-44; p. 539f.

71. See in particular Wedderburn, *Baptism*, pp. 37-69, which raises questions, and the balanced conclusions, p. 393ff., which also establish that before Paul it is difficult to find traces of the concept of a resurrection that has already occurred.

72. See Søren Agersnap, Rom 6,12 og det paulinske imperativ [Rom 6.12 and the Pauline imperative], *DTT* 43 (1980), pp. 36-47, cf. *Paulusstudier. 1. Kor 15 og Rom 2 (Tekst og Tolkning* 7) [Pauline Studies], Copenhagen 1979, pp. 7-100, a confrontation with a 'modification interpretation' of 1 Cor 15.45-46, where I also criticise the theological use of 'the eschatological reservation', p. 33ff., cf. also Agersnap, Gudsforståelsen, p. 98f. with n. 2, where I point out that the traditio-historical interpretation gives a shift in the perspective away from the positive: salvation enthusiasm and interest in the content of the new life.

73. See Traugott Holtz, Überlegungen zur Geschichte, in: *Geschichte und Theologie des Urchristentums (WUNT* 57), Tübingen 1991, pp. 31-44; p. 31f.

ditio-historical interpretation.[74] The sources seem rather to indicate the creation of a common Palestinian and Hellenistic Christian theology which involves a basic 'ecumenical' understanding of which Rom 6.3 is indeed an expression.[75]

Objections to this way of using traditio-history are also to be taken from discussion of other Pauline texts. If the difference between Paul's views and tradition is stressed, the negative and the polemics against the traditional concepts become the main issue.[76] Paul is described as one who is always against, and who dampens down all excitement in Hellenistic Christian communities. And it remains puzzling why in these contexts Paul uses the traditional concepts which he is in fact unable to accept.[77]

74. See Holtz, *Geschichte*, p. 35ff., Martin Hengel, Christologie und neutestamentliche Chronologie, in: Heinrich Baltensweiler and Bo Reicke, *Neues Testament und Geschichte*, Zürich 1972, pp. 43-67, where it is pointed out that there is only a period of about two years between the death of Christ and Paul's conversion, and that there is also a geographical proximity between the first Hellenistic and Palestinian communities. See also Martin Hengel, *Der Sohn Gottes*, Tübingen 1975, p. 32ff., 46ff., 53ff., where there is a sharp attack on the lack of religio-historical examples that make the thesis in Heitmüller, Problem, p. 330ff., Bultmann, *Theologie*, p. 66f., cf. notes 17 and 45 above, concerning a syncretistic pre-Pauline Christianity to a pure construction.

75. See Hengel, *Christologie*, p. 51, which asks whether it is not more reasonable to explain the Christological development until the meeting of apostles 'aus den innerjüdischen Voraussetzungen', cf. Holtz, *Geschichte*, p. 37ff. This opens up a different form of traditio-history where one works instead with common Christian teaching traditions as something that Paul has helped to develop, as was already the case in Alfred Seeberg, *Der Katechismus der Urchristenheit*, Leipzig 1903, a working method also to be found in Hejne Simonsen, Traditionshistoriske overvejelser til Romerbrevet [Traditio-historical considerations concerning Romans], in: Sigfred Pedersen (ed.), *Nytestamentlige Studier*, Århus 1976, pp. 181-213.

76. In the course of the thesis, we encounter other passages interpreted according to the same model. In Chapter III, section 2.1: Gal 3.27-29; Chapter III, section 3.3: Rom 8 and Phil 2.6-11; in Chapter III, section 4, various passages in 1 Cor, where Paul is to modifiy Corinthian enthusiasm. In Chapter V, section 2: Rom 5.12-21.

77. The methodical objection inherent in this question is raised in Eberhard Jüngel, Das Gesetz zwischen Adam und Christus, in: *Unterwegs zur Sache* (BEvTh 61), Munich 1972, pp. 145-72; p. 147, against a fanatical use of the interpretation model on Rom 5.12-21, cf. below Chapter V, section 4.3. See also Seyoon Kim, *The Origin of Paul's Gospel* (WUNT 2. Reihe 4), Tübingen 1981, p. 303, about similar problems. Methodically, it can indeed be criticised that this interpretation model is convenient and apologetic, because it is always Paul who brushes away the religious aspect. Moreover, what the interpretation rests upon is questionable. All the features in Rom 6 originally used as substantiation of a Hellenistic background can be interpreted differently. But even if the mysterious interpretation of the details is abandoned and it is admitted that the few passages where the mystery-religious concepts are to show through deviate strongly from the assumed model, the theory concerning the background is adhered to; as in Gäumann, *Taufe*, the deviations are interpreted as merely Pauline modifications, cf. note 38 above. An unfalsifiable hypothesis has thus been constructed, which is maintained after the substantiation has been withdrawn little by little.

2.5. Non-mysterious interpretations of Rom 6.1-14

The view has thus gradually gained greater recognition that Rom 6 must be interpreted without consideration for theories concerning a mystery-religious background.

This occurs not only in the works referred to, in which the religio- and traditio-historical interpretation models are directly rejected. Some presentations completely ignore the question of the religio- and traditio-historical background in interpreting Rom 6.1-14.[78] Others allow the problem of any mystery-religious influence to remain open. An influence is not directly rejected, but is apparently seen as nothing crucial, and is not allowed to affect the interpretation.[79]

No definite interpretation model has emerged, but instead there are various interpretations. I wish below to set out important points of view, and then to look at the remaining problems.

As concerns *the intention in Rom 6.1-11*, the stage is set for a simpler and more positive description of Paul's point of view. Having liberated oneself from the idea of a mysterious background to the text, there is no reason to assume that Paul is dealing with a perception of salvation as immediate apotheosis. Therefore, there should be no need for eschatological reservations. Instead, it seems that Paul intensifies the awareness of salvation and of a new life.[80]

Nevertheless, in interpreting the text there is a tendency to preoccupy

---

78. This applies in particular to brief comments and works of systematic theology such as C.H. Dodd, *The Epistle of Paul to the Romans*, (paperback ed.), London 1959, p. 106ff., Ernst Percy, *Der Leib Christi (Σῶμα Χριστοῦ) in den paulinischen Homologumena und Antilegomena (AUL NS 38,1)*, Lund 1942, p. 25ff., F.F. Bruce, *The Epistle of Paul to the Romans*, London 1963, p. 134ff., John Murray, *The Epistle to the Romans (NLC)²*, London 1970, p. 211ff., James D.G. Dunn, *Baptism in the Holy Spirit (SBT 2,15)²*, London 1973, p. 139ff., André Viard, *Saint Paul. Épitre aux Romains (SBi)*, Paris 1975, p. 140ff.

79. Thus Otto Michel, *Der Brief an die Römer (KEK 4)¹³*, Göttingen 1966, p. 150ff., C.K. Barrett, *The Epistle to the Romans (BNTC)²*, London 1962, p. 122, Georg Braumann, *Vorpaulinische christliche Taufverkündigung bei Paulus (BWMANT 82)*, Stuttgart 1962, p. 1ff., 15ff., G.R. Beasley-Murray, *Baptism in the New Testament*, London 1962, p. 127, Jacob Jervell, *Gud og hans fiender. Forsøk på å tolke Romerbrevet* [God and his enemies. An attempt to interpret Romans], Oslo 1973, p. 94 (cf., however, note 81 below), Heinrich Schlier, *Der Römerbrief (HThKNT 6)*, Freiburg 1977, p. 190ff., Hans Halter, *Taufe und Ethos (FThSt 106)*, Freiburg 1977, p. 42ff. (cf., however, note 81 below), Ulrich Wilckens, *Der Brief an die Römer. 2. Teilband (KEK VI/2)*, Zürich 1980, p. 54ff., Aage Pilgaard, *Dåbsteologien i Romerbrevet* [Baptism Theology in Romans], in: Sigfred Pedersen (ed.), *Dåben i Ny Testamente* [Baptism in the New Testament], Århus 1982, pp. 118-40; n. 39 p. 138f. (cf., however, note 81 below), Leon Morris, *The Epistle to the Romans*, Grand Rapids 1988, 243ff., Hans Hübner, *Biblische Theologie des Neuen Testaments II: Die Theologie des Paulus*, Göttingen 1993, p. 291.

80. See Sellin, Auferstehung, pp. 228-30, cf. Wedderburn, Baptism, p. 44ff.

oneself with features which can be interpreted to mean that final salvation is not yet certain. Even Hubert Frankemölle, who is opposed to the modification interpretation, brings out the details which have been interpreted as Pauline modifications of the Hellenistic perception of baptism. And he sees in them a confrontation with the Hellenistic enthusiasm. There is still seen to be in the Pauline intention a dialectic between those aspects of salvation which have already occurred and those which have not as yet done so.[81]

The relationship between the indicative and the imperatives in Rom 6.12-14 can also be presented differently if the starting point is not an enthusiastic perception of salvation involving a total renewal, which would make any demand superfluous.

I have tried earlier to describe this very simply: 'The indicative says that the new life is a reality, the imperative indicates what it contains'.[82] Similarly, Hans Halter has suggested that the struggle which is called for concerns primarily *the world*, whether it is to belong to one or other of the two powers, God or sin.[83] The imperatives must thus be turned outward against the tasks of the new life, and indeed concern something other than

---

81. See Frankemölle, *Taufverständnis*, p. 72f. Something similar is happening with other interpreters who are not in favour of the traditio-historical background but nevertheless anticipate modifications, thus Jervell, *Gud*, p. 93 (different in the later article: Dåpen til døden [Baptism into death], *Pr.F.Bl* 75 (1985), pp. 525-29), Halter, *Taufe*, who is working with a general 'schon-noch-nicht' structure in the text, especially p. 49, Pilgaard, Dåbsteologien, n. 32 p. 137, cf. also Horacio E. Lona, *Die Eschatologie im Kolosser- und Epheserbrief* (FzB 48), Würzburg 1984, p. 157ff. There is thus a gradual transition to the modification interpretation.
82. Agersnap, Rom 6,12, p. 47.
83. See Halter, *Taufe*, p. 69f., and similarly Käsemann, *Römer* p. 169f., who despite this starting point sees it, however, as crucial in the verses that the Christian's attitude towards the battle is: it becomes a battle about 'das Stück Welt, das wir in unserm Leibe sind'. Cf. Wolfgang Schrage, *Die konkreten Einzelgebote in der paulinischen Paränese*, Gütersloh 1961, p. 82ff., which underlines that the demands in Paul are not a call for 'Selbstverwirklichung' and 'Selbstgesetzgebung'; God's will continues to be a standard which confronts man as a voluntas externa, the Christian encounter in the paraenesis; nevertheless a traditional understanding of the indicative-imperative tension is maintained as the crucial motif in the paraenesis, although separated from the specific individual demands. A consistent denial of the indicative-imperative tension is to be found in Peter Steensgaard, Erwägungen zum Problem Evangelium und Paränese bei Paulus, *ASTI* 10 (1975-76), pp. 110-28, who rejects that the imperatives in Paul always have the character of a demand in the absolute sense; in Rom 6 the function is to highlight God's will as regards the believer, who has received new life and is therefore motivated to act accordingly (p. 124f.).

the acquisition of salvation. There should thus be no inherent coincidence with the indicative, and the tension would disappear.[84]

But the conclusion almost everywhere is nevertheless that the emphasis is on Rom 6.12, which is interpreted to mean that the Christians still have a mortal body.[85] And the tension still to be found between the indicative and the imperative is thus explained.

The historical background to the concepts in Rom 6.1-14 is to be found in various contexts.

The most marked is the theory that the background must be found in a collective line of thought from the Old Testament, which is called the 'conception of corporate personality'.[86] H. Wheeler Robinson originally tried to define this.[87] It is a special Semitic-Hebrew mode of thought. It is said to be characteristic of a Semitic way of thinking that it makes no sharp distinction between the individual and the group it represents. This is to be seen part-

---

84. An uncomplicated connection between indicative and imperative in a different way is also conceivable: the indicative concerns the fact that one is already bound and favoured, so that there is no wavering between several possibilities — one can only do that which is demanded — thus von Soden, *Urchristentum*, p. 274 with n. 1, cf. however p. 266ff., where the emphasis is that dialectics and a tension relationship are present between soteriology and paraenesis. Similarly, Tachau, *Einst*, p. 118, construes the antithesis in Rom 6.19bc to mean that in principle only one possibility remains; but using the argument that a demand would be superfluous if there were only the one necessary possibility Tachau rejects that it was meant seriously on Paul's part. Murray, *Romans*, p. 226f., is consistent, establishing that the supremacy of sin by virtue of the mortal body has definitively come to an end for the believer, and only therefore does the imperative make sense: only to the liberated can it be said that he must not act like a slave.

85. Thus Michel, *Römer*, p. 254, Nygren, *Romarna*, p. 254, Kuss, *Römerbrief*, p. 382ff., Frankemölle, *Taufverständnis*, p. 114f., Jervell, *Gud*, p. 102ff., Halter, *Taufe*, p. 88, Wilckens, *Römer* II, p. 20, Viard, *Romains*, p. 147, Pilgaard, Dåbsteologien, p. 128, Dunn, *Romans*, p. 335f.

86. Således Hanson, *Unity*, p. 84, Schnackenburg, Todes- und Lebensgemeinschaft, pp. 32-53, Wagner, *Problem*, p. 305f., Larsson, *Christus*, p. 24f., 50, Thüsing, *Per Christum*, p. 65f., 69, Frankemölle, *Taufverständnis*, p. 37f., Ridderbos, *Paulus*, pp. 45-49 etc., cf. M. Barth, *Taufe*, p. 228ff., 267-83, Delling, *Taufe*, p. 128f.

87. There are references normally to the definitions of the concept in H. Wheeler Robinson, The Hebrew Conception of Corporate Personality, in: J. Hempel (ed.), *Werden und Wesen des Alten Testaments* (BZAW 66), Berlin 1936, pp. 49-62. But before that Robinson had worked on this subject in several Old Testament treatises, see *The Doctrine of Man*, Edinburgh 1911, p. 8ff., The Cross of the Servant (originally 1926), in: *The Cross in the Old Testament*, London 1955, pp. 53-115. And already in Dodd, *Romans*, p. 106ff. (originally 1932), Christ is referred to as 'corporate personality' and 'representative' in the interpretation of Rom 6. The most comprehensive description of the motif in both the Old and New Testaments is to be found in Josef de Fraine, *Adam et son lignage*, Bruges 1959 (I have had access only to the German translation, *Adam und seine Nachkommen*, Cologne 1962).

icularly in the relationship between the progenitor and his descendants: the progenitor represents the subsequent generations at the decisive events, and they therefore participate in them. This can be seen in association with the Adam-Christ typology in Rom 5.12-21, and with the fellowship with Christ in death and in life to be found in the σὺν Χριστῷ concepts here in Rom 6. At his death on Golgotha, Christ was the representative of the Christians who in this sense died with him — and similarly at the other events: burial and resurrection.

Reference may still be made to the tradition rendered by Paul in 1 Cor 15.3-5 about Christ's death, burial and resurrection. Paul therefore alludes in Rom 6,3-11 precisely to a Christian tradition.[88] And this can be seen as a part of the creed or proclamation which early in Christian history was declared at baptism.[89]

In addition, a different set of intrinsic Christian traditions are included in the picture. Edvin Larsson and Ulrich Wilckens have drawn attention to concepts from the gospel narratives about Jesus. They reflect on the disciple relationship and the demand to follow Jesus in suffering and in death. The concepts of a common fate which we have in the σὺν Χριστῷ statements in Rom 6 may have been developed from this.[90]

Christology and the baptism concept in Rom 6 can also be given a distinctive formulation if one assumes the 'progenitor concept' that the corporate-personality concept involves. By virtue of faith, the Christians must be included in Christ's death and resurrection, and participate in the effects of the acts of salvation. Baptism is then often presented non-sacramentally, or even anti-sacramentally.

What is decisive does not occur in the act of baptism. It occurred at the time when Christ as a corporate personality died, was buried and arose. It did not occur to him alone, but in one event for all his descendants. Christ's crucifixion is the actual turning point in the life of Christians. Baptism is merely a presentation of the event or a creed in which the faith is manifested. Frankemölle maintains that the Christians actually died, were buried and arose at the time of and at Golgotha — it is merely put into force at baptism.[91] Markus Barth has a drastic interpretation of 'buried with him' in

---

88. See Wagner, *Problem*, p. 299, Larsson, *Christus*, p. 56, Werner Kramer, *Christos Kyrios Gottessohn* (AThANT 44), Zürich 1963, p. 24, 60, Beasley-Murray, *Baptism*, p. 127, Frankemölle, *Taufverständnis*, p. 27ff., 56f., Jervell, *Gud*, p. 94f., Wilckens, *Römer* II, p. 12.

89. See Wagner, *Problem*, p. 299, Beasley-Murray, *Baptism*, p. 127, Jervell, *Gud*, p. 94f.

90. Larsson, *Christus*, p. 74ff., Wilckens, *Römer* II, pp. 60-62.

91. Frankemölle, *Taufverständnis*, p. 54f., which emphasises that διὰ τοῦ βαπτίσματος in Rom 6.4 has no temporal significance but merely instrumental significance. Cf. Ridderbos,

Rom 6.4: death with Christ, which took place at Golgotha, is the true baptism, and therefore the act of baptism is only a burial with Christ, a confirmation of this, the creed of the believer.[92] Wagner emphasises that it reads 'we believe' in Rom 6.8, and he interprets this as an expression of the importance of faith in this context.[93]

2.6. Criticism of the alternative attempts at interpretation

As the non-mysterious interpretations are so varied they cannot be subjected to an overall review. But one can indicate questionable tendencies.

Most remarkable is the strange perception of baptism and Christology to be found in the most notable interpretations: one is incorporated into Christ and has thus participated in the decisive event of the Cross, which occurred much earlier and in an entirely different place. Halter in particular has indicated the speculative nature which makes it impossible for these ideas ever to be intelligibly coherent; it reminds one forcibly of the mysterious merging with Christ, which was earlier seen as the background; and the entire idea rests on a rigid, temporal understanding of the term 'with Christ' in Rom 6.4-8.[94]

It then becomes clear that the fundamental 'corporate personality interpretation' presents problems. It becomes merely another religio-historical explanation of the concepts in the text. It comes to resemble the concept that the background must be a gnostic myth about a mystical incorporation in a

Paulus, p. 285f. See also Oscar Cullmann, *Die Tauflehre des Neuen Testaments* (*AThANT* 12), Zürich 1948, p. 14ff., which refers to the Golgotha event as 'Generaltaufe'.

92. M. Barth, *Taufe*, p. 228ff., 267-83, cf. Delling, *Taufe*, p. 128f. Markus Barth's book is an attempt to provide an exegetic foundation for the anti-sacramentalist view of baptism, which was advanced by his father Karl Barth in his later works.

93. Wagner, *Problem*, p. 298 n. 112, cf. Gäumann, *Taufe*, p. 84, Frankemölle, *Taufverständnis*, p. 81f., Beasley-Murray, *Baptism*, p. 156, recognises that the term πιστεύομεν cannot support this interpretation, but on the other hand interprets λογίζεσθε in Rom 6.11 in this way (p. 145), cf. Hübner, *Theologie*, p. 245.

94. See Halter, *Taufe*, pp. 43-48 with notes where he turns towards the opinion in Hahn, *Mitsterben*, p. 90ff., which has a special Kierkegaardian concept of 'contemporaneity', and in Cullmann, M. Barth, Delling, Frankemölle, cf. notes 91-92 above. Halter also finds analogous viewpoints (n. 36 on p. 534) in, inter alia, Bornkamm, *Ende*, p. 39, 41, Erhardt Güttgemanns, *Der leidende Apostel und sein Herr* (*FRLANT* 90), Göttingen 1966, p. 213ff., Tannehill, *Dying*, p. 39ff., and especially Thyen, *Studien*, p. 194ff., where the text is seen against the background of a gnostic continuation of the mysteries. Halter also points out (p. 45f.) that the consistent execution of the idea means that any exterior act of baptism becomes superfluous, which is however contradicted by other Pauline passages on baptism. Cf. Kümmel, *Theologie*, p. 192, Käsemann, *Römer*, p. 157.

cosmic redeemer figure.[95] The consequences are in general terms the same, although the concepts are said to originate from several places. And the same methodical problems remain.[96] Can it be proved that this 'primitive' complex of concepts was still wide-spread and comprehensible in New Testament times? It is said to have been an original idea that one enters into a corporative unity with progenitor, tribe and family to such a degree that individuality becomes of no insignificance.[97] And how can this be transferred to the relationship with Christ? This does not indeed depend on a family-related link but on faith and baptism.[98] The viewpoint is indeed gradually weakened, so that it becomes a matter merely of wide-spread concepts of solidarity and representation.[99]

Finally, a further problem is in my opinion that there has not been a sufficiently consistent break with earlier interpretations. Tensions and dialectic are still to be seen in the text, probably because one clings to old subjects of discussion.[100]

---

95. An indication of the closeness of the theories to one another is given by Frankemölle, *Taufverständnis*, p. 37f., 102-7, who asserts that Hellenistic communities' knowledge of gnostic Adam-Anthropos speculation has had a conducive effect on the understanding of the Hebrew idea of a corporate personality.

96. As in the religio-historical school's interpretation, the main emphasis is placed on the explanation of the idea's origin — which is merely labelled. But how the ideas are to be understood remains unclear, as is to be seen from the questions referred to below and the following notes.

97. See in particular the critical review of the concept in J.W. Rogerson, The Hebrew Conception of Corporate Personality: A Re-Examination, *JThS NS* 21 (1970), pp. 1-16. Cf. also J.R. Porter, The Legal Aspect of the Concept of 'Corporate Personality' in the Old Testament, *VT* 15 (1965), pp. 361-80. There is scarcely any specific textual instance in the context of the New Testament, cf. the most detailed description, de Fraine, *Adam*, pp. 201-30 (which merely refers to the σῶμα Χριστοῦ idea and by implication to the Adam-Christ typology in Rom 5,12-21, and otherwise indicates a mutual connection with family, race, ancestors, and stylistic means such as personification and personal address), and Ridderbos, *Paulus*, p. 45ff. (where the reference to Rom 5,12-21 is the only specific point).

98. Cf. G. Barth, *Taufe*, p. 98 n. 223, which emphasises especially that this patriarch-descendants connection is not indeed associated with the concept that one is adopted into this through a cultic-sacramental act. For the same reason, he also turns against the suggestion in Wilckens, cf. note 90 above, concerning a background in the gospels' concepts of the Imitation of Christ, which is not of course dependent upon cultic-sacramental participation. Cf. also Rudolf Schnackenburg, Die Adam-Christus-Typologie (Röm 5,12-21) als Voraussetzung für die Taufverständnis in Röm 6,1-14, in: Lorenzo de Lorenzi (ed.), *Battesimo e giustizia in Rom 6 e 8*, Rome 1974, p. 37-55; p. 48, where it is indeed taken into account that belief in Christ is different from the fundamental concepts.

99. Cf. Schnackenburg, Adam-Christus-Typologie, p. 46ff., Wedderburn, Soteriology, p. 71f., *Baptism*, p. 351ff.

100. Cf. above in connection with notes 81 and 85. It appears to be the confrontation with the mysterious interpretation of the text which comes to the fore in such a way that all the features opposing this background are over-emphasised.

3. Guidelines for the discussion of Rom 6.1-14

3.1. Considerations in regard to methodical practice

The research-historical survey has shown that major methodical considerations play a part in the interpretation of Rom 6. Criticism has been raised against a one-sided religio-historical interpretation model and a dialectic traditio-historical procedure. There may consequently be reason to consider how the text can be interpreted with a valid use of religio- and traditio-historical material.

In the context of the indicative-imperative discussion, Bultmann opposed to an attempt at an objective, purely historical criticism in which one explains the background to the texts and refrains from going more deeply into their subject-matter.[101] Bultmann therefore introduces the term 'understanding' into the theological debate. This has led to a hermeneutic position which has since characterised the debate.[102] Work on the New Testament becomes broader — and more complicated — if the target is understanding: distance in time, language and world picture present problems. Bultmann has emphasised the hermeneutic circle, in which understanding demands pre-understanding; it becomes a more subjective empathy which must be presented in an 'existential interpretation'.[103]

This problem area has been of crucial importance to theological hermeneutics for many years. Correctives have been added to the existential interpretation, and in particular the significance of the language has been taken into consideration. This leads to an intensification of the circle of her-

---

101. Cf. above sections 2.2 and 2.3. This is a link in a justified confrontation with a strictly empirical (positivistic and thus scepticistic) scholarly ideal. The religio-historical school aimed at a purely descriptive treatment of the New Testament texts, which were made to stand in their historical strangeness, cf. Gunkel, *Verständnis*, p. V f., 13ff., Heitmüller, *Taufe*, 1903, p. 53ff. In fact this contribution was a fertile challenge to the church's theological work.

102. This is built up in a number of weighty articles: Die liberale Theologen und die jüngste theologische Bewegung (originally 1924), in: *Glauben und Verstehen* I⁴, Tübingen 1961, pp. 1-25, Die Bedeutung der 'dialektischen Theologie' für die neutestamentliche Wissenschaft (originally 1928), loc. cit., pp. 114-33, Das Problem der 'Natürlichen Theologie', loc. cit., pp. 294-312, Das Problem der Hermeneutik (originally 1950), in: *Glauben und Verstehen* II³, Tübingen 1961, pp. 211-35, Ist voraussetzungslose Exegese möglich? (originally 1957), in: *Glauben und Verstehen* III², Tübingen 1962, pp. 142-50, Jesus Christus und die Mythologie (originally 1958), in: *Glauben und Verstehen* IV, Tübingen 1965, pp. 141-89, Mythologie, p. 15ff.

103. See Bultmann, *Glauben* II, p. 226f., where there is a reference to the analysis of the understanding as existential in Martin Heidegger, *Sein und Zeit* I, Tübingen 1927, § 31f., and especially *Glauben* IV, p. 168ff., and Mythologie, p. 33f., where all of Heidegger's existential analysis is indicated as basis.

meneutic problems, since there should be no neutral attitude beyond the language and history from which the past can be observed.[104] The result of this development is a chaotic situation characterised by hermeneutic scepticism.[105]

On the one hand, there has been a concentration on the predominant, understanding, 'hermeneutic' interpretation, for which it is thought no actual rules can be given.[106] It was merely demanded that the understanding interpretation must be submitted as clearly and as evidently as possible.[107]

On the other hand, work on specific exegetic problems of method has for that reason long been neglected. Exegetes have merely referred to the 'historical-critical exegesis', as if this was a definite and well-defined method.[108] It has therefore become unclear how individual critical methods such as literary criticism, form criticism and the history of tradition relate to

104. Cf. the survey of the debate and points of criticism in Peter Stuhlmacher, *Vom Verstehen des Neuen Testaments* (NTD Erg. 6)[1], Göttingen 1979, p. 186ff., *Vom Verstehen des Neuen Testaments* (NTD Erg. 6)[2], Göttingen 1986, p. 198ff., Claus V. Bormann, Hermeneutik I. Philosophisch-theologisch, *TRE* 15 (1986), pp. 109-37; p. 127ff. Bultmann's use of the purely formal structures are accused of providing an abstract and intrinsically narrow kerygma where the individual's relationship to God is insulated from the relationship to the surrounding world, the social and political circumstances and the material reality. Where the language is taken into consideration, it is emphasised that one cannot go behind the language to a neutral pre-linguistic reality, but one is already oneself part of the texts' effect-history (Wirkungsgeschichte) and is involved. In theology this is underlined in 'the new hermeneutics' in Ernst Fuchs, *Marburger Hermeneutik*, Tübingen 1968, Was wird in der Exegese interpretiert? in: *Zur Frage nach dem historischen Jesus*, Tübingen 1960, pp. 219-37, Was ist ein Sprachereignis? loc. cit., pp. 424-30, Gerhard Ebeling, Wort Gottes und Hermeneutik, in: *Wort und Glaube* I, Tübingen 1960, pp. 319-48. The object of hermeneutics is that the original 'Sprachereignis' (speech event) which is fixed in the text is to become language again and prevail in a translation process in which readers are interpreted by the text rather than vice versa. Similarly, Paul Ricoeur, *Interpretation Theory. Discourse and Surplus of Meaning*, Fort Worth 1976, p. 45f., emphasises 'a semantic surplus of meaning', which prevails.
105. As emphasised by Wolfgang Schenk, Hermeneutik III. Neues Testament, *TRE* 15 (1986), pp. 144-50.
106. See Fuchs, *Marburger Hermeneutik*, p. 25, which speaks of methodology as a decay phenomenon compared to true hermeneutics; this is probably associated with the fact that what is crucial is that the speech act itself must prevail; therefore it should not concern specific methodic notions. Another example is Stuhlmacher, *Verstehen*[1], p. 205ff., which in extension of Bultmann's interest in preconception develops a 'Hermeneutik des Einverständnisses' and stresses that all interpretation methods will be encumbered by faults. Cf. the criticism of this scepticism in Schenk, *TRE* 15, p. 145f., where it is pointed out 'dass es gar keinen anderen Weg zur Überwindung von Irrtümern gibt als wissenschaftliche Methoden ...'
107. Cf. the conclusion in Stuhlmacher, *Verstehen*[1], p. 219.
108. Thus Fuchs, *Marburger Hermeneutik*, p. 207.

the basic exegetic work.[109] This has contributed to the methodical uncertainty which, as far as I can judge, is the cause of the criticisable use of traditio-historical arguments in the interpretation of Rom 6.

In view of the methodical scepticism which applied when I began this work, I have chosen to justify a methodical practice on a common-sense level. I can take as my point of reference the actual circumstances: in practical work everyone assumes that it is meaningful to interpret the New Testament texts and to argue conclusively for definite views. The large amount of secondary literature bears witness to this. It must also be possible to make the understanding of the text's content the subject of methodical analysis, and I believe that a clear historical exegesis gives the best foundation for presenting a valid understanding. And it seems to me that at the practical level some simple solutions to the hermeneutic problems may be given.

First, it should be established that a distinction must be made between exegesis, where one questions the text's content and meaning, and historical criticism, where one assesses the text in relation to contemporary currents and events. This is a classical distinction which Bultmann also used in the confrontation regarding the indicative-imperative understanding. Before the texts can be used as a source for other matters, one must first have understood the text's own meaning and intention.[110] For this reason he disputes the approach to the texts in which one contents oneself with an historical explanation. The same recognition now again comes to the fore, in that the first stage in the discussion of the New Testament texts must be an elementary interpretation of the texts that can be presented and tested.[111]

109. Frederik Torm, *Nytestamentlig Hermenevtik*[2], Copenhagen 1938, p. 204ff., still distinguishes between exegesis which is primary, and historical criticism, which comes in when necessary. Bultmann also has this differentiation in certain passages, cf. note 110 below. This differentiation was subsequently out of the picture. Heinrich Zimmermann, *Neutestamentliche Methodenlehre*[2], Stuttgart 1967, p. 17, is typical, where the historical-critical method is presented as 'der Weg der Exegese', which is followed by an introduction to textual criticism, literary criticism, and the history of form and redaction. Only recently has the necessity of an elementary text interpretation been rediscovered, cf. note 111 below.
110. See Bultmann, Problem, p. 124, *Glauben* II, p. 213f., 222f., where it seems that the work of understanding the text's 'Sinn' or 'Intention', which must precede the historical-critical application, is at least included as an exegesis which makes use of formal analysis and philological method, so that we arrive at the same classical division as in Torm, cf. note 109 above. Cf. also Bultmann, *Glauben* I, p. 123f.
111. See Klaus Berger, *Exegese des Neuen Testaments*[2], Heidelberg 1977, p. 11ff., (about text linguistics), Georg Strecker and Udo Schnelle, *Einführung in die neutestamentliche Exegese*, Göttingen 1983, pp. 40-44 (about text analysis), cf. also Sigfred Pedersen (ed.), *Skriftsyn og metode. Om den nytestamentlige hermeneutik* [View of scripture and method. On the New Testament hermeneutics], Århus 1989, where Chapter 14, pp. 289-307, is an article by Johannes Nissen, Tekst og kontekst. Om teksten som kommunikation [Text and Context. On Text as Communication]. Especially clear consideration is given to the principle in

If we then look at the exegetic work of understanding the subject-matter of the text, a distinction must be made between the two aspects of the hermeneutic problem-complex. The problem-complex is partly historical: one must understand a text which is alien by virtue of the time-related, environmental and linguistic distance. And partly there is a general problem of understanding, which becomes acute in theology: how something which is alien in the sense that it is new and unknown (like the effects of God's act of salvation) can be made understandable if understanding assumes preunderstanding. And how can this be presented linguistically if language's possibilities of expression are tied up with normal usage and thus with what is generally occurring?[112]

This distinction is important, since the problems are in principle resolved in two widely different ways.

The interpreter must resolve the problem of the text's historical aspect. One must obtain knowledge of the circumstances of the time, become failiar with the language and with ideas of the time. This is a translation problem.

Wilhelm Egger, *Methodenlehre zum Neuen Testament. Einführung in linguistische und historisch-kritischen Methoden*[2], Freiburg 1990, p. 13ff., where it is also (p. 25) established that these synchronous methods are a prerequisite for diachronous (historical-critical) methods — which is also carried through in the structure of the book. Also in Stuhlmacher, *Verstehen*[2], p. 219, is there receptivity to the recognition that a treatment of the text itself must precede all textual and traditio-historical reconstructions, and it is sought to incorporate this in the specific work (p. 240ff.), so that a slide has occurred in relation to the earlier position, cf. note 106 above. Schenk, *TRE* 15, p. 147f., indicates in principle the problems associated with the lack of a theory of interpretation and the necessity of working both exegetically and critically; he also considers, like many others, that this lack can be redressed by reorientation towards semiotics or communications theory, p. 144. But since such a generally accessible theory, which can form the basis of exegetic discussion, has not yet been prepared, it in any case continues necessary to present one's interpretations on a common-sense level.

112. In Bultmann also one can find a differentiation between these two aspect of the problem-complex, although to him they are so closely associated that they can never be isolated from one another, but are resolved together by means of the existential interpretation. See thus Bultmann, *Glauben* II, p. 211ff. (Das Problem der Hermeneutik), where the point of reference is clearly the first problem that can be resolved because present-day man has a pre-understanding by virtue of the fact that he lives in the same historical world as the author, marked by the fact that human existence is 'ein Sein in einer Umwelt, im verstehenden Umgang mit Gegenständen und mit Mitmenschen' (p. 219); this common horizon of understanding can be described by the existentials. The other problem emerges later (p. 231ff.) and it discussed separately in other articles, thus *Glauben* I, p. 294ff., 117ff.; the question here is whether natural man can have a pre-understanding of divine reality. He has a certain limited pre-understanding of who God is — not actual knowledge but merely the question of God who in the pre-Christian existence is reflected in a strained endeavour towards salvation. This and the true perception of existence, which rests upon belief in God, can be described by existentials, cf. *Glauben* II, p. 82, 231f., *Glauben* I, p. 126f.

It involves overcoming the distance with the aid of historical study in a broad sense.

The second problem also has initially quite a simple solution: it was the author's task to resolve it. It is he who wishes to communicate something, or persuade about something. One must therefore assume that he has done everything to make the matter clear. This applies when something transcendent or revolutionary is to be asserted, and when views must be presented of a more down-to-earth nature. He can use many means: underlinings, a clearly marked structuring, certain forms which signal what he intends, images whenever existing linguistic terms are insufficient, frequent repetitions, and so on. The author will characteristically express himself by using an abundance of information in order that the message can sink in, even if the recipient should be unable to comprehend some of the ways and means.[113] In principle, only interest, a ready response and an open mind are required on the part of the recipient. And here what is concerned is indeed not to remove the alien aspect from the content.

In practice, the two problems are contiguous in interpreting the New Testament, and this makes matters difficult. The interpreter must overcome the historical distance simultaneously with understanding the author's intention. This sets a limit to direct understanding, so that often one must proceed by analysis of the work, and frequently understanding must take on the nature of a draft. But this is precisely why it is important to distinguish between the two aspects of the task, so that one can know what to do, and do it in the correct sequence.

A number of points follow from these considerations: that the simplest, least complicated interpretation of a section of text is generally the most probable; that interpretation of Paul's intention must be the starting point in

---

113. This is the pragmatic explanation of the fact that there are linguistic dynamics in the texts, so that the reader becomes interpreted by the text, as stressed in 'the new hermeneutics', and that there is a 'semantic surplus of meaning' in the texts, as assumed by Ricoeur, cf. note 104. This also means that *the author* has sought to include the readers' pre-understanding and prepared the way for the understanding which is so important in the hermeneutic interpretation principle, cf. notes 102-6 above. On the one hand, this means that there is no longer the same basis for hermeneutic scepticism — it becomes possible to analyse the means the author uses to speak to the recipients' pre-understanding — and on the other hand it then becomes clear that the use of religious terminology and traditional usage is not necessarily an expression of the background to the concepts; there may also be a 'foreground', in the sense that the author must use the recipients' conceptual world to make his message understood, cf. again the idea of 'Anknüpfung und Widerspruch' in Bultmann, *Glauben* II, p. 117ff.

dealing with the individual texts;[114] that important aids here include philo-logy[115] and an understanding of the historical period in the general religious, social and other circumstances; and also that, when interpreting the intention, it is normally *not* relevant to use historical methods concerned with the development which preceded the genesis of the text, i.e. a form-, religio- or traditio-historical reconstruction of the concept's prehistory, or source-critical distinctions between concepts adopted and Pauline redaction. The aim of the text cannot lie in the specific trend or the special nuances one finds when comparing possible originals and parallels, since the recipients were not trained in historical criticism and had no parallel material, but had to rely on what is directly expressed in the text. If it comes to light that Paul modifies and distances himself from an adopted tradition, this must be emphasised; otherwise it will be overlooked.[116]

Apart from interpretation of the intention, there is *in the second place* yet another task in dealing with the text — i.e. to delve back into the text and investigate its basis.

In practice, it is not reasonable simply to restrict oneself to the available text.[117] After the work of understanding the text's subject-matter, one can

114. It must be emphasised that this promotion of the Pauline intention should not be confused with the romantic interest in the author's personality in Schleiermacher (Fr.D.E. Schleiermacher (Heinz Kimmerle ed.), *Hermeneutik²*, Heidelberg 1974, p. 147, 165f.), Wilhelm Dilthey (*Gesammelte Schriften V*, Leipzig 1924, p. 332 etc.) and Torm (*Hermeneutik*, p. 8, 15f.), cf. Bultmann's confrontation (*Glauben* II, p. 211ff.). Paul's psyche is wholly subordinate in this context — one must merely assume that he is reasonably normal, so that he wishes to make himself understood in his letters. The intention is then what is actually written in the texts, and as is shown there is an orientation towards the recipient's situation.

115. Cf. Bultmann, *Glauben* II, p. 212ff.

116. This is the reason for my scepticism towards the modification interpretation of Rom 6. It cannot be denied that in some instances Paul may have made use of the technique of playing on concepts that the adversary has employed or agrees with, twisting them so that a new point arises — cf. Berger, *Exegese*, p. 95ff., where this becomes the actual communication model. But in that case we can no longer regain this point with sufficient certainty. This will scarcely occur in the Letter to the Romans, since there is not a high degree of mutual knowledge between Paul and the Romans, which is a precondition for understanding a modification not directly indicated.

117. The request for textual autonomy, which played an important part in the breakthrough of structuralism and semiotics, cf. Geert Hallbäck, *Strukturalisme og eksegese* [Structuralism and Exegesis], Copenhagen 1983, p. 152f., may provide meaning as regards the gospel texts. But this becomes something different when the request is extended to apply to Paul's Letters as in Ricoeur, *Theory*. For him, the reference in the text does not concern the contemporary world but a world 'before the text', a world to which the text is an opening (cf. in particular p. 37, 94). 'The letters of Paul are no less adressed to me than to the Romans, the Galatians, the Corinthians, and the Ephesians' (p. 93). As it is emphasised in this connection that the decisive point is the text's intention, and that in this con-

use it as a source in regard to matters which are not its actual subject but is implied in the text.[118] By this means one can obtain further historical understanding.

In Paul's letters especially, it is important to go behind the text in a re-constructing way, since our theological interest does not coincide directly with what is the specific Pauline intention. In a given situation, Paul ad-dresses the communities with a definite aim and with arguments supporting his views. This is not direct proclamation of the new message; the letters are directed at people who are already Christians. Paul often starts from a fun-damental Christian doctrine common to him and the community, referring to it and using it as a conclusive basis for his arguments. Points are adduced which are used relative to the community's situation, and that means in par-ticular ethical, social and other consequences that can be adduced from the gospel in the early days of the church. These consequences are relatively simple to understand, since this is where Paul wishes to go. But it is not this that most interests us. The aim is to find our way to where Paul comes from — that is, the common faith and perception of existence which he takes as his starting point. Paul often refers very briefly to Christianity's central content, which he shares with the communities. We must therefore get behind the text in a reconstructing way if we wish to gain a true insight into the principal point. And here we will need to use historico-critical methods.

From these considerations it follows: that after the exegesis must come an examination of the text's historical background and possible origin; that this second, reconstructive part of the work on the text may be quite com-plicated, with a certain margin of uncertainty and attempts at resolution in the nature of a draft; and that religio- and traditio-historical considerations have their place in this second part of the discussion of the text — and really come into their own here. Once one has understood the text and its in-tention, one has a reasonable basis for further analyses. One has a more pre-cise evaluation as regards which religio-historical texts and concepts may be valid as parallels to those of Paul. And the traditio-historical work becomes more certain — both that part of it in which a comparison is made with pa-rallel New Testament texts and that part in which one refers back from the available text to the possible sources, assumed traditions, formulae and the like.[119]

---

nection it is a misunderstanding to take into consideration the recipients' opportunities for understanding, the practical consequence becomes a reversion to a misunderstood reading of the letters as epistles.

118. Cf. again Bultmann, *Glauben* II, pp. 213-23.

119. There are thus two different sides to the work on the history of tradition, as is also to be seen from the discussion of Rom 6; cf. above in association with note 45 and note 48.

3.2. The procedure in this work

These guidelines should be used when interpreting Rom 6.1-14, as well as texts included as we go along.

In the second main part of the thesis, the text and its context are treated in two stages. First, interpretation of the Pauline intention, where the emphasis is on the structure and other measures. This is prepared by way of a chapter on the preceding context, Rom 5, and a separate chapter on the introductory verses in Rom 6, where the structure is made clear. Otherwise, the examination of each section of text begins with an interpretation of its aim and points. Thereafter I search back passage by passage to the conceptual background and the presumed Christology and understanding of baptism.

The exegesis is preceded by some preparatory studies of the historical background. In context, these serve a dual purpose.

Since much parallel material and many theories concerning the conceptual background of Rom 6 have been presented in the course of time, a preliminary (critical) presentation of the material is useful. As already emphasised, the final treatment of the question of preconditions and background can take place only as a second stage in the actual discussion of the text. But then this can be done more simply and clearly if the material has already been presented and to some extent processed. In this way a clear basis is provided for religio- and traditio-historical comparisons.

At the same time, these preparatory studies will also throw light on the general religious currents in and around the primitive Christian communities. This is an important part of the period-historical background to Rom 6, and thus a precondition for the exegesis. And this is in fact why I wish to deal with the historical material in the first major part.

I begin with a religio-historical chapter on Hellenistic mystery religion as a possible precondition for the Pauline understanding of baptism. This is followed by a chapter on the concepts of baptism in the Hellenistic communities. Then comes a chapter on the primitive Christian communities' baptismal practice and its premises in the Judeo-Christian environment.

Part One
Preparatory studies
of the historical background

II
Hellenistic mystery religion as a background to baptism

1. Problem complex

The starting point must therefore be the consideration of certain mysteries as a background to Rom 6, and I shall then move on to a more general description of Hellenistic religion. This also corresponds to the development of the debate.

Theories on the connection between the mysteries and Christian baptism gradually emerged on the basis of studies of many different religious contexts. This led to the religio-historical school's conviction that Rom 6 had parallels in the contemporary mystery religions. These scholars assumed that baptism was perceived as a symbolic submergence into death with Christ and a corresponding emergence to resurrection and apotheosis. They meant to find in the mysteries similar acts of baptism with a ritual repetition of a god's death and resurrection, leading to the rebirth and divinity of the initiate. The original loose and general theories have been expanded by more religio-historical material.[1]

The Eleusinian mysteries are said to include ideas on rebirth and the ritual repetition of a deity's journey to the kingdom of the dead and back again.[2] The most frequent references are to the Isis mysteries of Apuleius, Metamorphoses 11, with baptism, absolution, descent into the kingdom of the dead and subsequently divinity as the crucial elements.[3] There is a

---

1. See Holtzmann, *Lehrbuch* II¹, p. 178ff., Pfleiderer, *Urchristentum* I², p. 294ff., 333f., Gunkel, *Verständnis*, p. 83ff. Development from the first general references to the increasing documentation can be observed in Heitmüller, in *Taufe*, 1903, p. 14ff., the mystical is emphasised in the primitive Christians' sacraments, whereas the dependence of the mysteries as regards baptism is merely indicated (p. 23) and postulated (p. 52f.); in *Taufe*, 1911, p. 23f., there are references to specific cultic connections.
2. Thus Dieterich, *Mithrasliturgie*, p. 163f., 167, cf. p. 176f., Lietzmann, *Römer*, p. 67, Loisy, *Mystères*, p. 275, Leipoldt, *Taufe*, p. 64ff., 38ff., Fritz Wehrli, Die Mysterien von Eleusis, *ARW* 31 (1934), pp. 77-104; p. 100f., Lohse, *Umwelt*, p. 174f., cf. Gäumann, *Taufe*, p. 40.
3. Thus Dibelius, *Botschaft* II, p. 30ff., Bousset, *Kyrios*, p. 113ff., Reitzenstein, *Mysterienreligionen*, p. 20ff., 41ff., 220ff., Gäumann, *Taufe*, p. 41ff., Lohse, *Umwelt*, p. 176, Betz, *Nachfolge*, p. 172ff., Käsemann, *Römer*, p. 153, J. Gwyn Griffiths, *Apuleius of Madauros, The*

general reference to the Osiris, Attis and Adonis mysteries, which are said to have their centre in the dying and resurrected vegetation deities.[4] The Attis cult in particular has attracted interest because of attempts to reconstruct a cult festival in March with bloody rites in which the mystes celebrates resurrection united with Attis, and also a blood-baptism which is associated with rebirth.[5] In addition, three individual texts play a part in the reasoning, the 'Themistios fragment',[6] the 'Mithras liturgy'[7] and the 'Naasene sermon', the most important evidence of the gnostic development of mystery religiousness.[8]

In the latest phase of development, the theories have again become more general. The descriptions of mystery-religious parallel concepts seem remarkably vague. This has several reasons.

It is to some extent a consequence of the debate on the interpretation of Rom 6 described in the introductory chapter. The interpretation of the religio-historical material has been challenged; in no place is it possible to demonstrate a consolidated understanding of mystical baptism which is parallel to New Testament concepts. This was attested by Wagner,[9] and in

---

Isis-Book (*EPRO* 39), Leiden 1975, p. 52, Helmut Köster, *Einführung in das Neue Testament*, Berlin 1980, p. 195f., Schnelle, *Gerechtigkeit*, p. 77.

4. Thus Otto Pfleiderer, *Die Entstehung des Christentums*, Berlin 1907, p. 147f., Paul Wendland, *Die hellenistisch-römische Kultur* (*HNT* 1.2), Tübingen 1912, p. 155f., Bultmann, *Theologie*, p. 142, Lohse, *Umwelt*, p. 173, 176f. But there is no relevant specific material from the Adonis cult to refer to; it is merely asserted that it is a dying and resurrecting God such as Attis and Osiris. Dionysus and Mithras are also mentioned in this context but with no parallels to New Testament baptism concepts.

5. Cf. Hugo Hepding, *Attis seine Mythen und sein Kult* (*RGGV* 1), Giessen 1902, p. 196ff., Bousset, *Kyrios*, p. 114, 138, Reitzenstein, *Mysterienreligionen*, p. 22, 45f., 81f., Leipoldt, *Taufe*, p. 43f., 63, Lohse, *Umwelt*, p. 177.

6. The fragment, to be found in Johannes Stobaeus, Anthologium 52.49, is said, according to Dieterich, *Mithrasliturgie*, p. 163f., Hepding, *Attis*, p. 196, Braun, *Studien*, p. 149, Gäumann, *Taufe*, p. 44f., to show that the mysteries were generally celebrated as a ritual death and transition to a new life.

7. The item from a magical papyrus is thus defined in Dieterich, *Mithrasliturgie*, which is presented as a version of and comment on it. According to him and Reitzenstein, *Mysterienreligionen*, p. 46ff., Braun, *Studien*, p. 148ff., Gäumann, *Taufe*, p. 44, it is said to contain an original cultic immortality magic in which death and rebirth again play an important part.

8. Especially Dibelius, *Botschaft* II, p. 68f., Bousset, *Kyrios*, p. 137ff., Bultmann, *Theologie*, p. 171, 298 (indirectly), refer to this text handed down in Hippolytus (Elenchus 5.7.3-5.9.11). There are only rare references to other specific gnostic material, especially texts from Corpus Hermeticum, cf. below, section 3.2, with notes 178 and 182.

9. In Wagner, *Problem*, the external position of baptism is consistently pointed out (p. 78ff.: against Eleusinian baptism: p. 109ff.: against the significance of Isis baptism; p. 257ff.: against interpretation of the Taurobolium as blood-baptism); only exceptionally is there a ritual imitation of the fate of a deity, i.e. in the Tammuz cult in which a sick disciple

general terms this appears to be the opinion of religio-historical research. As is shown by examination of the specific material, no one any longer wishes to assert that the whole of the assumed mystery-religious complex is to be found in a single cult. This is not however intended to be sufficient to form a refutation. It is still possible that there was a common mystery-theology in the Hellenistic syncretistic environment, or merely a mystical way of thinking with this content.[10] Also, Paul is said to be indirectly and to some extent negatively dependent upon the mysteries, and a direct accordance should not therefore be expected.[11]

But in any case there has always been a strange ambiguity when mystical concepts are interpreted as parallels to New Testament baptism texts. This is true of the effects the mysteries are said to have. Is it worldly happiness and certainty of a better lot in the life to come?[12] Or is it a matter of immediate salvation and apotheosis by virtue of the rituals?[13] Do the initia-

can go through a ritual death to become free of his sickness (cf. p. 160ff.), and the Egyptian death-cult in which the events surrounding the death of Osiris are imitated (p. 131ff.), but nowhere associated with an actual resurrection as regards the god (p. 149ff. and p. 126ff.). Concerning all religions he rejects that the initiation was in the form of the mystes's death and resurrection (p. 280), except the Isis mystery in which it is not excluded that death symbolism exists as the introduction to a new period of life, but an imitation of Osiris is sharply rejected (cf. p. 113ff.).

10. This plays a crucial part in the reasoning in Gäumann, *Taufe*, p. 39f., 44f., in which there are polemics against Wagner's method of concentrating on the individual cult connections, cf. Lohse, *Umwelt*, pp. 171-79, Thyen, *Studien*, p. 197 n. 1, and the criticism in Conzelmann (rec.), Wagner, p. 171f. But Wagner does not overlook this possibility. He characterises it in *Problem*, p. 281, as an arbitrary hypothesis which can be neither proved nor disproved, cf. also Martin P. Nilsson, *Geschichte der griechischen Religion* II (*HAW* V 2. Teil 2. Band)², Munich 1961, p. 685ff., Marcel Simon, Á propos de l' École comparatiste, in: R. Hamerton-Kelly and R. Scroggs, *Jews, Greeks and Christians* (*StJLA* 21), Leiden 1976, pp. 261-70; p. 269, Köster, *Einführung*, p. 202ff. This reference thus cannot in itself shake Wagner's assertion. It must be substantiated — or at least made probable — that such an association of ideas existed in the mystery-religious environment. In any case it may be profitable to examine the syncretistic environment, since it may give a more subtle picture of the religious currents and opportunities for exerting influence, cf. Wedderburn, *Baptism*, p. 139ff.

11. There remains, then, a complicated transmission process via the common environment by way of Hellenistic community theology (as emphasised by Gäumann, *Taufe*, p. 38f., 46ff., Schnelle, *Gerechtigkeit*, p. 78, 80f.) to Paul who adopts critical and modifying (cf. Chapter 1, section 2.3 on this wide-spread interpretation). Wedderburn also thinks it means that Wagner's criticism does not entirely hit the target, Paul, p. 817f., *Baptism*, p. 38.

12. Thus are the effects typically presented when the individual mysteries are examined — cf. Gäumann, *Taufe*, p. 41, 43 with n. 62 and p. 45 with n. 95, Lohse, *Umwelt*, p. 174.

13. Thus are the effects of the mysteries often presented when generalised (and when there is direct comparison with Rom 6) — Lietzmann, *Römer*, p. 65f., Leipoldt, *Taufe*, p. 62f., Bultmann, *Theologie*, p. 297f., Gäumann, *Taufe*, p. 49, 75f. with n. 66, Lohse, *Umwelt*, p. 173.

tion rites give rise to a repetition of the deity's struggle with life and death, and does the mystes participate in the same fate as the god?[14] Or is it simply that fusion with the deity occurs[15]? A different question is how can one imagine that these rites achieve their effect. Is the effective aspect the external process only, i.e. that the god's death and resurrection are played out or imitated by the mystes?[16] Or is the cult drama and cult myth simply the frame around a content consisting of different traditional agents which create the contact with and insight into the divine?

In the following, the cults and rites referred to will be discussed — not in depth but in regard to their relevance to the New Testament understanding of baptism. This material has been intensively studied, but there are several reasons for presenting it as clearly as possible.

A survey of the specific material is in itself of importance to the evaluation of any connection with the New Testament understanding of baptism, since the confusion probably means that many hesitate to adopt a definitive attitude towards the problem.

Once the actual material has been presented in the following section, one has a basis for the submission and evaluation of various interpretations of the individual mysteries and their effects.

Finally, the material can set the stage for the considerations that follow in section 3. This is the open question of what the common Hellenistic-syncretistic environment may signify.

2. Material and interpretations

2.1. The Eleusinian mysteries

Although many sources deal with the Eleusinian mysteries, it should be noted that our knowledge of their central features is restricted and uncertain. This results from the universally respected imposition of secrecy, the fact that the sources cover a period of more than a millennium, and that the history of the mysteries can be traced back further centuries. This makes reconstruction difficult.

---

14. The emphasis lies in the analogy between deity and mystes in Lietzmann, *Römer*, p. 67, Leipoldt, *Taufe*, p. 62, Gäumann, *Taufe*, p. 45f.
15. A unio mystica is assumed by Gunkel, *Verständnis*, p. 84, Reitzenstein, *Mysterienreligionen*, p. 22, and especially Bousset, *Kyrios*, p. 138 etc., Karl-Werner Tröger, *Mysterienglaube und Gnosis in Corpus Hermeticum* XIII (*TU* 110), Berlin 1971, p. 80.
16. Thus especially Heitmüller, *Taufe*, 1903, p. 14, Bousset, *Kyrios*, in which the sacramentalistic automatic is emphasised, cf. Lohse, *Umwelt*, p. 179, Tröger, *Mysterienglaube*, p. 13.

The exterior framework of the main sequence of events is reasonably clear.

We are aware of the mythological basis of the Homeric Hymn to Demeter, which also deals with the establishment of the Eleusinian mysteries.[17] The narrative's framework, verses 1-89 and verses 301-473, is the legend of Kore's (or Persephone's) abduction, which we also know about from other sources.[18] Aidoneus, the lord of the underworld, captures the grain-goddess' daughter and takes her to his subterranean kingdom. Demeter mourns her daughter and fights to get her back by halting the growth of grain. The other gods intervene and reach a settlement under which Kore is to stay one-third of the year with Aidoneus as queen of the underworld and the rest of the year on the earth with her mother. The central part of the hymn, verses 90-300, which takes place within this framework, is concerned with what happened when, during her search, Demeter arrives at Eleusis, unrecognised in the form of an old woman. She is accepted into King Celeus' house and is employed as nurse to the baby son Demophon. Several strange episodes are recounted, which apparently correspond to the rites of the Eleusinian cult, probably the introductory part of the sequence of events.[19] Verses 192-211 tell how the mourning Demeter is encouraged by the servant girl Iambe. She refuses to sit down until Iambe arrives with a simple footstool, over which she spreads a ram's hide. Demeter then sits with a veil over her face and in deep sorrow. But Iambe makes her break her fast and enjoy a special mixed drink, κυκεών. The sequence of events as described in verses 231-300 is of special importance. In her duties with Demophon the goddess tries to make him immortal by feeding him ambrosia and causing him to undergo rites at night, during which he is placed in the fire. Since Demeter is surprised by the horrified mother the attempt partly fails; Demophon does not become immortal, but outdoes others in growth, strength, etc. In her anger the goddess reveals herself as Demeter. To placate her, Celeus arranges for a temple to be built to her. The end of the hymn, verses 473-89, also tells that after the settlement in regard to Kore Demeter returns to Eleusis and establishes her mysteries, which improve the initiates' fortunes.

The public part of the great mysteries, which were celebrated annually

---

17. The Homeric Hymn 2 dates from about 600 BC, cf. George E. Mylonas, *Eleusis and the Eleusinian Mysteries*, Princeton 1961, p. 41, N.J. Richardson (ed.), *The Homeric Hymn to Demeter*, Oxford 1974, p. 5ff. The hymn probably relates secondarily to the cult. See the survey in Richardson (p. 121ff.) as regards the cult's obscure origin and possible background in harvest festival and fertility rites.
18. For example Cicero, Verr. 4.106ff., Ovid, Fasti 6.393-620, Diodor, 5.2-5, Firmicus Maternus De err. 7.1-7; 8.3 (euhemeristic version), Arnobius, Adv. nat. 5.24-25.
19. Cf. Richardson, *Hymn*, p. 22.

from the 15th day to the 23rd day of the autumn month of Boëdromion, can be reconstructed in some detail.[20] The following is quoted here. On the 16th day, named after the cry ἅλαδε μύσται, the mystes had to wash themselves in the sea off Athens, together with the pig they were to sacrifice. Following the great procession on the 19th day, when the participants moved on 22 kilometres to Eleusis, the initiation itself took place during the night of 20th and 21st and continued the following night. We know from a number of inscriptions that a chosen child had a special, honourable role somewhere in the sequence of events.[21]

The physical surroundings are known from excavations. The spot where the rites themselves took place, the Telesterium, together with the most sacred place, the Anactoron, has also been excavated. It may be noted that the Telesterium was at no time very large in relation to the number of people participating — about 50 metres by 50 metres when at its largest — and that it included no crypt or basin.[22] A relief from Eleusis has also attracted attention. It depicts a large figure of a woman holding her right hand over a small naked man. The hand is probably holding a bowl. The image might represent a baptism in which the goddess herself pours water over the mystes.[23]

We are also given a reasonable amount of information about the effect of the mysteries, not only as regards the expectations concerning the mysteries' power but also as regards the immediate pleasure of participating in the celebrations. One was permitted to give free expression to this.

The Homeric Demeter hymn reads thus, 'Happy is he among all people on earth who has seen the mysteries. But he who is not initiated into them and who has no part in them never attains a share in anything similar when after death he finds himself in murky darkness ... All those among the people of the earth whom these goddesses love are abundantly happy. They immediately sent as guest to the great house Plutus, who gives immortal people riches'.[24]

---

20. Much source material has been collected in Nicolaus Turchi (ed.), *Fontes historiae mysteriorum aevi hellenistici*, Rome 1930, §§ 94ff., cf. Mylonas, *Eleusis*, p. 243ff., Kuss, *Römerbrief*, p. 346f.
21. See in particular *Inscriptiones Graecae* I², 6, cf. Walter Burkert, *Homo necans* (RGVV 32), Berlin 1972, p. 309f., Wedderburn, *Baptism*, p. 319.
22. See Mylonas, *Eleusis*, plate 6 and p. 268ff., 314, Wagner, *Problem*, p. 89.
23. Cf. Johannes Leipoldt, Darstellungen von Mysterientaufen, Ἄγγελος 1 (1925), p. 46 and Tafel 1, Taufe, Abb. 1 and p. 38ff., Mylonas, *Eleusis*, plate 70.
24. Hom. hymn 2.480-82,486-89:
    ὄλβιος ὃς τάδ' ὄπωπην ἐπιχθονίων ἀνθρώπων·
    ὃς δ' ἀτελὴς ἱερῶν, ὅς τ' ἄμμορος, οὔ ποθ' ὁμοίων
    αἶσαν ἔχει φθίμενός περ ὑπὸ ζόφῳ εὐρώεντι ...

It reads in Pindar: 'Happy is he who has seen these mysteries and goes below the earth. He knows the end of life, and he knows the god-given beginning'.[25]

Philosophers have also felt drawn to the Eleusinian mysteries. Plato leans on them when he has to describe the awareness of the true being which the soul has entered in its pre-existent life. He describes it as an initiation 'into the mysteries which can in truth be called the most happy'; the emphasis is on the pure, serene experience.[26] Cicero praises the Eleusinian mysteries directly (the Athens' mysteries), which are seen as the direct opposite to the wild Bacchanalian festivals: '... by virtue of the so-called initiation we have in fact obtained knowledge of the principles of life, and we have not only obtained knowledge of how to live happily but also of how to die with a better hope'.[27]

Problems arise as regards the initiation rite itself.

From contemporary pagan sources we know only a few external facts. We know that the initiation contained three elements: δρώμενα, dramatic incidents, λεγόμενα, sacred words, and δεικνύμενα, display of sacred objects.[28] We also know that besides the actual and general initiation degree, τελέτη, there was a further initiation degree, ἐποπτεία = the vision, which could be achieved the following year.[29] From the designation of the supreme priest, the hierophant, we can conclude that great importance was given to visual impressions. It is clear from a comment by Plutarch that a strong light appeared when the door to the holy of holies was opened.[30]

A passage from Hadrian's time tells us that the sacred fire played a crucial part in Eleusis.[31] A fragment from Apollodorus of Athens reads:

... μεγ' ὄλβιος ὄν τιν' ἐκεῖναι
προφονέως φίλωνται ἐπιχθονίων ἀνθρώπων·
αἶψα δ' οἱ πέμπουσιν ἐφέστιον ἐς μέγα δῶμα
Πλοῦτον, ὃς ἀνθρώποις ἄφενος θνητοῖσι δίδωσιν.

25. Fragment 137 = Clement of Alexandria, Strom. 3.17.2:
    ὄλβιος ὅστις ἰδὼν <ἐ>κεῖνα <κοινὰ> εἶσ' ὑπὸ χθόνα·
    οἶδε μὲν βίου τελευτάν,
    οἶδεν δὲ διόσδοτον ἀρχάν.
    Cf. also Sophocles, Fragment 753 = Turchi, *Fontes*, § 152.
26. See Plato, Phaidr. 250 BC. That the Eleusinian mysteries are concerned is to be seen from the terminology, which corresponds to the Eleusinian (for example, ἐποπτεύοντες).
27. Cicero, De leg. 2.14.36.
28. Cf. Mylonas, *Eleusis*, p. 261ff., Richardson, *Hymn*, p. 26, 302f.
29. Plutarch, Demetr. 26,2.
30. Plutarch, De profect. virt. 81 E = Turchi, *Fontes*, § 140: ὁ δ' ἐντὸς γενόμενος καὶ μέγα φῶς ἰδών, οἷον ἀνακτόρων ἀνοιγομένων.
31. *Papiri della R. Universita di Milano* I (ed. Achille Vogliano), Milan 1937, p. 176f.: <λόγοι ' Ηρ>ακλέους μὴ ἐωμέ<νους τελ>εῖσθαι τὰ ' Ελευσίνια. <πάλαι μ>εμ<ύ>ημαι. ἀπόκλει-<σον τὴν ' Ε>λευσεῖνα καὶ τὸ πῦρ <τὸ ἱερόν,> δᾳδοῦχε, πῦρ φθό<νει νυκ>τὸς ἱερᾶς·

'When Kore is called upon, the hierophant beats the so-called bronze cymbals'.[32]

Two friezes dating from imperial times have been associated with the Eleusinian mysteries.[33] They are said to represent Hercules' initiation into the mysteries, and include three scenes: in the first a pig is sacrificed; in the second the mystes sits with a veil over his head on a strange stool on which a ram's skin is spread, while a woman holds an object (a torch or a cleaning sieve) behind him;[34] in the third scene, the mystes is participating in a procession which moves towards the goddess who sits on a basket around which winds a snake.

In evaluating these sources, the secrecy injunction presents us with the dilemma which is also present when evaluating the other mysteries: that everything we come to know, we know at the same time is of no real significance.

Fuller information comes only from the Christian fathers. But what they know is scarcely first-hand; none of the fathers say that they have been initiated into the mysteries. And these are markedly tendentious sources.

Most of the information comes from Clement of Alexandria. In Protrepticus 12.2 he gives us the more neutral information that Deo and Kore became the subjects of a mystical drama in which their wanderings, abduction and sorrow were played out with torches in Eleusis.[35] But in Protrepticus 20.1-22.5 he is very polemical, and tries to demonstrate that the rites' true nature is sexual and shameful. The Iambe episode from the Homeric hymn is to be found in a vulgarised version. The girl, here called Baubo, achieves her goal by displaying her genitalia to Demeter. An Orphic

μυστήρια <πολλῷ ἀ>ληθέστερα μεμύημαι ... τὴν Κόρην εἶδον. The text has been brought to light by W.F. Otto, Der Sinn der eleusinischen Mysterien, *Eranos* 7 (1939), pp. 83-112; p. 105f. Cf. also Burkert, *Homo*, p. 315f., K. Kerényi, *Die Mysterien von Eleusis*, Zürich 1962, p. 90f.

32. *Fragmenta graecae historicae* (ed. Jacoby), p. 244 fragment 110, cf. Burkert, *Homo*, p. 315f., Wedderburn, *Baptism*, p. 317.

33. One of these on a sarcophagus from Nova Terra, actually an 'ostothek' from the 2nd century — cf. Mylonas, *Eleusis*, fig. 84, Kerényi, *Mysterien*, Tafel 7. The other, the 'Lovatelle urn' — cf. Kerényi, *Mysterien*, Tafel 8-11. Cf. as to the interpretation Burkert, *Homo*, p. 294ff., Dieter Sänger, *Antikes Judentum und die Mysterien* (WUNT 2. Reihe 5), Tübingen 1980, p. 104f.

34. This scene is linked to the Iambe scene in the Homeric hymn, and to Aristophanes, The Clouds 254-66, which parodies the scene. There appears to be accord between the myth and the rite. See as to this W.K.C. Guthrie, *Orpheus and the Greek Religion*[2], London 1952, p. 210-12, Burkert, *Homo*, p. 295f., Sänger, *Judentum*, p. 104f.

35. Δηὼ καὶ Κόρη δρᾶμα ἤδη ἐγενέσθην μυστικὸν καὶ τὴν πλάνην καὶ τὴν ἁρπαγὴ καὶ τὸ πένθος αὐταῖν Ἐλευσὶς δᾳδουχεῖ.

hymn about this is quoted. In addition, the Eleusinian mysteries' σύνθημα[36] is given: 'I fasted, I drank the cyceon; I took from the chest, and when I had done my deed (? — ἐργασάμενος), I lay in the basket and from the basket into the chest'.[37] Clement later mentions the contents of the mystical chest in other cults. These are said to be very vulgar: objects partly trivial and partly obscene.[38] In Protrepticus 15.1, Clement says that Demeter's mystery implies a love relationship between Demeter and Zeus, like indications of a hieros gamos in the Eleusinian mysteries in other sources.[39]

Other, more obscure information about the Eleusinian mysteries is to be seen from the Naasene sermon in Hippolytus. Elenchus 5.7.34 refers to τὸ μέγα καὶ ἄρρητον 'Ελευσινίον μυστήριον 'ὕε κύε'.[40] Elenchus 5.8.39-40 asserts that in Eleusis the initiated (τοῖς ἐποπτεύουσι) were shown an ear of corn, cut off in silence, as the great, wonderful and most perfect initiation secret. The great light is mentioned, and it is said that in executing the great and ineffable mysteries the hierophant cried: 'The Mighty One has borne the holy child — Brimo has borne Brimos'.[41]

---

36. This cult symbol has been considered by Dibelius, *Botschaft* II, p. 35ff., together with similar short formulae from other cults, cf. notes 68 and 100 below. Dibelius wishes to conclude from the past-tense form that the words were not used liturgically in the initiation but subsequently as code words, parole, whereby the initiated could make themselves known to one another without disclosing anything to outsiders. Also Burkert, *Homo*, p. 303, sees it as a reference to the central sequence of events. But this does not fit as a matter of course into the Eleusis cult in which no communities or supporter groups were formed. It is more likely an admission card to the great mysteries themselves following the introductory exercises, or to the later ἐποπτεία, cf. Mylonas, *Eleusis*, p. 295, Ludwig Deubner, *Attische Feste²*, Berlin 1966, p. 80, Sänger, *Judentum*, p. 111.

37. Protr. 21.2: ἐνήστευσα, ἔπιον τὸν κυκεῶνα, ἔλαβον ἐκ κίστης, ἐργασάμενος ἀπεθέμην εἰς κάλαθον καὶ ἐκ καλάθου εἰς κίστην. Particularly enigmatic is the term ἐργασάμενος, which is perhaps for this reason in particular absent in Arnobius, Adv. nat. 5.26. This has occasioned corrections to the text, cf. Paul Foucart, *Les mystères d'Eleusis*, Paris 1914, p. 379, who reads ἐγγευσάμενος, which makes it relate to a cultic meal. This has also occasioned guesses, especially about obscene acts, cf. below.

38. In Protr. 22.4 the typical content of cultic chests is listed: various forms of pastry, salt, a snake, which is a sacred symbol for Dionysus Bassaros, and also various plants. Cultic objects in the Ge Themis cult are mentioned in particular in Protr. 22.5: ὀρίγανον, λύχνος, ξίφος, κτεὶς γυναικεῖος, ὅς ἐστιν, εὐφήμως καὶ μυστικῶς εἰπεῖν, μόριον γυναικεῖον.

39. Tertullian, Ad. nat. 2.7 = Turchi, *Fontes*, § 128, Asterius, Hom. 10 = Turchi, *Fontes*, § 133, Scholia til Gorg. = Turchi, *Fontes*, § 135.

40. The mystical expression 'rain, conceive' has also been passed down in Proclos, In Tim. 40 E = Turchi, *Fontes*, § 134, which is a cry from the Eleusinian mysteries — one must have looked towards heaven at the first word and to the earth at the second. Also, on a *public* well in Athens there is the inscription: ὕε κύε ὑπέρχυε, cf. Mylonas, *Eleusis*, p. 270.

41. Elench. 5.8.40: ἱερὸν ἔτεκε πότνια κοῦρον Βριμὼ Βριμόν. Brimos is probably a manifestation of Dionysus, cf. Burkert, *Homo*, p. 318f, against Tröger, *Mysterienglaube*, p. 16, which wishes to contend that it may be Kore despite the masculine form.

An abundance of possibilities is available if one wishes to understand the Eleusinian mysteries and their secret core. They are not mutually exclusive and must probably be combined, since a long and eventful sequence of events is concerned.[42]

One approach is to perceive the initiation as an acting-out of the goddess' sorrow or descent into the kingdom of the dead and return to life.[43] The emphasis is then on the myth and the cultic drama. Reliable information about an imitation of Kore and Demeter in the mysteries supports this interpretation, and it is clear that life and death themselves are a crucial theme in the initiation, as well as in the underlying fertility cult.[44] But an imitation of Kore does not appear to be central,[45] and it is scarcely likely that an imitation of Demeter's journey to Hades was the central part of the rite and the part from which its effect is to be perceived. The physical preconditions for this are indeed absent in the telestery in which the initiation rites themselves took place.[46] But in the course of this Demeter's sorrow has been imitated: the mystes have drunk cyceon like Demeter and, like her, sitting with head covered.[47]

Another form of interpretation is that the mystes is given new life as a child of the goddess. It is reasonable to interpret the Demophon episode from the cultic myth as an adoption rite.[48] The interpretation can also be

42. Apart from the types of interpretation below, other suggestions are also listed in Burkert, *Homo*, pp. 292-326.
43. Wehrli, *Mysterien*, p. 84ff., has indicated a Demeter imitation as the core of the mystery, seen as a death-resurrection symbolism which gives the initiate rebirth to a new life. The rebirth idea is taken from Hippolytus, Elench. 5.8.40, where it is associated not with an imitation but with a different ritual; furthermore, the theory is based on New Testament texts which are said to be dependent upon Eleusian ideas (p. 99ff.). Aimo T. Nikolainen, *Der Auferstehungsglauben in der Bibel und in ihrer Umwelt* I, Helsinki 1944, p. 78ff., sees Kore as a dying and resurrecting vegetation deity, and the imitation as a transfer of a similar fate to the initiate. Cf. also Tröger, *Mysterienglaube*, p. 13ff.
44. But the crux of the matter is of course whether the two motifs have been linked. But if one assumes that the initiate has gone through a death-resurrection process, this must not be interpreted factually as if the initiate had already arisen. The expectation concerned only a future improvement of the fate in the kingdom of the dead. What is concerned is rather a demonstration of the deity's power over life and death, giving guarantees of happiness also in the life hereafter — cf. Foucart, *Mystères*, p. 471ff., Wedderburn, *Baptism*, p. 319.
45. Cf. Wedderburn, *Baptism*, p. 317.
46. Thus Mylonas, *Eleusis*, p. 314, Wagner, *Problem*, p. 89, cf. however Burkert, *Homo*, p. 308f., in which the darkness surrounding the mystes is interpreted as a Hades experience.
47. Cf. Burkert, *Homo*, p. 295, who thinks that the mystes has also experienced blind wanderings, Wedderburn, *Baptism*, p. 319.
48. Cf. Plato, Theaet. 160 E, in which a similar rite is described as an initiation ritual when a child is born into the family, cf. Robinson, *Hymn*, p. 231, Burkert, *Homo*, p. 326, 309, Wedderburn, *Baptism*, p. 318f.

seen in the context of the cultic cry for the birth of a god-child, which thus must be the mystes. The boy chosen may have been of significance in this context.[49] As child of Demeter the mystes is within her sphere of power, and is encompassed by the same strength as she has. This is frequently associated with the σύνθημα, which Clement provides as well as information on the sexual content of the rites. The obscure term ἐργασάμενος is said to concern a manipulation of sexual symbols, especially symbols representing the female genitalia.[50] Through contact with the goddess's genitalia, the mystes was supposed to count as her new-born child. But this sexual interpretation is uncertain. It is an arbitrary interpretation of the word ἐργασάμενος which may just as well apply to acts of any other kind,[51] and it is unwise to hold to Clement's information which may be consciously distorted.[52]

A third path is to emphasise the perception of and contact with the divine achieved through participation in the rites, and whatever else is experienced in the cult.[53] The central point may have been the presentation of the ear of corn resulting from a growth miracle. There may have been cleansing fire in the anactoron.[54] The experience of the mystical scene, words and objects may have been strengthened by the intoxication that must result from imbibing the fermented cyceon after a long period of fasting.[55]

---

49. Cf. Burkert, *Homo*, p. 310, who also considers whether it is a relict of an original sacrifice, Wedderburn, *Baptism*, p. 319.
50. This sexual interpretation on the basis of Clement, Protr. 20.1ff. is widespread; thus Dieterich, *Mithrasliturgie*, p. 125, who is thinking of a phallus, Alfred Körte, Zu den eleusinischen Mysterien, *ARW* 18 (1915), pp. 116-26, who points to the female genitalia, Otto Kern, *Die griechischen Mysterien der klassischen Zeit*, Berlin 1927, p. 10f., who combines the two suggestions, Nock, *Essays*, p. 101f., cf. Burkert, *Homo*, p. 298f. If it is the case that the synthema is the admission card to the initiation, cf. note 36 above, the sexual rites asserted cannot belong to the central part of the initiation but must be an earlier, non-central rite, cf. Deubner, *Feste*, p. 83, Joseph Dey, Παλιγγενεσία (*NTA* 17.5), Münster 1937, p. 59.
51. Cf. Dey, Παλιγγενεσία, p. 59f, Deubner, *Feste*, p. 79ff., Mylonas, *Eleusis*, p. 269, 287ff., Burkert, *Homo*, p. 300, which indicates crafts such as weaving or spinning or making κυκεών, cf. note 55 below.
52. This shows itself in Protr. 20.2ff., in which Clement, apparently intentionally, seeks to give the impression that the Baubo scene, which is Orphic, and the content of the Ge Themis' cultic chest belongs to the Eleusinian cult, cf. Mylonas, *Eleusis*, p. 292, 297.
53. Cf. on this Otto, Sinn, p. 102f., Martin P. Nilsson, *Geschichte der griechischen Religion* I (*HAW* V 2. Teil, 2. Band)², Munich 1955, p. 661f., Wagner, *Problem*, p. 87, 95, Mylonas, *Eleusis*, p. 282ff., Sänger, *Judentum*, p. 112f.
54. This is indicated by the information about the strong ray of light and torch/cleaning sieve symbolism in the depictions of the sequence of the cult, cf. Burkert, *Homo*, p. 295.
55. The possibility is apparent from the synthema, cf. K. Kerényi, Voraussetzungen der Einweihung in Eleusis, in: C.J. Bleeker (ed.), *Initiation*, Leiden 1965, pp. 59-64, Burkert, *Homo*, p. 301, Sänger, *Judentum*, p. 110f. Ἐργασάμενος can thus concern participation in the

But apart from that one can abandon detailed understanding of the many individual features, since the content of the mysteries should not be reduced to an individual primitive rite with magical effects. One arrives at this more cautious interpretation if one keeps to the safest of the general features which emerge from the myth itself, from the scanty direct information, where immediate enthusiasm is expressed. What is important is vision, experience, insight, and thus close relationship with the divine.

We will now summarise the reasonably certain knowledge we have of those features of the Eleusinian mysteries which are included in theories regarding an association with the New Testament understanding of baptism.

There have been cleansing rites in the public part of the sequence of events, but a baptism cannot have been crucial to the act of initiation itself. The topography of the location is against this.[56]

The mysteries were not effective exclusively by virtue of a single ritual which, by magic, transfers the fate of the deity to whoever imitates it. The emphasis is on explanatory experience and various obscure means which may well have been attributed to magical effects, including possibly a sexually slanted fertility cult. But the crucial point was that the entire sequence of the initiation rites gave insight into and contact with the divine.

There was no concept of an immediate rebirth into divine life. The reference is unambiguously to temporary improvements of life on earth and a happier lot after death.

2.2. The Osiris and Isis mysteries

In Hellenistic times, there were both Isis mysteries and Osiris mysteries. The two deities belong in the same Egyptian mythological context. But the closeness of the connection between the mysteries bearing Osiris' name and those bearing Isis' name is not clear.

According to the myth, Osiris lived as king of Egypt. His helper was his

---

making of this κυκεών (for later use) from the grain, which may have been in the basket and chest.

56. Cf. the information above in connection with note 22. It should also be noted that the text, used in particular as proof of the central importance of baptism in the Eleusinian cult, must be disregarded here. There is Tertullian, De bapt. 5: ... certe ludis Apollinaribus et Eleusiniis tinguuntur, idque se in regenerationem et impunitatem perjuriorum suorum agere praesumunt. This is the reading of the text by Dieterich, *Mithrasliturgie*, p. 164, Lietzmann, *Römer*, p. 67, Leipoldt, *Taufe*, p. 39. But it has been demonstrated that the word Eleusiniis is formed through a conjecture of the manuscripts' Pelusiis. The groundless correction goes back to the publisher Rigaltius, with Ursinus as authority (17th century), and results from lack of knowledge of the Pelusian games. Cf. A.D. Nock, Pagan Baptism in Tertullian, *JTS* 23 (1927), pp. 281-82, Franz Joseph Dölger, *Antike und Christentum* I, Münster 1929, p. 147ff.

wife and sister, the wise Isis. In her absence, the brother Seth/Typhon lures
Osiris into a box, which he throws into the Nile. Osiris drowns. He is subsequently cut up into 14 pieces. Isis first looks for the body; later she looks for
the many pieces. She assembles the body, and Osiris continues to live with
Isis and in the underworld, whereas the son Hor(us) avenges his father. The
legend is told mainly unchanged from early pyramid texts up to Plutarch's
description in De Iside et Osiride.[57]

The myth forms the background to the Egyptian death cult. Each death
is treated as an Osiris NN. He/she is called Osiris in an imploring way; the
same practical measures are taken, in particular embalming, with the same
rites as those of which Osiris was the subject when eternal life after death
was to be ensured.[58] An old text expresses the objective as follows: 'As truly
as Osiris lives, you also live. As truly as he will not die, you also will not
die. As truly as he will not perish, you also will not perish'.[59] The remedies
that give Osiris continued life give the other dead the same lot.[60]

Similar ideas apparently played an important part in the Osiris mysteries. One of the few — but obscure — items of information on this is to be
found in Firmicus Maternus' De errore 22.1, which describes the nocturnal
cult in which there is mourning over an idol placed on a bier. After
anointing the mourners, the priest whispers:

> θαρρεῖτε, μύσται, τοῦ θεοῦ σεσωσμένου·
> ἔσται γὰρ ἡμῖν ἐκ πόνων σωτηρία.

---

57. See the account of the pyramid texts in Theodor Hopfner, *Plutarch über Isis und Osiris* I
    (*MOU* 9), Praque 1940, p. 16f. Plutarch's edition of the myth is to be found in De Iside et
    Osiride 12-21, while the other chapters render a series of 'philosophical' rationalistic int-
    erpretations to which the legend has been exposed.
58. This originally concerned the king only, but gradually it was democratised, cf. Hermann
    Kees, *Totenglauben und Jenseitsvorstellungen der alten Ägypter*, Leipzig 1926, p. 188f., Sigfred
    Morenz, *Ägyptische Religion*, Stuttgart 1960, p. 68f.
59. Pyr. 219, rendered according to Kees, *Totenglauben*, p. 226.
60. Thus Franz Cumont, *Die orientalischen Religionen im römischen Heidentum*[4], Stuttgart 1959,
    p. 91f., Wagner, *Problem* p. 131f. Sigfred Morenz, Das Problem des Werdens zu Osiris in
    der griechisch-römischer Zeit Ägyptens, in: *Religions en Égypte hellénistique et romaine*,
    Strasbourg 1969, pp. 75-91, consider that in Hellenistic times also a kind of unio mystica
    between Osiris and Osiris NN was assumed in life in the kingdom of the dead. But the
    main view is that the basis is a sharp and pervasive distinction between Osiris and Osiris
    NN in ancient times (p. 77f.). This was maintained into Hellenistic times when the clear
    distinction disappears. It is interpreted as expressing a concept of complete identification
    (p. 79ff.). But this is to happen only as a result of influence from Greek cult, since it
    marks an entirely new departure compared to the former position (p. 84f.). Cf. also Erik
    Hornung, *Der Eine und die Vielen*, Darmstadt 1971, p. 87, Wedderburn, *Baptism*, p. 305f.
    Brandon, *History*, p. 21f., Technique, p. 32 and n. 48, assume, however, a direct identi-
    fication as the consistent concept.

Later there follows Firmicus Maternus' ironic comment:

You extricate your god; you assemble the scattered stone limbs; you put the unfeeling stone in its place. Your god should thank you, give you similar gifts, want you as a companion. You should die as he dies, and live as he lives.[61]

The background to this may be an attempt to obtain while still alive the certainty of an end similar to that of Osiris.[62] Plutarch says directly that mystery initiations were established in which the entire mythical sequence of events was acted out to console men and women affected by similar misfortune.[63] The shout of joy which survives in several passages, εὑρήκαμεν, συγχαίρωμεν probably also originates from this.[64]

If we look at the Osiris mysteries in isolation, there is a connection between the fate of the deity and of the mystes; but it cannot be concluded that there was a fusion with the deity or an immediate transition to a life of divine resurrection.[65]

61. De err. 22.3. That the scattered limbs are assembled indicates the Osiris cult — an opinion that has now prevailed; thus Cumont, *Religionen*, p. 228 n. 26, Nilsson, *Geschichte* II, p. 639, Giulia Sfameni Gasparro, *Soteriology and Mystic Aspects in the Cult of Cybele and Attis (EPRO 130)*, Leiden 1985, p. 85, Wedderburn, *Baptism*, p. 208 (hesitantly). In isolation, De err. 22,1 might otherwise be interpreted in connection with the Attis cult's lamentation, as earlier assumed, thus Dieterich, *Mithrasliturgie*, p. 174, Hepding, *Attis*, p. 167, Bousset, *Kyrios*, p. 138, Reitzenstein, *Mysterienreligionen*, p. 400f., Leipoldt, *Taufe*, p. 62f., Tröger, *Mysterienglauben*, p. 29.

62. There has been a tendency to read the passage as meaning that a ritual is concerned which causes the participants to participate immediately in the deity's death and resurrection; thus Bousset, *Kyrios* p. 138, cf. Robert Turcan (ed.), *Julius Firmicus Maternus: L'erreur des religions paiennes*, Paris 1982, p. 319. 'You should die as he dies, and live as he lives!' is Firmicus Maternus' ironic comment, cf. Wagner, *Problem*, p. 238, Wedderburn, *Baptism*, p. 313.

63. In Plutarch, De Iside 27, it is said that Isis did not permit one to forget her struggle, her wanderings, her many wise and courageous acts, and it continues: ἀλλὰ ταῖς ἁγιωτάταις ἀναμίξασα τελεταῖς εἰκόνας καὶ ὑπονοίας καὶ μιμήματα τῶν τότε παθημάτων εὐσεβείας ὁμοῦ δίδαγμα καὶ παραμύθιον ἀνδράσι καὶ γυναιξὶν ὑπὸ συμφορῶν ἐχομένοις ὁμοίων καθωσίωσεν.

64. Seneca, Apocol. 13.4, Firmicus Maternus, De err. 2.9, cf. Bousset, *Kyrios*, p. 138, Lohse, *Umwelt*, p. 175, Gasparro, *Soteriology*, p. 60 n. 143.

65. Thus Wagner, *Problem*, p. 106, which despite scepticism against assuming an actual connection perceives the deity's redemption as 'typos' of that of men. In Dieterich, *Mithrasliturgie*, p. 174, Hepding, *Attis*, p. 167, Leipoldt, *Taufe*, p. 62f., cf. note 61 above, too much is read into Firmicus Maternus' evidence, especially because it is inserted into an Attis context, which also seems to be very fabricated.

The Isis mysteries became widely distributed in the second century AD.[66] We know them fairly thoroughly from Apuleius' treatment in Metamorphoses Book 11, which concerns the adoption into the Isis cult of the main character Lucius.

The initiation itself is described in the latter part of the book. But the first part presumably also reflects the nature of the Isis initiation. It speaks of Lucius' being transformed into a man again, having previously become an ass as punishment for a depraved life — and as a result of magical experiments. The goddess appears in a nocturnal vision (Metamorphoses 11.5-6). She promises Lucius that he will recover his human form when he meets her procession. When he is rid of the ass' form he must serve the goddess for the rest of his life. This will be a happy life, which will continue in the underworld in which Isis is also worshipped. As a reward for his faithful service, his earthly life will also be prolonged. Lucius is transformed as predicted (Metamorphoses 11.13). He is ordered to report to the sacred military service, whose oath of allegiance (sacramentum) he had already been requested to swear (Metamorphoses 11.15). The crowds praise Lucius. It is said that in a certain sense he is reborn — renatus quodam modo (Metamorphoses 11.16).

The initiation is preceded by a waiting period when Lucius is prepared by way of rites and teaching, which he receives direct from the goddess in dreams and from the priest Mithras, who is responsible for him. He warns Lucius against pressing for an acceleration of the initiation, which is determined by Isis alone. This would lead to certain death. 'Since (he said) the gates of hell and a guarantee of salvation were both within the scope of the goddess — indeed, the initiation itself was celebrated like a voluntary death and a merciful deliverance. In her divine power, Isis indeed selected people who had lived their lives, people whose thread of life was about to be cut (but to whom one could entrust the cult's great secrets), and in her divine providence she replaced these people on the chariot of salvation, in a certain sense reborn'.[67]

When the time comes, Lucius is informed of the further preparations, and is led from the temple to a bath-hall. After general ablutions, the priest requests forgiveness for Lucius and washes him quite clean by spraying him

---

66. Cf. Ladislav Vidman, *Isis und Sarapis bei den Griechen und Römern* (*RGVV* 29), Berlin 1970, p. 169.

67. Metam. 11.21: nam et inferum claustra et salutis tutelam in deae manu posita ipsamque traditionem ad instar voluntariae mortis et precariae salutis celebrari, quippe cum transactis vitae temporibus iam in ipso finitae lucis limine constitutos, quis tamen tuto possint magna religionis committi silentia, numen deae soleat eligere et sua providentia quodam modo renatos ad novae reponere rursus salutis curricula.

all over. For nine days Lucius must then refrain from meat and wine (Metamorphoses 11.22-23).

After this period, the initiation takes place one night between sunset and sunrise. The initiation is carried out in the holy of holies, to which only the initiated have access. There are very strict limits to what Lucius/Apuleius can recount, but there seems to be a set of scanty hints which the uninitiated are allowed to hear. Despite the limited insight it provides, this is the most important source for understanding the mystery: 'I went to the frontier of death, and when I had stepped over Proserpina's threshold and had been led through all the elements I returned. In the middle of the night I saw the sun shine with a flashing light. I stepped before the gods of the underworld and of the world of men, and I worshipped them at close quarters'.[68]

From dawn everything is in the open again. In the course of the night Lucius was arrayed in twelve stoles, and now stands arrayed in the richly ornamented Olympic stole. He holds a torch in his hand and has a crown of palm-leaves on his head, so that he looks like an idol — ad instar solis exornatus. He can celebrate the day as his happy initiation birthday (natalis sacrorum) with a banquet — and further rites on the following day (Metamorphoses 11.24). A crucial feature is the initiate's deep affection for Isis and his total dependence upon her power. This is expressed by Lucius in a eulogy which he recites on his departure (Metamorphoses 11.25). Back in Rome Lucius participates in the local Isis cult, and must go through further costly initiation rites to acquire knowledge of Osiris also.

Against this background, the essential in the Isis mystery and the importance to be attributed to it in our context must be assessed.

The main issue is the link with the deity achieved through the cult. The emphasis here is particularly on the absorption in and perception of the divine and Isis' all-embracing domain.[69] Following the preparations, this is communicated by the nocturnal vision which was presumably experienced within the framework of a symbolic journey down to the underworld and up again to life — along the path of the sun.[70] Various unknown magical rites may have had their part in this process.

---

68. Metam. 11.23: Accessi confinium mortis et calcato Proserpinae limine per omnia vectus elementa remeavi, nocte media vidi solem candido coruscantem lumine, deos inferos et superos accessi coram et adoravi de proxumo. This probably again (cf. note 36 above) concerns a synthema, as shown by Dibelius, *Botschaft* II, p. 35ff., cf. Griffiths, *Isis-Book*, p. 296, differently Wedderburn, *Baptism*, p. 303.

69. This corresponds to the general picture of Isis' role in Egyptian religion. See France Le Corsu, *Isis. Mythe et mystères*, Paris 1977, pp. 20-25, cf. C.J. Bleeker, Isis as Saviour Goddess, in: S.G.F. Brandon (ed.), *The Saviour God*, Manchester 1963, pp. 1-16; p. 8f., Sänger, *Judentum*, p. 133f., Wedderburn, *Baptism*, p. 310, cf. also Gäumann, *Taufe*, p. 43.

70. Cf. Griffiths, *Isis-Book*, p. 297, Wedderburn, *Baptism*, p. 309f.

Purification rites (not an actual baptism) were of importance in the cult — and were even associated with concepts of forgiveness of sins. They are not part of the initiation itself, but take place outside the temple ten days earlier. There is no reason to assert that the purification was associated with the life-death symbolism of the central sequence of events.[71]

There also appears to be no reason to assume that in his journey to the underworld and back the mystes repeats the fate of Osiris or of another god, thus securing immediate rebirth to a divine life fused with the god.[72] It is clear, however, that after the initiation the initiate Lucius appears as a divine figure. But this does not mean that there has been a fusion with a deity.[73] We hear nothing of the mystes sharing the lot of the deity,[74] and an Osiris imitation is unlikely since only later does Lucius obtain direct knowledge of Osiris.

Divinity is more probably granted to him by virtue of his newly-won link with Isis.[75] And this divinity should not be perceived as absolute.[76] The term *ad instar* solis directly emphasises that it is a figurative expression, in the same way as the concept of a rebirth is used in a figurative sense (both read *quodam modo* renatus).[77] This is confirmed when we see what the effect of the initiation is to be. It is indeed not a life beyond death. Lucius

71. Despite the difficulties, ablution and initiation rite are directly linked in Reitzenstein, *Mysterienreligionen*, p. 41, 221, 229f., Leipoldt, *Taufe*, p. 54, Griffiths, *Isis-Book*, p. 287ff., 298, in which it is perceived as a repetition of Osiris' death by drowning. Cf. however Dibelius, *Botschaft* II, p. 32 n. 4, Wagner, *Problem*, p. 109ff., Braun, *Studien*, p. 146, Gäumann, *Taufe*, p. 42 n. 53, Sänger, *Judentum*, p. 126, Wedderburn, *Baptism*, p. 307.

72. Contrary to Bousset, *Kyrios*, p. 113f., Hugo Gressmann, *Die orientalischen Religionen im hellenistisch-römischen Zeitalter*, Berlin 1930, p. 43 (which however speaks of rebirth and union with Osiris as an anticipation of the fate after death), Betz, *Nachfolge*, p. 72f., Tröger, *Mysterienglauben*, p. 26, cf. Griffiths, *Isis-Book*, p. 297ff., 315ff., Simon, École, p. 265, Köster, *Einführung*, p. 195f., which speaks of the mystes's symbolic death as corresponding to the New Testament term, 'death with Christ'. But note that nowhere is there a reference to a death with a deity, let alone a resurrection, cf. also Nilsson, *Geschichte* II, p. 636f., cf. p. 686, which points out that such a new existence with immortality would have been so great a gift of grace that Apuleius would not have passed it over in silence; the reference to 'death' in the ritual is interpreted as an image of the complete break with the former life.

73. There seems to be no logic that compels us to assume, with the interpreters referred to in the previous note, that one fuses together with another person because one does the same as he does, cf. on this Nock, *Essays*, p. 92.

74. Contrary to Dibelius, *Botschaft* II, p. 77.

75. Cf. note 69 above. If the Osiris myth was part of the picture during the ritual, it may have been as a reference to Isis' power over death, cf. Wedderburn, *Baptism*, p. 310.

76. Cf. Nilsson, *Geschichte* II, p. 690, Braun, *Studien*, p. 147, Gäumann, *Taufe*, p. 43 n. 62.

77. Emphasised by Wagner, *Problem*, p. 121, J. Ysebaert, *Greek Baptismal Terminology*, Nijmegen 1962, p. 115, Wedderburn, *Baptism*, p. 333.

has been given a better, more moral life, a 'militia Isiacis';[78] affiliation with the supreme god will also lead to a better lot after death.[79]

2.3. The Attis cult

The flowering and the wide spread of Attis worship beyond Asia Minor fell late in the Hellenistic period. The Cybele cult to which the Attis figure belongs was formerly wide-spread. In the year 204 BC Cybele arrived in Rome;[80] but we hear nothing of Attis worship there until imperial times[81] when the Attis mysteries were revived throughout the Hellenistic world. During this period, the cult was in continual rivalry with Christianity. This means that we have many sources which refer to Attis.[82] But since the most important sources are clearly later than the New Testament texts it is very probable that the common features here result from a spill-over from Christianity into the Attis cult.[83] In addition there is the difficulty that the material is very diffuse. On the one hand the cultic myth is to be found in different and highly varying versions, and on the other hand there are three different cultic connections associated with the mythic material: the public festival celebrated in Rome in March, culminating in the Hilaria festival; the mysteries that may have been linked to this festival;[84] and the Taurobolium, which appears to have been celebrated at all other times of the year.[85]

The best-known form of the Attis myth is probably that to be found in Ovid, Fasti 4,221-244. Briefly, this concerns Cybele who falls in love with the young and virginal Attis. She takes him into her service, and extorts from him a vow of chastity. This he breaks — with the nymph Sangistis. Both are

---

78. See Apuleius, Metam. 11.15-16. Cf. Betz, *Nachfolge*, p. 173, Griffiths, *Isis-Book*, p. 254ff., which also points out the parallelity with Rom 6.12-13,16-19.
79. Cf. especially Apuleius, Metam. 11.6, Plutarch, De Iside 27 (see note 63 above), cf. Ladislav Vidman, Isis und Sarapis, in: Maarten J. Vermaseren (ed.), *Die orientalischen Religionen im Römerreich* (OrRR) (EPRO 93), Leiden 1981, pp. 121-56; p. 142, Wedderburn, *Baptism*, p. 301.
80. During troubles in the Second Punic War, the meteorite in whose form Cybele was worshipped was taken from Phrygia to Rome as described in Ovid, Fasti 4.247f., and Livy, 29.10-11. Cf. Hepding, *Attis*, p. 142, Maarten J. Vermaseren, *Cybele and Attis the Myth and the Cult*, London 1977, p. 38ff.
81. According to Johannes Lydus (6th cent. AD), De mensibus 4.49,59 = Hepding, *Attis*, p. 75, the March festival and Dendophorion were already celebrated under Claudius.
82. Collected in Hepding, *Attis*, pp. 5-96. The complexity of the material is emphasised in Gasparro, *Soteriology*, especially in the conclusion, p. 119ff.
83. Cf. Hepding, *Attis*, p. 200 n. 7, Vermaseren, *Cybele*, p. 106.
84. Cf. the Emperor Julian, Or. 5.169 A.
85. Cf. the collection of inscriptions etc. in Robert Duthoy, *The Taurobolium* (EPRO 10), Leiden 1969, pp. 5-56. See especially p. 70 n. 5.

exposed to the wrath of the goddess. Sangistis is killed. Attis is overcome by madness. He believes that he is pursued by hostile beings with torches and whips. On the mountain of Dindyma he removes, using a sharp stone, the parts of his body which have brought him into misfortune. This is the episode which is said to be the model for the Cybele priests' ecstasies and self-castration. Nothing is said about Attis' end in the version of the myth referred to here.

In some sources Attis continues to live as a eunuch, and serves Cybele.[86] Other passages — including Ovid — assume that Attis dies: he is transformed into a pine-tree, which is the sacred tree in the Cybele cult.[87] A number of other passages say directly that Attis bleeds to death following the castration.[88] Only later, in Firmicus Maternus (fourth century AD), are there expressions which may relate to continued life.[89] This is sometimes associated with the winged Attis depicted in the second century BC.[90]

Attis' death is also central in an euhemeristic version in Diodorus, which deviates considerably from the former version.[91] Here the king's daughter Cybele is the main character. Her father kills her lover and throws away the body. Cybele rushes frenziedly to find the body of her beloved, with lamentations and noisy kettledrums, followed by other mourners.

A version of the myth from the cultic centre in Pessinus is of great significance. A short version is to be found in Pausanias, De descriptione 7.17. 10-12:[92]

86. Salustius, De diis 4.7ff., Julian, Or. 5.169 C, Lukian, De syr. dea 15.
87. Ovid, Metam. 10.103-5, Ovid, Ibis 505-6, Firmicus Maternus, De err. 27,1, Arnobius, Adv. nat. 5.39.
88. Firmicus Maternus, De err. 3.1ff., Pausanias, Descr. 7.17.10ff., Arnobius, Adv. nat. 5.7. Herodotus 1.34-35, speaks of a Lydian version in which the king's son Atys dies as a result of a hunting accident. This version was also known by Pausanias, Descr. 7.17.9.
89. De err. 3.1, in which we see the word 'revixisse' used. But it is uncertain what significance is to be attached to this word, which can mean many things from purely vegetative continued life to an existence of resurrection. Cf. Nilsson, Geschichte II, p. 648f., Wedderburn, Baptism, p. 204. See also Plutarch, De Iside 69, in which there is information that the Phrygians believed that their god sleeps during the winter and awakes during the summer.
90. See Maarten J. Vermaseren, The Legend of Attis in Roman and Greek Art (EPRO 9), Leiden 1966, p. 47. Cf. Wedderburn, Baptism, p. 205.
91. Diodorus Siculus, Biblioth. histor. 3.58 = Hepding, Attis, p. 16f.
92. Pausanias' rendering (from the 2nd. cent.) corresponds to a long version in Arnobius, Adv. nat. 5.5-7 (from the 4th cent.), cf. the synoptic presentation in Hepding, Attis, p. 37ff. Arnobius recounts far more details, partly piquant matters, partly, as stressed by Gasparro, Soteriology, p. 38ff., an interest in the various fruits, flowers and plants which form part of the sequence of events.

(It is told) that the sleeping Zeus spilled semen on the ground, and in time this produced a demon with two sets of genitalia, part male and part female. They gave it the name of Agdistis. But the gods who feared Agdistis cut off the male genitalia. An almond tree grew from them which bore ripe fruit, and the daughter of the Sangarius river — it is said — took some of the fruit. But the fruit disappeared into the lap of her clothing and she was shown to be pregnant. When she has given birth a goat cares for the discarded child. When he had grown up and in his appearance had greater beauty than a human being, Agdistis was overcome by love for the boy. But when Attis became adult his kinsmen sent him to Pessinus so that he could marry the king's daughter. When the wedding hymn was sung, Agdistis forced her way in. Attis became insane and cut of his genitalia. The bride's father also castrated himself. Agdistis repented of everything she had done to Attis, and by praying to Zeus she ensured that nothing of Attis' body putrefied or decomposed.

Apart from the indirect information available from the Attis myths, there are some sources which directly concern the cultic correlations and include Attis worship.

From the oldest times ecstatic madness has been the main characteristic of the cult. I wish here to refer in particular to a poem by Catullus which describes the arrival of a stranger at Phrygia,[93] who like another Attis is seized by madness,[94] castrates himself — and changes sex[95] — scratches himself until he draws blood and rushes about frenziedly with cymbals and tambourines, playing a flute and screaming piercingly.

In the Roman cult interest is concentrated on the Hilaria festival. We learn from Macrobius and an inscription that this was celebrated on 25 March as a festival of jubilation after a period of mourning and a 'dies sanguinis'.[96] Salustius provides important information in De diis et mundo 4.7-11.[97] A version of the myth similar to that of Ovid is made the subject

93. Catul, Cant. 63 has been placed in Attis' homeland — the madness is apparently linked to the location. The poem originates from a time when Attis was not worshipped in Rome, presumably because of the wildness the cult contained — cf. Vermaseren, *Cybele*, p. 96, 177f. Note also how it can be seen from all versions of the cult myth that the fury was a special characteristic of the cultic contexts, which is reflected upon.

94. Attis is not a true proper name but a designation for the Attis worshipper, cf. Hepding, *Attis*, p. 140, against Turchi, *Fontes*, § 246, in which this text is placed in the De Attide Mytho section.

95. This change of sex is dramatically emphasised in the text by a change from the masculine gender in v. 4 to the feminine gender in v. 8. Note also the intensity in v. 44ff. in describing the remorse over the lost sex and the desired but unsuccessful femininity.

96. Macrobius, Saturn. 1.21,10 (5th cent. AD), cf. Julian, Or. 5.168 C. The inscription CIL I², 312 (AD 354) = Hepding, *Attis*, p. 51.

97. Cf. the long description from the contemporary Emperor Julian, Or. 5.165ff., which Salustius is perhaps using.

of a philosophical, allegorical interpretation, turning the myth into cosmology:[98] the mother-god Cybele is the origin of everything; Attis is the
demiurge giving power to everything created; this he delivers to the nymph
in the form of the severed reproductive organs (this macabre variant of the
myth is to be found in Salustius); the nymph presides over the continued
process of genesis; thereafter Attis returns to the heavenly deity. The significance of the myth is then interpreted in 4.10-11:

Since the myth is thus closely associated with the world order, we celebrate the
festival imitating the world order (for how otherwise would we ourselves secure
order?). First we, too, fall down from heaven and are together with the nymph. Then
we are dejected and abstain from wheat and other rich and coarse foods, for both are
against the soul. Then follows tree-felling and fasting, as if we had also abstained
from the further process of propagation. Thereafter milk foods as if for people reborn
(ὥσπερ ἀναγεννωμένων). Then rejoicing (ἱλαρεῖα or ἱλαρεῖαι) and wreaths and
something similiar to an ascent to the gods. Indeed, the date of the dramatic incidents confirms this, since the incidents take place in spring and around the equinox,
on the one hand when what is created ceases to be created, and on the other hand
when the day becomes longer than the night, which suits uplifted souls.

Of more doubtful value as a source is a late and obscure note in the neoplatonic Damaskios, which it has been possible to interpret as a statement
that the climax of the Hilaria festival was the participants' imaginary
experience of Attis' death and deliverance from Hades.[99]

---

98. Salustius' basic view is that the gods are unchangeable and eternal (De diis 1-2); myths
    about the deity's experiences and vicissitudes must therefore have a deeper meaning (De
    diis 3) — cf. Arthur Darby Nock (ed.), *Sallustius Concerning the Gods and the Universe*,
    Cambridge 1926, p. xliii, Wedderburn, *Baptism*, p. 126ff. Lohse, *Umwelt*, p. 173, overlooks
    that Salustius carried out this re-interpretation, and therefore arrives at the misunder-
    standing of the passage to the effect that it expresses an official opinion of the cult as
    something unchangeable and eternal!
99. Thus is the text is interpreted by Hepding, *Attis*, p. 197, Bousset, *Kyrios*, p. 114, Ver-
    maseren, *Cybele*, p. 117f. The text originates from Damaskios, De vita Isidori (5th cent.
    AD), which is known however only in an account in Photius, Bibl. 242,344 B-345 A. Here
    Damaskios tells that when they were in the temple of Apollo at Hierapolis in Phrygia he
    and Doros succeeded in entering a crypt which was filled with deadly gases and that
    they returned unharmed, which was otherwise only possible for the initiated. It then con-
    tinues, Τότε τῇ Ἱεραπόλει ἐγκαθευδήσας ἐδόκουν ὄναρ ὁ Ἄττης γενέσθαι, καί μοι ἐπι-
    τελεῖσθαι παρὰ τῆς μητρὸς τῶν θεῶν τὴν τῶν Ἱλαρίων καλουμένων ἑορτήν· ὅπερ ἐδή-
    λου τὴν ἐξ Ἅιδου γεγονυῖαν σωτηρίαν. Note that this does not pretend to be authentic
    information about the Attis-Cybele cult but is the dream of an uninitiated associated with
    an experience at the temple of another deity. Nothing is said to the effect that the dream
    relates to what happens to all Attis worshippers at the Hilaria festival. Cf. Gasparro, *So-
    teriology*, p. 63, who sees it as evidence of a late understanding of the Hilaria festival as

Knowledge of the mysteries themselves is very limited. In De errore 18.1 Firmicus Maternus explains the signs and symbols used by the superstitious in their diabolical activities: for admittance to the inner parts of a certain temple, the person who is to die (homo moriturus) says:

de tympano manducavi, de cymbalo bibi et religionis secreta perdidici,

which means in Greek:

ἐκ τυμπάνου βέβρωκα, ἐκ κυμβάλου πέπωκα, γέγονα μύστης Ἄττεως.[100]

Clement of Alexandria also has — in Protrepticus 15.3 — a rendering of the symbols of the Attis mysteries:

ἐκ τυμπάνου ἔφαγον, ἐκ κυμβάλου ἔπινον, ἐκερνοφόρησα, ὑπὸ τὸν πάστον ὑπέδυν.

There is also information in Prudentius to the effect that the initiation also involved a sealing — a stigmatisation or tattooing with the sacred signs.[101]

We are better informed about the Taurobolium. Prudentius, Peristephanon 10.1011-1061, explains how this was carried out: In his most sacred vestments, the high priest descends into a pit in the ground, excavated for the purpose. Loosely-joined boards are placed across the trench, in which holes have been drilled. A bull is slaughtered on this. The blood penetrates through the holes into the pit, and the priest's clothing becomes covered in it. He turns his face towards the blood, gets it into his eyes and drinks all he can. The priest's ascent is described as an appalling sight. Everyone greets him reverently at a distance after the bloodbath.[102]

Further information about the Taurobolium can be gathered from, in particular, a number of inscriptions — and the similar sacrifice of a ram, the Kriobolium. We know that from at least AD 160 this was associated with the Attis-Cybele cult,[103] and that it was used partly as a collective propitiatory

---

a celebration of the initiate's hope for the same goodwill from the goddess as Attis received, i.e. hope for a continued life in death (not resurrection).

100. This again seems to concern a synthema, see Dibelius, *Botschaft* II, p. 35ff., cf. note 36 above.

101. Prudentius, Peristephanon 10.1076-1080. Dieterich, *Mithrasliturgie*, p. 165, presents the following verses which concern the initiate's funeral, after he had given up the spirit, as a clear example of a simulated death. But this is probably an incorrect interpretation. It is more likely to be physical death, perhaps as a result of sufferings during the tattooing. Cf. Hepding, *Attis*, p. 163 with n. 4.

102. Peristefanon 10.1048: omnes salutant atque adorant eminus.

103. CIL 13.1751 = Duthoy, *Taurobolium*, text 126. Vermaseren, *Cybele*, p. 102, considers an inscription from AD 134, which does not however refer to Cybele but to Venus.

sacrifice and partly (from the fourth century) as a personal purification.[104] Deliverance and fortifying effects were attributed to it, and it could be repeated after a period (perhaps every twentieth year).[105] A number of inscriptions refer to the day of the Taurobolium as a birthday.[106] One inscription (from the fourth century AD) refers to 'rebirth' — about Sextilius Agesilaos Aedasius it reads, inter alia, '... taurobolio crioboliog(ue) in aeternum renatus ...'[107]

This material gives no possibility of certain and precise interpretation.[108]

But we do gain sufficient information to adopt an opinion on the most distinctive and comprehensive theories in which March festival, mystery and Taurobolium are seen as one great whole, the crucial point being that the initiate's blood baptism is perceived as a ritual imitation of the dying and arising god, with divinity resulting as a consequence.[109] All this must be considered as unconvincing.

As regards the Taurobolium, it should be emphasised that its interpretation as a symbolic blood baptism, in which the mystes's descent into the pit corresponds to Attis' death and rising to resurrection is based on present-day speculation alone.[110] No such idea is expressed or implied in any source from antiquity. A hole in the ground is not necessarily a grave, but is required for practical reasons if the blood from a slaughtered bull is to run over a person without his being crushed.[111] The Taurobolium should rather be seen as a sacrifice in which the blood can have a strengthening and

---

104. See Hepding, *Attis*, p. 199f., Duthoy, *Taurobolium*, p. 118ff. The earliest example of the latter type is CIL 6.497 = Duthoy, *Taurobolium*, text 11, cf. Wagner, *Problem*, p. 261.
105. See Duthoy, *Taurobolium*, pp. 102-4. Text 25 = CIL 6.512 (AD 390) refers to the 20 years in the same way as Carmen contra paganos 57-62 = Hepding, *Attis*, p. 61.
106. See Duthoy, *Taurobolium*, p. 106 n. 2.
107. CIL 6. 510 (AD 376) = Duthoy, *Taurobolium*, text 126.
108. Cf. Gasparro, *Soteriology*, p. 38, 119ff.
109. Cf. especially the comprehensive construction in Hepding, *Attis*, pp. 196-98, where texts and ideas are used which originate from all sorts of places, Firmicus Maternus, De err. 22 (about Osiris), the Themistios Fragment, Apuleius, Metam. 11, and Christian ideas, 'Er [the mystes] hat dasselbe erlebt wie Attis, "der Erstling derer die sterben und wieder auferstehen zu einem neuen Leben"'.
110. In addition to Hepding, the symbolic explanation of the Taurobolium is found in Reitzenstein, *Mysterienreligionen*, p. 45f., 81f., Loisy, *Mystères*, p. 111f., Leipoldt, *Taufe*, p. 43f., Betz, *Nachfolge*, p. 67, Tröger, *Mysterienglauben*, p. 31, Lohse, *Umwelt*, p. 177 (who presents the case as if the idea is found to be expressed in the text Prudentius, Peristephanon 10.1011-50), Schneider, *Mysterien*, p. 47.
111. Cf. Nilsson, *Geschichte* II, p. 652ff., Wagner, *Problem*, p. 264.

cleansing effect attributed to it, or perhaps compensate for self-mutilation.[112] The fact that there is a reference to rebirth in just one late source is probably a spill-over from Christianity.[113] Under no circumstances can the Taurobolium's effect have been perceived as final salvation and apotheosis.[114] This is contradicted by much evidence of a repetition of the rite. It should be added that the Taurobolium was not chronologically linked to the March festival, and it has no demonstrable association with the mysteries. This must therefore definitively be disregarded when trying to understand these events.

The March festival and mystery initiation of the Cybele-Attis cult is characterised by the participants' intense experience. In this religious environment, elements such as vision and perception play a negligible part. They come into the picture only secondarily through a philosophical reinterpretation in Salustius. The crucial feature is the ecstatic savagery: the crowds' noisy chase through the countryside and the culmination in castration and other bloody rites. In Salustius and in the cultic symbol we hear of further rites which form part of the sequence of events, some with a sexual content, others revolving around the intake of food.

The cultic sequence of events was probably also perceived as an imitation of the divine acts. This especially applies to the ecstatic obsession which is the main characteristic of the religion. The cultic myth revolves around the wild chase and the self-mutilation. The reason given is dual: both Agdistis and Attis are castrated, both Cybele and Attis chase around insanely. The imitation thus seems to apply not only to Attis but also to Agdistis-Cybele.[115]

---

112. This interpretation can be considered because the animal's 'vires' has apparently been exposed to special treatment, cf. Gasparro, *Soteriology*, p. 82, 109, Wedderburn, *Baptism*, p. 328f.

113. The Aedesius, who according to CIL 6.510 will appear as 'reborn in eternity', is indeed known as a bitter enemy of Christianity, cf. Vermaseren, *Cybele*, p. 106, Simon, *École*, p. 263.

114. The assumption is frequently based on Prudentius, Peristephanon 10.1048, where there is a reference to respectful admiration — which is said to result from 'the mystes' having been made divine — thus Bousset, *Kyrios*, p. 114, Hepding, *Attis*, p. 198, Tröger, *Mysterienglauben*, p. 31f. with n. 7 (who tries to get around the problem that the text in fact concerns a high priest and not an mystes in a secret cult). But others besides gods can be held in veneration, as is incisively demonstrated by Nock, *Essays*, p. 92 with n. 181. Cf. also Gabriel Sanders, Kybele und Attis, in: Maarten J. Vermaseren (ed.), *Die orientalischen Religionen im Römerreich (OrRR) (EPRO 93)*, Leiden 1981, pp. 264-97; p. 285, Gasparro, *Soteriology*, p. 107ff.

115. Cf. Wagner, *Problem*, p. 250, who points out that the true purpose of the castration is to come to be like the goddess, cf. Carsten Colpe, Zur mythologischen Struktur der Adonis-Attis- und Osiris-Überlieferungen, in: W. Röllig (ed.), *lišān mithurti. Festschrift Wolfram Freiherr von Soden*, Neukirchen-Vluyn 1969, pp. 23-44; p. 33ff., who points out that the

But there is no firm evidence that the cult-participants have undergone Attis' death and resurrection.[116] In the first place, it is questionable whether Attis in his true being is a dying and arising deity. It is clear that he has gradually come to be considered as such in a line with Adonis in the rationalistic Hellenistic view of religion. But in earlier versions of the myth one hears nothing of Attis' resurrection (but of a further life as a tree or as a 'living corpse'). If Attis is perceived as a vegetation deity, a different interpretation pushes its way to the fore: Attis' death and blood are said to give strength to nature, to flowers and trees; the deity as guarantor of cosmic existence is then concerned.[117]

There is also no basis for assuming that the rite ended with the rebirth — understood as reality — of the initiate. Although it is possible to include the text which shows that the cult-participants were given milk ὥσπερ ἀνα-γεννωμένων,[118] Salustius is not referring here to a firmly-established tradition of a ritual rebirth. He concludes from the milk rite that a new birth takes place in the cult, and thereby he achieves accord with the cosmological interpretation of the cultic myth he has produced.[119] The rebirth idea is thus introduced as a secondary interpretation of the cultic events.

myth revolves around Agdistis' bisexuality, which she seeks to re-establish in the relationship with Attis. Castration is also seen as an attempt to abolish the differences between the sexes, cf. Catullus, Carm. 63. Cf. also Wayne A. Meeks, The Image of the Androgyne, HR 13 (1974), pp. 165-208; p. 170.

116. If this is maintained, it is not based upon information from the Attis cult but upon dubious analogy with other mystery religions; thus Hepding, *Attis*, pp. 196-98, cf. Bousset, *Kyrios*, p. 114, Vermaseren, *Cybele*, p. 116f., and also upon the Damaskios text referred to in note 99, and upon Firmicus Maternus, De err. 18.1, in which 'homo moriturus' is interpreted as expressing that the mystes experiences a death-symbolism. But the term is better understood as Firmicus' comment on this human being and its end — 'condemned to death' — he presents such terms again and again. See the survey in Wagner, *Problem*, p. 254 n. 237, cf. note 62 above.

117. Cf. Gasparro, *Soteriology*, pp. 43-49, cf. the observations referred to in note 92 above concerning Arnobius, Adv. nat. 5.5-7. She therefore emphasises the worldly effects of the Attis-Cybele cult — including the healing power (p. 84).

118. Salustius, De diis 4.10, referred to among others by Hepding, *Attis*, p. 197.

119. Cf. Dey, Παλιγγενεσία, p. 78f., Wagner, *Problem*, p. 247, Gasparro, *Soteriology*, p. 61f. There is every indication that the rebirth idea originates from the Neoplatonic cosmological and anthropological re-interpretation of the myth, and not from the myth itself. Dey has shown (p. 6ff.) that παλιγγενεσία is primarily and most distinctively used on the one hand in the doctrine of the transmigration of souls and on the other hand (since 1st cent. BC) in stoic cosmology as a term for the world renewal which occurs following the ever-recurrent world fire, whereas examples from the mystery religions are later.

2.4. 'The Themistios fragment'

A fragment attributed to Themistios in Johannes Stobaeus' Anthologium 52.49[120] is frequently used as proof that the mysteries were designed as an analogy of death.

In translation, the text concerned reads as follows:

Thus we say that the soul, when it has gone over to the hereafter, has 'come to an end' (ὀλωλέναι) in order to express the entire (εἰς τὸ ὅλον[121]) change and improvement. But here (in life on earth) the soul is ignorant until it is about to die. Then it is exposed to suffering like that experienced by those who celebrate great initiation mysteries. Therefore 'to die' (τελευτᾶν) and 'to be initiated' (τελεῖσθαι) resemble one another, both as regards the word and as regards the content. First there is tiring and bewildered roaming and anxious and futile (or uninitiated — ἀτέλεστος) wandering through darkness, and then — before the end — come all the horrors: shivering, shaking, sweat and terror. But then one encounters a wonderful light, and one is received by open landscapes and meadows where there are voices, dancing and a sublime atmosphere borne by sacred sounds and holy visions. Here, whoever is already perfect and initiated walks about liberated and relieved with a wreath on his head, celebrating mystery rites, and he is together with sublime and holy men, while he can watch over the uninitiated and unclean multitude who live here on earth trampled down by one another and driven together in a terrible mire and fog, remaining in wickedness because of fear of death and because they disbelieve in the good things in the hereafter.

The term τελεταὶ μεγάλαι does not take for granted the mysteries one must contemplate.[122] The indefinite form may imply that it was intended as a general reference to the mysteries.[123]

It must be asserted that the text primarily concerns the fate of the soul after death. To appreciate this subject, an image is introduced in which the unknown is explained by a reference to what is better known, the initiation

---

120. It is not unlikely that the text can be traced back to Plutarch — see F.H. Sandbach (ed.), *Plutarch's Moralia* XV (*Loeb*), London 1969, p. 306ff.
121. Differently in Braun, *Studien*, p. 152, who has the strained local understanding 'in das All', and then concludes that this is gnosticising thought, since 'a change into the All' must be concerned. But the simple and natural understanding is that it is an established term, 'completely' (my translation is an attempt to render the play on words). The passage is normally understood in this way, cf. Sandbach's translation in *Plutarch's Moralia* XV, p. 317, Henry George Liddell and Robert Scott, *A Greek-English Lexicon*[9], Oxford 1940, p. 1218.
122. Cf. Foucart, *Mystères*, p. 392f. Dieterich, *Mithrasliturgie*, p. 163f., points to the Eleusinian mysteries, Mylonas, *Eleusis*, p. 265f., to Orphism.
123. Cf. Nilsson, *Geschichte* II, p. 680.

rites.[124] At no time does this become more than a parable. The text shows that death can be compared to an initiation. But this is substantiated separately with the linguistic argument that the words τελευτᾶν and τελεῖσθαι correspond to one another in several ways. It does not indicate that the death analogy was absolutely vital to the mysteries, or even to the official interpretation of the mystery concerned.[125] If the initiation were generally considered as an acting-out of the death situation, it would make the substantiation superfluous. It had to be expected that there would be a direct reference to the known connection.

In any case, however, it is a fact that there is analogy and similarity between initiation rites and death concepts. This makes it possible to interpret the initiation as a kind of death. But this is not directly evidenced in this context.

2.5. 'The Mithras liturgy'

A passage from a Greek magical papyrus has become known under this name.[126] It is very doubtful whether the text has the origin which Albrecht Dieterich has ascribed to it by giving it the name 'Mithras liturgy';[127] but the text is still evidence of the way in which it was subsequently possible to employ mystery-religious ideas.

In its present form the text appears as a prescription for the achievement of immortality by magical means (line 478: ἀθανασία, line 741: ἀπαθαν<ατ>-ίσμῳ). This is introduced by quite a long prayer (lines 487-537), and later there are further prayers, some with fairly intelligible magical words, others with formulae that may be just a large number of different vowels (e.g. lines 559-60, cf. lines 575-76, lines 587-633 and lines 640-55). They are prayers to be removed for a brief period from the human, psychical sphere of power in order to attain contact with the immortal and divine upper world (e.g. lines 501-35). And this event is linked to the concept of rebirth and the granting

---

124. Cf. Wedderburn, *Baptism*, p. 152f.
125. Contrary to Dieterich, *Mithrasliturgie*, p. 164, Braun, *Studien*, p. 148f., Gäumann, *Taufe*, p. 44.
126. Lines 475-824 in Pap. Bibl. Nat. suppl. gr. 574, published as Papyrus 4 in Karl Preisendanz (ed.), *Papyri Graecae Magicae* I, Leipzig 1928; see pp. 88-101.
127. Dieterich himself also modified this later in *Eine Mithrasliturgie²*, Leipzig 1909, p. 228. Cf. Alan F. Segal, Hellenistic Magic: Some Questions of Definition, in: R. van den Broek and M.J. Vermaseren, *Studies in Gnosticism and Hellenistic Religions* (EPRO 81), Leiden 1981, pp. 349-75; p. 353ff., which indicate the passage is not merely magic but also genuine religion, which Dieterich demonstrated in his original definition of the text, cf. also note 188 below.

of immortality (lines 645-49 and lines 501-35). In addition, the text includes a description of the sequence of events one must traverse. One is raised up to a vision of heavenly immortality: sun, stars and gods. During this, various incantations and magical cultic cries must be provided, apart from the long prayers. The concluding invocation to the god (lines 709-24) leads to the climax of the ritual. It ends as follows:

κύριε, παλιγγενόμενος ἀπογίγνομαι, αὐξόμενος καὶ αὐξηθεὶς τελευτῶ, ἀπὸ γενένεως ζωογόνου εἰς ἀπογενεσίαν ἀναλυθεὶς πορεύομαι, ὡς σὺ ἔκτισας, ὡς σὺ ἐνομο-θέτησας καὶ ἐποίησας μυστήριων. ἐγώ εἰμι φερουρα μιουρι (lines 718-24).

One is then released from one's soul and the god proclaims an oracle in verse, which one can afterwards remember literally whatever the length (lines 724-33). Finally, rules are given for its performance: everything is to be said aloud with ecstatic enthusiasm, there are certain conditions for sharing the experience with others, and the process can be repeated three times a year (lines 733-50). Instruction is also given on the making of the magical agents and amulets to be used during the process (lines 751-824).

In general terms, the text contains many uncertainties. In particular, its climax in lines 718-24 quoted above is problematic. We have three parallel finite verbs which can all be used as a euphemism for dying (ἀπογίγνομαι, τελευτῶ, εἰς ἀπογενεσίαν ἀναλυθεὶς πορεύομαι). Each of these verbs is preceded by a participial expression concerned with creation and growth, and therefore in a relationship of tension with the main verbs. Since aorist participles are concerned, the sequence is as follows: first rebirth, then death. At the extreme, there may be simultaneity between the events. But the sequence cannot be reversed. There can be no direct use of a mystery-religious reference to death with subsequent rebirth.[128] A quite natural interpretation is that the 'rebirth' expresses the momentary release from the earthly which is the ecstasy, and that 'death' expresses the return to earthly life which follows immediately — cf. the introductory prayer (especially lines 501-35).[129]

But otherwise there is undoubtedly a link back to the mystery religions. The entire magical ritual is referred to as a mystery, even if it is a cult-less 'mystery', and the distance from the mysteries themselves is great. The particular interest in a deeper insight into the fact of existence (expressed in line

---

128. Note, however, that Dieterich, *Mithrasliturgie*, p. 166, writes about these very verses, 'Das ist die klarste und weitgehendste Anwendung des Bildes von Tod und Wiedergeburt, die wir in einem liturgischen Texte des Altertums besitzen.' Cf. also Braun, *Studien*, p. 148ff., Gäumann, *Taufe*, p. 44.

129. Cf. Dey, Παλιγγενεσία, pp. 103-9, Nilsson, *Geschichte* II, p. 687, Wagner, *Problem*, p. 76, Wedderburn, *Baptism*, p. 385.

504 by the verb ἐποπτεύσω), the religious ecstasy, the various magical agents and the concept of the future overcoming of death are crucial features here, as in the mysteries. Later magic has used the ideas and rituals of the mystery religions as sources to be drawn upon.

2.6. The Naasene sermon

The Naasene sermon, passed on by Hippolytus in Elenchus 5.7.3-5.9.10, shows the way in which the gnostics used mystery-religious material, and the way in which they could relate to the cult of the mysteries.

The text of which Hippolytus gives an account is concerned with describing the correct relationship between the human soul and the supreme divine principle from which the soul originates and from which it should also be controlled. The description consists of violent allegorisations of Bible passages, of pagan mythological ideas and of the cultic phenomena to which they were linked.[130] Attis and the deities to which he has been linked in the syncretistic environment (Osiris, Adonis, Hermes and Adamas) are of central significance. This is indeed also Hippolytus' most essential point of criticism, that the Naassenes teaching does not stem from Christianity but has been taken from the mysteries' teaching (Elenchus 5.7.1). Several passages reflect on phenomena from mystery cults. Elenchus 5.7.13 reads:

But they say when the god-mother castrates Attis, who was even her own lover, then, they say, it is the blissful nature of the superhuman, eternal things that summons the male power, which is the soul.

The Eleusinian cultic cry referred to earlier, ἱερὸν ἔτεκε πότνια κοῦρον Βριμὼ Βριμόν, is interpreted as follows in Elenchus 5.8.40-41:

This means that the strong one has given birth to the strong one. And 'the mighty one' is, they say, the spiritual, heavenly, superhuman creation; 'the strong one' is he who is born in this way.

The interpretation is supported by the terms Eleusis and anactorion (the

---

130. The history of the origin of the text is disputed. In R. Reitzenstein and H.H. Schaeder, *Studien zum antiken Synkretismus aus Iran und Griechenland* (SBW 7), Leipzig 1926, Reitzenstein has sought, by literary-critical discussion, to distinguish a pre-Christian gnostic text. This attempt is not convincing, cf. Agersnap, *Paulusstudier*, p. 65ff. with n. 79. Also Josef Frickel, *Hellenistische Erlösung in christlicher Deutung* (Nag. Ham. 19), Leiden 1984, is concerned with a development consisting of several layers. But this is of no significance to the present considerations.

innermost cult-room in Eleusis). Eleusis is linked to the verb Ἐλθεῖν, and is said to express that spiritual humans come from the heavenly Adamas. Anactorion is associated with ἄνω, and is understood as a description of their striving upwards towards the source. There are also a number of corresponding interpretations of the circumstances surrounding the mystery religions.

At the end of the account, in Elenchus 5.9.7, it is said that the Naasenes think that people praise the (*truly*) great mysteries without in fact knowing what they are doing when they sing the syncretistic Attis hymn quoted in Elenchus 5.9.8-9. In addition, 5.9.10 about the Naasenes' relationship with the cult to which the hymn belongs now reads:

Because of these and similar words they attend the so-called Great Mother mysteries in the belief that the primary concern is to *see* the whole mystery through the thing acted-out there, since they have no other benefit from what is acted-out there than that, without being castrated, they are able to act like the castrated.

These extracts show that gnostic circles can also continue to apply mystery concepts and see themselves as the heirs and true interpreters of not only just one mystery but of the entire mystery system.[131] It is also clear that this effect, to be achieved with the aid of mystery concepts, is a unio mystica which involves divine life. But one should not immediately draw the conclusion that proof is thereby provided that this may be the effect of the mysteries' rituals. If the final point in the gnosticising development of the mysteries is a fusion with the divine, this is because of the basis in the special anthropology to be found here, which cannot generally be assumed for the mysteries.[132] For the gnostics, there is already in man part of the divine, the soul, that must be released for men to become one with the deity. This happens through a recognition of the eternal connections, and true recognition is to be found behind the various primitive mythologies and ritual acts if one understands them correctly — i.e. wholly allegorically. The effect is indeed imagined as *not* having been achieved through any form of ritual cultic magic. The cultic acts as well as the mythological material is exposed to a re-

---

131. Cf. Bornkamm, μυστήριον, *ThWNT* IV (1938-42), pp. 809-34; p. 818f.
132. In gnosticism, (the important part of) man is basically divine, and what happens at the redemption is not, as in the mysteries, a change and improvement of man but a release of the divine within man. See Carsten Colpe, *Die religionsgeschichtliche Schule* (FRLANT 78), Göttingen 1961, p. 190, Hegermann, *Vorstellung*, p. 4, Hans-Martin Schenke, Hauptprobleme der Gnosis (originally 1965), in: Kurt Rudolph (ed.), *Gnosis und Gnostizismus*, Darmstadt 1975, pp. 585-600; p. 590, Die Gnosis, in: Johannes Leipoldt and Walter Grundmann, *Umwelt des Urchristentums* I, Berlin 1967, pp. 371-415; p. 379, Tröger, *Mysterienglaube*, p. 4, 12, 70ff., 99ff. and 169f. Cf. also the considerations in section 3.2 below.

interpretation. As in the apologetic philosophical re-interpretations of which we have seen an example in Salustius, this is entirely random and can be contrary to any original content. There is a purely symbolic perception of all cultic features which cannot be ascribed to any inherent continuity with the original cult.

Something similar applies to the few other texts that may be relevant as proof of a gnosticising continuation of the pagan mysteries. Thus in Hippolytus, Elenchus 5.20, concerning the Sethians who saw their teaching confirmed in mysteries in Phlius. The Orphic Bacchus mysteries are re-interpreted on the lines of what occurs in the Naasene sermon. Elenchus 5.24.27 speaks of an initiation act whereby one is introduced into the gnostic Justin's mysteries. But this is not concerned with the continuation of a certain cult. One relates to a speculative, symbolically perceived myth about man's creation and yearnings based on a Herodotus narrative combined with Gen 1-3. If gnosis and speculative contemplation is emphasised as the way of salvation, there is no true place for a cultic-ritual mediation of salvation.[133]

If we look at the specific source material, there is no clear, inherent continuity between the mystery religions and this gnosticising mystery. The assumption of a gnostic continuation of the mysteries' *cult* is particularly questionable.

2.7. Summary

It can be confirmed that there is no one overall mystery-religious concept of a baptism which is perceived as a death and resurrection with the deity.

But a certain clarity has been achieved about the general features of the mysteries investigated:

1. The effect of the mysteries is described throughout as an improved life on earth with hope of a postmortal future. In no mystery cult is the new life described as an apotheosis.

2. From several passages we can see that the mystes uses the same mystical agents as the deities to achieve similar effects. But there is no viable

---

133. See Epiphanius, Haer. 31.7.8, in which it is stressed that in connection with the mysteries the spiritual gnostic is interested only in τὰ ἐπιρρήματα. Cf. Werner Foerster, Das Wesen der Gnosis, in: Kurt Rudolph (ed.), *Gnosis und Gnostizismus*, Darmstadt 1975, pp. 438-62; p. 456: 'Vielmehr ist die eigentliche, der Gnosis allein adäquate Form des Sakraments der Vollzug von symbolischen Handlungen, die das erwachende Göttliche stärken soll; sie sind gehandelte Teile des "Rufes".'

evidence that the result of the initiation rite is an actual fusion with the deity imitated, and generally the imitation is not concerned with a dying and re-surrecting deity.[134]

3. In general, it seems that there was a marked feature in the mystery initiations, that one has experienced a struggle involving life and death. But it is also characteristic of the rites, as they are described, that many things occur and various means are employed to gain contact with the divine (in-cluding the purification rites in the initial sequence of events). In some my-steries, what is crucial is the sublime vision and the awareness of and con-nection with the gods achieved thereby (Demeter and Isis). In others, ecstatic emotion and the possession of divine madness are the most prominent (the Attis cult, Dionysus). But throughout what is important is that the mystes experiences a series of strange things in the cultic sequence of events, and is thereby linked to the powerful deity. There is thus no basis for the in-terpretation that the content of the cult can be reduced to just one external ritual in which a symbolic repetition of the god's death and resurrection in itself leads to the transfer of salvation to the mystes. The sources have no traces of such a symbolic, magically operative cult.

It has now been shown that the mysteries have important common features — including some of those involved in theories about a connection between the mystery initiations and the Christian baptism. On this basis, one can consider the possibility of a development of ideas in the Hellenistic en-vironment, which was characterised by syncretism.

---

134. The closest we came to this motif was in the Osiris death-cult, and perhaps in the Osiris mysteries. Demeter's sorrows and wanderings are imitated in Eleusis, and Attis' and Cybele's wanderings and the self-mutilation in the Attis cult. This conclusion thus confirms the main point in Wagner, *Problem*, cf. note 9 above, the clash with the theories about the dying and arising gods as the core of these religions. The theories, which date back to Frazer's work *The Golden Bough* (originally from 1890, cf. James George Frazer, *The Golden Bough* V-VI³ = *Adonis. Attis. Osiris* I-II, London 1906, *The Golden Bough* VII³ = Spirits of the Corn and of the Wild I, London 1912, p. 1, 33 etc.) and have been adopted by the religio-historical school, have thus also been the subject of serious criticism by scholars who have researched the specific cultic connections. Cf. Nilsson, *Geschichte* II, p. 685ff., Hengel, *Sohn*, p. 41ff., Gasparro, *Soteriology*, p. 28ff. See especially Colpe, Struktur, p. 23ff., who shows that there are Hellenistic-philosophical speculations about a primitive religion which was adopted uncritically by critics of religion and Christianity in the 18th and 19th centuries, whereby theories of the worship of Nature's cycle has obtained great significance; Adonis, Attis and Osiris were linked only later in time, and the connection does not arise on the direct mythical level; it had already become mythology before then.

3. Mysteries and the Hellenistic syncretism

3.1. Connection and common characteristics

Several features support the possibility that there may have been a special mystery-religious environment in which certain theological ideas were held in common. One can indicate mutual connections between the religions, and one can also consider the impact the mysteries together had on contemporary minds. There are two important assertions here: that there is a widespread form of mystical thought in the syncretistic environment, and that there was a connection between the mystery rituals and the magic which is important in Hellenism. Dealing with these comprehensive problem complexes must remain quite summary and be based on significant accounts of the subjects. But in several places the observations which have been made in connection with the specific mystery cults can be employed.

A relationship between the mystery religions is in the first place supported by the fact that there appears to be a certain connection between the various deities.

The Demeter cult existed not only in Eleusis but also in other locations in Greece with similar cultic myths.[135] We have heard about a male deity associated with Demeter, Brimo, who is probably a manifestation of Dionysus.[136] It is also clear that the speculations of Orphism concern the same deities and myths as are to be found in Eleusis.[137]

The deities could be identified with one another: Dionysus with Osiris[138] and Demeter with Isis and the various Asiatic mother-deities.[139] This opens up the possibility that the various cult-associations could influence one another.

And we know that the mysteries were exported. Inspired by the Eleusinian mysteries in particular, new cults were founded.[140] The Egyptian Sara-

---

135. See Nilsson, *Geschichte* I, p. 463ff., *Geschichte* II, p. 352ff., Bernhard Dietrich, The religious prehistory of Demeter's Eleusinian mysteries, in: U. Bianchi and M.J. Vermaseren (ed.), *La soteriologi dei culti orientali nell' impero romano (EPRO 92)*, Leiden 1982, pp. 445-67.

136. See note 41 above; it is even more obvious that the deity Iacchus, to whom the crowds pay homage during the procession according to Aristophanes, The Clouds 254ff., must be identified with Dionysus, cf. Burkert, *Homo*, p. 307ff.

137. Cf. especially Graf, *Eleusis*, p. 1ff. Cf. note 52 above.

138. This has taken place since Herodotus, 2.42, and is particularly prominent in Plutarch, De Iside 13, 35 etc.

139. Concerning the identification of Demeter and Isis, see already Herodotus, 2.59,171, cf. Nilsson, *Geschichte* II, p. 629, Graf, *Eleusis*, p. 37f., 155 n. 24. Demeter is probably related via her origin to other Mother deities, cf. Dietrich, Prehistory, p. 458ff.

140. Cf. especially Betz, Transferring, p. 87ff., where it is particularly emphasised that great personalities have founded new cults by transforming rituals from other cultic contexts.

pis worship resulted from a religious-policy initiative, perhaps an artificially created cult in which the ancient Egyptian deities Osiris and Apis were transformed according to a Greek model.[141] Also from Egypt, the mysteries, Isis being the main figure, spread to Greece and Italy.[142] It was thus in Corinth that Lucius of Apuleius, Metamorphoses 11, encountered the goddess. This also indicates a significant connection between the various mysteries.

We certainly also know that the various mystery religions are of most varied origin. As we have seen, dying and resurrecting vegetation deities are not crucial to the mysteries; this is a late and secondary theory that emerges in Hellenistic critiques of religion.[143] But nevertheless there were people in Hellenistic times who thought that such a connection existed between the deities. And there is found (at least gradually) a syncretism at the direct religious level in which local gods are also seen as manifestations of a universal deity.[144]

It is clear, then, that we are dealing with religions that had externally and in broad terms a markedly common character which has affected Hellenistic thought and usage.

The common characteristic was so strong that it had a linguistic impact. Contemporary awareness has bound the religions together under the common term μυστήρια. The same words were used in the description of religious phenomena such as τελετή, τελεῖσθαι, τέλος, ὄργια, ἐνθουσιάζειν, μύστης, μυσταγωγός, ἱεροφάντης.[145]

It is also remarkable that there is a pervading basic structure in the mysteries: the personal initiation act with mystical rituals and acts incomprehensible to outsiders; the intense religious experience; and the sudden re-

---

141. One thought that the deity was an artefact already in Antiquity — see Aelius Aristides, Or. 49.98, cf. Köster, *Einführung*, p. 191f., Klauck, *Herrenmahl*, p. 133, Wedderburn, *Baptism*, p. 313. See also, however, Vidman, Isis, p. 121ff., cf. *Isis*, p. 15ff., who points out that the basis was an already-existing Egyptian deity, which may then have been given a new life and to some extent a new content.

142. See Nilsson, *Geschichte* II, p. 624ff., Vidman, *Isis*, p. 27ff., 106ff., Köster, *Einführung*, p. 191f., Wedderburn, *Baptism*, p. 109ff.

143. Cf. the conclusion of the examination of the various cultic connections, section 2.7 above, with note 134. See also section 3.2 below, where an account is given of the re-interpretation of the mysteries among philosophers and other intellectuals.

144. This is the case with the Attis hymn in Hippolytus, Elench. 5.9.8-9, which compares Attis with a number of deities from other fields. According to the text, this hymn is said to belong to the Attis cult from which the Naasenes distance themselves but to which the masses have a directly religious relationship. It should also be noted that Sarapis worship in fact became important as a religion despite its constructed origin. Cf. Köster, *Einführung*, p. 192f.

145. Cf. Nock, *Essays*, p. 342f., Wedderburn, *Baptism*, p. 149ff.

newal of life by virtue of the cognition conveyed and association with the deity. At the same time, there are points of resemblance in structure and organisation.

There are perhaps also common inherent features. There is a purification, and frequently there is an element of imitation of the divine sequence of events.[146] Another common feature from the initiation rites has left its mark on the general awareness: the initiate's experience of death-like dangers which changes into joy and hope. This is perceived as a general feature of the mysteries, and is used proverbially to illustrate other matters.[147]

As regards the question of a pervasive mystery theology and a common interpretation of the rituals, however, there is reason for some caution. Conclusions reaching too far should not be drawn from the similarity between the mystery cults in external manifestations.

First, we know nothing of how far the mutual influence extended into the mysteries' secret core. One must use caution in assuming true openness in this field, at least as regards the mystery religions in which the original religious atmosphere is maintained. Secrets have been guarded here against contact with the outside world. This has had a dampening effect upon syncretism.[148]

Second, it therefore also become important to distinguish between the public part of the cult in the various locations and the mysteries associated with it. If at the time people sought a connection between the various religions, it is probable that the point of reference was the public part of the cult, which had its roots in the old fertility rites.[149]

Finally, we should show caution in interpreting the features which recur in all the mysteries as expressing interdependence, since they are features which are to be found not only here. Many forms of religious cult include an imitation of mythical events.[150] Ablutions are a particularly wide-spread

---

146. In Betz, *Nachfolge*, p. 48ff., there is an examination of this μίμησις concept. It is sought to show the origin of the term in the Dionysus cult, from which it spread to other religions. It can also be employed in a philosophical context (p. 107ff.). It is said in particular to have stamped Alexander the Great's self-knowledge and posterity's description of him; Alexander's background — mystery piety and constant participation in cultic connections in the role of the god — has stamped all his activities, which thus must be perceived as an imitation of god-figures, especially Dionysus and Hercules (p. 54ff.).

147. See in particular the Themistios fragment section 2.5 above, in which this feature illustrates the soul's fate after death. Cf. also Aristides 47.28, which speaks of an experience ὥσπερ ἐν τελετῇ ... παρεστώσας ἅμα τῷ φόβῳ τῆς ἀγαθῆς ἐλπίδος.

148. Cf. Frankemölle, *Taufverständnis*, p. 106 n. 44, Wedderburn, *Baptism*, p. 91.

149. See Wedderburn, *Baptism*, p. 148f., 158f., 394.

150. Betz, *Nachfolge*, p. 54ff., in establishing that Alexander the Great often played the role of the god in a cultic context, indicates a general feature in archaic religions in which the king had that role. Thus it is also disclaimed that the mimesis concept has its origin in one definite mystery, cf. note 146 above.

rite — perhaps the most universal. And the battle against the powers of death and the victory of life are the core of every religion. The pervasive features can thus also result from pure analogy, or dependence on more fundamental religious phenomena. Here, Wedderburn in particular has indicated 'rites of passage'. These elements can be included in all transitional phases of existence — birth, puberty, adoption into a new group, marriage, burial.[151]

3.2. Mystery thought

As has been asserted, there was widespread mystery thought in Hellenism. Whether or not the mysteries were interdependent or associated, the external similarities played an important part in popular awareness — especially the enigmatic features and the great experiences. Therefore life and its climaxes can be imagined and described as a mystery.[152]

But now this mystery thought penetrates beyond the area we directly perceive as belonging to religion.

This is indeed particularly demonstrated in the use philosophers make of the terminology and main features of the mysteries. We have already seen that philosophers from Plato and Cicero to Plutarch and Salustius use vocabulary and ideas from the mysteries. This is no accident. The philosophers perceived their activity as an extension of religion.

Plato used mystery terminology to describe central features of his thought: the soul's pre-existence and the awareness of true being.[153] The link is the mysteries' sublime cognition, insight into life's correlations and affiliation to the divine. For Plato, this is precisely the objective of philosophy.[154] It can be presented as a rational surpassing of the mysteries.[155]

---

151. See Wedderburn, *Baptism*, p. 363ff., which indicates a classical religio-phenomenological insight developed in Arnold van Gennep, *The Rites of Passage*[6], Chigago 1960 (French original, 1909), cf. John Cuthbert Lawson, *Modern Greek Folklore and Ancient Greek Religion*, Cambridge 1910, p. 546ff., Jane Ellen Harrison, *Themis. A Study of the Social Origins of Greek Religion*[2], Cambridge 1927, p. 20ff., Mircea Eliade, *Die Religionen und das Profane*, Darmstadt 1976, p. 225, Karl Albert, *Vom Kult zu Logos*, Hamburg 1982, p. 35f., Dunn, *Romans*, p. 310f.

152. See (in addition to the examples referred to in notes 146-47 above) Galen, De usu partium 17.1, in which 'mystery' is used about a cognitive break-through one can experience when one immerses oneself in scientific matters, cf. Nock, *Essays*, p. 800f. In that sense, the assertions about a mystery thinking are confirmed, cf. Gäumann, *Taufe*, p. 39f., 44f., Lohse, *Umwelt*, pp. 171-79, Thyen, *Studien*, p. 197 n. 1, Conzelmann (rec.), Wagner, p. 171f.

153. Faidr. 250 BC. Cf. section 2.1 above, with note 26.

154. Cf. Karl Albert, *Griechische Religion und Platonische Philosophie*, Hamburg 1980, p. 98ff., Wedderburn, *Baptism*, p. 149f.

The less rational aspects, the Dionysian, the experiences and the enchantment, can also be used as a link.[156] Both this and philosophy are seen as methods of rediscovering true existence. Something similar is to be found in Cicero and other stoics, where the true mystery is to gain knowledge of the divine rational correlation in life and the world.[157]

This tendency is further developed and strengthened by subsequent Hellenistic philosophers, as we have seen in Plutarch and Salustius.[158] Syncretism intrudes seriously at this time — simultaneously with the flourishing of the Hellenistic mysteries. There is a religious atmosphere in which it is wished to immerse oneself in the one divine principle, the eternal true being.[159] This is a philosophical task in which insight into the divine is emphasised. The philosophers can connect with all kinds of features from the mythical narratives, and even with the wildest barbaric features of the rites. But this does not mean true approval. The attitude is if not critical then at least distanced from the primitive form of religion in which myth and rituals are understood literally. It is a mystical or simplified rendering of the true insight that the philosophy conveys. There must be a re-interpretation — allegorising, de-mythologising, sublimating.[160] If the mysteries' myths and rites are interpreted in this way, this need have nothing to do with what was the cult's content originally.

The development that takes place has been described by various forms

155. See Faidr. 249 C about the objectives of philosophy, τελέους ἀεὶ τελετὰς τελούμενος, τέλεος ὄντως μόνος γίγνεται.
156. Especially Plato, Symposion 209ff., in which the enthusiasm characteristic of Dionysian religion is developed (see in particular Symposion 218 B, cf. Faidr. 249 D), cf. Wedderburn, *Baptism*, p. 149f. Even more marked is the trend in Aristotle; see fragment 15 (Rose), handed down in Synesios, Dion. 8,6: ᾿Αριστοτέλης ἀξιοῖ τοὺς τελουμένους οὐ μαθεῖν τι δεῖν, ἀλλὰ παθεῖν καὶ διατεθῆναι, δηλονότι γενομένους ἐπιδηδείους.
157. See section 2.1 above, with note 27. Cf. Ioannes ab Arnim (ed.), *Stoicorum veterum fragmenta* II, 42.1008 (Chrysip), Seneca, Ep. 90.28.
158. As regards Plutarch, cf. note 57 above; the whole of De Iside is a philosophical re-interpretation of Hellenistic mystery religion; the 'Themistios fragment' may also be an example of Plutarch's criticism of religion, cf. note 120 above. As regards Salustius (and Julian), see in particular the discussion of the Attis cult in section 2.3 above, with notes 97-98 and 119.
159. Thus clearly in Salustius, De diis 1-5. Also in Plutarch, De Iside, a fundamental monotheism and monism is initially expressed. This does not however prevent him from speaking of various mutually contending deities and demons — typical of his eclecticism, cf. the survey in J. Gwyn Griffiths, *Plutarch's De Iside et Osiride*, Cardiff 1970, p. 18ff.
160. See Salustius, De diis 1-5 (cf. note 98 above), Plutarch, De Iside 20, cf. the use of a play on words and 'etymological' arguments in the 'Themistios fragment', section 2.4 above.

of terminology in research. But the trend in the interpretations seems to me to be the same.

Mircea Eliade describes the core of the original archaic religions as 'ontophani'.[161] The world of the myths is the true world, the ontological; that which tells of gods, heroes and ancestors is the true reality. It is re-actualised ritually, and thereby a surplus of being enters the human world. The mythical events become models for human life, and prevail there. From here occurs, according to Eliade, an intellectualisation and rationalisation of the syncretistic environment, so that myths become ideas, cosmology and anthropology.[162] When the myth has in this way become mythology,[163] it can be emptied of religious content in the long term. But at the same time it is clear that there is a close connection between religion and philosophy, between myth and logos.[164]

Ugo Bianchi has introduced and developed, in a series of theses and articles, the term 'mysteriosophy' as an element in the explanation of the phenomenon.[165] He works with a development consisting of four stages. First there is the original public cult from which the mysteries emanated, revolving around the experiences and fertility rites of nature deities. Then there emerge the esoteric mysteries in which one seeks an individual salvation and contact with the deities. As a third element in the development comes the mysteriosophy, which is the re-interpretation of the mysteries one finds in Orphism, in Plato and in the philosophical development towards Neoplatonism; here interest turns away from the cult towards the human self, the soul, which traverses the same sequence of events as the cultic deities, from divine origin down into the 'grave' in the corporeal state and from there back towards redemption and divinity. Gnosticism can then be seen as the fourth element of the development; here the interest in the soul coming from above is intensified, and earthly shadow-life is regarded so

---

161. See Mircea Eliade, *Det hellige og det profane* [The Sacred and the Profane], Oslo 1969 (German original 1957), especially p. 56ff. The term 'ontophany' emphasises that the myths and the rituals associated therewith are at the same level as ontology in philosophical thought (cf. p. 40). Cf. also Albert, *Religion*, p. 3ff.

162. Eliade, *Det hellige*, p. 64f., 92f. etc. In the long term the result of this process is a pessimistic view of life, because the original religious content is exhausted.

163. Cf. Colpe, Struktur, p. 23ff., which also emphasises that syncretism is associated with the development away from the direct religious relationship with the cult, cf. note 134 above.

164. Cf. Albert, *Religion*, p. 10ff.

165. These works have been collected in Ugo Bianchi, *Selected Essays on Gnosticism, Dualism and Mysteriosophy* (SHR 38), Leiden 1978. See in particular pp. 159-76, Initiation, mystères, gnose, pp. 196-207, Psyche and Destiny, pp. 219-36, Le problème des origines du gnosticisme et l'histoire des religions.

negatively that the gnostic must distance himself entirely from the original cult, with its interest in fertility and propagation.[166]

The development can also be described as a transition from cultic mysteries to 'literary mysteries'.[167]

Whichever approach is used the main thought remains the same: a significant transformation of individual religions occurs when they enter the syncretistic environment. In the first stage there is an _intensification_, because one searches from the many gods to the one deity, an _intellectualisation_, since a symbolic re-interpretation of original religious features occurs, an _individualisation_, since salvation concerns the individual soul to an even higher degree than in the mysteries, and an _introversion_ in which the external cult is relativised. During the second stage, severance from the cultic context may pave the way for the detachment of the mysteries' terminology and set of ideas from the original religious content.

This image of Hellenism's syncretistic environment is endorsed when it is considered how Judaism, Christianity and gnosticism can relate to it.

In Hellenistic Judaism also, one can speak of the true mystery in which one must be absorbed with intensity.[168] And terminology from the mysteries can be used quite extensively — especially in Philo. He can present Judaism as the true mystery religion. He is initiated into the great mysteries, for which Moses is hierophant.[169] Enthusiasm can also be spoken of in this

---

166. This explanation model, as is clearly apparent from _Essays_, p. 196ff., and p. 227ff., enables Bianchi to affirm that mystery thought is a crucial basis of gnosticism, despite the marked differences: in the mysteries, man is transformed into something he has not been before; in gnosticism, man is redeemed by becoming the divine being he originally was — cf. note 132 above. Mysteriosophy's re-interpretation of the mysteries is the transitional link between the two entities. Cf. also Endre V. Ivánka, Religion, Philosophie und Gnosis: Grenzfällen und Pseudomorphosen in der Spätantike, in: Ugo Bianchi (ed.), _Le origini dello gnosticismo_ (_SHR_ 12), Leiden 1967, pp. 317-22.

167. See Reitzenstein, _Mysterienreligionen_, p. 51f., which describes Corpus Hermeticum 13 as a 'Lese-mysterium', and on p. 64 it is also described in Philo texts as 'literarische Mysterien', cf. Tröger, _Mysterienglauben_, p. 21, 82, which use the same term, Rudolf Bultmann, _Das Urchristentum im Rahmen der antiken Religionen_, Zürich 1949, p. 179, which, referring to Reitzenstein, speaks of a spiritualistic mystical piety that interprets the cultic acts as pure symbolism. A.J. Festugière, _L'idéal religieux des Grecs et l'évangile_[2], Paris 1932, p. 116ff., uses the term 'mystères litéraires' about Pythagorean, Platonic, Aristotelian and other philosophers' development of the mysteries, cf. also Larry J. Alderink, _Creation and Salvation in Ancient Orphism_, Chico 1981, p. 95f., about the Orpheans. All passages describe the same development in the syncretistic environment.

168. Thus already Sap 2.22; 6.22; 8.4.

169. See Philo, De cher. 49, De virt. 178, De gig. 54, etc., cf. Hegermann, _Vorstellung_, p. 9ff., Wedderburn, _Baptism_, p. 155f.

connection, and ineffable mysteries which are only for those who can observe the secrecy injunction.[170] But this cannot be taken as support for the
fact that Philo in any way links up with the mystery-religious cult.[171] He
holds fast to the Jewish rejection of participation in an alien religious
cult.[172] He adopts a philosophical usage. Like Plato, Philo can use mystery
terminology to describe the absorption in the true divine connections. For
Philo, this is the revealed Jewish faith. By this means he surpasses all philosophy and mystery thought. He also employs the same means — an allegorising and sublimating re-interpretation of mythical narratives and ritual
practice; but he always relates to Jewish narratives and rituals — never to
pagan myth and cult. If there is any inherent connection with mystery
thought, this is exclusively at the level of 'mysteriosophy'.

Neither is it possible to demonstrate a 'Jewish mystery' in connection
with the lately-attested Hellenistic-Jewish manuscript 'Joseph and Asenath'.
Asenath experiences a sequence of events that makes the pagan woman a
suitable wife for Joseph. In this connection it is said that she must 'eat the
bread of life and drink from the chalice of immortality and be anointed with
the ointment of indestructability'. The turning point comes when an angel
gives her honeycake to eat. The sequence of events is interpreted as mystical
and sacramental acts which are to lead to a true resurrection.[173] But taking
everything into account all that is concerned is a proselyte ritual described

170. Se especially Philo, De migr. Abr. 34-35, De vit. cont. 12, De leg. alleg. 2.57, De somn.
1.164, cf. also the references in Wedderburn, *Baptism*, p. 155f.
171. As Gäumann, *Taufe*, pp. 37-39 with nn. 10 and 20, appears to believe. It is tried to reconstruct such a Jewish mystery in Joseph Pascher, Ἡ βασιλικὴ ὁδός. *Der Königsweg zu
Wiedergeburt und Vergottung bei Philon von Alexandreia* (StGA 17.3-4), Paderborn 1931,
especially p. 261ff. Also Erwin R. Goodenough, *By Light, Light*, New Haven 1935, p. 8,
259ff., has been perceived as an assertion of a Jewish continuation of a pagan mystery
cult, cf. however Goodenough's definition in the later work, *An Introduction to Philo
Judæus*, New Haven 1940, p. 203ff.
172. Cf. for example Philo, De spec. leg. 1.319ff., cf. Arthur Darby Nock, The Question of
Jewish Mysteries, in, *Essays on Religion and the Ancient World* II, Oxford 1972, pp. 459-68;
p. 464ff., Hegermann, *Vorstellung*, p. 11.
173. Thus Reitzenstein, *Mysterienreligionen*, p. 248f., Brandenburger, Auferstehung, p. 24ff., cf.
Marc Philonenko, Initiation et mystère dans Joseph et Aséneth, in: C.J. Bleeker (ed.),
Initiation (SHR 10), Leiden 1965, pp. 147-53, and pp. 89-98 in the introduction in Marc
Philonenko (ed.), *Joseph et Aséneth* (SPB 13), Leiden 1968. The core passages are JosAs 8.6-
11; 15.1-16.9.

by borrowing mystery terms[174] — and perhaps also material from Christian thought.[175]

Within Christianity, one has if anything been even more intolerant towards pagan cults. Nevertheless, it has been possible to use words whose origin goes back to the mysteries, especially μυστήριον and τέλειος. But there is much to indicate that this was because it was these very words which became general usage to such a degree that they are no longer encumbered with the original religious content. It is indeed remarkable that the New Testament lacks the more technically loaded words associated with the mystery religions, such as μύστης, μυσταγωγός and ἱεροφάντης.[176]

Only in Clement of Alexandria is there a reference to Jesus as a hierophant, but indeed at the end of a ruthless criticism of all mystery religion.[177] Christianity is thus seen as an 'anti-mystery'.

Gnosticism — and other later forms of mysticism associated therewith — fit into the same pattern.

The above discussion of Hippolytus' account of the 'Naasene sermon' and other gnostic texts established that these gnostics, when concerned with the mysteries' myths and rituals, subjected them to severe re-interpretation. This was an a-cultic, allegorising and sublimating exposition similar to that of the philosophers. And these few passages are in general the only places in which the gnostics are concerned with the cult of the mysteries.

Mystery terminology is used in Corpus hermeticum, especially Tract 13

---

174. Thus Sänger, *Judentum*, p. 188ff., cf. Wedderburn, *Baptism*, p. 157f. In Christoph Burchard, *Untersuchungen zu Joseph und Aseneth* (WUNT 8), Tübingen 1965, pp. 121-33, in which it is also seen as a purely Jewish text, it is asserted that the terms about bread, chalice and anointment in no way refer to a ritual but are an expression for everyday meals; the Pagans eat impure meals infected by idol worship; after Asenat has received by mystical means the divine honey meal (manna!), she becomes pure, and any meal thereafter is celebrated with the bread of life, the chalice of immortality and the ointment of imperishability.

175. Cf. Traugott Holtz, Christliche Interpolationen in 'Joseph und Aseneth', in: *Geschichte und Theologie des Urchristentum* (WUNT 57), Tübingen 1991, pp. 55-71; the best argument that terms such as ἄρθον ζωῆς and πωτήριον εὐλογίας are interpolations taken from the Christian understanding of Communion is that such terms are in the New Testament but are not to be found in Jewish usage prior to 'Joseph and Asenath' (as conceded by Burchard, *Untersuchungen*, p. 130, 133 n. 1, cf. Holtz, *Geschichte*, p. 60 n. 28) — and it is very audacious to consider this a pre-Christian text. Another possibility is that a Jewish author has used terms originating from Christian usage.

176. This also applies to words such as ὄργια, τέλος and all words of the root used as the name for a ritual initiation. See especially Arthur Darby Nock, The Vocabulary of the New Testament, in: *Essays on Religion and the Ancient World* I, Oxford 1972, pp. 341-47, cf. Bornkamm, *ThWNT* IV, p. 830f., Wedderburn, *Baptism*, p. 158ff.

177. Clement, Protr. 2.120.1. Cf. Nock, *Essays*, p. 815f.

(about AD 200), which is however a 'reading mystery' without external cult.[178] Otherwise, the term 'mystery' alone is used together with other terms which have become general usage.[179]

This distance between gnosticism and the mystery-religious cult is not surprising. If gnosticism is to be understood as a dualistic, world-hostile, development of mystery thought, it follows naturally to shed everything that concerns an original fertility cult.[180] And if gnosis, recognition of the soul's divine origin, is the path to salvation there is in the first place no room for a mystery cult.[181] This may also be influenced by Christianity and its dismissive attitude towards the mysteries. It has indeed been shown that in later gnostic sources magical rites can be found which are to serve as relative improvements of worldly life; here it is largely on Christian baptism and anointing that work continues.[182]

3.3. Mysteries and magic

In describing the mysteries, the importance of the purely ritual is frequently emphasised — it has a magical or sacramental effect 'ex opere operato'.[183] One may therefore consider the way in which mystery rites are associated with the wide-spread magic of the time.

The first problem here is that in fact it has never been possible to define

---

178. Cf. note 167 above. The text is difficult to place from a religio-historical aspect. See the survey of the complicated discussion, which also involves taking a position on the difficult question of the origin of gnosticism, in Tröger, *Mysterienglauben*, p. 6ff.

179. Cf. R. McL. Wilson, Gnosis and the Mysteries, in: R. van den Broek and M.J. Vermaseren (ed.), *Studies in gnosticism and Hellenistic Religion* (EPRO 91), Leiden 1981, pp. 451-57; p. 454f., Wedderburn, *Baptism*, p. 120ff.

180. Cf. Bianchi's explanation model above in connection with notes 165-66.

181. Se especially Foerster, Wesen, p. 456, cf. note 133 above.

182. See Tröger, *Mysterienglauben*, p. 69, 139, which refers to Irenæus, Adv. haer. 1.21.3ff.; 1.25,3, which concerns baptism and anointment (which is however seen as expressing influence from the mystery religions!). As an example of magic processing of Christian rituals, Jeu's 2nd Book (ed. C. Schmidt), p. 102ff., should also be mentioned, cf. Søren Giversen, Dåb i Ny Testamentes omverden [Baptism in the surroundings of New Testament], in: Sigfred Pedersen (ed.), *Dåben i Ny Testamente* [Baptism in The New Testament], Århus 1982, pp. 3-13; p. 7. Cf. also Bornkamm, *ThWNT* IV, p. 819 n. 103.

183. This happens in particular where it is reasoned that New Testament baptism concepts are dependent upon the mystery religions. If traces of sacramentalism or magic can be found in the New Testament, this is immediately taken as a sign of a mystical background. Cf. Heitmüller, *Taufe*, 1903, p. 14f., *Taufe*, 1911, pp. 17-26, Bousset, *Kyrios*, p. 139, Bultmann, *Theologie*, p. 137ff., Gäumann, *Taufe*, p. 38f., 46., Conzelmann, *Grundriss*, p. 67, 296ff., Tröger, *Mysterienglauben*, p. 69.

the term 'magic' unambiguously.[184] Very different features are emphasised, and it is difficult to distinguish magic from 'religion'. One can try to identify particular trends which are more wide-spread in magic than in the religions of Hellenistic times, and it is then a matter of in what way the mystery rites fit into this picture.

Magic has been seen as a primitive cultural form, a kind of false science by means of which it is sought to obtain power over events. Religion, however, must be something higher and more developed. This is the opinion in James G. Frazer's pioneering work, which is strongly contested on this point.[185] There is also a basic division to be found here, and still maintained, between 'contagious magic', in which something is done with the person of another, property or images, and 'imitative magic', in which one imitates what one wishes to achieve, or as an agent against a problem one can use something similar thereto.[186] As regards Hellenistic times, it is indeed clear that magic and religion are *not* two stages of development. This proved to be the case as regards the 'Mithras liturgy', where development was in the opposite direction: mystery-religious rites have been reformed and made part of a recipe for immortality magic.[187] Religion and magic are found side by side — and this is general in the magical papyri from the third and fourth centuries, which are the main source of our knowledge of magic in late-Hellenism.[188] The same applies to the Neoplatonic

---

184. It is precisely the confusing and the fundamentally impossible in a complete definition which is stressed in more recent descriptions of the subject, Georg Luck, *Arcana Mundi*, Baltimore 1985, p. 1ff., Segal, Magic, pp. 349-75, Carl Heinz Ratschow, Magie I. Religionsgeschichtlich, *TRE* 21 (1991), pp. 686-91.

185. See James George Frazer, *The Golden Bough* I³ = *The Magic Art and the Evolution of Kings* I, London 1911, p. 53ff., 220ff., cf. L. Levy-Bruhl, *Les fonctions mentales dans les sociétés inférieures*, Paris 1918, p. 78ff., 111ff., which speaks of pre-logical thought (without this having necessarily to be understood as disparaging). It is indeed the perception of primitive people as stupid which is an important point of criticism against Frazer. Cf. John Hull, *Hellenistic Magic and the Synoptic Tradition* (*SBT0* 2, p. 28), London 1974, p. 54, Ugo Bianchi, *The History of Religions*, Leiden 1975, p. 46f., Ratschow, *TRE* 21, p. 687.

186. See the distinction between 'imitative' or 'homoeopathic' and 'contagious' magic in Frazer, *Bough* I, p. 52ff., cf. Geo Widengren, *Religionsphänomenologie*, Berlin 1969, p. 5, Bianchi, *History*, p. 47, Ratschow, *TRE* 21, p. 687.

187. See section 2.5 above, cf. also note 182, which indicates a corresponding development in gnosticism.

188. See especially Arthur Darby Nock, Greek Magical Papyri, in: *Essays on Religion and the Ancient World* I, Oxford 1972, pp. 176-94, Martin P. Nilsson, Die Religion in den griechischen Zauberpapyri, in: *Opuscula Selecta* III, Lund 1960, pp. 129-66, which works on theories that the magicians employed Hellenistic religious texts, cf. Segal, Magic, p. 351ff., which indicates the alternative possibility that the magicians were creative religious personalities.

philosophers, who cultivate magic in a sublime form which they refer to as 'theurgy'.[189]

Another difference indicated is that magic is associated with the control of things, whereas religion expresses dependence on the divine.[190] The technical aspect is then also emphasised in describing magic. Certain techniques can have an objective effect — the term 'ex opere operato' can be used here.[191] Such a characteristic fits a large part of the material. From Hellenistic magic we know of many different tools: charms, ostraka and small disks with magical formulae and the name of the person to be influenced negatively or positively;[192] the magical papyri contain recipes for action, and powerful names and symbols which are believed to act on supernatural forces.[193] The use of magical drinks and poison is also seen as a form of magic.[194] But other passages emphasise ecstasy and the magician's personality, will and charisma.[195] Prayers and invocations are also used in the practice of magic.[196] And then it becomes complicated again — with fluid boundaries. Whether something is religion or magic depends largely on interpretation.[197] There is great similarity between means, manner and expectations. Imitation of the divine is also a wide-spread religious rite, and cult objects are to be found in any religion. There is no sharp borderline between magic and symbolism or symbolic acts. For this reason magical techniques and religious rituals are similar to one another, when viewed from the outside. In the same way, descriptions of great magicians and religious personalities resemble one another.[198] And if one looks at what is to come from the act, it cannot always be determined whether one has a humble re-

---

189. See Segal, *Magic*, p. 361ff. Cf. also Apuleius' relationship to magic.
190. Thus Nathan Söderblom, *Den levande Guden*², Stockholm 1932, p. 31ff., Widengren, *Religionsphänomenologie*, p. 8ff., Bianchi, *History*, p. 46.
191. See Ratschow, *TRE* 21, p. 686, 690, cf. Bianchi, *History*, p. 46, Köster, *Einführung*, p. 391.
192. See the survey in Hull, *Magic*, p. 9ff., Luck, *Arcana*, p. 17ff.
193. Cf. Nilsson, *Opuscula* III, p. 134ff., Hull, *Magic*, p. 5ff., 42ff., Luck, *Arcana*, p. 16f.
194. Cf. Luck, *Arcana*, p. 8, 38.
195. See Henri Delacroix, La *religion et la foi*, Paris 1922, p. 27ff., which emphasises the subjective, the wish which is so strong that it abolishes the difference between the impossible and real, cf. Hull, *Magic*, p. 54f., 57, which also indicates examples where technique is not enough to carry out and control magical miracles, including Lactantius, Philopseudes 36, about the sorcerer's apprentice who can make an object scoop up water but cannot make it stop.
196. Cf. Hull, *Magic*, p. 42f.
197. Cf. Hull, *Magic*, p. 56f., which poses the question, whether faith in divine omnipotence can be separated from belief in magic.
198. Attention has been drawn to this in more recent works, which see Jesus in association with contemporary magic, thus Hull, *Magic*, p. 1ff., cf. the conclusion p. 142ff., Morton Smith, *Jesus, the Magician*, San Francisco 1978, p. 45ff., Segal, Magic, p. 367ff.

ligious hope of one's prayer being answered or whether one is thinking in terms of compelling the deity.[199]

It may thus often appear to depend upon the evaluation of the surroundings whether something is to be classified as magic or as religion. One may therefore also try to find the difference between the two entities as regards their social significance. In some circles, magic was considered immoral, aggressive and utterly negative.[200] One typically accuses religious opponents of being magicians.[201] Magic and sorcery were indeed seen as criminal in the Roman Empire; they were considered subversive.[202] But at the same time magic was a popular occupation — perhaps precisely because it was forbidden and rebellious. And it gradually spread to all layers of society; we have seen that an intellectual such as Apuleius experimented with magic, and that it became something sublime among Neoplatonic philosophers. That is to say, there is also a positive perception of magic which brings it into line with religion.

Yet another difference can be considered; this has to do with the social context. Whereas religion is concerned with community and is led by priests, magic is something individual and the magician is a private practitioner.[203] This means that magic becomes less conservative and more uncontrollable, so that it becomes an obvious hotbed for developments towards syncretism.[204] It also becomes clear that we are seeing the same development in the mystery thought as earlier towards the individual and the private, which is expressed in philosophy, mysticism and magic.[205] It is again demonstrated that there is continuity between religion and magic.

This brings us at last to the final, crucial characteristic of Hellenistic magic: it is associated with a particular world picture. The mainstay is a perception of cosmic 'sympatheia': all creations and phenomena in the world,

---

199. Cf. H. Riesenfeld, Remarques sur les hymnes magiques, *Er* 44 (1946), pp. 153-60, Hull, *Magic*, p. 43, in which the practice of magic is examined with special reference to Pap. mag. 36, where a development takes place from liturgically-sounding invocation and prayer to even greater pressure on the deity, which finally is to be compelled, by the symbolic content of the ritual, to subject itself to the will of the person performing. But there is at most a subtle difference compared with a situation in which the deity accepts the person's faith and grants his prayer.

200. Cf. Smith, *Jesus*, p. 81ff., Segal, *Magic*, p. 355f.; especially during early imperial times, the term is used pejoratively in line with the word γοητεία.

201. We have seen Firmicus Maternus and other Christian apologists deal thus with the mystery religions, in the same way as the early Christians were themselves accused of being magicians, cf. Segal, *Magic*, p. 370f.

202. Cf. Segal, *Magic*, p. 358.

203. Cf. Köster, *Einführung*, p. 391ff.

204. Cf. Nilsson, *Opuscula* III, p. 155, 166, Köster, *Einführung*, p. 392, Segal, *Magic*, p. 371f.

205. Cf. section 3.2 above.

including demons and powers, are interdependent in a system of action and reaction. Again, this is an idea Frazer has pioneered.[206] It is thus an inspired world in which one must try to understand and influence the powers by means of both magic and religion. There is thus a kind of difference of degree between magic and religion.[207] Magic is mostly concerned with immediate problems and the demonic powers to be influenced. Religion is mostly concerned with the sublime and the universal, which cannot be controlled.

If we then turn to the mystery religions, they can be called magical in the latter sense, since it is clear that they also presuppose the world picture upon which magic rests.

But if we look more closely at the content of the individual mystery rites the magical aspect fades into the background. Means are employed which can be compared to the techniques of magic. It is, however, difficult in the mysteries to demonstrate a purely objective mechanical effect. Imitative rites are to be found and the manipulation of particular divine objects, but it cannot be demonstrated that the mere imitation and contact with objects gives a share in supernatural powers. Experience, vision and insight are associated with the dramatic incidents and the handling of the sacred objects, and the same phenomena can be made the subject of profound symbolic interpretations. One may also see as magical agents the mysteries' ecstasy and the consumption of 'cyceon' and other substances, which are perhaps mind-expanding. But ecstasy and the cultic consumption of food are also general religious phenomena. Similarly, purification rituals can be invested with a special magical power. But religious symbolism is also associated with ablutions: one removes old dirt and begins again — not only upon entering the mysteries but at the transition to every new period of life.[208]

As concerns the basic atmosphere itself in the general mysteries, the trend seems even clearer. If magic is perceived as an attempt to control, the mysteries examined are not magic, since what is crucial is the emphasis on the deity's unrestricted power — most clearly in the case of Demeter and Isis

---

206. Cf. Frazer, *Bough* I, p. 52ff. It is a widespread view that there is this fundamental outlook on the world, cf. Günter Haufe, Hellenistische Volksfrömmigkeit, in: Johannes Leipold and Walter Grundmann, *Umwelt des Urchristentums* I², Berlin 1967, pp. 68-100; p. 77ff., Bianchi, *History*, p. 47, Hull, *Magic*, p. 37ff., Luck, *Arcana*, p. 3ff., Ratschow, *TRE* 21, p. 690, Dieter Harmening, Magie III. Historisch, *TRE* 21 (1991), pp. 695-701; p. 696f.

207. Cf. Segal, *Magic*, p. 372ff.

208. Cf. the rites of passage referred to in note 151 above. The rites of passage are described in Ratschow, *TRE* 21, p. 690, as magic rites with an 'ex opere operata' effect; but this can be compared with the description in Wedderburn, *Baptism*, pp. 363-71, where it is presented as religious symbolism and a way of relating to the unknown and borderline experiences.

but also as regards Cybele. What is important is to come into contact with the supreme deity. This is to be seen almost programmatically in Apuleius' narrative about Lucius, who with all his magic lived under blind fate but was freed by his obedience and loyalty to Isis.[209]

There is a vital connection between Hellenistic religion and magic. But magic is a comprehensive phenomenon which is not especially bound to the mysteries' ritual practice.

3.4. Summary

A motley picture results from investigation of the Hellenistic religious environment. Several possibilities exist to explain parallelity and accordance between mystery rites and Christian baptism.

1. It has been possible to show common features as regards structure and the public part of the cults' programming. This is not a true mystery theology, not the mystery religions' common official understanding of the cults' secret core. There is thus nothing immediately to support the suggestion that the Christian view of baptism is directly dependent upon the mysteries' theology.

2. The mystery thought which is evidenced appears only when the original religions are re-interpreted intellectually, symbolically and a-cultically. This mystical-symbolic thought may then have influenced the Christian idea of baptism.

3. But at the same time it has been established that mystery terminology and certain images from the mysteries can be used entirely detached from the original religious content. For this reason the influence may have been of a purely external, linguistic nature.

4. Finally, it has been shown that the features common to the mysteries are widespread outside the mysteries and are based on religious phenomena: imitation, purification rites, struggle against death-like dangers, and new life. This also opens up the possibility that the parallelity between mystery rites and the Christian baptism results from pure analogy, or that both have been developed from the same basis.

---

209. Thus Segal, Magic, pp. 362-64. See especially Apuleius, Metam. 11.15, cf. section 2.2 above.

III
Baptismal concepts in Hellenistic-Christian communities

1. Problem-complex involved

We shall here review traditional Hellenistic concepts and terms in Paul's letters which may have an association with baptism. The aim is to give an idea of the understanding of baptism in Hellenistic communities.

The point of reference will be the attempts to find marked pre-Pauline baptismal traditions whose content may point back to an origin in the mystery religions, the mysterious environment and in particular mythological concepts. But there are alternative theories which must be included in the discussion. The chapter thus becomes a broad investigation of passages on baptism in the Pauline letters (apart from Rom 6).

The Hellenistic-Christian communities' concepts of baptism are said to be reflected in three points in particular in Paul's reasoning.

First, there is a general reference to the enthusiasm which Paul must combat in the Hellenistic communities — especially in Corinth. Enthusiasm is associated with a sacramentalistic attitude, and a connection may be seen with the religious attitude described in the preceding chapter. Only rarely is this assertion challenged.[1]

Second, there is the assumption of the special Hellenistic tradition-complex in which the baptismal rite is a mystical repetition of Christ's death and resurrection. In addition to Rom 6, a number of other Pauline texts concern death and resurrection with Christ. It is often assumed that the texts reflect the same sacramentalistic basic plan under which the baptised has in

---

1. Cf. Käsemann, *Versuche* II, p. 120f., *Römer*, p. 153, Gäumann, *Taufe*, p. 48f. n. 115, p. 128 n. 28, Frankemölle, *Taufverständnis*, p. 72, Conzelmann, *Grundriss*, p. 67, Schule, p. 91 with n. 37, G. Barth, *Taufe*, p. 81ff., Schnelle, *Gerechtigkeit*, p. 79ff., Wedderburn, *Baptism*, p. 234ff., 278ff. There is no great difference between the views of supporters and opponents of the theory about mysterious dependence. See, however, Søren Agersnap, Paulinsk dåbsteologi ud fra Første Korinterbrev [Pauline baptismal theology on the basis of 1 Corinthians] in: Sigfred Pedersen (ed.), *Dåben i Ny Testamente* [Baptism in the New Testament], Århus 1982, pp. 99-117, in which I question the Corinthians sacramentalism, cf. *Paulusstudier*, p. 32f., in which I also point out that Paul uses the sacraments positively to guide the Corinthian enthusiasm for salvation.

fact experienced a death and resurrection.[2] Since Paul is said to have had his reservations about the Hellenistic view of baptism, this is merely hinted at in his letters. But it is often assumed that the consistent fundamental form without Pauline corrections is to be found in Deutero-Pauline texts, and particularly in Col 2.11-3.4.[3]

Some of the passages contain the term σὺν Χριστῷ. This expresses, sometimes in a marked manner, a connection between the events in the life of Christ and the life experienced by the Christians. This can therefore be perceived as a special formula which expresses mystical contemporaneity and association with Christ.[4] This is said to have been originally a baptismal formula relating to a ritual reliving of the Christ-event.[5]

There are, however, other views of the term σὺν Χριστῷ and of the concepts associated therewith. Its origin may have been in an apocalyptic context.[6] Σὺν Χριστῷ may be Paul's own usage.[7] Some scholars also see a backward link to the gospels' account of Jesus and the disciples as his followers.[8]

Third, there is a widespread theory about an established pre-Pauline tradition, that through baptism the baptised is incorporated into a community fellowship which arose from a collective union with Christ.

The term ἐν Χριστῷ is used in connection with baptism (Gal 3.28 and Rom 6.11). From this it is often concluded that after baptism the Christians

2. Thus Braun, *Studien*, p. 152ff., Tannehill, *Dying*, p. 2, 10-12, Gäumann, *Taufe*, p. 48f., 57f., Käsemann, *Römer*, p. 153f. (in which the traditions' background is, however, described in a more complex way).

3. Thus Käsemann, *Versuche* II, p. 120, *Römer*, p. 158, Tannehill, *Dying*, p. 10, 47f., Gäumann, *Taufe*, p. 48f., Dinkler, Taufaussagen, p. 98ff., Schnelle, *Gerechtigkeit*, p. 80, cf. also Lohse, Taufe, p. 314, Brandenburger, Auferstehung, p. 21, who assumes that the text is an adaptation of Rom 6, but in such a way that because of his knowledge of the original tradition the author of the Letter to the Colossians has overlooked the assumed Pauline reservation.

4. Specially emphasised in Karl Mittring, *Heilswirklichkeit bei Paulus. Ein Beitrag zum Verständnis der unio cum Christo* (NTF I 5), Gütersloh 1929, p. 37ff. and in particular p. 38, n. 3, in which it is concluded only from the repeated σὺν Χριστῷ in Rom 6 and other passages that baptism causes a union mystica.

5. See Kuss, *Römerbrief*, p. 376ff., Gäumann, *Taufe*, p. 57f., Conzelmann, *Grundriss*, p. 299, Käsemann, *Römer*, p. 153f.

6. See in particular Ernst Lohmeyer, Σὺν Χριστῷ, in: K.L. Schmidt (ed.), *Festgabe für Adolf Deissmann*, Göttingen 1927, pp. 218-57; p. 229ff. Similarily Jaques Dupont, Σὺν Χριστῷ, *L'union avec le Christ suivant Saint Paul* I, Bruges 1952, p. 12ff. In others, it is seen as one aspect of the origin, Gäumann, *Taufe*, p. 55ff., Käsemann, *Römer*, p. 154.

7. Thus Schnackenburg, *Heilsgeschehen*, p. 172f., Adam-Christus-Typologie, p. 46ff., Siber, *Mit Christus*, p. 251ff., Hans-Heinrich Schade, *Apokalyptische Christologie bei Paulus* (GThA 18), Göttingen 1981, p. 145. Cf. also Grundmann, σὺν — μετά, *ThWNT* VII (1960-64), pp. 766-98; p. 781, Frankemölle, *Taufverständnis*, p. 102, in which the background is to be seen in the 'corporate-personality concept'.

8. Thus Larsson, *Christus*, p. 72ff., Jervell, *Gud*, p. 95, Wilckens, *Römer* II, pp. 60-62.

are located within Christ. In an important investigation, Adolf Deissmann has asserted that throughout Paul 'the formula ἐν Χριστῷ' must be understood locally — and mystically — and refers to the Christian incorporated into Christ.[9] Käsemann in particular has developed the idea that the formula must be understood locally in a collective ecclesiological sense, so that it concerns the community of all Christians 'in Christ', which continues to be effected by baptism.[10] An alternative understanding of 'the formula ἐν Χριστῷ' has been prepared by Fritz Neugebauer; this rests upon the fact that ἐν Χριστῷ may have the function of introducing an often important 'definition of circumstances', so that the formula expresses an *affiliation* to Christ.[11] It may also be doubted whether this is a formula at all.[12]

The term βαπτίζεσθαι εἰς Χριστόν (Gal 3.27; Rom 6.5, cf. 1 Cor 12.13) may also be seen as an instance of mystery-religious thought, in that it is understood literally as an incorporation into Christ believed to be real.[13] And in this way baptism becomes an implanting into σῶμα Χριστοῦ, which is also thought to be a generally widespread Hellenistic concept of baptism to be found in 1 Cor 12.13 and behind Gal 3.27.[14] But as an alternative baptism εἰς Χριστόν may be interpreted as an expression of the affiliation to Christ which baptism gives.[15] And the background to the σῶμα Χριστοῦ concept

9. G. Adolf Deissmann, *Die neutestamentliche Formel 'in Christo Jesu'*, Marburg 1892, in which it is perceived as an individual mysticism that is particular to Paul; similarly Schneider, *Passionsmystik*, p. 9ff. Jf. Heitmüller, *Taufe*, 1903, p. 20, Bousset, *Kyrios*, p. 110, in which it is associated with the mystery religions.
10. Ernst Käsemann, *Leib und Leib Christi* (*BHTh* 9), Tübingen 1933, p. 159ff., p. 183ff., Percy, *Leib*, p. 25ff., Bultmann, *Theologie*, p. 312, Tannehill, *Dying*, p. 19f., Conzelmann, *Grundriss*, p. 291, cf. Best, *Body*, p. 20ff.
11. Fritz Neugebauer, *In Christus*, Göttingen 1961. Endorsement in Wagner, *Problem*, p. 303, Kramer, *Christos*, p. 141, Gäumann, *Taufe*, pp. 58-61 (where ἐν Χριστῷ is seen as a genuine Pauline term which is a corrective to the mysterious concepts adopted), Frankemölle, *Taufverständnis*, p. 117.
12. See in particular Friedrich Büchsel, 'In Christus' bei Paulus, *ZNW* 42 (1949), pp. 141-58, cf. Johannes Weiss, *Paulinische Probleme* II, *ThStKr* 69 (1896), pp. 7-33.
13. This can be described to the effect that the submergence into the baptismal water is no less than a movement into Christ, thus Wilhelm Heitmüller, *'Im Namen Jesu'* (*FRLANT* 2), Göttingen 1903, p. 320, *Taufe*, 1911, p. 16, Lietzmann, *Römer*, p. 65, Schneider, *Passionsmystik*, p. 37ff. Cf. also Oepke, *ThWNT* I, p. 537, Bornkamm, *Ende*, p. 37, Tannehill, *Dying*, p. 22f.
14. See Alfred Wikenhauser, *Die Kirche als das mystische Leib Christi nach dem Apostel Paulus*[2], Münster 1940, p. 99ff., 124ff., Käsemann, *Leib*, p. 159ff., Bultmann, *Theologie* p. 182, 298f., 312f., Egon Brandenburger, *Adam und Christus* (*WMANT* 7), Neukirchen 1962, p. 151ff., Tannehill, *Dying*, p. 20, 23ff., Dinkler, *Taufaussagen*, p. 70, 86.
15. See Schnackenburg, *Todes- und Lebensgemeinschaft*, s. 41, Larsson, *Christus*, s. 55, Gerhard Delling, *Die Zueignung des Heils in der Taufe*, Berlin 1961, s. 71ff., Gäumann, *Taufe*, s. 73f., Frankemölle, *Taufverständnis*, s. 41ff., Wedderburn, *Baptism*, s. 342ff. The term is then understood in line with the expression βαπτίζεσθαι εἰς τὸ ὄνομα Χριστοῦ.

may also be sought in the Old Testament 'corporate-personality concept'[16] or in Christian tradition.[17]

2. Baptism as incorporation into Christ

2.1. The union of the baptised with Christ — Gal 3.27-29

I wish to begin with the general opinion that Paul assumes a widespread Hellenistic tradition about baptism as an incorporation into Christ. The baptism reference in Gal 3.27 is an important element in this concept. We are in a reasoning process which is both complicated and wholly crucial to the context of the Letter to the Galatians.

In the struggle against the Galatians' inclination to allow themselves to be circumcised, Paul wishes to show in *Gal 3.6-4.7* that life is no longer based on justification by law but on justification by faith. The section is arranged on the basis of the rhetorical question in Gal 3.5, whether the Galatians received the spirit and salvation through legal acts or through faith.

The thesis is to be found in Gal 3.6-9: Abraham's faith was reckoned to him as righteousness (according to Gen 15.6), and the heathen peoples must also have been encompassed by this righteousness, since it says in Gen 12.3; 18.8: ἐνευλογηθήσονται ἐν σοί (Abraham) πάντα τὰ ἔθνη.[18]

Then follow the reasons; negative in Gal 3.10-12, where it is shown that the promise did not apply to the Jewish law-abiding: there is a curse only on those who are under the law, according to the law itself;[19] positive in Gal

16. See Alfred Edward John Rawlinson, Corpus Christi, in: G.K.A. Bell and Adolf Deissmann (ed.), *Mysterium Christi*, Berlin 1931, pp. 273-96; p. 286f., Schnackenburg, Todes- und Lebensgemeinschaft, p. 46, Best, *Body*, p. 99ff., Wagner, *Problem*, p. 305, Thüsing, *Per Christum*, p. 116f., Neugebauer, *In Christus*, p. 94ff., A.J.M. Wedderburn, The Body of Christ and Related Concepts in 1 Corinthians, *SJTh* 24 (1971), pp. 74-96.

17. See in particular Rawlinson, Corpus, p. 277ff., John A.T. Robinson, *The Body* (SBT 5), London 1952, p. 55ff., which points towards the Eucharist, cf. Percy, *Leib*, p. 42ff., in which the origin is seen in the locally-understood ἐν Χριστῷ which indicates Christ's vicarious self-devotion.

18. Where the Jewish interpretation of these passages emphasises that the crucial point was Abraham's fidelity to the law (see Hermann Strack and Paul Billerbeck, *Kommentar zum Neuen Testament aus Talmud und Midrasch* III⁵, Munich 1969, p. 18f.), Paul interprets them as expressing justification by faith, cf. Rom 4, and also interprets τὰ ἔθνη as meaning 'Gentiles' The final point becomes a fellowship between Abraham and the Gentile Christians, which is expressed by the terms ἐν σοί in Gal 3.8 and σὺν τῷ πιστῷ 'Αβραάμ in Gal 3.9, cf. Wedderburn, Body, p. 88f., Baptism, p. 349, in which it is established that Abraham obtains a function as 'representative', corresponding to Christ in Gal 3.16.

19. The evidence is based on Deut 27.26, interpreted with the aid of Hab 2.4 and Lev 18.5. A problem is how the verses can have evidential force, cf. Hans Lietzmann, *An die Galater* (HNT 10)⁴, Tübingen 1971, p. 19, Betz, *Galatians*, p. 145f., Christopher D. Stanley, 'Under

3.13-14, which emphasises that the Christians have been redeemed from the curse of the law by virtue of Christ's crucifixion.[20] The objective is 'that Abraham's blessing can come to the Gentiles ἐν Χριστῷ Ἰησοῦ'. This latter term is ambiguous: immediately, it will be understood instrumentally: by virtue of Jesus; but there may also be a play on the local meaning.[21] But the central assertion is clear: the Christians are included with Christ in the promise to Abraham. This will be evidenced in the remaining part of the section.

In Gal 3.15-25 this occurs particularly negatively. It is shown in various ways that the promise did not apply to the followers of law-abiding Judaism. One of the arguments, in Gal 3.16, rests on one — in our opinion laboured — exegesis of Gen 13.15: the promise was to apply only to Abraham 'and his offspring — in the singular — and not his descendants — in the plural — and this one person can only be Christ'.[22] The incontestability of the established 'testament' and the lack of freedom imposed by the law in the time before Christ is also indicated.

Opposed to this is the positive in Gal 3.26-4.7: that the Christians are the free children of the promise. It is established in Gal 3.26 that the Galatians are the sons of God through faith ἐν Χριστῷ Ἰησοῦ — the last part is ambiguous as in Gal 3.14, which is taken up again here.[23] Gal 3.27-29 does in-

a Curse': A Fresh Reading of Gal. III, 10-14, *NTS* 36 (1990), pp. 481-511. But this is of no significance to the problems here concerned.

20. The emphatic character of the central verse, Gal 3.13, is marked formally by the introductory asyndeton, cf. Albrecht Oepke, *Der Brief des Paulus an die Galater* (THkNT 9)², Berlin 1957, p. 73, Stanley, Curse, p. 505, and by the compact brevity, cf. Heinrich Schlier, *Der Brief an die Galater* (KEK 7)¹⁴, Göttingen 1971, p. 136. Here (as in vv. 10-12) the content is further emphasised by the style: it is a preceding interpretation of the quotation from Deut 21.23, 'anyone hung on a tree is under God's curse', which is interpreted as a statement that Christ has vicariously taken over the curse.

21. The instrumental interpretation is supported by the context, in which Christ's efforts are decisive; also, the adverbial member ἐν Χριστῷ Ἰησοῦ in Gal 3.14 is parallel to διὰ τῆς πίστεως and antithetical to ἐν νόμῳ in Gal 3.10. Cf. Friedr. Sieffert, *Kritisch-exegetisches Handbuch über den Brief an die Galater* (KEK 7)⁶, Göttingen 1880, p. 162, Weiss, Probleme, p. 26, Betz, Galatians, p. 154 n. 137. That the local interpretation should also be considered is because of the association with Gal 3.26-28, in which there is clearly a play on the ambiguity. It should be stressed that ἐν Χριστῷ Ἰησοῦ cannot exclusively be understood locally and as an adjectival member linked to ἔθνη (= 'Gentiles who are in Christ'), as suggested by Deissmann, Formel, p. 102; the distance is too great, and a repeat article is missing.

22. Cf. Volker Stolle, Die Eins in Gal 3, 15-29, in: Wolfgang Dietrich (ed.), *Theokratia* II, Leiden 1973, pp. 204-13. Note how clearly Paul can indicate in Gal 3.16 the grammatical form upon which he builds his reasoning.

23. Cf. note 21 above. It may also be considered here whether ἐν Χριστῷ Ἰησοῦ should be linked to the immediately preceding text, so that 'faith in Christ' is concerned, cf. Sieffert, Galater, p. 212, Lietzmann, Galater, p. 22, Dinkler, Taufaussagen, p. 85. But Paul does not

deed give an explanation of how the Gentile-Christian Galatians may have been included in the promise to Abraham and have a share in the redemption which Christ's crucifixion involved, according to the central assertion in Gal 3.13-14. At the same time, it must be explained how the Galatians can be sons — in the plural — when the promise according to Gal 3.16 applied to one person only: Christ.[24] In Gal 4.1-7 the new adoption as sons is then expanded, in contrast to the old slave-circumstances. And here there is in verses 5-6 yet another reference to the turning-point from the old existence to the new: 'When the fullness of time had come, God sent his Son, born of a woman, born under the law, in order to redeem those who were under the law, so that we might receive adoption as sons.' Both formally and inherently there is a link with Gal 3.13-14, which is again elaborated upon.

Gal 3.27-29 is in this way closely associated with Gal 3.13-14 and Gal 4.5-6, and concerns the same turning-point. But the emphasis is on the soteriological, the procurement of salvation.

Gal 3.27 reads: ὅσοι γὰρ εἰς Χριστὸν ἐβαπτίσθητε, Χριστὸν ἐνεδύσασθε.

This is a reason. The assertion in Gal 3.26 that all Galatians are sons of God by virtue of faith is substantiated. This is effected by reference to baptism as a clothing with Christ. In this context, it is certain that Paul operates with the idea that those baptised are included in Christ. But this is scarcely by reason of a quite literal understanding of εἰς Χριστὸν ἐβαπτίσθητε, where εἰς is understood in a strictly local sense. It is not the actual immersion during baptism that is in fact thought of as an implanting into Christ.[25] This would involve a strange and analogy-less identification of Christ and the

---

otherwise express himself in this way, cf. Deissmann, *Formel*, p. 103, Halter, *Taufe*, p. 109, 563 n. 2, Franz Mussner, *Der Galaterbrief* (HThKNT 9), Freiburg 1974, p. 261f.

24. This is explained by what becomes the concluding point in Gal 3.29, cf. note 35 below. Another problem is that the Galatians must all be sons, if a large part of them are women, cf. note 50 below.

25. Against Heitmüller, *Im Namen*, p. 320, *Taufe*, 1911, p. 16, Schneider, *Passionsmystik*, p. 37ff., Dibelius, *Botschaft* II, p. 142, where the interpretation is based on the German translation: '... in Christus getauft'. Cf. also Oepke, *ThWNT* I, p. 537, Tannehill, *Dying*, p. 22f. Schnelle, *Gerechtigkeit*, p. 59, 109f., polemicises against a metaphorical and 'nur bildhafte Bedeutung' of the terms Χριστὸν ἐνεδύσασθε and εἰς Χριστὸν ἐβαπτίσθητε in Gal 3.27 and of ἐν Χριστῷ 'Ιησοῦ in v. 28. He calls the identification with Christ 'tatsächlich' and speaks of a 'real' Christ-clothing, but nevertheless cannot avoid the metaphorical: 'Ist ἐνδύεσθαι sprachlich auch eine Metapher, so wird durch sie sehr wohl eine neue, sakramental begründete Wirklichkeit angezeigt' (p. 59). But this is basically the very point of all metaphors: they express a reality but do so by means of concepts taken from a different area; a term is then intended either metaphorically or literally — there are no compromises; at the same time it is clear that a metaphorical understanding of a text does not involve a weakening of the content, as is often asserted. Cf. also Deissmann, *Formel*, p. 95ff., where it is maintained that Gal 3.27-28 must be understood figuratively.

baptismal water.[26] But the main sentence in verse 27b shows that the result of baptism is intended to be a kind of 'inclusion in Christ', and thus the local sense of εἰς Χριστόν comes into the picture.[27] But at the same time it is clear that this is imagery, and that the term also (and perhaps primarily) expresses an affiliation to Christ; this is the point which is deduced in Gal 3.29, which is concerned with belonging to Christ.[28]

The more specific meaning of Χριστὸν ἐνεδύσασθε also causes problems. The term can be understood in various ways. It may refer to the fact that one receives new clothing after baptism.[29] It may be the Old Testament usage which is also found in Paul, where one clothes oneself in special power and strength.[30] Another possibility is the symbolism we met in the Isis cult, where the initiated appeared in a divine attire.[31] The term may also have been taken from the world of drama, where one clothes oneself as a specific person when playing a part as him.[32] These possibilities are not mutually

26. As a realistically-intended description of what occurs at baptism, the whole thing will collapse: the Christian does not indeed remain in the baptismal water. It cannot be denied that it is a metaphorical description of baptism, cf. Schnackenburg, *Heilsgeschichte*, p. 22f., Beasley-Murray, *Baptism*, p. 147f., Mussner, *Galaterbrief*, p. 263, Halter, *Taufe*, p. 565, and especially Dunn, *Baptism*, p. 109f., where the various literal interpretations are described as resulting from 'a pedantic and unimaginative literalism'; he also shows what it will mean if one interprets baptism as a literal Christ-clothing; then Rom 13.12,14 presumably becomes a demand to repeat the baptism event?

27. Cf. Tannehill, *Dying*, p. 23, Halter, *Taufe*, p. 112f.

28. Cf. Schnackenburg, *Todes- und Lebensgemeinschaft*, p. 41f., Neugebauer, *In Christus*, p. 103f., Halter, *Taufe*, 112f., Frankemölle, *Taufverständnis*, p. 41ff.

29. Thus Dunn, *Baptism*, p. 110, Meeks, *Image*, p. 183.

30. Thus Delling, *Zueignung*, p. 76, Mussner, *Galaterbrief*, p. 265, Oepke, ἐνδύω, *ThWNT* II (1935), pp. 319-21, in which a number of example-passages are given. The same image is to be found in Paul: Rom 13.12,14; 1 Thess 5.8, cf. 1 Cor 15.47-49.

31. This refers to Apuleius, Metam. 11.24. Thus Leipoldt, *Taufe*, p. 60, Dibelius, *Botschaft* II, p. 142, Lohse, Taufe, p. 316. Betz, *Galatians*, p. 188, interprets the Apuleius passage about a clothing into a divine redeemer-figure (which seems to be an over-interpretation). It is also connected with a gnostic concept of a clothing into a macro-cosmic redeemer-figure. An elaboration of this is to be found in Käsemann, *Leib*, p. 87ff., cf. p. 147ff., cf. also Oepke, *Galater*, p. 89f., Hanson, *Unity*, p. 79f., Schlier, *Galater*, p. 173f., Braumann, *Taufverkündigung*, p. 24, Dinkler, Taufaussagen, p. 86. This widespread interpretation will be evaluated below during examination of the religio-historical assumptions.

32. Thus Theodor Zahn, *Der Brief des Paulus an die Galater* (*KNT* 9)², Leipzig 1907, p. 186, with reference to Dionysius Hal., Ant. Rom. 11.5, cf. Oepke, *ThWNT* II, p. 321, who, however, expressly rejects the indicative use of the image. This interpretation is often disputed, e.g. Schlier, *Galater*, p. 173 n. 5, in which it is asserted that this reduces baptism to a transition to an ethical relationship in which what is concerned is to imitate Christ. But this criticism does not hit the mark as regards the viewpoint in which the concept is seen merely as a background and starting point for a figurative expression which is not to be squeezed in all its details.

exclusive, but point in the same direction: an image that every Christian begins a new section of life, characterised by Christ.

Gal 3.28a-c: οὐκ ἔνι Ἰουδαῖος οὐδὲ Ἕλλην, οὐκ ἔνι δοῦλος οὐδὲ ἐλεύθερος, οὐκ ἔνι ἄρσεν καὶ θῆλυ, makes it clear that ethnic, social and gender characteristics are of no significance after clothing in Christ. The result of the clothing is uniformity: each individual Christian is stamped by the new clothing. It wipes out differences.

Further reasons for the abolition of the differences are to be found in *Gal 3.28d*: πάντες γὰρ ὑμεῖς εἷς ἐστε ἐν Χριστῷ Ἰησοῦ. Upon incorporation, all have become equal to the one Christ. The supporting argument is the member ἐν Χριστῷ Ἰησοῦ. In isolation it can be seen as instrumentalis, or as an adverbial member expressing a link.[33] But in this context, where clothing oneself as Christ is concerned, it is undoubtedly a play on the local meaning.[34] If the Christians are each individually incorporated into Christ in this way, they can be identified with this one person.

The verse is thereby given a vital function in the context. In Gal 3.16, the promise to Abraham was limited to the one offspring. Here all are made equal to the one, and the promise can thus be extended to apply to them also. This is indeed the conclusion to be drawn in *Gal 3.29*: εἰ δὲ ὑμεῖς Χριστοῦ, ἄρα τοῦ Ἀβραὰμ σπέρμα ἐστέ, κατ' ἐπαγγελίαν κληρονόμοι.[35]

It is thus the link to Christ which is crucial in Gal 3.26-29. The Christians are incorporated into the same existence as Christ lived — which corresponds to the concept that dominates the parallel verses, Gal 4.4-5.

The question now remains, what are the concepts which form the basis of the central verses, Gal 3.27-28. Considerations of a religio-historical and traditio-historical nature lead to theories that pre-formulated, pre-Pauline material is used, or even anti-Pauline traditions.[36]

---

33. Cf. Weiss, *Probleme*, p. 26, Neugebauer, *In Christus*, p. 103f. See also section 2.4 below.
34. But this does not mean that ἐν Χριστῷ Ἰησοῦ is a formula which says that the Christians are in fact within Christ, cf. Mussner, *Galaterbrief*, p. 265f. See also section 2.4 below concerning the term ἐν Χριστῷ.
35. Cf. Sieffert, *Galater*, p. 215f., Lietzmann, *Galater*, p. 24, Oepke, *Galater*, p. 91, Schlier, *Galater*, p. 175f., Herman N. Ridderbos, *The Epistle of Paul to the Churches of Galatia* (NLC)[3], London 1961, p. 150, Jürgen Becker, Der Brief an die Galater, in: Jürgen Becker, Hans Conzelmann and Gerhard Friedrich, *Die Briefe an die Galater, Epheser, Philipper, Kolosser, Thessalonicher und an Filemon* (NTD 8), Göttingen 1976, pp. 1-85; p. 46, Halter, *Taufe*, p. 116, Betz, *Galatians*, p. 201, Stolle, *Eins*, p. 211. Different in this respect is L.J. Koch, *Fortolkning til Galaterbrevet* [Interpretation of Galatians], Copenhagen 1958, p. 109.
36. Form-critical considerations are also sometimes included to support such assertions. Gal 3.26-28 appears to be rigidly composed: verse 26 and verse 28d are corresponding statements about everyone's bonding with Christ, and at the same time the framework of verses 27-28c, which are a marked expression of the basis of baptism and the consequent

A number of terms in the text can be interpreted as expressing an incorporation into Christ.

Baptism 'into Christ' and Christians 'in Christ' have been seen as expressing a personal Christ-mysticism which can lead the thoughts towards Hellenistic religiosity.[37] But in this context no literal fusion can have been imagined between Christ and the Christians; as we have seen, Gal 3.29 continues to speak of Christians as belonging to Christ.

A more widespread theory about the background is based on the clothing concept from Gal 3.27; its origin is to be found particularly in gnostic concepts. And then it is maintained that it is basically a collective idea in which the redeemer embraces the redeemed like clothing, and so delivers them from the evil aeon.[38] This is not an obvious theory. First, a quite simple observation is opposed to this: the clothing idea cannot have its origin in concepts of a collective incorporation. This one sees if one keeps for a moment to the image aspect. Any clothing applies to individual persons;

abolition of differences, cf. Betz, *Galatians*, p. 181ff., Becker, *Auferstehung*, p. 57, Meeks, Image, p. 181, Johannes Nissen, Den urkristne dåb som kirke-sociologisk faktor [Primitive Christian baptism as a church-sociological factor], in: Sigfred Pedersen (ed.), *Dåben i Ny Testamente* [Baptism in the New Testament], Århus 1982, pp. 202-29; p. 206f., Schnelle, *Gerechtichkeit*, p. 50. Betz in particular has tried to classify the passage form-critically, and has associated it with a number of other proclamations from the New Testament which are expressed by the second person plural, such as 1 Thess 5.5, Mt 23.8, and Jesus' beatitudes from Mt 5, in Geist, p. 81f., *Galatians*, p. 182ff., which include, however, a long series of statements that are not kept in the second person plural. These is meant to be statements concerning an eschatological turn which has occurred in which past conditions have been turned upside down. 'Sitz im Leben' may have been the baptismal liturgy. As regards this theory, it must be pointed out that there are no marked formal similarities between the texts it is sought to link together form-historically, cf. Schnelle, *Gerechtigkeit*, p. 58. But it is clear that there is an intellectual relationship with the said features from Jesus' preaching.

37. See Heitmüller, *Im Namen*, p. 320, *Taufe*, 1911, p. 16, Schneider, *Passionsmystik*, p. 37ff., Dibelius, *Botschaft* II, p. 142. Cf. also Schnelle, *Gerechtigkeit*, p. 59 and 109f. with notes, although he wishes to avoid the designation 'mystical' and any idea that the 'I-you relationship' is abolished, he tries the term 'lokal-seinshaft'; but he nevertheless maintains that there is a genuine and literal connection to Christ, cf. note 25 above and the counterargument in note 26. In addition, the passage can be associated with the 'corporate-personality idea', cf. Thüsing, *Per Christum*, p. 116f.

38. Thus Oepke, *Galater*, p. 89f., Dinkler, Taufaussagen, p. 86, Betz, *Galatians*, p. 188. This 'Gewand-Vorstellung' is often referred to in Reitzenstein, *Mysterienreligionen*, who asserts, particularly on p. 179, that this is general in all mystery cults, including gnosticism which in his opinion is closely related to the mysteries. The idea is further elaborated in Käsemann, *Leib*, p. 88ff., 147ff. Different here is Schlier, *Galater*, p. 173f., who does not wish to assume a gnostic background but nevertheless presupposes a collective clothing in the heavenly being and an entry into the new aeon with reference to the concepts in Rom 13.12,14; Col 3.9-14; Eph 4.24; 6.11,14.

each receives his own clothes.[39] The image is in fact individual, and thus it is also used in Gal 3.27 and all earlier examples. Second, the clothing idea is in evidence late in gnosticism, and is not particularly widespread.[40] The gnostics use the clothing image individually, especially anthropologically: the human body is compared to a clothing, whereby the negative and transient nature of corporeality is expressed.[41] A concept of collective clothing can at most be sensed in late Mandaean texts.[42] Third, a strange confusion occurs if one wishes to associate this motif with early cosmological concepts. It is true that in Orphism and in Philo an idea can be detected that a divine person puts on the universe as an attire.[43] This comes from the widespread

39. Exceptions, in which several persons put on the same clothing, belong exclusively to the entertainment industry.

40. The example-passages referred to in the following notes are to be found in post-Christian gnostic texts which all presumably have a Christian influence, whereas the passages referred to in note 30 and 32 were Christian and pre-Christian.

41. Thus Acta Thomae 111; 147, Odes of Solomo 11.10-11; 15.8; 25.8, cf. Käsemann, *Leib*, p. 57, Meeks, Image, p. 187, Per Beskow and Sten Hidal, *Salomos oden*, Stockholm 1980, p. 88f. There is a connection with a widespread Jewish and Christian interpretation of Gen 3.21: that the garments of skins God made for Adam and Eve were the earthly bodies to replace the previous heavenly clothing. More surprising are the concepts of heavenly clothing, a glorious body, so that salvation does not consist in release from the corporeal; this might indicate that the concepts have been adopted from elsewhere (perhaps from 1 Cor 15.53-54; 2 Cor 5.1-5; Col 3.9). Gospel of Philip 101 thus speaks of clothing oneself in a living man after having undressed to go down into the water (cf. Betz, *Galatians*, p. 189, who quotes this rather late and clearly Christian-influenced gnostic text as 'background' to Gal 3.27). 'The Pearl Hymn' passed down in Acta Thomae 112-13 concerns the son of a king who take off his precious costume to travel in disguise to Egypt after a precious pearl; there he forgets his origin, has to be recalled to his task, and finally returns home to the royal castle in which he is given back the costume which resembles him like a mirror image, cf. Reitzenstein, *Mysterienreligionen*, p. 60f., 179, Käsemann, *Leib*, p. 90ff., Alfred Adam, *Die Psalmen des Thomas und das Perlenlied als Zeugnisse vor-christlicher Gnosis* (*BZNW* 24), Berlin 1959, p. 55ff., Jervell, *Imago*, p. 168, Betz, *Galatians*, p. 188. At the narrative level, it is a single person who is dressed in a costume, and a natural interpretation is that the story concerns the human spirit which is caught in the physical world and freed therefrom. There are no features in the story directly to indicate that it concerns a collective redeemer-figure or an anima generalis, as asserted by Adam, *Psalmen*, p. 56f. (in which the interpretation cannot be supported by features in the text itself but is derived from the assumed origin in old-Iranian ideas and the parellelism with Sap 18).

42. See Käsemann, *Leib*, p. 88f., 91, in which there is a reference to Ginza. But a forced interpretation of Ginza 491.12-16 is required if the collective clothing is to be found at all.

43. Fragment 192 (Kern), passed down in Pherekydes, tells that Zeus creates a large and beautiful cloak on which the earth and Oceanus are embroidered, cf. Käsemann, *Leib*, p. 87. Philo, De fug. 110, tells that logos as a divine person puts on the world as attire, corresponding to Sap 18.24, which in the same way elaborates on the description of the high-priestly costume in Ex 28; cf. on this Adam, *Psalmen*, p. 66f. See also the Christian-gnostic text UAW 16, which includes ideas about a costume containing cosmic forces and powers, cf. Pistis Sophia 10,10 (in which 1 Cor 12 is implied).

Hellenistic concept that the divine as anima generalis pervades everything. But if one wishes to use these concepts as parallels to Gal 3.27 and as an argument for a collective-clothing concept this is a misunderstanding. If the concept were to be a parallel to Gal 3.27 it would have to concern the dressing of a collective entity, the universe, in a divine person as clothing. But this concerns the opposite: that the divine person dresses himself in the universe as clothing! this is an entirely different clothing-image.[44] The texts are not therefore relevant to an understanding of Gal 3.27. The idea of putting on a divine person as clothing is found only in Gal 3.27 and texts dependent thereon.[45]

The individual character of this train of thought becomes of significance when discussing the next important member: that all are *one* in Christ (Gal 3.28d). The great majority of interpreters see the basis of this in a concept relating to σῶμα Χριστοῦ — often perceived as an established tradition in the context of baptism.[46] But there is reason for a certain amount of caution here.[47] The verses do not emphasise that the baptised amount together to a collective entity. What is important in the context is only the close link between Christ and the individual Christian, not the nature of the link. No σῶμα Χριστοῦ ecclesiology is displayed, and pre-knowledge of this idea is not necessary for understanding the term. If Paul has played on an idea of the Christians' mutual connection in σῶμα Χριστοῦ, one may be surprised that he does not make use of this idea in other places in the letter where he appeals for solidarity in the community (Gal 6.1-2) and seeks to rebuild the fellow-feeling he himself has had with the Galatians (Gal 4,12-19). That one wishes to find an established σῶμα Χριστοῦ concept behind the text is perhaps particularly because of the parallelism with 1 Cor 12.13, in which this idea is expanded. As in Gal 3.28a-c (and Col 3.10-11), differences are con-

44. This confusion of the two images emerges clearly in Hanson, *Unity*, p. 80, where he asserts that the closest religio-historical parallel of the concept that the Christians clothe themselves in Christ is the gnostic myth in which primal man is clothed in attire (= the body) which is at the same time the redeemed spirits.

45. Apuleius, Metam. 11.25 does not concern clothing in a divine person; only divine costume. One should be careful not to over-interpret, cf. Käsemann, *Leib*, p. 88, who considers the passage to be a statement from a gnostic 'Eikon-Theologie'.

46. Cf. Walter Bauer, *Wörterbuch zu den Schriften des Neuen Testaments⁶*, Berlin 1963, col. 457, Oepke, *Galater*, p. 126, Koch, *Galaterbrevet*, p. 108, Schlier, *Galater*, p. 175, Robinson, *Body*, p. 79, Conzelmann, *Grundriss*, p. 287, 297, 299, Becker, Galater, p. 45f., Betz, *Galatians*, p. 181ff., Henning Paulsen, Einheit und Freiheit der Söhne Gottes — Gal 3,26-27, ZNW 71 (1980), pp. 74-95.

47. Cf. Robert H. Gundry, *Sōma in Biblical Theology* (SNTS.MS 29), Cambridge 1976, p. 232 (where it is emphasised that it is a gross over-interpretation for Robinson, *Body*, s. 79, to state that the Christians 'have put on (the Body) of Christ'), Halter, *Taufe*, p. 116, 567.

cerned which become insignificant because of the new link with Christ.[48] But it should then be noted that 1 Cor 12.13 formally and clearly distinguishes itself from Gal 3.28: there are only two members, expressed in the plural and not denied. This is apparently a way of thinking to which Paul can freely relate.

Many interpreters find a further argument to support that Paul used a tradition in Gal 3.28a-c. Verse 28a about equality between Jews and heathens directly fits the crucial point at issue in the Letter to the Galatians. Verse 28bc — that there is no longer slave or free, male and female — is said to have no function in the larger context, and the placing of the members here can only be because they are a link in an established tradition, which Paul uses.[49] But this reasoning does not hold good. The two opposite pairs are highly relevant to the subject of the Letter to the Galatians. The contrast between existence as a slave under the law and the free life of the Spirit stamps the remainder of the Letter. And since circumcision is the specific point of dispute the equality of male and female is of great fundamental importance. In the nature of things, circumcision can apply only to the male section of the community. By using the opposites of male and female, Paul indeed indicates the risk of creating a new dividing line in the community if one uses circumcision as a sign of covenant in the new life.[50]

To summarise, I consider it reasonable to assume that we are dealing with pre-formulated material — particularly in view of its taut form and the

---

48. See Siber, *Mit Christus*, p. 192f. n. 4, cf. also the interpreters referred to in the next note.
49. Thus Meeks, Image, p. 181, Halter, *Taufe*, p. 114, Hans Dieter Betz, Geist, Freiheit und Gesetz, *ZThK* 71 (1974), pp. 78-93; p. 81, *Galatians*, p. 195, Nissen, *Dåb*, p. 207, cf. Jost Eckert, *Die urchristliche Verkündigung im Streit zwischen Paulus und seinen Gegnern*, Regensburg 1971, p. 88. Dieter Lührmann, *Der Brief an die Galater* (ZB.NT 7), Zürich 1978, pp. 65-68, decides that it is a basic rule for the Christian community that the three most important differences in society are abolished. See also Oepke, *Galater*, p. 90f., Mussner, *Galaterbrief*, p. 264f., which gives explanations of the members not considered to be directly relevant in the context.
50. Cf. F.F. Bruce, *The Epistle to the Galatians*, Grand Rapids 1982, p. 189. This contribution to the debate can be considered in two ways. From a humorous aspect it is a coarse taunt: when Paul indicates the difference between man and woman he forces the recipients to think about the tangible, physical aspect of the matter; and circumcision is an unpleasant, not wholly safe, operation. He employs similarly coarse allusions in Gal 5.12, where he plays on the fact that there is no great distance between circumcision and castration, and in Gal 6.13, in which he makes circumcision a cultic stigmatisation applied to the flesh of others, cf. the discussion of this passage in Chapter 4, section 3.3 below. But at the same time it can be seen as a fundamental, important part of the theological discussion. In both Gal 3.26 and in 4.6-7, Paul speaks of all Christians as υἱοὶ θεοῦ. He does not use, as in the parallel passage, Rom 8.16-17, the gender-neutral term τέκνα θεοῦ. The emphasis is that all Christians have the same status as sons: they are free and independent. And here circumcision must make no distinction between first-rank and second-rank Christians.

thought-laden central content. There is still a possibility that they are merely favourite Pauline formulations.[51] If a tradition is being used, there is no reason to consider whether Paul is opposing an enthusiastic Hellenistic attitude.[52] It may be a pre-Pauline tradition, or rather a Pauline tradition since Paul is assumed to have influenced the traditions which arose in the communities he built up.[53] As regards the content of the baptism concept which we encounter in Gal 3.26-29, what is crucial is the bonding with Christ — radically expressed as a new identity. It is not necessary to assume specific Hellenistic mythological thought processes to understand the text.

2.2. 1 Cor 12.12-13 and the σῶμα Χριστοῦ idea

We have here a context in which there is no doubt that baptism is associated with an ecclesiological use of an idea concerning σῶμα Χριστοῦ.

In 1 Cor 12-14, Paul deals with the question of the charismatics, 'spiritual gifts'. He turns particularly against a trend within the community towards competition with one another and a preference for the ecstatic gift of tongues. What must be decisive is not the intensity of the experience but its quality: whether the gifts serve Christ and the community. In 1 Cor 12.4-11, Paul points out the many charismatics in the community, but at the same time emphasises the unity: one Spirit, one Lord, one God. That there must be this unity within the multiplicity is substantiated in *1 Cor 12.12-27*: using an image of the community as one body in which every member has its specific function, it is argued that there is profit in the existence of various and unevenly distributed gifts of grace. This simile of the community as a living organism corresponds to a known and widespread image in popular philosophy which illustrates that a society functions by virtue of many parts with different functions.[54] The simile is thus developed quite traditionally in 1 Cor. 12.14-26.

But something remarkable happens in *1 Cor 12.12*. The image is in-

---

51. Thus Lietzmann, *Galater*, p. 23, cf. Mussner, *Galaterbrief*, p. 264f., Halter, *Taufe*, p. 114f.
52. Since in that case Paul would not have used it! It is nevertheless asserted that it is an expression of the enthusiastic attitude Paul is opposing in the Letters to the Corinthians — Käsemann, *Versuche* II, p. 124f., Betz, *Geist*, p. 80ff., Becker, *Auferstehung*, p. 57, 63, Siegfried Schultz, Die Charismenlehre des Paulus, in: Johannes Friedrich, Wolfgang Pöhlmann and Peter Stuhlmacher (ed.), *Rechtfertigung. Festschrift für Ernst Käsemann*, Tübingen 1976, pp. 443-60; p. 455, cf. against this Halter, *Taufe*, p. 566f., Betz, *Transferring*, p. 107.
53. Cf. Bruce, *Galatians*, p. 187.
54. Best known is a fable by Menesius Agrippa, quoted in Livy 2. 32.9-12. An outline of other examples is to be found in Hans Lietzmann, *An die Korinther* I/II (*HNT* 9)⁵ (ergänzt von Werner Georg Kümmel), Tübingen 1969, p. 62, Jacobus Johannes Meuzelar, *Der Leib des Messias*, Assen 1961, p. 149ff.

troduced not merely as a comparison; it is said to be a direct and pertinent description of the Church. First comes the image part: 'For just as the body is one and has many members, and all the members of the body, though many, are one body ...' One might then expect that the object part concerned the community: 'thus also the various members of the Church form an entity' or the like.[55] But instead it reads: οὕτως καὶ ὁ Χριστός. What happens is that the community, which is imagined as a body, is simply on a par with Christ. Similarly, following the development of the image in 1 Cor 12.14-26, this is directly emphasised in 1 Cor 12,27: 'You are the body of Christ'.

There may perhaps be some doubt about the precise meaning of these statements. Is there a direct identification between the community and Christ in 1 Cor 12.12, or should one choose a softer rendering: 'this is how it is where Christ is'?[56] And how indeed is the term σῶμα Χριστοῦ to be understood? It may be that the Christians are 'the body that belongs to Christ'.[57] Or that they are 'the body which Christ constitutes'.[58]

But there should be no doubt about the function of these striking terms. They intensify the representation of the matter. This effect in fact arises because this is so surprising a turn of phrase. And the term is understandable even without special prerequisites,[59] since immediately thereafter Paul gives a reason for speaking in this way.

The reason appears in *1 Cor 12.13:* καὶ γὰρ ἐν ἑνὶ πνεύματι ἡμεῖς πάντες

---

55. Cf. Johannes Weiss, *Der erste Korintherbrief* (KEK 5)[10], Göttingen 1925, p. 302f., Heinz-Dietrich Wendland, *Die Briefe an die Korinther* (NTD 7)[13], Göttingen 1972, p. 111, Lietzmann, *Korinther*, p. 63, Hans Conzelmann, *Der erste Brief an die Korinther* (KEK 5)[11], Göttingen 1969, p. 249, Halter, *Taufe*, p. 167.

56. Thus Heinrich Schlier, *Christus und die Kirche im Epheserbrief* (BHTh 6), Tübingen 1930, p. 40f. (in an attempt to establish that Paul reaches no further than the analogy between the community and a body). Cf. against this Käsemann, *Leib*, p. 162, Percy, *Leib*, p. 5, Kümmel i Lietzmann, *Korinther*, p. 187, who (justly) holds to what is sharp and pointed in the term.

57. Thus Schlier, *Christus*, p. 41, who understands the genitive as the possessive, and in turn achieves a distance between Christ and the Christians.

58. That is to say an epexegetic genitive, which is the most widespread solution, cf. Käsemann, *Leib*, p. 162, Wikenhauser, *Kirche*, p. 101, Percy, *Leib*, p. 4f., Meuzelar, *Leib*, p. 5ff., Ridderbos, *Paulus*, p. 264, Halter, *Taufe*, p. 167. There is thus a more direct identity between Christ and the Christians.

59. Contrary to Käsemann, *Leib*, p. 159ff., Percy, *Leib*, p. 4f., Schweizer, σῶμα κτλ., *ThWNT* VII (1960-64), pp. 1024-91; p. 1068f., in which it is maintained that the use of Christ as an expression of communal fellowship is understandable only if one already agreed with the concept of Christ as such a collective figure, cf. the discussion below on the religiohistorical background. But it should be remembered here that it may be a member in a compositional technique which Paul also employs elsewhere: a surprising, puzzling statement is introduced, which is later shown to be quite reasonable and obvious — thus for example in Rom 10.4 and Rom 6,2, cf. Chapter VI below.

εἰς ἓν σῶμα ἐβαπτίσθημεν, εἴτε Ἰουδαῖος εἴτε Ἕλληνες εἴτε δοῦλοι εἴτε ἐλεύθεροι, καὶ πάντες ἓν πνεῦμα ἐποτίσθημεν.

The vital argument lies in the phrase πάντες εἰς ἓν σῶμα ἐβαπτίσθημεν. It appears to be an ambiguous term. There may be a play on the term βαπτί- ζεσθαι εἰς Χριστόν (finally understood). Through baptism, all Christians have achieved a close connection with Christ, and Christ is he who died for their sake, he whose body was sacrificed. Therefore one can also say that baptism gives connection with this one body (or corpse). One has then the term πάντες εἰς ἓν σῶμα ἐβαπτίσθημεν.[60] But this can also be understood in another way, which also intrudes into the context. It can be read to mean that through baptism all Christians are incorporated into the one body which Christ constitutes. Grammatically, this interpretation can be made in two ways: either εἰς can be understood locally, so that the limbs, those baptised, are incorporated into a body, which is thus already in existence;[61] or εἰς can be more specifically defined as consecutive — the body has arisen by an as- sociation of the many baptised.[62] In neither case does it become a smooth and coherent concept.[63] It should thus not be understood literally. But the term and the play on words is striking as a reason for presenting the com- munity as an organism which is so comprehensively determined by Christ that it is simply called the body of Christ.[64]

Additionally, the reason for the close fellowship between the members

---

60. Cf. L. Cerfaux, *La Théologie de l'Eglise suivant Saint Paul* (*Unam sanctam* 10)², Paris 1948, p. 207f., Halter, *Taufe*, p. 168, 590f., Wedderburn, *Body*, p. 79, *Baptism*, p. 62f. with n. 9.

61. Thus Bultmann, *Glauben* I, p. 166, *Theologie*, p. 312, Hanson, *Unity*, p. 75ff., Percy, *Leib*, p. 16, Kümmel i Lietzmann, *Korinther*, p. 187, Conzelmann, *1. Korinther*, p. 249f., Lohse, *Taufe*, p. 318, Schnelle, *Gerechtigkeit*, p. 121.

62. Thus Weiss, *1. Korinther*, p. 303, Archibald Robertson and Alfred Plummer, *A Critical and Exegetical Commentary on the First Epistle of St. Paul to the Corinthians* (*ICC*)², Edinburgh 1914, p. 272, Lietzmann, *Korinther*, p. 63, Wendland, *Korinther*, p. 111, Wikenhauser, *Kirche*, p. 102, Schnackenburg, *Heilsgeschehen*, p. 23f.

63. Cf. as to these difficulties, the discussion between Jeremias, Benoit, Dinkler, de la Pot- terie, Schnackenburg and Cambier i Dinkler, *Römer* 6,1-14, pp. 111-14. In the first case we have a body that existed before the parts of which it consists. The second opinion is directly supported by the subsequent context, where on the image side several references speak of God's creation of the body, 1 Cor 12.18,24,28. But as a direct description of bap- tism itself it is of no use. Strictly speaking, there must then have been simultaneity be- tween everyone's baptism, and Christ would have come into existence only on that oc- casion.

64. Thus also Ridderbos, *Paulus*, p. 267f., who, following a discussion about literal or meta- phorical interpretation, concludes: 'Die Bezeichnung der Gemeinde als Leib Christi hat also eine uneigentliche, metaphorische Bedeutung, so real und eigentlich die darin ausge- drückte Gemeinschaft mit Christus auch ist.' This discussion is associated with the question of the religio-historical background, cf. below in connection with notes 76-77 and 82-90.

of the community is given in the other parts of 1 Cor 12.13. There is not only the common link to the one Christ, but also the common arming with the one Spirit, as it says at the beginning of verse 13a.[65] And it is repeated in verse 13c that 'we have all received the one Spirit to drink' — at baptism or perhaps at the Eucharist.[66] Verse 13b establishes that the ethnic and social differences in the Church are of no great importance compared with the mutual fellowship; this emphasises how much is meant by the common link with Christ and the Spirit.[67]

By giving this comprehensive reason for using the concept of an organism in regard to the Christian community, Paul gives the image a special intensity. He develops the image part of the simile accordingly in 1 Cor 12.14-26 and uses it directly of the community's situation in 1 Cor 12.28. Then (in 1 Cor 13) love is included as the crucial principle to be utilised in building up the fellowship (1 Cor 14).

It is thus a central idea here that baptism is seen as an incorporation into the body of Christ.

65. The term ἐν ἑνὶ πνεύματι is scarcely to be understood locally about the baptism elements as assumed by Weiss, *1. Korinther*, p. 303, Robertson and Plummer, *1 Corinthians*, p. 272, Lietzmann, *Korinther*, p. 63, Percy, *Leib*, p. 15, but rather instrumentally about the force active at baptism, cf. Halter, *Taufe*, p. 169, William F. Orr and James Arthur Walther, *1 Corinthians* (*AncB* 32), Garden City New York 1976, p. 277, 284, who indicates the difficulty of distinguishing strictly between local and instrumental meaning.

66. Most interpreters believe that the reference is only to baptism, since the aorist form ἐποτίσθημεν must concern a one-off event, and the image can easily be understood in accordance with the context: the Christians have been watered (like plants) by baptism; see Weiss, *1. Korinther*, p. 303, Robertson and Plummer, *1 Corinthians*, p. 272, Wendland, *Korinther*, p. 112, F.F. Bruce, *1 and 2 Corinthians* (*NCB*), London 1971, p. 121, Orr and Walther, *1 Corinthians*, p. 284, Halter, *Taufe*, p. 172f., who also indicates the strongly formal parallelism between 1 Cor 12.13a and 1 Cor 12.13c. But it is precisely this conscious, formal parallelism which can also be used as an argument that the aorist form should not be pressed too hard (it is well-known that aorist can also refer to the action repeated in the past). Some also point to the Eucharist, such as Rawlinson, *Corpus*, p. 286f., Käsemann, *Leib*, p. 176, Cerfaux, *Théologie*, p. 207. Others consider that both baptism and the Eucharist may have been intended, Lietzmann, *Korinther*, p. 63, Ernst Käsemann, Anliegen und Eigenart der paulinischen Abendmahlslehre, in: *Exegetische Versuche und Besinnungen* I³, Göttingen 1964, pp. 11-34; p. 15f. (with reference to 1 Cor 10.3-4), Conzelmann, *1. Korinther*, p. 250, Schnelle, *Gerechtigkeit*, p. 244.

67. Cf. Lietzmann, *Korinther*, p. 63, who considers 1 Cor 12.13b to be a disturbing insertion; the corresponding members in Gal 3.28 and Col 3.11 are part of a context in which the point is that all differences have been abolished by baptism; in 1 Cor 12, the main point is that differences are necessary. Halter, *Taufe*, p. 170f., refines the assertion: verse 13b is a parenthesis with a form and function different from the parallels: it is to show the unity despite all differences. But then perhaps all of verse 13 is a parenthesis with this objective.

But now the question arises, whether the background to the concept is an established and widespread Hellenistic-Christian baptismal tradition. This is the general opinion, resting upon various redactio-historical and traditio-historical considerations.

The first consideration relates to the background to the concept, which has been sought in particular in Hellenistic thought.

The comparison itself between the community and a body is, as indicated, in line with the image of society as an organism, which is widespread in popular Hellenistic philosophy.[68]

But it is a widespread assumption that the more direct presentation of the community as the body of Christ must have its roots in a special gnostic mythology. Käsemann in particular has looked back to the gnostics' cosmological speculations, the 'Aion doctrine' and the 'Anthropos myth'.[69] The main idea here is said to be that redemption consists in the pneumatics' incorporation into the macrocosmic redeemer-figure. But direct parallels, in which the redeemed are seen as limbs on the redeemer's body, are not to be found until the second century, and then only in *Christian* gnosticism where Christ is normally seen as the body's head.[70] If one also takes into account

---

68. Cf. note 54 above.
69. Käsemann, *Leib*, p. 50ff., where the position is elaborated, is very largely dependent upon Reitzenstein, *Mysterienreligionen*, and his other works, where — on the basis of texts from the first post-Christian centuries — he tries to reconstruct a very early gnosticism which goes back to Indo-Iranian concepts from the 5th century before Christ. Käsemann's position then becomes more radical than the contemporary work of Schlier, *Christus*, p. 39ff., where it is asserted that only the Deutero-Pauline passages depend upon gnostic concepts, not the Pauline texts, cf. Wikenhauser, *Kirche*, p. 239, who sees the primal man-redeemer myth as a probable linguistic and figurative background, whereas Paul himself has developed the theological-objective content. Käsemann's viewpoint has met with support, and has become the basis of further discussion, cf. Rudolf Bultmann, Johanneischen Schriften und Gnosis, in: *Exegetica*, Tübingen 1967, pp. 230-54; p. 250, *Theologie*, p. 182f., Hegermann, *Vorstellung*, p. 153 (which indicates, however, a pre-gnostic Aion concept which is said to be particularly visible in Philo, cf. note 74 below), Brandenburger, *Adam*, pp. 151-53, Conzelmann, *Grundriss*, p. 287. Later, Käsemann himself has become much more restrained — cf. Ernst Käsemann, Das theologische Problem des Motivs vom Leibe Christi, in: *Paulinische Perspektiven*, Tübingen 1969, pp. 178-210; p. 179ff., where, in addition to the Anthropos myth, there is a reference to the Stoic metaphor and the Jewish corporate-personality concept as a possible background, and *Römer*, p. 324f., on the parallel in Rom 12.4-5, where the only religio-historical concept which is given any weight is an original pre-Platonic concept of cosmos as a giant body pervaded by divine power, and here there is even a reservation as regards the viewpoint that the concept is used directly in Paul, cf. notes 76-77 below.
70. See exemplary material in Käsemann, *Leib*, p. 80f., cf. p. 169. The oldest is from the 2nd cent. AD, The Odes of Solomon 17.15-17: 'They accepted my blessing and were given life; they gathered around me and were saved. For they became my limbs and I their head. Praise be to you, our head, O Lord Christ.' It should be noted that it is disputed in

that to the gnostics 'the body' is generally something negative, it indicates far more that on this point gnosticism depends on the Pauline texts.[71]

But there are some older Greek cosmological concepts which may be the source of the Pauline concepts. Heinrich Schlier has indicated a widespread Greek idea that the universe can be represented as a living organism.[72] Plato and the stoics speak of cosmos as a body, and the idea can be transferred to the polis-society.[73] This concept is also widespread in the religious

research whether The Odes of Solomon are gnostic, see James Hamilton Charlesworth, The Odes of Solomon — Not Gnostic, *CBQ* 31 (1969), pp. 357-69, Beskow and Hidal, *Oden*, p. 77f.; but it is impossible to ignore the Christian strain in this passage in particular. In about AD 200, Clement, Exerpta ex Theodoto 42, quotes gnostic concepts, in which there is a distinction between Jesus and Christ, referred to as the head, and in which it is said that Christ adopted Jesus' body, which is of the same being as the Church. This is influenced by the Christian idea of taking up the cross and following Jesus (Mark 8.24, with parallels, and Mt 10.38, with parallel), cf. also Percy, *Leib*, p. 39ff. Clement, Eclogae Propheticae 56,2f., quotes a corporative concept, which may be gnostic; here there occurs an incorporation into another divine figure, i.e. Helios/the sun; but we are again in a Christian context — '... since a body is constituted of all those who received the same belief and justification — who are introduced into the same entity; but some were placed shining upon the sun as head, some as eyes, some as ears, some as hands, some as breasts, some as feet.' This is a reference to a statement by Pantainos, a Stoic who became a Christian and perhaps a gnostic. The accordance with 1 Cor 12.12-27 (same parts of the body) should be noted; also the terms 'belief' and 'justification' imply a dependence upon Paul; the passage comes as a comment on Ps 19.5b(4b): 'In the heavens he has set out a tent for the sun', and 'tent' equates to 'body' as in 2 Cor 5.1-2. Cf. Schweizer, *ThWNT* VII, p. 1089, Best, *Body*, p. 224, 85. The other gnostic parallels, such as those cited by Käsemann, are to be found only in Mandaean and Manichaean texts even centuries later.

71. Cf. Percy, *Leib*, p. 41, Best, *Body*, p. 223ff., Karl Martin Fischer, *Tendenz und Absicht des Epheserbriefes* (FRLANT 111), Göttingen 1973, p. 74f., Wedderburn, Body, p. 85.

72. See Heinrich Schlier, Corpus Christi, in: Theodor Klauser (ed.), *Reallexicon für Antike und Christentum* III, Stuttgart 1957, cols. 437-53, cf. Eduard Schweizer, Die Kirche als Leib Christi in den paulinischen Antilegomena, in: *Neotestamentica*, Zürich 1963, pp. 293-316; p. 296, *ThWNT* VII, p. 1034, 1041. In Käsemann, *Leib*, p. 87f., the earlier ideas are incorporated in the arguments in support of a gnostic background. This is an inheritance from the religio-historical school, and Reizenstein in particular, in which gnosticism was seen as a precondition also for the mysteries and Orphism — a theory with no secure foundation, cf. Arthur Darby Nock, Gnosticism, in: *Essays on Religion and the Ancient World* II, Oxford 1972, pp. 940-59, Hengel, *Sohn*, p. 53ff.

73. Cf. Schlier, *RAC* III, col. 439ff. In Plato, Timaios 30B, 34B, there is a reference to τὸ ζῷον as σῶμα τοῦ πάντος or σῶμα τοῦ κόσμου. A leading idea in stoicism is that the divine, logos, as an anima generalis pervades cosmos; cf. Diogenes Laërtius 7.143, and especially Seneca, Ep. 92,30: ... unum est deus; et socii sumus ejus et mebra, and Ep. 95,52: omne hoc, quod vides, quo divina atque humana conclusa sunt, unum est; membra sumus corpore magni. The idea of society as macro-cosmos is to be found in Plato, Resp. 5, 464B. The popular image of society as a body with limbs, cf. note 54 above, can then be seen as an offshoot of this concept. Schlier, indicates (col. 441) that this usage can be more than a comparison — an established idiom. T.W. Manson, A parallel to a N.T. Use of

field. In such different contexts as Orphism and Hellenistic Judaism, cosmos can be conceived as a giant body with a deity as the controlling principle, or simply identified with the deity.[74] A connection can also be seen with the idea of 'cosmic sympathy': the basis of Hellenistic religious and magical thought is that the world is a coherent and animated whole with demons and divine powers that can be influenced.[75] This material shows that we are dealing with usage and thought which are related to 1 Cor 12. But nevertheless it is unlikely that this concept is something Paul adopts or uses directly as point of reference for his σῶμα Χριστοῦ idea. For this is a pantheistic cosmology which rests on a dualistic concept of the body in which the divine is the soul — the controlling principle in the world — while the body itself and thus the material things of the world are something external and temporary. Transferred to 1 Cor 12.12-27, this would mean that Christ must be the Spirit who as controlling principle pervades the body and the limbs, which are the community and its members. This corresponds to the older perception of the σῶμα Χριστοῦ idea as pure mysticism.[76] Relative to this, it will be maintained that Paul does not have this dualism between body and spirit; that the body of Christ is to be understood as the body which is Christ himself; and that what is crucial is the Christians' link to the body.[77]

Alternatively, an Old Testament-Jewish background has been suggested for the σῶμα Χριστοῦ idea. In this context a 'corporate personality' is referred to, and it is emphasised that this is a special Hebrew mode of thought

---

σῶμα, *JThS* 37 (1935), p. 385, has pointed to Augustus' 3rd Edict, in which the term Ἑλλήνων σῶματι occurs. But doubts have arisen about whether this really means 'the Hellenes' society', cf. Cerfaux, *Théologie*, p. 208ff., Schlier, loc.cit.

74. It is relevant here to introduce the cosmological clothing-concept, which had to be seen as misleading in connection with Gal 3.27, cf. note 43 above. In addition to Orphic Fragment 192, which concerns cosmos as the clothing which encircles the divine, Orphic Fragment (Kern) 168 may also be indicated, in which Zeus is identified with the universe and in particular is the head of the gigantic body, cf. Schlier, *Christus*, p. 46, Best, *Body*, p. 224. Hegermann, *Vorstellung*, p. 47ff., 153f., especially has emphasised the Philonic concepts about a macro-cosmic body pervaded by divine power, with the emphasis on Philo, De somn. 1.128, that speaks of logos, which is 'like the head on a united body' (p. 66). Schlier, *RAC* III, sp. 445, connects the thoughts with the primal-man myth, which comes into the picture in other contexts. See in particular Chapter 5, section 4.3 below on Rom 5.12-21 and the primal-man concept.

75. Cf. the considerations on the nature of magic in Chapter II, section 3.3 above.

76. Cf. Traugott Schmidt, *Der Leib Christi*, Leipzig 1919, p. 142ff., Karl Ludwig Schmidt, Die Kirche des Urchristentums, in: K.L. Schmidt (ed.), *Festgabe für Adolph Deissmann*, Tübingen 1927, pp. 258-319; p. 312, Wikenhauser, *Kirche*, p. 87f.

77. Cf. as regards the interpretation of 1 Cor 12.27 above notes 61-62. Cf. also Best, *Body*, p. 97, Käsemann, *Römer*, p. 324. Cf. in addition the discussion of parallel passages below, in which what is crucial seems to be this affiliation to Christ.

where the individual sees himself primarily as part of a collective.[78] But the description seems misleading. The term indicates that there should be a Hebrew usage in which a collective can be referred to as a 'corporate personality'. But this is exclusively an antique Greek and modern European metaphor.[79] It transpires that nowhere in the Old Testament or other antique Semitic texts can one find 'the body' used as an image of the connection between several people.[80] One must be content with more general references to concepts of collective responsibility, progenitor ideas, primal-man concepts, Israel as the elect and as a vine.[81] Although there is this idea of solidarity, true parallels to the Pauline means of expression are thus lacking.

The religio-historical material shows that at the time there were clear points of contact for the σῶμα Χριστοῦ idea. On the basis of the widespread use of the σῶμα metaphor in the Hellenistic world (and perhaps also the Jewish solidarity idea), Paul could indeed anticipate that his mode of thought would be understood. But one cannot by this means point to a specific, established complex of ideas which Paul adopts.

By reference back from the available text, one can argue that Paul had to employ a widespread set of mythological ideas.

It is indicated here in particular that there is not only the figurative idea in 1 Cor 12.14-26, in which the community is *like* a body; there is also a direct description of the community as the body of Christ in 1 Cor 12.12-13,27.

78. Cf. Rawlinson, *Corpus*, p. 286f., Percy, *Leib*, p. 38f., 41ff., Robinson, *Body*, p. 59ff., Schnackenburg, Todes- und Lebensgemeinschaft, p. 44ff.
79. Cf. Rogerson, *Conception*, p. 2f., who has shown that the term 'corporate personality' has been taken from present-day English legislation.
80. Cf. the emphasis on this in Best, *Body*, p. 221f., cf. p. 112. Robinson, *Body*, p. 11ff., cf. p. 112, contains a strange attempt to substantiate the concept of 'corporate personality' with linguistic arguments; this indeed takes its point of reference in the very fact that Hebrew lacks a clear equivalent to the Greek σῶμα, and it is maintained that the Hebraic בשׂר does not refer to anything that separates a man from his neighbour but to something that binds him to other people and to nature (p. 15). Cf. the criticism of the method of reasoning in James Barr, *The Semantics of Biblical Language*, Oxford 1961, p. 35ff., Gundry, *Sōma*, p. 22f., 118 etc. Other scholars try to show that Judaism also was aware of a macrocosmic primal man by the reference to Ex Rabba 40.5, which speaks of Adam as he in whom all later generations are contained, cf. Percy, *Leib*, p. 41, W.D. Davies, *Paul and Rabbinic Judaism*, London, 1955, p. 57, Schlier, *RAC* III, col.
81. See Best, *Body*, p. 20ff., 93f, 99f., Eduard Schweizer, Die Kirche als Leib Christi in den paulinischen Homologumena, in: *Neotestamentica*, Zürich 1963, pp. 272-92, Wedderburn, *Body*, p. 80ff. (cf. p. 85, 95f., in which he modifies and defines, so that 'corporate personality' does not become an alien concept but a more down-to-earth idea about solidarity and representation). This complex of ideas comes into the picture several times, cf. in particular Chapter V, section 4.2 below.

But this cannot be used as an argument that the latter idea must then have a different and quite separate background.[82] There may be merely a difference in the form and intensity of the statements.[83]

There is also no basis for this formal reasoning: in 1 Cor 12.12-13,27, Paul does not say that the Christians are *like* the body of Christ; it is not therefore a metaphor; but it literally points to a specific reality.[84] This is mistaken, particularly at the formal level. That the word ὡς is absent in connection with σῶμα Χριστοῦ does not go against understanding it as a metaphor. It is indeed characteristic of the metaphor, in contrast to the comparison, that an image is introduced without the use of this particle. In this way, Paul often speaks metaphorically: about the community as a chaste virgin (2 Cor 11.2), or as olive branches (Rom 11.17-24).[85] And inherently it collapses if σῶμα Χριστοῦ is to be interpreted literally. It has already been shown that the mode of thought cannot be entirely smooth in 1 Cor 12.13.[86] There will also be serious discrepancies in Paul's theology if the verse is understood to mean literally and mythologically that the Christians are quite factually incorporated in the body of Christ at baptism. Then there will no longer be any distance between Christ and the Christians. Since Christ has risen, Paul must also think that at baptism the Christians have already taken part in the life of resurrection.[87] And how can it be understood literally that all Christians are parts of the body of Christ? Presumably only if this is an ecstatic-mystical-mythological concept in which the Christians' actual selves are to be found in a supernatural fusion with Christ — and the

---

82. Against Käsemann, *Römer*, p. 323, Percy, *Leib*, p. 45f., Hegermann, *Vorstellung*, p. 148.

83. Cf. below in connection with note 90.

84. Thus Robinson, *Body*, p. 51, cf. p. 59f., cf. Käsemann, *Römer*, p. 323. There is in general a marked tendency to treat all talk of a figurative understanding as a weakening of the statement, and to insist that Paul is speaking literally and realistically, cf. Weiss, *1. Korinther*, p. 302, Lietzmann, *Korinther*, p. 52, Hansson, *Unity*, p. 76f., Conzelmann, *1. Korinther*, p. 249, Käsemann, *Perspektiven*, p. 181f., Jewett, *Terms*, p. 303, Halter, *Taufe*, p. 168, Schnelle, *Gerechtigkeit*, p. 121, 139f.

85. Gundry, *Sōma*, p. 234, incisively asks why these terms also (which are likewise not introduced by ὡς) should not be understood literally, cf. Best, *Body*, p. 99. Gundry has also indicated that it becomes nonsense if one assumes that a precondition in 1 Cor 12 is that the community is in fact the body of Christ. For then in 1 Cor 12.12,14-26 Paul is comparing the community to something they in fact *are* (p. 238).

86. Cf. notes 63-64 above.

87. As far as I can see, it is precisely such dogmatic consequences of the σῶμα Χριστοῦ concept that are to be combated in Käsemann, *Perspektiven*, pp. 178-210. The mythological and literal understanding of the concept is nevertheless maintained, which has these consequences (p. 182f.). Cf. Wedderburn, *Body*, p. 83. Gundry, *Sōma*, p. 233, contains a corresponding criticism of the dogmatic problems in Robinson, *Body*.

present earthly life is understood as a sham existence — that is, pure mysticism.[88]

Accordingly, the last argument also disappears: that the mode of thought surrounding 1 Cor 12.12-13, in which the community is equated to the body of Christ, is so complicated that only the Corinthians could understand it, provided they already knew the concept of Christ as a universal personality.[89] It becomes a circular argument. The verses become complicated because of the attempts to understand them literally and mythologically. If the verses do not contain the supposed mythological complex of ideas, no special assumptions are called for on the part of the recipients. It has indeed been shown that the mode of thought can be developed on the basis of widespread concepts and general usage. Thus the text makes good sense: Paul first begins with a comparison between the community and a living organism. The description is then intensified, and we get a metaphor — it is said that there is a strong structural accordance between a body and the community if it is bound to Christ.[90] A reason is given for this, with a play on words and a reference to baptism and the Eucharist. This does not signify that these are stable ecclesiological concepts, since Paul would then be able simply to refer to them. And neither did he need to develop comparisons so painstakingly. The mode of thought may be under construction.

But it is still possible that a separate Hellenistic baptismal tradition can be demonstrated on the basis of parallel terms in other Pauline texts.

The First Letter to the Corinthians speaks directly of the body of Christ in two contexts, in connection with the Eucharist, and two other texts from this can be considered, together with two passages in the Letter to the Romans.

The traditional words instituting the Eucharist are quoted in *1 Cor 11.23-29* — where Jesus interprets the bread as his body — and the following commentary speaks of the obligation relative to the 'body of the Lord'. This is the crucial argument in the matter of the divine-service meetings which has

---

88. This means that the consistent interpretation is that to be found in Schmidt, *Leib*, p. 142ff., cf. note 76 above. See also Conzelmann, *Grundriss*, p. 287, which speaks of a mythological, not realistic, concept of the body.

89. As assumed by Käsemann, *Leib*, p. 159ff., Percy, *Leib*, p. 4f., Schweizer, *ThWNT* VII, p. 1068f.

90. Cf. Käsemann, *Perspektiven*, p. 182: 'Der Apostel bedient sich des Ausdrucks "Christusleib", weil er tatsächlich eines Leibes aufzeigen will ...' He thus, as far as I can see, expresses what is the essence of the metaphor: it expresses an isomorphism in the strongest way by taking an image from another aspect of reality. Similarly, Conzelmann, *1. Korinther*, p. 249, agrees de facto with the metaphorical interpretation when he writes, 'das nicht nur ein Bild vorliegt, sondern der "eigentliche" Gebrauch.'

been given an unfair character. Paul says nothing about the background. One has guessed at theological motifs for the conflict — anti-sacramentalism or unadulterated sacramentalism; but it may also be merely disorder and thoughtlessness.[91] Paul thinks he can resolve the conflict by imprinting the traditional words instituting the Eucharist. By the word 'bread', the member τὸ ὑπὲρ ὑμῶν emphasises Jesus' sacrifice for the sake of the community. The chalice is similarly interpreted as a covenant sacrifice. There follows in 1 Cor 11.26 a traditional-sounding interpretation of the Eucharist: it is a proclamation of the Lord's death until he comes. In 1 Cor 11.27-28 Paul exhorts that, through self-examination, unworthiness and guilt should be avoided in the face of the Lord's body and blood. He warns in 1 Cor 11.29 against eating and drinking without discernment τὸ σῶμα. What Paul is using is a main feature from the Eucharistic tradition: Jesus' self-devoted death for the sake of the Christians.[92] Selfishness and absence of solidarity are in contrast to this. The Christians' dependence upon Jesus' acts of solidarity is thus emphasised. It is remarkable that in this connection there is no trace

---

91. Particularly in the past, the conflict was seen in an anti-sacramentalism in which one felt oneself superior to the Eucharist — thus W. Lütgert, *Freiheitspredigt und Schwarmgeister in Korinth* (BFChTh 13,3), Gütersloh 1908, p. 131ff., Weiss, *1. Korinther*, p. 283, Hans Lietzmann, *Messe und Herrenmahl* (AKG 8), Bonn 1926, p. 254, Walter Schmithals, *Die Gnosis in Korinth* (FRLANT 66)³, Göttingen 1969, p. 238ff. And in support of this it may be noted that Paul in fact impresses on them the words of institution and the holy nature of the Eucharist. But normally the background is to be found in the opposite theological attitude, and the Corinthians are referred to as unadulterated sacramentalists — Ernst von Dobschütz, *Die urchristlichen Gemeinden*, Leipzig 1902, p. 24, von Soden, *Urchristentum*, p. 263, Käsemann, *Versuche* I, p. 18f., Günther Bornkamm, Zum Verständnis des Gottesdienstes bei Paulus, in: *Das Ende des Gestzes. Gesammelte Aufsätze* I (BEvTh 16)⁵, Munich 1966, pp. 113-32; p. 119ff., Herrenmahl und Kirche bei Paulus, in: *Studien zu Antike und Christentum. Gesammelte Aufsätze* II (BEvTh 28)², Munich 1963, pp. 138-76, Conzelmann, *1. Korinther*, p. 328f., Klauck, *Herrenmahl*, p. 297; the problem is that nothing in 1 Cor 11.17-33 points positively in the direction of a sacramentalistic opposing view — it is argued indirectly that Paul does not stress respect for the sacramental elements (argumentatio e silentio), and much is put into the individual members, cf. notes 92-93 below. If the background is false theology, why then does Paul not attack it? The conflict is in fact treated like an instance of disorder and egoism, cf. Lietzmann, *Korinther*, p. 56 ('nicht Parteimeinungen, sondern schlechte Manieren'), Gerd Theissen, Soziale Integration und sakramentales Handeln, in: *Studien zur Soziologie des Urchristentums* (WUNT 19), Tübingen 1979, pp. 290-317; p. 291 (social conflict).

92. Throughout the text Jesus' death is emphasised. It seems to me an arbitrary interpretation when Conzelmann, *1. Korinther*, p. 238, indicates that the reminder of Christ's death in 1 Cor 11.26 and the eschatological reservation are '... die Kriterien gegen den sakramentalen Enthusiasmus, der sich auf eine Erhöhungschristologie stützt'. There is no trace in the section of such an attitude or of a Pauline dissociation.

of an idea of the body of Christ as an expression of community fellowship.[93] It would have been a telling argument in this context had Paul thought of it.

The other passage is *1 Cor 10.16-17:* 'The cup of blessing that we bless, is it not κοινωνία τοῦ αἵματος τοῦ Χριστοῦ? The bread that we break, is it not κοινωνία τοῦ σώματος τοῦ Χριστοῦ? Because there is one bread, we who are many are one body, for we all partake of the one bread.' Several features of the verses are discussed: the precise meaning of κοινωνία,[94] the connection between the two verses and between tradition and use?[95] But the function the verses have in the larger context is not a problem. They are included in a sharp rejection of participation in a heathen cult, 1 Cor 10.1-22. The main view is the Christians' bonding to the Lord. The promise of sal-

---

93. Agains Käsemann, *Versuche* I, p. 32, Bornkamm, *Ende,* p. 121f., *Studien,* p. 169, cf. Klauck, *Herrenmahl,* p. 329, it must be asserted that there is nothing to support the theory that Paul mentions only 'the body' and not 'the blood' in 1 Cor 11.29, because he indicates the concept of the community as 'the body of Christ'. If Paul had this evident argument in mind, it is inexplicable that he is content to imply it so covertly, and does not develop it forcefully. That Paul only mentions τὸ σῶμα in verse 29 may be accidental, or it may be because it is the Host in particular that is interpreted as an expression of Jesus' self-sacrifice for the sake of the community.

94. Κοινωνία can mean 'participation'. If one chooses to understand it as participation in the element of the Eucharist, there is an opening for very primitive sacramentalistic ideas — thus Lietzmann, *Korinther,* p. 48, and in particular Klauck, *Herrenmahl,* p. 260f., in which it is asserted that it is a Greek sacred-meal terminology — because the word can be used in such a context! It can also be used in many other contexts, cf. the criticism in Karl-Gustav Sandelin, Gemenskap med Kristi kropp. Realpresens hos Paulus? [Fellowship with Christ's Body. Real presence in Paul?], *TA/TT* 95 (1990), pp. 378-86. Κοινωνία may refer to participation in Christ's blood and body, understood as participation in the consequences of his death, cf. von Soden, *Urchristentum,* p. 263, Kümmel in Lietzmann, *Korinther,* p. 181f. Finally, κοινωνία means 'fellowship', that is to say 'fellowship with Christ's blood/body', which is an even more open interpretation, cf. Weiss, *1. Korinther,* p. 258.

95. There is a tendency to consider the context to mean as a matter of course that 1 Cor 10.16 is a traditional statement and 1 Cor 10.17 is a Pauline point, cf. Käsemann, *Versuche* I, p. 12f., Bornkamm, *Ende,* p. 121f., *Studien,* p. 164, Kümmel in Lietzmann, *Korinther,* p. 182, Klauck, *Herrenmahl,* p. 260ff., Wolfgang Schrage, *Der erste Brief an die Korinther. 2. Teilband* (*EKK* VII/2), Solothurn 1995, p. 431ff. But this is questionable, since verse 17 is asyndetically linked to verse 16, which is a rhetorical question to which an affirmative answer is expected. On the face of it, one might believe that verse 17 supported this answer, cf. Weiss, *1. Korinther,* p. 259, Lietzmann, *Korinther,* p. 48. If verse 17 is to express a consequence, it would have been more difficult to do without a syndeton. In addition, as will be shown below, it is verse 16 which is utilised in the context, whereas verse 17 is not developed as an actual argument. It is of course possible that both verses contain traditional viewpoints. But the surprising and somewhat uncomfortable result of traditio-historical considerations, which seem to be unavoidable, is that verse 17 is a tradition used only to substantiate verse 16.

vation in baptism and the Eucharist does not bind the Lord to the Christians but, conversely, the Christians to the Lord (1 Cor 10.1-13). And this absolute bonding excludes a simultaneous bonding to idols. This crucial idea is supported in 1 Cor 10.16 by a reference to the Eucharist's fellowship with Christ. 1 Cor 10.17 gives a reason for this fellowship — the mutual fellowship symbolised by the bread. It refers to the tradition of the fellowship of the meal, which is certainly part of the Eucharist's pre-history. But this is a subsidiary motif which is not utilised in the context.

There is a reference in *1 Cor 6.15* to the Christians' bodies being members of Christ. The image probably presupposes that Christ is seen as the comprehensive body to which each individual Christian is linked.[96] But no idea is developed about Christ as a collective entity. The bonding with Christ is crucial — it excludes a simultaneous bonding to prostitutes. It is possible that these bondings are associated with baptism, which is alluded to in 1 Cor 6.11.[97] It is less certain in *1 Cor 1.13c* that a σῶμα Χριστοῦ concept was in mind.[98] In the context of the party disputes, Paul establishes that Christ is not divided. It is therefore absurd that Christians acknowledge different persons. What this primarily concerns is that the community's unity is based on the link to the one Lord.

Rom 7.4 mentions σῶμα Χριστοῦ directly, and the context may be understood as a condensed summary of Rom 6,4-11. By σῶμα Χριστοῦ, there is a reference to Christ's crucified body, to which each individual Christian is linked. But there is no demonstrable concept of a Christian fellowship.[99] *Rom 12.4-5*, on the other hand, is concerned with the fellowship, but without the term σῶμα Χριστοῦ and without reference to baptism. 'For as in one body we have many members, and not all the members have the same function, so we, who are many, are one "body" ἐν Χριστῷ and "members" one of another.' The statement operates as a re-use of 1 Cor 12.12-27. It is a pure comparison.[100] The community is seen as one body, which is not iden-

---

96. Cf. Wendland, *Korinther*, p. 51, Conzelmann, *1. Korinther*, p. 134, Kümmel, *Theologie*, p. 187.
97. Cf. section 4 below.
98. This is often assumed, cf. Hanson, *Unity*, p. 74f., Conzelmann, *1. Korinther*, p. 49. Against the assumption of an ecclesiological σῶμα Χριστοῦ idea, it may however be asked here whether it would not be as good an argument in the matter itself that Paul's failure to develop this is inexplicable if it merely crossed his mind. Cf. section 4 below, with note 272.
99. Cf. section 3.2 below, with note 189.
100. Cf. Cranfield, *Romans*, p. 617f. This is a clear construction, where Rom 12.4 is the image part and Rom 12.5 the subject part of a simile; in the subject part, the word 'body' emerges in the figurative sense, which is introduced in the image part. This is not remarkable in normal usage. But Käsemann, *Römer*, p. 323, overlooks the construction and emphasises this feature, maintaining that it is a transition from a comparison 'zu der

tified with Christ. The reason for using this image about the Christian community is to be found in the phrase ἐν Χριστῷ, whose function corresponds to 1 Cor 12.13. It would be reasonable to understand 'in Christ' spatially (in a metaphorical sense), so that Paul plays on the idea that the Christians are encompassed by Christ and by his reality.[101]

Only later in Col 1.18; 2.19, Eph 4.11-16 is there an obvious ecclesiological use of the motif σῶμα Χριστοῦ — presumably a development of 1 Cor 12.[102]

On the basis of the parallel material, which includes Gal 3.27-28, an established ecclesiological σῶμα Χριστοῦ tradition, as is universally assumed, cannot be proved. There are changing motifs with a certain connection; there may be a reference to the death of Jesus, to baptism and the Eucharist, sometimes also to a collective concept. The pervasive feature is the Christians' bonding with Christ.[103]

2.3. The phrase βαπτίζεσθαι εἰς ...

This phrase appears in both texts now examined, and in both passages it was reasonable to understand the term as meaning that through baptism one was incorporated into Christ. But this was not seen in the same way in Gal 3.27, where it was an individual identification with Christ, and in 1 Cor 12.13, where it was a collective inclusion.

It does not indeed depend upon a universal local meaning being the true meaning of the preposition εἰς. This is immediately apparent from other known connections such as πιστεύειν εἰς and ἐλπίζειν εἰς; the basic meaning

---

theologischen Feststellung in [V.] 5 mit dem Realität bekundenen Prädikat ...' This formalistic argument is intended to support that it is the corpus-Christi-mysticum concept which makes the comparison possible, and not the metaphorical understanding of the context.

101. Cf. in particular Percy, *Leib*, p. 18ff., who considers that the (literally) local-spatial ἐν Χριστῷ is the origin of the σῶμα Χριστοῦ concept, Wedderburn, *Body*, p. 86f., who establishes that ἐν Χριστῷ is the basis of the idea of ἐν σῶμά ἐσμεν, rather than the opposite, and thus opposes, inter alia, Käsemann, *Leib*, p. 138ff., where the ἐν Χριστῷ formulation is derived from cosmological aeon-concepts, cf. Käsemann, *Römer*, p. 323.

102. Most clearly in Eph 4.11-16, which is a stage in a context in which other concepts from 1 Cor 12 and Rom 12 are also to be found, cf. Käsemann, *Römer*, p. 323, Rudolf Schnackenburg, *Der Brief an die Epheser* (EKK X), Zürich 1982, p. 175f. In Col 1.18; 2.19, the idea of σῶμα Χριστοῦ appears to have been combined with concepts of Christ as the head of man from 1 Cor 11.3 and baptism concepts of the same type as Rom 6, cf. section 3.5 below.

103. Cf. Best, *Body*, p. 93f.: 'The primary emphasis of the phrase is on the unity of the believers with Christ rather than on their mutual interdepedence.'

is not to 'believe into' and 'to hope into'.[104] Εἰς represents an affiliation just as naturally, and can also express finality. Only in special verbs of motion is the local meaning the most obvious. Then arises the question of whether βαπτίζεσθαι is such a verb. Etymologically, it is an intensive form of βάπτειν, to dip. But this does not necessarily mean that the original meaning is still pervasive.

This does not happen everywhere. In 1 Cor 10.2, βαπτίζεσθαι εἰς cannot possibly refer to an inclusion. The Israelites' exodus is seen as a counterpart to the Christian baptism with the Spirit and water: πάντες εἰς τὸν Μωϋσῆν ἐβαπτίσθημεν ἐν τῇ νεφέλῃ καὶ ἐν τῇ θαλάσσῃ. It is out of the question for the prepositional member εἰς τὸν Μωϋσῆν to refer to the element of baptism which is designated in the sentence with the prepositional members introduced by ἐν. Also, the result of baptism cannot be an incorporation into Moses, who is never seen as a mystical universal person. This is a baptism 'in regard to Moses'. Εἰς refers to the connection which becomes the result of baptism.[105]

This accords with the general usage in the New Testament. Where βαπτίζεσθαι otherwise occurs, it refers not to a single movement but to the entire sequence of events associated with baptism. Εἰς thus always indicates the result to which the entire act of baptism leads: εἰς ἄφεσιν ἁμαρτίων — Mark 1.4, cf. Lk 3.3; Acts 2.38 — εἰς μετάνοιαν — Mt 3.11.[106] Similarly, the established phrase βαπτίζεσθαι εἰς τὸ ὄνομα Ἰησοῦ referred to below concerns the link that arises at baptism. If the element with which one comes into contact during the act of baptism is to be indicated, this is expressed by the instrumental dative or by the preposition ἐν.[107] It is thus normal that εἰς

---

104. See Schnackenburg, *Heilsgeschehen*, p. 20, Gerhard Delling, Die Bezugnahme von neutestamentlichem εἰς auf Vorgegebenes, in: Otto Böcher and Klaus Haacker (ed.), *Verborum Veritas. Festschrift für Gustav Stählin zum 70. Geburtstag*, Wuppertal 1970, pp. 211-23; p. 218ff., cf. de la Potterie in the discussion of Dinkler, Römer 6,1-14, p. 106.

105. See Schnackenburg, *Heilsgeschehen*, p. 19f., Delling, *Zueignung*, p. 79. Similarily also Tannehill, *Dying*, p. 23, who points out, however, that this perception applies only to the concept in which baptism is seen as a movement directly into Christ (= the baptismal water), whereas it cannot be employed to reject the concept that baptism as a whole leads the Christians into Christ (cf. note 27 above). But apparently he fails to see that the local interpretation has thereby lost the primateship, and that it will accordingly be necessary to argue separately for the local concept in each individual case.

106. The only exception is Mark 1.9: ... εἰς τὸν Ἰορδάνην, which is probably, however, because the general tendency at that time was to replace the local ἐν by εἰς, cf. Friedrich Blass, Albert Debrunner and Friedrich Rehkopf, *Grammatik des neutestamentlichen Griechisch*[15], Göttingen 1979, § 205 with n. 4. Note also the correct term in Mark 1.5: ἐν τῷ Ἰορδάνῃ ποταμῷ. It should be noted that this tendency is not to be found in Paul.

107. The terms are used indiscriminately; according to Mark 1.8; Acts 1.5; 11.16, John baptised ὕδατι and Jesus ἐν πνεύματι ἁγίῳ, cf. Lk 3.16; according to Mt 3.11, they respectively baptised ἐν ὕδατι and ἐν πνεύματι ἁγίῳ καὶ πυρί.

should not be understood as local in connection with βαπτίζεσθαι. The literal meaning 'to be immersed' has given way to the technical use, where the word refers to the entire act of baptism — at least to the extent that the original meaning has no influence upon the syntactic construction.

The local meaning can be played on where the context sets the scene. But the phrase itself does not indicate an established concept about baptism as inclusion in Christ. What is crucial seems again to be the close connection to Christ.

The phrase βαπτίζεσθαι εἰς τὸ ὄνομα τοῦ κυρίου Ἰησοῦ is of further significance to an understanding of baptism in the Hellenistic communities. It is to be found in Acts 8.16; 19.5 and is clearly implied in 1 Cor 1.13,15.[108] In Mt 28.19 there is a Trinitarian formulation; in Acts 2.38; 10.48 there is the variant βαπτίζεσθαι ἐν/ἐπὶ τῷ ὀνόματι Ἰησοῦ Χριστοῦ, which is also implied in 1 Cor 6.11.

Most attempts to understand the term assume εἰς τὸ ὄνομα to be an established idiom, whose origin it is sought to trace.

Wilhelm Heitmüller's 'Im Namen Jesu' is fundamental. A linguistic-historical investigation is said to demonstrate that εἰς τὸ ὄνομα is an acquisition formula from a Hellenistic transfer practice, known in particular from Egyptian texts of the 2nd and 3rd centuries AD.[109] Baptism in the name of Jesus then means the establishment of ownership.[110] Baptism is seen as a baptism in which the mention of the name is a crucial factor.[111] Religio-historically, Heitmüller sees the use of 'the name' as a reflection of world-encompassing name-magic, where the divine name is a charm and a means of binding the named god.[112] It is said to be found in magic papyri and in the Old Testament cultic use of the name Yahweh.[113] This is

108. Cf. 1 Cor 1.10 and the discussion in section 4 below.
109. See Heitmüller, *Im Namen*, pp. 94-127. Cf. Friederich Preisigke, *Girowesen im griechischen Ägypten*, Strasbourg 1910, p. 149.
110. Heitmüller, *Im Namen*, p. 127. The viewpoint has gained broad acceptance, cf. Oepke, *ThWNT* I, p. 537, Schnackenburg, *Heilsgeschehen*, p. 16f., Eduard Stommel, Das 'Abbild seines Todes' und der Taufritus, *RQ* 50 (1955), pp. 1-21; p. 4f., Kertelge, *Rechtfertigung*, p. 231, Conzelmann, *1. Korinther*, p. 50. Lietzmann, *Korinther*, p. 7f., interprets similarly, but takes his point of reference in the term ὀμνύναι εἰς τὸ ὄνομα, which is to be found in Herodian, 2.2.10; 2.13.2.
111. Heitmüller, *Im Namen*, p. 88ff.
112. Heitmüller, *Im Namen*, p. 132ff.
113. See Heitmüller, *Im Namen*, p. 171ff., in which it is indicated that he over whom the name of Yahweh is mentioned will be placed in a proprietary relationship to Yahweh and be subject to his protection — this is interpreted as a mystical connection with Yahweh! In this context, passages from the Old Testament are included which relate that the righteous are marked by a special sign, Ezek 9.4; Isa 44.5, cf. Rev 7.2-8; 9.4; 14.1; 22.4; Gal

reflected in primitive Christianity in a circling around the name of Jesus, which is used as a power in exorcisms.[114] Also, through the baptism, the Jesus-name is said to be a magical agency giving membership and ensuring protection.[115] Baptism in the name of Jesus is thus placed in a religious environment characterised by sacramental mysticism and magic. Against this interpretation is the fact that the 'acquisition formula' adopted cannot be found in other contexts in the New Testament or its immediate environment. The distance is too great for a term from the field of accounting.[116]

An alternative explanation of εἰς τὸ ὄνομα as an established phrase assumes Semitic usage. It is said to correspond to ΠΨ ?, which means 'concerning'. Transferred to the baptismal passages, βαπτίζεσθαι εἰς τὸ ὄνομα Ἰησοῦ becomes equivalent βαπτίζεσθαι εἰς Ἰησοῦν.[117] On the other hand, ΠΨ in this connection has a weakened meaning and has no article. In the New Testament passages, special emphasis is indeed given to τὸ ὄνομα.[118]

On the whole, it seems to be unnecessary and arbitrary to isolate the prepositional members and to make precisely them special formulae, as is done in the lingustic-historical approach. The emphasis is not upon the prepositions, which indeed change, whereas the connection between the Jesus-name and baptism is constant.

If one abandons the idea of a formula coming from outside, one arrives

---

6.17. Tattooed property marks are said to be concerned, corresponding to the stigmatisation and sealing practices of the mysteries (pp. 173-76).

114. Heitmüller, *Im Namen*, p. 224ff.

115. See Heitmüller, *Im Namen*, p. 12. In Paul, however, the concept is said to have been sublimated and less primitive (p. 326).

116. Also, εἰς τὸ ὄνομα here refers not to an acquisition — in itself, apart from the context. If something is entered 'in someone's name' a bonding is created. But it is the verbal term which gives this meaning. That εἰς τὸ ὄνομα τοῦ δεῖνα can be used on its own in transfer documents is because it is implied that an entry of the amount is made in the books under the name concerned. Cf. Preisigke, *Girowesen*, p. 149. The words εἰς τὸ ὄνομα retain their general, broader meaning, and are not a formula in the sense that a new established content is created. Cf. Delling, *Zueignung*, p. 31ff., Frankemölle, *Taufverständnis*, p. 45ff., Wilckens, *Römer* II, p. 49. Similarly, as regards the term ὀμνύναι εἰς τὸ ὄνομα, cf. note 110 above. That a bonding is created here is solely because of the oath by which one binds oneself to the master whose name is mentioned.

117. Thus Bietenhard, ὄνομα, *ThWNT* V (1944-54), pp. 242-83; p. 274, Joachim Jeremias, *Die Kindertaufe in den ersten vier Jahrhunderten*, Göttingen 1958, p. 35.

118. See 1 Cor 1.10,13 (cf. section 4 below, with note 278); also in Acts special emphasis is given to the term τὸ ὄνομα, not only to the baptismal passages but also, for example, in Acts 3.16, which speaks of belief in the name of Jesus as a healing power, and Acts 8.12 on Philip's proclamation of the kingdom of God and the name of Jesus Christ, cf. Heitmüller, *Im Namen*, p. 224ff. Cf. also against the 'Semitic' interpretation Delling, *Zueignung*, p. 40ff., Frankemölle, *Taufverständnis*, p. 46f.

at a simple interpretation. A vital, recognisable feature of baptism has been that the name of Jesus is pronounced over whoever is baptised. Thereby the person concerned is put into contact with the power the name expresses. In the light of passages such as Acts 3.6; 4.30 and 1 Cor 5.4, there is no doubt that the name of the Lord in New Testament contexts may be understood as a special power which becomes present when the name is pronounced, as maintained by Heitmüller. And this is associated with the Old Testament concept of the name as an independent reality which participates in the being named.[119] This may in fact mean that Jesus' name is made present through baptism. But this should not immediately be understood as magic, in which the power in the name is made independent and becomes something of which one can take possession. That the concept can be utilised in this way does not prove that this always happens. If Jesus' name can achieve the central significance in the New Testament, even associated with the Old Testament god-predicate κύριος, the background is undoubtedly reflections on Jesus' person and works. His name gains significance because it is an expression of the power that prevailed in his life and especially in his death and resurrection, as is to be seen from Phil 2.6-11 and Acts 4.10,12; 8.12 where Jesus' name refers to the centre of the preaching. The use of Jesus' name at baptism may be a reference to and a proclamation of the crucial events in the history of salvation.

Βαπτίζεσθαι εἰς τὸ ὄνομα ᾽Ιησοῦ expresses that baptism provides a link to Christ, and is close in meaning to βαπτίζεσθαι εἰς ᾽Ιησοῦν. Whether, from the historical aspect, this latter term has been created as an abbreviation[120] is, as far as I can judge, of no significance to an understanding.

2.4. The term ἐν Χριστῷ

The texts already examined can again give important hints in regard to an understanding of this mode of expression, which has no clear pre-Pauline analogies.[121] If it is wished to interpret ἐν Χριστῷ as a formula, there are, as indicated, three models, and for all of them arguments can be picked up from the specific material.

1. If, like Deissmann, one assumes a formula of 'local mystical' significance,

---

119. Cf. Johs. Pedersen, *Israel* I-II³, Copenhagen 1958, p. 190ff., Gerhard von Rad, *Theologie des Alten Testaments* I⁶, Munich 1969, p. 193ff., Bietenhard, *ThWNT* V, p. 254ff.
120. Cf. Jervell, *Gud*, p. 97, Wedderburn, *Baptism*, p. 54ff., Wilckens, *Römer* II, p. 11. But most interpreters maintain, probably correctly, that they are parallel terms with different origins.
121. Cf. Deissmann, *Formel*, p. 70ff.

one may invoke Gal 3.14,26,28.[122] We have seen that the metaphorical background to Gal 3.28 is baptism as a clothing in Christ, so that each individual Christian finds himself 'within Christ' at the metaphorical level.[123] The local meaning may also be the basis if ἐν Χριστῷ is used adjectivally. Thus the central passage in 2 Cor 5.17: 'If anyone is *in Christ*, there is a new creation'.[124] Rom 8.2 can be read similarly: 'There is therefore now no condemnation for those who are in Christ Jesus'.[125] This passage reads 'in Christ' and 'in the Spirit' in contrast to 'in the flesh', which can be understood as local in a wholly literal sense. In this way we arrive at a figurative meaning of the term which is based on the local meaning.

A true and literal local understanding of ἐν Χριστῷ is arrived at only if one considers, together with Deissmann, an 'immaterial' understanding of the formula, which must then be equated to ἐν πνεύματι and indicate an all-pervading mystical pneumatic reality.[126]

A (figurative) local meaning is also reasonable in the large group of passages in which there is reference to brothers, sisters, colleagues, holy 'in Christ' or 'in the Lord'. This may concern those who have personally made contact with Christ; the phrase is employed more weakly, equivalent to our term 'Christian'.[127]

But the mode of expression can also be understood as referring to those who are 'within the sphere of Christ'. This is the next type of interpretation.

2. If, with Käsemann and others, one wishes to understand ἐν Χριστῷ as a 'local-spatial' ecclesiological formula,[128] one can point to Rom 12.4-5 and behind this the concepts displayed in 1 Cor 12.12-27, since here one operates

---

122. See in particular Deissmann, *Formel*, pp. 102-5, cf. notes 21, 23 and 34 above.
123. See Deissmann, *Formel*, p. 95ff., in which it is acknowledged that ἐν Χριστῷ is used figuratively here in connection with Paul's imagery. But it is maintained that it is precisely this imagery which may have been furthered by Paul's already having had an idea to the effect that the Christians were within the pneumatic Christ in a real local sense, cf. note 126 below.
124. Cf. Deissmann, *Formel*, p. 79, 108.
125. Cf. Deissmann, *Formel*, p. 79.
126. See Deissmann, *Formel*, pp. 84-98, in which it is very subtly considered whether the formula is to be understood factually or figuratively, as in Gal 3.28. Deissmann himself stresses that no final decision is possible. However, he inclines towards believing in this factual pneumatic-mystical interpretation, supported inter alia by 2 Cor 3.17 which is read as an identification of Christ with the Holy Spirit (p. 84f.), and by the fact that Christ and the Holy Spirit act as alternatives, for example in Rom 8 (pp. 85-87).
127. See in particular Rom 16.3-14, in which the accumulation of these terms shows the weakened and undramatic nature of the terms. Note also οἱ νεκροὶ ἐν Χριστῷ in 1 Thess 4.16, νήπιοι ἐν Χριστῷ in 1 Cor 3.1, ὁδοὶ ἐν Χριστῷ i 1 Cor 4.17. Cf. Deissmann, *Formel*, p. 79, 108, Weiss, *Probleme*, p. 13.
128. See Käsemann, *Leib*, p. 183, cf. note 10 above.

with an idea that all Christians collectively find themselves 'within Christ'. The same idea is to be found again in the passages referred to, where ἐν Χριστῷ can be interpreted as a designation for those who belong 'within the sphere of Christ' — the community.[129]

But the problem with all the assertions about a local formula is the passages in which ἐν Χριστῷ reads adverbally.[130] This cannot mean directly that the Christians are within Christ. It is actions and events that take place ἐν Χριστῷ. Only in a few cases is it possible to understand the term locally (but not literally) as referring to something in which the Christians participate in the Christ-sphere.[131] But there are many passages in which the local meaning is excluded. This applies in particular where ἐν Χριστῷ is involved firmly linked to verbs — such as ἐλπίζειν, πείθειν or καυχᾶσθαι ἐν Χριστῷ (or κυρίῳ).[132] Most natural here is an instrumental interpretation.

3. We have now arrived at the last way of understanding the 'ἐν Χριστῷ formula'. The Semitic background is emphasised, in which the preposition ב can also express the instrumental and modal.[133] 'Εν Χριστῷ can then be perceived as an 'Umstandsbestimmung', as Neugebauer has expressed it.[134] In support of this viewpoint, reference may be made to Gal 3.14, which may be directly rendered as: 'Abraham's blessing was to come to the Gentiles by virtue of Christ Jesus (ἐν Χριστῷ 'Ιησοῦ)', corresponding to Gal 3.1 where it reads that no one is justified by virtue of the law.[135] Yet another passage

---

129. The passages referred to in note 127 above and 2 Cor 5.17; Rom 8.1, are meaningful if ἐν Χριστῷ here means 'within Christ's sphere'. Cf. Weiss, Probleme, p. 15ff.

130. Or — even more clearly — adjectivally connected to a noun, which does not refer to the Christians, as in Rom 3.24, where it expressly says that it is redemption which occurs ἐν Χριστῷ, and in Rom 8.39, where it is God's love that is 'in Christ'. These passages exclude definitively that ἐν Χριστῷ is everywhere a mystical or ecclesiological formula, as emphasised in Weiss, Probleme, p. 27. Cf. also the laboured interpretation of Rom 3.24 in Deissmann, Formel, p. 112f., in which 'the redemption' is said to be an everlasting condition which includes the Christians 'in Christ'.

131. As in 2 Cor 2.12 where Paul experiences open doors 'in the Lord', and 1 Cor 9.1, where Paul speaks of his work 'in the Lord'.

132. Cf. the survey in Weiss, Probleme, p. 18f., Büchsel, 'In Christus', p. 144.

133. See Blass, Debrunner and Rehkopf, Grammatik, § 219. Cf. also Büchsel, 'In Christus', p. 144. 1 Cor 7.14 shows that this also applies to persons in the singular: ἐν τῇ γυναικί and ἐν τῷ ἀδελφῷ, which is denied in Deissmann, Formel, p. 124, perhaps in order to exclude the instrumental interpretation of ἐν Χριστῷ — 1 Cor 7.14 is said to be a spill-over from the ἐν Χριστῷ formula.

134. Cf. note 11 above. The primary adverbial use is seen not only in the context of Paul's Semitic background; it can also be found in genuinely Greek texts, Neugebauer, In Christus, p. 34ff.

135. Cf. note 21 above. In other passages also, this general instrumental use is natural — for example the passages Rom 3.24; 8.39 referred to in note 130 above.

should be remembered — Gal 3.9: 'All the Gentiles shall be blessed ἐν σοί (= Abraham)'.[136] 'In Abraham', which must probably be understood modally or in a figurative local sense,[137] appears here as a parallel concept to 'in Christ'. And it concerns an idea that the progenitor is a kind of representative of his descendants. It can be used to support a connection with Semitic concepts about a 'corporate personality', with which Neugebauer also agrees.[138]

The problem with this interpretation of the term is especially the passages in which ἐν Χριστῷ is used adjectivally.[139]

The idea of one unambiguous formula must be abandoned for the very reason that we can put forward strong grounds in support of all three views.[140] We can then modify the theory by assuming that one of the meanings is the true and original meaning. But this becomes a discussion of limited relevance, since there is no one definite meaning which is the true meaning with the preposition εἰς — neither is it the local meaning. The word is used just as naturally about a number of other circumstances.[141] For the user who has a non-theoretical relationship with the language, the various meanings merge into one another.

This is confirmed when we see how the mode of expression ἐν Χριστῷ actually functions. The broadest meaning can be taken as a point of reference. The crucial aspect is the connection with Christ which is expressed throughout — not the nature of the link, which varies. We can imagine that ἐν Χριστῷ becomes a favourite term because it points broadly to the link with Christ, which was of such great importance to the life of Paul and the other Christians. In the various contexts, Paul can thus play on the varying nuances of meaning to express particular thoughts.

In addition, methodical considerations which lead to the assumption that

---

136. Cf. note 18 above, and in particular the interpretation in Wedderburn, *Body*, p. 88f.
137. Cf. Wedderburn, *Body*, p. 89.
138. See Neugebauer, *In Christus*, p. 94ff.
139. Cf. the passages referred to above, Gal 3.28; 2 Cor 5.17; Rom 8.2. Neugebauer, *In Christus*, generally uses the laboured rendering 'Christusmässig'. See the criticism in Wedderburn, *Body*, p. 87; it is pointed out that 'Umstandsbestimmung', taken at face value, must be a broad category which may include local circumstances. Cf. Schnelle, *Gerechtigkeit*, p. 107 n. 11.
140. With Weiss, *Probleme*, p. 7ff., Büchsel, 'In Christus', p. 141, Oepke, ἐν, *ThWNT* II (1935), pp. 534-39, Schnelle, *Gerechtigkeit*, p. 107 n. 1. Cf. also Kümmel, *Theologie*, p. 195, Käsemann, *Römer*, p. 213: 'Jeder Text muss daraufhin befragt werden, ob lokale, instrumentale oder modale Bedeutung vorliegt.'
141. Cf. merely the introduction to the article on ἐν in Bauer, *Wörterbuch*, col. 511f.: 'D. Gebr. dieser Präp. ist so vielseitig, aber auch oft so verschwommen, das e. genaue Systematik unmöglich ist.' The same applies to many other prepositions.

ἐν Χριστῷ is a formula with a constant local or particular adverbial meaning are untenable. This can be substantiated by examining the method used by Deissmann, which Neugebauer evaluates.

Deissmann's investigation shows that ἐν Χριστῷ followed by a personal singular is rare in 'profane Graecism', whereas it is relatively much more frequent in the Septuagint.[142] That it is a much used construction in Paul, and that the preposition ἐν is so often used in the New Testament as a whole, leads to the natural conclusion that this use was influenced by the Semitic background of Paul and the other New Testament authors. Deissmann avoids this conclusion by toning down the importance of the Hebraic background — and especially by asking, as a methodical principle, (a) how the Greek-speaking reader, whom Paul is in fact addressing, had to understand this ἐν. The answer is that, with his background, he could only understand it *locally*.[143] For Deissmann makes use of yet another methodical assumption (b): that prepositions — viewed as linguistic particles, which are the crucial meaning-bearing elements in the language — have a constant and quite precisely established meaning. ʼΕν must therefore always be understood in the basic, local sense.[144] And one may therefore conclude in advance that ἐν Χριστῷ, with variants, is always a formula with this constant meaning.

In his consideration of the problem-complex, Neugebauer objects to the first methodical principle in Deissmann (a). Using a strange argument, he rejects that the interpreter might have an interest in the recipient-situation: 'Kann der "Griechisch redende Leser" Paulus nicht gerade missverstehen? Uns geht es doch nicht um das Verständnis eines Lesers, sondern um die Meinung des Paulus'.[145] This appears to be hasty. Throughout 20 years of work among the Greeks, Paul is said to have held to a mode of expression that they simply had to misunderstand! If it is to make sense to read Paul, we must assume that he could make himself understood. And this is at the same time an important argument against Deissmann's strictly local inter-

---

142. Deissmann, *Formel*, p. 16ff., especially the summary p. 55.

143. See Deissmann, *Formel*, pp. 79-81. This is meant to apply, even if it is recognised that no true analogies exist in profane Greek and the formula must be assumed to be Paul's own usage (pp. 70-74).

144. See Deissmann, *Formel*, p. 4f. There is yet another assumption: he restricts himself to dealing with ἐν, followed by a personal singular (p. 8, cf. note 133 above). Passages are thereby excluded which show that ἐν has a far more varied meaning. Cf. also Weiss, *Probleme*, p. 10f.

145. Neugebauer, *In Christus*, p. 19, cf. p. 31 n. 2. Gäumann, *Taufe*, p. 59 n. 8, also has this strange point of criticism.

pretation. Paul and other New Testament writers, addressing the same circle of readers, can use ἐν Χριστῷ everywhere in this 'un-Greek' way — adverbally, modally, instrumentally — and nevertheless expect to be understood. Consideration for the recipient-situation is a sound principle, which shows that the word could be understood in its entire breadth of meaning.

Neugebauer agrees, however, with Deissmann's other methodical principle (b): that ἐν Χριστῷ with variants is to be seen in advance as a formula: 'Ausserdem sollte man zugeben, dass ein uneinheitliches Verständnis nur ein Notbehelf ist, der erst vertreten werden kann, wenn der Versuch eines einheitliches Verständnisses gescheitert ist'.[146] The assumption is therefore that ἐν Χριστῷ has a constant and precise meaning everywhere. This rests upon a simplified linguistic understanding.[147] And examination of the specific occurrences shows that there is great variance.[148] That ἐν Χριστῷ has the broad meaning in fact becomes Neugebauer's main result, despite the point of reference. He indeed concludes that this 'einheitliche Verständnis' is that ἐν Χριστῷ is 'allgemeine Umstandsbestimmung'. The term must thus indicate the crucial link to Christ, but as concerns the content in general he gives the preposition so vague a definition that any talk of a formula becomes meaningless. Neugebauer then himself also modifies this expression: it is a formulised term.[149] The open and varying interpretation of ἐν Χριστῷ is thus confirmed.

As regards the term ἐν Χριστῷ, like σῶμα Χριστοῦ and βαπτίζεσθαι εἰς Χριστόν a background in a specific pre-Pauline mythological concept-complex cannot be indicated. But this is again an expression of the Christians' link to Christ, which can be used in various contexts including baptism.

3. Death and resurrection with Christ in baptism?

3.1. The phrase σὺν Χριστῷ

There is also reason for reservation as regards what has been called the σὺν Χριστῷ formula.[150] First, there are only fourteen passages which refer to

---

146. Neugebauer, *In Christus*, p. 20, cf. p. 18. Cf. Best, *Body*, p. 19 n. 2.
147. Cf. note 141 above. See in particular Barr, *Semantics*, p. 107ff., 213f., where he ridicules the idea that the words have a 'proper' meaning independent of the context.
148. Cf. Schnelle, *Gerechtigkeit*, p. 107f.
149. See in particular Neugebauer, *In Christus*, pp. 37-48.
150. Thus Lohmeyer, Σὺν Χριστῷ, p. 218, Dupont, Σὺν Χριστῷ, p. 7ff.

the Christians' acts, sufferings or being σὺν Χριστῷ.[151] Second, it becomes
clear that this material is diverse.

This relates to *the form*. In half the incidents we have σύν as a preposition. In the rest, σύν is a prefix to verbs or a noun. In two places only
does the term σὺν Χριστῷ itself occur: Rom 6.8; Phil 1.23; σὺν Ἰησοῦ is
found once: 2 Cor 4.14; and σὺν κυρίῳ once: 1 Thess 4.17. In Gal 2.19 the
term Χριστῷ συνεσταύρωμαι occurs. In the other cases the personal pronoun
is used to signify Christ: 1 Thess 4.14; 5.10; 2 Cor 13.4; Rom 6.4,8; 8.17,32, or
the Christ designation is implied: Rom 6.6 and 8.17.

It also applies *inherently* that the material is diverse:

Particular attention has been given to the fact that there are differences
as regards the time aspect. It is relatively easy here to establish that a group
of occurrences concern the Christians' future-eschatological bonding with
Christ in resurrection and glorious life — this is clear in 1 Thess 4.14,17; 5.10;
2 Cor 4.14; Rom 8.17d. Other passages concern situations and events in the
Christian life or at its beginning.[152]

The question of contemporaneity and the time aspect belong together.
There is a widespread opinion that the use of the preposition or preverb σύν
involves contemporaneity. If one does something with another or are exposed to something together, they will normally be simultaneous events.
This also follows as a matter of course in the future-eschatological passages
in which the life of resurrection and glory is shared with Christ. But not as
regards the past and present contexts. The passages concerning the Christians' death with Christ have been found to be particularly remarkable. On the
face of it, there is a time difference between Christ's death and the Christians' death. Ideas are considered here regarding a contemporaneity of a paradoxical nature, timeless mystery-thought and a mystical connection between
Christ and the Christians.[153] But one can also consider the simple ex-

---

151. In addition to the passages which will be mentioned below, the following passages might
also be considered: Phil 3.10 (συμμορφιζόμενος τῷ θανάτῳ αὐτοῦ), Phil 3.21 (σύμμορφον
τῷ σώματι τῆς δόξης αὐτοῦ), Rom 6.5 (σύμφυτοι ... τῷ ὁμοιώματι τοῦ θανάτου αὐτοῦ)
and Rom 8.29 (συμμόρφους τῆς εἰκόνος τοῦ υἱοῦ αὐτοῦ). But formally they do not
belong directly to the group, since here the prefix σύν does not form a direct connection
between Christ and the Christians.

152. Such a division of the material is common, cf. Dupont, Σὺν Χριστῷ, p. 11ff. (the work referred to is the first part which concerns 'with Christ' in the future life; the second part
which was to concern 'with Christ' in the present life has, as far as I know, never been
completed), Gäumann, *Taufe*, p. 57f., Käsemann, *Römer*, p. 153f.

153. Cf. notes 4-8 above. Roughly speaking, there are three ways to explain this contemporaneity: (a) Christ's death and resurrection are repeated in the cult, so that Christ
becomes contemporary with the Christians, cf. Heitmüller, *Taufe*, 1911, p. 22, Lietzmann,
Römer, p. 67f., Mittring, *Heilswirklichkeit*, p. 37ff. (b) The Christians are incorporated in
Christ who is a mystical collective person or 'corporate personality', and has thus become

planation, that in these passages σὺν Χριστῷ primarily expresses connection and accord.[154] This can be confirmed when we come to the meaning of the preposition.

The preposition σύν also has a wide breadth of meaning, and it must be established that it expresses contemporaneity far from always. The word σύν can have instrumental meaning, as in the widespread term (σὺν θεῷ or σὺν θεοῖς, with a god's or the gods' help).[155] It can also appear weakened, almost equivalent to καί.[156] Σύν can be used in the sense 'similar to', where what is concerned is merely that one does the same or is exposed to the same as another.[157] It can also have a more figurative meaning, indicating an agreement with a principle.[158] In such cases there is no need for contemporaneity. And along those lines several of the Pauline passages can be directly understood. 2 Cor 13.4: '... but in dealing with you we will live with him (= with Christ's help) ...' Rom 8.17c: 'we suffer with (= like or in association with) Christ.' A corresponding meaning can also be considered as regards the statements relating to crucifixion and death with Christ.[159] It should also be noted that σύν is used nowhere in contemporary mystery-religiosity or mysticism to express a ritual contemporaneity or mystical bonding with a deity.[160] But there is a widespread use of

contemporary with the past Christ-events, cf. Dibelius, *Botschaft* II, p. 72f., M. Barth, *Taufe*, p. 276ff., Tannehill, *Dying*, p. 11f., 29f. (c) The Christ-events and baptism took place at various times, but there is a paradoxical contemporaneity between them, cf. Hahn, *Mitsterben*, p. 111, Güttgemanns, *Apostel*, p. 219f. See also the concluding discussion in Chapter VIII, section 2, below.

154. See Halter, *Taufe*, p. 43f., who emphasises that σύν should not primarily be understood temporally, cf. Schnackenburg, *Heilsgeschehen*, p. 31.

155. See Tycho Mommsen, *Beiträge zu der Lehre von den griechischen Präpositionen*, Berlin 1895, p. 3ff., which shows that σύν is rare in Attic prose, apart from such established terms. Cf. Lohmeyer, Σὺν Χριστῷ, p. 226ff., Dupont, Σὺν Χριστῷ, pp. 19-21, Grundmann, *ThWNT* VII, p. 767f.

156. Thus, for example, Lk 20.1; Phil 1.1, cf. Bauer, *Wörterbuch*, col. 1548. In Rom 8.32 also, σὺν (αὐτῷ) appears to have such an additive function, cf. Lohmeyer, Σὺν Χριστῷ, p. 219 n. 4.

157. Thus clearly with συμπάσχειν, which can mean 'suffer like', Plato, Charm. 169 C, cf. Bauer, *Wörterbuch*, col. 1543. See also 2 Cor 1.21; 4.14 (cf. note 245 below); Gal. 3.9, where σύν is used to combine elements which are similarly exposed, but not at the same time.

158. For example in Plato, Nom. 11 924 A: ποιείσθω σὺν νόμῳ. Cf. Grundmann, *ThWNT* VII, p. 771.

159. Paul uses συναποθνῄσκειν elsewhere in a sense where no one wishes to interpret a mystical contemporaneity into it — in 2 Cor 7.3, Paul says that he and the Corinthians will die together, cf. note 250 below.

160. See for example Gäumann, *Taufe*, p. 55 with n. 7, where it is established that the σύν terms cannot be adduced from the Hellenistic mystery-liturgies (but cf. p. 58 n. 31). Lohmeyer, Σὺν Χριστῷ, p. 234ff., tries, via Johnian traditions, to reach back to gnostic, apocalyptic concepts of Iranian origin about a unification with the Lord. But the parallel

σύν in the gospels where the disciples' affiliation to Jesus is concerned.[161]

One should also note the differences as regards to the *degree of fellowship* the term σύν implies.

When σύν is used in connection with verbal concepts, it expresses that a certain action or event is common to several parties. But one must distinguish between two, in principle very different, ways of conceiving this fellowship. (a) In some cases, a close connection between the two parties is concerned: either a contact which arises as a result of the event to which the verb refers — thus συγκάλειν, συνάγειν, συλλογισμός — or a more prolonged fellowship as with συζῆν or εἶναι σύν. Here there is considerable emphasis on σύν. (b) In other cases, merely a temporary fellowship of action or the like is concerned. This applies to terms such as συνεσθίειν, συνοδεύειν, συγχαίρειν. Here the emphasis is on the verbal action. Then can nothing be assumed about a closer connection or association between the parties who participate in the common action. This can be a matter of merely acting in the same way in a given situation. This distinction is generally ignored in the treatment of the particle σύν, but it is nevertheless a real and very important difference.[162]

terms are found only in Mandaean texts and the Odes of Solomon. Dupont, Σὺν Χριστῷ, p. 21ff., seeks to find a similar concept of a unification with God in the hereafter by going back to Greek concepts about death as a quest for God and to the Old Testament, where in particular one finds the concept of 'God with us'; but in none of the passages are there σύν terms which correspond to the Pauline terms, cf. the conclusion in Dupont, p. 57f. Also, the 'corporate-personality interpretation' has no linguistic connection with the term, cf. Schnackenburg, Adam-Christus-Typologie, p. 52, who suggests that σὺν Χριστῷ is a distinct Pauline usage in connection with the solidarity and representational idea. Cf. also Wedderburn, *Baptism*, p. 342ff., in which there is also a reference to the term σὺν τῷ πιστῷ 'Αβραάμ in Gal 3.9.

161. See Lohmeyer, Σὺν Χριστῷ, p. 231f., who asserts that a linguistically-close parallel to the Pauline term is οἱ σὺν 'Ιησοῦ ὄντες, which is said to be found in Mark 2.26; Lk 5.9; 8.45; 9.32; 22.56; Acts 4.13; but apart from Acts 4.13 they are incidental and misleading references, and Lohmeyer rejects these passages as true background because they are far removed from the markedly Pauline σὺν Χριστῷ, which is said to have its origin in ideas concerning Jesus' transcendental divinity, cf. next note. But more precise reference may be made to passages such as Mark 14.31; Lk 5.15; 7.11; 8.1.38; 14.25-27; 15.2; 23.49; 24.29-30; Acts 1.4; 10.41, in which σύν (preferred by Luke in particular, whereas the other evangelists use μετά) is used to describe the connection between Jesus and those who are disciples, follow him and eat together with him, cf. Schnackenburg, *Heilsgeschehen*, p. 169, Larsson, *Christus*, p. 72ff., Jervell, *Gud*, p. 60f., Wilckens, *Römer* II, p. 60f.

162. See Henricus Stephanus, *Thesaurus Graecae linguae* VII³, Paris 1848-54, col. 1169, which notes that in compounds σύν can mean on the one hand 'simul, una, pariter, communiter', as in σύσσιτος, συστράγητος, and on the other hand refer to a 'contractio' or 'coitio' as in σύνοξυς, σύστομος. Lohmeyer, Σὺν Χριστῷ, p. 222ff., distinguishes between σὺν Χριστῷ εἶναι and all other contexts which merely express 'ein einmahliges Geschehen'; 'Sein mit Christus' however, refers to something all-embracing and eternal —

If we look at the σὺν Χριστῷ occurrences in Paul, there are only a few passages of the type (a) in which a connection or an everlasting fellowship with Christ is concerned: 1 Thess 4.14 concerns God's wishing to bring the Christians *together* with Christ; 1 Thess 4.17; 5.10; Phil 1.23 concern the everlasting life with Christ. There is otherwise the type (b) with the more toneless σύν we are dealing with: one *suffers, dies, is glorified* with Christ. These formulations does not, in themselves, say that the events result in an association with Christ.

To summarise, it can be established that there is not the common characteristic which makes it meaningful to speak of σύν as a formula. And if we go deeper into the intrinsic aspect of the matter it will be seen that the formulation can be associated with two quite different motifs. In the first group of passages, the death of Christ is connected in a remarkably loaded manner to the Christians' transition to the new life. In the other and larger group, there is a more direct connection between Christ's suffering, death and raising up, and a similar sequence of events for the Christians.

3.2. 'Death with Christ' in Gal 2.19-20 and other passages

In Gal 2.19-20 the motif of 'death with Christ' is to be found in the strictest and most pronounced form.

This is a crucial passage in the Letter to the Galatians. In Gal 2.14-21, Paul quotes from an address he himself once gave in Antioch, when Peter wished as a Jew to break away from the Gentile converts in the community.[163] Paul wishes to hold to the truth of the gospel. He points out that belief in Christ and the resulting justification is a breach with Jewish life and its demands. Paul is thereby in the centre of the letter's subject, the dispute about circumcision and other demands of the law. Gal 2.19-20 concerns the basic principle itself.

Gal 2.19a looks back to the crucial break with Judaism which the preceding verses deal with: 'For through the law I died to the law, so that I

---

to be together with him as friend and companion and to be united with him; therefore is this futuristic-eschatological aspect also seen as the true and original content of the 'formula'.

163. That the entire section Gal 2.14-21 belongs to the Antiochian speech is evident; it reads 'we Jews' in v. 15-17, and thereafter 'I' (former belief in the law), whereas it is emphasised in Gal 3.1 that Paul is now again directly addressing the Galatians. Cf. Sieffert, *Galater*, p. 116, Oepke, *Galater*, p. 56f., Schlier, *Galater*, p. 87, Ridderbos, *Galatians*, p. 98. This is different in Betz, *Galatians*, p. 113f., who considers it possible that the speech already ended in v. 15.

might live to God.' A transfer of power has occurred.[164] The earlier bonding to the law has been replaced by a bonding to God. But this is expressed paradoxically in a dual sense. It may appear puzzling that the breach with the law occurs by virtue of the law itself; this is explained in Gal 3.6-29 where Paul proves by means of the law that the law is not a way to salvation.[165] It sounds even more paradoxical that the Christian has obtained new life precisely by way of a 'death'. There should now be no doubt that the verb ἀποθνῄσκειν is used metaphorically of a break which is so strong that it must be equivalent to death.[166] Nevertheless, the stage is set for an amplification, and this soon comes.[167]

But *Gal 2.19b*: Χριστῷ συνεσταύρωμαι, seems to be even more remarkable when considered directly. It is a linking together of two different events that occurred at two different times: the death of Christ as a salvation event, and the Christian's transition to a new life. The statement then contains simultaneously a loaded christological reference and a loaded soteriological reference, which are interwoven. Since we have a perfect form of the verb the emphasis is on the new situation, which is the result of 'crucifixion with Christ'.[168]

This, then, is indeed the consequence of the break which has occurred and which is explained more specifically in *Gal 2.20a*: 'and it is no longer I who live, but it is Christ who lives in me.' Once again we have a markedly figurative usage. Where in the preceding verse there was a break with the law, the break is now with an 'I'. It must be so understood that the 'I' which no longer lives is the old Paul, who was tied to the law. That Christ lives in him expresses that he is entirely dependent upon Christ in his new life.[169]

This is also what is said in *Gal 2.20b*: 'And the life I now live in the flesh I live by faith in the Son of God who loved me and gave himself for me.' Paul has thus amplified what is inherent in the complex expression: 'I am crucified with Christ'. On Christ's side, the self-sacrificing redeemer-death is pointed out. Soteriologically, the emphasis is on a 'death' in which the old personality with its bonding to the law is spent, so that it has been possible to create a new bonding and a new purpose in life. This is an optimistic

---

164. Cf. Tannehill, *Dying*, p. 57ff., Siber, *Mit Christus*, p. 227ff.
165. Cf. the discussion of Gal 3.6-29 above, and especially note 18, cf. Sieffert, *Galater*, p. 130, Schlier, *Galater*, p. 101, Tannehill, *Dying*, p. 58f., Schnelle, *Gerechtichkeit*, p. 55.
166. Thus clearly Ernest de Witt Burton, *The Epistle to the Galatians (ICC)*, Edinburgh 1921, p. 135f., cf. Betz, *Galatians*, p. 122.
167. Cf. Sieffert, *Galater*, p. 130, Betz, *Galatians*, p. 122, Lührmann, *Galater*, p. 45, Hans Weder, *Das Kreuz Jesu bei Paulus (FRLANT 125)*, Göttingen 1981, p. 179.
168. Cf. Mussner, *Galaterbrief*, p. 181. The perfect form shows that the term is used quite metaphorically. The continued effect of the crucifixion provides no meaning at a direct level.
169. Cf. Betz, *Galatians*, p. 121f., Schlier, *Galater*, p. 100.

statement: Christ is the vital force in the new existence, it says in verse 20a, and it now indicates this by solemn references to faith in the Son of God, his love and sacrifice.[170]

In this way, it seems to me that it becomes possible to follow Paul's thought and to see what it is that is concerning him.

But the question then arises, what concepts and traditions can form the basis of Paul's exposition.

Most people point out directly that the concept we encounter here must be a baptism concept.[171] In support of this is the fact that the verse concerns a decisive turning-point which leads to the Christian life (and in the parallel Rom 6.6 there is a connection with baptism). This is a possibility which cannot be excluded.

Another theory, however, is questionable. Exegetes often speak of 'death and resurrection with Christ' in Gal 2.19-20.[172] But in fact these verses speak only of 'death' with Christ.[173] And if one looks at the structure it transpires that there is only one event which is significant, a momentary turning-point. 'Death' is a break with the old bondings, and this break is the transition to the new life. There is no direct place for resurrection as yet another salvation event.

170. Burton, *Galatians*, p. 135ff., speaks of 'enthusiastic joy' and of Paul's being knocked down when he comes to the basis and object of belief, the son of God, so that we have the distinctive terms about Christ-acts. Schlier, *Galater*, p. 103: 'Der Glaubende glaubt also daran, dass sein Leben von der Liebe Christi geliebt ist.' Weder, *Kreuz*, p. 181, speaks of a movement from death to life.

171. Thus Reitzenstein, *Mysterienreligionen*, p. 261, Lietzmann, *Galater*, p. 17, Schnackenburg, *Heilsgeschehen*, p. 57ff., Todes- und Lebensgemeinschaft, p. 46, Schlier, *Galater*, p. 100ff., Oepke, *Galater*, p. 62, Gäumann, *Taufe*, p. 57, Thüsing, *Per Christum*, p. 110, Mussner, *Galaterbrief*, p. 179f., Halter, *Taufe*, p. 102ff., Schnelle, *Gerechtigkeit*, p. 55. This is rejected by Braun, *Studien*, p. 156, Tannehill, *Dying*, p. 59 (because here death occurs by virtue of the law), Kümmel, *Theologie*, p. 191, Siber, *Mit Christus*, p. 192, 218, Betz, *Galatians*, p. 122f.

172. Thus Oepke, *ThWNT* I, p. 539, *ThWNT* II, p. 334, *Galater*, p. 62, Tannehill, *Dying*, p. 70, Kümmel, *Theologie*, p. 191, Mussner, *Galaterbrief*, p. 181, Halter, *Taufe*, p. 102ff., Lührmann, *Galater*, p. 45, Schnelle, *Gerechtigkeit*, p. 55, jf. Schlier, *Galater*, p. 101.

173. It may appear that some interpreters think that there must be a reason for omitting the resurrection here. Conzelmann, *Grundriss*, p. 308, says that life is not yet there in the form of resurrection-δόξα. Schnelle, *Gerechtigkeit*, p. 55f., understands the term 'death — in order to live to God' in Gal 2.19 as a parallel to Rom 6.8; in Gal 2.20 there is said to be tension between the forceful 'Christusgegenwart' (he also speaks of belief in the resurrected son of God) and the human conditions of existence 'in the flesh' and 'by faith'; this latter is said to be Paul's attempt to avoid enthusiastic misunderstanding, cf. also Halter, *Taufe*, p. 106. But it is difficult to detect this tension directly in the wording of the verses. It also seems to be incomprehensible in the context of Galatians that Paul should take up an enthusiastic statement immediately to contradict it. Finally, it is shown that the structure is also against such an opinion.

This becomes of significance to the question of a religio-historical background. There is no basis as in the past to claim a connection backwards to the mysteries' dying and resurrecting deities[174] or other specific concepts. One must be content with more general references to contemporary religiosity, either Hellenistic mysticism[175] or Old Testament-inspired ideas of a representative redeemer-figure.[176] There are no true parallels outside Christianity.

It is possible that in Gal 2.19-20 Paul is dependent upon a separate primitive Christian tradition. Here one can indicate the possible connection to baptism and to traditionally-sounding formulations.[177] In addition, the central statement in verse 19, Χριστῷ συνεσταύρωμαι, is so provocative and paradoxical that, it is asserted, it can only be understood with certain advance knowledge.[178] Finally, there are also a number of parallels in Paul.

In *Gal 6.14*, in the final appeal to the Galatians not to listen to those who preach circumcision, Paul draws attention to himself: 'May *I* never boast of anything except the cross of our Lord Jesus Christ, by which the world has been crucified to me and I to the world.'

The mode of expression is less compressed here. It thus becomes more clear that there is the dual reference which could be observed in Gal 2.19-20. First, by using the term σταυρός Χριστοῦ there is a reference to the death of Jesus as the central salvation event. Then the relative sentence states the significance to the Christian. And here the verb σταυροῦν, is used, again in a loaded, figurative sense.[179] It expresses the break between the Christian and the world. Other elements also appear once again, if the following verses are included. The optimistic point is found in Gal 6.15, which reads that what is important is neither circumcision nor uncircumcision but καινὴ κτίσις. This is the principle to follow according to Gal 6.16, so there seems to be a demand associated with the motif. Finally, it is also said that there is a new

---

174. Thus in particular Reitzenstein, *Mysterienreligionen*, p. 261, cf. Oepke, *Galater*, p. 63.
175. See Martin Dibelius, Paulus und die Mystik, in: *Botschaft und Geschichte* II, Tübingen 1956, pp. 134-59; p. 150f., Lietzmann, *Galater*, p. 17, Oepke, *Galater*, p. 64, which points to a Hellenistic mysticism. In Schneider, *Passionsmystik*, pp. 32-36, it is a mysticism which Paul himself creates. Tannehill, *Dying*, p. 57ff., refuses to speak of mysticism, but says instead that the Christians are included in Christ's crucifixion.
176. Thus Schnackenburg, Todes- und Lebensgemeinschaft, p. 46, who speaks of a 'progenitor' idea, corporate personality and baptism as an incorporation into Christ's past death, Frankemölle, *Taufverständnis*, p. 65, 73f., 91f.
177. Especially Gal 2.20: 'the Son of God, who loved me and gave himself for me' reads like a traditional statement, cf. above.
178. Cf. Wedderburn, *Baptism*, p. 345, who calls it 'a daring statement' and expresses doubt about whether it was in any way understandable to the Galatians.
179. Cf. Tannehill, *Dying*, p. 64, who also speaks of crucifixion as an 'inclusive event'.

bonding with Christ. He is referred to in Gal 6.14 with special emphasis as our Lord Jesus Christ, and Gal 6.17 says that Paul bears 'stigmata' on his body.[180]

Gal 5.24 contains only parts of this thought process. As a member in a paraenesis, the acts of the flesh and the fruits of the Spirit are recited. It then reads: 'And those who belong to Jesus Christ have crucified the flesh with its passions and desires.' The explicit reference to Christ's death on the cross is lacking here. But that it is part of the picture is taken for granted when the verb σταυροῦν is used.[181] The emphasis is on the effect of Christ's death on the Christians. Again, this is a decisive break: the bonding with the flesh is abolished.[182] It seems that the word σταυροῦν has an established and recognisable metaphorical meaning.[183] It points in the direction of what is moral and almost ascetic. That the ethical is stressed is also to be seen from the subsequent verse, Gal 5.25: 'If we live by the Spirit, let us also be guided by the Spirit'.[184] The new bonding with Christ is given by the term οἱ τοῦ Χριστοῦ.

The formal parallelism is not so pronounced in *2 Cor 5.14-15*. Paul is about to demonstrate that his apostolic work has been honest and unselfish. It is a service to God and the community. 'For the love of Christ urges us on, because we are convinced that one has died for all (or on behalf of all, ὑπὲρ παντῶν); therefore all have died. And he died for all, so that those who live might live no longer for themselves, but for him who died and was raised for them.'

This corresponds inherently to the earlier passages. It speaks of death in two ways, which in turn are interlinked. 2 Cor 5.14b speaks literally of Christ's self-sacrificing death. In verse 14c, where it speaks of everyone's 'death', a figurative meaning must be concerned. Here also there is not the

---

180. See more specifically on this term and the whole passage in Chapter IV, section 3.3. below.
181. Cf. Burton, *Galatians*, p. 320, Halter, *Taufe*, p. 131.
182. The occasion on which the break occurred is also discussed here. Baptism is frequently indicated: Sieffert, *Galater*, p. 313, Oepke, *Galater*, p. 143, Merk, *Handeln*, p. 74f., Schlier, *Galater*, p. 263, Eckert, *Verkündigung*, p. 141f., Halter, *Taufe*, p. 130 with n. 32. The reference to baptism is contested by Burton, *Galatians*, p. 320, Mussner, *Galaterbrief*, p. 390 (which, with a reference to the active form, indicates a decision of faith), Weder, *Kreuz*, p. 199f. .
183. Cf. Burton, *Galatians*, p. 320.
184. This is one of those passages on whose basis the indicative-imperative problem was originally formulated. Cf. Wernle, *Christ*, p. 103ff., cf. Chapter I, section 2.1 above and Chapter X, section 2.3 below.

strict form as in Gal 2.19, where there is a reference with the same verb to two different events. But we get more information on how the death of Christ may be crucially important to the Christians. It becomes a vicarious death, whereby the power and threat of death have been removed from the Christians — therefore the strong expression that the Christians have put death behind them.[185]

The consequences of this 'death' correspond to those we have seen earlier. This is shown in 2 Cor 5.15. There is a break with the old existence — here it is the selfish life that has disappeared (corresponding to Gal 2.20). And the break becomes the crucial turning-point which leads to life. We have again the enthusiastic point which is carried on in the following, where in 2 Cor 5.17 it speaks of καινὴ κτίσις as in Gal 6.15. And what is still concerned is that after the final break with the old life there comes a new bonding and a new service. This is expressed here (as in Gal 2,20b) in solemn terms: 'so that those who live might live ... for him who died and was raised for them.' Here we can establish for the first time that the resurrection comes into the picture. But that does *not* mean that the motif becomes two-fold, so that a 'resurrection with Christ' must also be contemplated. It is still the same motif as earlier, in which the liberating, redeeming death is the one central event which initiates the new life. It includes as an extra advantage that Christ was not only he who died for the Christians but that he also arose. This may underline that he is present as Lord of the new life. It opens up new trains of thought. But there is no reference here to the Christians' resurrection.[186]

185. Hans Windisch, *Der zweite Korintherbrief* (KEK 6)[9], Göttingen 1924, p. 182, indicates the change of meaning which occurs in 2 Cor 5.14 (in which the member ὑπὲρ πάντων, as given in my translation above, is ambiguous): it seems initially that Christ's death is interpreted as 'vicarious', so that it must be concluded that everyone can thank Christ for existence; but instead it becomes 'representative', so that everyone is mystically encompassed by Christ's death, cf. also Tannehill, *Dying*, p. 66, Philip E. Hughes, *Commentary to the Second Epistle to the Corinthians (NIC)*, Grand Rapids 1962, p. 193f., Victor Paul Furnish, *II Corinthians (AncB 32A)*, Garden City, New York 1984, p. 327, Ralph P. Martin, *2 Corinthians (WBC 40)*, Waco, Texas 1986, p. 129ff. Rudolf Bultmann, *Der zweite Brief an die Korinther (KEK Sonderband)*, Göttingen 1976, p. 153, indicates a legal (not sacramental or mystical) vicarial concept.

186. There is certainly a tendency to interpret οἱ ζῶντες in 2 Cor 5.15 as a statement that the Christians have arisen with Christ, cf. Windisch, *2. Korintherbrief*, p. 183, Bruce, *Corinthians*, p. 207f., Bultmann, *2. Korinther*, p. 154, Furnish, *2 Corinthians*, p. 311. But this seems to be an over-interpretation, in the same way as the idea in Thüsing, *Per Christum*, p. 103: '... insofern sie durch die Taufe in das Leben des erhöhten Christus einbezogen sind.' It is more natural to understand the term, corresponding to Gal 2.19-20, as about the newly-created life which follows the deliverance from death and sin, cf. Alfred Plummer, *A Critical and Exegetical Commentary on the Second Epistle of St. Paul to the Corinthians (ICC)*, Edinburgh 1915, p. 175, Wendland, *Korinther*, p. 202, Tannehill, *Dying*, p. 66, Mar-

There is a connection from *Rom 7.4* to Rom 6.1-14, so that in this way the passage is to be found in a 'baptism context'.[187] Rom 7.1-6 shows that there has been a final break with the sinful existence under the law. Rom 7.4 describes the decisive turning-point: 'In the same way, my friends, you have also died to the law through τὸ σῶμα Χριστοῦ so that you may belong to another, to him who has been raised from the dead in order that we may bear fruit for God.'

Christ's crucified body, Christ's corpse, must have been intended by σῶμα Χριστοῦ.[188] Then again it is Christ's death on the cross that leads to the Christians' 'death'. The question is whether one should also be mindful of the other loaded meanings of σῶμα Χριστοῦ, the Eucharistic symbolism and the ecclesiological use of the concept.[189] It is obvious that Paul does not utilise these meanings in this context.

Here again (as in Gal 2,19) there is a break with the existence which was characterised by the law. And by virtue of this there is a definitive opening for the new life. Once again the crucial point is a new bonding with Christ expressed by a marriage metaphor. And where the significance of this is to be emphasised Christ is described as the resurrected Lord. 'Death with Christ' is still the decisive turning-point. But now it is stressed, even more strongly than in 2 Cor 5.15, that Christ is present in the new life. The ethical dimension is also clearly to be seen in the last member of the verse, where it says that what is important is to bear fruit for God.

It has been established that the pattern is the same in these texts. One marked turning-point is described as a 'death with Christ', who is seen as the redeemer. There is a break with various old powers: the law, the ego, the

---

tin, *2 Corinthians*, p. 132. This means that 2 Cor 5.15 must be listed among the many resurrection statements whose soteriological function is to indicate the divine confirmation of the central faith-content — as in 1 Thess 1.10; Gal 1.1; Rom 1.4; 4.25; 7.4; 8.34; 10.9; 14.9. Cf. Wengst, *Formeln*, p. 27ff., Kegel, *Auferstehung*, p. 33, Becker, *Auferstehung*, p. 14ff., 30f., Hoffmann, *TRE* 4, p. 478ff.

187. Cf. Thüsing, *Per Christum*, p. 96, Halter, *Taufe*, p. 92f.

188. Cf. Michel, *Römer*, p. 167, Best, *Body*, p. 53, Jervell, *Gud*, p. 112, Cranfield, *Romans*, p. 336, Halter, *Taufe*, p. 92.

189. There is reference to Eucharistic symbolism in Schweizer, *ThWNT* VII, p. 1064, Käsemann, *Römer*, p. 181, Halter, *Taufe*, p. 92; the ecclesiological concept is brought into the picture by Dodd, *Romans*, p. 120, Nygren, *Romarna*, p. 281, Kümmel, *Theologie*, p. 190f.; particularly problematic in this connection are the references to a mystical, pneumatic or corporative association between Christ and the Christians, as in Schweizer, *Mystik*, p. 186, von Soden, *Urchristentum*, p. 263 n. 1, Percy, *Leib*, p. 29, Robinson, *Body*, p. 47, Tannehill, *Dying*, p. 46; this association between the Christians and Christ is denied in the subsequent context, where the Christians are placed in front of Christ in a relationship of service and dependence.

self, the flesh, the world. The new bonding to Christ and the new demand are described using various terms, and here the resurrection may come into the picture. There may be a connection with baptism, but this is not directly expressed.

It does not point unambiguously in the direction of a firmly formulated baptismal tradition. But the main idea itself behind all the passages appears to be well-known and widespread, since the remarkable, loaded formulations assume a certain knowledge of the way of thinking.

3.3. Suffering and resurrection with Christ in Rom 8.17; Phil 3.9-10; 1 Thess 4.14 and 2 Cor 4.10-11

In these four significant contexts, the conviction is expressed that the Christians' suffering and death with Christ will lead towards resurrection and glory with Christ. As regards both form and content, this motif is less complicated than the previous motif. But it is included everywhere in a context with other central Christological motifs.

The motif is to be found in *Rom 8.17* in a strict and simple form. It establishes that as children of God the Christians are his heirs and Christ's joint heirs, and it explains why this is so: εἴπερ συμπάσχομεν ἵνα καὶ συνδοξασθῶμεν.

The principle is that there is an accord and a connection between what happens to the Christians and what happened to Christ. This is expressed by the prefix σύν, which must be linked to an implicit Christ: the Christians suffer and are glorified 'in conformity with the pattern of His earthly life'.[190] Εἴπερ, followed by the indicative, indicates the fulfilled condition;[191] the sufferings are a factual reality for the Christians, and these are interpreted as Christ-sufferings. The final ἵνα then indicates that the divine intention of these sufferings is future glory.[192] The direction of the thought thus moves

---

190. Thus Cranfield, *Romans*, p. 408. See also notes 157 and 159 above.

191. See Blass, Debrunner and Rehkopf, *Grammatik*, § 454,2, cf. also Kühl, *Römerbrief*, p. 288, Michel, *Römer*, p. 199, Siber, *Mit Christus*, p. 139f., Schlier, *Römerbrief*, p. 255, von der Osten-Sacken, *Römer 8*, p. 135 n. 18. Against Kuss, *Römerbrief*, p. 706, Otto, *Formulierungen*, p. 84, Käsemann, *Römer*, p. 221, in which the εἴπερ sentence is understood conditionally and becomes an indirect request, as is seen in the context of the paraenesis in Rom 8.12f.

192. Thus Kühl, *Römerbrief*, p. 288: 'ἵνα der göttlichen Absicht'. Cf. also Siber, *Mit Christus*, p. 140: 'Es geht ... um dasjenige Ziel, welches Kraft des Weges Jesu vom Leiden zur Herrlichkeit und nun auch im Mitleid des Christen objektiv gesetzt ist, nicht um ein subjektiv vom Christen angestrebtes Ziel.' This subjective interpretation is to be found in the authorised Danish translation of 1992: 'så sandt vi er med i hans lidelser for også at være med i hans herlighed' [as truly as we are with him in his suffering so as also to be with him in his glory]. The idea here is apparently that Christians imitate or identify themselves with Christ's suffering in order thereby to attain Christ's glory.

from the present tribulations to the coming glory following the resurrection, which is the expected 'inheritance'.[193]

That there is reason for hope and not fear about the transient tribulations is also emphasised in the context, since in the whole of Rom 8 there is a series of fundamental christological and soteriological concepts where the life of Christ and the life of the Christians are linked together in such a way that an assured sequence is concerned. And here there are a number of parallels to Gal 3-4, where it is also emphasised that the Christians will participate in Christ's 'inheritance'.[194]

This begins in Rom 8.3-4 with a mission-of-Christ statement to explain that the Christians ἐν Χριστῷ will be released from 'the law of sin and death' into 'the law of the Spirit of life'. The central statement is introduced by saying that God sent his son 'in the likeness of sinful flesh'.[195] As in Gal 4.4, it is emphasised that Christ came to live under the conditions of human life. There is thus the first similarity between the Christians' life and Christ's life. The result is that the sin of the flesh is condemned. How this comes about is not quite clear because of the elliptical construction of the sentence. Rom 8.3a proposes that Christ's mission and life mean that whatever was impossible under the law is implemented.[196] It often points out the widespread concept of Christ's death of atonement.[197] But it is quite clear that the consequence for the Christians is a spiritual life in which the law's demands

---

193. Cf. von der Osten-Sacken, *Römer 8*, p. 137, Schlier, *Römerbrief*, p. 255, Siber, *Mit Christus*, p. 139f. That the emphasis is upon the positive — the glory of resurrection — is apparent not only from consideration of the christological background below; I shall return to the question of the direction of the thought-process in Chapter VI, section 2.3.

194. See the examination of Gal 3-4, section 2.1 above. As regards the parallel features, cf. Tannehill, *Dying*, p. 113f., Siber, *Mit Christus*, p. 135ff., von der Osten-Sacken, *Römer 8*, p. 129ff., Paulsen, *Überlieferung*, p. 98ff., Wilckens, *Römer II*, p. 138f., Gerd Theissen, *Psychologische Aspekte paulinischer Theologie* (FRLANT 131), Göttingen 1983, p. 264f. In Simonsen, *Overvejelser*, p. 200f., the observations are used to stress that Paul uses baptismal terminology.

195. This translation of ἐν ὁμοιώματι σαρκὸς ἁμαρτίας must be maintained despite the discussion about the precise meaning of the word ὁμοίωμα, cf. Chapter VII, section 3.5 below in connection with the interpretation of Rom 6.5. The word refers to something (concrete) which is similar to what is stated by the objective genitive. What is crucial is the similarity of Christ to mankind, i.e. in the exterior manifestation; but at the same time there are also differences, since he indeed did not live this life in sin, cf. Bornkamm, *Ende*, p. 42, Käsemann, *Römer*, p. 209, Schlier, *Römerbrief*, p. 241, Cranfield, *Romans*, p. 381.

196. Cf. Schmidt, *Römer*, p. 137, who emphasises that the condemnation is shown by the false judgement, in which the truly righteous is condemned to death as godless, and the delusion of sin has reached its end.

197. The reason for this is that it must be possible to use the term περὶ τῆς ἁμαρτίας in Septuagint as a fixed term meaning propitiatory sacrifice — cf. Käsemann, *Römer*, p. 209, Schlier, *Römerbrief*, p. 241, Wilckens, *Römer II*, p. 126ff., Morris, *Romans*, p. 303; different in Barrett, *Romans*, p. 156, Michel, *Römer*, p. 190, Murray, *Romans*, p. 280.

are met.[198] There is thus another similarity between Christ and the Christians, who are to live life spiritually as he did.

Rom 8.9-11 expresses a very close connection between the Christians, Christ and the Spirit. It is emphasised by four conditional clauses almost like a refrain, Rom 8.9bc,10a,11a, that it is crucially significant that God's spirit resides in the Christians, that they have the Spirit of Christ, that Christ is within them, and that the Spirit which resurrected Christ resides in them. Rom 8.9 then reads the Christians are in the Spirit and that the Spirit is in the Christians. And if the ἐν Χριστῷ which chimes in from Rom 8.1-2 is combined with Rom 8.10 it reads similarly that the Christians are in Christ and Christ in the Christians. This mode of expression has been perceived as mystical: that the Christians are merged together with the sublime Christ and the Spirit.[199] But it may also be merely an attempt to express as intensely as possible the Christians' bonding with Christ. This is described as meaning, as in Gal 2.20; 3.27, that the Christians have received a new identity.[200] But closer examination shows that there is in fact distance between Christ and the Christians, which is maintained quite naturally and evidently. Rom 8.10b reads that the Christians' body is certainly 'dead', presumably as a result of sinfulness in the old existence.[201] But, emphasises Rom 8.10c, the Spirit is life by virtue of righteousness; in the context of the Letter to the Romans, one must think of justification by faith, which rests on God's act of salvation that comes from without.[202] Rom 8.11 reads that the Christians have the same Spirit as Christ, and will therefore go through the same process via death to resurrection as Christ has already experienced.[203] This is the

198. One must understand δικαίωμα in this rather broad sense, cf. Karl Kertelge, *'Rechtfertigung' bei Paulus* (NTA.NF 3), Münster 1967, p. 217, J.A. Ziesler, *The Meaning of Righteousness in Paul* (SNTS.MS 20), Cambridge 1972, p. 204, Schlier, *Römerbrief*, p. 243.
199. See in particular Deissmann, *Formel*, p. 91ff., Schweitzer, *Mystik*, p. 123. Cf. against this Käsemann, *Römer*, p. 212ff., who indicates the eschatology and 'Christi Herrschaftsbereich', Jervell, *Gud*, p. 142f.
200. See Theissen, *Aspekte*, p. 262ff., cf. Käsemann, *Römer*, p. 214.
201. The understanding of Rom 8.10b is not quite certain. But the best meaning of the sentence is given if σῶμα νεκρόν is perceived negatively in line with Rom 7.25 about the mortality to which the body is subject as a result of the old sin, and then to understand the introductory μέν concessively, so that this circumstance is relativised because of the new vital force; cf. Dodd, *Romans*, p. 140f., Michel, *Römer*, p. 193, Murray, *Romans*, p. 289, Siber, *Mit Christus*, p. 82f., von der Osten-Sacken, *Römer 8*, p. 327f, Cranfield, *Romans*, p. 389. The alternative interpretation, to be found in Schmidt, *Römer*, p. 139, Paulsen, *Überlieferung*, p. 72ff., Käsemann, *Römer*, p. 216, Wilckens, *Römer II*, p. 132f., makes the death of the body something positive, 'death' from the old existence, which by a reference to Rom 6.3-6 is identified with baptism; but it implies a loaded Christological idea, and the member διὰ δικαιοσύνην must have a laboured meaning: 'in regard to justification'.
202. Cf. Kertelge, *Rechtfertigung*, p. 155ff., Ziesler, *Meaning*, p. 204.
203. Cf. Cranfield, *Romans*, p. 390.

thought which is continued in Rom 8.17. Christ's resurrection is given the special function that it confirms the expectation of the Christians' resurrection. But this is also linked to the Christians' confrontation with external demands in the following verses.

Rom 8.14-17 states that arming with the Spirit gives filial adoption and thus the same status as Christ. As in Gal 4.5-6, the Spirit and the υἱοθεσία associated therewith represent a break with the former life of a slave; in family terms, the Christians are placed as is Christ.[204] The close relationship to God is stressed by the cry 'ἀββᾶ ὁ πατήρ'. It may be natural in Gal 4.6 to associate this with baptism, as a proclamation of the new filial relationship.[205] But it can also be understood as a 'Gebetsruf', perhaps the introduction to the Lord's Prayer;[206] and in Rom 8, in which it is indeed a crucial concept that the Christians are confronted with suffering in the same way as Christ, it is natural to see a reference to Jesus' prayer at Gethsemane in Mark 14.36, which includes the same term.[207] The family-law aspect of the way of thinking continues by presenting the Christians as Christ's joint heirs. The use of the image of the Christians as heirs here and in Gal 3.29-4,7 also indicates that, in addition to his present situation, the heir can expect more.[208]

The final point in Rom 8.28-30 is, then, that the sequence of events towards glory is so certain that it is described as having already taken place. According to Rom 8.29, the basis of this is that the Christians have been 'pre-

---

204. In Greco-Roman usage, υἱοθεσία refers to the adopted's rights as a son, cf. Kuss, *Römerbrief*, p. 601f.
205. Cf. Siber, *Mit Christus*, p. 137f., von der Osten-Sacken, *Römer 8*, p. 130f., Paulsen, *Überlieferung*, p. 87ff., Betz, *Galatians*, p. 210f.
206. Cf. Lietzmann, *Römer*, p. 83, Michel, *Römer*, p. 197f., Oscar Cullmann, *Die Christologie des Neuen Testaments*[2], Tübingen 1958, p. 215, Barrett, *Romans*, p. 163f. The reference to the Lord's Prayer is to be found in Seeberg, *Katechismus*, p. 240ff., who at the same time shows that it was used in baptism early in primitive Christianity, cf. Kittel, ἀββᾶ, *ThWNT* I (1933), pp. 4-6, Gerhard Delling, *Der Gottesdienst im Neuen Testament*, Göttingen 1952, p. 72f., Joachim Jeremias, Das Vaterunser im Lichte der neueren Forschung, in: 'Abba'. Studien zur neutestamentlichen Theologie und Zeitgeschichte, Göttingen 1966, pp. 152-71; p. 162ff., Abba, op. cit., pp. 15-67; p. 66 n. 73.
207. It thus expresses firm belief in God and certainty of salvation, as emphasised by Jeremias, *Abba*, p. 66f. Cf. also p. 163, Cranfield, *Romans*, p. 399f. Note that the various interpretations do not exclude one another, cf. Wilckens, *Römer II*, p. 137f. Also supporting this interpretation is Rom 8.27-28, in which the Holy Spirit is included in a prayer which says that God's will must have its way, just as in M.36d.
208. Cf. Paulsen, *Überlieferung*, p. 102ff., who rightly connects this with the duality to be seen from the term δόξα and from υἱοθεσία, which is both something topical (Rom 8.30 and Rom 8.15) and something in the future (Rom 8.17,23). If one accepts the consequence of this recognition, it is not tension-charged as indicated by Paulsen ('eschatologische Spannung'), but indeed a simple idea about an expected development.

destined to be conformed to the image of his Son, in order that he might be the firstborn within a large family'. In extension of Rom 8.4-16, an explanation is given here of how it happened that the Christians have received the same status as Christ. This may be seen as a parallel to being clothed with Christ in Gal 3.27. But here it is expressed with a concept of 'conformity' which is said to have linguistic parallels in Hellenistic thought and also comes to the fore in Pauline contexts;[209] also, the term εἰκών shows that there is a play on the Old Testament concept of God-imagery: Christ is God's image and thus a pre-image for the Christians.[210] In the following hymnic conclusion, in Rom 8.32, the certainty is confirmed that after Christ's sacrificial death God will give the Christians everything like him (σὺν αὐτῷ).

The chapter thus displays throughout a special christological line, which begins with Jesus showing solidarity with mankind and thus becoming their precursor in life, death and resurrection to glory. The parallels from Gal 3-4 are a first confirmation that Paul uses central primitive-Christian concepts. And they show that these themes can be associated with baptism.

Phil 3.10-11 has a less strict version of the motif. As a stage in the warning beginning in Phil 3,1 directed against some opponents with roots in Judaism,[211] Paul uses himself as an example: After having come to know Christ, he turned away from the earlier striving after his own justification through the law and looked to justification by faith — it then reads: τοῦ γνῶναι αὐτὸν καὶ τὴν δύναμιν τῆς ἀναστάσεως αὐτοῦ καὶ τὴν κοινωνίαν τῶν

---

209. Συμμόρφους is given as similar terms in Rom 12.2; 2 Cor 3.18; Phil 2.6-7; 3.10,21, in connection with Hellenistic ideas on metamorphosis, cf. Reitzenstein, *Mysterienreligionen*, p. 357f., Ernst Käsemann, Kritische Analyse von Phil. 2,5-11, in: *Exegetische Versuche und Besinnungen* I³, Göttingen 1964, pp. 51-95; p. 65ff., von der Osten-Sacken, *Römer 8*, p. 74, Bultmann, *2. Korinther*, p. 98, which points in particular to mystery religions; but the usage cannot be restricted to this; they are general Hellenistic terms.

210. The εἰκών concept, which is also to be found in 1 Cor 11.7; 15.49; 2 Cor 3.18; 4.4; Rom 1.23; Col 1.15, has a special Christological hierarchy in Paul: God — Christ as 'Urbild' — man as 'Abbild'. Thus Jervell, *Imago*, p. 276ff., Conzelmann, *1. Korinther*, p. 221f., 343, cf. also concerning the previous history of the term in Judaism and Hellenistic parallels Friedrich-Wilhelm Eltester, *Eikon im Neuen Testament* (BZNW 23), Berlin 1958, p. 130ff. Larsson, *Christus*, p. 18ff., 113ff., also associates Christ's 'Vorbildlichkeit' with the gospels' imitation concept and the development of the σὺν Χριστῷ concepts.

211. Cf. J.B. Lightfoot, *Saint Paul's Epistle to the Philippians*⁶, London 1881, p. 143ff., Ernst Lohmeyer, *Der Brief an die Philipper* (KEK 9.1)¹⁴, Göttingen 1974, p. 122ff., Tannehill, *Dying*, p. 114ff., Olof Linton, *Pauli mindre brev* (TNT 9)² [The smaller Letters of Paul], Stockholm 1970, p. 186ff. (Christian 'Judaists'), Niels Hyldahl, *Loven og Troen. En analyse af Filipperbrevets tredie kapitel* (AJut 15.6) [Law and Belief. An analysis of Chapter Three of the Letter to the Phillipians], Århus 1968, pp. 14-20 (which draws attention to non-Christian Jews).

παθημάτων αὐτοῦ συμμορφιζόμενος τῷ θανάτῳ αὐτοῦ, εἴ πως καταντήσω εἰς τὴν ἐξανάστασιν τὴν ἐκ νεκρῶν.

Despite the loose association with the foregoing, it is clear that the sentence shows what justification by faith involves.[212] The Christians' sufferings in the world are again linked to Christ's suffering and death, and again this is associated with the concept of a resurrection to glory related thereto. There is here a reduplication of the motif. Phil 3.10 emphasises beforehand the forces which are now involved: the power of resurrection and common suffering. Then comes the motif itself in Phil 3.11; not with the same strict wording as in Rom 8.17 but in the same sequence: conformity with Christ's suffering leads to conformity with Christ's resurrection.[213] This is the same two-phased sequence of events with the emphasis on the last member. The reference to Christ's resurrection is again used to safeguard the hope of the Christians' resurrection.[214]

212. The construction τοῦ + the infinitive either indicates a weak consecutive meaning or it is epexegetic, cf. Blass, Debrunner and Rehkopf, *Grammatik*, § 400.5,8; in any case justification by faith is amplified, and perhaps also the γνῶσις 'Ιησοῦ Χριστοῦ, which according to Phil 3.8 pervades at conversion. This makes it apparent that knowledge of the power of resurrection and common suffering is something topical and not a futuristic-eschatological benefit of salvation, as asserted by Lohmeyer, *Philipper*, p. 138, Peter Stuhlmacher, *Gerechtigkeit Gottes bei Paulus* (FRLANT 87)², Göttingen 1966, p. 99, cf. however C.F. Evans, *Resurrection and the New Testament*², London 1981, p. 164, Siber, *Mit Christus*, p. 111. It should also be noted that over-interpretations seems to be concerned, when Martin Dibelius, An die Philipper, in: *An die Thessalonicher I II. An die Philipper* (HNT 11)³, Tübingen 1937, pp. 59-98; p. 89, Lohmeyer, *Philipper*, p. 133f., Bultmann, *Theologie*, p. 184, Stuhlmacher, *Gerechtigkeit*, p. 99, treats γνῶσις 'Ιησοῦ Χριστοῦ as mystical or gnostic terminology and as an absolute recognition; this sentence indeed shows that what is concerned is the experience of something quite specific: the significance of Jesus' death and resurrection, cf. Tannehill, *Dying*, p. 119f., Siber, *Mit Christus*, p. 111.
213. This thus becomes a chiastic construction, as indicated in Siber, *Mit Christus*, p. 111. Since the motif is initially indicated in the reverse sequence, it is natural to interpret it as an expression of having to emphasise the power of resurrection in particular — differently in Siber, loc. cit. One should be aware, however, that the power of resurrection and common suffering in Phil 3.10 seem already to be active phenomena, whereas the fellowship of death and resurrection from the dead in Phil 3.11 is for the future, cf. Tannehill, *Dying*, p. 120, Evans, *Resurrection*, p. 164.
214. Against Siber, *Mit Christus*, p. 111ff., who tries to put the emphasis on the suffering and similarity to Christ's death, so that the point becomes a glory only in the future and thereby a dissociation from the opponents' enthusiasm which has gained a foothold among the Philippians. But this positioning of emphasis is not found in the text itself. On the contrary, in Phil 3.10 Paul emphasises the power of resurrection, which is referred to as something topical. The hypothesis rests on a widespread theory that the opponents were at the same time Judeo-Christian, law-abiding, circumcision preachers and enthusiastic libertarians, cf. Phil 3.12,18-19, a theory about which Siber himself has misgivings (p. 101ff.). It is also constructed upon a literary-critical operation in which Phil 3 is for no compelling reason removed from the context of the letter as an independent text

This motif also is linked to other 'precursor motifs'.

In Phil 3,17 comes the demand: Συμμίμηται μοῦ γίνεσθε. Paul makes use of a mimesis-concept, which he also uses elsewhere and incidentally has in common with the mystery religions.[215] Like Paul, the Philippians must imitate Christ. On the one hand this points backwards to Phil 3.10-16, where Paul spoke of a road of suffering which he follows with Christ as example and motive power. He admits that he has not achieved perfection, but with God's power he is on the way to this.[216] On the other hand this points forward: in the following context the Philippians are required to choose between the two ways of living: either like the earthly enemies of Christ's cross,[217] or like Paul and other Christians who belong among the heavenly and will therefore attain glory.[218]

Phil 3.21 is particularly important. It says of Christ that he will

transform the body of our humiliation that it may be conformed to the body of his glory, by the power that also enables him to make all things subject to himself.

It is again stressed here that the final target for the entire sequence of events is the conformity between the Christians and Christ in a state of glory. From here, there is not only a clear connection back to Phil 3.10-11[219] but also to

---

(p. 99ff.), so that it is not to be part of the trustful exhortation to the Philippians, which is the general line of the epistle, but a polemic against them. Cf. also Betz, *Nachfolge*, p. 145ff.

215. 1 Thess 1.6; 2.14; 1 Cor 4.16; 11.1. See as to this Betz, *Nachfolge*, p. 167ff. Cf. Chapter II, notes 146 and 150 above and note 238 below.

216. Paul therefore expresses a 'not yet' as far as he himself is concerned and expands it with Phil 3.17 to apply to the Philippians also. It is then assumed that in this section Paul introduces an eschatological reservation in a polemic against people who have considered themselves as τέλειοι — thus Betz, *Nachfolge*, p. 146f., Siber, *Mit Christe*, p. 109. But there is reason for some caution. On the one hand, it is questionable whether Paul makes a reservation; he admits the defects in the Christian existence, but in the context stresses the expectation of final glory; and in Phil 3.15 he refers to himself and at least some of the Philippians as τέλειοι with no form of demonstrable reservation. On the other hand, no polemic objective is emphasised. It might just as well concern an apology for Jewish accusations of libertine enthusiasm. Or Paul simply wishes to explain the matter as precisely as possible, cf. Hyldahl, *Loven*, p. 42.

217. Phil 3.18-19 refers to many who are enemies of the cross and perish. Who they are, whose belly is their god, who glory in their shame and who set their minds on earthly things, cannot be determined, cf. the varied considerations in Lohmeyer, *Philipper*, p. 153ff., Linton, *Brev*, p. 195ff., Hyldahl, *Loven*, p. 55f., Siber, *Mit Christus*, p. 105ff.

218. This is the final optimistic point, as already emphasised by Lohmeyer, *Philipper*, p. 159.

219. In addition to the parallel to σύμμορφον, the movement is again found where the Christian passes from (body of) humiliation to (body of) glory, cf. Lohmeyer, *Philipper*, p. 161, Siber, *Mit Christus*, p. 122ff.

the statement in Phil 1.23 about Paul's longing to leave the earthly and be σὺν Χριστῷ,[220] and to the Christological hymn in Phil 2.

Phil 2.5-13 includes the 'precursor Christology' in the context of a rigidly composed, hymn-like passage. From the Christ hymn[221] there is both an inherent and a word-related connection to Phil 3. The first part, Phil 2.6-8, concerns Christ, who did not abuse his divine origin but took on a servant's role in human form and obediently accepted the consequences: humiliation and crucifixion; as in Phil 3.10,21, the road is via degrading suffering. The second part of the hymn, Phil 2.9-11, concerns the movement in the opposite direction, which God initiates, towards exaltation, universal power and worship; this corresponds to resurrection in glory, which is the final objective in Phil 3.11,21. There is also remarkable accord in the choice of words. This is true in particular of the words from Hellenistic religious usage, which in Phil 2.7-8 express that Jesus received the form of a man: μορφή, σχῆμα and ἐταπείνωσεν. This is readopted in Phil 3.21 in describing how the Christians are to be given a splendour like that of Christ.[222] First, it shows that this is a

---

220. For Lohmeyer, *Philipper*, p. 159, this connection plays an important part, in that he interprets Phil 3.21 as expressing *the martyr's* fate in death, and is indeed intended to be the letter's main theme which is struck in Phil 1.22-26. It is however doubtful whether it relates to the martyrs' fate in particular, and not merely to the final end of all dead Christians.

221. The text and its hymnic nature has been thoroughly discussed in Ernst Lohmeyer, *Kyrios Jesus. Eine Untersuchung zu Phil. 2,5-11* (SAH 1927-28,4), Heidelberg 1928, p. 4ff., cf. *Philipper*, p. 90ff. Here it is also asserted that an incorporated pre-Pauline hymn is concerned, with its background in Jewish apocalyptics, Dan 7.13 and 'the Lord's suffering servant' from Deutero-Isaiah. In contrast to this concept of the background, Käsemann has sought in his 1950 critical analysis of Phil 2.5-11, *Versuche* I, p. 51ff., to demonstrate dependence upon a gnostic primitive mythology — with CH 1.13-14 as the only example-passage apart from New Testament passages such as Rom 5.12-21; Heb 5.8-10. Since then, the debate about the background has played a crucial part in the examination of this text, cf. the survey of research in R.P. Martin. *Carmen Christi. Philippians ii.5-11 in Recent Interpretation and in the Setting of Early Christian Worship* (SNTS.MS 4), Cambridge 1967, p. 74ff., Wengst, *Formeln*, p. 144, which incidentally seeks to support Käsemann's opinion by references to the 'The Pearl Hymn' (cf. note 41 above). But these religio-historical considerations are of limited relevance to interpretation of the text, partly because of its uncertain, hypothetical nature and partly for fundamental, methodical reasons, since in any case Paul is responsible for the final result, cf. Larsson, *Christus*, p. 230f., and also Chapter I, section 3.1 above, and note 226 below.

222. The words μορφή, σχήματι and ἐταπείνωσεν in Phil 2.6-8 correspond to συμμορφιζόμενος in Phil 3.10 and σύμμορφον, μετασχηματίσει and ταπεινώσεως in Phil 3.21; in Phil 2.10 every knee shall bend at the name of Jesus, in Phil 3.21 he can make all things subject to himself, cf. Lohmeyer, *Philipper*, p. 161, Güttgemanns, *Apostel*, p. 241. In addition, there is an emphasis on obedience to the cross in Phil 2.8, a counterpart to enmity towards the cross in Phil 3.18, which is again contrasted with what applies to the Christians according to Phil. 3.20-21. And there is a reference to ἐνεργεία in both Phil 2.13 and 3.21.

train of thought from the Christ-hymn, which is continued in Phil 3, whether or not Paul goes on working on the concepts from the hymn or perhaps uses several fragments of a longer Christ-hymn.[223] Second, we can see that here also there are several coherent precursor motifs. As in Rom 8.3, it begins again with Christ's arrival in the world, where he identifies himself wholly with human life.[224] And the accord between Christ and the Christians also emerges when the Christological hymn is used paraenetically in the context of the Christians;[225] it is clear that Phil 2.12, introduced by ὥστε, is a demand to show the same obedience and firmness as Christ, with salvation as the objective.[226] It is also emphasised that this is a power — as in Phil

---

223. Cf. on the one hand Lohmeyer, *Philipper*, p. 161, Güttgemanns, *Apostel*, p. 241, who uses the agreements as an argument to support that Phil 3.20-21 is a pre-Pauline hymn like Phil 2.6-11, and on the other hand Gundry, *Sōma*, p. 180, Andrew T. Lincoln, *Paradise Now and Not Yet* (SNTS.MS 43), Cambridge 1981, p. 88, which considers that Paul uses concepts from the Christ-hymn in Phil 3.20-21. Siber, *Mit Christus*, p. 123f. n. 88, underlines the differences in substance between the two passages in order to reject a tradition in Phil 3.20-21; but the connection between the two texts is evident.

224. Cf. Wengst, *Formeln*, p. 151 n. 32, which emphasises that no 'mission of Christ' is concerned. This is formally correct, and it is also probably a special intention that Christ himself is a subject for the road to degradation, whereas God is the power behind the exaltation. But the idea is nevertheless the same; since it is stressed that Christ follows his destiny — and this is to submit to God's will. According to Phil 2.6, whose function is to pave the way for the positive clause following, he does not revolt; Phil 2.7 concerns the necessary renunciation associated with becoming a human being, and this is developed in Phil 2.8, with the emphasis on obedience.

225. All of Phil 2 is obviously paraenetic, and several connections between Phil 2.1-4 and Phil 2.6-8 can be indicated, cf. Larsson, *Christus*, p. 249f.

226. Cf. Larsson, *Christus*, p. 263ff. Especially in Käsemann, *Versuche* I, p. 51ff., there is an attempt to refute that the hymn is used as an ethical model — with two main arguments. One of these (p. 90ff.) relies on the interpretation of the somewhat unclear introductory verse, Phil 2.5: Τοῦτο φρονεῖτε ἐν ὑμῖν ὃ καὶ ἐν Χριστῷ ᾽Ιησοῦ. On the basis of the preceding exhortation on agreement, this may be seen as a call to adopt the disposition of Christ (there is here an implied 'was' or 'you see'), cf. Lightfoot, *Philippians*, p. 110, Lohmeyer, *Philipper*, p. 90f., Larsson, *Christus*, p. 233, Linton, *Brev*, p. 170. Käsemann implied φρονεῖν δεῖ ('... the disposition which you should also have in Christ'), and perceives 'in Christ' as an ecclesiological formula, whereby it comes to concern the Christ sphere and its demands. But if Paul in the paraenetic context did not wish the hymn to be understood exemplarily but exclusively soteriologically, he had indeed to avoid such a loose and meagre formulation, which would invariably be misunderstood by readers unable to analyse the context from literary-critically or religio-historical aspects, cf. Käsemann's own findings in *Versuche* I, p. 53: 'Fast durchweg hatte man ja seit der Reformation, übrigens bestimmte altkirchliche Ansätze aufgreifend, die Perikope unter dem Gesichtspunkt gedeutet, dass sie am Beispiel Christi die rechte ethische Gesinnung in Demut und Selbstverleugnung erblicke ...' The second, formalistic argument rests on the assumption of a gnostic background: if the entire hymn is to be perceived as a cosmological-soteriological myth about the pre-existent Christ and his course of action, he cannot be a model for mortal man, according to Käsemann, *Versuche* I, p. 56, 70ff., cf.

2.9-11 — which enables the Christians to carry through this sequence of events. And the line is continued in Phil 3, where it says firmly that the secure end is a life in glory with Christ, which is also anticipated in Phil 1.23.

1 Thess 4.14 contains an early stage of the motif which may act as a pointer to its origin. It is an initial argument that a resurrection is in store for dead Christians: εἰ γὰρ πιστεύομεν ὅτι ᾽Ιησοῦς ἀπέθανεν καὶ ἀνέστη, οὕτως καὶ ὁ θεὸς τοὺς κοιμηθέντας διὰ τοῦ ᾽Ιησοῦ ἄξει σὺν αὐτῷ. Paul must argue in this way because death in the community threatened to reduce it to the hopelessness which, in Paul's opinion, marks 'the others', that is to say the surrounding Hellenistic world.[227]

The argument is in the nature of an analogic conclusion.[228] The premise in verse 14a is a central statement of faith regarding Jesus' death and re-

Betz, *Nachfolge*, p. 163ff., Wolfgang Schrage, *Ethik des Neuen Testaments* (NTD.Erg 4), Göttingen 1982, p. 162f., 168. See, however, Schade, *Christologie*, p. 125. Even if the point of reference in Phil 2.6-7 were a myth about the pre-existent's way to the world, Phil 2.8 at least concerns his obedient life in human form.

227. It is not clear what precisely was the problem. Some interpreters believe that Paul must convince the community of a resurrection of the dead before the parousia; thus J.E. Frame, *A Critical and Exegetical Commentary on the Epistles of St. Paul to the Thessalonians (ICC)*, Edinburgh 1912, p. 164, Paul Hoffmann, *Die Toten in Christus* (NTA.NF 2), Münster 1966, p. 208ff., Tannehill, *Dying*, p. 132, Linton, *Brev*, p. 303, A.F.J. Klijn, 1 Thessalonians 4.13-18 and its Background in Apocalyptic Literature, in: M.D. Hooker and S.G. Wilson (ed.), *Paul and Paulinism. Essays in honour of C.K. Barrett*, London 1982, pp. 67-73. Others believe that Paul must convince the Thessalonians that there is any hope at all of a resurrection of the dead, either because he had no need to or no time to explain it earlier, or because the Thessalonians has come to have doubts — see Martin Dibelius, An die Thessalonicher I, in: *An die Thessalonicher I II. An die Philipper* (HNT 11)³, Tübingen 1937, pp. 1-33; p. 23f., Bultmann, *Theologie*, p. 80, Albrecht Oepke, *Der erste Brief an die Thessalonicher* (NTD 8)¹¹, Göttingen 1968, p. 172, Ulrich Luz, *Das Geschichtsverständnis des Paulus* (BEvTh 49), Munich 1968, p. 318ff., Willy Marxsen, *Einleitung in das Neue Testament³*, Gütersloh 1964, p. 37, Bernhard Spörlein, *Die Leugnung der Auferstehung* (BU 7), Regensburg 1971, p. 125, Becker, *Auferstehung*, p. 46ff., Schade, *Christologie*, p. 158, Gerd Lüdemann, *Paulus, der Heidenapostel I. Studien zur Chronologie* (FRLANT 123), Göttingen 1980, p. 229f., Traugott Holtz, *Der erste Brief an die Thessalonicher* (EKK XIII), Zürich 1986, p. 186. One might also think that Paul must convince them that the parousia is possible, Niels Hyldahl, Auferstehung Christi — Auferstehung der Toten, in: Sigfred Pedersen (ed.), *Die Paulinische Literatur und Theologie*, Århus 1980, pp. 119-35; p. 129. Finally, there are some who think that Paul must convince gnostic opponents that not only the living are resurrected — Walther Schmithals-Marburg, *Paulus und die Gnostiker* (ThF 35), Hamburg-Bergstedt 1965, p. 118, Wolfgang Harnisch, *Eschatologische Existenz* (FRLANT 110), Göttingen 1973, p. 27ff.; but there is no evidence of gnostic opponents, and it is not clear that this hypothetical, enthusiastic group would have been disheartened, if it existed at all.

228. Cf. Dupont, Σὺν Χριστῷ, p. 42, 103f., Tannehill, *Dying*, p. 132f., Linton, *Brev*, p. 304, Siber, *Mit Christus*, p. 25f., Holtz, *1. Thessalonicher*, p. 192.

surrection.[229] This is followed by the appeal that something similar must apply to Christians who have died with a bonding to Jesus: corresponding to his resurrection, they will (after their resurrection) be brought together with him. This is said in a hesitant, somewhat clumsy way, so that it might appear to be a new formulation: there is an incongruity between the subordinate clause's εἰ and the main clause's οὕτως καὶ. Jesus' resurrection is paralleled with the Christians' 'parousia togetherness', and the accord between Christ and the Christians is expressed, a little unevenly, by διὰ τοῦ 'Ιησοῦ and σὺν αὐτῷ respectively.[230]

This hesitant nature is also found in another reasoning process, 1 Thess 4.15-17a. Paul expressly uses an apocalyptic tradition, which is said to go back to Jesus. It concerns the course of events at the parousia, when the dead Christians are to resurrect before the crucial events. But it is not quite clear what is tradition and what is pointed use.[231]

On the other hand, what Paul has in mind is absolutely clear. He wishes to confirm the expectation of an existence σὺν Χριστῷ after the parousia.

229. The introductory πιστεύομεν ὅτι renders it probable that this is a reference to a fundamental dogma, even if ἀνέστη, is employed where the traditional formulations would otherwise have ἠγέρθη. In Wengst, *Formeln*, p. 45, the deviation is used to support the hypothesis that Paul uses a Hellenistic mysterious formula. A more obvious explanation is to be found in Luz, *Geschichtsverständnis*, p. 325, Siber, *Mit Christus*, p. 24f., that Paul's formulation is influenced by the words of the prophet quoted in 1 Thess 4.16, cf. Becker, *Auferstehung*, p. 48f., Schade, *Christologie*, p. 158. In Kramer, *Christos*, p. 41ff., cf. Hoffmann, *TRE* 4, p. 487, it is assumed on no reasonable grounds that this dogma may have been associated with baptism.

230. Also, the understanding of the member διὰ τοῦ 'Ιησοῦ is not clear. Immediately, it is easiest to interpret it in a modal sense, linked to τοὺς κοιμηθέντας (and similarly to οἱ νεκροί ἐν Χριστῷ in 1 Thess 4.16); thus Dibelius, 1. *Thessalonicher*, p. 24, Oepke, 1. *Thessalonicher*, p. 172, Dupont, Σὺν Χριστῷ, p. 42. It is also possible (but more laboured), like Siber, *Mit Christus*, p. 26ff., Schade, *Christologie*, p. 158, Lüdemann, *Paulus*, p. 237ff., to understand the preposition member as instrumentally and adverbially linked to the verbal member, so that it expresses the basis of salvation. The unevenesses are listed especially in Becker, *Auferstehung*, p. 48ff., and this is justifiably seen as expressing that Paul has entered a new field, cf. Schade, *Christologie*, p. 158, which emphasises the distance from the later version of the 'death and resurrection with Christ' motif.

231. It is most probable that 1 Thess 4.15 is an advance emphasis on the use: living and dead Christians have become equal by way of the parousia; the Jesus-statement itself is then 1 Thess 4.16-17a on the Lord's sudden coming and the resurrection of dead Christians, after which all Christians meet the Lord in the air. Cf. Dibelius, 1. *Thessalonicher*, p. 25, Lars Hartman, *Prophecy Interpreted* (CB.NTS 1), Lund 1966, p. 188, Siber, *Mit Christus*, p. 36f., Becker, *Auferstehung*, p. 51f., Lüdemann, *Paulus*, p. 242ff., Hyldahl, Auferstehung, p. 121. Holtz, 1. *Thessalonicher*, p. 183ff., 196. is different. The word of the Lord cannot with certainty be specified more closely, cf. Dupont, Σὺν Χριστῷ, p. 45ff., Siber, *Mit Christus*, p. 35ff., Lüdemann, *Paulus*, p. 242ff., Holtz, 1. *Thessalonicher*, p. 203ff. Hartman, *Prophecy*, p. 190, Hyldahl, Auferstehung, p. 130f., identifies experimentally the word of the Lord with Mt 20.40-41, with parallels.

This is said not only in verse 14; in 1 Thess 4.17b-18 he impresses on the Thessalonians the certainty that they are to be σὺν κυρίῳ in eternity.[232] And in 1 Thess 5,10 comes a third σύν formulation. The exhortation to be vigilant in the final hours is supported by a renewed promise of salvation, with a reference to Christ 'who died for us, so that whether we are awake or asleep we may be σύν αὐτῷ'.[233]

Several aspects of the religio-historical and traditio-historical background to the development of thought are now clear.

The objective of the section's reasoning process is to underline the expectation of parousia, which meant everything to primitive Christianity. And it then seems that the precursor-motif's σὺν Χριστῷ formulations are, as often assumed, connected to this apocalyptic hope of salvation.[234] But another leading thought comes to the fore if the motif regarding death and resurrection with Christ is developed.

The crucial agent in the reasoning is the concept of the Christians' association and common destiny with Christ, which comes into existence in 1 Thess 4.14. A picture is emerging of the development, which can be confirmed by other observations. When Paul wishes to hold fast to the hope of parousia despite death, he sees the situation to the effect that in the heathen Hellenist world there is widespread scepticism as regards the concept of a resurrection of the dead, which is also to be seen in 1 Cor 15 and Acts 17.32. The main argument therefore does not become the Jewish-inspired tradition about the resurrection of the dead in 1 Thess 4.15-17; it becomes the special use of the fundamental dogma in 1 Thess 4.14a. Belief in the resurrection of Christ was apparently familiar throughout the Church — without being necessarily directly associated with the resurrection of the dead; it was a more general confirmation of the substance of faith. But it is natural to develop the thought to include the Christians' resurrection in the picture, since Christ's resurrection is proclaimed as God's crucial intervention. And if one thinks eschatologically, this must be seen as the first of the end-time's

---

232. Cf. Dupont, Σὺν Χριστῷ, p. 43, Hyldahl, Auferstehung, p. 121, Holtz, *1. Thessalonicher*, p. 204.

233. Whereas the resurrection of Jesus was the crucial salvation event in Thess 4.14, this is now his death of atonement. But it is still existence after the parousia which is determined by the term σὺν Χριστῷ, cf. Dupont, Σὺν Χριστῷ, p. 44, Siber, *Mit Christus*, p. 59f., Tannehill, *Dying*, p. 33f., since in the context, future wrath and salvation are clearly concerned. In isolation, the statement might well be understood, as in Rom 14.7-9, to be about the current situation for the Christians, cf. Schnackenburg, *Heilsgeschehen*, p. 169, 171, Schweizer, 'Mystik', p. 264f., Wilckens, *Römer* II, p. 45, which also assumes that the death of atonement is added because a baptismal concept is used.

234. As stressed by Lohmeyer, Σὺν Χριστῷ, p. 229ff., Dupont, Σὺν Χριστῷ, p. 12ff., Schade, *Christologie*, p. 145.

expected resurrections of the dead. The expectation of a resurrection is thereby intensified for those bonded to him.[235]

There is then no reason to see this motif of a future death-resurrection with Christ against the background of Hellenistic concepts of a cultic replica of the deity's fate. This is asserted with a reference to the fact that Judaism does not know that a Messiah-figure is resurrected as a precursor for the believers.[236] It is thus ignored here that Paul relates not to a Jewish concept but to a Christian belief in resurrection, which is probably an extension of Jewish concepts (as is also to be seen from 1 Thess 4.15-17) but which has a wholly new eschatological dimension. In addition, it is clear that the resurrection idea is alien to Hellenism. If the divine continued life of the mysteries was intended as a resurrection, this is lost in archaic darkness. And the problem is indeed to make Hellenistic Christians believe in the resurrection.[237]

235. That traditional references to Christ's resurrection have the general soteriological function is demonstrated above in the examination of 2 Cor 5.15 and Rom 7.4, cf. the additional Pauline examples and the descriptions referred to last in note 186. This can be further confirmed by glancing at the synoptic gospels' visions of resurrection; nowhere is Christ's resurrection linked to the Christians' resurrection, but this expresses the continued validity of the proclamation, and the resurrected Lord presents the disciples with new demands. The possible development from general belief in resurrection to the special concepts relating to the resurrection of the Christians as outlined here, cf. note 230 above, may also be seen as confirmed by the examination of 1 Cor 15, section 4 below. In my opinion, Paul is struggling here against the same Hellenistic scepticism towards the idea of the resurrection of the dead, and he can then in 1 Cor 15.3-8 refer to the tradition of Christ's resurrection, which is acknowledged as the basis of the promise of salvation. From this he derives the concept that the Christians may expect a corresponding resurrection, and indeed in 1 Cor 15.20,23 he uses the concept of Christ's resurrection as first fruits. Cf. also Evans, *Resurrection*, p. 161, 168, where the same two thought-processes are emphasised as something not systematically connected in Paul, so that a certain development cannot be reconstructed; but at the same time he draws attention to another possible line of development (which then moves in the opposite direction to that outlined above): that ever greater emphasis is given to the resurrection as the central salvation event and less to the resurrection as an 'adjunct at the end'. That there is also a development in this direction is confirmed by the next passage: 2 Cor 4.10-11, cf. below.
236. This is the argument in Wengst, *Formeln*, p. 37ff., 45, cf. Becker, *Auferstehung*, p. 49, which rejects the mystery framework here, but believes that it penetrates into Christianity as a parallel development (p. 55ff.). Also in Dibelius, *1. Thessalonicher*, p. 24f., the background is to be seen in the mysteries' ideas about dying and resurrecting gods.
237. If, as shown above in Chapter II, the resurrection idea was of no significance in contemporary Hellenistic religiosity, and if at the same time it is indisputable that it received ever-increasing importance in Judaism and was taken over by Christianity in an actualised form, it is astounding that attention can be given to a restricted, formal parallelism with the mystery cult. The background seems to be a methodical narrowing down which causes one to ignore the opportunities for development the new departure in Christianity involves.

If one wishes to find further reasons for the development of this precursor concept, another motif in 1 Thessalonians can be included. In two passages there is an idea that the Thessalonians have become μιμηταί, imitators of Christ and the earlier Christians. According to 1 Thess 2.14-15, they have come to resemble the community in Judaea, because they were pursued by their own people in the same way as the primitive church — and before this the prophets and the Lord Jesus. 1 Thess 1.6 shows the Thessalonians as imitators of the apostles and of the Lord himself, because they have received the word under tribulation but with joy. It then reads that they themselves have become prototypes for other communities, and 1 Thess 1.9-10 emphasises that they have turned away from idols 'to wait for his Son from heaven, whom he raised from the dead — Jesus, who rescues us from the wrath that is coming'. This may seem as if Paul begins here to work with ideas he returns to in 1 Thess 4.14: about resurrection and parousia, and a special pattern in which the Christians follow Christ through tribulation to joy.[238]

---

238. Also in Tannehill, *Dying*, p. 100ff., Wilckens, *Römer* II, p. 47, Holtz, *1. Thessalonicher*, p. 49f., these mimesis passages are to be seen in connection with the motif of death and resurrection with Christ. Wilckens also links them to the concept of 'Nachfolge Jesu' (p. 60ff.), cf. E. Lohse, Nachfolge Christi I. Im NT, *RGG* 4[3] (1960), cols. 1286-88, Larsson, *Christus*, p. 16f., who also sees the concept of 'Nachfolge' and mimesis as a whole, and Schade, *Christologie*, p. 124, which warns against any make-believe that a traditiohistorical line is concerned. The accordance is confirmed in several respects by Betz, *Nachfolge*, p. 27ff. But nevertheless he becomes the keenest advocate of the view that there must be discontinuity, because the historical Jesus cannot be a model in Paul's theology, cf. Rudolf Bultmann, Die Bedeutung des geschichtlichen Jesus für die Theologie des Paulus, in: *Glauben und Verstehen* I[4], Tübingen 1961, pp. 188-213; p. 206, Schrage, *Ethik*, p. 198ff., Otto Merk, Nachahmung Christi, in: Helmut Merklein (ed.), *Neues Testament und Ethik. Für Rudolf Schnackenburg*, Freiburg 1989, pp. 172-206. Betz denies continuity in principle by referring to the different terms ἀκολουθεῖν and μιμεῖσθαι, which are said to indicate entirely different worlds of ideas (p. 3, 137f., 186f.). Mimesis is described as an original cultic and mystery-religious concept (p. 48ff., cf. Chapter II, notes 146, 150 above). This cannot therefore concern an historical person, but a myth — the Christ myth (p. 167f., 186f., 144). It seems as if one is working here on an untenable linguistic theory, where the words have constant, context-independent meanings. And this understanding is contradicted by the passages 1 Thess 1.6; 2.14-15, in which Christ, in line with historical persons and groups such as Paul, the prophets and the primitive church, is the object of a mimesis, which therefore cannot be cultic. Cf. Anselm Schultz, *Nachfolgen und Nachahmen*, Munich 1962, p. 206ff., Benjamin Fiore, *The Function of Personal Example in the Socratic and Pastoral Epistles* (*AnBib* 105), Rome 1986, p. 164ff., in which it is shown that μιμεῖσθαι in Paul's paraenesis as in the surrounding world is used about an exemplary lifestyle. But at the same time it is clear, as is often emphasised, that the Thessalonians did not become 'imitators' by virtue of their own ethical achievements but because, through the evangelical proclamation, they had become drawn into this specific pattern. But there is accord thus with the very concept of 'Nachfolge', in which the Christ-vocation is decisive, and with what I have called the precursor idea in general. Μιμηταί may be an attempt to translate/render these ideas.

In *2 Cor 4.10-11*, the motif is to be found with a somewhat different content. As a step in his defence of his apostolic work, Paul describes it self-confidently as a revelation of God's creative and redemptive power, which is to be seen in particular in weakness, and he says of himself:

... πάντοτε τὴν νέκρωσιν τοῦ ᾽Ιησοῦ ἐν τῷ σώματι περιφέροντες, ἵνα καὶ ἡ ζωὴ τοῦ ᾽Ιησοῦ ἐν τῷ σώματι ἡμῶν φανερωθῇ. ἀεὶ γὰρ ἡμεῖς οἱ ζῶντες εἰς θάνατον παραδι-δόμεθα διὰ ᾽Ιησοῦν, ἵνα καὶ ἡ ζωὴ τοῦ ᾽Ιησοῦ φανερωθῇ ἐν τῇ θνητῇ σαρκὶ ἡμῶν.

It is important here to realise that this is a present-tense version of the motif.[239] Paul's present tribulations, which are mentioned in 2 Cor 4.8-9, are set in association with Jesus' death in the main clause. Similarly, the member ἡ ζωή τοῦ ᾽Ιησοῦ in the subsidiary clauses must concern the present life which is supported by the power of resurrection.[240] The association with Jesus' death and resurrection thus appears to have an effect in the midst of Christian existence when weakness is overcome. We get an enthusiastic-sounding expression of an actualised eschatology.

Once again there is a connection with other precursor motifs, and on this basis one can understand the development that occurs.

Preceding this are remarkable statements about God-imagery. The simplest is 2 Cor 4.4, where the same thought is expressed as in Rom 8,29: that Christ is God's true image, and that as a Christian one shares in the light from this glory.[241] This idea is developed in 2 Cor 4.6-7, in which Paul describes his own activities as the light from God's new creation — and him-self as the clay which is given life because God's power manifests itself in this.[242] But the fundamental εἰκών passage must be 2 Cor 3.18, where Paul says that the Christians 'see the glory of the Lord as though reflected in a mirror and are transformed into the same image from one degree of glory to another ...' There is doubt about the precise meaning of the word κατοπ-

239. The verb in the two subordinate clauses φανερωθῇ might grammatically relate to some-thing in the future as in other instances of the motif, cf. Lietzmann, *Korinther*, p. 116. But the connection with the preceding verses makes this unlikely. 2 Cor 4.8-9 relates to tri-bulations that are overcome as soon as they emerge.

240. Cf. L.J. Koch, *Fortolkning til Paulus' andet Brev til Korinthierne*[3] [Interpretation of Paul's Second Letter to the Corinthians], Copenhagen undated (originally 1914), 225f., Wend-land, *Korinther*, p. 189, Hughes, *2 Corinthians*, p. 143, Tannehill, *Dying*, p. 84, Siber, *Mit Christus*, p. 68f., 78, Bultmann, *2. Korinther*, p. 121, Furnish, *2 Corinthians*, p. 255f.

241. If we again have here the hierarchy in which Christ is God's 'Urbild' (prototype) and the Christians 'Abbild' (imitation) of it, cf. note 210 above, they are thus given a 'Christus-ebenbildlichkeit', as stated by Larsson, *Christus*, p. 280.

242. Cf. as regards the connection between 2 Cor 4.6 and Gen 1.3, especially Lietzmann, *Korinther*, p. 117, and as regards the connection between 2 Cor 4.7 and Gen 2,7, Windisch, *2. Korintherbrief*, p. 142, Hughes, *2 Corinthians*, p. 136, Furnish, *2 Corinthians*, p. 253.

τρίζεσθαι, which can also mean 'mirror' or 'reflect'.[243] But in any case the idea is that the Christians are affected by what they see, and receive the same glory and God-imagery as Christ. Christ is again associated with the divine purpose of human life. It is once again emphasised soteriologically that the Christians are included in Christ's pattern of life.[244]

The subsequent context also continues the precursor motif. In 2 Cor 4.13, Paul again indicates the power that makes it possible to overcome tribulations. This is 'the spirit of faith'. And 2 Cor 4.14 explains what faith involves: '... we know that the one who raised the Lord Jesus will raise us also with (= like) Jesus,[245] and will bring us with you into his presence.' We have thus slipped back to the normal futuristic version of the motif,[246] and this is again that the glory of the end-time is the certain objective of the sequence of events that has been initiated. This is also emphasised in the continuation: in 2 Cor 4.16-18, that the present tribulations are nothing compared to the coming glory; in 2 Cor 5.1-10, that a perfect state of glory with the Lord may be expected.[247]

---

243. See Bauer, *Wörterbuch*, col. 839f., which states the significance of the medium form as 'see oneself in a mirror', but perceiving 2 Cor 3.18 somewhat differently: 'etw. für sich selbst wie in e. Spiegel auffangen, etw. beschauen'; cf. Hughes, *2 Corinthians*, p. 118f. n. 19, Bultmann, *2. Korinther*, p. 93f., Furnish, *2 Corinthians*, p. 214, which indicates that the context is crucial to the understanding. The contrast to 2 Cor 3.13-15, which speaks of the hardening of Moses and Israel, covering up and lacking the ability to see, makes it clear that the Christians are transformed by virtue of what they see.
244. Here the present-tense verb μεταμορφούμεθα may express a continued process; thus Bultmann, *2. Korinther*, p. 98f., Wilckens, *Römer* II, p. 164, cf. Eltester, *Eikon*, p. 165, Wedderburn, *Baptism*, p. 44.
245. In Lietzmann, *Korinther*, p. 202, Kümmel tried to interpret σὺν 'Ἰησοῦ to mean that it concerns a resurrection to an everlasting union with Christ. But this is clearly an over-interpretation, as shown by Siber, *Mit Christus*, p. 72. That no form of contemporaneity can be associated with this term is evident, cf. Koch, *2. Korinthier*, p. 230, Lietzmann, *Korinther*, p. 116, Windisch, *2. Korintherbrief*, p. 149 (who otherwise tried to see it in connection with the mysteries' death and resurrection with the cult deity), Hughes, *2 Corinthians*, p. 148 (who also speaks of 'mystical union'), Bultmann, *2. Korinther*, p. 124, Wengst, *Formeln*, p. 35 (one event — temporally separated!). Norbert Baumert, *Täglich Sterben und Auferstehen (StANT 34)*, Munich 1973, p. 90ff., considers a special modal understanding of the future form ἐγερεῖ, said to relate to an event in the course of history, a (according to our concepts) metaphorical use of the word for an actual event in the Christian's life. This does not seem to be convincing, since in no other passage does Paul use the resurrection concept itself in this manner (note, however, 2 Cor 13.4, in which the verb ζῆν is used, cf. below), and since this understanding is in no way emphasised in the text.
246. Cf. Siber, *Mit Christus*, p. 71.
247. Note that there are parallels in connection with precursor motifs in other Pauline texts, and especially in Rom 8: Rom 8.18 corresponds to 2 Cor 4.17; ἀπαρχὴ τοῦ πνεύματος in Rom 8.23 is parallel to ἀρραβὼν τοῦ πνεύματος in 2 Cor 5.5; the end-time tribulations are expressed by στενάζομεν in both Rom 8.23 and 2 Cor 5.2,4; Rom 8.24 corresponds to two equally puzzling statements, 2 Cor 4.18 and 5.7. In addition, the use of the word ἐπεν-

It is thus also clear that the present-tense version of the 'death and resur-rection with Christ' motif has been developed from the futuristic version. The strength from faith in the glory to come now already prevails, and ac-cordingly the course of the end-time is pre-empted.[248] This traditio-historical cognition is also confirmed when we look at the other passages in the letter in which the motif is implied.

In 2 Cor 1.8-9 Paul, tells of an emergency situation in the Province of Asia. This was so stressful that he had abandoned hope of saving his life and had passed sentence of death upon himself in order to put his trust in God alone, who awakens the dead. Here also it is the end-time expectations that are actualised.[249] The expected death and resurrection (like Christ) becomes the pattern for what happens in Christian life, where suffering and tribula-tion lead to consolation. This is a general motif which is already given in the proem, 2 Cor 1.3-7: Paul's apostolic work is a constant movement through tribulation to consolation for the Corinthians' sake.[250]

The motif in 2 Cor 13.3-4 is especially noteworthy. Paul tells here that he will be merciless towards the Corinthians during the coming visit. It must be proven that Christ, who speaks through Paul, is strong towards them. This evidence is heralded in verse 4: 'For he was crucified in weakness, but lives by the power of God. For we are weak in him, but in dealing with you we will be alive with him (σὺν αὐτῷ) by the power of God.' There is here a clear parallelism between Christ's death and resurrection and whatever will confront Paul in Corinth; and there is also a direct interlinking. Thus once again it is said that the power behind Christ's resurrection will have immediate effect the next time Paul meets the Corinthians.[251]

δύσασθαι in 2 Cor 5.2,4 points in the direction of Gal 3.27 and 1 Cor 15.53-54, where there are also other parallels.

248. This is shown not only in 2 Cor 4.13-14 but also by the stressing in 2 Cor 4.16-18 of the actual renewal of the inner man which has its basis in the coming glory, cf. also note 244 above, in which the Christ imagery appears to be due to a continuous process.

249. Cf. Tannehill, *Dying*, p. 92, Siber, *Mit Christus*, p. 69.

250. Cf. Evans, *Resurrection*, p. 165. As well as in 2 Cor 1.8-11; 4.7-15, this general motif is to be found in 2 Cor 6.3-10, where in verse 9 Paul uses the distinctive term about his work: ὡς ἀποθνήσκοντες καὶ ἰδοὺ ζῶμεν; in 2 Cor 7.3, where Paul tells the Corinthians that they are in his heart εἰς τὸ συναποθανεῖν καὶ συζῆν; in 2 Cor 12.2-10 where it is made especially clear that it is in Paul's weakness that Christ's power is revealed; and in 2 Cor 13.3-4.

251. Thus Koch, *2. Korinthier*, p. 46f., Lietzmann, *Korinther*, p. 161 (Kümmel, op. cit., p. 213), Windisch, *2. Korintherbrief*, p. 419, Hughes, *2 Corinthians*, p. 481, Tannehill, *Dying*, p. 99, Güttgemanns, *Apostel*, p. 152, Siber, *Mit Christus*, p. 168ff., Frankemölle, *Taufverständnis*, p. 117, Bultmann, *2. Korinther*, p. 246, Furnish, *2 Corinthians*, p. 571, Helge Kjær Nielsen, *Paulus' Verwendung des Begriffes Δύναμις. Eine Replik zur Kreuzestheologie*, in: Sigfred Pedersen (ed.), *Die paulinische Literatur und Theologie*, Århus 1980, pp. 137-58; p. 145ff., Martin, *2 Corinthians*, p. 477. Gäumann, *Taufe*, p. 56 with n. 14, Fischer, *Tendenz*, p. 105,

3.4. Two different motifs

A series of texts that concern the Christians' suffering, death, resurrection and glory 'with Christ' have now been examined.

It can be established that there are indeed a number of obvious common features between the two groups into which the material has been divided: all passages build upon Christological reflections on the same central sequence of events. The ideas are employed soteriologically, and concern death and new life for the Christians. The term σὺν Χριστῷ may crop up in both types of text. And throughout certainty of salvation and excitement about salvation are expressed.

But the material nevertheless falls into two clearly separate groups. There are great differences of form. This relates to widely differing events in the Christians' life. And we are dealing with two different theological themes. Schematically, the two sets of motifs can be contrasted with one another as follows:

'Death with Christ':	*'Resurrection with Christ'*
1. one event in the Christian's life	1. two events in the Christian's life:
2. 'death' as a decisive break with the old life and transition to the new life,	2. suffering-death and resurrection-raising up with the emphasis on resurrection-raising up,
3. where 'death' is something good and positive,	3. where death is problematic and must be overcome,
4. a clear metaphorical usage	4. a quite simple usage
5. about a past turning-point,	5. about a present and future sequence of events,
6. an offshoot of a central Christological motif: Christ as the Christians' *redeemer* — especially through death.	6. an offshoot of an equally central Christological motif: Christ as *precursor* of the Christians' life.

Against the background of this survey, the importance of the material to the problems here discussed can be considered.

In association with Item 5, the possible connection of the ideas to baptism can be considered. The texts examined thus far do not in fact speak directly of baptism. But it is not unlikely that there may be a connection. The

---

wish, giving no reason, to have the verse relate to the apocalyptic future. This is impossible because of the member εἰς ὑμᾶς, which shows that Paul has in mind the impending confrontation in Corinth.

'death with Christ' motif, which indeed concerns the transition to the Christian life, fits in well when used directly in relation to baptism.[252] As regards the second motif, an indirect connection with baptism can be imagined in which baptism is seen as an introduction to the existence lived according to Christ's pattern and involving a future death as a transition to the life of resurrection.[253]

But what the many and great differences between the two types of motif show is also important. This is of significance to the evaluation of the essential question: whether on the basis of these texts one can reconstruct a fundamental pre-Pauline Hellenistic-Christian tradition of baptism as a ritual death and resurrection into glory with Christ.

Once the marked differences between the motifs have been established, it is futile to explain one motif as a development of the other. And neither of the two motifs can have been developed from a hypothetical, basic cultic tradition. What can be said about the development of these traditions directly contradicts this. In its basic form, the 'death with Christ' motif concerns one single event, but can be expanded by a reference to Christ's resurrection (without the Christians' resurrection having yet come into the picture). The two-phase 'death and resurrection with Christ' motif concerned from the outset the future of the Christians, but gradually this pattern may be seen to have been pre-empted at the centre of the Christians' life.[254]

But because the two motifs both reflect on the crucial Christ-events and the close connection between Christ and the Christians, there may have been a mutual spill-over-effect, and it may have been natural to combine them.

252. This is most evident in Gal 2.19-20; Rom 7.4, cf. section 3.2 above and the interpreters referred to in notes 171 and 187.
253. In interpreting Rom 8.17, a comparison with Gal 3-4 might show that baptism terminology is probably used in the context of the passage, cf. section 3.3 above, with notes 194 and 206. Less probable is the opinion in Wilckens, *Römer* II, p. 45f., that baptism is also included in the picture within the context of 1 Thess 4.14 and can therefore already be considered as a general precondition for this motif, cf. note 233 above. There is also no reason to assume, with Kramer, *Christos*, p. 41ff., cf. Hoffmann, *TRE* 4, p. 487, that the resurrection creed was generally associated with baptism.
254. Cf. Schade, *Christologie*, pp. 144-46, which similarly challenges the concept that the 'sacramental motif' (= death with Christ) is a precondition for the 'eschatological' motif (= resurrection with Christ), and emphasises that the two motifs are mutually independent. Against the hypothesis of a fundamental tradition about 'death and resurrection in baptism', it may be noted that as yet no passages have come to light in which baptism is directly and unambiguously connected to belief in resurrection, let alone the idea of the Christians' resurrection.

3.5. Death and resurrection with Christ in Col 2-3

These motifs or related motifs also crop up in the later New Testament letters.[255]

Three passages in particular in the Letter to the Colossians may be of significance here: Col 2.11-13; 2.20; 3.1. In regard to the first text especially, it is often assumed that the text concerns a death and resurrection with Christ performed ritually, and that it expresses an older, more primitive idea than that to be found in the undoubtedly Pauline texts — without the eschatological reservation which is said, according to this theory, to be particularly Pauline.[256] A brief review of the facts shows, however, that this assumption is questionable.

In Col 2 we are in a paraenetic section. This is clear from Col 2,6 in which Paul refers to the Colossians receiving Christ, and then requiring them to 'live their lives in Christ'. After a warning against philosophy and other human traditions,[257] there follows an emphasis on Christ's significance as

---

255. Apart from the passages in the Letter to the Colossians, Eph 2.1,5-6 (which appears to be a development of Col 2.12-13) and 1 Pet 4.13-14; 5.1, cf. 1.11, which are a looser rendering of the 'suffering and glory with Christ' motif. It is also considered here that this may be more original traditions which precede Paul's Letters — thus Siber, *Mit Christus*, p. 178f., 181, Berger, *Exegese*, p. 55ff., Wilckens, *Römer* II, p. 139; but since this letter is later than the Pauline letters and reveals knowledge of them, nothing reliable can be based upon this fact. It is even clearer that 2 Tim 2.11 is an echo of Pauline formulations, cf. Martin Dibelius (and Hans Conzelmann), *Die Pastoralbriefe* (HNT 13)[3], Tübingen 1955, p. 82, Siber, *Mit Christus*, p. 179f., Hejne Simonsen, Christologische Traditionselemente in den Pastoralbriefen, in: Sigfred Pedersen (ed.), *Die Paulinische Literatur und Theologie*, Århus 1980, pp. 51-62; p. 59, 62.
256. Cf. note 3 above.
257. Cf. on the comprehensive and difficult question of the heretics in Colossae, Martin Dibelius (and Heinrich Greeven), *An die Kolosser, Epheser, an Philemon* (HNT 12)[3], Tübingen 1953, p. 38ff., Günther Bornkamm, Die Häresie des Kolosserbriefes, in: *Das Ende des Gesetzes. Gesammelte Aufsätze* I (BEvTh 16)[5], Munich 1966, pp. 139-56, Eduard Lohse, *Die Briefe an die Kolosser und an Philemon* (KEK 9,2)[14], Göttingen 1968, p. 186ff., Eduard Schweizer, *Der Brief an die Kolosser* (EKK XII)[3], Zürich 1989, p. 100ff., Joachim Gnilka, *Der Kolosserbrief* (HThK X/1), Freiburg 1980, p. 163ff., which rightly urges scepticism towards over-confident reconstructions of the opponents' views. There is indeed a tendency towards a reading in which all important ideas and concepts in the letter reflect the opponents' view. The result is an all-embracing heresy which is said to involve not only wisdom-worship, pseudo-philosophy, awareness of divine fulfilment, worship of powers and authorities, asceticism and circumcision but also gnosticism, cosmological speculation and mystery cults. The possibility is generally ignored that it is the author, Paul or a disciple of Paul, who himself introduces some of the important ideas for combating heresy. And it is still incomprehensible that Paul or his pupil is to oppose heresy by always adopting heretical viewpoints and by closely identifying himself with them. In our context, there is special reason to warn against the assumption in Bornkamm, *Ende*, p. 141ff. (and others) that gnostic opponents have introduced the cosmic primal-man myth into the discussion. It

'the head of every ruler and authority' and as he in whom divine fulfilment lives, in which the Christians also share. We have thus arrived at *Col 2.11-13*, in which there is marked and complicated imagery expressing the connection between Christ and the Christians.

Col 2.11 is a reminder of the Christ-circumcision the Colossians have experienced when they put off the body of the flesh.[258] Col 2.12 continues: συνταφέντες αὐτῷ ἐν τῷ βαπτισμῷ, ἐν ᾧ[259] καὶ συνηγέρθητε διὰ τῆς πίστεως τῆς ἐνεργείας τοῦ θεοῦ τοῦ ἐγείραντος αὐτὸν ἐκ νεκρῶν. Using an imagery probably assumed to be known to the reader, the effects of baptism are illustrated here: it does away with the old mortal form of existence and opens up a new life based upon belief in the resurrection.[260]

is the author who uses positively the idea of Christ as the new man into whom all Christians are incorporated. Similarly, the assumption of a Colossian mystery cult must be approached with scepticism. This relies in particular on the word μυστήριον which occurs in Col 1.26-27; 2.2; 4.3, cf. Dibelius, *Kolosser*, p. 39. As is shown in Chapter II, section 3, above, this word has a far wider meaning and dissemination in circles which are indeed strong opponents of mystery cults. It should also be noted that it is the author himself who positively presents his doctrine as a mystery; cf. also Gnilka, *Kolosserbrief*, p. 135, which finds that Paul uses ideas characterised by mystery, and therefore seems indeed *not* to attack the opponents of mystery religion. Also in Halter, *Taufe*, p. 190f., there is a very cautious description of heresy, but with a thought-provoking addition: the author appears to have meant that the Colossian heretics had a deficiency in enthusiasm — too much 'Noch-nicht' — and therefore he preaches the 'Schon', which is associated with the realised part of eschatology.

258. Cf. as to this Dibelius, *Kolosser*, p. 30, Linton, *Brev*, p. 239f., Halter, *Taufe*, p. 195f., Gnilka, *Kolosserbrief*, p. 131, in which this circumcision metaphor is connected with baptism. This can also be supported by the fact that the disrobing metaphor via Col 2.15 indicates Col 3.9-14, where a disrobing and robing metaphor is used which leads the mind onwards towards Gal 3.27-28, combined with Rom 6.6. Also, the term 'the body of the flesh' has been the subjected of various considerations. In C.F.D. Moule, *The Epistles of Paul the Apostle to the Colossians and to Philemon (CGTC)*, Cambridge 1957, p. 95f., Tannehill, *Dying*, p. 48, it is suggested that the flesh of sin which is removed is Christ's body, in whose death on the cross the Christians are given a share when baptised. But this is far too complicated an idea for the recipients to have any chance of understanding it, cf. Gnilka, *Kolosserbrief*, p. 132. Nevertheless, he also considers that a death of the old mankind (with Christ) is concerned as in Rom 6, cf. Hegermann, *Vorstellung*, p. 144 n. 2, Halter, *Taufe*, p. But this still seems to be a laboured interpretation of 'circumcision', which at the figurative level can only be understood as the removal of some flesh.

259. The term ἐν ᾧ in Col 2.12b is naturally understood as referring to what occurred immediately before ἐν τῷ βαπτισμῷ, cf. Oepke, *ThWNT* I, p. 543, Jervell, *Imago*, p. 233 n. 226, Beasley-Murray, *Baptism*, p. 153, Lona, *Eschatologie*, p. 156f., Schweizer, *Kolosser*, p. 113. It is not a matter of course, as in Dibelius, *Kolosser*, p. 30f., Schnackenburg, *Heilsgeschehen*, p. 63, Lohse, *Kolosser*, p. 140f., 156 n. 4, Halter, *Taufe*, p. 196f., Gnilka, *Kolosserbrief*, p. 134f., Schnelle, *Gerechtigkeit*, p. 210, n. 436, to perceive the member as a parallel to ἐν ᾧ in Col 2.11 — and thus a reference to Christ; there must be compelling reasons not to allow the relative pronoun to refer to the immediately preceding member, which fits grammatically. But inherently it does not make much difference.

Col 2.13 continues to consider the metaphors from the two previous verses. Verse 13a concerns the situation that precedes 'circumcision', 'burial' and 'resurrection'. The Colossians 'died' because of transgressions and 'uncircumcision'. 'Death' and 'uncircumcision' are thus seen as the situation of sinfulness which precedes baptism.[261] Verse 13b concerns the new departure itself: '... God made you alive together with him, when he forgave us all our trespasses.' All that has led to the new life is summarised by the decisive term συνεζωοποίησεν ὑμᾶς σὺν αὐτῷ, not only 'resurrection' but also 'circumcision' and 'burial', which indeed have led to the elimination of the mortal body.

Col 2.14-15 then amplifies how the forgiveness came about — by the cross of Christ,[262] which represents a triumph over powers and authorities. The Colossians must therefore, according to Col 2.16-19, break with these authorities and their earthly decisions, which do not subordinate themselves to Christ (who is the true head of the whole body).

This exhortation is varied in *Col 2,20*: 'If with Christ you died to the elemental spirits of the universe (στοιχεῖα), why do you live as if you still belonged to the world?'. This is followed by a polemic against human commands which serve only the lusts of the body.

Col 3.1 begins with a new exhortation: 'So if you have been raised with Christ, seek the things that are above, where Christ is, seated at the right hand of God.' Later, in Col 3.3-4, the exhortation is explained by the fact that the Colossians are 'dead' and their life is hidden 'with Christ in God'; life comes only with the revelation of Christ.[263] There follows from Col 3.5 a demand to allow the earthly in them to die, and it ends with a demand in Col 3.9-11 to strip off the old self and to clothe oneself in the new.

As regards the traditio-historical background, there are several considerations against a sacrament-realistic idea behind the text, that in baptism the Christians are already dead and resurrected with Christ.

---

260. Note that, also here, there is no reference to the Christians having 'died with Christ', as recognised by Dinkler, Taufaussagen, p. 100f., Schweizer, *Kolosser*, p. 113f. n. 352, Siber, *Mit Christus*, p. 197, who considers, however, that the idea is implied in the 'burial with Christ'. But at the figurative level on which we find ourselves the concept of a burial with Christ makes just as good sense if here, as in Col 2.13, it is assumed that the Christians 'died' because of sin: the burial then removes the dead body.
261. Cf. Dibelius, *Kolosser*, p. 31, Linton, *Brev*, p. 204f., Lohse, *Kolosser*, p. 156, 160f., Dinkler, Taufaussagen, p. 102, Schweizer, *Kolosser*, p. 163, Gnilka, *Kolosserbrief*, p. 135. Here, however a development from Col 2.11f. is assumed, but this is only because an idea of death with Christ is read into the verses. This, as shown in notes 258 and 260 above, is unnecessary.
262. That is, a reference to Christ's death of atonement, cf. Lohse, *Kolosser*, p. 165.
263. Cf. Dibelius, *Kolosser*, p. 40.

First, the central passage in Col 2.11-13 speaks neither of the Christians' dying in baptism nor of their dying together with Christ! As is shown, 'death' is the sinfulness which precedes baptism, and Christ has indeed no part in this. Thus a somewhat different idea is introduced here. It corresponds to Rom 7.10-11; 8.10,[264] where 'death' has also smitten the old self because of sin; this idea is also expressed in Eph 2.1,5-7, which is an early comment on this passage.[265]

Second, the continuation contains variations and changes of meaning. The idea of 'death' continues to receive a new content. As indicated, in Col 2.13 death expresses that the sinner is lost. Col 2.14 alludes to the idea of Christ's death of atonement on the cross, and Col 2.20 perceives 'death with Christ' as the break with the old life.[266] The theme in Col 3.1-4 is different and not wholly clear: following 'resurrection with Christ' the Christians are still dead and their life hidden, however this is understood. It cannot all be referred back to the same motif.

Third, there is a clear metaphorical stamp to the whole context. When in Col 2.12 one meets a concept of baptism as a burial and resurrection with Christ, the metaphorical aspect is already marked: it is indeed directly apparent that the Christ-circumcision in Col 2.11 is to be understood neither literally nor mystically. It also transpires that the prominent expressions do not stand alone but are continually explained. As regards 'circumcision', it is added that this consists of a removal of the mortal body. As regards 'resurrection with Christ' in Col 2.12, it is explained that this occurs in the context of belief in God's power of resurrection. Col 2.13 clarifies that 'death' is associated with trespasses, and that 'alive together with Christ' is connected with the forgiveness of trespasses. We do not encounter a primitive sacramentalism here.[267]

264. Cf. note 201 above.
265. Cf. Tannehill, *Dying*, p. 48, Lona, *Eschatologie*, p. 168, 360f., Schnackenburg, *Epheser*, p. 90, 95.
266. When Christ's death of atonement and the Christians' 'death' from sin are linked together, we have the same single-phase concept as in Gal 2.19-20. Cf. Halter, *Taufe*, p. 201, Gnilka, *Kolosserbrief*, p. 156.
267. It is thus an incorrect interpretation and an undervaluation of the letter's author for Güttgemanns, *Apostel*, p. 68 with n. 79, to assert that in his opinion the Christian is in fact resurrected etc. In addition, Güttgemanns sees it as an argument against the letter's authenticity, because Paul (in 1 Cor 15) cannot so radically oppose something he himself advocates here. But it would be just as inexplicable that a pupil of Paul plays with an idea of a true resurrection with Christ if this is what Paul has opposed in 1 Cor 15, cf. Wedderburn, *Traditions*, p. 339, *Baptism*, p. 71f. Cf. also Lona, *Eschatologie*, 158f., who writes as follows about Rom 6.1-11 and Col 2.12: 'Beiden Texten gemeinsam ist die übertragene Sprache in der Rede von Tod und Leben. Es handelt sich um eine Sprachebene, wo nicht das faktische Leben und Sterben gemeint sind, sonmdern eine andere

Everything suggests that we are concerned with a later, quite subtle and varied rendering of thoughts from other Pauline letters, perhaps particularly from Rom 6.[268]

4. A sacramentalistic opposition in Corinth?

There now remain important considerations about the attitudes Paul faces, especially in the First Letter to the Corinthians. It is useful to have an insight into a Hellenistic community's way of thinking. But a position must also be taken on the theories mentioned in the introduction, that the Corinthian opponents are said to be characterised by an exaggerated certainty of salvation, which in turn is said to be associated with a sacramentalism that can further be combined with contemporary mystery-religiosity.

It is thought-provoking that baptism comes into the picture a total of five times in the First Letter to the Corinthians, and that ideas about celebrating the Eucharist are employed twice.[269]

1 Cor 1.10-17 emphasises from the outset that the question to be tackled it important: 'I appeal to you, brothers and sisters, by the name of our Lord Jesus Christ ...'[270] Paul calls for unity, and thereby shows what the problem is, and this is elaborated in the two following verses. Paul has received reliable information about disputes, which are particularly evident in that members of the community feel themselves tied to certain leader-figures,

---

Wirklichkeit.' Lona, however, continues to reject the term 'figurative', since it restricts reality to the factual (?). It can also be established that the author does not skip the so-called 'eschatological reservation' which is to be found in the genuine Pauline letters. Col 3.1-4 contains in fact the tension between 'already' and 'not yet' which is said to be especially Pauline, cf. Bornkamm, *Ende*, p. 43f., Dinkler, *Taufaussagen*, p. 101. It can thus be seen that this dialectic is to be found in the Letter to the Colossians, whereas in my opinion it is questionable in the undoubtedly genuine Pauline letters.

268. That we find ourselves in a context in which other themes from the Pauline letters are taken up and re-interpreted also supports this: sublimation of circumcision, the idea of Christ as the head, the Christ-body concept and the clothing idea. Cf. Ed Parish Sanders, Literary Dependence in Colossians, *JBL* 85 (1966), pp. 28-45; p. 40ff., Siber, *Mit Christus*, p. 191ff., Lohse, *Kolosser*, p. 156 n. 1, Halter, *Taufe*, p. 194, Lona, *Eschatologie*, p. 171, Wedderburn, *Baptism*, p. 70ff., Betz, Transferring, p. 110 n. 92.

269. I have discussed most of these passages in earlier studies — Agersnap, *Dåbsteologi*, 101ff., *Paulusstudier*, p. 7ff. I shall refer to this and then elaborate my views where it is of special importance to the question to hand: whether these passages can support the theory of a sacramentalistic opposition.

270. See in particular Carl J. Bjerkelund, *Parakalô*, Oslo 1967, p. 141ff., who stresses that παρακαλῶ sentences introduce a main purpose in Paul, and that the other members in the sentences operate as further strengthening.

even admitting to a special disciple-relationship with them: Paul, Apollos, Cephas and Christ.[271]

1 Cor 1.13 in fact begins to deal with the problem. By using three rhetorical questions, it indicates (a) that Christ cannot be divided, (b) that Paul was not crucified for the Corinthians and (c) that it is not in Paul's name that they are baptised. Paul stresses in 1 Cor 1.14-16 that he is fortunate in having baptised so few in the community. He cannot have meant in any way to imply that they were said to have been baptised in Paul's name. On the contrary, Paul's real work was to proclaim the gospel of Christ's cross, as it says in 1 Cor 1.17, so preparing the way for the reasoning that follows.

There are three main viewpoints here, which are interwoven. First, Paul defines the Corinthians' situation on the basis of the crucial cross-theology: their position is due not to their own gifts and wisdom but solely to the paradoxical power of Christ's cross, thus in particular 1 Cor 1.18-31; 3.18-23; 4.7-8, cf. 1 Cor 1.13b. Second, he defines the apostles' situation, with himself as an example: the humble appearance also corresponds to the cross, which is the content of the proclamation: that God's power reveals itself in powerlessness, thus especially 1 Cor 2.1-5; 4.6,9-13, cf. 1 Cor 1.13c. Third, he establishes that there is only one foundation to build upon and one Lord to serve, namely Christ, thus 1 Cor 3.5-17; 4.1-5, cf. 1 Cor 1.13a.[272]

If the background to the party conflict is assessed, it becomes clear that the Christian Corinthians considered themselves wise and grand, especially because of the power their teacher has passed on to them.

But apart from this there is almost a consensus that an enthusiastic view of baptism played a part: that baptism was perceived as a sacrament according to a pattern corresponding to Hellenistic mystery-thought, where one envisaged a mystical connection arising between initiate and mystagogue following initiation into the mystery.[273] But this theory is in fact unsup-

---

271. Cf. on this Agersnap, *Dåbsteologi*, p. 101f. in which it is indicated that it is not crucial to an understanding of the context that one tries to reconstruct the theology of the various groups, as has happened traditionally, or one rejects that there has been significant theological accord with Johannes Munck, *Menigheden uden partier* [Community without Parties], *DTT* 15 (1952), p. 215-33, cf. *Paulus und die Heilsgeschichte* (AJut 26,1), Århus 1954, p. 127ff.

272. Since the stressing of Christ's oneness in Cor 1.13a must thus be seen in the context of the motif of this one edifice and one Lord, σῶμα Χριστοῦ is not necessarily included in the picture here, cf. note 98 above. This would result in a very complicated use of imagery.

273. Thus Weiss, *1. Korintherbrief*, p. 19, Lietzmann, *Korinther*, p. 8, Ulrich Wilckens, *Weisheit und Torheit* (BHTh 26), Tübingen 1959, p. 12ff., Lohse, *Taufe*, p. 314f., Conzelmann, *1. Korinther*, p. 50, Halter, *Taufe*, p. 135 with n. 6 on p. 575f., p. 139ff. (with caution), Schnelle, *Gerechtigkeit*, p. 137, Wedderburn, *Baptism*, p. 248 (in which it is, however, rejected that the background is mystery-religious. It is more probably the laying on of

ported. A mystical connection between the initiated and the mystagogue is unknown in the mysteries.[274] In addition the theory does not fit the situation in Corinth where one also felt oneself linked to Paul, Peter and Christ, who according to what we know cannot have been very active in the baptism field among the Corinthians.[275] One should also be aware that Paul uses the idea of baptism positively in his reasoning: baptism in the name of Christ leads the thoughts towards his death on the cross for the Christians' sake, and this is the thought Paul employs in what follows.[276]

A simpler explanation, therefore, is that it is Paul who introduces baptism into the discussion. He has been provoked by the various individual professions: to Paul, Apollos, Peter and Christ. He begins to speak ironically about this in 1 Cor 1.13. If one professes to different persons, Christ must be split up; one must also perhaps be baptised in the name one professes, and believe that this person has died for one's sake.[277] But the positive aspect of the matter is already clear. The beginning of 1 Cor 1.10 says 'by the name of our Lord Jesus Christ'. The emphasis is therefore immediately apparent,

hands at baptism which was pondered over). Cf. against this Schmithals, *Gnosis*, p. 243f., 374ff., Agersnap, Dåbsteologi, p. 103ff., Wolfgang Schrage, *Der erste Brief an die Korinther. 1. Teilband (EKK VII/1)*, Zürich 1991, p. 146ff.

274. Cf. the examination in Chapter II above, in which it can be seen that the important aspect of the mysteries is the ritual followed and the experiences this includes. The only passage which appears to concern a personal bonding to the mystagogue is in Apuleius, Metam. 11.25, in which Lucius calls the priest Mithras his father, but this primarily concerns a teaching-father figure, cf. Dieterich, *Mithrasliturgie*, p. 146ff., which is the passage one consults to find the material to form the basis of the theory of a baptism mysticism behind 1 Cor 1.13-16, cf. against this Agersnap, Dåbsteologi, p. 103f., Schrage, *1. Korinther* I, p. 149 n. 301. Also, the problems in Corinth cannot have arisen on the basis of such a teaching-father tradition, since then Paul would destroy his entire argument when in 1 Cor 4.14-15 he indeed impresses upon the Corinthians that he is 'father' of them all.

275. See as to this Schmithals, *Gnosis*, p. 243f., Agersnap, Dåbsteologi, p. 104, Schrage, *1. Korinther* I, p. 149, p. 104, cf. the considerations in Halter, *Taufe*, p. 140. In Schnelle, *Gerechtigkeit*, p. 137f., there is an attempt to rescue the theory, which instead leads ad absurdum. He believes that the bonding with Paul was said to arise because a group of Corinthians were baptised by Paul's assistant, as it were 'in Paul's name'. That is to say, the question in 1 Cor 1.13c was a genuine question to which the Corinthians were quite able to answer 'yes', whereas the first two questions were obviously absurd!

276. Cf. Schrage, *1. Korinther* I, p. 153. If the mystery-religious background to 1 Cor 1.13c is accepted, this again expresses the tendency to interpret everything that Paul writes as directly reflecting an opponent's viewpoint. If it is wished to uphold these interpretations, a quite amazing ability to use opponents' concepts brilliantly for his own purposes must be attributed to Paul.

277. Cf. Wendland, *Korinther*, p. 19, Agersnap, Dåbsteologi, p. 104ff. Paul continues to use irony in 1 Cor 1.14-16, where he shows how absurd it is that anyone should believe he has been baptised to Paul, cf. also Schmithals, *Gnosis*, p. 243, who stresses that Paul's argument is indeed based on this absurdity.

that Christ is the one Lord to whom one must profess, the one in whose name one is baptised, and the one who is crucified.[278] And so it is upon these thoughts that Paul constructs his reasoning.

But the Corinthians whom Paul rebukes are enthusiastic. According to 1 Cor 4.8 they have mentioned an 'already', they were already replete, rich, kings, and all this without apostles.[279] But it should be noted here that Paul does *not* rebuke them by asserting a 'not yet'. He merely says: if only it were so that the humble and wretched apostles might also share in the regal dignity. This corresponds to 1 Cor 3.21-23, where Paul apparently adopts a Corinthian slogan: 'For all things are yours!'. Then a number of persons and phenomena are mentioned over which they have sovereignty, and then it concludes: 'and you belong to Christ, and Christ belongs to God.' That is to say, Paul is not correcting an exaggerated conviction of salvation but the incorrect perception of salvation which is associated with self-sufficiency and boastfulness.

1 Cor 6.11 also has a reference to baptism in a context that may be associated with Corinthian enthusiasm.

In 1 Cor 5-6, Paul rebukes the Corinthians in two areas: sexual immorality (1 Cor 5; 6.12-20) and reciprocal litigation (1 Cor 6.1-8). Where sexual problems are concerned the background may be enthusiasm. In any case, certain Corinthians have a supercilious and dissociated attitude towards cohabitation by a member of the community with his father's wife. And as regards the matter of relations with prostitutes it seems that someone has used the slogan: 'All things are lawful' (1 Cor 6.12); in this connection, this must express a libertarianism which contrasts with the almost ascetic reserve we encounter in 1 Cor 7.[280] But there is no reason to assume enthusiasm

---

278. That the prepositional member with διά, to be found in association with the παρακαλῶ terms in Rom 12.1; 15.30; 1 Cor 1.10; 2 Cor 10.1, contains a reference to a crucial theological reason for the exhortation has been emphasised by Schmitz, παρακαλέω κτλ., *ThWNT* V (1944-54), pp. 771-77, 790-98; p. 793, cf. Oepke, διά, *ThWNT* II (1935), pp. 64-69; p. 67, Bjerkelund, *Parakalô*, p. 161f. That the reference to the name of Christ in 1 Cor 1.10 must be seen as a preparation for 1 Cor 1.13 has been acknowledged by Frankemölle, *Taufverständnis*, p. 46f., and developed in Agersnap, *Dåbsteologi*, p. 106.
279. Cf. Lincoln, *Paradise*, p. 33, Schnelle, *Gerechtigkeit*, p. 80, Wedderburn, *Baptism*, p. 34ff.
280. According to Lietzmann, *Korinther*, p. 27, this may be Paul's own slogan turned against Jewish dietary regulations (cf. 1 Cor 8; 10.23), which the Corinthians have transferred to the sexual field, cf. Traugott Holtz, Zur Frage der inhaltlichen Weisungen bei Paulus, in: *Geschichte und Theologie des Urchristentums (WUNT 57)*, Tübingen 1991, pp. 205-22; p. 207. Lietzmann also points out that in the same way as occurred both before (1 Cor 5.9-13) and after Paul may be reacting to enquiries from the Corinthians. It does not then follow that Paul, as is generally taken for granted, in 1 Cor 6.12ff. is reacting to specific abuses. This may merely be a stage in the main considerations on the boundaries of sexual activ-

for members of the community who take proceedings against one another in heathen courts.[281]

1 Cor 6.9-11 is Paul's concluding expression of his views on litigation within the community. But the sharp warning to be found here is probably also a reaction to the sexual abuses. The warning in 1 Cor 6.9-10 has three elements: verse 9a is a reference to the awareness that 'wrongdoers will not inherit the kingdom of God'; verse 9b is a direct rejection of delusion; and verses 9c-10 catalogue the depravities which signify exclusion from the kingdom of God, emphasising indeed sexual impurity and crimes of enrichment.[282] This is followed in 1 Cor 6.11 by an underlining that all this is in the past for the Corinthians, and this is because of baptism. Although the term itself is not used, baptism is undoubtedly in mind, since it is established that the Corinthians 'were washed, sanctified and justified in the name of the Lord Jesus Christ and the Spirit of our God'.[283]

It seems that Paul makes use of known perceptions of baptism, with roots deep in tradition. They relate to baptism as the definitive break with the past. Immediately they are used negatively, in particular to warn against relapse and to show the limits within which the new life must be kept. Similarly, in 1 Cor 5.7, Paul indicates the definitive break with the sins of the past by virtue of Christ's death, and he uses this as a basis for his exhortation against unclean sinfulness and 'the incestuous person'.

It may also be considered whether the reference to baptism is used po-

ity, which continues in the following chapter, cf. Dieter Lührmann, Freundschaftsbrief trotz Spannungen, in: Wolfgang Schrage (ed.), *Studien zum Text und zur Ethik des Neuen Testaments. Festschrift zum 80. Geburtstag von Heinrich Greeven*, Berlin 1986, pp. 298-314; p. 307.

281. Cf. however Halter, *Taufe*, p. 146, who perceives it as expressing their aloof distance, and Schultz, *Charismenlehre*, p. 455, who postulates this viewpoint: 'das Weltliche Recht ... (hat) nichts mit der oberen Lichtwelt zu tun.'

282. Relative to the list depravities in 1 Cor 5.11, the member πόρνοι is then supplemented by μοιχοί, μαλακοί and ἀρσενοκοῖται, and κλέπται is added to πλεονέκται and ἅρπαγες. These extensions may obviously arise because of the actual points of discussion. Cf. Eduard Schweizer, Gottesgerechtigkeit und Lasterkataloge bei Paulus (inkl. Kol und Eph), in: Johannes Friedrich, Wolfgang Pöhlmann and Peter Stuhlmacher (ed.), *Rechtfertigung. Festschrift für Ernst Käsemann*, Tübingen 1976, pp. 461-77, Halter, *Taufe*, p. 147.

283. The understanding of ἐδικαιώθητε is under discussion. Heitmüller, *Taufe*, 1903, p. 12, Bultmann, *Theologie*, p. 138f., Kertelge, *Rechtfertigung*, p. 244f., Halter, *Taufe*, p. 150, Schnelle, *Gerechtigkeit*, p. 40, wishes to understand it in a traditional pre-Pauline sense in terms of 'forgiveness of sins', corresponding to 'sanctified'. Conzelmann, *1. Korinther*, p. 129, sees in the term the entire Pauline doctrine of justification by faith alone, cf. Philipp Bachmann, *Der erste Brief des Paulus an die Korinther* (KNT 7), Leipzig 1905, p. 243, Dinkler, *Signum*, p. 226f., Wendland, *Korinther*, p. 49f., Ziesler, *Meaning*, p. 157ff. But it is generally agreed that it relates to baptism, and that the content is characterised by the traditional and universal perception within the primitive Christian communities.

sitively in 1 Cor 6.12-20. Paul denounces any relations with prostitutes, still by referring to perceptions known to the Corinthians. As a basis for this exhortation, he emphasises the link to Christ, whose limbs the Christians are, and that they have become a temple of the Holy Spirit. Both aspects may relate to baptism.[284]

In this passage, it is evident that Paul introduces baptism into the discussion, and uses this and the perceptions linked to it against the Corinthian abuses. It may also be noted that Paul does not oppose the enthusiasts' certainty of salvation, but on the contrary himself stresses the definitive in salvation.[285]

In *1 Cor 10.1-22*, Paul denounces idolatry and refers to baptism and the Eucharist.

1 Cor 10.1-11 is a warning presented by Paul with a reference to the Exodus narrative from the Old Testament. That the Israelites had baptism is established in 1 Cor 10.1-2, where passing through the sea and under the cloud is interpreted as a 'Moses baptism'. And they received spiritual food and drink (corresponding to the Eucharist), it says in 1 Cor 10.3-4, where there is a play on the manna-miracle and Moses' spring-miracles. But nevertheless 1 Cor 10.5 points out that things went wrong with most of them, and this is used in the following verses as a general warning to Christians (kept in the first person plural) to avoid the Israelites' infringements. This interpretation of the Scriptures is used in two ways in what follows.

In 1 Cor 10.12, the warning is directly asserted in the imperative. Everyone must take care not to fall. But immediately afterwards, in 1 Cor 10.13, it is emphasised that God himself will be on the side of the Corinthians so that they do not fall.

1 Cor 10.14-22 therefore demands that they keep away from idols. 1 Cor 10.16-17 establishes that participation in the Eucharist binds the Christian to the body and blood of Christ.[286] Similarly, according to 1 Cor 10.18-20, idol-worshippers are bound to the idol.[287] 1 Cor 10.21-22 can then establish

---

284. Cf. Gaümann, *Taufe*, p. 118 n. 76 and 86, Halter, *Taufe*, s. 150, Agersnap, Dåbsteologi, p. 108f. This is different in Dinkler, *Signum*, p. 210, cf. however p. 233 n. 60, in which 1 Cor 6.19f. is considered to be a renewed reference to baptism.

285. Something similar occurs when in 1 Cor 6.12b Paul corrects the Corinthian slogan: 'All things are lawful for me, but I will not be dominated by anything.' Paul does not reject the desire for freedom; on the contrary, he draws attention to the danger of losing freedom through renewed bonding to a sinful power. Cf. Lührmann, Freundschaftsbrief, p. 307.

286. Cf. the examination of these verses in section 2.2 and note 95 above.

287. I follow here the interpretation in von Soden, *Urchristentum*, p. 245ff., where it is contended that 1 Cor 10.18 reflects the golden calf episode and especially Ex 32.5-6, which

that the two ties exclude one another, because God is a jealous God who demands absolute obedience.

It is again a complicated matter to penetrate the text to the Corinthian viewpoints on which Paul expresses an opinion.

But this is part of a wider context, 1 Cor 8.1-11.1.[288] And in the remainder of this section Paul has to admonish some of the 'strong ones' in the community who have emphasised their knowledge (γνῶσις) and their power (ἐχουσία). What is decisive is a monotheistic knowledge which to them means that there is no reason to be afraid of idols and other powers; therefore they have absolute freedom, which they display particularly when without scruple they eat meat sacrificed to an idol.[289] In contrast to this, Paul enjoins love, edification and renunciation. He is apparently facing an enthusiasm of the same nature as in 1 Cor 1-4, a supercilious, intellectualist attitude. The question is then whether this is part of a sacramentalism which Paul must also warn against.[290]

Since Paul indeed concentrates on baptism and the celebration of the Eucharist, it is evident that the sacraments may have played a part in the Corinthians' understanding of salvation. Baptism and the Eucharist may well have contributed to a cocksure awareness of salvation as something they possess. But it must be seen in association with an intellectual attitude which is the most remarkable aspect. It is not at all probable that we are dealing with a primitive sacramentalism.[291]

---

forms part of the picture in 1 Cor 10.7, cf. also Ridderbos, *Paulus*, p. 299f.; if this is said to reflect the legitimate cult (cf. Lev 7.6,15 as stated in the margin in Nestle and Aland, *Novum Testamentum*, which is on this point followed by almost all commentators), which concerns a fellowship with God, the objection in 1 Cor 10.19 is incomprehensible. It should, however, be noted that whether one interpretation or the other is chosen is not crucial to the overall understanding.

288. See again von Soden, *Urchristentum*, p. 239ff., who has argued convincingly against literary-critical division hypotheses, cf. Halter, *Taufe*, p. 152.

289. See in particular 1 Cor 8.1a,2,4-6,8; 10.19,23-24.

290. This is the opinion of Lietzmann, *Korinther*, p. 46, von Soden, *Urchristentum*, p. 259f., Käsemann, *Versuche* I, p. 19, Dinkler, Taufaussagen, p. 90f., Conzelmann, *1. Korinther*, p. 199, Halter, *Taufe*, p. 154, Wedderburn, *Baptism*, p. 241ff. (who, however, sees above all such a utilisation of the Eucharist).

291. Cf. the examination of the Hellenistic religious environment relative to Chapter II, section 3.2, which shows that the main tendency in intellectually-characterised religiosity is a symbolic re-interpretation of external cultic religiosity; cf. also Schmithals, *Gnosis*, p. 371. It should also be noted that there is no evidence in this section that the Corinthians have given as their reason for this attitude that they are pneumatics. The only passage in which πνεῦμα, is concerned is 1 Cor 10.3-4, where the Israelites' food and drink is described as 'spiritual', presumably to ensure accordance with the Christian Eucharist; cf. Wedderburn, *Baptism*, p. 241ff., who assumes, however, that the description 'pneumatic' may be based on the Corinthians' perception of the Eucharist.

What is also thought-provoking here is the way in which Paul opposes the ideas on the possession of salvation. There is much to indicate that in 1 Cor 10.1-11 he uses a pre-formulated doctrine[292] that indeed warns against perceiving the salvation promised by the sacraments as something of which one has gained possession. As regards the first use of this in 1 Cor 10.12-13, Paul's reticence may be noted in expressing the 'not yet' for which the instructions employed are setting the stage. He contents himself with a brief warning, and then emphasises God's help when tempted. He thereby stresses salvation's dependence upon God. This leads to a different and crucial use in 1 Cor 10.14-22. Here Paul uses the Eucharist positively in his argument in support of the bonding with Christ and with God. Paul's intention is not, therefore, to tone down the significance of the sacraments. On the contrary, he asserts that the Eucharist is a true bonding with the Lord which is crucial to the specific life of the Christian.[293]

Paul also refers to the Eucharistic traditions in *1 Cor 11.23-29*. Although it is true that the theological background to the absence of solidarity during services it is not clear, it is apparent that it is Paul who implants the Eucharistic words of institution and respect for Christ's body and blood.[294]

1 Cor 12.13 refers to baptism (and perhaps to the Eucharist) in a context in which it is apparent that pneumatic enthusiasm is the problem. But at the same time it is again obvious that it is Paul who introduces baptism as an argument. This helps to substantiate the idea of joint fellowship in the body of Christ, which Paul uses in his struggle against the pneumatics' reciprocal competition.[295]

1 Cor 15.29 contains a peripheral and not readily comprehensible comment, to which nevertheless great importance is often attributed in understanding

---

292. This is generally referred to as a midrash or a midrash-like item. Some see the background in pre-Christian Jewish teaching traditions; thus Leipoldt, *Taufe*, p. 64ff., Joachim Jeremias, Der Ursprung der Johannestaufe, ZNW 28 (1929), pp. 312-20, Oepke, *ThWNT* I, p. 533, von Soden, *Urchristentum*, p. 25 n. 2, cf. also Chapter IV, note 1 below. Others indicate concepts developed within Christianity, thus Conzelmann, *1. Korinther*, p. 194ff., Klauck, *Herrenmahl*, p. 253, Schrage, *1. Korinther* II, p. 384. Halter, *Taufe*, p. 155f., stresses the Pauline characteristic and rejects that this is pre-formulated material. A decisive sign that the material was pre-formulated (by Paul) is, in my opinion, the general form using first person plural where it would have been natural to put the whole paragraph in second person plural, if it were expressed directly to the Corinthians in the given situation.
293. Cf. Agersnap, Dåbsteologi, p. 110f.
294. Cf. the examination above in section 2.2 and notes 91-93.
295. Cf. section 2.2 above.

the Hellenistic view of baptism and the Corinthian conflict. 'Otherwise, what will those people do who receive baptism on behalf of the dead? If the dead are not raised at all, why are people baptised on their behalf?'.

This is a step in Paul's long argument in support of the resurrection of the dead. 1 Cor 15.12 shows that the problem lies in a group within the community which denies the resurrection of the dead. It is also clear how Paul opposes the problem. 1 Cor 15.1-11 refers to the fundamental tradition of Jesus' death and resurrection as crucial salvation events; 1 Cor 15.12-28 argues both negatively and positively that Christians who die will be resurrected in the same way as Christ; 1 Cor 15.29-34 again has negative arguments: vicarious baptism, which was apparently practised in Corinth, and the Christians' struggle are meaningless without faith in the resurrection of the dead; in 1 Cor 15.35-58, Paul explains that the resurrection of the body is possible, and concludes with a demand that the Corinthians remain steadfast. It seems immediately that, as in 1 Thess 4.13-5.10, Paul wishes to console and encourage members of the community who have come to doubt the resurrection.[296]

But there is a tendency to interpret this baptismal practice as expressing a Corinthian enthusiasm and a sacramental magic,[297] but in my opinion this is because of an uncertain interpretation of the situation and of the text.

First, the passage itself in 1 Cor 15.29.

It cannot be denied that Paul is here speaking of a vicarious baptism: one is baptised for the dead to ensure for them a share in the effect of baptism, and this must relate to a post-mortal life.[298] It is also clear that Paul

296. I have also argued is support of this understanding in Agersnap, *Paulusstudier*, p. 9ff. That Paul is confronted with sceptics is also assumed by Schweitzer, *Mystik*, p. 94, Conzelmann, *1. Korinther*, p. 309f., Spörlein, *Leugnung*, p. 190ff. Cf. also the clarification of my viewpoint in note 310 below.

297. Thus Heitmüller, *Taufe*, 1903, p. 52, Reitzenstein, *Mysterienreligionen*, p. 343, cf. p. 233, Güttgemanns, *Apostel*, p. 77f., Dinkler, *Taufaussagen*, p. 92f., Lohse, *Taufe*, p. 310, Jewett, *Terms*, p. 38f. It is often assumed that the opponents maintain the same assertion as in 2 Tim 2.18: that they are already resurrected (so that resurrection from the dead in this manner is superfluous). These opponents were originally seen as gnostics; later, when it was difficult to find religio-historical examples, Hellenistic Judaism was indicated. Here the general viewpoint has otherwise traditionally been that only the spirit continues to live, cf. Agersnap, *Paulusstudier*, p. 52, cf. p. 12 with n. 5. This theory still enjoys approval in a form in which the background is seen as a Hellenistic-Jewish meditation on wisdom: Sellin, *Streit*, cf. especially the conclusion p. 290ff., cf. also A.J.M. Wedderburn, The Problem of the Denial of the Resurrection in I Corinthians XV, *Nov.Tes* 23 (1981), pp. 229-41; p. 234ff.

298. This is the overriding opinion, cf. Weiss, *1. Korintherbrief*, pp. 362-64, Lietzmann, *Korinther*, p. 82, Wendland, *Korinther*, p. 150, Oepke, *ThWNT* I, p. 540, Schnackenburg, *Heilsgeschehen*, p. 90ff., Wagner, *Problem*, p. 284f., Rissi, *Taufe*, p. 57, Ridderbos, *Paulus*, p. 18f., Spörlein, *Leugnung*, p. 79ff., Orr and Walter, *1 Corinthians*, p. 337.

himself refers to this baptismal practice, and without distancing himself from it.[299] Finally, it can be seen that Paul's argument is effective only if the Corinthians, who have rejected the resurrection of the dead, have themselves recognised this practice.[300]

It is this awareness which is meant to be unavoidable evidence of a magical view of baptism which points in the direction of the mystery religions.[301]

But the mystery religions lack true analogies to vicarious baptism.[302] One can certainly find evidence of the performance of sacrifices and other rituals for benefit of the deceased and to atone for their guilt, but these texts do not directly state that the rituals were carried out in place of the dead.[303] In addition, there is reason to ask more critically how such a

---

299. This is the embarrassing perception which is the reason for some (comparatively few) interpreters making an imaginative attempt to ignore that this relates to a vicarious baptism. Cf. the survey in Rissi, *Taufe*, p. 40f., Conzelmann, *1. Korinther*, p. 328.

300. Again a widespread perception, cf. Weiss, *1. Korintherbrief*, p. 363f., Rissi, *Taufe*, p. 91, Conzelmann, *1. Korinther*, p. 327, Wedderburn, Problem, p. 230, *Baptism*, p. 8, Sellin, *Streit*, p. 281. Different in Spörlein, *Leugner*, p. 84.

301. Cf. note 297 above.

302. As already emphasised by Albert Schweitzer, *Geschichte der paulinischen Forschung*, Tübingen 1911, p. 164ff.

303. Three passages in particular are given when there is argument about a mystery-religious background to vicarious baptism; see Oepke, *ThWNT* I, p. 540, Conzelmann, *1. Korinther*, p. 327 n. 116, Wedderburn, *Baptism*, p. 288f., cf., however, Schweitzer, *Mystik*, p. 276f., Rissi, *Taufe*, p. 62f. — 1. Plato, Resp 2.364-65 concerns religious cheats who by means of Orphic texts succeed in convincing people that there '... are atonements and purifications for injustice through sacrifices and festivals, not only for those still living but also for the dead, which they call τελεταί ...' The crux of the matter here is the last word; in the singular it means initiation; in the plural merely rituals associated with an initiation. It cannot therefore be concluded from this that one has imagined that the dead have experienced a mystery-initiation. — 2. Orphic Fragment 232 (Kern) is about people who annually send hecatombs and carry out rituals to obtain release for lawless ancestors (?) — ὄργια τ' ἐκτελέσουσι, λύσιν προγόνων ἀθεμίστων μαιόμενοι. It is questionable whether it is correct to understand the genitive as an objective genitive; in connection with λύσις, a separate understanding is more natural (and the dative should have been used to safeguard the translation 'for lawless ancestors'); the sentence should therefore probably be understood as stated by M.L. West, *The Orphic Poems*, Oxford 1983, p. 99: '... perform the rites, seeking release from their forefathers' unrighteousness.' But even if the first rendering is correct, it is not inherent in the word ὄργια, that it is mystery-initiations which are carried out; ὄργια, can mean any kind of rite, here probably sacrifices. — 3. An inscription of AD 163, quoted by Oepke, loc. cit., relates to a certain Apollonius who, when his brother went through purifications (κατελύσετο) and did not observe the goddess' (Magna Mater's) time limit, gave satisfaction for him (ἀπετελέσετο αὐτόν). That the word κατελύσετο refers to something comparable to a baptism need not be discussed. The crucial point is what ἀπετελέσετο αὐτόν means: to pay what is owed, often used in connection with financial obligations; a vicarious initiation is thus a doubtful interpretation. What may be concerned in these passages is an attempt (by sacrifices) to appease

vicarious ritual is to be understood. The terms 'magic' or 'quasi-magic' give no precise understanding, since magic is an almost undefinable phenomenon.[304] If one can by magical means convey salvation to a deceased person, one may well immediately think of rituals in which one takes some action with the corpse or with objects that belonged to the deceased; but then one ends up with a death cult, which is something entirely different from a vicarious ritual.[305] The ritual must be perceived as an attempt to influence the divine to the benefit of the deceased; and so we have arrived at an area in which one cannot distinguish between religion and magic. But it is difficult to combine a vicarious ritual with mystery religion, since in the mystery rites what is crucial is experiences and insights that give the initiate contact with the divine.[306] And one cannot experience and comprehend something on behalf of another. A pneumatic understanding of baptism must be excluded as a background; since how can one receive the Spirit on behalf of another? There is also the possibility of perceiving it as a symbolic phenomenon, where by appeal (or invocation) one seeks to emphasise that the deceased has a bonding with Christ.[307] Or one can perceive the vicarious baptism 'quasi-juridically': since God has promised to save the baptised, one attempts to obligate God by allowing oneself to be baptised on another's behalf.[308] Here one can still speak of sacramentalism and an 'ex opere operatum' effect without magic being concerned.[309] But it should be pointed out that it is Paul who argues to this effect — not Corinthian enthusiasts.

1 Cor 15.29 thus, on the contrary, excludes that the opponents are enthusiasts. The argument only fits those who have doubts and no longer dare

and placate the deity relative to the deceased as in 2 Macc 12.39-45, which is also mentioned.

304. Cf. Chapter II, section 3.3 above.

305. It may also be noted that frequently, when a magical vicarious baptism is to be substantiated previous to 1 Cor 15.29, the reference is to a death cult — thus Reitzenstein, *Mysterienreligionen*, p. 220ff., and especially p. 232f., Leipoldt, *Taufe*, p. 47ff., cf. against this Schweitzer, *Mystik*, p. 277, Rissi, *Taufe*, p. 62. Also note that the late gnostic texts, which in Lietzmann, *Korinther*, p. 82, are stated as parallels (and are probably repercussions of 1 Cor 15.29), relate to the dead being baptised, after others have merely responded on their behalf.

306. See Chapter II, section 2, and the summary in section 2.7.

307. This is the direction taken by the somewhat ridiculed attempts at a solution in Rissi, *Taufe*, p. 89ff., where the vicarious baptism is said to be a proclamation and a creed of a hope of resurrection for certain deceased people. Cf. Schweitzer, *Mystik*, p. 277, Schnelle, *Gerechtigkeit*, p. 151f.

308. The only vicarious ritual to which one can immediately refer is of a legal nature: the custom from medieval princely weddings in which a delegate from the groom carried out the wedding ceremony by fetching the bride from her parents.

309. Cf. W. Heitmüller, Taufe I im Urchristentum, *RGG* V¹ (1913), cols. 1086-1102; col. 1093.

to believe that the dead arise; then it is a good argument that in the past they allowed themselves to be baptised for the dead without misgivings.[310] If the opponents are convinced pneumatics their vicarious baptism becomes incomprehensible, not only because pneumatic, vicarious baptism is an impossibility but also because it is contrary to their present-tense eschatology.[311]

We are thus back at the situation lying behind 1 Cor 15.

The other arguments in favour of an enthusiastic group of opponents also do not hold good.

The interpretation rests originally on a theory that the religio-historical background is a gnostic primal-man redeemer-figure; but this is only to be found in late, post-Christian sources.[312]

And the decisive argument is accordingly a sophistic interpretation of 1 Cor 15.45-46 as anti-enthusiastic polemics: Paul must prove by Holy Writ that there is not only a psychical body but also a spiritual (resurrection) body. This occurs with an Adam-Christ typology. It is introduced in verse 45: ἐγένετο ὁ πρῶτος ἄνθρωπος Ἀδὰμ εἰς ψυχὴν ζῶσαν, ὁ ἔσχατος Ἀδὰμ εἰς πνεῦμα ζῳοποιοῦν. The problem now is that only the words underlined are to be found in Gen 2.7, which is quoted. In addition, it is the other sentence about the spiritual Adam (= Christ) that contains the assertion which must be proved. It is then maintained that the evidence is valid only if the

---

310. Cf. Agersnap, *Paulusstudier*, p. 44f. In Wedderburn, Problem, p. 230, in which the concept in Spörlein, *Leugner*, is contested, cf. note 295 above, it is asserted as inconceivable that convinced 'Epicureans' or 'Saducees' might be guilty of the self-contradiction of practising baptism with a post-mortal objective. But it must indeed be stressed that Paul is not contesting a triumphant, convinced attitude but scruples. Wedderburn also touches upon the possibility that the resurrection-deniers are an isolated group compared with those polemised against in the letter generally; but he thinks that it would be an otherwise unrepresented group, and that it would be more satisfactory if it could be shown that the viewpoint accords with other ideas in the letter (Problem, p. 233). But it is in fact apparent from the letter that there are several groups and opposing viewpoints within the community: followers of various persons in 1 Cor 1-4, the strong and the weak in 1 Cor 8-10, libertines in 1 Cor 6 and ascetics in 1 Cor 7. The shaky attitude towards resurrection from the dead would suit the weak in 1 Cor 8.7,10-12, cf. Agersnap, *Paulusstudier*, p. 30ff., 36f.

311. Cf. Agersnap, *Paulusstudier*, pp. 12-14, 35ff.

312. Cf. Agersnap, *Paulusstudier*, p. 55ff., where I have examined the religio-historical material presented in Brandenburger, *Adam*, p. 68ff., as the fundamental presentation. Ulrich Wilckens, Zu 1Kor 2,1-16, in: Carl Andresen and Günther Klein (ed.), *Theologia crucis — signum crucis. Festschrift für Erich Dinkler*, Tübingen 1979, pp. 501-37; p. 531ff., has however a different version of the interpretation in which the tendency is the same, but in which the religio-historical background is said to be not gnostic but ideas in Philo, especially Opif. 128 and Leg. alleg. 1.31, about two types of people who are seen in the context of the two narratives about the creation of man in Gen 1.26-27; 2.7 (passages also included in the earlier reconstruction of a gnostic background). Cf. Hoffmann, TRE 4, p. 454.

Corinthians knew of the speculations about two primal beings (cf. Gen 1.27 and Gen 2.6) and envisaged that the first primal being (to whom they belong) was spiritual while the other was the psychical, fallen, primal being. Paul must then reverse the sequence, as indicated in verse 46, which is perceived polemically: 'But it is not the spiritual that is first, but the physical, and then the spiritual'.[313] This is a flimsy basis for a comprehensive theory. It is not a foregone conclusion that 1 Cor 15.46 polemises against precisely this specific idea; this may also have merely a defining and developing function.[314] And the proof of Holy Writ is still not tenable — on the contrary; since the Corinthians, if subjected to this polemic, could point out that the word πρῶτος is not to be found in Gen 2.7, and that the first man was the man referred to in Gen 1.27.[315] There must be independent evidential weight in 1 Cor 15.45b.[316] The subtle interpretation of the evidence is not convincing.

Yet another counter-argument may be indicated. And it shows how improbable it is that Paul in Corinth had to combat an enthusiasm which asserted that one is already resurrected by way of baptism. As we have seen,[317] in the Second Letter to the Corinthians and especially in 2 Cor 13.4 Paul himself states that the vital force of the resurrected Lord works quite topically in him. This he would not be able to do if shortly before in 1 Cor 15 or in some other passage in the First Letter to the Corinthians he would have had to combat the same assertion among some opponents.

To summarise, it can be established that the Corinthians had in general an enthusiastic expectation of salvation which may remind one of a contemporary

313. This interpretation, introduced by Reitzenstein, *Mysterienreligionen*, p. 346, is continued with special emphasis by Brandenburger, *Adam*, p. 74, Lengsfeld, *Adam*, p. 59ff., cf. the criticism in Agersnap, *Paulusstudier*, p. 23ff. and Schade, *Christologie*, p. 82, in which it is indicated that the interpretation demands an implied ἄνθρωπος in 1 Cor 15.46, which is grammatically impossible.

314. Cf. Agersnap, *Paulusstudier*, p. 26ff., in which other possibilities are mentioned. Again one is confronted with an interpretation in which Paul's description can only be understood as a complete reflection of a very distinctive (hypothetical) opposing position.

315. Cf. Agersnap, *Paulusstudier*, p. 25f. Similarly, Dunn, *Romans*, p. 278, has indicated that in 1 Cor 15.45-49 Paul cannot adopt a polemical attitude towards an idea concerning a pre-existent primal man (= Christ), since he will then deny a concept with which he otherwise consistently identifies himself. The idea of a polemic in this verse thus creates more problems than it resolves.

316. In the thesis referred to, Agersnap, *Paulusstudier*, p. 93ff., I have argued that 1 Cor 15.45b must be an abbreviated rendering of Ezek 37.1-14 (or a lost text). I have subsequently found a similar opinion in Claudio Farina, *Die Leiblichkeit der Auferstandenen* (typed dissertation), Würzburg 1971, p. 145ff., Cf. also Schade, *Christologie*, p. 79.

317. Section 3.3 above, with note 251.

Hellenistic religiosity. Paul upbraids them about this, but not about the intensity. What disgusts him is self-sufficiency and lack of humble gratitude.

Paul mentions baptism and the Eucharist on several occasions. But on each occasion he uses it positively in his reasoning. This does not imply that the sacraments are the subject at issue. On the contrary, the sacraments are always something to which Paul can refer as the common conclusive basis of any discussion.

IV
Baptismal Practice in the Primitive Church and Judeo-Christian prerequisites

1. Problem-complex

We have now established that the bonding with Christ for Paul and the Pauline communities is a crucial feature of the Christian existence. Baptism helps to provide this affiliation to Christ and the vital salvation events, and here the death of Christ can be particularly emphasised as what is happening in 1 Cor 1 (and 12) in addition to Rom 6. We have also examined whether there is a dependence here on concepts from Hellenistic religion. This chapter will examine an aspect which is certainly among the historical prerequisites as regards the view of baptism: primitive Christianity's practice of baptism and its background in the baptism by John and perhaps other Jewish purification rites.

Here also one cannot find a marked death-baptism.

It is true that attempts have been made to arrive at tangible ideas in regard to this. According to Franz Dibelius a death-symbolism is fundamental to the baptism by John, that the Messiah is to come through water as the element of death, and Per Lundberg finds behind 1 Cor 10.1-2 an analogous primitive-Christian concept of baptism as a walk through the sea of death.[1] Oscar Cullmann interprets the words from Isa 42.1 that are heard at the baptism of Jesus as a pointer towards the task of the Lord's suffering servant which will lead to his death.[2] But these connections

---

1. See Franz Dibelius, *Das Abendmahl*, Leipzig 1911, p. 54ff., Per Lundberg, *La typologie baptismal dans l'ancienne eglise* (*ASNU* 10), Leipzig 1942, p. 135ff., who also sees behind Mark 10.38; Lk 12.49-50 the idea of a walk through the sea of death. Jeremias, Ursprung, p. 314f., sees the background to the typology in a rabbinical defence of the proselyte baptism's scripturalism. According to R. Reitzenstein, *Die Vorgeschichte der christlichen Taufe*, Leipzig 1929, both John and the Christians are dependent upon Mandaean baptismal sects with mysterious baptismal concepts. Cf. as regards these theories the justly critical survey in Otto Kuss, Zur Frage einer vorpaulinischen Todestaufe, in: *Auslegung und Verkündigung* I, Regensburg 1963, pp. 162-86.
2. See Cullmann, *Tauflehre*, p. 11ff., where it is assumed that Jesus' awareness is said to have been decisively affected by the audition, rendered in Mark 1.11, which is a quotation from an Ebed-Yahweh song which leads the thoughts in the direction of the later Ebed-

between baptism and death cannot be demonstrated directly and positively.

Broader lines and possible linkages must be kept to. First, it may be asked whether there are in the baptism by John and its historical preconditions features which later tradition can associate with death.[3] Second, the idea of an imitation of Jesus in life and death that we have encountered can be examined, and a connection with baptism can be considered.[4] Third, there are features in the earliest Christian baptismal practice which can be associated with ideas about Jesus' death and its significance: in baptism forgiveness of sins is mediated, and forgiveness of sins is also linked to Jesus' death.[5] At an early date baptism involved a profession to Christ, and his death will evidently form part of this.[6]

A brief outline of these three fields will be given first.

2. Features from the development of Christian baptism

2.1. The baptism by John and other Jewish purification rites

John the Baptist's work can mainly be described on the basis of the few, rather scanty sources in the gospels and in Josephus.[7]

The Baptist is described as the heir to the Old Testament prophets. His judgmatical preaching is especially noteworthy. It is sustained by the conviction that the final ending of the passage of time hitherto is at hand. He sees himself as the last precursor-figure before the end-time events. Judgement is directed in particular toward the Jewish people, who have not been able to live the life that should be lived but have simply asserted their de-

Yahweh song, Isa 53, about the servant's sacrificial death of atonement. Cf. against this: Otto Kuss, *Zur vorpaulinischen Tauflehre im Neuen Testament*, in: *Auslegung und Verkündigung* I, Regensburg 1963, pp. 98-120; p. 114f., where it is argued that according to this theory Jesus is to comprehend his task by literary-critical consideration of the Book of Isaiah.

3. That is, more cautious considerations than those referred to in note 1 above.

4. These concepts are also pointed out by Larsson, *Christus*, p. 72ff., and Wilckens, *Römer* II, p. 60f., cf. Chapter III above, notes 161 and 238.

5. Cf. Cullmann, *Tauflehre*, p. 15 etc., Wagner, *Problem*, p. 305, Thyen, *Studien*, pp. 131-94, Wilckens, *Römer* II, p. 50.

6. Thus Schnackenburg, *Heilsgeschehen*, p. 119f., Bultmann, *Theologie*, p. 313, Wagner, *Problem*, p. 299f., Beasley-Murray, *Baptism*, p. 127.

7. See in particular Mt 3.1-17; Mark 1.1-11; Lk 3.1-22; John 1.15-36 and Josephus, *Ant.* 18.117-19, which has special relevance to the subject here. Cf. Martin Dibelius, *Die urchristliche Überlieferung von Johannes dem Täufer* (FRLANT 15), Göttingen 1911, p. 46ff., Jürgen Becker, *Johannes der Täufer und Jesus von Nazareth* (BSt 63), Neukirchen-Vluyn 1972, p. 16ff., Friederich Lang, *Erwägungen zur eschatologischen Verkündigung Johannes des Täufers*, in: Georg Strecker (ed.), *Jesus Christus in Historie und Theologie*, Tübingen 1975, pp. 459-73, Josef Ernst, *Johannes der Täufer* (BZNW 53), Berlin 1989, especially p. 278ff.

scent from Abraham. John therefore preaches a 'baptism of repentance for the forgiveness of sins'. In view of the late hour, there appears to remain only one possibility: for each to submit himself individually to a penitential baptism which can efface the sinfulness that preceded it. This is a baptism in the running water of the River Jordan, in which the baptised is passively recipient. John contrasts his own baptism with what is to happen when the more powerful one arrives: 'I baptise you with water ... He will baptise your with the Holy Spirit and fire'.[8] By virtue of the change that baptism will mean, the life that can avert the threatening judgement becomes possible. This is a life characterised by solidarity and righteousness.[9]

The baptism which has given him his appellation thus stands at the centre of John's work. It is scarcely possible to arrive at a wholly precise understanding of the nature of his baptism, and how it was imagined that it would have the revolutionising effect ascribed to it. But what was most characteristic is reasonably clear.

That the baptised is passively recipient must be understood to mean that the Baptist acts on behalf of God. Baptism is then presented as God's own act, whereby whoever subjects himself penitentially to baptism is freed from the burden of guilt. Whether this is to be perceived exclusively as a proph-

---

8. Thus Mt 3.11; Lk 3.16. Mark 1.8 mentions only baptism with the Holy Spirit. Which of the two versions is the most original is a complicated literary-critical question. Some believe that the baptism by water-baptism by fire contrast comes closest to the historical John, cf. Dibelius, *Überlieferung*, p. 54ff., Rudolf Bultmann, *Die Geschichte der synoptischen Tradition* (FRLANT 29)[8], Göttingen 1970, p. 261f., Lang, Erwägungen, p. 467f., François Bovon, *Das Evangelium nach Lukas — 1. Teilband* (EKK III/1), Zürich 1989, p. 167, 177; others indicate spiritual baptism, or both fire and spiritual baptism, as the original, cf. Schweizer, πνεῦμα, πνευματικός, ThWNT VI (1959), pp. 330-456; p. 397, Heinz Schürmann, *Das Lukasevangelium* (HThK III/1), Freiburg 1969, p. 176f., Joachim Gnilka, *Das Evangelium nach Markus. 1. Teilband* (EKK II/1), Zürich 1978, p. 48, Ernst, *Johannes*, p. 13ff., 305f. In Olof Linton, Johannes Døber, Johannesdåb og åndsdåb i Lukasskrifterne [John the Baptist, Baptism by John and Spiritual Baptism in the Luke texts], in: Niels Hyldahl and Eduard Nielsen (ed.), *Hilsen til Noack* [Greetings to Noack], Copenhagen 1975, pp. 151-67; p. 153f, it is pointed out that both fire and πνεῦμα in the sense of 'wind' fit the image of the winnowing shovel and the threshing floor.
9. Thus Lk 3.10-14, which has no parallels in other gospels, cf. Josephus, Ant. 18.117. Here also the question of the source situation is disputed. For example, it is referred to as a late Christian catechism-like community tradition in Bultmann, *Geschichte*, p. 155, cf. Hans Conzelmann, *Die Mitte der Zeit* (BHTh 17)[5], Tübingen 1964, p. 93f., Thyen, *Studien*, p. 138, Bovon, *Lukas* I, p. 173. Against this, it can be argued that it is indeed the positive, ethical content which might have been suppressed by the other evangelists, who wished to avoid competing with Jesus' radical preaching, cf. also Schürmann, *Lukasevangelium* I, p. 169, Ernst, *Johannes*, p. 93ff., Cf. also Otto Böcher, Johannes der Täufer, TRE 17 (1988), pp. 172-81; p. 179, Traugott Holtz, Die Standespredigt Johannes des Täufers, in: *Geschichte und Theologie des Urchristentums*, Tübingen 1991, pp. 45-54, who points out that the content distinguishes itself from the later Christian ethical preaching.

etic act of symbolism or whether it is also of a sacramental nature must remain an open question in this context. But it is certain that baptism does not — apart from the conduct of the baptised — automatically avert the coming judgement.[10] Baptism with water denotes a break with the old life and salvation from the baptism of fire with which it will end. It is the judgement of fire and thus the eschatological death that is averted.[11] Thus, in this indirect way, an idea of death enters into the understanding of baptism.

But we cannot go much further — even though we search back into the historical prerequisites.

Somewhere in the background are to be found the many Old Testament-Jewish purification rites, going back to Lev 16; but the baptism by John is once-and-for-all.[12] It is also distinct from the Essene baptist sects and the Qumram community; repeated baths are again concerned here, and this is a 'self-baptism'.[13] Similarly, the proselyte baptism is a self-baptism. There is late evidence of this. It serves as entry into the religious fellowship and applies only to non-Jews, whereas the baptism by John concerns Jews especially.[14] Against this background, the baptism by John can be seen as a new departure: a provoking and final surpassing of the prevalent purification rites, an eschatological, once-and-for-all event, which was perhaps seen as a fulfilment of the prophecy in Ezek 36.25-26.[15]

It might also be considered whether the baptism by John was a kind of

---

10. There is a tendency towards a purely sacramentalistic interpretation in Dibelius, *Überlieferung*, p. 135ff., Thyen, *Studien*, p. 138. But that the ethical aspect is significant in the new life is shown not only in the (disputed) passages referred to in the previous note but also in Mt 3.7; Lk 3.7, where the Baptist stresses that it is not sufficient to allow oneself to be baptised, cf. Ernst Haenchen, *Der Weg Jesu*², Berlin 1968, p. 42f., Becker, *Johannes*, p. 21ff., Ernst, *Johannes*, p. 308.

11. Cf. Schürmann, *Lukasevangelium* I, p. 177, Ulrich Luz, *Das Evangelium nach Matthäus — 1. Teilband* (EKK III/1), Zürich 1985, p. 149, Ernst, *Johannes*, p. 305f.

12. Cf. Peter Steensgaard, *Dåbsforestillinger i den tidlige jødedom* [Baptismal concepts in early Judaism], in: Sigfred Pedersen (ed.), *Dåben i Ny Testament* [Baptism in the New Testament], Århus 1982, pp. 14-28, Ernst, *Johannes*, p. 320ff. In Delling, *Taufe*, p. 22, the corresponding injunctions in Ex 30.17-21 are pointed out, where the lustrations are to avert the priests' death. In Gnilka, *Markus*, p. 46, it is assumed that John with his once-and-for-all baptism is in opposition to these external rites.

13. Cf. Becker, *Johannes*, p. 38, Steensgaard, *Dåbsforestillinger*, p. 15ff., Ernst, *Johannes*, p. 325ff.

14. Cf. Dibelius, *Überlieferung*, p. 137, Oepke, *ThWNT* I, p. 535, Becker, *Johannes*, p. 38, Steensgaard, *Dåbsforestillinger*, p. 21ff., Ernst, *Johannes*, p. 322ff. In Böcher, *TRE* 17, p. 172, 177, it is considered that it is the proselyte baptism (which is considered as early) that is conveyed provokingly to the Jews.

15. Cf. Delling, *Taufe*, p. 22ff., 53f., Schweizer, *ThWNT* VI, p. 397, Lang, *Erwägungen*, p. 464.

initiation.[16] But the sources include no clear evidence that from the outset baptism was an entry into a new fellowship. There may, however, be a development in this direction.

2.2. The baptism of Jesus and the imitation concept

The gospels' narrative of John the Baptist gives the impression that its centre is located elsewhere — in the baptism of Jesus.

One of the most certain facts concerning the historical Jesus is that he was baptised by John, and that this was the introduction to his work on earth which ended with death on the cross. The sources show this unambiguously. What gives it a special certainty is the difficulties the Christian community had with this fact soon afterwards — not only because of reluctance to see Jesus as a disciple of John but also because it was disagreeable that he began his work by subjecting himself to a baptism of repentance for the forgiveness of sins.[17]

Jesus' baptism is thus the starting point of the gospel narrative in its oldest form. This is to be seen from the Gospel of Mark and from the preaching plan we encounter in Acts 10.37-43.[18] But the original penitential baptism retreats into the background at the baptism of Jesus. The crucial point becomes the arming with the Holy Spirit which follows, and the proclamation of Jesus as the son of God. This is seen as a fulfilment of John's prediction about baptism with the Holy Spirit.[19] The baptism of Jesus becomes the introduction to the works that proceed onwards to death and resurrection. That the baptism of Jesus is traditionally associated with the temptation narrative is emphasised by this line: Jesus begins to struggle against human expectations as regards the son of God; this is continued in the 'the secret Messiah motif' and the predictions of suffering, especially in Mark 8.33.[20]

16. Thus Oepke, *ThWNT* I, p. 535, cf. against this Lang, Erwägungen, p. 462.
17. Cf. Bultmann, *Geschichte*, p. 263, 270, Carl H. Kraeling, *John the Baptist*, New York 1951, p. 240, Bent Noack, *Det nye Testamente og de første kristne årtier³* [The New Testament and the early Christian decades], Copenhagen 1973, p. 186, Schürmann, *Lukasevangelium* I, p. 197, Becker, *Johannes*, p. 15, Gnilka, *Markus* I, p. 51, Ernst, *Johannes*, p. 337, Böcher, *TRE* 17, p. 177.
18. Cf. Haenchen, *Weg*, p. 47, 49f., Noack, *Testamente*, p. 186, Gnilka, *Markus* I, p. 51, Rudolf Pesch, *Die Apostelgeschichte. 1. Teilband (EKK V/1)*, Zürich 1986, p. 343.
19. Mark 1.8 parr. Cf. Haenchen, *Weg*, p. 51ff., Sigfred Pedersen, Dåbsteologien i Markusevangeliet [Baptismal Theology in the Gospel of Mark], in: Sigfred Pedersen (ed.), *Dåben i Ny Testamente* [Baptism in the New Testament], Århus 1982, pp. 49-78; p. 55f., 66f., Ernst, *Johannes*, p. 15ff.
20. Cf. Pedersen, Dåbsteologien, p. 67f.

In this way there is in the oldest layers of the gospels a connection between baptism and death where Jesus is concerned.[21]

But it is evident that the baptism of Jesus also has another meaning: this is the institution of Christian baptism.[22] The crucial new feature in the baptism of Jesus to which evangelical tradition attached itself is passed on in the baptism of the Christians. John the Baptist's prophecy of a spiritual baptism, which in the gospels forms the prelude to the baptism of Jesus, also heralds Christian baptismal practice, which according to Acts 2 was initiated on Whitsunday.[23] The spiritual outpouring becomes a central feature in Christian baptism. It becomes the armour for the Christians' new life in the same way as the baptism of Jesus became the introduction to his works.

There is parallelism at this point between events in the life of Christ and in the Christians' life.

But in the gospels there are also ideas of parallelism between later events in Christ's life and the fate of the Christians. Jesus' disciples are those who are together with Jesus and must follow him; later Christians are also included in the term disciple.[24] What becomes crucial in this concept of following is that the disciples follow Jesus in suffering. 'If any want to become my followers, let them deny themselves and take up their cross and follow me.' So said Jesus in the context of the prediction of suffering and in the commissioning discourse.[25] The motif is also to be found in the final process, especially in the prediction of Peter's denial. In Mark 14.31, Peter speaks directly about his wish to die with Jesus. This is presented as the

21. There is a line from the two most certain facts about Jesus' work on earth, the beginning in baptism and the end in death, cf. Gnilka, *Markus* I, p. 25, 51.
22. Cf. Bultmann, *Geschichte*, p. 269, Schürmann, *Lukasevangelium* I, p. 196f., Kurt Aland, *Taufe und Kindertaufe*, Gütersloh 1971, p. 10, Gnilka, *Markus* I, p. 48.
23. See also Acts 1.5, where the same prophecy is put into Jesus' mouth. Cf. Bultmann, *Geschichte*, p. 262 with n. 2, Schürmann, *Lukasevangelium* I, p. 196f., Ernst, *Johannes*, p. 141.
24. See as regards the ideas of Christians as the followers of Christ especially Larsson, *Christus*, p. 72ff., Wilckens, *Römer* II, p. 60f., cf. Chapter III, note 161 above. Cf. also Betz, *Nachfolge*, p. 27ff., who expresses scepticism concerning the age of the ideas.
25. These passages, Mt 10.38; 16.24; Mark 8.34; Lk 9.23; 14.27, are significant, whether or not this is an historical core or only reflects primitive-Christian traditions. In J. Wellhausen, *Das Evangelium Marci*, Berlin 1903, p. 72, Bultmann, *Geschichte*, p. 176 (cf. however p. 172f.), Haenchen, *Weg*, p. 296f., the logia is considered to be secondary. It is treated as a possible saying of Jesus about readiness to die in Erich Klostermann, *Das Markusevangelium* (HNT 3)[5], Tübingen 1971, p. 84, Joh. Schneider, σταυρός κτλ., *ThWNT* VII (1960-64), pp. 572-84; p. 577ff., Larsson, *Christus*, p. 41, Schürmann, *Lukasevangelium* I, p. 542f., Joachim Gnilka, *Das Evangelium nach Markus 2. Teilband* (EKK II/2), Zürich 1979, p. 24, and (more definitively) *Das Matthäusevangelium 1* (HThK I/1), Freiburg 1986, p. 398, Luz, *Matthäus* I, p. 142ff. Cf. Betz, *Nachfolge*, p. 27ff., and Dinkler's interpretation note 56 below.

consistent imitation which Peter and the other disciples were not in a position to carry out immediately.[26]

The question now is whether these different forms of parallelism have been combined, so that the Christians' baptism is seen as the introduction to an existence which can proceed to suffering, death and resurrection.

A single text points in this direction. During the episode with the sons of Zebedee, Jesus sets out in Mark 10.38 the conditions for sharing his glory: 'Are you able to drink the cup that I drink, or be baptised with the baptism that I am baptised with?' Here baptism is used as an image of the death that Jesus expects for himself, and in Mark 10.39 also in regard to the disciples' fate. The background may be an Old Testament metaphor, in which one is 'overwhelmed' by adversity and anxiety and about to drown in them. Or it may be a play on words coming from the Greek, where βαπτίζεσθαι in the passive has the widespread meaning of 'going under', 'drowning'.[27] In any event, concepts of baptism and death are linked closely together in the life of Christ and the Christians.

The age of the traditions which can here be detected may be open to question. But what is crucial is not the chronological aspect but that it can be explained as an internal-Christian development. And the final result is parallel to the concepts we have encountered in Paul: Christ is the precursor for

---

26. Similarly in Mt 26.35; Lk 22.33; John 11.16. See especially Lohmeyer, *Markus*, p. 312, Wilckens, *Römer* II, p. 60f., who associates this with σὺν Χριστῷ in Paul. Cf. as regards the age of the traditions Martin Dibelius, *Die Formgeschichte des Evangeliums*[6], Tübingen 1971, pp. 215-18, Bultmann, *Geschichte*, p. 287, who refers to it as 'legendarisch gefärbten Geschichtsbericht', Klostermann, *Markusevangelium*, p. 148f. In the Gospel of John there is further reflection on the possibility of following Christ in suffering. In John 13.36d, Jesus says to Peter: 'Where I am going, you cannot follow me now', and this sets the stage for the prediction of Peter's denial in John 13.38 and the denial itself in John 18.15-27. But it is added in John 13.36d: 'but you will follow me afterward', and this motif is developed in John 14.1-4, where Jesus speaks of going away and preparing the road. And in John 21.15-19 it is made clear that after the death and resurrection of Christ Peter can follow him all the way to martyrdom. Cf. Bultmann, *Johannes*, p. 460ff., Larsson, *Christus*, p. 42ff.

27. Cf. also Lk 12.50. In Oepke, *ThWNT* I, p. 534, 536, it is established that the dual meaning 'to drown'/'be baptised' only arises when the logia is translated into Greek (טבל, the Aramaic equivalent to βαπτίζεσθαι, does not have the meaning 'to drown'). Perceived as a genuine saying of Jesus, it must have concerned, as in Ps 42.6; 62.2; Isa 43.2, difficulties and dangers described as threatening waves, without baptism having originally been part of the picture, cf. Kuss, *Auslegung* I, p. 162. In Dunn, *Romans*, p. 312, 328, it is considered that Jesus referred to the Baptist's statement about the Holy Spirit and baptism by fire (Mt 3.11, with parallels). The passage is treated as vaticinium ex eventu in Dibelius, *Formgeschichte*, p. 57f., Bultmann, *Geschichte*, p. 23, Lohmeyer, *Markus*, p. 223, Haenchen, *Weg*, p. 367. But even if it is a community tradition it confirms that for the community there is a fundamental connection between baptism and death as far as Jesus is concerned — and also as concerns his successors.

the Christians in a process through suffering and death to resurrection in glory.

2.3. The death of Jesus and the forgiveness of sins in baptism

There is thus a line from Jesus' baptism and death to the spiritual baptism which is the introduction to the Christian life.

But the death of Jesus can also be linked to baptism in another way. Christian baptism is a break with the old, sinful life. In this way there is a clear connection back to the baptism by John, which was indeed a baptism for the forgiveness of sins. But this gives rise to a problem, since at the same time, according to the very oldest traditions that can be traced, Christian forgiveness of sins is to an eminent degree connected to the person of Jesus, and especially to his death which is seen as a sacrificial death of atonement. In 1 Cor 15.3-5, Paul stresses the first fundamental tradition with which both he and the Corinthians became acquainted, and the first part is indeed the death of Christ for the sake of the Christians' sins.[28] Such dual reasons are untenable.[29] But there is an obvious solution. If the act of baptism points towards the person of Jesus and his sacrificial death, the forgiveness of sins may at the same time be due to the death of Christ, as the Christians' redeemer, and mediated through baptism. Everything considered this was precisely what occurred at an early date in the history of the church. This seems to be reflected in John 1.29-34. John the Evangelist avoids both mentioning Jesus' baptism and saying that forgiveness of sins is the substance of John's baptism. On the other hand, he allows the Baptist to proclaim that Jesus is the lamb of God who bears the sins of the world. Indirectly, then, the Baptist's baptism becomes a baptism for the forgiveness of sins. This and all his works points towards Jesus and his death of atonement.[30]

This connection between baptism and the death of Christ may also arise because the characteristic of the Christian baptism quickly became that it was a baptism to Christ's name.[31] It can be imagined that this name was an ex-

---

28. Cf. Kramer, *Christos*, p. 15f., Wengst, *Formeln*, p. 81. Other major passages are Lk 24.47; Rom 3.25.
29. This is apparently reflected in the Gospel of Matthew's narrative on the Baptist, which does not mention that there is forgiveness of sins in the baptism by John, cf. Günther Bornkamm, Enderwartung und Kirche im Matthäusevangelium, in: Günther Bornkamm, Gerhard Barth and Heinz Joachim Held, *Überlieferung und Auslegung im Matthäusevangelium* (WMANT 1)[6], Neukirchen-Vluyn 1970, pp. 13-47; p. 13, Thyen, *Studien*, p. 139f., Mogens Müller, *Mattæusevangeliet fortolket* [The Gospel of Matthew Interpreted], Copenhagen 1988, p. 47. Something similar occurs in the Gospel of John, cf. below.
30. Cf. Oepke, *ThWNT* I, p. 536, Bultmann, *Johannes*, p. 66ff., where it is also established that the term 'lamb of God' must originate from an earlier tradition.

pression of the power which appeared in Jesus' acts of redemption.[32] Baptism thus involved submission to this power, and this alone meant that it became a profession to Jesus Christ. And, as we have seen, a central point in Jesus' acts of redemption and in the earliest professions to Christ is his death. This renders it probable that from the very outset there was a profession to baptism which had its centre in the death of Christ, as is still the case.

In primitive Christian baptismal practice and reflections on the content of baptism there is thus a basis for the development of ideas about a 'baptism to the death of Christ', as is to be found in Paul. I wish below to consider a further possibility of a connection between the earliest baptismal practice and the death of Christ. This is even more hypothetical; but potentially there will be a close and evident connection.

3. Baptism and the sign of the cross

3.1. Observations

A number of archaeological, religio-historical and liturgic-historical observations render it probable that a symbolic stigmatisation involving the sign of the cross was used in the earliest Christian baptismal practice.

Erich Dinkler in particular has indicated this in a number of articles collected in the book *'Signum crucis'*.[33] Earlier, Franz Joseph Dölger also worked on the same subject.[34]

An initial observation is that at the time of Jesus cross-markings were used as a symbol of protection.[35]

This is based on an ossuary find at Talpioth near Jerusalem dating from the second half of the first century after Christ. Apart from inscriptions, which in two cases included the name ᾿Ιησοῦς, the sign of the cross written in charcoal was also found on the ossuaries. Jesus was a common name at that time, and there is no compelling reason to believe that these are

---

31. See 1 Cor 1.13,15; 6.11; Acts 2.38; 8.16; 10.48; especially programmatical in Acts 19.1-7. Cf. Heitmüller, *Im Namen*, p. 224ff., Delling, *Zueignung*, p. 40ff., Frankemölle, *Taufverständnis*, p. 46f. See also Chapter III, section 2.3 above.

32. See especially Phil 2.6-11; Acts 8.12; 10.38-43.

33. See the following articles from Erich Dinkler's *Signum crucis*, Tübingen 1967: Zur Geschichte des Kreuzsymbols, pp. 1-25, Kreuzzeichen und Kreuz. Tav, Chi und Stauros, pp. 26-54, Jesu Wort vom Kreuztragen, pp. 77-98, Die Taufterminologie in 2Kor 1,21 f, pp. 99-117, Älteste christliche Denkmahler — Bestand und Chronologie, pp. 134-78.

34. See in particular the posthumously published work Beiträge zur Geschichte des Kreuzzeichen I-VI, in *JbAC* 1-6 (1958-63).

35. See especially Dinkler, *Signum*, p. 1-25.

Christian burials.[36] But since this is a Jewish form of burial the Jews must have used the sign of the cross. It may have been a magic sign in Judaism on a line with a widespread heathen use of cross-like protection marks.[37]

Dinkler, however, associates it with the following perception.

The other observation is that contemporary Judaism had living traditions of a cultic marking using the letter tav; this is based particularly on Ezek 9.4.[38]

The background is a marking practice that was widespread in the heathen world.[39] The words σφραγίς and στίγματα, which were generally used synonymously, referred to the tattooed or branded markings by which slaves might be marked. Ownership was marked in this way. It might also be used in a religious context: followers of a deity allowed themselves to be marked with its sign, and they were then the god's property and as such the object of its favour and protection.[40] Pictures show that these στίγματα might take the form of a cross, and in general terms the cross-sign is quite a widespread form of marking and sealing.[41]

Similar marks are encountered in the Old Testament: thus the mark of Cain (Gen 4.15). The most striking passage is to be found in Ezek 9. In a vision of a massacre in Jerusalem, a person appears who is ordered by God to go through the centre of the city putting a mark (תו) on the forehead of those who sorrowfully distance themselves from the idol worship in the city; these people will be protected in the subsequent slaughter. The Hebrew word תו means both 'mark' and the letter 'tav', which at the time as well as later was written as a lying or standing cross: x or +. It is in the nature of a protection mark and is perhaps also Yahweh's property mark, as mentioned in Isa 44.5.[42]

36. Thus Dinkler, *Signum*, p. 3, Erwin R. Goodenough, *Jewish Symbols in the Graeco-Roman Period* I, New York 1953, p. 131ff. Against E.L. Sukenik, The Earliest Records of Christianity, *AJA* 51 (1947), pp. 351-65; p. 365.
37. Thus Goodenough, *Symbols* I, p. 131ff., Dölger, Beiträge II, p. 22ff.
38. Dinkler, *Signum*, especially p. 15ff., 26-54, cf. Franz Jos. Dölger, *Sphragis*, Paderborn 1911, p. 55ff.
39. Cf. on this Dölger, *Sphragis*, p. 39f., Wilhelm Heitmüller, Σφραγίς, in: *Neutestamentliche Studien Georg Heinrici dargebracht (UNT 6)*, Leipzig 1914, pp. 40-59; p. 45ff. As regards the term στίγματα, see below.
40. The best-known evidence of this is Herodotus 2.113: Ἦν δὲ ... Ἡρακλέους ἱρὸν, ἐς τὸ ἢν καταφυγὼν οἰκέτης ὅτευ ὦν ἀνθρώπων ἐπιβάλεται στίγματα ἱρὰ, ἑωυτὸν διδοὺς τῷ θεῷ, οὐκ ἔξεστι τούτου ἄψεσθαι. Cultic signing in the Mithras cult is dealt with in Tertullian, De praescr. haer. 40, about something equivalent in the Attis cult, Prudentius, Peristefanon 10,1076-80, cf. Chapter II, section 2.3 above, with note 101.
41. See Dölger, *Sphragis*, Tafel I and II, Beiträge II, p. 18ff., Hadar Lilliebjörn, *Über religiöse Signierung in der Antike*, Uppsala 1933, p. 39ff., 63ff.
42. Cf. Dinkler, *Signum*, p. 17.

The Old Testament in general has a dual attitude towards these markings. In Lev 19.28; 21.5-6; Deut 14.1 one finds absolute prohibitions against this heathen-inspired religious tattooing custom. But there is also a more positive connection: a figurative, sublimated use of the terminology that stems from this practice. Ex 13.9 (cf. 12.22-23) uses the expression about the Passover: 'It shall serve for you as a sign on your (Israel's) hand and as a reminder on your forehead'.[43]

A reference to the Damascus Manuscript 19.12; Ps 15; Rev 7.3-4; 9.4; 14.1; 22.4 shows that the Ezek 9 concepts were still alive at the time of Jesus (presumably in the spiritualised form).[44]

As with Dinkler, the crosses on the ossuaries can then be understood as Jewish protection signs to protect the dead until and throughout resurrection and eschatological judgement.[45]

The third point to be observed is that at an early date in the history of the Church the sign of the cross is associated with a loaded symbolism and is used liturgically in baptism.[46]

The sign of the cross has been associated with several symbolic meanings in religious meditations. It has not been merely a reference to Jesus' manner of death. In addition to this, it can be understood as the letter tav as in Ezek 9.4. In this connection, one can imagine both the Greek letter T (ταῦ) and the corresponding Hebrew letter which was written as + or x. In Greek, T is also a numerical character for 300, for which reason this figure when encountered in the Old Testament is in many cases interpreted allegorically as a term for the cross of Christ.[47] The sign of the cross is also understood as the Greek letter X (chi), which was written in the same way as the old Hebrew tav. It can then be taken as an abbreviation of Χριστός.[48]

For these reasons it is clear that at an early stage the sign of the cross played an important role as a distinctive mark and a protection symbol. In particular, it was drawn on the forehead of the baptised, analogous to the

---

43. Cf. Dinkler, *Signum*, p. 18f. Note however that the word 'tav' is used only in Ezek 9.4; the other passages refer to the religious stigmatisation using other words. But indeed from Ex 12.22-23; 13.9, which concern the Passover there is a connection to Ezek 9.4-11, which is described as a repetition of the Passover event.

44. See Dinkler, *Signum*, pp. 18-20, Heitmüller, *Im Namen*, p. 173ff.

45. Cf. however Goodenough, *Symbols*, p. 131ff., which expresses doubt about understanding the protection marks on the basis of this one passage where the mark is called a tav.

46. Thus Dinkler, *Signum*, especially pp. 26-54, 134-78.

47. See Barn 9.8, Tertullian, Adv. Marc. 3.2, Clement of Alexandria, Strom. 6.84. Cf. Dölger, *Sphragis*, pp. 174-78, Beiträge I, p. 13ff., Dinkler, *Signum*, p. 40, 113, Hugo Rahner, *Symbole der Kirche*, Salzburg 1964, p. 413ff.

48. See Tertullian, De bapt. 8.2, Justin, Apol. 60,1-4, Ambrosius, De valent. consol. 58, cf. Dölger, Beiträge III, pp. 5-14, Dinkler, *Signum*, p. 38ff.

present liturgical use of the sign of the cross. It might be seen as a signing with the name of Christ as a property mark.[49]

The question is now, how early in history did the cross have the loaded meaning and the liturgical application. In my opinion, evidence is to be found as far back as sources stretch.[50]

Literary instances are early. Tertullian evidenced (about the year 200) that the cross was significant in the act of baptism: during baptism the Christians were marked on the forehead, and all Christians have a sign on the forehead in the form of a cross.[51] Even earlier, among the Apostolic Fathers, there is a loaded symbolic use of the cross and evidence of an association with baptism.[52]

In the visual arts, the Christian sign of the cross is not found until the third or fourth century; there is no Christian visual art until then.[53] But epigraphically there is early evidence of the central Christian cross-symbolism. The papyrus fragments P^{66} and P^{75} dating from about the year 200, which include parts of the gospels of Luke and John, contain the contraction form

$$\sigma\rlap{\,\text{\raisebox{2pt}{P}}}{\text{f}}ο\varsigma = \sigma\text{-}\tau\alpha\upsilon\text{-}\rho\text{-}ο\varsigma,$$

where τ and ρ together form a stylised representation of a crucifixion.[54]

The crux of the matter is whether, as *a fourth observation*, one can show that baptism was already associated with a cross-marking symbolism at the time of the New Testament.

---

49. Cf. Dölger, Beiträge III, pp. 5-14, Dinkler, *Signum*, p. 38ff., cf. the passages referred to in the previous note.
50. Dinkler displays far more caution on this point in certain contexts. Cf. below.
51. Tertullian, De bapt. 8.2, shows that the sign of the cross is associated with baptism, in that the laying on of hands which takes place during baptism is associated with the crossed hands at Jacob's blessing of Ephraim and Manasseh. It can be seen from De carn. res. 8 that during baptism a specific imaginary mark was placed upon the body. De praescr. haer. 40 shows that the signing at baptism was a spiritualised counterpart to the cultic stigmatisation in the Mithras cult, cf. also De bapt. 6.13. Adv. Marc. 3.22 makes it clear that the mark on the forehead is a cross.
52. It is assumed in Barn 9.8 as a self-evident matter calling for no explanation that 300 = T refers to ὁ σταυρός, which in turn refers to grace. We have in Barn 11 an interpretation of Ps 1.3-6 in which it is asserted that since water is described in association with the cross ('the tree') this psalm expresses a blessing on those who have linked their hope to the cross and descended into the water, cf. Lundberg, *Typologie*, p. 179ff. The connection between baptism and the term σφραγίς is found in Hermes' shepherd 7.16.2.
53. Cf. Dinkler, *Signum*, p. 150ff. Note however that there is an earlier depiction of Christ on the cross — the well-known satirical crucifix from Palatinum (2nd cent.) where the crucified god is depicted with an ass's head, loc.cit. Plate XIII.
54. This is the oldest figurative illustration of the cross of Christ, as pointed out by Dinkler, *Signum*, p. 177f., in continuation of Kurt Aland, Neue Neutestamentliche Papyri II, *NTS* 10 (1963-64), pp. 62-79; p. 78f.

Dinkler believes this is so.[55]

Bearing in mind that both before, in the Jewish environment, and after, in the very earliest history of the Church, cultic acts using a protective sign of the cross were known, it would not be improbable that this was also known during the intervening period. Ezek 9.4 is in fact also used directly in the New Testament, i.e. in Rev 7.3-4; 9.4; 14.1; 22.4.

This is elaborated in the interpretation of other New Testament texts.

According to Dinkler, the words about carrying one's cross can be understood as a genuine saying of Jesus and associated with the idea of a cultic marking-act and Ezek 9.4. The statement would then concern the carrying of the eschatological 'tav'. When translating into Greek σημεῖον was not chosen but, in the light of Jesus' death, the other possibility σταυρός.[56]

2 Cor 1.21-22 is also set in such a context. It is probably a baptism statement, and the word σφραγισάμενος can be interpreted as expressing a specific act in baptism, a symbolic sealing with a depicted sign of the cross.[57]

Finally, τὰ στίγματα τοῦ ᾿Ιησοῦ in Gal 6.17 is seen as describing a symbolic signing with the cross using water (or ointment).[58]

3.2. Interpretation

Dinkler thus considers that at the time of the New Testament signing with the cross was already practised in the context of the act of baptism. But strangely enough he does not draw the conclusion that it must then be established that baptism involved signing with a cross as a symbol of Christ's redeeming death. He thinks that the signing with the cross which had its place in the process of baptism was merely the eschatological mark and was not associated with the manner of Jesus' death.[59]

---

55. Cautiously in *Signum*, p. 111ff., more unreservedly in *Signum*, p. 93f.
56. This interpretation of Mt 10.38; 16.24; Mark 8.34; Lk 9.23; 14.27 is drafted by Dinkler, *Signum*, pp. 77-98, cf. Rudolf Bultmann, *Die Geschichte der synoptischen Tradition. Ergänzungsheft³*, Göttingen 1966, p. 27, and critically to the contrary Schneider, *ThWNT* VII, p. 379, Luz, *Matthäus* I, p. 142f.
57. See in particular Dinkler, *Signum*, pp. 99-117. But against this there are other interpretations in which, although the term is understood as baptismal terminology, it is perceived in an implied sense and is not seen as expressing a specific act during baptism. Heitmüller, Σφραγίς, p. 40ff., Bousset, *Kyrios*, p. 227, sees it as meaning that it is the name pronounced over the baptised which becomes a seal of property. Dölger, *Sphragis*, p. 76f., believes that baptism as a whole is the seal = confirmation of faith.
58. See Dinkler, *Signum*, p. 112. In connection with a reference to anointing and sealing practice in the 2nd cent., Ysebaert, *Terminology*, p. 411ff., provides material for understanding Gal 6.17 similarly as about a cross-anointing during baptism, cf. p. 284ff.
59. See Dinkler, *Signum*, p. 86, 94, 113, 144, cf. against this Wilckens, *Römer* II, p. 60 n. 23.

But this viewpoint is not convincing. It is suddenly asserted that the sign of the cross became a decisive Christological symbol only in the third and fourth centuries,[60] and that the connection between signum crucis and the cross of Calvary emerges only after New Testament times.[61]

If a sign of the cross was in fact used during baptism in New Testament times, it is quite inconceivable that it was not associated with the — for Christianity — wholly central motif: Jesus' death on the cross.

Dinkler's own investigations make this connection probable. Some scepticism should perhaps be exercised in regard to the interpretation of the New Testament texts upon which Dinkler in particular bases his assertion.[62] In my opinion, there are New Testament texts which give a better basis for assuming that marking with a cross forms part of the baptism ritual.

As we have seen, in 1 Cor 1.10-17 there is the close connection between baptism in the name of Jesus and the cross as an expression of the central basis of redemption. In addition, I shall try to indicate the significance the sign of the cross appears to have in the Letter to the Galatians.

3.3. The cross in the Letter to the Galatians

It is immediately significant that there is a pervasive line of statements about the cross: Gal 2.19; 3.1,13; 5.11,24; 6.12-14. Otherwise, statements about the cross in Paul occur in only a few (but central) passages: 1 Cor 1-2; Rom 6.6; 2 Cor 13.4; Phil 2.8; 3.18. The accumulation is to be found precisely in the context of Paul's combating circumcision, which is the symbol of the old fleshly covenant. It might be because the sign of the cross is the sign of the new pneumatic covenant.

We saw in *Gal 2.19-20* that the term 'crucified with Christ' was as-

---

60. Dinkler points out that the sign of the cross emerges in Christian art only in the 3rd cent. — e.g. in *Signum*, p. 113 — or in the 4th cent. — e.g. in *Signum*, p. 91f. n. 61, p. 145. But he himself has demonstrated that not only the Christian cross but also Christian art in general is absent — *Signum*, p. 176. Moreover, he has indicated the cross symbolism in the papyrus manuscripts' Ϸ-contraction form — *Signum*, p. 77f. Cf. above.

61. According to Dinkler, *Signum*, p. 115, 94 n. 70, 42f., this first occurs with the Barnabas Letter. The connection is said to have arisen as a result of a later reflection in which Paul's cross christology, 1 Cor 1.18-2.16, penetrates into this field, see *Signum*, p. 144, 42f., 56f. It is possible that we have here an explanation of Dinkler's general reluctance to assume an earlier connection: if it existed prior to Paul, his cross theology would not have been as unique as is normally emphasised. But according to Dinkler himself the sign of the cross is understood as an expression of the manner of Jesus' death at the latest when the traditions in Mt 10.38; 16.24 parr. were translated into Greek by using the word σταυρός, cf. note 56 above.

62. Dinkler's interpretation is disputed in regard to both 2 Cor 1.22 and Mt 10.38; 16.24 parr., cf. notes 57 and 56 above.

sociated with a dual, very loaded symbolism which referred both to Christ's act of redemption and the crucial turning point in the Christian's life. It becomes evident that Paul can use so complicated a reference if any marking with the cross took place at the transition to Christianity.[63]

It might be considered whether *Gal 3.1b* can also be understood along these lines. It is included in Paul's accusatory outburst against 'the bewitched Galatians': οἷς κατ' ὀφθαλμοὺς 'Ιησοῦς προεγράφη ἐσταυρωμένος. It is a puzzling expression. A widespread concept of the verb προγράφειν does not hold water. It cannot mean to 'describe (vividly) in front of' and the sentence cannot relate to Paul's preaching, which is said to describe vividly this central event in particular.[64] Προγράφειν is not evidenced in this sense. The only known use of the word which may be relevant here is that correspond- ing to the Latin proscribere: 'to write (or draw) publicly', 'make known by advertisement'.[65] Rather than broadly-painted, emotive preaching, it refers to something brief and official. But would it not be a strange image of Paul's preaching if Christ were publicly written or depicted before the eyes of the Galatians?[66] This would indeed be so. But it is not certain that Paul's preaching was in mind. The intention might be a different official act during which Christ was proclaimed by being depicted or written about as crucified. It might be a sign of the cross during baptism! This would fit the context perfectly. Paul asked in Gal 3.1a who had bewitched the Galatians. If the cross is the sign before their eyes as a property and protection sign, it indeed becomes quite incredible that such magic could be performed on them. Gal 3.2 also speaks of recieving the Spirit, which is frequently associated with baptism.

It should be noted that there is a clear connection from *Gal 3.13*, where there is an allusion to the crucifixion, to the baptism statement in Gal 3.26- 29.[67]

The idea in *Gal 5.11* is that if one preaches circumcision one betrays the cross. Circumcision and the cross are presented as alternatives, which is also the case in Gal 6.12-14.

Gal 5.24 again assumes that the crucifixion is a known metaphor for the Christians' almost ascetically perceived farewell to the world of the flesh.

---

63. Cf. the examination above, Chapter III, section 3.2, and note 168, where the established metaphorical use of the term is shown.
64. Against Zahn, *Galater*, p. 139f., Lietzmann, *Galater*, p. 16f., Koch, *Galaterbrevet*, p. 78, Betz, *Galatians*, p. 131, Lührmann, *Galater*, p. 47f. — and also Bauer, *Wörterbuch*, col. 1397 (despite the absence of examples).
65. Thus Burton, *Galatians*, p. 144f., Oepke, *Galater*, p. 100, Schlier, *Galater*, p. 119ff., Ridderbos, *Galatians*, p. 112, Mussner, *Galaterbrief*, p. 207.
66. As rightly pointed out by Zahn, *Galater*, p. 139f., Koch, *Galaterbrevet*, p. 78.
67. Cf. the examination above, Chapter III, section 2.1.

The same is true of *Gal 6.14*. But this verse forms part of a larger context in *Gal 6.12-17*, where the sign of the cross plays a pervasive part.

In Gal 6.12-13, Paul emphatically tackles the characterisation of his Judaistic adversaries. They are cowards; they dare not accept the consequences of the cross, and revert to circumcision (verse 12). They will boast of the flesh, and not even their own but the Galatians' — which they interfere with in circumcision (verse 13).

In Gal 6.14-17, Paul sets himself up demonstratively as the absolute antithesis to the preachers of circumcision — initially in verse 14 with the accentuated ἐμοί, later in verse 17b, with the explicit ἐγώ. According to verses 14-15, it is to Paul's credit that he has totally and consistently subjected himself to the cross, so that it has become of revolutionary significance to his life: he has broken completely with the old world and its circumcision problems, so that what is all-important is the new creation. After the conditional greeting in verse 16, Paul stresses that there can be no more problems with which to trouble him. This is said in verse 17, with a marked reference to Jesus' wounds. It becomes a crucial concluding remark, in which Paul points out that he is bearing the sufferings on his own body — and does not attempt to shift them onto others, as do the preachers of circumcision according to verse 13.

We have now arrived at the content of Gal 6.17b: ἐγὼ γὰρ τὰ στίγματα τοῦ ᾽Ιησοῦ ἐν τῷ σώματι μου βαστάζω. This verse also contains a cross for the exegete. But in my opinion it contains an argument for the connection between baptism and the sign of the cross at the time of Paul.

Τὰ στίγματα τοῦ ᾽Ιησοῦ in particular is a puzzling term, which has occasioned many explanations over time.[68] Two of these are worthy of consideration.

The general opinion is that στίγματα means 'scars', 'marks of injury', and that the term refers to marks resulting from sufferings analogous to Jesus' sufferings, which Paul has had to endure in his work.[69]

Another interpretation is that the word στίγματα means 'tattooing', so that we are dealing with a (symbolic) cultic mark which has been set upon Paul.[70]

---

68. See the survey in Güttgemanns, *Apostel*, pp. 126-35.
69. Thus Oepke, *Galater*, p. 205ff., Schlier, *Galater*, p. 284f., Koch, *Galaterbrevet*, p. 173ff., Ridderbos, *Galatians*, p. 229, Betz, στίγμα, *ThWNT* VII (1960-64), pp. 657-64; p. 663, Mussner, *Galaterbrief*, pp. 418-20.
70. Thus Dinkler, *Signum*, p. 93, 112, Dölger, *Sphragis*, p. 49f., cf. Ysebaert, *Terminology*, p. 284, Burton, *Galatians*, p. 361f., Betz, *Galatians*, p. 324, Lührmann, *Galater*, p. 102, who consider a figurative meaning, 'slave marks' or 'tattooing', with reference to the basic meaning.

The basic meaning is 'prick', and the word is used exclusively as terminus technicus for 'tattooing' (that is, the mark produced by the tattooing technique).[71] Where there is no special emphasis on the technical aspect, however, it can be used indiscriminately with terms for marks produced by other techniques: χάραγμα (brand) and σφράγις (seal, stamp). The meaning never varies very much from this starting point. The marks can have various functions: property marks, punishment marks for thieves, and slave marks, which include the religious slave- and protection-mark which was widespread in the Orient.[72] The word itself does not therefore mean 'scars' in general, but 'scars resulting from a marking'.[73]

The basic meaning of the word suggests directly that it concerns cultic marks, made at Paul's entry into the Christian life. Tattooing itself is of course excluded in this context, where there is indeed a distancing from physical, 'fleshly' markings in Gal 6.13. Problems also arise if it is thought to be a marking in a more figurative sense, purely a symbolic act or a marking with a cross using water or oil as suggested by Dinkler,[74] for marks that Paul continues to bear on his body are in fact concerned.[75]

It is therefore reasonable to consider whether στίγματα may be an expression for signs made in the course of the Christian existence — the first-mentioned possible interpretation. But in view of the word's ordinary

71. Cf. as to this especially Betz, *ThWNT* VII, p. 659ff., Ysebaert, *Terminology*, p. 182f., 187ff.
72. See Herodotus 2.113, cf. note 40 above, Prudentius, Peristefanon 10.1076-80, cf. Chapter II, note 101 above. Cf. Dölger, *Sphragis*, p. 25ff., 40ff., Lilliebjörn, *Signierung*, p. 14ff. and the text material p. 4ff.
73. In *Sylloge inscriptionum Graecarum* (ed. Dittenberger), No. 1168 line 48f., 53ff., no general scar formations are concerned as assumed by Oepke, *Galater*, p. 205f., who uses this as evidence for a completely non-terminological meaning of στίγμα. A divine healing, a miraculous removal of a burdensome slave tattoo or punishment tattoo is probably concerned, cf. Dölger, *Sphragis*, p. 29 with n. 4.
74. Dinkler, *Signum*, p. 93ff., 112, cf. Dölger, *Sphragis*, p. 51, Ysebaert, *Terminology*, p. 412.
75. Cf. as to this pertinent objection, Güttgemanns, *Apostel*, p. 131 n. 33. Other objections in loc. cit. are off the mark. Güttgemanns asserts secondly, in continuation of Schlier, *Galater*, p. 285 n. 1, cf. also Mussner, *Galaterbrief*, p. 418f., that the plural form στίγματα excludes the sign of the cross being intended. But the plural form is also used, and to an extensive degree, about a single marking, which is natural since one tattoo consists of many pricks. This is also to be seen from the text referred to in note 40 above, Herodotus 2.113 (which Schlier quotes incorrectly). Cf. also Bauer, *Wörterbuch*, col. 1522. A third objection must also be rejected. It is asserted that the marks borne by Paul cannot have had anything to do with cultic marking during baptism, because in that event they would not have been something to distinguish Paul from other Christians. But there is nothing whatsoever to say that this should be so. As regards this mark, Paul does not need to differ from Christians in general. He can certainly have this in common with the true Israel of God in Gal 6.16. But he differs from those who preach circumcision, since in his opinion they have denied the cross out of cowardly selfishness.

meaning it must be asserted that it was then used in a figurative sense, and is in fact a reference to a cultic sign.[76]

But how then can the original readers have arrived at this meaning when they read the text? It would require them to have associated an expression referring to a cultic marking with the scars left by Paul's sufferings, and also, if it is to have any meaning as a badge of honour, with Jesus' sufferings.

It assumes at least that the context sets the scene for this complex association of ideas. And this it may well do! Here at all events we have *the cross*, which has the fixed, dual metaphoric and symbolic significance: for Christ, suffering and death; for the Christians, new life by virtue of this suffering. That is, στίγματα must be perceived as synonymous with σταυρός, also to the Galatians. This must be so if it was a spiritual mark set upon the Christian on a certain occasion, and then most probably during baptism. This then becomes the new covenant's mark, in contrast to the old covenant's circumcision.[77] But upholding this mark involves risk of suffering. In contrast to the preachers of circumcision, Paul has consistently won through, and of this he has visible marks. This is emphasised in Gal 6.17, which underlines Paul's true Christian attitude — as opposed to that of the Judaists.

That is to say, neither of the two interpretations of τὰ στίγματα τοῦ Ἰησοῦ which we took as our point of reference makes any sense in itself. But if they are combined they do. So, remarkably enough, we arrive at an interpretation of the word στίγματα which is very close to the basic meaning: 'scars which are — although indirect — a result of a cultic marking'. And one gets a good, coherent understanding of the whole section Gal 6.12-17. In my opinion the text is then clear and intelligible — but only if the sign of the cross was already at that time an established, recognisable part of the liturgy of baptism.

This is clearly indirect, hypothetical reasoning. But here also it can be seen that the preconditions for a development in which baptism is associated with concepts of the death of Christ were already present in Paul's time.

---

76. Cf. note 70 above. Against Thyen, *Studien*, p. 212 n. 4, where it is maintained that the word is wholly non-sacramental in its basic meaning, with an incorrect reference to Schlier, *Galater*, where it is asserted that the background is a cultic way of thinking, p. 284f.

77. Cf. Lührmann, *Galater*, p. 102, who indeed sees στιγμάτα as an antithesis to circumcision, since it is on a par with other religions' cultic marking.

Part Two
Review of the text

V
Rom 5 as Prelude to Rom 6

1. Introductory considerations

Rom 5 will be discussed as a preceding context to the actual subject of our investigation, Rom 6.1-14. Nevertheless, the discussion must be quite comprehensive.

First, there are crucial structural features pursued in the subsequent context and therefore of importance to an understanding of the structure and intention of Rom 6-8.

Second, christological and soteriological concepts are emphasised which will still be part of the picture when we arrive at Rom 6.

Third, it is discussed whether the background lies in particular mythological concepts, which are also considered as background to the following chapter.

In addition to this, there are complicated exegetic problems in connection with Rom 5.12, and these are bound up with all three points referred to. There is a sentence break which is of significance to an understanding of the dominant structure. There are difficulties in discerning the relationship between Adam, Christ and their respective successors, and here the religio-historical background will also be involved. This gives rise to quite a confused debate — with some markedly extreme opinions.

On the one hand there is the traditional idea that Rom 5.12 states that all people sinned 'in Adam' — corresponding to restoration 'in Christ'. Then there is a doctrine of original sin with a Jewish background which Paul is supposed to pursue.[1] This has later been developed, so that it is seen as a link in the 'Hebrew-Old Testament concept of corporate personality', which has already been considered in several contexts.[2]

On the other hand, there is the concept presented by Günther Bornkamm

---

1. The religio-historical prerequisites for the concept of original sin have been fundamentally described in Joseph Freundorfer, *Erbsünde und Erbtod beim Apostel Paulus* (NTA 13,1-2), Münster 1927.
2. The concept has been drawn into the debate about Rom 6 and the Pauline understanding of baptism via the connection to Rom 5.12-21 by Dodd, *Romans*, p. 106f., p. 100ff., cf. Schnackenburg, *Heilsgeschehen*, pp. 106-15, Todes- und Lebensgemeinschaft, p. 44ff., de Fraine, *Adam*, p. 134, Larsson, *Christus*, p. 24f., Shedd, *Man*, p. 97ff.

and Egon Brandenburger in particular. The sentence break in Rom 5.12 is said to arise because Paul gives two reasons for man's sinfulness: on the one hand Adam's sin (Rom 5.12a-c) and on the other man's own guilt (Rom 5.12d). This is interpreted to mean that Paul wishes to modify a concept of collective guilt and redemption. And the background to this concept is said to be a gnostic, primal-man mythology.[3]

There are many variations between these viewpoints. For this reason also, examination of the text becomes complicated.

2. Rom 5.1-11

2.1. A survey of the thought-process

From the beginning in *Rom 5.1-2*, Paul emphasises what is now the crux of the matter. He wishes to show the consequences that justification by faith has for the life of the Christians now and in the future.

The participial construction Δικαιωθέντες οὖν ἐκ πίστεως creates a link to the foregoing. Justification through faith in Christ alone is the subject in the first main section of the Letter to the Romans, Rom 1.16-4.25.[4] Δικαιοσύνη θεοῦ is emphasised in Rom 1.17; 3.21-26. This does not express a characteristic of God but God's way of acting; as in Old Testament thought it is a power that prevails. And the leading principle in the entire context is that God creates justice when he intervenes and declares that the godless are righteous.[5] Accordingly, God's righteousness also expresses the gift the be-

---

3. The religio-historical material has been submitted in Brandenburger, *Adam*, who continues to work on the viewpoints in Rudolf Bultmann, Adam und Christus nach Römer 5, in: *Exegetica*, Tübingen 1967, pp. 424-44, *Theologie*, p. 251ff., and Günther Bornkamm, Paulinische Anakoluthe, in: *Das Ende des Gesetzes. Paulusstudien. Gesammelte Aufsätze* I (*BEvTh* 16)[5], pp. 76-92; p. 80ff., cf. the continuation in Jüngel, *Unterwegs*, pp. 145-72, Peter Lengsfeld, *Adam und Christus* (*KSN* 9), Essen 1965, p. 46ff., 65ff. See also Bousset, *Kyrios*, p. 125f., Tannehill, *Dying*, p. 26ff., Käsemann, *Römer*, p. 154, where the concept of the primal-man redeemer is associated with Rom 6 by virtue of the preceding context.
4. This is already apparent from the choice of words: the term δικαιοσύνη θεοῦ (or αὐτοῦ) occurs six times, δικαιοσύνη (used alone) seven times, the verb δικαιοῦν nine times, the adjective δίκαιος four times, and there are four other words from the stem.
5. That God's righteousness is here a power that prevails is emphasised in Ernst Käsemann, Gottesgerechtigkeit bei Paulus, in: *Exegetische Versuche und Besinnungen* II[3], Göttingen 1968, pp. 181-93. But this is not because δικαιοσύνη θεοῦ can be isolated as a fixed formula with a special content (which is present automatically): the Old Testament-Jewish concept of God's fidelity to the covenant and apocalyptic act of redemption as assumed by Käsemann (p. 185) and elaborated in Stuhlmacher, *Gerechtigkeit*, p. 106ff., cf. Kümmel, *Theologie*, p. 175f., Käsemann, *Römer*, p. 27. This concept-historical interpretation model has rightly been rejected, cf. Rudolf Bultmann, Δικαιοσύνη θεοῦ, in: *Exegetica*, Tübingen 1967, pp. 470-75, Günter Klein, Gottes Gerechtigkeit als Thema der neuesten Paulus-

lievers have received.[6] This righteousness is above all a new relationship with God, but it probably also involves a new (ethical) quality in the life that can now be lived after the break with the former sinfulness, which is described in Rom 1.18-3.20.[7]

Other members from Rom 5.1-2 also show that the main thoughts from

Forschung, *VF* 12 (1967), pp. 1-11, Erhardt Güttgemanns, Gottesgerechtigkeit und strukturale Semantik, in: *Studia linguistica neotestamentica* (*BEvTh* 60)², Munich 1973, pp. 59-98, Ziesler, *Meaning*, p. 9f., 169f., 186., Schnelle, *Gerechtigkeit*, p. 93ff., Dieter Lührmann, Gerechtigkeit. III. Neues Testament, *TRE* 12 (1984), pp. 414-20; it rests upon too flimsy a material and is methodically untenable; how could Paul expect that the Gentile-convert Romans could understand such a loaded Jewish idea? From the context, one must instead show that δικαιοσύνη θεοῦ must be understood as expressing this divine power and strength; in Rom 1.16f. one can point out that the term amplifies δύναμις θεοῦ and represents an antithesis to ὀργή θεοῦ in Rom 1.18, which is clearly an expression of God's acts; similarly, δικαιοσύνη θεοῦ is a key concept in Rom 3.21-26, where the emphasis is on God's mercy and supreme act of redemption, which is also stressed in the scriptural evidence in Rom 4, especially in Rom 4.5,17. The context also shows that δικαιοῦν and δικαιοσύνη in Rom 3.21-4.25 are used in a very special forensic-eschatological and effective sense; what is concerned is not that the judge evaluates certain acts impartially in order either to pass judgement or to acquit. Despite the incorrect mode of action, God as judge has intervened and has testified to man's righteousness, and thus made him so, cf. Kertelge, *Rechtfertigung*, p. 123, Schlier, *Römerbrief*, p. 136. It is not the Pauline usage and the words in themselves that have this content. As regards the future judgement according to the deeds Paul can use the words in the ordinary sense, so that it is assumed that God as judge evaluates the specific actions; the group of words is also used in this way in the section here: Rom 2.5-16, cf. 3.20.

6. As will be seen from the previous note, δικαιοσύνη θεοῦ can be understood as subjective genitive: the leading principle is that God is just, cf. Käsemann, *Versuche* II, p. 182ff., Stuhlmacher, *Gerechtigkeit*, p. 78ff., Jervell, *Gud*, p. 36f., 65, Schlier, *Römerbrief*, p. 44 (primarily but not exclusively). But it must be clear that at the same time there is a nuance of genitivus auctoris; when in Rom 1.17; 3.21-22,26; 4.3,5-6,9,11,13,22-23 there is a reference to 'the righteousness of faith', 'righteousness to believers' and 'reckoned as righteousness', this clearly concerns the gift the believers have received by virtue of God's act of redemption; cf. Nygren, *Romarna*, p. 82ff., Bultmann, *Theologie*, pp. 271-85 (especially p. 278), *Exegetica*, p. 471f., Conzelmann, *Grundriss*, p. 242f., Gäumann, *Taufe*, p. 146ff., Ridderbos, *Paulus*, p. 121ff., Michael Wolter, *Rechtfertigung und zukünftiges Heil* (*BZNW* 43), Berlin 1978, p. 26ff., Schnelle, *Gerechtigkeit*, p. 89f., Willi Marxsen, '*Christliche*' *und christliche Ethik im Neuen Testament*, Gütersloh 1989, p. 146f. (who sees the genitivus-auctoris interpretation as expressing that God's sovereign power prevails).

7. Although it is clear that Rom 4 entirely concerns the new relationship with God, it is not possible everywhere to understand righteousness in purely relational terms, as in Bultmann, *Theologie*, pp. 271-85, Barrett, *Romans*, p. 75f. The section Rom 3.21-26 must also be seen in the context of what immediately precedes, where Rom 3.10-19 reels off the specific sins which the non-righteous practice according to the Scriptures; cf. also the idea of judgement according to deeds in Rom 2.5-16. In the light of this, it accords that those justified by faith are not embraced by these sins. Cf. Ziesler, *Meaning*, p. 190ff. This also corresponds to the general, broad meaning of the Greek stem, which includes the ethically correct.

the preceding section are continued. It is stated by the term εἰρήνην ἔχομεν πρὸς τὸν θεόν that the Christians have been given a new status:[8] they have been freed from God's wrath — thus the new relationship to God is also emphasised here. The relative subordinate clause in Rom 5.2a further emphasises the merciful situation in which the Christians now find themselves. The word χάρις points back to the central verse, Rom 3.24 (and Rom 4.4-5), and thus to God's act of redemption.

But something new and important also occurs. This is to be seen on the formal level from the main verbs, ἔχομεν in Rom 5.1, and καυχώμεθα in Rom 5.2.[9] Whereas the past forms and the timeless present have predominated hitherto, the present is used hereafter (and later the future). And a shift in person has taken place. Paul now uses the first person plural (later second person also). From Rom 1.16, Paul has spoken in the third person — in principle — about the gospel's power and about the crucial turning-point for all believers. These instructions on fundamental principles dominate until Rom 4.23-25; here it is established that the statement about Abraham's justification by faith has validity also for 'us' who believe in he who raised Jesus from the dead; that is to say, for all Christians and in particular Paul and the Romans.[10] The stage is set for a direct use of the principle. And at the same time Paul has returned to the more personal tone of the proem, Rom 1.8-15, where he stressed his wish to strengthen the Romans' faith — or rather that he and they must strengthen one another. This is probably what he is begin-

8. Cf. Cranfield, *Romans*, p. 258, who establishes that 'peace' is not a subjective feeling but an objective status; on p. 266 he emphasises, with Bultmann, *Theologie*, p. 285, the connection between the concepts of 'peace with God' and 'reconciliation' in Rom 5.10-11, a connection which is developed in Wolter, *Rechtfertigung*, p. 35ff.
9. See Schlier, *Römerbrief*, p. 138f., cf. Jervell, *Gud*, p. 77, Cranfield, *Romans*, p. 257.
10. Cf. Gäumann, *Taufe*, p. 25, 150, Schlier, *Römerbrief*, p. 135f. It may be noted that the resurrection concept is given central importance in the scriptural evidence in Rom 4, where it is justification of faith by virtue of Jesus' sacrificial death that must be proven. There is reference to Abraham's justifying faith, which preceded circumcision and deeds. Rom 4.17 speaks of the content of faith: the creative dead-awakening God. According to Rom 4.18-22, Abraham's faith was a faith in the awakening of the dead — because both his body and Sarah's womb were dead, and nevertheless he believed that life could be given to a son, cf. Evans, *Resurrection*, p. 167f. In this way, Abraham's faith has the same content as the Christians' faith, and therefore the scriptural evidence also applies to 'us', who believe that God awakened Christ from the dead, Rom 4.23-25. These verses have a dual function. On the one hand they give the hermeneutic basis for the scriptural evidence: that the text applies to the eschatological events which have Christ as their centre. On the other hand it is specified to whom the evidence applies: 'us', Jews and gentile converts. The transition thus occurs to the use of the first person, which was prepared for in Rom 4.1,16.

ning in Rom 5.1.[11] And therefore he changes to speaking more intensely, i.e. topically and personally, about what the turning-point means for the Christians now and in the future.

One senses in Rom 5.1-2a the liberation and enthusiasm which is to characterise the new life. The future enters into the picture in Rom 5.2b. It is said that the Christians can boast of the hope of eschatological glory. The Christians' existence is thus determined by the new, direct relationship with God, which will develop further.

Rom 5.3-5 begins with οὐ μόνον δέ, ἀλλά ... It signals an increase compared to the foregoing, which speaks of 'boasting' about hopes for the future. Then there is also an inherent advance. The talk is now of boasting about (the present) adversities. This is a paradoxical expression which therefore stands out as strongly emphasised.[12] It calls for a reason, although there is probably a clear sense of what is intended, i.e. that the joys and hopes are so vigorous that suffering cannot shake them but only emphasise them even more. In this way Paul also progresses. He expresses his certainty that this is what will happen. This is effected in the period in Rom 5.3b-5a: 'Knowing that suffering produces endurance, and endurance produces character, and character produces hope, and hope does not disappoint us'. After the three first members we are back with hope, and at the fourth comes a further climax which again points ahead to the certain glory. But this certainty must also be substantiated. This happens with the ὅτι sentence in Rom 5.5b, which thus supports the whole of the preceding context, both the present overcoming of adversities and the expectations for the future.[13]

Rom 5.5b contains a striking statement: 'because God's love has been poured into our hearts through the Holy Spirit that has been given to us'. But the intention is clear enough. The following context shows that the genitive in ἀγάπη θεοῦ is of a subjective nature. The decisive point in Rom 5.6-10 is that God loves mankind.

But this love is also intended as something concrete and present in the Christians' existence, not only as a characteristic of God. What is intended by the formulation that love has been poured into our hearts is in fact the Holy

---

11. Rom 1.8-15 certainly concerns the purpose of Paul's coming visit to Rome. But since according to Rom 15.14-16 the letter must have a corresponding purpose, it is reasonable to assume that an important objective of the letter was to prepare the strengthening in which the visit was supposed to result, cf. Cranfield, *Romans*, p. 22f., 814ff., Schlier, *Römerbrief*, p. 6ff., Simonsen, *Overvejelser*, p. 209ff.

12. Cf. John Paul Heil, *Romans. Paul's Letter of Hope (AnBib* 112), Rome 1987, p. 36f.

13. Cf. also Martin Dibelius, Vier Worte des Römerbriefes, *SyBU* 4 (1944), pp. 3-17; p. 4, von der Osten-Sacken, *Römer* 8, p. 262, Wolter, *Rechtfertigung*, p. 153, Schlier, *Römerbrief*, p. 150.

Spirit's outpouring — the word ἐκχέειν is normally used about the Spirit.[14] God's love has manifested itself in the Christians in the form of the Spirit, which is their distinctive mark. In this way Rom 5.5b refers back to the turning-point in the Christians' existence. The outpouring of the Spirit is seen as the event in which salvation is mediated.

In *Rom 5.6-10*, Paul continues to elaborate upon what the radical renewal of the relationship to God means as expressed here in Rom 5.5b, and he again indicates the quite overwhelming consequences it will continue to have.

Rom 5.6 is introduced by γάρ as reason for or amplification of the preceding context.[15] God's unrestricted love is emphasised. Paul speaks of Christ's death for our sake, and refers back to Rom 3.24. He now wishes to stress once again that Christ's sacrifice took place at a time when man was weak and godless, as was shown in Rom 1.18-3.20. This makes Christ's conduct totally surprising. But this stressing of the time also creates disarray in the sentence, which contains pleonasms and grammatical clumsinesses.[16] First we have a dual ἔτι, made even stronger by a κατὰ καιρόν. This leads to an interruption of the thought-process in Rom 5.7, which should further emphasise the astounding and the analogy-less in Christ's acts. In the ordinary way, one would shrink from sacrificing oneself — even for the righteous.[17] This shows Christ's acts in relief. Rom 5.8 resumes the line from Rom 5.6 — and again the emphasised ἔτι is repeated. But now God becomes the subject, and is seen as he who stands behind the death of Jesus for the sake of the Christians. It is seen as expressing God's love (cf. Rom 5.5b). It is presented as the boundary-overstepping action which is wholly incomprehensible if the preceding situation was that man was ἁμαρτωλοί, which corresponds to ἀσθενεῖς and ἀσεβεῖς in Rom 5.6.[18]

Thus Rom 5.5b is substantiated in Rom 5.6-8. But in the context this is not the crucial function of these verses. What is most important is that they

---

14. Thus Dibelius, Worte, p. 5f., Michel, *Römer*, p. 133, cf. Schlier, *Römerbrief*, p. 150f, Ulrich Wilckens, *Der Brief an die Römer. 1. Teilband* (KEK VI/1), Zürich 1978, p. 293, who also sees a baptism motif here. Different in Cranfield, *Romans*, p. 262f.

15. The reading in Nestle and Aland, *Novum Testamentum Graece*[26], Stuttgart 1979: ῎Ετι γὰρ ... ἔτι, is to be preferred because of the external attestation alone. In addition, it is lectio difficilior with the pleonastic ἔτι. Cf. Bornkamm, *Ende*, p. 78f., Schlier, *Römerbrief*, p. 152, Cranfield, *Romans*, p. 263, Wilckens, *Römer* I, p. 294.

16. See in particular Bornkamm, *Ende*, p. 78f.

17. The precise understanding of Rom 5.7 is uncertain, but there is no doubt about the verse's function, cf. Cranfield, *Romans*, p. 264, Schlier, *Römerbrief*, p. 153, Wilckens, *Römer* I, p. 259.

18. Thus clearly in Bornkamm, *Ende*, p. 79.

set the stage for the πολλῷ-μᾶλλον conclusion which follows in 5.9.[19] It is this that provides the disorder in the previous sentence. The repeated ἔτι corresponds to νῦν in Rom 5.9. It is emphasised that the former situation and the present situation are diametrically opposed. And upon this is the conclusion based.

The term πολλῷ μᾶλλον is characteristic of the 'a fortiori conclusion'. It is perhaps most easy to describe it as an analogical conclusion with a built-in rise. An analogical conclusion maintains that whatever has validity in a given case also has validity in a similar case. A conclusion a fortiori reaches a higher degree of validity, since the conclusion proceeds from the less obvious case to a more obvious case. The conclusion receives extra weight. The absolute certainty is emphasised.[20]

In Rom 5.6-8, God's love and the new departure by way of justification appear to be surprising and miraculous because the situation before is the sinfulness of man.

In the light of this, Rom 5.9 concludes that God's help must be even more certain in the future, since now the situation is the direct opposite: the Christians are justified. And God will therefore lead them safely through the wrath to come. The member δικαιωθέντες νῦν ἐν τῷ αἵματι αὐτοῦ thus obtains an important dual function in the context. On a line with the corresponding member in Rom 5.1, it refers back to the decisive turning-point described in Rom 3.21-26. It also becomes a summary of the premise in Rom 5.6-8, which emphasises that the moral corruption of the past has been replaced by a proper relationship with God.[21] It strengthens the certainty of

---

19. Cf. Käsemann, *Römer*, p. 130, Schlier, *Römerbrief*, p. 154, Wilckens, *Römer* I, p. 294.
20. Cf. as to this Wolter, *Rechtfertigung*, p. 170ff., Heinrich Müller, Der rabbinische Qal-Wachomer-Schluss in paulinischer Typologie, *ZNW* 58 (1967), pp. 73-92. Although the conclusion is widespread among rabbis and known under the Hebrew designation, it is a generally understood way of concluding which is also used elsewhere. It is quite superfluous to emphasis, like Wilckens, *Römer* I, p. 298, that rabbis also can use this conclusion in the reverse way, from the smaller to the greater, in the Torah interpretation because the prerequisite is complete harmony in God's creation. Here Paul clearly concludes from the difficult instance to the easy instance.
21. Seen in this way, δικαιωθέντες continues to express God's act of mercy and the new relationship with God, cf. Nygren, *Romarna*, p. 209, Bultmann, *Theologie*, p. 282, Käsemann, *Römer*, p. 130, Schlier, *Römerbrief*, p. 154, Ziesler, *Meaning*, p. 197; and this is confirmed in that it is a parallel to καταλλαγέντες in Rom 5.10, which also deals with God's action and the new relationship. But now the ethical content also enters into the picture, because δικαιωθέντες is the marked contrast to ἀσθενοί, ἀσεβοί and ἁμαρτωλοί in Rom 5.6,8, which expresses both the earlier, perverted relationship with God and the moral corruption associated therewith. Although one may also not wish here to speak of righteousness as a new quality of existence, one must at least recognise that it involves an inherent change in existence that the Christians have been removed from the sphere in which the hostility towards God releases further delusion and sinfulness, cf. Rom 1.18-32. See Victor

God's continued help. The conclusion is thus from the new departure which has already occurred to the even more certain salvation in the end-time.

Because of the unevenness described in the premise in Rom 5.6-8, this first conclusion becomes somewhat incomprehensible. Perhaps this is why it is repeated in a clear form in Rom 5.10. Here the Christians are described as God's enemies during the time before Christ's death, and as reconciled with God in the time following. But otherwise the conclusion is again from help in the past situation to salvation from the future crisis. But something new is also happening in relation to Rom 5.6-9. According to Rom 5.10b, future salvation is secured 'by his (Christ's) life'. This gives an extra rise. This was not necessary for the logic in the πολλῷ-μᾶλλον conclusion. It may have come about for purely stylistic reasons, as a contrast to and a surpassing of death as referred to in Rom 5.10. Probability suggests, however, that something intrinsic must also be implied in the word. Many think that this points towards the resurrection of Christ.[22] But now there is a reference to his life, and it must be reasonable also to consider whether his substance of life and vitality are in mind. In Rom 5.12-21, a decisive importance to the Christians' new life is in fact attributed to Jesus' life and the obedience which characterised it. And a new life-death contrast arises.

Rom 5.6-10 thus strongly underlines the general theme: the certainty of salvation which the Christians have by virtue of the new departure that has occurred.

Rom 5.11 has the same term as in Rom 5.3: οὐ μόνον δὲ, ἀλλά ..., and here also, as in verse 3, we have a shift in the interest from the future to the present salvation effects. And again there is a clear reference to the event which led to the present salvation position: the reason for the Christians' boasting is Christ, δι' οὗ νῦν τὴν καταλλαγὴν ἐλάβομεν.

But it should also be borne in mind that Rom 5.11 is not a new, independent, main clause. It reads οὐ μόνον δὲ, ἀλλὰ <u>καυχώμενοι</u> ... Formally, the verb is thus not parallel to σωθησόμεθα in Rom 5.10 but to καταλλαγέντες, and it is thus in principle subordinate to σωθησόμεθα.[23] Literally,

---

Paul Furnish, *Theology and Ethics in Paul*, Nashville 1968, p. 154, 148f.: 'The concept of δικαιοσύνη ... is therefore not a purely formal one, but has a specific content and meaning'.

22. See as to this Michel, *Römer*, p. 135, Bultmann, *Exegetica*, p. 429, Barrett, *Romans*, p. 108, Wolter, *Rechtfertigung*, p. 194f., Wilckens, *Römer* I, p. 295, Morris, *Romans*, p. 226. Cf. Murray, *Romans*, p. 174f., Jervell, *Gud*, p. 83, Schlier, *Römerbrief*, p. 156, where Jesus' life of resurrection is pointed out. Dodd, *Romans*, p. 98f., alone draws attention to the Christians' new life 'in Christ' and 'in the Spirit'.

23. See Heinr. Aug. Wilh. Meyer, *Kritisch exegetisches Handbuch über den Brief des Paulus an die Römer* (KEK 4)[4], Göttingen 1865, p. 196, Bernhard Weiss, *Der Brief an die Römer* (KEK 4)[9], Göttingen 1899, p. 229. This recognition has been missed in later research but taken up

the sentence would then have to be translated: 'But not only (being reconciled), but also boasting about God ...'

This clarification of the syntactic context is important, although not for an understanding of the point. It is in any case clear that it is the rejoicing over the present effects of the renewal of life which is emphasised. But this shows quite precisely the way in which the thought progresses from Rom 5.10 to Rom 5.11, and this is important to an understanding of the linking of the subsequent context to these verses. We shall return to this.

2.2. The text's meaning in the context

It is now clear what Rom 5.1-11 has to say in the context. Paul himself makes it unmistakably clear that what is concerned is establishing the certainty which characterises the Christians' life now and in the future, after God has become reconciled with them. This he does by the continuous repetition of the theme, and especially by the a fortiori conclusions in Rom 5.6-10, which shows that the real turning-point in existence was God's act of love, atonement. This removed the threatening element from the expected end-time crisis and created confidence that God will allow the new life to continue uninterrupted throughout adversities. In my opinion, Bultmann has rightly maintained that this a fortiori conclusion is the basic structure, not only in these verses but in the entire section, Rom 5.1-11.[24] There is indeed general agreement that the purpose of the text is to stress the present effects of redemption: life and hope.[25]

For this reason, I also think with most interpreters that this is the accentuated introduction to the main section which goes as far as Rom 8.39.[26] Others have wished to see Rom 5.12[27] or Rom 6.1[28] as the new input. It is

---

again by Wolter, *Rechtfertigung*, p. 196ff., who emphasises that there is always complete congruence between the two members which are linked together by οὐ μόνον δέ ... After οὐ μόνον δέ ... in verse 11, καταλλαγέντες is thus also implied. Cf. Murray, *Romans*, p. 268, Schlier, *Römerbrief*, p. 156f., Cilliers Breytenbach, *Versöhnung* (WMANT 60), Neukirchen-Vluyn 1989, p. 152f., 172.

24. Bultmann, *Exegetica*, p. 425. Cf. the triumphant rise in Rom 5.3 and Rom 5.11, and the period in Rom 5.3-5.

25. See Althaus, *Römer*, p. 52, Dodd, *Romans*, s. 99, Michel, *Römer*, p. 130 with n. 1, Kuss, *Römerbrief*, p. 198f., Bruce, *Romans*, p. 122, Jervell, *Gud*, p. 76ff., Cranfield, *Romans*, p. 260, Schlier, *Römerbrief*, p. 157, Wilckens, *Römer* I, p. 300. Different here Käsemann, *Römer*, p. 124ff.

26. Thus Lietzmann, *Römer*, p. 58, cf. p. 89, Dodd, *Romans*, p. 93, Nygren, *Romarna*, p. 196f., Michel, *Römer*, p. 129, Schmidt, *Römer*, p. 89, Käsemann, *Römer*, p. 123, Jervell, *Gud*, p. 76f., Schlier, *Römerbrief*, p. 137f., Cranfield, *Romans*, p. 252ff., Heil, *Romans*, p. 35ff.

27. Thus Theodor Zahn, *Der Brief des Paulus an die Römer* (KNT 6), Leipzig 1910, p. 259ff., Henning Paulsen, *Überlieferung und Auslegung in Römer 8* (WMANT 43), Neukirchen-

clear that such subdivisions are arguable. There is often a backwards connection, even where new inputs are concerned. It is thus clear that Rom 5.1-11 passes on major concepts from Rom 3.21-4.25 about justification by virtue of Jesus' death, and that it concerns liberation from the sinfulness and wrath of God which dominated the former existence according to Rom 1.18-3.20. But here I wish to emphasise the enthusiastic and preceptive tone which from now on characterises the presentation.

In addition, there is an important thematic connection from the beginning of Rom 5 to the end of Rom 8. Hope and certainty are stressed from first to last.[29] And there is a crucial 'before-now structure' which marks the entire section. As will be shown below, there begins in the a fortiori conclusion in Rom 5.6-10 a before-now contrast which is passed on via Rom 5.11 in the Adam-Christ typology and continues right up to Rom 8.17. This before-now structure thus also binds Rom 6 together with Rom 5.12-21 (as will be seen from the next chapter).

2.3. The transition to Rom 5.12-21

If we are to understand the transition from Rom 5.11 to 5.12, the central a fortiori conclusions in Rom 5.6-10 become crucial. They contain four elements: the premise takes its point of departure in 1: a past situation (sinfulness, enmity towards God), which is the background to 2: the utterly surprising and incomprehensible past event (justification, reconciliation by virtue of Christ's death); the conclusion takes its point of departure in 3: the present situation created thereby (righteousness, peace with God), which is the background to 4: the future event which now becomes quite obvious (salvation from the coming wrath). In Rom 5.6-9 and Rom 5.10, the emphasis has been on the eschatological event and the certainty which the Christians now have in relation to this event (Item 4).

In Rom 5.11, Paul continues triumphantly to praise also the present situation (Item 3). He places this at the centre, whereas in Rom 5.9 and Rom 5.10b it was only the background to the point. It is clearly to be seen grammatically that in Rom 5.11 Paul concentrates on what has hitherto been only a prerequisite for the conclusion. Καυχώμενοι is formally subordinate to the

Vluyn 1974, p. 13ff.

28. Thus J. Huby, *Saint Paul: Épitre aux Romains*[2], Paris 1957, p. 27, Bruce, *Romans*, p. 68, 134, Matthew Black, *Romans (NCeB)*, London 1973, p. 92, Wilckens, *Römer* I, p. 17ff. etc., Morris, *Romans*, p. 243, Stuhlmacher, *Römer*, p. 83.

29. See in particular N.A. Dahl, Two notes on Romans 5, *StTh* 5 (1951), pp. 37-40, who has demonstrated a series of connecting lines between Rom 5 and 8, and von der Osten-Sacken, *Römer* 8, pp. 57-60, 124ff., where the viewpoint is elaborated.

main verb in Rom 5.10a and parallel to καταλλαγέντες, although it is quite clear that there is an independent interest in the Christians' current situation.[30] In Rom 5.6-10, this situation (Item 3) stood in marked contrast to the previous sinful situation (Item 1), and therefore the stage is now set for an independent comparison between the pre-Christian and the Christian existence.

What has happened simultaneously is that Christ's act (Item 2), which was considered as the ending of the previous situation in Rom 5.6-10, is now also emphasised as the cause of the new situation (Item 3). This has been prepared in Rom 5.10b, which tells of the importance of Christ's life to the future salvation, and it is stressed in Rom 5.11: ... διὰ τοῦ κυρίου ἡμῶν 'Ιησοῦ Χριστοῦ, δι' οὗ νῦν τὴν καταλλαγὴν ἐλάβομεν. This means that the stage is set not only for a comparison between the new Christian life and the old pre-Christian life but also for a comparison between Christ and the cause of the old situation. We thus arrive at the Adam-Christ typology, in which Adam is set up as an antipole to Christ and the Adamic existence as a contrast to the Christian life.[31]

It thus transpires that Rom 5.12-21 is a consequence and a continuation of the train of thought in Rom 5.11 and the preceding verses. What is important is still Christ's significance to the current life of the Christians, but

---

30. Cf. note 23 above.
31. The complicated development of thought can be shown diagrammatically: Rom 5.6-9 and Rom 5.10 thus contain four members which can be placed on a time line; points 1 and 3 are contrasts:

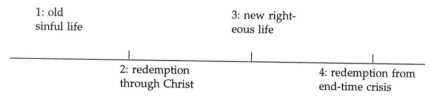

The a fortiori conclusion has the form: if 1 results in 2, 3 must all the more result in 4. The point is item 4.
After the shift in emphasis in Rom 5.11, where 3 becomes the chief concern with 2 as prerequisite, and still in contrast to 1, the prerequisite for 1 also comes into the picture:

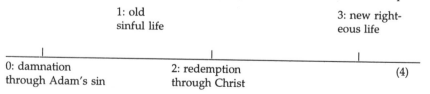

The comparison in Rom 5.12-21 has the form: that 0 results in 1, corresponds to 2 resulting in 3.

this is now presented against the background of Adam's importance to the Adamic life. This means first that the Διὰ τοῦτο which introduces Rom 5.12 can really be taken at face value.[32] Second, the closeness of the connection between Rom 5.11 and Rom 5.12 is confirmed, as well as the development here of the before-now structure.

3. The intention of Rom 5.12-21

3.1. The anacoluthon in Rom 5.12

Paul begins immediately in Rom 5.12 by comparing the 'Adam event' and the 'Christ event', for which the term in Rom 5.11 sets the stage. But this is not carried through. The verse ends with a broken sentence.

It begins with a ὥσπερ: 'Therefore, just as sin came into the world through one man, and death came through sin, and so death spread to all because all have sinned...' There is thus no second member in the period. A sentence introduced by οὕτως, which is to present the corresponding Christ side, is lacking. It appears only when the comparison is finally implemented in Rom 5.18.

This anacoluthon is crucial to the structure of the entire passage:[33] After the interruption, Rom 5.13-14 is a parenthesis about the actual dominion of sin and death over Adamic mankind. In the conclusion to Rom 5.14, where it says that Adam is a 'type' of 'the one who was to come' — and that of course is Christ — Paul tries to return to the comparison intended. But a new parenthesis, Rom 5.15-15, explains that the antithetic paralleling of the Adam side and the Christ side is nevertheless not quite adequate for the relationship between the two sides. At last in Rom 5.18-21 the comparison between the effects of Adam's sin and of Christ's act of justification is accomplished — three times.

But the anacoluthon also causes problems. Why does it arise? Or is there

---

32. It is important to see that the close connection between Christ and the Christians is already given ahead of the complicated comparison with Adam-Adamites, cf. Freundorfer, *Erbsünde*, p. 217, L. Cerfaux, *Le Christ dans la Theologie de saint Paul*, Paris 1951, p. 117f., Cranfield, *Romans*, p. 271. Otherwise, the term merely becomes a colourless transitional particle as in Lietzmann, *Römer*, p. 26, Bultmann, *Exegetica*, p. 433, Paulsen, *Überlieferung*, p. 14, Benedict Englezakis, Rom 5,12-15 and the Pauline Teaching on the Lord's Death, *Biblica* 58 (1977), pp. 231-36; p. 231, Schlier, *Römerbrief*, p. 159.
33. See in particular Bornkamm, *Ende*, 80ff., Brandenburger, *Adam*, p. 10, 158ff. Cf. also Huby, *Romains*, p. 188, Bultmann, *Exegetica*, p. 432, Murray, *Romans*, p. 180f., Jervell, *Gud*, p. 84, Wilckens, *Römer* I, p. 307f., Schlier, *Römerbrief*, p. 164, 166, 172, Morris, *Romans*, p. 228f., Dunn, *Romans*, p. 272.

any anacoluthon at all? These questions must be considered in the context of the other problems in the verse.

3.2. The causes of sin and death according to Rom 5.12

At first, Rom 5.12ab appears to be simple and to present no problems.

'Therefore, just as sin came into the world through one man, and death came through sin ...' This merely concerns how sin and death initially emerged. But then the problems come in Rom 5.12c, and especially in Rom 5.12d: καὶ οὕτως εἰς πάντας ἀνθρώπους ὁ θάνατος διῆλθεν, ἐφ' ᾧ πάντες ἥμαρτον. Discussion has often revolved around concepts of 'original sin', and have linked up with ἐφ' ᾧ which introduces Rom 5.12d.[34]

A number of attempts have been made to understand the term quite simply as a preposition following upon the relative pronoun. Most notable is Augustine's perception, that it corresponds to the Latin 'in quo', refers back to Adam (= 'one man' in Rom 5.12a), and thus indicates that all are part of Adam's sin and are collectively embraced by its effects.[35] It may be immediately objected as regards this interpretation that the distance from the word which must be referred back to is too great for an impartial reader to apprehend, and in addition that it is an imprecise rendering of the preposition.[36] The latter objection can be avoided by the correct causal translation of ἐπί + the dative: '... because of whom (i.e. Adam) all have sinned'.[37] But the first objection still applies. It has therefore also been attempted to allow the relative pronoun to refer back to other members — either to 'death' in Rom 5.12c or, perceived in the neuter, to the entire preceding context: 'because of which all sinned'.[38] The idea is then that it is the existence of (sin and) death which causes mankind's sin. There is still a fateful dependence upon Adam's Fall. But these are laboured attempts at interpretation. Against them all it can be said that there is a more obvious understanding of the term under discussion.

---

34. Cf. the survey in Cranfield, *Romans*, pp. 274-79.
35. Thus still W. Manson, Notes on the Argument of Romans 1-8, in: A.J.B. Higgins (ed.), *New Testament Essays. Studies in Memory of Thomas Walter Manson*, Manchester 1959, pp. 150-64; p. 159.
36. See the opposing reasoning in Cranfield, *Romans*, p. 276f., Huby, *Romains*, p. 190.
37. Thus Cerfaux, *Christ*, p. 179, J. Cambier, Péchés des hommes et péché d'Adam en Rom. V. 12, *NTS* 11 (1965), pp. 217-55; p. 242ff., 253.
38. Thus Zahn, *Römer*, p. 265, Nygren, *Romarna*, p. 220f., Schmidt, *Römer*, p. 98, A. Feuillet, Le règne de la mort et le règne de la vie (Rom V, 12-21), *RB* 77 (1970), pp. 481-520; p. 489ff., Black, *Romans*, p. 88f. ('wherefore'). Cf. F.W. Danker, Romans V. 12. Sin under Law, *NTS* 14 (1968), pp. 424-39, who thinks that the relative pronoun must refer back to an implied word, 'the law' — an interpretation which seems somewhat arbitrary.

Normally, ἐφ' ᾧ functions as an established expression, a causal conjunction: 'because', 'since'.[39] This is also natural here, and is indeed the interpretation chosen by the great majority:[40] '... death penetrated to all men, because they all sinned'.

But there may still be a tendency to understand the verb ἥμαρτον collectively, so that in the context it is still intended to express that men sin as a consequence of Adam's original sin. This can be achieved if the verb is to mean that all were sinning simultaneously.[41] Or it can be done simply by implying an 'in Adam' in the sentence.[42] But the objection to this is that in such a case much is left to the reader's imagination. And normally the verb is used individually about the specific sins which man independently commits.[43]

Nevertheless many recoil from the wholly individual interpretation, probably not only for dogmatic reasons: it is the Pelagian view that man sins independently (merely following Adam's example).[44] There are two other weighty reasons to be included in the considerations.

(a) The structure of the entire Rom 5.12-21 section should require the

---

39. Cf. Blass, Debrunner and Rehkopf, *Grammatik*, § 294 n. 6, cf. § 235 n. 3, Bauer, *Wörterbuch*, col. 569. This corresponds to the meaning in other Pauline incidences: 2 Cor 5.4; Phil 3.12; 4.10.

40. See Lietzmann, *Römer*, p. 60ff., F. Prat, *La Theologie de saint Paul* I, Paris 1924, p. 256f., n. 1, Freundorfer, *Erbsünde*, p. 232ff., Lagrange, *Romains*, p. 106, Michel, *Römer*, p. 138, Kuss, *Römerbrief*, p. 232ff., Huby, *Romains*, p. 190, Murray, *Romans*, p. 183, Larsson, *Christus*, p. 177, Brandenburger, *Adam*, p. 175, Käsemann, *Römer*, p. 140, Cranfield, *Romans*, p. 274ff., Schlier, *Römerbrief*, p. 162, Wilckens, *Römer* I, p. 315f. S. Lyonnet: Le sens de ἐφ' ᾧ en Rom 5,12 et l'exégèse des Pères grecs, *Biblica* 36 (1955), pp. 436-56, is in agreement with James Hope Moulton, *A Grammar of New Testament Greek* I³, Edinburgh 1908, p. 107, pleading that it expresses the (fulfilled) condition ('sous la condition que ...', 'on condition that ...'); but this corresponds to the causal meaning ('since'), cf. A.J.M. Wedderburn, The Theological Structure of Romans V. 12, *NTS* 19 (1973), pp. 339-54; p. 349f.; and it can therefore not be used as an argument for the translation 'wherefore' as in Black, *Romans*, p. 389.

41. See Lagrange, *Romains*, p. 105ff., Shedd, *Man*, p. 108f., Morris, *Romans*, p. 231ff., in which the aorist form is interpreted to mean that all must have sinned, as a once-and-for-all event. Grammatically this is untenable, which is immediately shown by the earlier incidences of the word: Rom 2.12; 3.23. It is an aorist of the complexive type, cf. Blass, Debrunner and Rehkopf, *Grammatik*, § 332,2.

42. See Freundorfer, *Erbsünde*, p. 239ff., who despite great misgivings chooses this expedient — but in his opinion anything else will destroy the understanding. Cf. also Prat, *Théologie* I, p. 256f. n. 1, Huby, *Romains*, p. 191, Murray, *Romans*, p. 182ff., Larsson, *Christus*, p. 178, Bruce, *Romans*, p. 130.

43. As is also clearly acknowledged in Freundorfer, *Erbsünde*, p. 239, Murray, *Romans*, p. 182f.

44. Cf. Murray, *Romans*, p. 182f., Cranfield, *Romans*, p. 275f. His solution is that every man sins as a result of the corrupting nature inherited from Adam, p. 275, cf. p. 279.

more integrated understanding of Rom 5.12d. The viewpoint is that from the Christ side there is complete dependence upon Christ's act of redemption (according to the justification doctrine); similarly, the Adamites must be completely dependent upon Adam's Fall.[45] I shall return to this viewpoint.

(b) There should be tension-charged, dual reasons for man's sinfulness, if Rom 5.12d is concerned with individual transgressions. The viewpoint here is that a reason has already been given in Rom 5.12a-c: i.e. that Adam brought sin and death into the world, and that death thus came to all men. Only by the collective interpretation of Rom 5.12d can this tension be avoided.[46] The matter might also, however, be presented from the aspect that Paul's view of the cause of sin is so complex and dialectic that it must be expressed by this duality.[47] But these considerations can also lead to a different, significant perception of the verse.

Bornkamm and Brandenburger have an explanation for the tension between the two reasons, which at the same time suggests why the anacoluthon arises.[48]

The two widely differing reasons for the emergence of sin are said to originate respectively from the gnostic tradition employed by Paul and from his rectifying modification. In Rom 5.12b, Paul is said to begin by expressing a main idea from a gnostic myth, i.e. that Adam by his transgression was guilty of causing sin and death to dominate the entire world of man. Rom 5.12c establishes that for this reason death is the fate of all mankind. On the other hand, Rom 5.12d gives a different explanation of the universality of death. Thereby tension arises. Paul cannot accept the fate-related aspect on the Adam side — since this would mean that redemption would also have to be intended as a new and inescapable natural force.

Therefore comes the modification, which establishes against Rom 5.12a-c that sin is man's own guilt and responsibility. This new idea in Rom 5.12d must then be further substantiated in Rom 5.13-14. But thereby comes an interruption which is so long that Paul cannot carry through the line in the sentence. In this way the sentence break is understood as resulting from the

---

45. See in particular Freundorfer, *Erbsünde*, p. 241ff., Murray, *Romans*, p. 183ff., Black, *Romans*, p. 88, Morris, *Romans*, p. 332. It is also pointed out that the Adamites are collectively encompassed by Adam's sin according to Rom 5.17-19, and that this is assumed in Rom 5.13-14.

46. Thus Freundorfer, *Erbsünde*, p. 240f., Larsson, *Christus* p. 177, Schmidt, *Römer*, p. 99, Black, *Romans*, p. 86.

47. Such a dual causality is suggested in Wedderburn, Structure, p. 351f., Dunn, *Romans*, p. 273f., Wilckens, *Römer* I, p. 316, where it is pointed out that there is accordance on this point with the Jewish perception. Cf. also Käsemann, *Römer*, p. 141, Schlier, *Römerbrief*, p. 163f., Ziesler, *Romans*, p. 147.

48. Bornkamm, *Ende*, p. 83ff., Brandenburger, *Adam*, p. 175ff., cf. Jüngel, *Unterwegs*, p. 154, Schlier, *Römerbrief*, p. 163f.

breaking up of the thought-context by Paul himself to correct the gnostic, original-sin concepts adopted, with all this involves.

This means that the break, which arises at the syntactic level, is not meant to be accidental but almost intentional, because it corresponds with a break in the actual matter described.

But this is quite a complicated perception. For the time being I shall disregard problems of religio-historical prerequisites and methodical considerations.[49] But the question is whether the recipients would have had any chance of understanding that this was the specific point of this tension-charged, self-contradictory period. Would they not rather try to understand the sentence more simply and straightforwardly?

For it transpires that a definite, quite restricted understanding of the members in Rom 5.12a-c must be presupposed for tension to be in any way concerned in relation to Rom 5.12d.

If εἰς τὸν κόσμον εἰσῆλθεν in Rom 5.12a is read directly, it seems merely to express that that sin appeared in the world for the first time. If tension is to arise, loaded meanings of the words must be chosen. The word κόσμος is intended to relate only to mankind.[50] And the verb εἰσῆλθεν, which is also implied in Rom 5.12b, is to be understood as meaning that sin and death spread completely and had overall implications.[51] But it also means that εἰς τὸν κόσμον εἰσῆλθεν comes to mean precisely the same as εἰς πάντας ἀνθρώπους ... διῆλθεν in Rom 5.12c. This means that there is no advance in thought in Rom 5.12c, despite that the word εἰσῆλθεν does not directly have the same meaning as διῆλθεν. It would be more natural to understand it as an advance from merely 'to enter into', 'appear to be', to 'to prevail', 'to spread to everyone'.[52] Also, οὕτως must be perceived unambiguously as a consecutive particle ('in this way', 'thus'),[53] where in the context emphasis can also be given to the comparative function ('in the same way', 'so').[54]

In the light of this, it seems unlikely that a reader will simply arrive at the understanding of Rom 5.12a-c which will involve a contradiction relative to Rom 5.12d. A simpler understanding of the verse would have been chosen instead, if this were possible.

---

49. They will be discussed below in section 4.3.
50. See Bornkamm, *Ende*, p. 83, Brandenburger, *Adam*, p. 161ff., Käsemann, *Römer*, p. 139.
51. See Bornkamm, *Ende*, p. 83 n. 2, Brandenburger, *Adam*, p. 160.
52. Thus Sanday and Headlam, *Romans*, p. 133 ('contains the force of distribution; made its way to each individual member of the race'), Freundorfer, *Erbsünde*, p. 230, Michel, *Römer*, p. 138, Murray, *Romans*, p. 182, Wilckens, *Römer I*, p. 315, cf. Morris, *Romans*, p. 230, n. 46.
53. Clearly in Brandenburger, *Adam*, p. 164f., cf. Weiss, *Römer*, p. 236, Freundorfer, *Erbsünde*, p. 230f.
54. Cf. Murray, *Romans*, p. 182. See note 57 below.

In my opinion, it is possible to understand Rom 5.12b without the tension.

The word οὗτως must be understood in a broader sense, so that the meaning 'in the same way' also rings true. This meaning has been used in an attempt to understand Rom 5.12 as a complete sentence, entirely without anacoluthon: 'As death came into the world through one man, and through sin, death, so death spread to all people, because they all sinned'.[55] But this attempt at interpretation is excluded for inherent reasons. It cannot be evaded that the stage is set in the context for a comparison between Christ and Adam.[56] But grammatically there is no objection to emphasising that οὗτως primarily expresses accordance.[57] If we are content with this latter part of the reasoning, in my opinion we arrive at quite a simple understanding of the text and of the anacoluthon.

Rom 5.12ab is concerned with sin's entering the world by Adam's transgression and death's arrival as a result. Rom 5.12cd is concerned with the fact that all subsequent people also suffered death because they also sinned. It may be noted that there is a beautiful chiastic structure (sin-death-death-sin).[58] The two sides are bound together — Adam and the Adamites — by οὗτως. First and foremost, an accordance is established between the two sides. The way is also prepared for a kind of connection between them. But

55. The viewpoint is to be found in very few places in the modern debate: Cerfaux, *Christ*, p. 178 (hesitatingly, it concerns 'en premier lieu'), Barrett, *Romans*, p. 109f. (in the translation), Robin Scroggs, *The Last Adam*, Philadelphia 1966, p. 79f., n. 13, Niels Hyldahl, *Paulus' breve* [The Letters of Paul], Copenhagen 1977, p. 169 (in the translation), John T. Kirby, The Syntax of Romans 5,12: A Rhetorical Approach, *NTS* 33 (1987), pp. 283-86. When the word οὗτως is no longer perceived as 'thus' in the sense 'in *this* way' (which indicates a causality), but in the sense 'in the *same* way', the tension is released. Rom 5.12ab now merely states that sin showed itself for the first time with Adam, who therefore died. Rom 5.12cd says that something similar will come to apply to all other people, that they have sinned and must die.
56. Cf. the explanation of the connection between Rom 5.11 and 5.12, section 2.3 above. The introductory Διὰ τοῦτο becomes meaningless if it was intended as an introduction to a passage which exclusively concerns the Adam side. Pointing in the same direction is the demonstratively preceding 'through one man' in Rom 5.12a, which requires that the following sentence be introduced in the same way, as is also the case in Rom 5.18.
57. The understanding of οὗτως in the sense 'in the same way' is not only possible but is very obvious directly. The introductory ὥσπερ creates an expectation of a subsequent οὗτως sentence to such a degree that there is in the first instance a temptation to perceive Rom 5.12cd as the expected sentence, cf. below. The term καὶ οὗτως can also be synonymous with οὗτως καί, which the interpretation requires, cf. Kirby, Syntax, p. 283f., Scroggs, *Adam*, p. 79f. n. 13, Cerfaux, *Christ*, p. 178.
58. Cf. Dibelius, Worte, p. 8, Scroggs, *Adam*, p. 79 n. 13., Cranfield, *Romans*, p. 274, Englezakis, Rom 5,12-15, p. 231, Wedderburn, Structure, p. 351f., Wilckens, *Römer* I, p. 315, Dunn, *Romans*, p. 273.

of what this consists is not yet specified in detail.[59] This is perhaps what Paul is about to do from Rom 5.13 onwards — and thus we have a reason for the broken sentence.

But there is also another reason for the anacoluthon. The sentence is already impossible to carry through when Paul uses the word οὕτως in Rom 5.12c because it was by this very word that the main clause expected was to be introduced. Confusion would be created if Paul continued. The problem is that there is an 'as-so structure' on two levels. Adam and Christ correspond to one another, and there is an accordance between respectively Adam and the Adamites, Christ and the Christians.[60] Had Paul completed the train of thought, it would have had to be according to the pattern: 'In the same way as it applies to the Adam side, that in the same way as it applies to Adam, so is the case with the Adamites, so it also applies to the Christ side, that in the same way as it applies to Christ, so it is also the case with the Christians'. There is thus an obvious reason for Paul to break off. He has made his intention clear, but he would have lost clarity had he completed the train of thought.[61]

It can be established that there is quite a simple way to understand Rom 5.12, if at first one allows to remain open the question of what kind of connection there is between the sin of Adam and that of the Adamites. There is no doubt about Paul's intention: he wishes to begin the broadly imagined Adam-Adamite-Christ-Christian comparison. And in the course of this he will allow the connection between all these members to become clear.[62]

3.3. Rom 5.13-14 — the factual dominion of death and sin

It is pointed out that a rationale begins in Rom 5.13, and the text that follows is concerned with the factual dominion of death over the whole of mankind.

---

59. Cf. Dibelius, *Worte*, p. 7f. See also Murray, *Romans*, pp. 182-86, who admits that this simple ('Pelagian') interpretation is the natural, direct understanding of Rom 5.12, but he rejects this (cf. notes 42-44 above) because it is in contrast to the line in the letter, especially the following context. A frequent argument is that the close connection between Adam and the Adamites is advanced later in the section and must also therefore be assumed in Rom 5.12; thus Freundorfer, *Erbsünde*, p. 241ff., Brandenburger, *Adam*, p. 162ff., Black, *Romans*, p. 88, Morris, *Romans*, p. 332. But it does not apply to the interpretation here presented. The possibility is under discussion that an advance in thinking and a tightening-up of the formulation occurs in the course of the section, cf. Dunn, *Romans*, p. 290.
60. Cf. Jüngel, *Unterwegs*, p. 154, Cerfaux, *Christ*, p. 178 n. 1.
61. It may also be noted that in the following verses Paul avoids the use of ὥσπερ-οὕτως. The word ὁμοίωμα is used in Rom 5.14 about the relationship between Adam and the Adamites and the word τύπος about the relationship between Adam and Christ.
62. Cf. Schnackenburg, Adam-Christus-Typologie, p. 39.

It is probably therefore to be expected that the chief concern is to expand and amplify the assertion in Rom 5.12 about universal sinfulness.[63]

But problems arise in understanding the precise connection.[64] There is thus reason for caution. Rom 5.13a emphasises that sin was in the world before the law came. Thus sin was also present during the time from Adam to Moses, as is also said in Rom 5.14. Rom 5.13b, ἁμαρτία οὐκ ἐλλογεῖται μὴ ὄντος νόμου, can be interpreted in two ways. The verb ἐλλογεῖται, 'charged to one's account', can be understood as divine bookkeeping which stamps something as sin. Then the sentence expresses, as in Rom 4.15b, that there is no violation without law. This is the opposite to Rom 5.13a, and may be understood as an imagined objection which is rejected by Rom 5.14.[65] But the verb can probably also be understood in a broader meaning as about a human registration of sin, i.e. that sin is not perceived if there is no law.[66] In any event, Rom 5.14 establishes that death has dominion over everyone. All things considered, the factuality of death is evidence of universal sinfulness. This also applies to those who lived before Moses and could not sin 'like Adam' (who certainly had a specific commandment to transgress). But apparently it must be brought out that they sinned in a different way, so that sin's universality applies irrespective of the law.[67]

3.4. Rom 5.15-17 — an abundance of grace and redemption

Paul has tried to return to the Adam-Christ typology in Rom 5.14b, where it says that Adam is the type of the one to come. But the comparison is still not implemented in the form intended.

First there comes in Rom 5.15-17 a clarification of the differences between the two sides. It is emphasised in the two parallels expressed in Rom

---

63. On this point there is widespread agreement among interpreters, cf. Freundorfer, *Erbsünde*, p. 247ff., Bornkamm, *Ende*, p. 84, Brandenburger, *Adam*, p. 201, Murray, *Romans*, p. 189, von der Osten-Sacken, *Römer 8*, p. 166f., Wilckens, *Römer I*, p. 318f.

64. Cf. Bultmann, *Exegetica*, p. 433, Heikki Räisänen, *Paul and the Law* (WUNT 29), Tübingen 1983, p. 146, n. 91.

65. Thus Black, *Romans*, p. 89f., Englezakis, Rom 5,12-15, p. 232f., Morris, *Romans*, p. 233. Cf. Gerhard Friedrich, 'Ἁμαρτία οὐκ ἐλλογεῖται. Röm 5,13, *ThLZ* 9 (1952), cols. 523-28, in which the opinion is that sinfulness is punished by physical death, but is not maintained on the Day of Judgement.

66. Cf. Schlier, *Römerbrief*, p. 165, Hyldahl, *Breve*, p. 189.

67. Thus explicitly Dunn, *Romans*, p. 275, cf. Michel, *Römer*, p. 139, Schlier, *Römerbrief*, p. 166. Different in Freundorfer, *Erbsünde*, pp. 247-53 (who maintains that on the contrary the intention in Rom 5.13a is that there are some who have not sinned personally; they die as punishment for Adam's sin), Dahl, Notes, p. 43ff., Jüngel, *Unterwegs*, p. 155f. (where it is asserted that only the law gives sin and death eschatological power), cf. Wilckens, *Römer* I, p. 317f.

5.15a and Rom 5.16a that there is a difference between 'the fall' and 'the gift of grace' and between 'the fall of the one' and 'the gift'. This is amplified in the reasons that follow. But although the difference is now emphasised there is no démenti of the connection.[68] Quite the reverse. Since the crucial difference is merely that if from the Adam side it was given that the consequences for the successors would be powerful, then it is even more obvious that the consequences for Christ's successors will be overwhelming. This is a matter of the new exceeding the old. This is the evident point of the two πολλῷ-μᾶλλον conclusions in Rom 5.15b and Rom 5.17b.

But the immediate effect is as if there are difficulties about these a fortiori conclusions. Rom 5.15b goes from the death of the many as a result of the fall of the one to the fact that God's grace and gift will come in abundance to the many by virtue of Christ's act. And it must be more apparent that the restoration has eternal consequences than was the case with the disintegration. There seems to be a movement from what is relatively easy to imagine, that one man can infect all his descendants with sin and death, to what is far more difficult, that one man might overcome sin and death among all people.[69] It is even said directly in Rom 5.16b that restoration is far more difficult because the status of many people must be changed, from fall to δικαίωμα (which presumably means the justification of all[70]). And this is precisely why the a fortiori conclusion in Rom 5.17 must have validity.

It is possible that there is the hidden premise, that God has power everywhere. Destruction is therefore surprising and incredible, whereas restoration is obvious.[71]

But one can maintain the logic at the direct level if one defines what the subject of the conclusion is. It is not certain that what must be evidenced is the restoration itself — that Christ's act, like Adam's, has consequences for successors. This has already been established. The soteriological consequences of Christ events have been emphasised in Rom 5.6-11 precisely as a

---

68. Against Bornkamm, *Ende*, pp. 85-87, Brandenburger, *Adam*, pp. 219-31. Cf. Murray, *Romans*, p. 192, Schlier, *Römerbrief*, p. 166.

69. In Rom 5.15-16, cf. 5.18-19, οἱ πολλοί is used synonymously with πάντες, cf. Jeremias, πολλοί, *ThWNT* VI, pp. 536-45, Barrett, *Romans*, p. 114, Black, *Romans*, p. 90, Schlier, *Römerbrief*, p. 169, Morris, *Romans*, p. 235, M. Eugene Boring, The Language of Universal Salvation in Paul, *JBL* 105 (1986), pp. 269-92; p. 284ff. Different in Sanders, *Paul*, p. 473.

70. In Greek, verbal nouns can vary somewhat in meaning. Here, δικαίωμα appears to mean the same as δικαίωσις; the form using -μα may have been chosen because all other nouns in the sentence have this ending. Cf. Bauer, *Wörterbuch*, col. 392, Barrett, *Romans*, p. 115, Käsemann, *Römer*, p. 146, Ziesler, *Meaning*, p. 198.

71. Cf. Bultmann, *Exegetica*, p. 435, Bornkamm, *Ende*, p. 85f., Michel, *Römer*, p. 140f., Brandenburger, *Adam*, p. 228f., Schlier, *Römerbrief*, p. 167f., Wilckens, *Römer* I, p. 323f.

prelude to this section (and similar consequences on the Adam side in Rom 5.12-14). One may therefore consider whether the restoration is a prerequisite for the conclusion. If this crucial event forms part of the premise, the objective of the conclusion is to show that the restoration which took place and the consequences which occurred will prove to be overwhelming and prevail invincibly. It is then fully comprehensible that Rom 5.16b stresses that the restoration occurring is far greater than the destruction, since if the destruction were of violent and lasting significance this must be so to an even greater degree in regard to the new situation, which is due to a far greater power.[72]

This understanding is especially confirmed by the other implementation of the conclusion in Rom 5.17, where the core is not to be seen in the Christians' having been made the object of grace but in the dominion they have thereby commenced. In the a fortiori conclusion in Rom 5.17, there is no complete parallelism between the members on the Adam side and on the Christ side. Rom 5.17a says that 'because of the one man's trespass, death exercised dominion through that one'. Rom 5.17b states that 'those who receive the abundance of grace and the free gift of righteousness exercise dominion in life through the one man, Jesus Christ'. This can be explained as stylistic variation, but it may also have a deeper meaning. The participial member οἱ τὴν περισσείαν τῆς χάριτος καὶ τῆς δωρεᾶς τῆς δικαιοσύνης λαμβάνοντες apparently has the same function as the corresponding members in Rom 5.9-10 (δικαιωθέντες νῦν ἐν τῷ αἵματι αὐτοῦ ..., καταλλαγέντες ...), which summarise the premise of the a fortiori conclusion. The restoration is thus looked back upon as that which is given. And it is emphasised what an abundance of grace and what a gift are to be found in the justification that has occurred.[73] A dominion of the vital force can therefore be looked forward to. The future form βασιλεύσουσιν is probably meant to express that the new dominion is certain to extend into the future.[74]

But the very same members have been interpreted as expressing directly opposing points, reservations. Thus, λαμβάνοντες has been understood as a condition: 'only in so far as they receive it'.[75] But it must be stressed that

---

72. Cf. Brandenburger, *Adam*, pp. 228-30.
73. Here δικαιοσύνη has quite expressly the 'nature of a gift', and at the same time it is God's power that comes to the fore, cf. Käsemann, *Versuche* II, p. 182f., *Römer*, p. 147, and in particular Ziesler, *Meaning*, p. 198, where it is pointed out that here the term has not merely a forensic-relational meaning but must also concern the Christian person's 'manner of life'.
74. Thus Murray, *Romans*, p. 198, Schnackenburg, Adam-Christus-Typologie, p. 40, cf. the future forms in Rom 6.2,5,8,14, and the discussion in Chapter VII, section 3.6, below.
75. Thus Bornkamm, *Ende*, p. 87, Sanders, *Paul*, p. 473, cf. Schlier, *Römerbrief*, p. 174f., 'Dies natürlich nur, wenn der Mensch zu den λαμβάνοντες von v. 17b gehört'.

normally λαμβάνειν has a passive meaning, so that one can scarcely see anything special in this detail.[76] Similarly, a reservation has been seen in the future form βασιλεύσουσιν; it is meant to stress that the final dominion is something eschatological in the future.[77] But it will be difficult for a reader to perceive such a hidden point if the main tendency of the section is the opposite — to stress the power of the justification which has occurred.

3.5. The comparison in Rom 5.18-21

At long last the comparison is made between the effects of Adam's sin and the effects of Christ's act of righteousness. This occurs in three rounds: Rom 5.18,19,21. The repetition stresses the section's intention: dependence on Adam and his sin has been replaced by dependence on Christ and the righteousness he represents. That the emphasis is on righteousness is stressed by the fact that four different words from the stem δικαι- occur in this short section.

The introductory ἄρα οὖν presents Rom 5.18 as the conclusion of the preceding discussion about the connection between Adam-Adamites and Christ-Christians. The sentence is elliptical. Both subject and verb are lacking in the subordinate clause about the Adam side, as well as in the main clause about the Christ side. The clauses consist of only three prepositional groups each. In the first group, introduced by διά, the point of departure is stated for the previous situation and present situation respectively: Adam's Fall, his faulty conduct and the diametrically opposite conduct: Christ's δικαίωμα, 'act of righteousness'.[78] The last two prepositional groups in each sentence introduced by εἰς, state the end-point of the two sides. Εἰς πάντας ἀνθρώπους (in both the subordinate and in the main clause) emphasises that the

---

76. Cf. Murray, *Romans*, p. 198, Boring, Language, p. 286f.
77. Cf. Bultmann, *Exegetica*, p. 437, Bornkamm, *Ende*, p. 87, Brandenburger, *Adam*, p. 230, Klaiber, *Rechtfertigung*, p. 119. More subtle here is Käsemann, *Römer*, p. 147, Andrie B. du Toit, Dikaiosyne in Röm 6, ZThK 76 (1979), pp. 261-91; p. 290. Precisely because the definitive turning-point which has occurred is the consequence of the overwhelming grace and gift of righteousness, it is difficult to see how the point can be that this vital force will commence only someday.
78. From the position in the context, where παράπτωμα stands as an antithesis and ὑπακοή in Rom 5.19 as a parallel, it is clear that δικαίωμα, which normally has a certain breadth of meaning, must have this (ethical) content in this passage, cf. Bauer, *Wörterbuch*, col. 392, Bornkamm, *Ende*, p. 88, Ziesler, *Meaning*, p. 199, 205, Schlier, *Römerbrief*, p. 173. In addition, as stated in Brandenburger, *Adam*, p. 232, it is debatable whether ἑνός in δι' ἑνὸς παραπτώματος / δικαιώματος is to be understood as neuter and as an adjective ('through the one trespass / the one act of righteousness') or as masculine and substantive ('through one person's trespass / act of righteousness'); but it is unimportant to an understanding of the main point of the context.

result applies universally, to all Adamites, to all Christians. Εἰς κατάκριμα in Rom 5.18a gives us the result for the Adamites. Rom 5.18b gives the result for the Christians: εἰς δικαίωσιν ζωῆς. According to our concepts the sentence is indeed defective, and it is indeed still vague how the Christian boons of salvation, justification and life are to be linked together more closely.[79] But despite these defects the main matter in the period can be understood perfectly: by virtue of Christ, righteousness and life have broken through. This is indeed a summary of the preceding discussion.

In addition, the matter is explicated in the following verse, Rom 5.19, which is syntactically complete: 'For just as by the one man's disobedience the many were made sinners, so by the one man's obedience the many will be made righteous'. The status of the Christians as righteous is opposed to sinfulness in the former life and is the result of Christ's obedience.[80] This in-

---

79. It is discussed how the genitive connection δικαίωσις ζωῆς is to be analysed, cf. Blass, Debrunner and Rehkopf, *Grammatik*, § 166, n. 1, Bornkamm, *Ende*, p. 88, Brandenburger, *Adam*, p. 233, Ziesler, *Meaning*, p. 199, who indicate an 'intentional genitive' (justification for life); Lietzmann, *Römer*, p. 64, Bauer, *Wörterbuch*, col. 393, Käsemann, *Römer*, p. 148, who interpret it as genitivus qualitatis (life-giving justification); Nygren, *Romarna*, p. 230, who sees it as objective genitive (justification of life); Wilckens, *Römer* I, p. 326, who indicates an epexegetic genitive (justification, which is life), in the same way as Schlier, *Römerbrief*, p. 174, who rightly establishes that for understanding the meaning of the term it is immaterial which is chosen.

80. There is no doubt that here, as in the context generally, these two forms of existence are opposed to one another. The emphasis is not therefore on the verbs, and it is less remarkable that κατασταθήσονται in Rom 5.19b is in the future tense. It may simply be a logical future tense, cf. Bultmann, *Theologie*, p. 274f., Stuhlmacher, *Gerechtigkeit*, p. 223f., Jervell, *Gud*, p. 90, Wilckens, *Römer* I, p. 328. The form is perceived as an eschatological future tense in Bornkamm, *Ende*, p. 88, Schrenk, δίκαιος, *ThWNT* II (1935), pp. 189-93; p. 193, Oepke, καθίστημι, *ThWNT* III (1938), pp. 447-48, Lengsfeld, *Adam*, p. 94f., Käsemann, *Römer*, p. 149, Schlier, *Römerbrief*, p. 175. But then there is a problem that καθιστάναι with object and predicate, means 'to make someone into something', in the passive 'to become something'; it does not relate to anything forensic ('accepted as') but (as particularly emphasised by Oepke) a factual situation, as is also clear as regards the Adam side's sin. Strictly speaking, the effects of justification would then not occur until the futuristic-eschatological event. But to avoid this consequence, the interpreters referred to assume that it is also a current (pre-empted) reality (different in Brandenburger, *Adam*, p. 234, who maintains that Paul has used a 'genuine' future to avoid an enthusiastic misunderstanding of righteousness as 'ein naturhaft-unverlierbarer Besitz', and thereby contradicts the structure of the entire section). A third (and absolutely tenable) possibility is to see the future form as time-related but not eschatological; that is to say, it is intended that the universal spread of righteousness is not yet accomplished; there are still many who by virtue of the missionary activities taking place must be included in the effects of Christ's obedience; cf. Sanday and Headlam, *Romans*, p. 142, Murray, *Romans*, p. 206, Klein, *Gerechtigkeit*, p. 4 n. 6.

dicates that δίκαιοι is also a description of the new life's content, and is thus concerned with the ethical.[81]

This is also indicated in Rom 5.20, in which the law again comes into the picture. Rom 5.13-14 asserts that sin prevailed in the old world, whether or not the law was there. It is now said that the law entered at a certain time, and some importance is attributed to this. But only quantitatively: it sharpens the contrast between the old existence and the new existence. This means in the context that sin becomes greater and thus also the grace that overcomes it.[82] Verse 20 is thus given a first function in the context: the stage is set for the third and definitive implementation of the ὥσπερ-οὕτως contrast. It receives another function at the transition to Rom 6.

In Rom 5.21, Paul concentrates on the consequences of the crucial events. For the Adam descendants, it was the dominion of sin by virtue of death. For the Christians, grace now dominates 'through justification leading to eternal life through Jesus Christ our Lord'. It is presented as the absolutely certain path to eternal life. The concluding eulogy emphasises the intensity of the statement, and extra emphasis is given to strength and certainty in the new life.[83]

In addition, it can thus be established that in the course of the passage something intrinsic occurs in regard to the recurrent ideas about justification and righteousness. Rom 5.21 still says, and with emphasis, that δικαιοσύνη

---

81. It must be a natural expectation that the word δίκαιοι is associated with Christ's δικαίωμα and ὑπακοή and the eschatological life he brings, and is at the same time a contrast to ἁμαρτωλοί, which has been used until now in the letter about the old Adamite existence and its hopelessness and immorality (cf. notes 7 and 21 above). Cf. especially Ziesler, *Meaning*, p. 199, who states cautiously that it expresses more than something forensic and more than a status, and also Morris, *Romans*, p. 238f. Otherwise it is notable how rarely the commentators explain what the word involves. When this occurs it is negative, an attempt to evade an inherently ethical understanding: Brandenburger, *Adam*, p. 235ff., stresses that righteousness is (exclusively) because of Christ's act of justification, Schlier, *Römerbrief*, p. 175, Wilckens, *Römer I*, p. 327, that it is not because of one's own qualities, Murray, *Romans*, p. 205f., that the term is purely forensic, Barrett, *Romans*, p. 117, that 'relationship, not character' is concerned. Important points are indicated, but it is not denied that the word δίκαιοι is *also* concerned with the content of the new life, cf. further in Chapter X below, section 1.3 in particular.
82. Cf. Nygren, *Romarna*, p. 231ff., Michel, *Römer*, p. 143, Brandenburger, *Adam*, p. 247ff., Käsemann, *Römer*, p. 150, Schlier, *Römerbrief*, p. 177. Different in Jüngel, *Unterwegs*, p. 155f., cf. note 67 above.
83. Cf. Nygren, *Romarna*, p. 235f., Schmidt, *Römer*, p. 104, Schlier, *Römerbrief*, p. 178. — Käsemann, *Römer*, p. 150, defines the verb βασιλεύσῃ (which is in the aorist conjunctive) as the logical future, but then pertinently continues: 'Gnade, Gerechtigkeit, ewiges Leben sind nicht mehr zeitlich oder kausal zu trennen. In ihnen begegnet unter verschiedenem Aspekt der gleiche Sachverhalt der Basileia Christi.' Cf. also Lengsfeld, *Adam*, p. 99, du Toit, Dikaiosyne, p. 290.

expresses God's grace and a power that prevails. But from now on there is clearly more than this.

First, it involves a new content in life to be encompassed by this power; an ethical aspect is added.[84] And there is basically little disagreement about this. Some scholars are, however, content to speak cautiously of righteousness as something normative, or about the new obedience and service towards the power of righteousness.[85] Others take the view that righteousness becomes reality in the Christians' actions and is a vital force — in contrast to the destructive course of action of sin.[86]

Second, there is a development in the direction of the Christocentric. Up to the present, God was the subject of the breakthrough of righteousness; Rom 3.25; 5.6-8 makes it clear that God's acts go through Christ and his self-sacrifice. This section still concerns God's grace and gift, but here finally the emphasis is on the fact that it is Christ's effort, his act of righteousness, which leads to the Christians' life and righteousness, which becomes clear in Rom 5.18 and in the concluding doxology in Rom 5.21. Grace is, as it were, given a face.[87] And if Christ's course of action is linked together with the Christians' righteousness the impression is strengthened that righteousness is concerned with ethics and the purpose of life.

It is in fact the structure itself in the large-scale Adam-Christ typology which comes to the fore in the development which occurs in the righteousness concepts. Here, as we have seen, four entities are brought into close association with one another: Adam-Adamites-Christ-and Christians, and we have the complicated structure with ὥσπερ-οὕτως on several levels. On the one hand this means that the Adamitic life is compared with the Christian life, and on the other hand that the connection and accordance which is between Adam and the Adamites according to Rom 5.12 corresponds to a connection between Christ and the Christians. The way has already been pre-

---

84. As emphasised by Jervell, *Gud*, p. 91, Ziesler, *Meaning*, p. 199.
85. Cf. du Toit, Dikaiosyne, p. 290 ('lebensgestaltende Norm'), Käsemann, *Versuche* II, p. 184, Stuhlmacher, *Gerechtigkeit*, p. 224, Jervell, *Gud*, p. 91.
86. Thus Schrenk, δικαιοσύνη, *ThWNT* II (1935), pp. 194-214; p. 213, who in connection with Rom 5.2, stresses that righteousness as an expression of God's act may not be separated from Christ's life-creating dominion which causes the community to be alive, and in connection with the continuation in Rom 6.13,17,18,20 speaks of 'der Gerechtigkeit als der Lebensmacht, welche die Sünde überwindet'; cf. du Toit, Dikaiosyne, p. 290f., Lührmann, *TRE* 12, p. 417f.: 'Gerechtichkeit ist aber von ihrem Opposita Ungerechtigkeit wie Sünde auch ethisch definiert, und Rechtfertigung des Sünders ist zugleich Rechtfertigung des Handelnden'. Indeed, the sharp contrast of the old sin and the new righteousness is a contributory reason for the ethical gradually being given greater emphasis in this context, cf. Ziesler, *Meaning*, pp. 197-200, and the considerations above in notes 7, 21, 78 and 81.
87. Cf. Wilckens, *Römer* I, pp. 327-30, Nygren, *Romarna*, p. 235f.

pared for this in Rom 5.6-11, where the Christians are dependent upon Christ's act of redemption. And so it is natural to understand Rom 5.18-21 as meaning that there is also inherent accord between Christ and the life of the Christians — that there is a precursor Christology — although not expressed directly by a ὥσπερ-οὕτως connection.[88]

To summarise, it may be said that the Pauline intention in Rom 5.12-21 appears to be clear: Paul wishes to continue to stress the Christians' certainty of salvation. He does this by contrasting redemption with Adam's Fall and damnation, and gradually sharpens the contrast so that as regards the two sides there are somewhat fateful consequences. It becomes a sharp before-now contrast in which death and life face one another. The certainty and the enthusiasm for redemption of the Christians is thereby emphasised. At the same time, it becomes clear that in their life and its content they are dependent upon Christ's life and acts. We have a motif I have called 'precursor Christology'.

In my opinion, this perception of the facts can also be maintained and confirmed when the religio-historical background to the section is considered below.

4. The background to the concepts in Rom 5.12-21

4.1 Jewish concepts of original sin?

The search was at first for Old Testament-Jewish concepts of original sin as a background to Rom 5.12-21. But here the problem immediately arises that they cannot be verified. At most, a concept of original death can be reached: Adam and Eve's Fall led to death for mankind.[89]

Sir 25.24 reads as follows: 'From a woman sin had its beginning, and because of her we all die'. 4 Ezra 7.116-31 reads that it would have been better that the earth had not produced Adam or had forced him not to sin; since now it is man's lot to live with sorrow and to expect punishment. It is also emphasised that man himself has committed death-provoking acts. And the answer to the complaint is that man has an opportunity for victory by

---

88. As regards the structure, see sections 2.3-3.2 above. It may also be pointed out that we have an expression of a ὥσπερ-οὕτως correspondence between Christ and the Christians in the continuation in Rom 6.4,(5),11.

89. So recognised in Freundorfer, *Erbsünde*, p. 264, Larsson, *Christus*, p. 139ff., 179, who sees it as a sign that Paul has tightened-up the traditional ideas. Cf. Brandenburger, *Adam*, p. 15ff., where it is used to reject the Old Testament-Jewish background.

struggle, that there is a way Moses has shown, so that destruction is his own fault.[90]

There is an even clearer trend in Rabbinic Judaism, that Adam's transgression has at most physical — not moral — consequences for his descendants.[91] Even the viewpoint in Ezek 18.4 has been clearly emphasised, that there is no death without (one's own) sin.[92]

It must therefore be said that there is a significant distance between Jewish development of the Fall concepts and Paul's train of thought in Rom 5.

4.2. 'Corporate personality' in Rom 5.12-21?

The broader concept of 'corporate personality' has instead been turned towards, here seen as a progenitor concept in which both Adam and Christ are regarded as progenitors of those who follow after and experience the same fate.

But difficulties are associated with the theory of corporate personality. The loose definition of the concept and the lack of specific textual models has been indicated in general terms.[93] These difficulties will also be significant in discussion of this passage.

The corporate-personality concept has been presented most notably as a quite alien psychology, a primitive mentality, deeply embedded in the Semitic Hebrew language; it is said to lack the ability to distinguish between the individual and the collective, a way of thinking wholly different from modern Western individualism.[94] For people who think in this way, the connection to others must be a physical reality. So alien is the concept in its primitiveness that it becomes questionable whether the phenomenon can have played any part whatsoever in New Testament times and be understood today.[95] And it is strange that the term 'corporate personality' it-

---

90. See also Sap 2.24; Vit. Ad. 35.3; Apoc. Mos. 14.2; 44.1ff.; Syr. Bar. 17.3; 23.4; 48.2; 54.15-19, cf. on this Freundorfer, *Erbsünde*, pp. 52-93, Larsson, *Christus*, p. 140ff., Brandenburger, *Adam*, p. 20ff., Lengsfeld, *Adam*, p. 40ff.

91. Cf. Freundorfer, *Erbsünde*, pp. 93-104, Brandenburger, *Adam*, p. 58ff.

92. Thus Rabbi Ammi according to Lazarus Goldschmidt (ed.), *Der Babylonische Talmud mit Einschluss der vollständigen Midrasj* I, (repr.) the Hague 1933, p. 445, cf. Freundorfer, *Erbsünde*, p. 95, Brandenburger, *Adam*, p. 61.

93. See especially Rogerson, Conception, pp. 1-16, cf. Porter, Aspect, p. 361ff., Lengsfeld, *Adam*, p. 62, Wedderburn, *Baptism*, p. 351ff.

94. Cf. Robinson, *Cross*, p. 77, *Doctrine*, p. 11ff., de Fraine, *Adam*, p. 30ff.

95. A blurred concept of 'primitiveness' is used which approaches an 'Urdummheit' theory. Anthropologically, the Hebrew texts would scarcely be described as 'primitive' in this sense, cf. Rogerson, Conception, p. 7f. Epistemologically it is a whorfianism, in which the

self is a modern Western concept with no linguistic equivalent in Hebrew.[96]

More restrainedly, an idea about collective guilt and punishment has been suggested, which is said to have characterised the old Israelite society.[97] The episode in Josh 7 is particularly emphasised, in which Achan takes the tabooed booty and incurs Yahweh's wrath. When things go wrong during the next battle, Achan is exposed and is taken to the Valley of Achor with all his property and his sons and daughters; there they are all burnt and stoned. It may appear as if there is a special common destiny among those who belong to the same family or clan, but it should be noted that what is concerned is not that one cannot distinguish between the individual and the collective. This episode involves primarily punishment for the individual, Achan.[98] One should also be aware of the revolt against punishment of the innocent, which is reflected in Ezek 18. This presumably had such an impact that ideas about collective guilt and punishment were suspect several centuries before New Testament times.[99]

This brings us to an even more modified form of the concept. Attention is simply drawn to the relationship between ancestor and descendant. Descendants identify themselves with the ancestor. The ancestor represents the descendants who are by fate dependent upon his actions. It may be especially emphasised here that Israel is both the person (Jacob) and the

96. In Rogerson, Conception, p. 2f., it is pointed out that Robinson takes the concept from English law. And the concept of the corporative (= the body used as an imagine of a fellowship) originates from Western Graeco-Roman thought, cf. the discussion of σῶμα Χριστοῦ in 1 Cor 12 above, Chapter III, section 2.2 (in connection with note 79), where I have also pointed out that talk of a Hebrew idea of 'corporate personality' creates a wrong expectation, that a corporate connection between participants in a fellowship is known in Hebrew.

97. Cf. Robinson, *Deuteronomy*, p. 266, *Doctrine*, p. 8, Conception, p. 49, where in addition to the Achan story the Gibeonites' revenge on Saul's descendants is indicated, 2 Sam 21.1-9, the decision regarding the entire town's liability for an undetected murder, Deut 21.1-9, the demand for revenge on the third and fourth generations under the Second Commandment, Ex 20.5; Deut 5.9, and the unrestricted blood feud in Gen 4.15,24.

98. The Achan story indeed involves that Achan's transgression is not to harm Israel collectively. For this reason he must be wiped out with everything that belongs to him, and here his family is considered as property. Cf. Rogerson, Conception, p. 4ff., which points out that a lack of awareness of individuality cannot be concluded from the lack of individual rights; Porter, Aspects, p. 367ff., who points out that following his crime all that belonged to Achan had to fall to he who was wronged, Yahweh, who receives it as a burnt offering. It may also be noted that the punishment's deterrent effect increases if innocent family members are also affected. In this way the present-day Mafia and other terrorist organisations operate without regard in any way for concepts of collective guilt or corporate personality.

99. Cf. Robinson, *Doctrine*, p. 30ff., Rogerson, Conception, p. 6.

people.[100] Along this road we end with the concept that a person cannot be treated as an isolated individual but must be seen as a member of the social community.[101] This is an evident perception which corresponds entirely to modern Western thought.[102]

Applied to Rom 5.12-21, the 'corporate-personality concept' accordingly becomes of limited importance.

On the Adam side of the comparison, it has already been established that Judaism has no demonstrable concepts that subsequent mankind is included in Adam's sin. Thus the theory of corporate personality and collective guilt and punishment can evidence no more than the specific material.

On the Christ side, it must be established that the parallelism itself is absent. No biological or family connection between ancestor and descendants is of course concerned, but potentially a further development of the idea.[103]

It is thus a vague version of the idea which can be considered here. One speaks of 'solidarity', 'representation' and 'vicariousness'.[104] It is not a true exemplar but merely a general reference to a widespread way of thinking.

4.3. A Hellenistic primal-man redeemer idea behind Rom 5.12-21?

If it is wished to find the background to a gnostic Anthropos myth, the religio-historical substantiation must be decisive: that before Christianity there existed a mythological complex in which a primal-man figure will come to redeem fallen mankind from the prison of the body and the material world.[105]

But this view is also supported by a series of more indirect arguments.

There are two negative reasonings which should show that the concepts cannot be derived from elsewhere. (a) It is said to be unknown in the Old

---

100. Cf. de Fraine, *Adam*, p. 79ff., Shedd, *Man*, p. 102f., Wedderburn, *Baptism*, p. 352, 349 (where it is emphasised that the ideas are developed in Gal 3.9: the peoples are to be blessed 'with Abraham', cf. Chapter II above, note 18).
101. Cf. Robinson, *Doctrine*, p. 34.
102. Cf. Rogerson, Conception, p. 7, Bruce, *Romans*, p. 126f., Wedderburn, *Baptism*, p. 353.
103. Cf. Wedderburn, *Baptism*, p. 352f., Lengsfeld, *Adam*, p. 39 n. 62, where it is pointed out that this is primarily a religious concept.
104. Cf. Bruce, *Romans*, p. 126f., Wedderburn, *Baptism*, p. 352, Schnackenburg, Adam-Christus-Typologie, pp. 46-50, where it is called 'Denkweise', and where it is also pointed out that the ideas are associated with the widespread Anthropos myth which are repeated in the σὺν-Χριστῷ ideas.
105. See especially Brandenburger, *Adam*, pp. 77-157, cf. Bultmann, *Theologie*, p. 177f., Lengsfeld, *Adam*, p. 48ff.

Testament and in Judaism that a second Adam is to come as redeemer.[106] (b) Neither can the concept of original sin be attributed to an Old Testament Jewish concept about fateful dependence on Adam.[107] (c) The parallels in 1 Cor 15, which can only be understood as a polemic against concepts of a primal-man redeemer, are also pointed out.[108] (d) And finally the structure of Rom 5.12-21 and the tensions in the text, which it is said can only be explained as a reaction against gnostic fatalism, are emphasised.[109]

It is certainly correct that gnosticism contains cosmological primal-man myths which may perhaps be associated with old Greek mysteriosophy and other forms of dualism.[110] But if indeed a closer look is taken at the indirect arguments, the weaknesses of the theory of a gnostic background come to light:

If we look at the first point (a), it is not only Judaism that lacks a primal-man redeemer figure: this is true of gnosticism to an equally high degree. No redeemer figure can be evidenced prior to the influence of Christianity.[111] A feature crucial to the theory of dependence upon gnosticism is thus lacking.

Something similar applies to the second point (b). It seems that the original-sin concept is questionable not only in Judaism but also in gnosticism. The individual's decision is of great significance. What is important is to choose the spiritual existence.[6] And wickedness is not seen as

---

106. Thus Brandenburger, *Adam*, p. 69, where there is also (p. 69f. with n. 6) a subtle argument, incomprehensible to me, that it is otherwise impossible to explain that the coming Adam (= Christ) in Rom 5.15c is called ἄνθρωπος.

107. Thus Brandenburger, *Adam*, p. 69, 15ff., cf. section 4.1 above.

108. Thus Brandenburger, *Adam*, pp. 70-75.

109. Thus Brandenburger, *Adam*, p. 158ff., Bornkamm, *Ende*, p. 83ff.

110. A primal-man myth is to be found in the (Christian) gnostic Naasene sermon in Hippolytus, *Elench.* 5.7.3ff., in Apocryphon John and in CH I, as stated in Brandenburger, *Adam*, pp. 83-95. As regards the possible connection back to Greek concepts, see my discussion of mystery religion and gnosticism in Chapter II, section 3.2, above, and of the Anthropos myth as a possible background to 1 Cor 12, Chapter III, section 2.2 above, with notes 69-74, cf. notes 41-43.

111. A widespread scepticism has gradually arisen against theories of a redeemer figure as the centre of pre-Christian gnosticism, cf. Colpe, *Schule*, p. 203ff., Nock, Gnosticism, pp. 940-59, Hengel, *Sohn*, p. 53, Käsemann, *Römer*, p. 136. Cf. Agersnap, *Paulusstudier*, p. 63ff., where I show that in Brandenburger, *Adam*, p. 155 n. 3, there is a faulty interpretation of the few specific passages in which Adam-Anthropos is said to have a soteriological function: Naassene sermon and Pap. mag. 1.195ff., 4.1167ff.

6. See Apoc. Ioh. 67,7-18, Hippolytus, *Elench.* 5.26.24-31; 6.17.1, cf. Ernst Haenchen, Gab es eine vorchristliche Gnosis? in: *Gott und Mensch*, Tübingen 1965, pp. 265-98; p. 279f., Das Buch Baruch, op. cit, pp. 299-334; p. 327, Luise Schottroff, *Der Glaubende und die Feindliche Welt* (WMANT 37), Neukirchen 1970, p. 12, 96ff., Wedderburn, Structure, p. 342f.

human guilt but as oppression under the authorities.[7] This also does not correspond to Rom 5.12.

As regards the third point (c), where there is a reference to the parallel-sounding concepts in 1 Cor 15, I wish to refer to the earlier discussion.[8] It is not a natural interpretation to see this text as a polemic against a specific, enthusiastic, gnostic primal-man redeemer mythology. On the contrary, it can be seen that Paul himself uses positively references to the Adam-Christ correspondence in his reasoning in 1 Cor 15.21-22,45-49 and in Rom 5.12-21. A comparison between Rom 5.12-21 and the parallel passages in 1 Cor 15 also shows that Paul employs the concepts in a varied way.[9] In 1 Cor 15.45-49, there is an outbidding relationship between the first Adam's creation and the even more glorious one who is to appear by virtue of the other Adam. In 1 Cor 15.21-22 there is a comparison between destruction through the one man's death and restoration through resurrection from the dead, which has also come through one man. In Rom 5 also there is a comparison; but here, as we have seen, there are other features which are contrasted with one another: sin and death through Adam versus obedience and eternal life through Christ. This variation does not suggest that the background is a large and firmly formulated mythological complex, as is assumed by the theories regarding a gnostic origin.[10] These are myths in a different sense, narratives about universal conditions. They appear to be free adaptations of Old Testament protohistory.

But as concerns the last point (d), tensions in the text, there is a risk of the interpretation becoming arbitrary. We have already seen that the interpretation which Bornkamm and Brandenburger have chosen in an attempt to demonstrate a gnostic background is far from the simplest:[11] first, Paul is meant to undertake in Rom 5.12a-c a comparison between Adam and Christ based upon a gnostic fatalism; this then is contradicted in Rom 5.12d and further modified in the following verses; nevertheless, the comparison is effected in Rom 5.18-19, and quite sharply without reservation in Rom 5.21. This raises questions of both a methodical and an inherent nature. Why does Paul adopt an idea which he cannot in fact use?[12] It is also surprising

---

7. Cf. Wedderburn, Structure, p. 342f.
8. Chapter III, section 4 above, with notes 312-16, cf. also the more detailed discussion in Agersnap, *Paulusstudier*, p. 25f., 35-52.
9. Cf. Schnackenburg, Adam-Christus-Typologie, p. 47.
10. Cf. Brandenburger, *Adam*, p. 153ff., Bultmann, *Theologie*, p. 177f., Bornkamm, *Ende*, p. 89, Lengsfeld, *Adam*, p. 50.
11. Cf. the discussion of this in section 3.2 above.
12. This pertinent objection is to be found in Jüngel, *Unterwegs*, p. 147, against the fanatical implementation of the interpretation to be found in Brandenburger, *Adam*, p. 243 in particular.

that he is content with modifications and an implied distancing from the concept employed; it will be difficult for impartial readers to understand what he means. If there is tension and development in the text, it goes rather in the opposite direction. Interpretation of the section of text has shown — and the history of interpretation has confirmed — that Rom 5.12 is expressed quite broadly and vaguely, so that many possible interpretations are considered while the process of thought is gradually intensified by a specific point in Rom 5.21. This indicates a different and simpler explanation of the text's genesis.

4.4. Rom 5.12-21, perceived as Adam-Christ typology

This simple perception of the text's background and origin becomes apparent when the passage is directly defined as an 'Adam-Christ typology', as is often the case.[13]

This involves using the Old Testament's protohistory to understand what happens to Christ, and to put it into perspective.[14] The universal exegetic model in primal Christianity is associated with the belief that Old Testament expectations are initiated through Christ. The typological way of thinking is particularly widespread in the Letter to the Hebrews and in Paul. In addition to the Adam-Christ typologies, reference may be made in particular to the typological use of the Abraham story in Rom 4 and of the Moses story in 1 Cor 10.1-13; 2 Cor 3.7-18, where the rendering of protohistory is embellished by topical use.

Thus there is no argument that Judaism knows of no other Adam figure with a redeemer role. This concept is added because it is Jesus Christ who is connected with the narrative of the earliest times. No prerequisites are needed other than the general expectation that the consequences of Adam's Fall must be mitigated in the end-time. Added to this is the Christians' experience that the conditions of human life have been renewed through Christ. Christ's obedience and the consequences of this become therefore a natural contrast to Adam's Fall. It is also deep in the evangelical tradition

---

13. Thus Rudolf Bultmann, *Ursprung und Sinn der Typologie als hermeneutischer Methode*, in: *Exegetica*, Tübingen 1966, pp. 369-80; p. 374, Brandenburger, *Adam*, p. 240f., Lengsfeld, *Adam*, p. 26ff., Black, *Romans*, p. 84, Käsemann, *Römer*, p. 136, Schnackenburg, Adam-Christus-Typologie, p. 38ff.
14. Cf. the somewhat different definitions of the typology concept in Leonard Goppelt, *Typos. Die typologische Deutung des Alten Testamentes im Neuen*, Gütersloh 1939, p. 5ff., Bultmann, *Exegetica*, p. 369ff. It is in any event crucial in New Testament typologies that the Old Testament events are repeated and completed in the eschatological redemption events. The leading aspect is the connection between the proto-events and the topical redemption story.

that Jesus resists all temptation. This occurs not only in the temptation narratives themselves (Mt 4.1-11; Mark 1.12-13; Lk 4.1-13) but also at later key events such as the feeding in the desert (John 6.14-15) and Peter's confession of faith (Mark 8.32-33; Mt 16.22-23).[15]

This point of view is also no longer vulnerable to the objection that the Old Testament and Judaism lack a true concept of original sin. The almost fatalistic dependence may evidently originate from the Christ side. An eschatologisation is taking place. The connection with Christ becomes all-determining. He is the saviour and the precursor figure who draws his successors along with him. And because Christ obtains such a crucially positive significance for the Christians the old existence comes to represent something thoroughly negative and unpleasant. This has already been emphasised in Rom 1.18-3.20, and it indeed comes to the fore in Rom 5.6-11 as a prelude to the Adam-Christ typology.[16] The dominant context thus seems to confirm that the train of thought is being formed here in Rom 5.12-21.

In this fashion there are thus two sources of the Adam-Christ typology: the Old Testament narratives and the Christological reappraisal, which is the true incentive. And we are again dealing with what I have called a 'precursor Christology'. The Christians are to live a life of the same type as Christ's (obedience and righteousness), and with the same hope for the future.

15. Cf. Agersnap, *Paulusstudier*, p. 91ff.
16. Cf. section 2.3 above.

VI

The leading questions in Rom 6.1-2
and the dominant structure

1. Rom 6.1-2: new form and new theme

1.1. The change in style

At the transition from Rom 5 to Rom 6 there is a change of style. From now on Paul uses a living form of a dialogic nature. The line of thought is guided by rhetorical questions and counter-questions, as is to be seen in Rom 6.1-2.

These verses are quite simple to understand — in contrast to what follows in Rom 6.3-14 where the exegetic problems accumulate. But it is important to pay some attention to these early verses and their meaning in the context, for Paul uses the leading questions to begin to employ a special compositional technique. This has striking parallels in the following sections up to Rom 8, and results in a form and a structure which are at least broadly clear. An examination of the parallel reasoning processes may help to clarify Paul's compositional technique, and thus the entire context to be investigated.

Rom 6.1 begins with the question: Τί οὖν ἐροῦμεν; Formally, this in fact indicates that some new thoughts are about to be introduced. But it cannot be concluded from this that there has been a sudden transition to an entirely new subject, so that a strong caesura between Rom 5 and Rom 6 results.[1] For the crucial eschatological turning from the old life to the new life continues unremittingly as in Rom 5.21 viewed from a perspective in which sin and grace confront one another as personified powers.[2] And the particle οὖν emphasises formally that the line of thought from previously continues. But to what does Paul refers back?

Rom 5.21 ended with Paul's sharp contrast of the new life's unrestricted

---

1. As assumed by Huby, *Romains*, p. 27, Kuss, *Römerbrief*, Bruce, *Romans*, p. 68, 134, Black, *Romans*, p. 92, Wilckens, *Römer* I, p. 17ff., Morris, *Romans*, p. 243, Stuhlmacher, *Römer*, p. 83. The connection with the preceding text, which emerges when the development of the thought-process is made clear, does not support this.
2. Cf. Gäumann, *Taufe*, p. 69f., Tannehill, *Dying*, p. 14ff., Schnackenburg, Adam-Christus-Typologie, p. 42ff., Jervell, *Gud*, p. 196.

dominion by virtue of Christ with conditions in the old sinful life. This has the effect of a cue — a thematic indicator for the new section. It might now be expected that Paul would begin to amplify on how the dominion of life would unfold. But this does not happen. The quite unimportant comment in Rom 5.20 is taken up again. Here for a moment the law came into the picture with restricted function: since law led to a quantitative increase in sin the grace which initiated the new existence became even greater. This is so formulated that it may appear as a universal rule: the greater the sin, the greater the grace.

This comment gives rise to the objection in Rom 6.1b: ἐπιμένωμεν τῇ ἁμαρτίᾳ, ἵνα ἡ χάρις πλεονάσῃ; It is presented as a reply from an interlocutor. It asks whether it is a rule which can also be used in the new existence: i.e. to continue the close relationship to sin in order thus to experience grace even more intensely.

We therefore do not (immediately) receive the expected continuation of Rom 5.21. Instead a collateral circumstance is used as point of departure. But such a surprising turnabout has an effect: it sharpens attention. At the same time the objection is given a clear function. It in fact sets the theme for what follows — despite the lopsided angle of approach. For the question concerns the correct conduct of life in the renewed existence. And it will be shown that the line of thought develops so that ultimately it is the positive consequences of the turnabout that has occurred which are unfolded.[3]

The dialogic form which begins here also has quite a clear function. If a fictitious opponent who can be rebuked is introduced, it provides a lively argument with a strong appeal to listeners or letter-recipients. This is a common rhetorical style. It provides a personal emotional approach, and makes the viewpoints intensely topical. It is often seen as a parallel to the stoics' 'diatribe'; this is a form of argument very widespread within Hellenism.[4]

Matters become less clear when we arrive at the two associated questions about the background to the entire argument: Is it a purely ficti-

---

3. In this way one can nevertheless see Rom 5.21 as giving the theme for Rom 6.1-14, as is also emphasised in David Hellholm, Enthymemic Argumentation in Paul: The Case of Romans 6, in: Troels Engberg-Pedersen (ed.), *Paul in His Hellenistic Context*, Minneapolis 1995, pp. 119-79; p. 139f. This will be further confirmed in the survey of the entire course of reasoning and the parallel sections in what follows.

4. As regards the 'diatribe' phenomenon, see Rud. Bultmann, *Der Stil der paulinischen Predigt und die kynisch-stoische Diatribe* (FRLANT 13), Göttingen 1910, pp. 60-68, Stanley Kent Stowers, *The diatribe and Paul's letter to the Romans*, Chicago 1981, p. 125ff., cf. Barrett, *Romans*, p. 121, Gäumann, *Taufe*, p. 68, Frankemölle, *Taufverständnis*, p. 31ff., Halter, *Taufe*, p. 38. Hellholm, Argumentation, p. 119ff., seeks to define the form more precisely as 'enthymeme', an argumentative text not based on pure logic but on reasoning resting upon assumptions with which the recipients agree.

tious objection, or is it a true situation of dispute in which Paul intervenes? And what are the views Paul is arguing against?

If we first look at the last question, there are two possibilities to be considered. It may be seen as an exaggerated nomistic objection to the preceding Pauline statements which characterises their consequences as unrestrained libertinism.[5] Or perhaps it may be a libertinism, just as absurdly naive, that wishes to take credit for Paul's views.[6] Because Paul himself says in Rom 3.8 that he has met with the nomistic objection from other quarters, the first possibility is evident. In the following text, Paul's procedure is in any case to distance himself from any form of libertinism.

As concerns the question first referred to, it is clear that the objection is fictitious — in the sense that the entire conversational situation is of course imaginary. But this does not exclude that Paul may have adopted this very objection because there is an actual reason for it within the community to which he is writing. In that event, there must be in the Roman community Judeo-Christian opposition to him and accusations of libertinism against which he must defend himself — or perhaps libertines against whom he is polemising. But then there is a substantial burden of proof. This is a gentile-convert community of which, according to Paul's own information, he has no personal knowledge. There must therefore be strong indications that the letter is a contribution to an actual conflict with Judeo-Christianity (or libertinism).[7] Otherwise there is the obvious possibility that the dialogic form of

5. Because of the parallel in Rom 3.8, the objection is frequently identified as Judeo-Christian — thus Zahn, *Römer*, p. 293, Ernst Kühl, *Der Brief des Paulus an die Römer*, Leipzig 1913, p. 201, Michel, *Römer*, p. 152, Jeremias, *Abba*, p. 270, Käsemann, *Römer*, p. 156f., Schlier, *Römerbrief*, p. 190, Wilckens, *Römer* II, pp. 8-10, Dunn, *Romans*, p. 306f., Hellholm, Argumentation, p. 142ff.

6. Thus in particular W. Lütgert, *Der Römerbrief als historisches Problem* (BFChTh 17,2), Gütersloh 1913, p. 72ff., cf. Bruce, *Romans*, p. 134f., Gäumann, *Taufe*, p. 69 n. 7, Cranfield, *Romans*, p. 297 n. 1.

7. See especially Hellholm, Argumentation, p. 142ff., which establishes that the dialogue in a letter is inevitably fictitious, but also points out that the letter-writer can take up an objection actually raised — and according to Rom 3.8 Paul has been accused that the righteousness theory is libertinism. But there is still some way to the assertion that there is an actual conflict within the community which Hellholm holds in line with Zahn, *Römer*, p. 293f., Kühl, *Römer*, p. 201, Michel, *Römer*, p. 152, Wilckens, *Römer* II, pp. 8-10. This opinion assumes the hypothesis (with which Hellholm agrees, p. 144ff.) that the Letter to the Romans came into being in a crisis situation as a stage in a struggle with Judaism. The problem here is not only the obligation to demonstrate the situation of dispute. Hellholm himself agrees (p. 168) that it is questionable whether in the context of this (dogmatic) discussion about righteousness Paul uses paraenetic imperatives (in Rom 6.12-13,19). This would be more suited to an actual polemic against a libertinism — the view maintained in Lütgert, *Römerbrief*, p. 72f., and probably forming the basis of the 'modifying interpretation's' assertion that Paul is correcting an enthusiasm. But here the

discussion is a purely stylistic means which has above all a pedagogic, defining function — a means of bringing out the correct, positively expressed concept of the new existence; it stands out more sharply against the background of a fictitious opponent's views.[8]

Finally, the nature of the objection may also be considered. Can one say that the objection has formal — but diabolic — logic on its side?[9] This appears to be unreasonable. The point in Rom 5.12-21 is indeed that there has been a final break with the previous existence's sin by virtue of Christ and the victory of the new life. The increase in sin referred to in Rom 5.20 can therefore only occur in the old existence. The objection to the Pauline theology is absurd as soon as it is expressed.[10] Matters are thus pushed to extremes, and the attention of the letter's recipients is intensified.

The lively, temperamental style is continued in *Rom 6.2* with the strong denial, μὴ γένοιτο, for which the question is already preparing the way.

A new question arises in Rom 6.2b: οἵτινες ἀπέθανομεν τῇ ἁμαρτίᾳ, πῶς ἔτι ζήσομεν ἐν αὐτῇ; 'How can we who died to sin go on[11] living in it?' The counter-question here sets the scene for a reply such as: 'By no possible means!' to the extent that it is unnecessary to express it directly. If one has died relative to something, one cannot of course live connected to it. The counter-question in Rom 6.2b is thus a first definitive reply.

The point here emerges by virtue of the provocative statement that 'we', the Christians, have died. This is quite abrupt. It is a very striking expression about people who in the preceding text were characterised as especially alive. But it is now clear — and gradually becomes more so — that this is not meant literally. It expresses that such a radical break has occurred that

problem is that in the dialogue sections Paul then attacks in two different directions. For both theories, it is difficult to demonstrate that Paul finds himself in crucial conflict. Here he does not even address the issue clearly, as often noted, cf. Bornkamm, *Ende*, p. 36, Kuss, *Römerbrief*, p. 293f., Gäumann, *Taufe*, p. 71f., Frankemölle, *Taufverständnis*, p. 32, Jervell, *Gud*, p. 96, Schnelle, *Gerechtigkeit*, n. 379 p. 204. This indicates that the objection has merely a communicative function, cf. the continued survey of the thought-process in the entire context of the text.

8. This idea, which is specially emphasised in Stowers, *Diatribe*, p. 153f., is confirmed when the compositional technique is analysed and viewed in the context of the subsequent parts of the text, cf. note 21, and section 3, with note 67, below.

9. Like Bornkamm, *Ende*, p. 36f., cf. Kuss, *Römerbrief*, p. 293, Gäumann, *Taufe*, p. 71, Schnelle, *Gerechtigkeit*, p. 75 with n. 380.

10. Cf. Bultmann, *Stil*, p. 67f., Thyen, *Studien*, p. 197, Jervell, *Gud*, p. 96, Käsemann, *Römer*, p. 156f., Schlier, *Römerbrief*, p. 191.

11. Cf. Kuss, *Römerbrief*, p. 196, Käsemann, *Römer*, p. 157, Wilckens, *Römer II*, p. 11, n. 15, Schnelle, *Gerechtigkeit*, p. 75, who notes that the future form in Rom 6.2b is 'logical', since it has in mind the relative future, reckoned from the moment of death. But this is unnecessary. It is concerned with what must be the case also in the future (with certainty) — like the future form in Rom 6.14b.

it must be described in terms of a death. The violent contrast between the old life and the new life of Rom 5 is further radicalised. Only in the subsequent context does it also become clear that the dative τῇ ἁμαρτίᾳ is to be understood as a qualification of the statement: it is only in relation to sin that the Christians are 'dead'. But as it stands this does not appear directly to be the case. It merely says that the Christians are dead, and that sin in particular suffers.[12] This is sharply expressed therefore, bearing in mind that this death symbolism was not used earlier in the letter. The sharpness underlines the nature of the sentence as a first negatively-structured point: sin must have no influence in the life of the Christians.[13]

At the same time, life and death are caused to stand as striking opposites to one another. This also gives weight to the sentence.

1.2. Development of the new main idea

We can now see the significance of the leading questions. The thought-process is so constructed that Rom 6.2 has two crucial functions within the context.

First of all the keynote is sounded. Whereas in the Letter to the Romans the key-concept so far has been 'righteousness', it now becomes 'life' confronted with 'death'. There is a connection between the two benefits of redemption, and there is a gradual transition. Life and death are already confronted with one another (in connection with the contrast between righteousness and sin) by the Adam-Christ typology in Rom 5.12-21. But from now on life and death become the crucial opponents.[14] We shall see that the term

---

12. This must be seen immediately as the dativus incommodi described in Blass, Debrunner and Rehkopf, *Grammatik*, § 188, cf. Jervell, *Gud*, p. 96, Halter, *Taufe*, p. 38. But in the light of subsequent development of thought the 'Dativ der Beziehung' described in Blass, Debrunner and Rehkopf, *Grammatik*, § 197, may be considered. The metaphorical interpretation is however disputed, as it was in connection with Gal 3.27; Cor 12.12-13, cf. Chapter III, notes 25-26, 37, 63-64, 76-77, 82-90 and 126 above. See in particular Wrede, *Paulus*, p. 62, in which it is maintained that Rom 6.2 must be understood 'conventionally' and thus mystically. In connection with the following verses also there is a tendency to insist on a literal understanding, especially as regards terms which concern death, cf. below.

13. Cf. Dinkler, Taufaussagen, p. 71, Halter, *Taufe*, p. 38, who considers it the crucial thesis in the entire section. But it should be pointed out that it is merely an expression of the negative side of the matter. There is a corresponding positive point which must be considered as the main matter, as will be shown below. Cf. Schnelle, *Gerechtigkeit*, p. 75.

14. Cf. Schnackenburg, Adam-Christus-Typologie, p. 43, L. Schottroff, ζῶ, ExWNT I (1980), cols. 261-71, in particular col. 265f., Fitzmyer, *Romans*, p. 430. See also Kertelge, *Rechtfertigung*, p. 263, who also emphasises the connection with the 'righteousness' concept which expresses the same benefit of redemption, and Jervell, *Gud*, p. 76, which expresses it as follows: 'Chaps. 1-4: The righteous shall live *by faith* / Chaps. 5-8: The righteous *shall*

'life' has broad significance, so that physical life on earth (Rom 6.2), power of life (Rom 6.4), quality of life (Rom 6.11) and an eternal life of resurrection (Rom 6.13,23) must be contemplated.[15] There is a similar gradual change of meaning on the 'death side': the term 'death' moves away from being concerned with 'eternal death' as punishment for sin and with the 'power of death' to become a metaphorical expression for parting from the old life — and thus something positive. Later the negative meanings again dominate, and here also it is perceived as 'physical death'.[16]

In the second place, Rom 6.2's function is clearly to prepare the way for the following development of thought. There are several reasons why the assertion in this verse cannot stand alone. As we have seen, it is a striking and provocative statement which calls for an explanation. It includes certain weighty concepts, life and death, whose meaning is not established. And it is expressed negatively as a break with the old, and so one expects to hear what the new involves. The justification and amplification called for appear in the following verses. A new rhetorical question in Rom 6.3 refers to the basal, assumed knowledge of the association of baptism with Christ's death, and the argument then continues on this basis. Points of view are further sharpened, and 'death' to sin is now — from Rom 6.4 — also seen as the beginning of a new life.

The following development of thought includes the many problems to

---

live by faith'. This concept of development can be supported by some word-statistics: the words for 'life' (ζῆν and ζωή and compounds thereof) can be found scattered over the first four chapters: Rom 1.17; 2.7; 4.17. On the other hand, they are frequent in Rom 5-8, especially the central sections:

    Rom 5.10,17-18,21.

    Rom 6.2,4,8,10-11,13,22-23; 7.1-3.

    Rom 7.9; 8.2,6,10-13,38.

Thereafter it again becomes more scattered: Rom 9.26; 10.5; 11.15; 12.1; 14.7-9,11.

Similarly, the words for 'death' are frequent in the central parts of Rom 5-8:

    Rom 5.6-8,10,12,14-15,17,21.

    Rom 6.2-5,7-13,16,21-23; 7.2-6.

    Rom 7.8-11,13,24; 8.2,6,10-11,13,34,36,38.

This means that life and death confront one another in the very passages which will prove to be before-now antitheses. There is an opposite movement in the words on 'righteousness'. As pointed out in Chapter V, note 4, above, words of this stem are used 30 times in Rom 1-4. Thereafter the curve declines: Rom 5.1,9,16-19,21; 6,7,13,16,18-20; 7.12; 8.4,10,30,33; 9.30-31; 10.4-6,10; 14.17.

15. Cf. Schottroff, *ExWNT* I, col 263f., which establishes that the borderline between metaphorical and non-metaphorical use is difficult to draw.

16. The term 'death' is used absolutely negatively until Rom 6.2, after which it has a positive and metaphorical ring in Rom 6.2-8,11; 7.4, whereas it sounds negative in Rom 6.9-10,12-13,16,21-23 and again from Rom 7.6 onwards. A merely 'physical death' is clearly concerned in Rom 8.38; 14.9.

which we shall return. For the time being, we shall consider here how far the line of thought introduced by the questions in Rom 6.1-2 goes, and what the conclusion of this becomes.

It is clear that in any event the thought-process moves ahead to the statement emphasised in Rom 6.11, in which the negative term from Rom 6.2, 'death' to sin, and the positive term from Rom 6.4, about a new life to God, are connected and thereby further emphasised.

But something new happens in Rom 6.12-13. Paul now expresses himself in the imperative, whereas indicatives have so far been employed. There is also exhortation later in Rom 6. Some interpreters therefore wish to set the crucial distinction between Rom 6.11 and 6.12, so that the promise of redemption is received in a more dogmatically characterised section, Rom 6.1-11, which is followed by an imperative, paraenetic section in Rom 6.12-23.[17] But this appears to be rash. In the remaining part of the chapter, which constitutes the main part of this 'imperative section', only one imperative occurs — in Rom 6.19b.[18] New rhetorical questions emerge from Rom 6.15 onwards which formally mark the beginning of a new process of reasoning. And the central point here, Rom 6.16-19a, is a promise of redemption expressed just as indicatively as in Rom 6.1-11.

It is also emphasised with an οὖν in Rom 6.12 that the earlier thought-process is continued. Moreover, in Rom 6.12-14 there is also an antithetical structure corresponding to Rom 6.11. The old service characterised by sin and death is contrasted with the new service for righteousness. This establishes that these verses are linked to the preceding text.[19]

If we assume this, the thought-process ends with a request to serve righteousness and God. This final point is after all what must be expected on the basis of Rom 5.21: Paul indeed arrives at an amplification of the way in which life's dominion, as opposed to death's dominion, must

17. Thus Kuss, *Römerbrief*, p. 293ff., Bornkamm, *Ende*, p. 41, Murray, *Romans*, p. 226, Käsemann, *Römer*, p. 155, Halter, *Taufe*, p. 67, Dunn, *Romans*, p. 305f., Fitzmyer, *Romans*, p. 431f., Nestle and Aland, *Novum Testamentum*[26].

18. Against this background a violent generalisation occurs is Käsemann, *Römer*, p. 155: '[Rom 6.]12-14 bilden das Thema des zweiten, in 15-23 breit entfalteten Abschnittes. In ihm, der nicht grundlos von Imperativen beherrscht wird, geht es um die Konsequenz solcher Botschaft in ihrer praktischen Bewährung.' Cf. Schnelle, *Gerechtigkeit*, p. 85: '... das Vorherrschen des Imperativs in Röm 6,12ff.', in which the context clearly shows that Rom 6.12-23 is intended.

19. Thus most interpreters, Nestle, *Novum Testamentum*[25], Nygren, *Romarna*, p. 256, Michel, *Römer*, p. 148f., Schmidt, *Römer*, p. 114, Gäumann, *Taufe*, p. 27f., Jervell, *Gud*, p. 92f., Schlier, *Römerbrief*, p. 202 n. 21, Cranfield, *Romans*, p. 296f., Wilckens, *Römer* II, p. 6f., Stuhlmacher, *Römer*, p. 84, 87.

develop.[20] We can thus also see what Paul achieves by taking up the absurd objection. Although the question is linked to a peripheral and incidental circumstance in the preceding text, it nevertheless points in the right direction. By tackling the obviously incorrect consequence, Paul wishes to reach his goal: to convince recipients of the only correct consequence of the gospel.[21]

This perception of the thought-process can be confirmed by comparison with the following context.

2. Relationship to the subsequent sections

2.1. The parallel process of reasoning in Rom 6.15-23

There is a remarkable parallelism between the two halves of Rom 6. Clause by clause, they contain almost the same elements.

In both passages leading questions mark a new beginning. In *Rom 6.15a* we have a Τί οὖν; This corresponds to Rom 6.1a.

In Rom 6.15 there is a link with an incidental circumstance in the preceding text in the same way as Rom 6.1. In Rom 6.12-14 the emphasis is on the dominion of righteousness, which has replaced the dominion of sin and, according to Rom 6.14a, is not threatened by sin. It might then be expected that life's progress under the unrestricted dominion of righteousness would be unfolded. This does not happen. Paul refers back to Rom 6.14b, in which the reason for the statement about the powerlessness of sin is substantiated wholly parenthetically by a reference — surprising in the context — to the fact that the law no longer has any power because the Christians are under grace.

The leading question in *Rom 6.15b* corresponds to Rom 6.1b, as regards both content and tendency. 'Should we sin because we are not under law but under grace?' Behind this lies again the objection that unconditional grace will set the Christians completely free to throw themselves into a sinful life. In the first place, it is of no importance that the law is part of the picture. As

---

20. Note that by μὴ οὖν βασιλευέτω ἡ ἁμαρτία ἐν τῷ θνητῷ ὑμῶν σώματι in Rom 6.12 Paul resumes the formulation from Rom 5.21a: ὥσπερ ἐβασίλευσεν ἡ ἁμαρτία ἐν τῷ θανάτῳ, and thus sets the scene for the positive request in 6.13bc, which corresponds to 5.21b. Cf. Agersnap, Rom 6,12, p. 42.

21. Looked at in this way, the objective of the thought-process in Rom 6.1-14 is the positive, ethical consequences, and the cue in Rom 5.12 in fact gives the theme for the section, as emphasised in Hellholm, Argumentation, p. 139f., cf. note 3 above. But precisely for this reason it becomes questionable to assume, with Hellholm (p. 143), that this is a contribution to an ongoing, dogmatic discussion about sin and grace in which the emphasis is on rejection of the incorrect views, cf. note 7 above.

hitherto, the real point is the positive: what it means to be under grace. If the objection in Rom 6.1 was absurd, the same must apply directly to Rom 6.15 — and to a greater extent, for Paul has indeed rejected the objection, giving detailed reasons. It shows that the question is intended exclusively as an opportunity for Paul to define his position further.

Precisely as in Rom 6.2a, the reply in *Rom 6.15c* is introduced by μὴ γέ-νοιτο. Unlike Rom 6.2b, we have no counter-question here as a precedent point. But apart from this it can be established that the answer to the leading question follows the same path as before.

In *Rom 6.16* as in Rom 6.3, the reasoning is based upon information assumed to be already known, here introduced by the question οὐκ οἴδατε ....[22] And it continues with ὅτι ᾧ παριστάνετε ἑαυτοὺς δούλους εἰς ὑπακοήν, δοῦλοί ἐστε ᾧ ὑπακούετε, ἤτοι ἁμαρτίας εἰς θάνατον ἢ ὑπακοῆς εἰς δικαιοσύνην; Now, no special theological insight is concerned but rather general anthropological information. But the content corresponds to the words of Jesus, that one cannot serve two masters.[23] It is crucial that the master-servant relationship is exclusive. This was true in an entirely different sense when the servant was a slave who was his master's property and wholly in his power. This is further emphasised when the second half of the verse makes it clear that the two potential rulers are sin and obedience, which confront one another sharply and personified. This must be seen as a continuation of the image of struggle from Rom 6.13: one can be in the service of the power of evil or of the power of good with death and righteousness respectively as the result.[24] It then becomes again an absolute either-or between two possibilities of life. Any simultaneity is excluded.

Like Rom 6.4-11, *Rom 6.17-18* acts to emphasise the insight quoted. But the form is strikingly different. It is drafted as a eulogy to God. Paul give

---

22. It may be noted out that the corresponding term in Rom 7.1: ἢ ἀγνοεῖτε ὅτι ..., introduces a different answer to the question in Rom 6.15, cf. section 2.2 below.

23. See Mt 6.24; Lk 16.13, cf. Sanday and Headlam, *Romans*, p. 167f.

24. Interpreters are often surprised that the personified power which confronts sin is not righteousness, as it is later in Rom 6.18,20. Similarly, it has been considered remarkable that it does not read εἰς ζωήν as an antithesis to εἰς θάνατον. Cf. Käsemann, *Römer*, p. 172, Schlier, *Römerbrief*, p. 206f., Wilckens, *Römer* II, p. 34. But these are seen as quite natural variations. As antagonistic to sin, we have not only 'righteousness' and 'obedience' in the special meaning of being bound to God (cf. Schmidt, *Römer*, p. 115), but also 'grace' in Rom 5.20-21 and God himself in Rom 6.11,13,22; in all cases binding to God's power is expressed. And in this context 'death' is understood not merely as physical death but also as a destructive power which characterises life, Rom 5.21; 6.9; 7.13. In this connection, therefore, righteousness comes to express the content of the opposite-directed form of existence, cf. Schrenk, *ThWNT* II, p. 213, Ridderbos, *Paulus*, p. 181, Gäumann, *Taufe*, p. 93, Ziesler, *Meaning*, p. 202, du Toit, Dikaiosyne, p. 271 (which speaks of 'Lebensinhalt'). An ethically validated life also seems to be concerned.

thanks that the Roman community has been converted from slavery under sin to obedience to the new teaching and slavery for righteousness.[25] In this way the either-or which applies according to Rom 6.16 is immediately brought into use on the Christian Romans, and Paul rapidly arrives at the point he is to use. By virtue of God's grace alone, the Christians have entered a new relationship of service.[26] The break with the old sinful existence is total and final, because any simultaneity between the old and the new is impossible.

Rom 6.19a, 'I am speaking in human terms because of your natural limitations', has apparently no equivalent in Rom 6.1-14. But it is an insertion that belongs together with Rom 6.17-18. In a parenthesis (a meta-communicative comment), Paul defends his method of expression in verse 18 by a reference to the limitations of the Roman community's possibility of understanding.[27] To be a slave of righteousness is indeed so paradoxical an ex-

---

25. In connection with these verses, it is discussed whether Rom 6.17b: ὑπηκούσατε δὲ ἐκ καρδίας εἰς ὃν παρεδόθητε τύπον διδαχῆς, is a secondary insertion as maintained by Rudolf Bultmann, Glossen im Römerbrief, in: *Exegetica*, Tübingen 1967, pp. 278-84; p. 283, Bornkamm, *Ende*, p. 48, Gäumann, *Taufe*, p. 96. The context of the text would probably be smoother without v. 17b. But the unevenesses may be because Paul is fumbling and only gradually arrives at the precise term. A similarly hesitant and ornate style is found in the preceding verse, where Paul also cannot decide whether he must describe dependence as slavery or a relationship of obedience, and he therefore includes both parts twice. Although the content is unusual for Paul, there is nothing against his speaking in this way. Cf. Kuss, *Römerbrief*, p. 388, Käsemann, *Römer*, p. 172f., Schlier, *Römerbrief*, p. 209f., Wilckens, *Römer* II, p. 35 — and in particular Stuhlmacher, *Römer*, p. 88, who points to a formulated article of faith which was the guideline for the Christian's thought and life. He thus resumes the fundamental view in Seeberg, *Katechismus*, p. 1ff., that it is an expression of the Christian dogma which is to be the pattern for the life of the baptised.

26. Here we clearly have righteousness as a normative power, as emphasised by du Toit, Dikaiosyne, p. 270f., cf. Kertelge, *Rechtfertigung*, p. 271, Käsemann, *Römer*, p. 172ff., Jervell, *Gud*, p. 107.

27. Thus must the sentence be understood with Lietzmann, *Römer*, p. 71, Dodd, *Romans*, p. 117, Michel, *Römer*, p. 161, Kuss, *Römerbrief*, p. 390f., Barrett, *Romans*, p. 132, Bruce, *Romans*, p. 142, Wilckens, *Römer* II, p. 37, n. 148, Hellholm, Argumentation, p. 174, who calls it the 'metanarrative clause'. It must indeed be stressed that Rom 6.19a does not belong on the same level as the reasoning itself. The word λέγω marks that Paul is commenting on his own formulation. That the sentence is in parenthesis here is confirmed when it is seen how Rom 6.19bc is linked to the preceding text. Introduced by γάρ, it is intended as a justification. But v. 19bc is not obvious as a justification for v. 19a but fits in well with the statement in Rom 6.18, as will soon be shown. In some more recent interpretations, however, Schmidt, *Römer*, p. 166f., Käsemann, *Römer*, p. 174, Tachau, 'Einst', p. 118, Halter, *Taufe*, p. 81f., have shown a trend towards understanding Rom 6.19a as a crucial link in the section's reasoning. 'Weakness of the flesh' was intended to express moral weakness — an eschatological reservation directed towards enthusiastic misunderstandings of redemption as total autarchy. Looked at in this way, v. 19a would have to

pression that there may be reason to defend it, for it should not of course be slavery in the true sense to make an effort for righteousness; not compulsion but in fact fulfilment of life. Paul expresses himself in this way for pedagogic reasons — since it is wholly new. By adding verse 19a, Paul thus emphasises that Rom 6.17-18 is a sharp and paradoxical-sounding statement. It is thereby emphasised even more in the context as a decisive answer to the question in Rom 6.15b. After the final break with sin, it is simply impossible for the Christian to have anything to do with sin; all he can do is to serve righteousness.

In *Rom 6.19b-23* the section ends as in Rom 6.12-14. There is an antithetical structure, and the consequences are drawn of the break which has occurred, with special emphasis on the ethical and the certainty of redemption. Rom 6.19bc is close to Rom 6.12-13: 'For just as you once presented your members as slaves to impurity and to greater and greater iniquity, so now present your members as slaves to righteousness for sanctification.' Whereas Rom 6.12-13 is directly introduced as a consequence of what came before, a reason is apparently concerned here. The expression from Rom 6.18 about being righteousness' slave is explained when the radical new obligation in verse 19bc, to make oneself available to righteousness, is pointed out. It is then nevertheless a consequence of what came before which is emphasised. And thereby in two respects the course of argument becomes clearer than in Rom 6.1-14: in verse 19, the two aspects of the antithesis are linked together by a ὥσπερ-οὕτως as in Rom 5.21. At the same time the struggle for impurity and lawlessness is presented as something in the past (aorist form) and the struggle for righteousness emerges as the present situation (νυνί).[28] This continues in Rom 6.20-23, in which Rom 6.19bc is explicated with new, antithetically-structured statements about the old existence and the new existence. The precedence of ὅτε in verse 20 (cf. τότε in verse 21) and νυνί in verse 22 emphasises the absolute contrast between service under sin which results in death and service to God which leads to eternal life. Once again the latter becomes the chief concern: the new life and its reward of grace — Rom 6.23.

be linked to the request in the following text and substantiate that it is directed at the Roman community. But the interpretation does not hold water. 'Weakness of the flesh' may express a moral deficiency, but it does not necessarily do so. Here, where the Romans' total conversion to the service of righteousness is hinted at, no one would immediately think of perceiving it in this way (it appears unlikely that weakness of the flesh would be understood without further ado as referring in particular to 'the strong's' enthusiastic feeling of independence, as assumed by Käsemann, *Römer* p. 174).

28. Thus Bornkamm, *Ende*, p. 48f.: 'Die Entscheidung ist ja nicht mehr offen — ein Entweder-Oder, sondern es gilt das Einst — Jetzt, Damals — Jetzt (Röm 6 19-22; 7 5f.; Kol 1 21f. u. ö.). Paulus redet darum eindringend und triumphierend.' Cf. Tachau, *Einst*, p. 118.

Again we can see that Paul appears to adopt a subsidiary theme by the leading question, but nevertheless he continues the thought-process along that path. He in fact elaborates on what was preparing the way at the end of Rom 6.14: what it means to be under grace.

At the same time, as regards both form and content, there is a return (as in Rom 6.12-14) to the parallel concepts from Rom 5.18-21. In Rom 6.15-23 there is the same ὥσπερ-οὕτως correspondence between the old life and the new life. And here the ideas about righteousness have the same two aspects. Righteousness is still an expression of the divine power and grace.[29] But at the same time δικαιοσύνη also receives a clearly ethical content in this consistently paraenetic context. Not only the obligation associated with the powerful nature of righteousness is concerned.[30] The word δικαιοσύνη is also used in line with ἁγιασμός as a description of the new life into which the Christians have been introduced.[31] It concerns their practice, 'fruits', which must be specific actions that thus lead to eternal life following the eschatological judgement.[32]

29. There is still δικαιοσύνη used in the forensic-effective meaning, cf. Chapter V, note 5 above. This impression is reinforced in that χάρις also proves to be a cue in the context; cf. Rom 5.2,15-17,20-21; 6.1,14-15,17,23.
30. Thus Käsemann, *Versuche* II, p. 186, cf. note 26 above.
31. As shown in note 24 above, the member εἰς δικαιοσύνην in Rom 6.16 appears to apply to the content of the new life, where righteousness must come to the fore. This is confirmed by the parallel-placed member ἁγιασμός in Rom 6.19,22, which clearly concerns an ethically validated life, cf. Barrett, *Romans*, p. 133, Jervell, *Gud*, p. 107, Stuhlmacher, *Römer*, p. 90, and all interpreters referred to below. Originally, ἅγιός and other words of the same stem belong in the cultic area, but in the New Testament it becomes in particular a designation for the Christians, who have been made holy through baptism, 1 Cor 6.11, and the word ἁγιασμός is used in 1 Thess 4.3-8 about the new life as a moral life in which one abstains from impurity. In 1 Cor 1.30, ἁγιασμός is used as a personified parallel with δικαιοσύνη about Christ, as he who gives the new life. Like δικαιοσύνη, ἁγιασμός can therefore concern both the transition to and the unfolding of the new life. Cf. Ridderbos, *Paulus*, p. 180ff., Thüsing, *Per Christum*, p. 94, Furnish, *Theology*, p. 153ff., Gäumann, *Taufe*, p. 99, Kertelge, *Rechtfertigung*, p. 272f., du Toit, Dikaiosyne, p. 286f. There is thus no basis for the traditional perception, which is still discernible in Sanday and Headlam, *Romans*, p. 169, Procksch, ἅγιος κτλ., *ThWNT* I (1933), pp. 87-97, 101-16; p. 114f., that consecration is a process which follows righteousness and leads to final perfection. One can perhaps, like Ziesler, *Meaning*, p. 202f., speak of a process in a different sense, about the specific actualisation of righteousness, the daily task of living out righteousness, cf. Halter, *Taufe*, p. 83ff., Käsemann, *Römer*, p. 175, Karl Paul Donfried, Justification and Last Judgment in Paul, ZNW 67 (1976), pp. 90-110; p. 99.
32. There is thus still a power to be borne in mind, which is now also affecting the Christians' specific life. Cf. Thüsing, *Per Christum*, p. 93ff., Wilckens, *Römer* II, p. 40ff., Brendan Byrne, Living out the Righteousness of God. The Contribution of Rom 6:1-8:13 to an Understanding of Paul's Ethical Presuppositions, CBQ 43 (1981), pp. 557-81; p. 564.

2.2. Rom 7.1-6 as a further parallel

An important recognition is that Rom 7.1-6 is another answer to the question in Rom 6.15. The section is thus a direct extension of 6.15-23.[33] This must be established in the face of a competing opinion: that Rom 7.1-6 correlated with Rom 7.7-25 is one section — 'freedom from the law'.[34] Rom 7.1 then becomes an unintegrated new contribution relative to the end of Rom 6.[35]

Attention must be given to the introduction in *Rom 7.1*: ‛Η ἀγνοεῖτε ... ὅτι ... ‛Η signals that the thought-process is linked to something in the preceding text. Then thoughts are led in the direction of the parallel rhetorical question in Rom 6.16. At the same time, the content of the verse points back to the question in Rom 6.15. This concerns the law and the consequences of its being replaced by grace. In the first place, in Rom 6.16-23, this has been answered without mentioning the law at all (only implied in the word ἀνομία in Rom 6.19). But an expectation has been created that the subject of the law will be discussed directly. Rom 7.1 will therefore immediately be perceived as a fulfilment of this expectation when it makes a fundamental statement about the law's power. The connection back to Rom 6.15 is additionally seen formally and inherently, for essentially Rom 7.1-6 is parallel to Rom 6.16-23 and thus to 6.3-14.[36]

The question remains whether freedom from the law must lead to sin.

Just as in Rom 6.3 and Rom 6.16, the first answer in Rom 7.1 is a counter-question pointing towards a knowledge which Paul can assume. In this way, the form of what came before continues. It is still a fictitious discussion-situation, in which Paul takes a position on the views of an interlocutor. Rom 7.1a, in which Paul refers to the recipients' knowledge of the law, indicates that the nomistic objections he rejects are not wholly alien to the Roman community. But no true, topical polemic seems to be concerned; indeed he here addresses the Romans as his brothers.[37] It is maintained

---

33. Cf. Lietzmann, *Römer*, p. 19, Dodd, *Romans*, p. 105, 119, Ulrich Luz, Zum Aufbau von Röm 1-8, *ThZ* 25 (1969), pp. 161-81; p. 176f., von der Osten-Sacken, *Römer 8*, p. 188f., Cranfield, *Romans*, p. 332.

34. Thus especially Nygren, *Romarna*, p. 46f., 272ff., cf. Michel, *Römer*, p. 165ff., Murray, *Romans*, p. 239, Bruce, *Romans*, p. 134, Gäumann, *Taufe*, p. 23, Käsemann, *Römer*, p. 178ff., Cranfield, *Romans*, p. 330f.

35. This clearly in Michel, *Römer*, p. 166, Käsemann, *Römer*, p. 178f.

36. As emphasised in Luz, *Aufbau*, p. 176f.

37. Probability indicates that here 'the law' must be seen, as in the whole context, as the Law of Moses, cf. Lietzmann, *Römer*, p. 72, Murray, *Romans*, p. 240, Schmidt, *Römer*, p. 120, Jervell, *Gud*, p. 111f., Cranfield, *Romans*, p. 332f., against Käsemann, *Römer*, p. 179. But it does not follow from this that Paul is combating specific nomistic opponents in the Roman community, as assumed by Zahn, *Römer*, p. 329, and Wilckens, *Römer II*, p. 63. This is contradicted not only by the form of address, cf. the reinforced term 'my brothers'

inherently in Rom 7.1b that the law has power over a person for as long as that person lives. This is a principle all will be able to accept. But it is in fact ambiguous. At first the positive aspect would be emphasised, that the law has validity throughout life without exception; this is thus a principle about the law's total requirement. But the negative aspect of the matter can also be emphasised; the law prevails over a person only for as long as that person lives. It is said that the dead are not bound by the law. It is a strange principle, but of course correct, that one cannot obey the law when one is dead. In the course of the argument, it transpires that the principle is applied in this different, somewhat subtle, way.[38]

In *Rom 7.2-3*, this assumed fact is the basis for a further argument (parallel to what occurs in Rom 6.4, in which Paul is also working towards his point). Paul elaborates and exemplifies the Rom 7.1 principle. He uses an analogy from matrimonial legislation. A woman is bound by her marriage as long as her husband lives and cannot enter into any other relationship until her husband's death. But things go wrong if this example is applied. The Christians' situation is described by an absurd image: in the past they were married to the law but are now dead — and can therefore enter into a new marriage with Christ![39] Nevertheless, there is not doubt about Paul's intention.

Rom 7.4 represents Paul's arrival at the crucial point, which corresponds to Rom 6.11 and Rom 6.17-18. 'In the same way, my friends, you have died to the law through the body of Christ, so that you may belong to another, to him who has been raised from the dead in order that we may bear fruit for God.' What is crucial in the thought-process is again that the transition to Christianity is a total break with existence hitherto, a change of authority by virtue of Christ's death.[40] It is also described as a break with the law which characterised the old existence. Indeed, the law's cessation must

---

in Rom 7.4. It should also be noted that in Rom 7.4-6 Paul, purely indicatively and without reservation, places the Roman community among the group which has finally broken with existence under the law.

38. It is rarely noted that this lapse occurs in the text. But see Zahn, *Römer*, p. 329, von der Osten-Sacken, *Römer 8*, p. 189.

39. The logic is beyond recovery, cf. Dodd, *Romans*, p. 120, Lietzmann, *Römer*, p. 72, Murray, *Romans*, p. 240f., Jervell, *Gud*, p. 112. In isolation, Rom 7.2-3 might perhaps be perceived as an example not to be forced in all its details, but merely to illustrate one point: that death cancels a binding to the law — thus Nygren, *Romarna*, pp. 277-80, Schmidt, *Römer*, p. 120, Käsemann, *Römer*, p. 179, Cranfield, *Romans*, p. 334f. But in Rom 7.4, usage is continued from the example (especially the term γενέσθαι ἑτέρῳ), so that the impression is given that it is the marriage example which is used. Paul thus himself uses the illustration in the forced manner. Cf. however Chapter VII, note 189, below.

40. See the detailed interpretation of this motif, 'death with Christ', in Chapter III, section 3.2, above.

be a precondition for the arrival of the proper fruits of the new departure.

Rom 7.5-6 expresses the further consequences of this, presented antithetically, corresponding to Rom 6.12-14 and Rom 6.19-23. What the new fertile life for God involves in contrast to the old sinful life is again amplified. Differing from the parallels in Rom 6, it is expressed wholly indicatively. But this makes no difference. The active consequences are still maintained. Another difference is that the law has now adopted the role which sin had in Rom 6. According to Rom 7.5, the law aroused sinful desire. But this alteration also means nothing especial in regard to the matter, for the negative, the law and its effect, is not the subject. The emphasis is still on the positive, the new existence, which unfolds under grace. Rom 7.6 emphasises that this has finally replaced the reality known hitherto.[41]

A striking new motif is introduced at the end, where the Spirit comes into the picture. But this is only an intimation. Quite concisely, πνεῦμα, which is linked to the new existence, is contrasted with γράμμα, which is the distinctive mark of the old existence. We also encounter this pair of contrasts in other passages, where it strongly emphasises the relationship between a distorted and a true perception of the Old Testament.[42] It appears here quite like a cue — unintegrated and directly enigmatic.

2.3. Parallel features in Rom 7.7-8.39

Paul also employs in the subsequent context the compositional technique which in Rom 6.1-7.6 results in the sharp contrast of the past and present existences, in which the righteousness and the splendour of the new life are emphasised. But the description is longer and becomes more intense from Rom 7.7, where an emphasised 'I' is used in the description of the old existence.[43] The before-now antitheses are not perhaps so immediately ap-

---

41. If one keeps to the positive view in Rom 6 and Rom 7.1-6, there is thus a clear thematic connection. A division between Chapters 6 and 7 may appear to be natural from a direct consideration of the text. One allows oneself to become fixated on the negative in the text and to classify the chapters as 'freedom from sin' and 'freedom from the law', cf. note 34 above. But these negative aspects are not the matter itself. Their main function appears to be to lead up to the positive statements about the new life.

42. See in particular 2 Cor 3.6-18, also Rom 2.27-29. Cf. Ernst Käsemann, Geist und Buchstabe, in: *Paulinische Perspektiven*, Tübingen 1969, pp. 237-74, cf. Jervell, *Gud*, p. 114f.

43. This is a stylistic means which may be seen as an especially intense variation of the dialogic form. It anticipates that the recurrent ἐγώ in Rom 7.7-25 must be understood in a general sense. This is supported by the fact that the same (fictitious) person in Rom 8.2 is addressed in the second person (σέ). The most widespread opinion is that this is a general description of man in the power of sin, cf. Werner Georg Kümmel, Römer 7 und die Bekehrung des Paulus (originally 1929), in: *Römer 7 und das Bild des Menschen im Neuen Testament. Zwei Studien* (ThB NT 53), Munich 1974, pp. 1-160; p. 117ff., Günther

parent as in the preceding section. But the same pattern still recurs in the principal features, and Rom 7.7-8.39 is also thematically associated with Rom 6.1-14 and the intervening parts of the text.

I wish first to draw attention to the more formal aspect, the structure. The same elements are again to be found as in the previous section.

This is clear from the beginning, where there is again the dialogic form with leading questions.

Rom 7.7a: Τί οὖν ἐροῦμεν; is the same introductory question as Rom 6.1a, cf. Rom 6.15a.

Rom 7.7b, 'Is the law sin?', sets out the new problem, just as in Rom 6.1b and Rom 6.15b. And here also Paul does not directly tackle the matter for which the way has been prepared. One might well expect an amplification of the idea of the Spirit as the characteristic feature of the new existence, which was introduced by a cue in Rom 7.6. The question instead concerns the other side of the antithesis γράμμα-πνεῦμα — understanding of the law. There is again in the context an incidental circumstance — but now quite an important incidental circumstance, an urgent question. In Rom 7.1-6, and especially in verse 5, Paul has allowed the law to adopt the villain-role that sin had in the past. It therefore follows naturally to raise the question in Rom 7.7b, which introduces an apology for the law. Once again this appears to be an excursus, but nevertheless it proves to lead the thought-process in the right direction.

Rom 7.7c introduces the answer with a μὴ γένοιτο as in Rom 6.2a and Rom 6.15c. But here the reply becomes longer and more complicated. We can see a certain hesitation in Paul. He raises a new leading question in Rom 7.13a about the law: that however good it is it leads to death. The second at-

Bornkamm, Sünde, Gesetz und Tod, in: *Das Ende des Gesetzes. Gesammelte Aufsätze* I (BEvTh 16)[5], Munich 1966, pp. 51-69, p. 58f., Käsemann, *Römer*, p. 185, 188, Cranfield, *Romans*, p. 343f., Schlier, *Römerbrief*, p. 221, Wilckens, *Römer* II, p. 76ff., Morris, *Romans*, p. 276ff. Opposed to this is in particular the interpretation that it is an autobiographical 'I', cf. Dodd, *Romans*, p. 124f., Murray, *Romans*, p. 249f., Bruce, *Romans*, p. 147. This discussion is not crucial to the subject here. But in my opinion the interpretations are not absolute alternatives. The 'I' cannot be Paul himself as distinct from others; this is excluded by the use of 'you' in Rom 8.2. It is also questionable when it is maintained in Kümmel, *Römer* 7, p. 74ff., especially p. 84, cf. Bornkamm, *Ende*, p. 58f., that the 'I' is purely fictitious, and that Paul is not included in this. It is a step in the efforts to harmonise with Phil 3.4-11, and it appears forced that the only person who utters this 'I' is not to be included in it. It must be perceived as a 'typical I', cf. Karl Kertelge, Exegetische Überlegungen zum Verständnis der paulinischen Anthropologie nach Römer 7, in: *Grundthemen paulinischer Theologie*, Freiburg 1991, pp. 174-83; p. 176f., Theissen, *Aspekte*, p. 181ff. See also notes 48 and 51 below.

tempt at a reply is introduced in Rom 7.13b by a new μὴ γένοιτο. This divides the text into two sections: Rom 7.7-12 and Rom 7.13-25.[44]

In two instances, in Rom 7.14 and in Rom 7.18, there is a reference to a general knowledge, which as in Rom 6.3, Rom 6.16 and Rom 7.1 must be the basis of further discussion. Here, Paul does not use a question to introduce the insight which he makes the basis of the argument. But the introduction using οἴδαμεν ὅτι and οἶδα ὅτι respectively has the same function.[45] He indicates the well-known conflict between duty and inclination.

We find in Rom 8.1-4 emphasised statements about the crucial turning point by which the Christians, by virtue of Christ's deeds, have been taken out of the old form of existence and set in a new spiritual life. This corresponds to the points in Rom 6.4-11, Rom 6.17-18 and Rom 7.4.

This is followed from Rom 8.5 onwards by antithetical statements in which the new life of the Spirit is contrasted with the old sinful life and the life of the 'flesh'. This accords with the conclusions of the preceding sections, Rom 6.12-14, Rom 6.19b-23 and Rom 7.5-6, where the ethical consequences were in this way revived. Since Rom 5, the before-now contrasts have characterised the description. They continue up to Rom 8.15. In the remainder of the chapter the main emphasis appears to be on the security associated with the life of the Spirit. Apart from length, is corresponds to Rom 6.14 and Rom 6.23, which end by briefly emphasising the safe hope associated with the new life.

We thus again have the same process of an intended objection which in an apparent detour leads Paul to stress the power and splendour of the new life.

Going more deeply into the content, there are also features which confirm this development of thought and the parallelism with the preceding sections. I can present observations from three areas which support that the emphasis is again on the positive aspect: life and certainty of redemption.

First, there is reason to look more closely at the apology for the law which gives this passage so extensive a range, and which becomes so intense that one almost forgets what one is aiming at. I wish here to point out that the

---

44. Cf. Schmidt, *Römer*, p. 128, Jervell, *Gud*, p. 120, Cranfield, *Romans*, p. 354, Wilckens, *Römer* II, p. 74ff. The widespread alternative is a division between Rom 7.7-13 and Rom 7.14-25, as found in Kümmel, *Römer 7*, p. 56f., Bornkamm, *Ende*, p. 61ff., Käsemann, *Römer*, p. 191, Schlier, *Römerbrief*, p. 228f., Theissen, *Aspekte*, p. 187f.

45. Cf. Stowers, *Diatribe*, p. 121, 152, Jervell, *Gud*, p. 121, Cranfield, *Romans*, p. 355, Schlier, *Römerbrief*, p. 229, Morris, *Romans*, p. 290. Different in Wilckens, *Römer* II, p. 85, who wishes to read οἶδα μεν in Rom 7.14, so that the entire section is kept in the first person singular. See also Theissen, *Aspekte*, p. 213ff., where it is argued that the sentences in Rom 7.15b,19 are pre-coined thoughts.

apology has three members — not only the two paths of argument in Rom 7.7-12 and Rom 7.13-25 but also a third which begins in Rom 8.1.

The argument begins in Rom 7.7d: 'Yet, if it had not been for the law, I would not have known sin'. There is cause for hesitation — a certain ambiguity in the understanding of the crucial member: ἁμαρτίαν γινώσκειν. In a Pauline context, 'knowledge of sin' can mean two things: that one is aware of sinfulness (that is to say, the function of the law is to characterise sin as sin),[46] or that in practice one is familiar with sin (that is to say, the function of the law is to set sin going).[47] As far as I can see, Paul hesitates similarly.

The first course of argument clearly concerns a knowledge of the latter kind. Rom 7.7-12 is an account of the Fall:[48] the law is described, if not as the cause of sin, then at least as its catalyst.[49] The commandment not to covet provokes covetousness. It is in fact intended to stress the conditions of life and to lead to life, but instead it leads to death (verse 10). There is then a crucial distinction between the law's intention and the effect it has. It can therefore be maintained that the law is good enough, but has sin and death as its paradoxical and inexplicable actual effects. This conclusion is anticipated in Rom 7.12: ὥστε ὁ μὲν νόμος ἅγιος καὶ ἡ ἐντολὴ ἁγία καὶ δικαία καὶ ἀγαθή. But we are not given the continuation expected: τὸ δὲ ἀγαθὸν ἐμοὶ ἐγένετο θάνατος.[50] Paul checks himself — probably because the law would then have a strongly negative effect.

46. Cf. Rom 5.13,20 and (in my opinion also) Rom 3.20. Thus Dodd, *Romans*, p. 126f., Bruce, *Romans*, p. 149, Käsemann, *Römer*, p. 185 (who calls the concept dialectic, by which he probably means that it must be combined with the concept referred to in the next note), Cranfield, *Romans*, p. 348, Morris, *Romans*, p. 278f.

47. Cf. 2 Cor 5.21 and (in the opinion of many) Rom 3.20. Thus Rudolf Bultmann, Römer 7 und die Anthropologie des Paulus, in: *Exegetica*, Tübingen 1967, pp. 198-209; p. 200, γινώσκω κτλ., *ThWNT* I (1933), pp. 688-715; p. 703, Althaus, *Römer*, p. 73, Nygren, *Romarna*, p. 285f., Schmidt, *Römer*, p. 123, Bornkamm, *Ende*, pp. 51-69, p. 54, Michel, *Römer*, p. 172, Lagrange, *Romains*, p. 168, Barrett, *Romans*, p. 140f., Morris, *Romans*, p. 249, Jervell, *Gud*, p. 116f., Schlier, *Römerbrief*, p. 221, Wilckens, *Römer* II, p. 78.

48. This designation is used by Theissen, *Aspekte*, p. 204ff., cf. Bornkamm, *Ende*, p. 58f., Käsemann, *Römer*, p. 188, Cranfield, *Romans*, p. 343, Schlier, *Römerbrief*, p. 224, Wilckens, *Römer* II, p. 78f. In contrast, Kümmel, *Römer 7*, pp. 85-87, has tried to show that Adam cannot have been part of the picture. But the line from Rom 5.12-21 and the reminders of Gen 3 lead the thoughts towards the Adamite type of man. This does not concern Adam as a subject of the conflict in Rom 7.7-25 but as a model for it, cf. Theissen, *Aspekte*, p. 205.

49. Cf. Theissen, *Aspekte*, p. 224ff., who presents it as 'Das Gesetz als Stimulus der Sünde'.

50. Cf. Kümmel, *Römer 7*, p. 56f., who establishes that it must be supplemented in this way by the anacoluthon which arises because a corresponding μέν is lacking after δέ in Rom 7.12. Lagrange, *Romains*, p. 171, Wilckens, *Römer* II, p. 83 n. 335, indicates the possibility that the expected apodosis is included in Rom 7.13. This interpretation seems obvious to me.

The continuation is instead formulated in Rom 7.13a as a new rhetorical question: τὸ οὖν ἀγαθὸν ἐμοὶ ἐγένετο θάνατος; this introduces the other course of argument. In the other answer the law has a more positive function. If sin can create death by virtue of the law, this happens in order that sin can be made obvious and appear in all its horror, Rom 7.13c. According to this correction, what is concerned is a knowledge of sin of the type in which sin is made recognisable. Paul relies on the general knowledge of this effect. The conflict between duty and inclination described so vividly in these verses must be something recognisable.[51] This conflict gains significance in two ways in the context. In the first place it expresses two forces struggling within sinful man: on the one hand the law and the will to do good; on the other hand sin and the inclination towards evil. This underlines the distance between sin and the law, and shows that the law leads towards the good. This in fact produces a defence of the law. But in the second place the main consideration remains the hopelessness and despair which characterises the divided personality. This becomes acute in the cry of distress in Rom 7.24, in which man appears to be completely lost. But the problem of law and sin remains. The law's effect is still far from its intention.[52] In isolation, Rom 7.7-25 would be an unsuccessful defence of the law. But it should not in fact be seen in isolation.

In my opinion, Rom 8 is the crucial member in the context — the third and true answer to the question in Rom 7.7. The first answers distinguished between the law's good intentions and its unfortunate effect. But Rom 8.4 makes it clear that the law's intention is in fact achieved when the Christians walk in the Spirit by virtue of Christ's act of redemption. The law of sin and death has been replaced by the true law: the law of the Spirit of life — Rom 8.2.

These observations confirm that the main function of Rom 7.7-25 is to prepare the way for Rom 8.1-39. And if Rom 8.1 is the crucial turning point[53] this shows unambiguously that Rom 7.7-25 concerns the non-

---

51. Cf. note 43 above. This observation points in the direction of the 'typical' understanding of the 'I'.

52. It seems therefore to be a doubtful assertion, when it reads in Kümmel, *Römer 7*, p. 57: 'Mit diesem Satz [Rom 7,13] ist das Gesetz nun endgültig rehabiliert [sic].'

53. There is however an uncertainty at the transition to Rom 8, which may camouflage the dominant structure. The reversal from the dispersed situation to redemption comes in two stages (Rom 7.24/25a; 7.25b/8.1). The text may be in disarray, cf. Kümmel, *Römer 7*, p. 67f., Bultmann, *Exegetica*, p. 278ff. Note, however, that almost all members in Rom 7.7-25 are duplicated: Rom 7.8-10 is a parallel to Rom 7.11-12; Rom 7.14-17,18b is duplicated in Rom 7.18a,19-20a,22-23,20b,21. The thought-process apparently moves in a circle, which helps to present the situation as desperate and chaotic. In the context, the duplication in Rom 7.24-8.1 does not appear as surprising, and it is reasonable to assume that

Christian life which is now of the past.[54] It may seem at first that Paul has
returned to the factual situation when he begins to use the present tense in
Rom 7.14 and develops the conflict so intensively.[55] If this is the impression
given, it is contradicted when one arrives at Rom 8. But it is precisely this
long, present-tense, persistent description of the disruptive, sinful existence
that creates a special effect. It is stressed that this would still be the situation
were it not for God's contribution in Christ.[56] It sets the scene for a high degree of gratitude for what has occurred.

And in contrast to the despairing situation in Rom 7.7-25 the new life is
described in Rom 8. It is characterised by the sure hope — the problems of
sin have been overcome, and the threat of death has been replaced by the
prospect of eternal life.

Another inherent feature is the Christological line in Rom 8. As we have
seen, this is a general, precursive Christology.[57] Christ has identified himself
with mankind, so that they can live a life of the same kind as his (Rom 8.3-
4), with the same life-giving Spirit (Rom 8.11), the same child-circumstances
(Rom 8.15-16), the same way through suffering to glory (Rom 8.17) and the
same sure process of redemption (Rom 8.28-30). The emphasis is that the
Adamite life has finally been replaced by the life that comes to the fore with
Christ. In his psychological interpretation of the section, Gerd Theissen has
described it as a 'Rollenwechsel' from Adam's role to Christ's role. This was
prepared for in Rom 5.12-21; it is developed in Rom 6.1-7.6 by the symbolism

Paul is responsible for this also. In any case, it is clear that in these verses a crucial
reversal has occurred.
54. This interpretation holds the strongest position in research. See Kümmel, *Römer 7*, p. 74ff.,
Althaus, *Römerbrief*, p. 79ff., Dodd, *Romans* p. 125f., Bultmann, *Exegetica*, p. 198ff., Bornkamm, *Ende*, p. 51ff., Michel, *Römer*, p. 171, Schmidt, *Römer*, p. 127f., Jervell, *Gud*, 126ff.,
Wilckens, *Römer II*, p. 76. It may also be maintained that Rom 7.7-25 and Rom 8 are connected in the manner given in the γράμμα-πνεῦμα-antithesis in Rom 7.6, cf. above in connection with note 42.
55. See Nygren, *Romarna*, p. 295, Murray, *Romans*, p. 257ff., Bruce, *Romans*, p. 150f., Cranfield,
Romans, p. 344ff., Morris, *Romans*, p. 284ff., in which one can base oneself on the thought-
provoking features in Rom 7.14-25, which make it understandable that the text has been
used traditionally as a description of the Christian existence: the confessional nature, the
'I' form, gives the section the present-tense and the intensity, as well as the surprising
range the section has. But as referred to above not only the dominant structure is opposed to this assumption; it can also be said, with Theissen, *Aspekte*, p. 186, that there is
a striking antithesis between the statements in Rom 7.14,17,18,23 and in Rom 8.2,9b,9a,6,
and that the transition at around Rom 7.13 is too unmarked to be the crucial turning
point. Moreover, it is immediately shown that there is a quite obvious explanation for the
thought-provoking features.
56. Cf. Kertelge, *Grundthemen*, p. 182f.
57. Cf. the review above in Chapter III, section 3.3.

of burial, change of authority and marriage; here it comes intensively re-flected.[58]

A third consideration is the relationship between the certainty of redemption which is enjoined and the measures against sin and tribulation also mentioned in Rom 8.

Rom 8.10-11 reads that 'the body is dead because of sin', and that a 'mortal body' must be given life. Rom 8.12-13 has a demand to keep away from things mortal, followed by a promise of life if the deeds of the body are killed. According to Rom 8.17, Christians must suffer with Christ. In Rom 8.23 they groan inwardly and suffer. Rom 8.24 associates redemption with a hope, something not visible. And according to Rom 8.26 Christians need the help of the Spirit. All this has been interpreted as eschatological reservation, in which the body's mortality and external threats are meant to emphasise that this is not a final redemption, which makes any requests superfluous.[59]

The crucial considerations are about the direction of the thought-process. There is a marked difference between reservations and admissions. In both cases deficiencies and problems emerge.

If one makes *reservations*, one emphasises the deficiencies, for example in order to put an exaggerated certainty of redemption in its correct place. The aim is to pose problems. By an *admission*, problems arrive from the outside and become urgent, in particular when a certainty of redemption is expressed. A position must be adopted towards the deficiencies, and it must be shown that there is no threat against the new life. The aim is to overcome the problems.

It must be clear that we are dealing with an admission in Rom 8.10-14. The negative terms about the body's mortality are not the main line in the

---

58. See Theissen, *Aspekte*, p. 252ff., especially p. 266.
59. This line is particularly emphasised in Käsemann, *Römer*, p. 215ff. He sees in Rom 8.9-11 a confrontation with the enthusiasts' demand for a place apart, p. 215f., cf. Tannehill, *Dying*, p. 78ff. Rom 8.12-15 is said to be a warning against temptation, in which enthusiastic usage is employed, p. 216f. He perceives, p. 221f., the conclusion to Rom 8.17, '... if we suffer with him so that we may also be glorified with him', as a modification and an anti-enthusiastic polemic, cf. Paulsen, *Überlieferung*, p. 96. Käsemann also assumes, p. 230, as is often the case, that Rom 8.24-25 directly emphasises that the hope-category presupposes that final redemption is not yet fulfilled, cf. Michel, *Römer*, p. 206f., Schmidt, *Römer*, p. 149. According to Ernst Käsemann, Der gottesdienstliche Schrei nach der Freiheit, in: *Paulinische Perspektiven*, Tübingen 1969, pp. 211-36, *Römer*, p. 231f., the talk of 'unutterable longing' is said to polemicise against an enthusiastic pride in charismatic abilities.

context, and are not the point.[60] The emphasis is on the strength of the Spirit by which the Christians are seized, so that problems are overcome: According to Rom 8.10, 'though the body is dead because of sin, the Spirit is life because of righteousness';[61] Rom 8.11 is an assurance that the inherent Spirit is to give life to mortal body.[62] The call, 'by the Spirit you put to death the deeds of the body' (Rom 8.13), is continued in Rom 8.14 by a comment that it is the Spirit which drives the Christians, and this continues in an assurance that as God's children the Christians will (through suffering) achieve glory.[63] Finally, we may also note that Paul allows carnal weakness to emerge only after he has declared in Rom 8.18, with emphasis, that this problem is resolved.

Similarly, we can see that in the last half of Rom 8 Paul wishes to show that the problem of suffering is overcome, that the strength of the Spirit will help the Christians through to glory. Again, the direction of the thought-process shows that this is an admission in which the problem is produced so that it can be overcome. The point from the beginning in Rom 8.17 is that suffering leads to glory with Christ. Before the problems are developed, Rom 8.18 underlines the predominance of glory over suffering.[64] The emphasis in Rom 8.25 is on the perseverance which is associated with hope.[65] And

---

60. It is noteworthy that on the three occasions where 'the body' and 'death' are connected in Rom 8.10-14 the linking together takes place in a different way, and at first sight does not cohere logically: according to verse 10, the body is dead; in verse 11 the problem is that the body is mortal; and according to verse 13, the deeds of the body must be put to death. This must be interpreted to mean that these negative statements are neither the main matter nor the point.

61. As shown above in Chapter III, note 201, the introductory τὸ μὲν σῶμα ... in Rom 8.10b must probably be understood concessively, so that the sentence is entirely subordinate to what follows, cf. Bruce, *Romans*, p. 164. It is then accepted that the Christians have a mortal body as a result of the earlier sin (cf. Rom 5.12-14; 7.7-25), but this is indeed not crucial to the new life. The alternative interpretation is, as also referred to above in Chapter III, note 201, that death as in Rom 6.2-11; 7.4, is something good, deliverance from sin. The whole verse thus expresses an enthusiasm for redemption: the body is dead relative to sin, and is entirely characterised by the Spirit and life.

62. It is not disputed that this is the point. But Käsemann, *Römer*, p. 216, sees an eschatological reservation in the mere fact that the resurrection of the dead is in the future.

63. Cf. Michel, *Römer*, p. 197, Cranfield, *Romans*, p. 401, Wilckens, *Römer* II, p. 135f.

64. Thus also Käsemann, *Römer*, p. 223, cf. Wilckens, *Römer* II, p. 150f., where there is a rejection of von der Osten-Sacken, *Römer 8*, p. 78ff., who seeks to reconstruct an enthusiastic tradition, which Paul adopts, at the same time rejecting the enthusiastic trends.

65. As opposed to the interpretation of Rom 8.24-25 referred to in note 59 above, it is in fact said unreservedly that the Christians are redeemed, as emphasised by Murray, *Romans*, p. 308f., Wilckens, *Römer* II, p. 158. The dative τῇ ἐλπίδι is probably instrumentalis concerning the accompanying circumstance. The (anaphoric) article points to the certain hope — the body's delivery from mortality, Rom 8.23. It seems that in this hope there is a positive power. That one allows 'hope' to mean 'that which one hopes' or 'in the category of

Rom 8.26-27 says that the strength of the Spirit will truly help the Christians to persevere, so that all can end in triumph. This occurs on the one hand in Rom 8.28-30, in which the glory is described as something already realised, and on the other hand in the hymnic ending to Rom 8.31-39, where it is stressed that God's love is unshakeable and that the Christians have yet more to expect.[66]

The train of thought thus leads us from the misery of the old time to the glory of the new life. This direction is also anticipated by the form.

3. The compositional technique

The outline review of these chapters of the Letter to the Romans has shown them to fall into four sections: Rom 6.1-14, Rom 6.15-23, Rom 7.1-6 and Rom 7.7-8.39. The sections are held together by the common compositional technique which serves to continue the line of approach from Rom 5. This compositional technique means that both the structure and the main subject of these sections stand out clearly and are easy to grasp.

The same elements of form are repeated in all sections. It begins with a new contribution, asking the question Τί οὖν (ἐροῦμεν); The preceding context ended on a point of emphasis, and prepared the ground for an amplifying continuation. But instead, and surprisingly, an incidental circumstance is taken up. In an objection in the form of a question, some clearly incorrect ethical consequences of Paul's evangelism are inferred. These are sharply rejected by μὴ γένοιτο. There is reference to a basic understanding. On this basis the answer is given, first with a reasoned rejection of the leading question (a 'no'), then with a continuing positive emphasis (an

---

hope' (thus Hyldahl, *Breve*, p. 173), may perhaps be defended by the generic use of the article. But there is no basis for adding a restrictive 'only' as does Michel, *Römer*, p. 206f., Schmidt, *Römer*, p. 149, *The New English Bible*, Oxford 1970, The New Testament, p. 199. Rom 8.24b apparently defines the term 'hope' as a symptom of a lack — it is superfluous to hope for something one can see, cf. Michel and Wilckens in the passages stated, Käsemann, *Römer*, p. 230. But in Rom 8.25 this is turned into something positive: one gains strength when one's hope is directed towards something that goes beyond the merely visible, cf. 2 Cor 4.18.

66. Rom 8.30 serves as an almost enthusiastic point, cf. Schmidt, *Römer*, p. 153: 'unerschütterliche Gewissheit', Schade, *Christologie*, p. 102. Rom 8.32 can be perceived as a parallel to the a fortiori conclusion in Rom 5.9-10: from the eschatological events which have already occurred, it is concluded that there is even more to expect from the future consummation, cf. Wolter, *Rechtfertigung*, p. 183, von der Osten-Sacken, *Römer 8*, p. 51ff., 309ff. This must deny all consideration of a Pauline reservation in the verses. If it were really Paul's intention to renounce enthusiasm, it is incomprehensible that he does not do so directly and emphatically, and it is an impossible thought that he would then end by withdrawing everything.

'on the contrary') which is given the final emphasis. The true ethical consequences of the new departure which has occurred are amplified by antithetical formulations, in which they are contrasted with the old sinful existence. The continuation which was anticipated at the end of the preceding section is thus in fact achieved.

By this procedure Paul achieves, as shown, the continuation of the before-now structure from Rom 5.12-21 right up to Rom 8.

What is also happening is that almost the same point is stressed in several contexts. There is probably a certain development between the sections. But the main subject is repeated in every passage and thereby cemented: that the new departure which has occurred has finally placed the Christians in an existence ethically characterised by righteousness, and which without real threat will inevitably lead to eternal life.

It may also be noted that the before-now structure is preponderant: the main interest everywhere lay in the positive, continuing part. When Paul answers the introductory questions, the actual rejection of the objection is not of interest in itself but is merely of passing interest. The crucial point is not an apology or a polemic, not a repudiation of a false theology. In isolation, it might be considered whether Rom 6.1-14 was a current dispute, and that Paul had to defend himself or perhaps admonish his opponents. But when Paul uses the same procedure of rejection and clarification in the sections following the matter becomes of a different nature, since a universal, opposing viewpoint cannot be reconstructed.

The repeated structure seems therefore to be an instance of the general use in rhetoric of fictitious objections and incorrect conclusions to a defined and emphasised description of one's own views.[67] We are dealing with a clearly implemented, advanced version of a widespread stylistic means.

4. Survey of Rom 6.1-14

This perception of the compositional technique also provides a certain clarity in regard to the structure and main approach of the text.

An important means of interpreting the subsequent parts of the text is thus provided in advance. The great problems and the important points of

---

67. The analysis of the structure undertaken here therefore confirms that the dialogic form is primarily a stylistic means in which the objections are fictitious, cf. section 1.1, with notes 3-8, above. See in particular Stowers, *Diatribe*, p. 125ff., in which the diatribe figure, 'Objections and False Conclusions' is examined with the use of a large body of text-material, cf. also Bultmann, *Stil*, pp. 46-54. It may also be noted that this stylistic figure is a broad development of the so-called correctio which comes to be considered in connection with Rom 6.12-14, cf. Chapter X, section 1.2, below.

discussion are here. But the structure of the text is reasonably clear, and there should be no doubt about the direction of Paul's thought-process.

I try in the diagrammatic division of the text below to give a provisional, formal definition of the function of the individual parts. I wish also to emphasise the text's antithetical nature. There are statements about 'death with Christ' and a life with Christ. Only the beginning is not covered: Rom 6.1-2a: Τί οὖν ἐροῦμεν; ἐπιμένωμεν τῇ ἁμαρτίᾳ, ἵνα ἡ χάρις πλεονάσῃ; μὴ γένοιτο.

Apart from this, Rom 6.2-14 can be arranged in two columns. The first contains the statements about death; the other the statements about life:

Verse 2 — the emphasised counter-question:
οἵτινες ἀπεθάνομεν τῇ ἁμαρτίᾳ, πῶς
ἔτι ζήσομεν ἐν αὐτῇ;

Verse 3 refers to basic insight:
ἢ ἀγνοεῖτε ὅτι, ὅσοι ἐβαπτίσθημεν εἰς
Χριστὸν Ἰησοῦν, εἰς τὸν θάνατον
αὐτοῦ ἐβαπτίσθημεν;

Verse 4 amplifies the insight, and the consequences of this are emphasised:

συνετάφημεν οὖν αὐτῷ διὰ τοῦ βαπτίσματος εἰς τὸν θάνατον,	ἵνα ὥσπερ ἠγέρθη Χριστὸς ἐκ νεκρῶν διὰ τῆς δόξης τοῦ πατρός, οὕτως καὶ ἡμεῖς ἐν καινότητι ζωῆς περιπατήσω- μεν·

Verse 5 amplifies the conclusion in verse 4:

εἰ γὰρ σύμφυτοι γεγόναμεν τῷ ὁμοιώματι τοῦ θανάτου αὐτοῦ,	ἀλλὰ καὶ τῆς ἀναστάσεως ἐσόμεθα·

Verse 6a justifies, with a new reference to insight:
τοῦτο γινώσκοντες ὅτι ὁ παλαιὸς
ἡμῶν ἄνθρωπος συνεσταυρώθη,

Verse 6bc adduces the consequences of this:
ἵνα καταργηθῇ τὸ σῶμα τῆς
ἁμαρτίας, τοῦ μηκέτι δουλεύειν ἡμᾶς
τῇ ἁμαρτίᾳ·

Verse 7 is a parenthetic justification:
ὁ γὰρ ἀποθανὼν δεδικαίωται ἀπὸ τῆς
ἁμαρτίας·

Verse 8 summarises verses 6-7 and on this basis undertakes a new conclusion:
εἰ δὲ ἀπεθάνομεν σὺν Χριστῷ,   πιστεύομεν ὅτι καὶ συζήσομεν αὐτῷ,

Verse 9 introduces a justification with a new reference to an insight:
                                                     εἰδότες ὅτι Χριστὸς ἐγερθεὶς ἐκ
                                                     νεκρῶν οὐκέτι ἀποθνῄσκει, θάνατος
                                                     αὐτοῦ οὐκέτι κυριεύει·

Verse 10 amplifies the insight:
ὃ γὰρ ἀπέθανεν, τῇ ἁμαρτίᾳ ἀπέθανεν
ἐφάπαξ·   ὃ δὲ ζῇ, ζῇ τῷ θεῷ·

Verse 11 gives an emphasised use of the insight:
οὕτως καὶ ὑμεῖς λογίζεσθε
ἑαυτοὺς νεκροὺς μὲν τῇ ἁμαρτίᾳ   ζῶντας δὲ τῷ θεῷ ἐν Χριστῷ ᾿Ιησοῦ.

Verses 12-13a — negative request followed by a positive request in verse 13bc as a consequence of the foregoing:
μὴ οὖν βασιλευέτω ἡ ἁμαρτία ἐν τῷ   ἀλλὰ παραστήσατε ἑαυτοὺς τῷ θεῷ
θνητῷ ὑμῶν σώματι εἰς τὸ ὑπακούειν   ὡσεὶ ἐκ νεκρῶν ζῶντας
ταῖς ἐπιθυμίαις αὐτοῦ,
μηδὲ παριστάνετε τὰ μέλη ὑμῶν ὅπλα   καὶ τὰ μέλη ὑμῶν ὅπλα δικαιοσύνης
ἀδικίας τῇ ἁμαρτίᾳ,   τῷ θεῷ

Verse 14 — reasons for the request:
ἁμαρτία γὰρ ὑμῶν οὐ κυριεύσει·
οὐ γὰρ ἐστε ὑπὸ νόμον,   ἀλλὰ ὑπὸ χάριν.

Using this survey as a starting point, several important observations can be made — especially as concerns the reasoning in Rom 6.3-11.

1. First of all, it can clearly be seen that in Rom 6.3-11 there is a line from the statements about the Christians' 'death fellowship' with Christ to the statements about a life with Christ.

This is conspicuous in verse 4, verse 5 and verse 8, which are in the nature of analogic conclusions. Starting from the knowledge introduced in verse 3 about baptism, which gives a connection to the death of Christ, it is asserted that there must be a corresponding connection to Christ's resurrection and new life. This repeated conclusion clearly states the direction of the thought-process.

The other members also emphasise this. Verses 6-7 support the conclusion in verse 4 and verse 5, and at the same time form the prelude to the conclusion in verse 8. Verses 9-11 are to substantiate the conclusion in verse

8, and although the starting point is an insight different from that hitherto the concluding point in verse 11b again becomes the same.

There is no doubt therefore about what Paul intends by his reasoning. He wishes to emphasise the Christians' new life.

2. Next, this structure also means that a number of statements in Rom 6.3-11 are placed in parallel to one another.

There is thus a certain accordance and connection between the members which concern the association with the death of Christ (left column of the survey). Similarly, this also applies to the members which concern the Christians' connection with Christ's resurrection and new life (right column). Since analogic conclusions are concerned in verse 4, verse 5 and verse 8, a certain structural similarity and an inherent connection between premises and conclusions must be anticipated.

These different expressions and terms, which will be discussed in the following chapters, can thus enlighten on the basis of several parallels. In this way, the meaning, often strongly disputed, can be identified. It is precisely this coherence between the many disputed terms which complicates the exegetic discussion, because so many items must be considered. But it is also this which makes a precise understanding possible.

3. If we also look at the two series of parallel-arranged statements, a further development of thought in the course of Rom 6.3-11 can be observed — alongside that to be found in the principal conclusions. There is an increasing intensity in the expressions. A development occurs, asserting a continuously higher degree of connection between what the Christians have obtained through baptism and what happened to Christ at the end of his earthly life.

Let us first look at the statements about participation in Christ's death. If we disregard verse 2, which is the provocative, paradoxical expression that is gradually explained, there is a continuous rise. The Christians' 'death' is described with increasing intensity, and is gradually linked to Jesus' death quite unreservedly. Verse 3 merely expresses a connection, from the Christian's baptism to Jesus' death. In verse 4, according to the wording, the connection applies only to the burial in which the Christians participate. In verse 5a the baptismal event is linked to death, but the connection is indirect or cautious, in that the Christians are connected to τὸ ὁμοίωμα τοῦ θανάτου αὐτοῦ. In verse 6, we have the common crucifixion and thus a fellowship concerning the manner of death. But here we have seen that the crucifixion, used of the Christians, has a fixed, implied meaning which applies to the Christians' severance from the past content of life.[68] Only verse 8a, thus

---

68. Cf. Chapter III, section 3.2, above.

thoroughly prepared, speaks plainly of a death with Christ, in the same way as in verse 11a we finally return to the expression from verse 2 about the Christian's death to sin.

Similarly, this also applies to the statements which connect the Christians' new life to Christ's resurrection. In verse 4bc there is supposed to be a certain analogy between Christ's resurrection and the Christians' new life (ὥσπερ-οὕτως). According to verse 5, the Christians are connected to τὸ ὁμοίωμα τῆς ἀναστάσεως. Verse 8 plainly expresses that the Christians live with Christ, cf. also verse 11b and verse 13.

4. A further fact in Rom 6.3-11 can be read from the above presentation. In a few respects, the amplifying reasons in verses 9-11 fall somewhat outside the pattern which has characterised the preceding verses. In verses 3-8, Paul has taken his starting point in soteriological statements concerning 'death's' crucial importance to the Christians' life. From verse 9 the basic knowledge is expressed Christologically, at least formally, and it concerns both death and resurrection to a new life, with the emphasis on the latter.

This fact also shows that a development is taking place in the course of the section of text.

5. As the final point the division of Rom 6.3-11 may be considered (Rom 6.12-14 is clearly a subsection on its own).

Again, the survey presented illustrates the most important points. There is a coherent process of reasoning, with gradual transitions. This already begins in verse 2 with the preceded point, which is substantiated in verse 3 by the reference to the common insight, from which a new point is derived in verse 4, which is further underlined in verse 5 and substantiated in verse 6a by a new reference to a common insight, which comes to a head in verses 6b-7 and forms in verse 8 the basis of a new formulation of the point, which in turn is substantiated in verse 9 by yet another reference to a common insight, which is amplified in verse 10 and employed in verse 11 in a concluding emphasis of the point. The same crucial point indeed circles around. One returns several times to the same aspects, but not in such a way that the thought-process moves in circles. As we have seen, there is a continuous development by which the point is intensified.

In the light of this perception it is clear that the text can be divided in several ways, which need not be mutually exclusive.

It is usual to keep to the clear, formal parallelism between verse 5 and verse 8 and between the subsequent reasons given in verses 6-7, or verses 9-10, so that as the reasons for verses 3-4 two sections are given, verses 5-7 and verses 8-10, with verse 11 as a conclusion.[69] There are also other proposals:

verse, 3, verses 4-5, verses 6-10, verse 11 — or verse 3, verses 4-5, verses 8-10, verse 11.[70]

If the text is to be subdivided — and this must be done for practical reasons in the exegetic review — it seems to me natural to consider verses 6-8 as one particularly coherent phase in the reasoning and verses 9-11 as another, for in both passages there is a unified progress from the insight referred to forward to the point to be adduced. Similarly, verses 3-5 can also be seen as a progression from the basic insight to the point which is then adduced in two stages (in verse 4 and in verse 5).

The way has thus been prepared for the text-review which is now to follow.

The very intense debate about the text's background and the theological problems in connection therewith has led, as we have seen, to many problems of detail being turned upside down, and there appears to be an abundance of possible interpretations. An understanding of the text verse by verse can nevertheless be arrived at, thanks to the clarity of the dominant approach.

In each section the intention is first examined, and after this a position taken on the underlying concepts. This will in particular be a question of the concepts to which Paul directly refers and from which he takes his point of reference.

---

69. This division of the text is suggested in Bornkamm, *Ende*, p. 39, and has been adopted by many, see Michel, *Römer*, pp. 23-26, Güttgemanns, *Apostel*, p. 218f., Gäumann, *Taufe*, p. 31, Frankemölle, *Taufverständnis*, pp. 23-25, Käsemann, *Römer*, p. 159, Wilckens, *Römer* II, p. 7. As we have seen, there are reasonable grounds for emphasising the parallelism between Rom 6.5-7 and Rom 6.8-10. But one must warn against the inherent consequences from this purely formal parallelism. In particular, one must warn against isolating verse 11 relative to verses 8-10, cf. Chapter IX, section 2.1, below.

70. See Jervell, *Gud*, p. 92f., Pilgaard, Dåbsteologien, p. 120, which maintains that Rom 6.4-5, Rom 6.6-7 and Rom 6.8-10 are three structurally almost parallel clauses, which inherently continue the reasoning. Schnackenburg, *Heilsgeschehen* p. 27f., entirely refrains from a division of the passage, with a reference indeed to the fact that Paul is all the time circling around the same basic idea.

VII

Rom 6.3-5: the new life
as a consequence of baptism into death

1. Rom 6.3: baptism into death

1.1. The fundamental insight

Rom 6.3 is of fundamental importance to the entire reasoning.

The verse is formed as a new rhetorical question. It approximates closely to the preceding question in Rom 6.2b, as the introductory ἤ indicates, and it is directly apprehended as the justification necessary after the provocative statement about the Christians' 'death'. Verse 3 indeed refers to a certain insight about baptism and death.

And the οὖν which introduces Rom 6.4 shows that this insight is also the basis of the further thought-process.[1]

Paul asks the Roman community a question, which begins with the words ἤ ἀγνοεῖτε ὅτι ... Again (as in the preceding verses) the answer is given immediately: No, of course they cannot be ignorant on this point. Paul thus indicates some concepts which the Roman community cannot avoid knowing, and which they must immediately acknowledge so that he can use them as a conclusive basis for his reasoning. This corresponds to the function that terms such as: 'Do you not know ...' have in other passages in Paul, as was also clearly the case in Rom 6.16 and 7.1.[2]

The possibility is certainly considered that Paul is making use of so-called 'polite pedagogics', by which he wishes to convey new knowledge

---

1. Cf. Schnackenburg, Todes- und Lebensgemeinschaft, p. 39, Wagner, *Problem*, p. 292f., 297, Larsson, *Christus*, p. 52f., Frankemölle, *Taufverständnis*, p. 53, which all emphasise that this involves the insight which Paul refers to by ἤ ἀγνοεῖτε ὅτι ..., being found only in Rom 6.3. Rom 6.4 then becomes the genuine Pauline continuation of the thought-process.
2. Cf. Chapter VI, section 2.1 and 2.2 above. See also Rom 11.2; 1 Cor 3.16; 5.6; 6.2,3,9,15, 16,19; 9.13,24. This observation formed part of the reasoning of the religio-historical school in support of a mysterious background and has since become generally accepted. See Lietzmann, *Römer*, p. 67, Windisch, Taufe, p. 171, Heitmüller, Problem, p. 335, Bousset, *Kyrios*, p. 107, Bultmann, *Theologie*, p. 143f., Bornkamm, *Ende*, p. 37 n. 2, Tannehill, *Dying*, p. 12f., Gäumann, *Taufe*, p. 46, 72f., Käsemann, *Römer*, p. 157, Cranfield, *Romans*, p. 300, Wilckens, *Römer* II, p. 11, cf. however note 3 below.

without rebuking the Roman community for its ignorance.[3] But there is no basis for such an approach. It concerns Paul's subjective judgement, a judgement that should not indeed come to the fore in the text. What one can see, however, is that Paul is referring to a certain knowledge which is used as axiomatic in the continued reasoning. In any case, Paul assumes that the Roman community will accept it as general knowledge.

The insight assumed concerns the baptism to which all Christians have submitted themselves: ὅσοι ἐβαπτίσθημεν εἰς Χριστὸν ᾿Ιησοῦν, εἰς τὸν θάνατον αὐτοῦ ἐβαπτίσθημεν. This linkage to Christ provided by baptism is in particular a linkage to his death. It must therefore be general knowledge (or at least an immediately recognisable characteristic) that baptism provides an association with Christ's death.[4] And the last reference to Christ's death was in Rom 5.6-10, as the event when God in his boundless love reconciled sinful man with himself. The linkage from baptism to Christ's death therefore directly provides the expected grounds for Rom 6.2: that the Christians have finally broken with sin.

How this tradition of a connection between baptism and Christ's death has arisen is still an open question. But it is not necessary to clarify this to understand what Paul intends by his reasoning.

---

3. Thus Kuss, *Römerbrief*, p. 297, Wagner, *Problem*, p. 291f., Siber, *Mit Christus*, p. 195f., Frankemölle, *Taufverständnis*, p. 40. The term 'polite pedagogics' is due to Lietzmann, *Römer*, p. 72 (as regards Rom 7.1; he does not assume, as maintained by Käsemann, *Römer*, p. 156, polite pedagogics in Rom 6.3). The assumption of polite pedagogics is used to reject a mystery-religious background. By this assumption it can also be achieved that the 'Baptism doctrine' of Rom 6 can be seen as something especially Pauline — as in Sanday and Headlam, *Romans*, p. 156. Franz Mussner, 'Zusammengewachsen durch die Ähnlichkeit mit seinem Tod'. Der Gedankengang von Röm 6,1-6, *Trier ThZ* 63 (1956), pp. 257-65, goes a step further and wishes seriously to envisage the possibility that Paul would have expected an affirmative answer to the question. But that is excluded, if only because in that event Paul would have to explain how the connection between baptism and death in Rom 6.3 was to be understood before he could use it in his reasoning.

4. As assumed in 1 Cor 1.10-13 and perhaps also in 1 Cor 12.13, cf. Siber, *Mit Christus*, p. 208, Jeremias i Dinkler, Römer 6,1-14, p. 111f. Cf. Chapter III, section 4 and section 2.2, with note 60 above, where I have sought to substantiate this opinion. Different in Wilckens, *Römer* II, p. 11, who maintains that primal Christianity lacks other examples of baptism εἰς τὸν θάνατον αὐτοῦ. Wilckens' solution is that readers will understand βαπτίσθημεν in the specific meaning of 'immerse', so that they can comprehend baptism as a movement into death despite the lack of advance knowledge about this linkage. But Wilckens himself stresses that ἢ ἀγνοεῖτε ὅτι refers to a known tradition, and this can only be Rom 6.3b where the proper content of the sentence is to be found — not Rom 6.3a, cf. Hellholm, Argumentation, p. 153.

1.2. Βαπτίζεσθαι εἰς ...

There is in German exegesis in particular a debate here about a detail of no direct significance to an understanding of the Pauline matter, but which is strongly emphasised in discussion of the religio- and traditio-historical background. This is the precise interpretation of the preposition εἰς, which occurs twice in Rom 6.3. Does it concern a baptism 'in Christus', 'in seinen Tod' or 'auf Christus', 'auf seinen Tod'?[5]

If εἰς Χριστόν in Rom 6.3a is understood local-spatially, 'in Christus', we are dealing with an idea about a baptism which incorporates the Christians in Christ (and thereby gives participation in his death). If it is understood as the directing or final 'auf Christus', it concerns the (very close) linkage the baptised is given to Christ and his death.[6]

In the first place, this depends on the understanding of the verb βαπτίζειν. If we look at the other incidences in the New Testament, there are only two passages (Mark 7.4; Lk 11.38) where it is clearly used in the real sense of immersing or washing. In a few places it may also be a play-on-words, in that βαπτίζειν can mean 'go under', 'drown'. Otherwise, the word

---

5. That the question is especially discussed in German exegesis is undoubtedly because German has these two prepositions which can render two nuances of the Greek εἰς. In English, the word 'into', which has basically the local-spatial meaning (like the German 'in'), has such a large breadth of meaning that it can also be used with the other occurrences of the term. The problem is therefore discussed only in English-language concepts which relate to the German problem-complex. And it is generally assumed that the local meaning has the greatest weight, but no extreme conclusions are normally drawn from this, and it is open to shifts, different nuances and transferred meanings, cf. Murray, *Romans*, p. 214, Barrett, *Romans*, p. 123, Beasley-Murray, *Baptism*, p. 128, Morris, *Romans*, p. 247, Dunn, *Romans*, p. 311.

6. The first possibility is chosen by Heitmüller, *Im Namen*, p. 320, *Taufe*, 1903, p. 9, *Taufe*, 1911, p. 16, Lietzmann, *Römer*, p. 64f., Leipoldt, *Taufe*, p. 62f., Tannehill, *Dying*, p. 22ff., Käsemann, *Römer*, p. 157 (where the text is commentated upon; in the translation, p. 151, the preposition 'auf' is used), Bornkamm, *Ende*, p. 37f., G. Barth, *Taufe*, p. 99, who all think that Paul binds to a mystery-religious concept about incorporation in Christ at baptism; moreover Schneider, *Passionsmystik*, p. 40f., Warnach, Taufe, p. 295, who envisages a separate Pauline mysticism. The interpretation is also considered in Hellholm, Argumentation, p. 152, but is abandoned in favour of the broader meaning, cf. note 13 below. The other possibility is chosen by Loisy, *Mystères*, p. 270 n. 2, Mittring, *Heilswirklichkeit*, p. 39 n. 3, Schnackenburg, Todes- und Lebensgemeinschaft, p. 41ff., Wagner, *Problem*, p. 199f., Delling, *Taufe*, p. 125ff., Gäumann, *Taufe*, p. 74, Lohse, Taufe, p. 317, Siber, *Mit Christus*, p. 206f., Frankemölle, *Taufverständnis*, p. 43, Schlier, *Römerbrief*, p. 192, Halter, *Taufe*, p. 48f., cf. the discussion between Barrett, Dinkler, Schnackenburg, Jeremias and de la Potterie in Dinkler, Römer 6,1-14, pp. 104-6. The interpretation can be included in the reasoning against a mystery-religious background, but can also be combined with theories about this background, since the close connection to the deity is also emphasised in the mystery religions.

is used purely as a technical term for 'to baptise' and normally in the passive, because it is a principal idea that God is the true power in baptism.[7] Where the text reads βαπτίζεσθαι εἰς, finality and linkage are in most cases concerned: a baptism of repentance, of the forgiveness of sins, to Moses, in the name of Christ. And here a local-spatial understanding is not possible. Only two passages (Gal 3.27; 1 Cor 12.13) use an image of baptism as an inclusion in Christ or Christ's body; but linkage is also concerned here. The broad meaning ('taufen auf') can thus be taken as a point of reference throughout.[8]

But it may then be asked whether there is something in the context which indicates that the local understanding should be taken into consideration in this text (as in Gal 3.27; 1 Cor 12.13).

Here the σύν-Χριστῷ terms which appear in the following verses may be interpreted as expressing union together with Christ.[9] But as we shall see these terms may also be understood as referring to the close linkage.

A notable reason for the local meaning of εἰς Χριστόν is that the parallel expression, εἰς τὸν θάνατον αὐτοῦ, in the apodosis must be understood as local.[10] But on closer examination this is not an obvious argument.

Rom 6.3b thus emphasises εἰς τὸν θάνατον αὐτοῦ ἐβαπτίσθημεν. It can follow that this is understood to mean that the baptised are drawn into Christ's death, so that they share in its effects. This can be expressed in German as 'in seinen Tod getauft'. This is seen as evidence that εἰς must be perceived as 'local-real'.[11] But εἰς τὸν θάνατον αὐτοῦ cannot indeed be perceived locally in the real sense, since death is an abstractum without spatial extent (and this applies irrespective of however present, materially and realistically, Jesus' death is imagined to be). A transferred meaning of the preposition εἰς must be potentially concerned. And it is certainly possible that a shift in meaning occurs between verse 3a and verse 3b, so that there is now a play-on-words that baptism not only gives a linkage to Christ and his death but that the Christians are indeed included in this. Such a shift can

---

7. Thus Oepke, *ThWNT* I, p. 538. Cf. Chapter IV, section 2.1 above concerning the baptism by John, also in section 2.2, the discussions about Mark 10.38-39; Lk 12.50, where βαπτίζε-σθαι may have the secondary meaning of 'go under'.

8. Cf. Oepke, *ThWNT* I, p. 526ff., Schnackenburg, *Heilsgeschehen*, p. 19ff., Delling, *Zueignung*, p. 79, Halter, *Taufe*, p. 48. See also my discussion of the term βαπτίζεσθαι εἰς in Chapter III, section 2.3, above.

9. Thus Heitmüller, *Taufe*, 1911, p. 22, Lietzmann, *Römer*, p. 67f., Bornkamm, *Ende*, p. 37f., Tannehill, *Dying*, p. 21f., G. Barth, *Taufe*, p. 99.

10. Thus Käsemann, *Römer*, p. 157 ('Die Parallelität von "in Christus" und "in seinen Tod getauft" spricht wie in 1. Kor 12,13 für lokale Bedeutung des εἰς'), Tannehill, *Dying*, p. 22.

11. Thus Dinkler, Römer 6,1-14, p. 87, cf. Schnelle, *Gerechtigkeit*, p. 77 ('räumlich-real'), Käsemann, *Römer*, p. 157, Tannehill, *Dying*, p. 22.

easily occur between the different nuances of the preposition, which is not noticed by someone who has a direct relationship with the language.[12] This gliding transition between different meanings can indeed have a promotional effect upon the thought-process, and this must be taken into account in reasoning of a more rhetorical than logical nature.[13]

This means that in the first place one must choose the most neutral understanding, as expressing relation: that a baptism is concerned which gives a linkage to Christ. But one must still keep an open mind that, on the image level, there may be a play-on-words, that the Christian are drawn into the crucial salvation event.

2. Rom 6.4: the new life as the positive consequence

2.1. The continuation of the thought-process in Rom 6.4a

The function that Rom 6.4 has in the context is immediately clear. As already indicated, the introductory οὖν shows that Paul continues his thought-process on the basis of the preceding text. The content confirms this. In Rom 6.4a, συνετάφημεν οὖν αὐτῷ διὰ τοῦ βαπτίσματος εἰς τὸν θάνατον, the insight now introduced is elaborated, and on the basis of this an analogic conclusion is undertaken in Rom 6.4bc.[14]

The term συνετάφημεν αὐτῷ introduces a new element.

But otherwise Rom 6.4a contains the same elements as Rom 6.3b. It is said by διὰ τοῦ βαπτίσματος that burial with Christ occurs by virtue of bap-

---

12. Cf. the sentence by Käsemann quoted in note 10 above, where strictly speaking the preposition 'in' has two meanings. Only when it must be translated and a theoretical angle of approach is therefore employed does one become aware of the nuances, cf. note 5.

13. Cf. Dunn, *Romans*, p. 315, where it becomes clear that one must work with two different sets of ideas if one wishes to understand βαπτίζεσθαι εἰς Χριστόν and βαπτίζεσθαι εἰς τὸν θάνατον in Rom 6.3 as a term for baptismal symbolism. If a baptism is thought of which includes the baptised in Christ's death and is a 'burial with Christ' according to Rom 6.4, one can imagine that the subsequent movement upwards from baptism must be considered together with the resurrection, cf. section 2.2 with note 20 below. But if baptism is seen as a movement into Christ the emersion cannot come into the picture, since it would have to be a movement away from Christ. This observation supports that there are no concepts which must be understood literally and mystically, but pure imagery which must have a promotional effect upon the thought-process. Cf. also Schnackenburg, *Heilsgeschehen*, p. 22f., where it is concluded that an important interpretation principle is appearing: 'Das Paulus jeweils vorschwebende Bild ist aus der betreffenden Stelle selbst herauszuheben. Die Bilder bei ihm wechseln, die Sache bleibt.' These observations are now also confirmed by Hellholm, *Argumentation*, p. 152f., who speaks of 'polysemy'; Paul consciously chooses a term which can be understood broadly because it gives him an opportunity to lead the argument where he wishes it to go.

14. Cf. Halter, *Taufe*, p. 50, Dunn, *Romans*, p. 314.

tism, and thereby it becomes clear that this burial with Christ is another way of expressing the connection there is, according to verse 3, between baptism and Christ's death.[15] The last member in Rom 6.4a, εἰς τὸν θάνατον, must despite the missing article presumably be connected adjectivally to the preceding noun, 'baptism into death'.[16] The content of the sentence thus corresponds almost entirely to εἰς τὸν θάνατον αὐτοῦ ἐβαπτίσθημεν. Although the pronoun αὐτοῦ is omitted in verse 4, the term will still be understood to mean that a linkage to Christ's death is taking place. But it becomes more ambiguous. It becomes increasingly clear that there is a play-on-words, that it involves a 'death' for the Christians also[17]. The play-on-words that had to be considered in verse 3 is thus continued. Baptism into Christ's death is also something that leads the Christians into a 'death'. But it is still uncertain whether such a play-on-words will be sufficiently clear to have an effect upon the readers.

But in any event Rom 6.4a concerns the same connection between Christ's death and baptism as is established in Rom 6.3, and from this Paul concludes in Rom 6.4bc that there is a similar accordance between Christ's resurrection and the Christians' new life.

2.2. Burial with Christ

We again find ourselves in the situation that we can follow Paul's thought-process and arrive at what concerns him, although we do not immediately understand in every detail his method of expression. This also applies to the term συνετάφημεν αὐτῷ. We understand what Paul intends, but the problem is that we cannot immediately explain how he came upon the expression.

First, this applies to σὺν Χριστῷ which the formulation involves. 'Burial with Christ' commences the series of σὺν Χριστῷ terms. It continues with 'crucifixion with Christ' in Rom 6.6, 'death with Christ' in Rom 6.8a, and Rom 6.8b speaks of 'living with Christ'. In Paul the concept is found in its strictest form here only, and in Gal 2.19 (and in Col 2, where the thought-

---

15. The adverbial member διὰ τοῦ βαπτίσματος has instrumental significance. But this fact cannot be used, as maintained by Frankemölle, *Taufverständnis*, p. 55, to weaken the dating and show that burial does not occur in baptism. If baptism is the means by which one is buried, the time of the burial must still be baptism!

16. See Blass, Debrunner and Rehkopf, *Grammatik*, § 272,2, cf. Larsson, *Christus*, p. 56, Gäumann, *Taufe*, p. 74, Käsemann, *Römer*, p. 158. But it is also possible to interpret it adverbially, i.e. the member is linked to the verb or to the whole sentence: 'We were thus by baptism buried together with him into death', cf. Bornkamm, *Ende*, p. 38, Kuss, *Römerbrief*, p. 298. This gives no major difference as regards understanding.

17. See Merk, *Handeln*, p. 24. Cf. also Frankemölle, *Taufverständnis*, p. 54, where there is a warning against deriving vital points from the missing pronoun, Dunn, *Romans*, p. 315.

process from Rom 6 is developed). 'Burial with Christ' at baptism is an immediately striking expression that links together diverse events (Jesus' burial and the Christians' baptism) which have taken place in different places and at different times. Special emphasis is therefore given to σὺν Χριστῷ, and this gives cause for considerations of mystical simultaneity and the Christians' collective incorporation into Christ.[18] But the preposition can also be understood to mean 'like', or be perceived as a more figurative expression.[19] Initially, therefore, the broadest meaning of σὺν Χριστῷ should be chosen. How the term should be interpreted more precisely is best determined when the whole context in which it occurs is examined.

It may also seem puzzling that Paul describes baptism as a 'burial'. And the sequence of loaded terms is striking. Paul begins with 'burial with Christ', to continue with 'crucifixion', 'death' and 'the new life with Christ'. What is intended by producing the burial as the first salvation event?

A widespread explanation is that here Paul employs a baptism symbolism in which, by his immersion during baptism, the baptismal candidate repeats Christ's burial. Similarly, the emersion is said to be a repetition of Christ's resurrection.[20] But widespread scepticism against this repetition symbolism gradually arose.[21] It is doubted that the original meaning of βάπτισμα, 'immersion', was still heard after it had become a technical term for baptism.[22] In any case, the text is not interested in the emersion from the

---

18. Thus Heitmüller, *Taufe*, 1911, p. 22, Lietzmann, *Römer*, p. 67f., Bornkamm, *Ende*, p. 37f., Güttgemanns, *Apostel*, p. 216ff., Tannehill, *Dying*, p. 22ff., G. Barth, *Taufe*, p. 99 (who all envisage a background in mystery religion), M. Barth, *Taufe*, p. 276ff., Wagner, *Problem*, p. 305f., Frankemölle, *Taufverständnis*, p. 102ff. (who works on the basis of the 'corporate personality idea'). Cf. Chapter III, note 153, above.

19. Cf. Schnackenburg, *Heilsgeschehen*, p. 30f., 48f., Michel, *Römer*, p. 130, cf. Chapter III, section 3.1, above, with notes 154-58. See the final discussion in the next chapter.

20. This interpretation is frequently associated with a sacramentalist or mystery-religious interpretation of the text or its background. See Holtzmann, *Lehrbuch II²*, p. 196f., Pfleiderer, *Urchristentum I²*, p. 295, Gunkel, *Verständnis*, p. 83, Heitmüller, *Im Namen*, p. 319, Lietzmann, *Römer*, p. 65, Bousset, *Kyrios*, p. 107, Reitzenstein, *Mysterienreligionen*, p. 81f.; 230f., Kümmel, *Theologie*, p. 189f., Warnach, *Tauflehre*, p. 294ff., Schmithals, *Römerbrief*, p. 189. Cf. also Dodd, *Romans*, p. 107, Bruce, *Romans*, p. 136.

21. The rejection often forms part of a confrontation with mysterious interpretations (including in particular the Catholic cult-mystery theory developed in Warnach, *Tauflehre*), cf. Eduard Stommel, 'Begraben mit Christus' (Röm.6,4) und der Taufritus, *RQ* 49 (1954), pp. 1-20, Schnackenburg, *Todes- und Lebensgemeinschaft*, pp. 39-41, Frankemölle, *Taufverständnis*, p. 54ff., cf. p. 50ff. See also Schweitzer, *Mystik*, p. 119ff. But the rejection is also to be found in interpreters who assume dependence upon Hellenistic mystery religion: Bornkamm, *Ende*, p. 38, Gäumann, *Taufe*, p. 74f., Tannehill, *Dying*, p. 34, Käsemann, *Römer*, p. 156.

22. Cf. Schnackenburg, *Heilsgeschehen*, p. 23, Frankemölle, *Taufverständnis*, pp. 48-51, Siber, *Mit Christus*, p. 207, Pilgaard, *Dåbsteologien*, p. 122, and Chapter III, section 2.3 above concerning βαπτίζεσθαι εἰς ...

baptismal water.[23] It is also pointed out that such a symbolic perception of baptism is late evidence, and it is doubtful that baptism was practised as total immersion in New Testament times.[24] It may also be asked whether baptism can be perceived as a repetition of the death and burial of Christ, since Christ's death was not a death by drowning.[25] But even if the full 'immersion-emersion symbolism' must be abandoned, it may still be considered whether the term was chosen because the Christians in any case moved downwards during the baptism ceremony.[26] Perhaps there is also a play-on-words, since βαπτίζεσθαι can mean 'go under' or 'drown'.[27]

Without the assumption of symbolism, it becomes more difficult to understand why Paul produces the burial in this way. It is often sought to resolve this problem by a reference to 1 Cor 15.3-4. Here, Paul refers to a fundamental doctrine about the significance of Christ's death and about his resurrection. This is based on the verbs ἀπέθανεν, ἐτάφη, ἐγήγερται (and ὤφθη). The second member in the confession of faith, Christ's burial, is said to have the function of confirming the content of the first member, Christ's death. A vital idea at that time was that one is really dead only after interment. Burial then becomes a final confirmation of the reality of death. It

23. Thus Gäumann, *Taufe*, p. 75 n. 59, Frankemölle, *Taufverständnis*, p. 51ff. See also Dunn, *Romans*, p. 314, cf. note 13 above.

24. See Schnackenburg, *Heilsgeschehen*, p. 50ff., Stommel, Begraben, p. 12ff., where it is shown that the idea of baptism as a death and resurrection was not expressed until the 4th century. See also Eduard Stommel, Christliche und antike Badesitten, *JAC* 2 (1959), pp. 5-14, Begraben, p. 19f., where it is shown that baptismal basins were shallow and that pictures relate to sprinkling, and where the thought is presented that total immersion was introduced at a late date when the symbolism of immersion-emersion = burial-resurrection won through in the Church, cf. Frankemölle, *Taufverständnis*, p. 51ff., Bent Noack, Dåben i Didake [Baptism in Didache], in: Sigfred Pedersen (ed.), *Dåben i Ny Testamente* [Baptism in the New Testament], Århus 1982, pp. 246-265, pp. 252-254. Different in Wilckens, *Römer* II, p. 11, n. 22.

25. Thus Stommel, Begraben, p. 5, Tannehill, *Dying*, p. 34. The cognition goes back to Dibelius, *Botschaft* II, p. 71f., where the difference is pointed out between the burial-resurrection symbolism in baptism and the events at the death of Christ, which indeed was not a death by drowning. He uses it to argue that the symbolism of the mystery-religious initiation rite has been later transferred to baptism because it is the Christians' initiation rite. Similarly Bultmann, *Theologie*, p. 143, Gäumann, *Taufe*, p. 47. There is however also a possibility that in the context there is a play on the point that βαπτίζεσθαι can also mean 'drowning', cf. note 27 below.

26. Thus Kuss, *Römerbrief*, p. 298, Wagner, *Problem*, p. 302, Beasley-Murray, *Baptism*, p. 133, Larsson, *Christus*, p. 57, where it is pointed out that Stommel and others have exaggerated the justified clash with the symbolic interpretation. Cf. also Wilckens, *Römer* II, p. 11 n. 22.

27. As regards this meaning of βαπτίζεσθαι cf. Oepke, *ThWNT* I, p. 527f. See also the discussion in Chapter IV, section 2.2, with note 27, on the understanding of Mark 10.38-39, where this understanding intrudes.

is also maintained that this 'credo' is employed in Rom 6.3-8 — also the first and third members are to be found here. That baptism is described as a burial with Christ expresses the real nature of this death for the baptised.[28] The reference to 1 Cor 15 may give a contributory explanation for Paul's use of the term 'buried with Christ'. But this does not in itself explain everything. There remains the problem that Paul here makes Christ's burial a decisive, positive, soteriological motif. No other passages have an independent emphasis on Christ's burial — including 1 Cor 15.4 where the reference to burial has the function of showing that Christ was really dead, and that therefore the resurrection also was real. There is no need to stress the burial where Christ's death is otherwise emphasised in Paul.

But now the only real problem is what caused Paul to choose the term 'buried with Christ'. We can content ourselves by saying that it is one of the two concepts referred to, or a combination, or perhaps an accident. If we accordingly look at the term's function in the context, there is a clear meaning.

'Burial with Christ' acts as an excellent *image* of what happens during baptism, and it links baptism to death. At a burial, the corpse is got out of the way. The old person who was ruled by sin has been finally cleared away (cf. Rom 6.2,6).

The context indeed shows that 'burial with Christ' is a well-chosen metaphor.

This is to be seen in connection with Rom 6.4bc, for which it sets the scene. Paul here seems to wish to compare Christ's resurrection with the Christians' new life, because there is a connection between the two things.

---

28. The parallelism between 1 Cor 15.3-4 and Rom 6.3-8 has been discussed fundamentally in Seeberg, *Katechismus*, p. 52ff. It is adduced primarily by interpreters who reject the mystery-religious background and suggest as an alternative the concept of Christ as a 'corporate personality'; if the Christians can be envisaged as having been buried, this is because baptism and confession of faith bind them to a Lord who is dead, buried and resurrected; they are included in the events of the past — cf. Schnackenburg, *Heilsgeschehen*, p. 22, 204f., Todes- und Lebensgemeinschaft, p. 39ff., Adam-Christus-Typologie, p. 51, n. 19, Stommel, *Begraben*, p. 6ff., Wagner, *Problem*, p. 302, Frankemölle, *Taufverständnis*, p. 28f., 56f. In M. Barth, *Taufe*, pp. 267-83, Delling, *Taufe*, p. 127ff., Beasley-Murray, *Baptism*, p. 133, this is combined with the concept that death with Christ occurred at Golgotha and only burial at the act of baptism, as a confirmatory confession of faith — so that the interpretation becomes anti-sacramentalist. Also, interpreters who assume Pauline dependence upon the mysteries can use the reference to 1 Cor 15.3-4. Thus in particular Gäumann, *Taufe*, pp. 61-65, 75 and especially pp. 126-29. This feature then becomes Paul's own underlining of the Christian death and its definitive nature; then it is no longer by virtue of the external rite that the death of Jesus is being effected; the theological content of baptism is concerned; and it is the believers who participate in the useful effect; and it is considered important that 'a credo' is concerned — this means that one arrives at a non-sacramentalist interpretation. Cf. also Bornkamm, *Ende*, p. 38, Tannehill, *Dying*, p. 34, Conzelmann, *Grundriss*, p. 297ff., Wilckens, *Römer II*, p. 12, Dunn, *Romans*, p. 314, 329.

When in Rom 6.4a he chooses to describe baptism as a burial with Christ, he indeed achieves a comparison between the two events which precede the Christians' new life and Christ's resurrection.

This can also be seen in the context of the development which is demonstrated in the course of verses Rom 6.3,4a,5a,6,8.[29] There is an increasing intensity in these verses. They begin with just a connection between the baptised and Christ's baptism and they close with a statement that the Christian is 'dead with Christ', so that the preceding point in Rom 6.2 is substantiated. Rom 6.4a is the first link in this structure. Paul does not immediately jump to the radical statement about 'death with Christ'. He begins cautiously by finding in the burial image a similarity between baptism and Christ's death.

2.3. The point in Rom 6.4bc: the power of resurrection and the new life

In Rom 6.4bc the analogic conclusion is now expressed which was prepared for by Rom 6.4a.

It begins with the conjunction ἵνα. This does not introduce the subjective intention with the Christians' baptism but the objective result corresponding to the divine intention. The meaning is therefore close to the consecutive aspect.[30] And a consequence is indeed adduced here. Paul has been working with the traditional insight from Rom 6.3 with a view to the twofold statement now encountered: ἵνα ὥσπερ ἠγέρθη Χριστὸς ἐκ νεκρῶν διὰ τῆς δόξης τοῦ πατρός, οὕτως καὶ ἡμεῖς ἐν καινότητι ζωῆς περιπατήσωμεν. Here we have, linked together with a 'like so', what followed the burial as far as Christ is concerned, and what therefore became the consequence of the Christians' 'co-burial'. This is a resumption of the ὥσπερ-οὕτως linking from Rom 5.12-21, and correspondence is again expressed, and perhaps also connection between the two sides.[31]

---

29. Cf. Chapter VI, section 4, point 3, above.
30. Cf. Stauffer, ἵνα, *ThWNT* III (1938), pp. 324-34, Bornkamm, *Ende*, p. 38, Wilckens, *Römer* II, p. 12.
31. This linking together of ὥσπερ-οὕτως initially expresses an accordance, but also anticipates a connection as emphasised by καί in Rom 6.4c. Cf. Murray, *Romans*, p. 216. See also Wilckens, *Römer* II, p. 12: 'Wie besonders 5,18-21 zeigt, denkt Paulus das 'Wie-So' im Sinne wirksamer Entsprechung, so dass der Vergleich begründende Kraft hat.' Käsemann, *Römer*, p. 158, G. Barth, *Taufe*, p. 100, defines it more definitively as a reason and refers to Rom 5.12,15-21. In Rom 5.12 both meanings may be relevant, cf. Chapter V, section 3.2, above with notes 53, 54 and 57. But in Rom 5.15-21 the justifying function is excluded: here Adam's Fall and restoration through Christ are compared (Adam's Fall was not the reason for the restoration!).

The Christ side in Rom 6.4b points to the resurrection. Here one finds a solemn confession of creed-like style.[32] This is demonstrated in particular in the term διὰ τῆς δόξης τοῦ πατρός. Paul only refers to God as 'the Father' when he employs special liturgical-sounding usage.[33] Δόξα is also used in a special way; in both Old Testament and New Testament tradition, δόξα frequently concerns the appearance of the divine in the earthly sphere, and in some passages may therefore be an expression of God's power on a line with δύναμις.[34] It is thus stated that God's power is manifest, having broken through at Christ's resurrection from the dead.

That Paul says this using traditional, confession of creed-like terms is not surprising. Paul usually refers to the resurrection in this way, as do other passages in the New Testament.[35] This may indeed arise because the resurrection is the surprising and intangible break with all human conceptions, and at the same time a decisive event which must be fundamental to all Christians.[36]

It has already been established that the reference to Christ's resurrection in other contexts may have two different functions. In the first group of statements, the resurrection is more generally to confirm the promise of salvation, and it is therefore stressed that Christ is present with his power and is ruler over life: this is the case in, inter alia, a number of passages in

---

32. Cf. Michel, *Römer*, p. 153, Gäumann, *Taufe*, p. 76 n. 70, Käsemann, *Römer*, p. 158, Cranfield, *Romans*, p. 304 n. 3, Schlier, *Römerbrief*, p. 193f., Wilckens, *Römer* II, p. 12.
33. This occurs in letter introductions and thanksgivings (Gal 1.1; 1 Thess 1.1; 2 Cor 1.3) and in contexts in which Paul, everything considered, employs traditional material (1 Cor 8.6; 15.24; Phil 2.11); these passages contain πατήρ as attribute to θεός; as an independent reference to God the word is found only here and in the cry 'Abba! Father!' (Rom 8.15; Gal 4.6). Cf. Michel, *Römer*, p. 153, Käsemann, *Römer*, p. 158, Schlier, *Römerbrief*, p. 193f., Wilckens, *Römer* II, p. 12.
34. For example, Mark 8.38; 13.26; John 11.40. Cf. Kittel, δόξα, *ThWNT* II (1935), pp. 236-40, 245-56; p. 251, Michel, *Römer*, p. 153, Gäumann, *Taufe*, p. 76 n. 70, Käsemann, *Römer*, p. 158, Cranfield, *Romans*, p. 304, Schlier, *Römerbrief*, p. 193f., Wilckens, *Römer* II, p. 12, Morris, *Romans*, p. 249, Dunn, *Romans*, p. 315.
35. There have been examples of this earlier: 1 Thess 4.14; 1 Cor 15.3-4, cf. Chapter III, sections 3.3 and 4 above and note 229. And it is widely agreed that this is a general reference to Christ's resurrection using formularistic terms, cf. Bultmann, *Theologie*, p. 293, Kegel, *Auferstehung*, p. 33, Kramer, *Kyrios*, p. 41ff., Wengst, *Formeln*, p. 27ff., Hoffmann, *TRE* 4, p. 478.
36. Cf. Conzelmann, *Grundriss*, p. 227f., Ridderbos, *Paulus*, p. 43f., and my article Opstandelse [Resurrection], in: Geert Hallbäck and Hans Jørgen Lundager Jensen (ed.), *Gads Bibel Leksikon* [Gad's Biblical Encyclopaedia], Copenhagen 1998, pp. 338-39. The trend is different in Kegel, *Auferstehung*, pp. 33-56; here, Paul's use of transmitted formulas is seen as expressing that the resurrection idea does not belong in the centre of his theology, but that Paul merely considers himself to be in accordance with the early-Christian creed of resurrection; cf. to the contrary Hübner, *Kreuz*, pp. 266-68.

the Letter to the Romans: Rom 1.4; 4.17-25; 7.4; 8.34; 10.9; 14.9.[37] It is therefore directly anticipated that our passage primarily belongs in this category, which seems to be the most original; this is confirmed by the continuation. The other group consists of distinctive passages as in 1 Thess 4.14; 1 Cor 15.20-23,44-49; Phil 3.10-11 and Rom 8.11, where Christ's resurrection is linked to the Christians' resurrection. It is a natural consequence of the fundamental faith in resurection, and this aspect may be present here also.[38]

The Christian side, in Rom 6.4c, speaks of 'walking in newness of life'.

When Paul writes καινότης ζωῆς instead of merely speaking of the new life, he emphasises both members. And the stressed καινότης will in turn lead the thoughts towards an eschatological new departure.[39] There is clear parallelism with Rom 6.5b, which also concerns a decisive turning point. The verb περιπατεῖν also has something essential to say about the content of life after baptism. Paul always uses this term metaphorically, corresponding to the Hebrew הלך, about man's behaviour in an ethical respect.[40] The verse thus concerns correct moral conduct.

It seems, then, that ζωή is primarily a description of the life the Christians are to live in the world, and of its content.[41] This also corresponds to the preceding negative point in Rom 6.2, where it is asked how following

---

37. This group also includes 2 Cor 5.15; 1 Thess 1.10; Gal 1.1, cf. 2 Cor 13.4; Acts 10.40-43; 13.31-37; 17.31. Also the gospels' visions of resurrection have the same affirmative function, cf. Chapter III, sections 3.2, 3.3 and 4 above, and notes 186 and 235. A vital point here is that Christ appears as the present Lord who gives the disciples certain tasks: Mt 28.18-20; Lk 24.46-48; John 20.21-23; Gal 1.15-16.

38. Cf. also 1 Cor 6.14; 2 Cor 4.14; Acts 26.23. The construction of 1 Thess 4.13-17, cf. 1 Cor 15.1-19, seems to show a development from the fundamental creed of the death and resurrection of Jesus to faith in a similar destiny for the Christians, as outlined in the discussion in Chapter III, section 3.3 above, with notes 230 and 235. Cf. in particular Becker, *Auferstehung*, p. 14ff., 31, 46ff., 149ff.; also Wilckens, *Römer* I, p. 65, where it is pointed out that when the resurrection of Christ in Rom 1.4 is referred to as ἀνάστασις νεκρῶν, this is already seen as a step in the general resurrection of the dead.

39. Cf. Bornkamm, *Ende*, p. 38 n. 9, Nygren, *Romarna*, p. 242, Schnackenburg, *Heilsgeschehen*, p. 30f., Gäumann, *Taufe*, p. 76f., Käsemann, *Römer*, p. 158, Cranfield, *Romans*, p. 305f., Schlier, *Römerbrief*, p. 194, Wilckens, *Römer* II, p. 12f. n. 31, Dunn, *Romans*, p. 315. The word καινότης is also used with emphasis in Rom 7.6, and is often associated with the term καινὴ κτίσις in 2 Cor 5.17; Gal 6.15.

40. In the New Testament generally, the word is most frequently used in a literal sense. Paul uses it only metaphorically, but it occurs so frequently that it appears as an established term for the ethically-correct life. Cf. Seesemann, πατέω κτλ., *ThWNT* V (1944-54), pp. 940-41, 943-52; p. 944, Bertram, πατέω κτλ., *ThWNT* V (1944-54), pp. 941-43; p. 942, Gäumann, *Taufe*, p. 77, Schlier, *Römerbrief*, p. 195, Wilckens, *Römer* II, p. 12. Braun, *Studien*, p. 155, Eckert, *Taufe*, p. 217f., sees it as a polemic against people who have envisaged the new life as 'eine naturhafte Gegebenheit'!

41. Cf. Schnackenburg, *Heilsgeschehen*, p. 30f., Murray, *Romans*, p. 217, Gäumann, *Taufe*, p. 77.

death to sin the Christians can still live in it. It is now said that they can only live a wholly different life. This confirms the feeling that there is a correspondence and connection between the Christ side and the Christian side — that the power of Christ's resurrection also has an impact upon the content of the Christian life. This connection is not clearly expressed. It is associated with the form of reasoning which is not strictly logical but rather suggestive. Paul wishes to impress, convince and guide the readers' thought-process in the right direction by means of analogic conclusions, imagery and associations. It is therefore also possible that Paul here wishes the readers to include the Christians' resurrection in their thoughts, although this is not directly referred to.[42]

But although the precise connection between the members is not made clear, there is no doubt here about what it is that the verse is to stress: that the eschatological power has penetrated into the life of the baptised.

3. Rom 6.5: amplification of the conclusion

3.1. Function and problems of the verse

Although Rom 6.5 is the most complicated verse in the whole of this passage, there is again no problem about Paul's intention.

The introductory γάρ signals that the point adduced from Rom 6.4 is now to be substantiated. Rom 6.5a is a conditional sentence with εἰ + the indicative. It concerns a condition which seems to have been met. It is inherently clear that a connection between the Christians' situation and Christ's death as in Rom 6.4a is concerned.

The principal sentence in Rom 6.5b is introduced, strongly emphasised, by ἀλλὰ καί. The Christians' association with Christ's resurrection is now concerned. Paul thus wishes to conclude from a certain connection with Christ's death to an analogous connection with the resurrection. This is the same kind of conclusion as in Rom 6.4, which is substantiated by virtue of the amplifying repetition.

But a number of problems of detail remain.

There are questions about the syntax. Is Rom 6.5a, εἰ γὰρ σύμφυτοι γεγό-

---

42. Cf. the cautious and balanced evaluation in Schlier, *Römerbrief*, p. 194. Others assume more directly that this is a statement about the life of resurrection, cf. Bornkamm, *Ende*, p. 38, Barrett, *Romans*, p. 123. And it is a widespread assumption that Paul has the resurrection primarily in mind, but modifies the line of thought precisely to avoid speaking of the Christians' resurrection, cf. section 4.3, point 6 below and the interpreters given in note 166.

ναμεν τῷ ὁμοιώματι τοῦ θανάτου αὐτοῦ, syntactically complete? Or is a 'with Christ' implied? And can Rom 6.5b, ἀλλὰ καὶ τῆς ἀναστάσεως ἐσόμεθα, be understood without implied members? How is the future form in Rom 6.5b to be interpreted?

These questions are associated with the understanding of the words σύμφυτος and ὁμοίωμα, where it is considered whether this is a special baptismal terminology. What does it mean in the context? 'For if we are grown together (with Christ) by an imitation of his death, then are we so (i.e. grown together with him) also by (an imitation of) the resurrection'?[43] Or: 'For if we have grown together with the representation of his death (= Christ's sacramental presence), then must we also be part of his resurrection'?[44] Or: 'For if we are grown together with the form of his death, so shall we also be this (i.e. grown together) with (the form of) his resurrection'?[45]

---

43. Thus Weiss, *Römer*, p. 268, Windisch, *Taufe*, p. 170, Kühl, *Römer*, p. 204, Schneider, *Passionsmystik*, p. 44f., Dodd, *Romans*, p. 106ff., Schnackenburg, *Heilsgeschehen*, p. 32f., 40f., Heitmüller, *Taufe*, 1903, p. 10, Bousset, *Kyrios*, p. 107. The important aspect of this interpretation was originally that τῷ ὁμοιώματι was perceived as instrumentalis; since ὁμοίωμα was intended to mean 'replica' or 'imitation', it became a description of the baptismal rite as a means of fusion with Christ, a sacramentalism that could be seen as an instance of mystery-religious influence. But this interpretation can also result from other concepts of the syntax. Heinrich Schwarzmann, *Zur Tauftheologie des hl. Paulus in Röm 6*, Heidelberg 1950, p. 38ff., Schnelle, *Gerechtigkeit*, p. 82, wishes to have σύμφυτοι control the genitive τοῦ θανάτου αὐτοῦ, so that τῷ ὁμοιώματι (alone) becomes instrumentalis. According to Mussner, *Zusammengewachsen*, p. 260, Shedd, *Man*, p. 183, σύμφυτοι is meant to be understood in the absolute, so that it controls no other word in the sentence. σύμφυτοι γεγόναμεν means that the Christians are mutually bound to Christ, as is included in the implicit subject; ὁμοιώματι then again becomes instrumentalis. According to Lietzmann, *Römer*, p. 68, Bultmann, θάνατος κτλ., *ThWNT* III (1938), pp. 7-21; p. 19f., cf. *Theologie*, p. 299, it in fact reads: 'grown together with the imitation of his death'. But this is an abbreviated, logically inaccurate term for 'through imitation of his death grown together with his death'.

44. The verse is thus perceived in connection with the Catholic idea of a 'Christian cult-mystery' which originated in the circle around Odo Casel. Here, ὁμοίωμα is translated by the word 'Gleichbild', which can be rendered as representation — it is not meant to refer to abstract similarity but to something material, an image which does not differ from the original. This 'Gleichbild' is thus the mystical sacramental presence in the baptismal rite of Christ's actual death. The cult-mystical interpretation of Rom 6 was first developed by Simon Stricker, *Der Mysteriengedanke des hl. Paulus nach Römerbrief 6,2-11*, *LiLe* 1 (1934), pp. 285-296, obviously inspired by Casel. Casel's own opinion, emerges in *JLW* 14, p. 213, 245, 371ff. (especially in a complimentary review of Stricker's article). The concept is described with particular thoroughness in Warnach, *Taufe*, pp. 302-15, cf. Tauflehre, p. 299ff. See Chapter I, notes 19 and 21 above. This opinion is also to be found among Protestant interpreters, thus Schneider, ὁμοίωμα, *ThWNT* V (1944-54), pp. 186-198; p. 193ff., Peter Brunner, *Aus der Kraft des Werkes Christi*, München 1950, p. 20ff.

45. The interpretation, originally suggested in Bornkamm, *Ende*, pp. 41-43, perceives (very much like the above) ὁμοίωμα as a *concretum*, a 'Gleichgestalt', which may be like the

These are the most distinctive interpretations of the members. They can be combined differently. And there are further possibilities; there has in particular been a gradual tendency to assume less loaded meanings.[46]

3.2. Σύμφυτοι

The basic meaning of the word is 'grown together'. It has thus long been perceived as expressing a complete, organic growing together — and this is normally assumed to be a growing together with Christ, an associatively understood Χριστῷ being implied.[47] For it is assumed that only two homogeneous entities can grow together in this way.

That this interpretation has been entirely replaced by a more cautious idea of the word's meaning is due in particular to Otto Kuss. By means of example passages in Liddell and Scott, *A Greek-English Lexicon*, he has demonstrated that as a rule σύμφυτος has a far less loaded meaning, so that it may merely express a connection or association.[48] It is also shown that when using the word it is not necessary for what is to be connected to be homo-

---

reality it depicts (in English this is translated by the simpler 'form' — cf. note 62 below). If that is the case, the term has nothing to do with baptism and sacramentalism. This interpretation has had an impact among interpreters, who do not see the mysteries as a background, cf. Schnackenburg, Todes- und Lebensgemeinschaft, p. 35f., Wagner, *Problem*, p. 293f., Beasley-Murray, *Baptism*, p. 134f., Siber, *Mit Christus*, p. 220, Thüsing, *Per Christum*, p. 134ff., Frankemölle, *Taufverständnis*, p. 67ff., Wilckens, *Römer* II, p. 13f. It is also chosen by interpreters who envisage a modification of the mystery background, cf. Tannehill, *Dying*, p. 35f., Gäumann, *Taufe*, pp. 50-52, 78f., Conzelmann, *Grundriss*, p. 298, Merk, *Handeln*, p. 24.

46. On the one hand, this applies to σύμφυτοι, where it has been demonstrated especially in Otto Kuss, Zu Röm 6,5a, in: *Auslegung und Verkündigung* I, Regensburg 1963, pp. 151-61, that the meaning may be much more vague, 'linked to'. On the other hand, it applies to ὁμοίωμα, to which vaguer meanings are also attributed: 'something similar', cf. Jervell, *Gud*, p. 98, Bo Frid, Römer 6,4-5, *BZ* 30 (1986), pp. 188-203; p. 195f., 'Gleichheit', 'likeness', cf. Murray, *Romans*, p. 218, Käsemann, *Römer*, p. 160, Cranfield, *Romans*, p. 308, Morris, *Romans*, p. 250, Dunn, *Romans*, p. 316f., or 'Bild', 'Abbild', cf. Kuss, *Römerbrief*, p. 301ff., Josef Gewiess, Das Abbild des Todes Christi (Röm6,5), *HJ* 77 (1957), pp. 339-46, Larsson, *Christus*, p. 59, Michel, *Römer*, p. 154. Pilgaard, Dåbsteologien, p. 125, suggests that the 'image of Jesus' death' is the crucifixion, with reference to Rom 6.6; a similar interpretation is to be found in Schnackenburg, Todes- und Lebensgemeinschaft, p. 36f.: 'Weil Paulus an die besondere "Gestalt" des Todes Christi denkt, nämlich an die Kreuzigung, kann er in V. 6 fortfahren, dass unser alter Mensch (mit Christus) mitgekreuzigt wurde', cf. Dinkler, Taufaussagen, p. 73.

47. Cf. Kühl, *Römer*, p. 204, Schneider, *Passionsmystik*, p. 44f., Schnackenburg, *Heilsgeschehen*, p. 31ff., 41, 43, Strecker, Indicative, p. 64, who implies a Χριστῷ as the required associative dative. In the Catholic cult-mystical interpretation, σύμφυτοι can be linked to τῷ ὁμοιώματι, since Christ's sacramental presence is perceived as a personal entity, cf. Warnach, Taufe, p. 302ff.

geneous; it may be a person and something as abstract as a quality or inclination. This is a common use of the word; to characterise someone as, for example, cowardly or inclining towards imitation it could be expressed by saying that that they have 'grown together' with cowardice or imitation.[49] What is concerned therefore is a close connection and linkage.

This perception does not of course mean that a play on a distinctly literal meaning of σύμφυτος is excluded. But it does mean that this has lost its priority. Moreover, the perception has consequences for the understanding of the syntax in the sentence — and this will lead in the long term to σύμφυτος not being able to concern a growing together here in the strong, loaded sense.

3.3. Is Rom 6.5a syntactically complete?

The question is, in what way should σύμφυτος be connected to the other sentence members. Words combined with the preposition σύν normally govern the dative.[50] Naturally, therefore, one allows τῷ ὁμοιώματι to be the dative that σύμφυτος demands. The nearest word would automatically be linked thereto, if it has the expected form.[51] Τοῦ θανάτου αὐτοῦ becomes an objective genitive linked to ὁμοιώματι. The sentence must then cohere as follows: 'We have a linkage to his death's ὁμοίωμα ...' — however this last member is to be understood.

There is no reason to assume an implied Χριστῷ after σύμφυτοι for the sentence to have a meaning, if σύμφυτος does not, as assumed, demand a connection to another personal entity.[52]

Neither does the other argument for the implied Χριστῷ hold good. It is assumed that the context requires a direct connection between Christ and the

---

48. See Liddell and Scott, *Lexicon*, p. 1689, Kuss, *Auslegung* I, pp. 154-56, cf. *Römerbrief*, p. 299f. Of the many examples, see in particular Plato, Resp. 609 A: σχεδὸν πᾶσι σύμφυτον ἑαυτῷ κακόν τε καὶ νόσημα, and Plato, Tim. 71 C, which refers to a sweetness that has 'grown together' with the liver. Cf. Schnackenburg, Todes- und Lebensgemeinschaft, p. 35f., Tannehill, *Dying*, p. 31, Gäumann, *Taufe*, p. 78, Halter, *Taufe*, p. 63 n. 72, Schlier, *Römerbrief*, p. 194, Cranfield, *Romans*, p. 307, Wilckens, *Römer* II, p. 13.
49. See Lysias 28, οὕτω σύμφυτος αὐτοῖς ἡ δειλία, Aristotle, Poet. 1448 B 2: τό τε γὰρ μιμεῖσθαι σύμφυτον τοῖς ἀνθρώποις.
50. This applies especially to verbs, but also to adjectives (which can also control the genitive). See Blass, Debrunner and Rehkopf, *Grammatik*, § 202, cf. § 182, Kuss, *Auslegung* I, p. 153.
51. Cf. Kuss, *Auslegung* I, p. 153, Gewiess, *Abbild*, p. 339, Siber, *Mit Christus*, p. 219, Cranfield, *Romans*, p. 307, Wilckens, *Römer* II, p. 13, Dunn, *Romans*, p. 316.
52. This assumption has been a significant argument for perceiving Rom 6.5a as syntactically incomplete, cf. Kühl, *Römer*, p. 204, Schneider, *Passionsmystik*, p. 44f., Schnackenburg, *Heilsgeschehen*, p. 31, 41, 43, Frid, *Römer* 6,4-5, p. 196.

baptised; for all other σύν connections in the text are meant to concern a linkage between Christ and the Christians.[53] If we look at the other σύν composita, it is in fact correct that they relate to a linkage between Christ and the Christians (and in Rom 6.6 a Χριστῷ after συνεσταυρώθη must even be implied). But here one must be aware of the nature of the linkage. The important point as regards the other σὺν Χριστῷ passages is that the Christians share with Christ in an event and its effects; they are 'buried', 'crucified', 'die' and live with Christ. In the same way there is a fellowship as regards an event if the Christians obtain a linkage to Christ's death's ὁμοίωμα. It would be different if σύμφυτος were to be linked directly to Christ; it would then be a unique term for a unio mystica.[54] But then it is strange that the word upon which everything depends is merely implied.

It may also be added to this that strictly speaking this sentence period becomes meaningless if τῷ ὁμοιώματι τοῦ θανάτου αὐτοῦ and (τῷ ὁμοιώματι) τῆς ἀναστάσεως are seen as instrumental dative. What happens to the thought-process? From having a linkage to Christ *by virtue of* the imitation (or the like) of his death, it is concluded that this is also the case *by virtue of* the imitation of the resurrection. The conclusion becomes quite superfluous. If one has the decisive linkage to Christ, it is of no importance whether yet another agent is added.[55]

The main objection is therefore that, without it being stressed, a reader has not only to embark upon implying the decisive word in the sentence but also to overcome a number of other difficulties into the bargain.

The result of the review is thus clear on this point: Rom 6.5a must be understood as syntactically complete. Σύμφυτος cannot indicate a growing together with Christ, and the word is therefore presumably used in the broader, more figurative sense about the linkage the Christians have attained to Christ's death's ὁμοίωμα.

3.4. Is Rom 6.5b syntactically complete?

The problem presented is apparently parallel to the preceding text. Is the sentence to be supplemented so that it corresponds to the preceding text?[56]

---

53. Cf. Kühl, *Römer*, p. 204, Bauer, *Wörterbuch*, col. 1124, Schnackenburg, *Heilsgeschehen*, p. 41, Cranfield, *Romans*, p. 307.

54. Cf. the discussion of the various meanings of the particle σύν in Chapter III, section 3.1 above, with note 162. See also the discussion of the term σὺν Χριστῷ in Chapter VIII, section 2, below.

55. This objection also applies to the other attempts to make τῷ ὁμοιώματι instrumentalis, cf. note 47 above

56. Cf. Bornkamm, *Ende*, p. 43 n. 19, Gäumann, *Taufe*, p. 79, Michel, *Römer*, p. 154, Jervell, *Gud*, p. 99, Cranfield, *Romans*, p. 308, Wilckens, *Römer* II, p. 15.

Or, as is maintained in the context of Casel's theory concerning the Christian cult mystery, must one try to understand it absolutely as it stands?[57]

On the face of it, this should again support the latter opinion, that it keeps to the actual wording, so that one need not assume implied words in the sentence. The interpretation should normally be preferred in which the sentence is read as complete. One must assume that the author wishes to define his intention as precise as possible, and leave as little as possible to chance and the readers' imagination. The more there is implied the greater the risk of arbitrary interpretations.

But if we look more closely at the proposed interpretation two aspects emerge.

First, it becomes clear that if one wishes to perceive the sentence as complete, one in reality assumes a digression on the part of the reader which is far greater than implying a few words. The entire period must then be read as follows: 'For if we are grown together by the representation of his death (Gleichbild), then we must also belong to the resurrection.' A directly evident connection is lacking between the two parts of this conclusion. The problem is how to move from the premise in Rom 6.5a to the conclusion in Rom 6.5b, and how to understand the ἀλλὰ καί which somewhat confusingly links together subordinate sentence and principal sentence. The theory is that Rom 6.5a about growing together with the representation of Christ's death sets the scene for the main sentence: 'then we are dead'. But Paul has said this so many times in the preceding text that he omits it here, and instead, by the ἀλλά sentence, switches over to the positive consequences of this.[58] A complete sentence is thus meant to be implied!

It then emerges that this is a somewhat forced interpretation of Rom 6.5b. It is possible grammatically for a possessive genitive to stand as a subject predicate. Paul also uses this where an affiliation to persons is concerned (thus Gal 3.29; 1 Cor 3.22-23). It is striking, however, that something as abstract as a resurrection shall have a proprietary relationship over people, and it arrives completely unprepared for in the context.[59] It is a concept that

---

57. Cf., apart from the interpreters referred to in note 44 above, Stommel, *Abbild*, p. 14f., 20, Georg Eichholz, *Die Theologie des Paulus im Umriss*[2], Neukirchen-Vluyn 1977, p. 205f., Schlier, *Römerbrief*, p. 196. Sometimes an intermediate standpoint is asserted that only σύμφυτοι is to be implied: Blass, Debrunner and Rehkopf, *Grammatik*, § 194, n. 3, cf. Käsemann, *Römer*, p. 161. But this is very unlikely. One must then either assume that σύμφυτοι controls the dative in Rom 6.5a and the genitive in Rom 6.5b, which would be very confusing, or one must assume that σύμφυτοι also controls the genitive in Rom 6.5a, which has been shown to be impossible.

58. See Stricker, *Mysteriengedanke*, p. 292, Warnach, *Taufe*, p. 312.

59. Cf. Schnackenburg, *Todes- und Lebensgemeinschaft*, p. 34. Seen in isolation, 1 Thess 5.5b certainly reads: οὐκ ἐσμὲν νυκτὸς οὐδὲ σκότους, as stated by Warnach, *Taufe*, p. 313, in

calls for much imagination on the part of the reader; as we have seen a complete sentence must be implied.

Contrary to this, it is appears to follow naturally that σύμφυτοι τῷ ὁμο-ιώματι is implied. This can already be seen by a translation into modern languages. A rendering can be given here in which the very same words are implied and the sentence is nevertheless clear: 'For if we are linked to his death's ὁμοίωμα, then we must also be this to the resurrection's.' The close connection which would normally exist between the content of the premise and the conclusion in an analogic conclusion means that the missing member in the sentence structure of the conclusion is taken directly from the premise. The central point in Rom 6.5a is to be found in the member τοῦ θανάτου αὐ-τοῦ. It is the baptised's linkage to Christ's death that is established in verse 5a, in line with the preceding verses. Τῆς ἀναστάσεως in Rom 6.5b cor-responds to this term. It is emphasised by the preceding καί and by its position in the sentence, where it is as close as possible to τοῦ θανάτου αὐ-τοῦ. This is therefore seen as a pair of contrast, and the principal sentence is automatically supplemented so that it corresponds to the subsidiary sen-tence.[60] The pleonastic ἀλλά can also be explained on this basis. It indeed emphasises that τοῦ θανάτου and τῆς ἀναστάσεως are opposites (and at the same time an advance from the statement of the premise to that of the con-clusion). In this way no problems arise in implying a few members.

Rom 6.5b is supplemented in accordance with Rom 6.5a, as is normally assumed.

3.5. The meaning of ὁμοίωμα

Since it is now clear how the member τῷ ὁμοιώματι is located in both parts of Rom 6.5, we can return to the question of the word's content and try to isolate what in fact it means in this passage.

One of the more distinctive interpretations of ὁμοίωμα is already out of the picture: the abstract meaning 'imitation' which makes it express a bap-tismal symbolism is no longer relevant, because it requires an implied 'with Christ' in Rom 6.5b.[61]

Two loaded meanings remain. On the one hand 'Gleichbild', 'representa-tion', as suggested by Casel and mystery theology and as defined by Simon Stricker: ''Ομοίωμα (Gleichbild) besagt philologisch ein Abbild, das mit der

---

defence of this interpretation. But a υἱοί is clearly implied here from 1 Thess 5.5a: πάντες γὰρ ὑμεῖς υἱοὶ φωτός ἐστε καὶ υἱοὶ ἡμέρας. This still accords in the following sentence.
60. Cf. Wilckens, *Römer* II, p. 15, Frid, *Römer* 6,4-5, p. 194f.
61. Cf. note 43 above, and see section 3.3 with the discussion of the question of an implied word.

gleichen Wirklichkeit gefüllt ist wie sein Urbild'; it is based om this as-sumption: 'ὁμοίωμα bedeutet nicht die abstracte Aehnlichkeit, sondern das Concretum, das Aehnlich- oder Gleichgemachte'. On the other hand 'Gestalt', 'Gleichgestalt', as proposed by Bornkamm: '... Gleichgestalt, d.h. Bezeich-nung einer Gestalt, die der Gestalt eines andern nicht nur ähnlich ist, son-dern gleicht'; and it is stressed that in Paul 'ὁμοίωμα ein *concretum*, nicht die abstrakte Eigenschaft der Ähnlichkeit oder Gleicheit bezeichnet'. Al-though they are widely different in their tendency, both cases thus consider it im-portant that the word refers to a *concretum*. And in both cases it is main-tained that it corresponds to the basic meaning and normal usage, partic-ularly in the Septuagint, and that Paul uses the word in this way where it occurs in other passages.[62]

Opposed to this are the interpretations in which ὁμοίωμα is perceived as less loaded in regard to one or other form of similarity. Here it is maintained that neither the ordinary meaning nor the usage in other passages in Paul can be as narrow as asserted, and, as a third point, that in any case what the context has in mind becomes crucial.[63] If there is to be a wholly special meaning, there must be something that leads the readers' attention in this direction.

There are thus three points to be examined:

1. The general meaning. ῾Ομοίωμα is not overwhelmingly widespread in profane Greek literature.[64] It is a verbal noun to ὁμοιοῦν 'to imitate', and if it is formed regularly the meaning 'imitation', 'copy' (= the concrete which is the result of an imitation) must be assumed, since verbal nouns ending in -μα normally refer to something concrete which results from the verbal action (but these nouns can also refer to abstracta). This meaning we find in Plato, where the word can be used as a synonym for εἴδωλον and εἰκών to

---

62. See Stricker, Mysteriengedanke, p. 290, and Bornkamm, *Ende*, p. 41f., cf. Brunner, *Kraft*, pp. 20-25, 68-73 (where Plato's usage is also included), Warnach, Taufe, p. 303ff., Gäu-mann, *Taufe*, p. 50f., Frankemölle, *Taufverständnis*, p. 67ff., cf. notes 44-45 above. These words are not easily translated into English. 'Gleichbild' and 'Gleichgestalt' are not to be found in any dictionary. In particular there are problems concerning the word 'Gestalt'; it can be the equivalent of the English 'form' or 'appearance' — and of the Greek ὁμο-ίωμα; but 'Gestalt' has a broader meaning and can also be the equivalent of the English 'figure' — a meaning which scarcely corresponds to ὁμοίωμα. This causes confusion in German exegetic discussion, as will be shown. In order to follow this discussion, I will often have to use the German words in the text.
63. See especially Jervell, *Gud*, p. 99: 'It is important, exegetically, not to become hypnotised by concepts like, in this case, ὁμοίωμα or by ideas that are detached from the text instead of asking what Paul's intention is.' Cf. note 46 above.
64. As regards the word's background, cf. Schneider, *ThWNT* V, pp. 186-198, Brunner, *Kraft*, p. 22ff., 68-73, Gewiess, Abbild, p. 339ff.

refer to the earthly depictions of transcendental ideas.[65] But it should be
noted that ὁμοίωμα has a broader meaning than the other words. Where
εἰκών can only refer to that which is similar to something else because it has
been derived from it, ὁμοίωμα can also refer to that which is more coin-
cidentally similar to something else.[66] This can broadly mean 'something
which is similar'. This is the case in Aristotle, where it says about rhetoric
that it is μόριόν τι τῆς διαλεκτικῆς καὶ ὁμοίωμα.[67] Moreover, the term ἐξ
ὁμοιώματος has been in evidence with the meaning 'on the basis of a case
which is similar' = analogous.[68]

The word is quite widespread in the Septuagint, where it is found 44
times. The usage follows by and large the same guidelines. In most cases it
refers to an imitation and is used synonymously with εἴδωλον and εἰκών,
and in this connection it refers almost exclusively to idols.[69] In a number of
other cases it refers broadly to something with the characteristic of being
similar to something. This is particularly the case in the visions in the Book
of Ezekiel. The word is used to describe what Ezekiel's vision actually looks
like. In such a matter there are both similarities and differences. In some
cases, perhaps, so much importance is attributed to accordance that the German translation 'Gestalt' becomes evident, and it is then possible to speak of
'Tiergestalte' and 'Menschengestalte'.[70] One passage is especially noteworthy, Deut 4.12,15, where it is emphasised that there was no ὁμοίωμα when
God spoke to Israel in the fire. Here ὁμοίωμα stands as an absolute. Nothing
seems to be concerned which is similar to something else. This could support
the view that here ὁμοίωμα concerns something which is identical with the

---

65. Phaidr. 250 BC, Soph. 266 D, Parm. 132 D, 133 D. This of course does not necessarily
    mean that it is established terminology for precisely these phenomena, as assumed by
    Brunner, *Kraft*, p. 68f. n. 20, Dunn, *Romans*, p. 317. A similar usage is to be found in
    Aristotle, Herm. 16a.
66. It corresponds in this way to ὁμοίωσις, which signifies not only similarity resulting from
    an imitation but similarity in general. As emphasised by Richard Chenevix Trench, *Syno-
    nyms of the New Testament*, London 1886, p. 50, ὁμοίωμα may mean that two things are
    as similar to one another as two eggs or two people who are not related.
67. Rh. 1356 A: '... part of the dialectic and something which is similar thereto.'
68. *Orientis Graeci inscriptiones selectae* II² (ed. W. Dittenberger), Hildesheim 1970, no. 669, line
    52f. Cf. Brunner, *Kraft*, p. 72f. n. 27, Gewiess, Abbild, p. 340 n. 5.
69. Ὁμοίωμα however, differs from the other words in that it is almost always connected
    to an objective genitive (a possible exception is Deut 4.12,15, cf. below). It is presumably
    the word ὅμοιος, which comes to the fore, so that one hears that it is something which
    is similar to something else. The word is used, for example, about idols in Deut 4.16-18;
    1 Sam 6.5; 2 Chr 4.3; Ps 105.20 (LXX). In 2 Kings 16.10 it is used about a working
    drawing.
70. Ezek 1.4,5,16,22,26; 2,1; 8,2-3; 10,1,8,10,22. Also Ps 143,12 (LXX); Judg 8,18. Cf. Schneider,
    ThWNT V, p. 191, 196, Gewiess, Abbild, p. 340f.

reality it represents.[71] But in connection with the subsequent context it is perhaps better to choose the translation 'image'. Deut 4.12,15 justifies the warning against image worship, which follows in Deut 4.16-18. What this says is that the Lord did not announce himself by an image. There is thus no reason for the Israelites to worship images. No far-reaching conclusions can thus be drawn from this term.[72]

The survey shows that the broad meaning, 'something similar', can be used as a point of reference everywhere. Then ὁμοίωμα may come to mean 'imitation', 'likeness' and 'image', according to the context. Although the German translation 'Gestalt' may in some cases seem natural, it is not the basic meaning of the word. And nowhere can the assumed absolute meaning be demonstrated, where the word is meant to refer to a 'Gleichbild' or a 'Gleichgestalt', which does not differ from but is identical with the reality described.

2. Paul's use of ὁμοίωμα. The question is, then, whether the Pauline incidences can show that the word is generally used in a stricter meaning. The meaning of 'Gestalt' in particular is under consideration.

In the New Testament ὁμοίωμα is found six times, five of these in Paul.[73]

Rom 8.3 reads that God sent his son ἐν ὁμοιώματι σαρκὸς ἁμαρτίας. In this context one may choose the German translation 'in Gleichgestalt des Sündenfleisches'. It is pointed out that there is accordance between Christ's and other people's living conditions. Like other people, he has a material body of flesh and blood.[74] But at the same time it is clear that there is a

---

71. Perhaps correspondingly in Josh 22.28. Cf. as to this the generalisations, according to which ὁμοίωμα generally means 'Gleichbild' or 'Gestalt' in the Septuagint — thus Brunner, *Kraft*, p. 22 with n. 21ff. on p. 70f., Schneider, *ThWNT* V, p. 191, Schnackenburg, Todes- und Lebensgemeinschaft, p. 36.

72. Cf. Gewiess, Abbild, p. 341 n. 8.

73. The sixth passage is Rev 9.7 about the manifestation of some locusts: τὰ ὁμοιώματα τῶν ἀκρίδων ὅμοια ἵπποις ἡτοιμασμένοις εἰς πόλεμον. This is entirely the same style as in the Septuagint, in Ezek. cf. above note 70.

74. Cf. in particular Wilckens, *Römer* II, p. 118, 125, who emphasises the classical interpretation, that there is not only external similarity but that an actual incarnation is concerned. Similarly also Frankemölle, *Taufverständnis*, p. 68, who considers perceiving it to mean that there is no difference between Christ and others. But this is scarcely feasible, cf. next note. Note also that it is not ὁμοίωμα in itself which means a material figure, a *concretum*. It is shown only by the objective genitive σαρκὸς ἁμαρτίας: because Jesus comes in something similar to 'sinful flesh' it becomes clear that his manifestation is also corporeal.

crucial difference between him and others: he did not allow sin to develop. There is thus both similarity and difference.[75]

Phil 2.7c: ἐν ὁμοιώματι ἀνθρώπων γενόμενος, expresses the same Christological point as Rom 8.3: following the incarnation Jesus resembles other people completely. In this context, where μορφὴ θεοῦ and σχῆμα ὡς ἀνθρ-ώπος are also concerned, it is reasonable to render this to mean that Jesus 'in Gestalt' (= in appearence) was like other human beings. The plural form shows that there is again a comparison between Jesus and other people.[76] Although the emphasis is on the accordance with men, this is so expressed that there is (strong) similarity but not complete identity.[77]

Rom 1.23 concerns a Fall: καὶ ἤλλαξαν τὴν δόξαν τοῦ ἀφθάρτου θεοῦ ἐν ὁμοιώματι εἰκόνος φθαρτοῦ ἀνθρώπου καὶ πετεινῶν καὶ τετραπόδων καὶ ἐρ-πετῶν. Here the rendering of 'Gestalt' provides no evident meaning. Ὁμοί-ωμα would normally be translated as 'image' or the like, corresponding to the use in the Septuagint, since there is a play on Deut 4.15-18 and Ps 106.20 which concerns an image cult. But the word is therefore given precisely the same meaning as the subsequent εἰκών. The style becomes pleonastic and clumsy.[78] I wish therefore to suggest an alternative: to assume the broader understanding of ὁμοίωμα. The sentence can then be rendered quite simply,

75. Cf. Bornkamm, *Ende*, p. 42, Gewiess, Abbild, p. 342, Käsemann, *Römer*, p. 209, Schlier, *Römerbrief*, p. 195, 241, Cranfield, *Romans*, p. 381. Even Wilckens, *Römer* II, p. 126, cannot avoid speaking of 'Identität bei Nichtidentität'.

76. Contrary to Schnackenburg, Todes- und Lebensgemeinschaft, p. 37, where it is maintained that the parallelism with μορφή confirms that '... ὁμοίωμα 'Gestalt' in diesem Sinne, d.h. ohne den Charakter einer 'Abbildung', bedeuten kann'. But then it should have read ἐν ὁμοιώματι ἀνθρώπου — in the singular — 'a "Gestalt" which is (like) a person'. Cf. also Gnilka, *Philipperbrief*, p. 120, Frankemölle, *Taufverständnis*, p. 68, who emphasises the identity between Jesus and other people to stress the 'complete incarnation'. It can also be pointed out that the plural form ἀνθρώπων may be seen as expressing that Christ identified himself with all people, cf. Lightfoot, *Philippians*, p. 112. It should again be noted that it is this objective genitive which makes the translation 'Gestalt', possible; 'das konkrete Menschsein' is concerned here; it is then stated that Jesus' life has been given a similar form or 'Gestalt', cf. Gewiess, Abbild, p. 341. This opinion is also confirmed by the parallelism σχῆμα ὡς ἄνθρωπος in Phil 2.7d, where indeed a comparison particle is employed.

77. Cf. Käsemann, *Versuche* I, p. 76, who says that Christ behaved differently from other people, Gewiess, Abbild, p. 341, who considers that the difference is not made clear here, Wilckens, *Römer* II, p. 14, who notes that because of his origin Christ is different from all other people.

78. The reduplication in ἐν ὁμοιώματι εἰκόνος is explained either as epexegetic genitive or as an echo of Gen 1.26, which reads — also pleonastically — κατ' εἰκόνα and καθ' ὁμοίωσιν. Whereas ὁμοίωμα is perceived in the meaning 'image', it is normally εἰκών which is here accorded the nuance 'Gestalt'. Cf. Lietzmann, *Römer*, p. 32, Michel, *Römer*, p. 66, Kuss, *Auslegung* I, p. 155f., Jervell, *Imago*, p. 319ff., Käsemann, *Römer*, p. 41, Cranfield, *Romans*, p. 118, Schlier, *Römerbrief*, p. 57f., Wilckens, *Römer* I, p. 107f.

without pleonasm: 'And they exchanged the glory of the immortal God for the likeness of an image of a mortal man and of birds, four-legged animals and reptiles'.[79] This results in a problem-free understanding which fits the context. In this connection, the creation and the human possibilities resulting therefrom are emphasised; Gen 1.20-27 also forms part of the background.[80] Δόξα τοῦ θεοῦ concerns the original condition of man; in both a Jewish and a Pauline context, this δόξα is associated with the creation of man in God's image, and the term can indeed be used as a synonym for 'God-imagery'.[81] The God-imagery disappears when people go over to worshipping idols. The possibility of living a true life thereby also disappears. Instead there is likeness to idols which are ephemeral and bestial. This means that people adopt the form of their god and lose themselves in bestiality, as developed in Rom 1.24-27. In this way, the 'likeness' becomes almost material: the ephemeral and bestial life which fools live.[82]

Rom 5.14 also concerns the consequences of a Fall.[83] It is established that death ruled in the time from Adam to Moses, and thus also ἐπὶ τοὺς μὴ ἁμαρτήσαντες ἐπὶ τῷ ὁμοιώματι τῆς παραβάσεως ᾿Αδάμ ... This must be seen to mean that death also ruled over those whose sin did not correspond precisely to Adam's transgression (which was disobedience to a commandment specifically expressed). In this context, it gives no meaning to think of a *concretum*, a material 'Gestalt'.[84] The discussion concerns correspondence between two entities, similarity.[85]

These other Pauline incidences show that no passages anticipate that the word ὁμοίωμα should be understood in a specifically strict sense with com-

79. Thus also Murray, *Romans*, p. 42, cf. the interpretation in Jervell, *Gud*, p. 43.

80. Cf. Niels Hyldahl, A Reminiscence of the Old Testament at Romans i. 23, *NTS* 2 (1955-56), pp. 285-88, Jervell, *Gud*, p. 43, Käsemann, *Römer*, p. 41.

81. As shown by Jervell, *Imago*, p. 100ff., 175ff.; in Paul, δόξα and god-imagery are found linked in 2 Cor 3.18-4.6; 1 Cor 11.7.

82. As god-imagery is something material: the life where there is accordance and coherence with God also applies to 'similarity to idols': the perverted life of sin.

83. Cf. the review of the obscure passage in Chapter V, section 3.3, above.

84. Attempts are also made here to use terms such as 'konkrete Gleichgestalt', 'gleichgestaltig', 'Gleichgestaltigkeit', and 'die abstrakte Bedeutung "Gleichheit, Ähnlichkeit"' is rejected, cf. Gäumann, *Taufe*, p. 50, Käsemann, *Römer*, p. 131, 142f., Wilckens, *Römer* I, p. 318. But it can be noted here that 'Gleichgestaltigkeit' is just as abstract as 'Gleichheit'. In Schnackenburg, Todes- und Lebensgemeinschaft, p. 38, it is also explained how the word 'Gestalt' is used here about a phenomenon: 'Es braucht also nicht immer um eine anschauliche Gestalt zu handeln; auch ein Vorgang kan eine "Gestalt" haben ...' Cf. Gewiess, Abbild, p. 341, Frid, Römer 6,4-5, p. 196.

85. Cf. Bauer, *Wörterbuch*, col. 1124, Kuss, *Auslegung* I, p. 158f. ('Bei Röm 5,14 könnte man allerdings in der Tat auf den Gedanken kommen, es handle sich in dem ἐπὶ τῷ ὁμοιώματι um eine abgeschwächte Bedeutung "ebenso wie"'), Gewiess, Abbild, p. 342, Schlier, *Römerbrief*, p. 165.

plete accordance between the two entities compared. All passages relate to a comparison in which there are both similarities and differences, and the broader 'something similar' meaning can be assumed.

3. The passage itself. If one must then consider ὁμοίωμα in Rom 6.5 in the meaning 'Gleichbild' or 'Gleichgestalt', there must be something in the context which indicates this clearly and concisely, or without misunderstanding paves the way for this. But in fact making these interpretations fit the context presents a problem.

This evidently concerns the 'Gleichbild' interpretation, where ὁμοίωμα is meant to express the sacramental 'Vergegenwärtigung' of Christ's death which takes place at baptism. This is a complicated idea in which one has not only baptism and the repetition of Christ's death which baptism involves but also, as an independent third entity, ὁμοίωμα τοῦ θανάτου, which means that Christ's death becomes really — and mysteriously — present. It rests upon this one word in the context, and the concept cannot be found in any other passage in the text.[86] It then becomes definitive that ὁμοίωμα has no special emphasis in the sentence. Without the present Catholic interest in a baptismal mystery, one would not come to this interpretation.

This applies somewhat similarly to the interpretation 'Gleichgestalt', 'Gestalt', perceived as a material personal entity. It is wished to understand Rom 6.5a as concerning a 'Zusammenwachsen mit der Gestalt des Todes Christi'. If it is assumed that in the context this meaning must be evident and unmistakable, this rests upon Bornkamm's assumption that the sentence would then correspond to the other σύν connections in the text, which all refer to the person of Christ.[87] But in many respects this is a faulty argument.

First, it must still be established that σύμφυτοι differs from the other σύν formulations which apply to the fellowship in certain events.[88]

Second, it is a crucial misunderstanding that the translation 'zusammengewachsen mit der Gestalt des Todes Christi' causes the Christians' linkage directly to the person of Christ to be concerned. The term 'der Gestalt seines Todes' does not mean, as the translation might fool one into believing, 'the

---

86. It is true that Warnach, Taufe, p. 302ff., contains a further argument: that ὁμοίωμα as the sacramental presence of Christ's death becomes a personal entity, and that the word σύμφυτοι must concern a growing together with such a personal entity. But the latter does not hold good, as shown in section 3.2 above. Also, this interpretation is associated with the understanding of Rom 6.5b as syntactically complete, and it is laboured as shown in section 3.4 above.

87. See Bornkamm, *Ende*, p. 42, cf. note 45 above.

88. Cf. section 3.3 above, with note 54.

'Gestalt' (= figure) Christ has when dead'.[89] If one wishes to base oneself on the interpretation's premises, it means 'the 'Gestalt' (= form) Christ's death has'.[90]

Third, it shows at the same time that this interpretation of ὁμοίωμα rests upon an untenable alternative in which the meaning 'likeness' is meant to be abstract and the meaning 'Gestalt' material. One overlooks that the German 'Gestalt' has a dual meaning. It can refer to a factual, material personal entity similar to the English 'figure'. It can also refer to the appearance of a given phenomenon, and then not only material things but also phenomena and events; this corresponds to the English 'form'. It is only this second meaning of 'Gestalt' that can correspond to ὁμοίωμα, and then it can refer to something quite non-material and intangible. This applies here if what has to be concerned is 'the form of Christ's being dead'; this sounds very abstract.[91]

Finally, it is difficult to carry through in the interpretation the feature that there is a *'Gleich*gestalt', that it refers not merely to something similar to the model but that it is identical with it.[92] Why, then, does it read σύμφυτοι τῷ ὁμοιώματι τοῦ θανάτου? Why not merely: 'we are linked to his death'? Although the main point is the correspondence between Christ and the Christians, one cannot ignore that ὁμοίωμα expresses that there is also a difference and a distance.[93]

---

89. Bornkamm thus fools himself and others, Beasley-Murray, *Baptism*, p. 134f., Conzelmann, *Grundriss*, p. 298, Hahn, Taufe, p. 19 n. 50. In Bornkamm, *Ende*, p. 42, one can see how a shift occurs from ὁμοίωμα τοῦ θανάτου αὐτοῦ (= 'das Sterben Christi') via 'Christus als der Gekreuzigter' to 'die Person of Christus' — unnoticed and without giving a reason. But there is no support for these new meanings of the term, as shown by Kuss, *Auslegung* I, p. 126 n. 9, cf. *Römerbrief*, p. 301. In Gäumann, *Taufe*, p. 51, Kuss' objection is accepted, but it is nevertheless sought to make use of Bornkamm's argument, in that it is maintained (p. 79 with n. 97f.) that the intention of ὁμοίωμα τοῦ θανάτου is ultimately a linkage to the person of Christ. But by this the argument is diluted.
90. Cf. Tannehill, *Dying*, p. 35, Wilckens, *Römer* II, p. 14. It is consistently maintained, when in Schnackenburg, Todes- und Lebensgemeinschaft, p. 36f., Dinkler, Taufaussagen, p. 73, it is seen as a term for the special form of Jesus' death, that it was a death on the cross, cf. note 46 above.
91. Cf. the review of the parallel passages above, where it also emerged that 'likeness' or 'similarity' can be used about something material, and that not ὁμοίωμα in itself but the subsequent objective genitive determines whether something material or something abstract is concerned, cf. notes 74, 76, 82 and 84.
92. Cf. Bornkamm, *Ende*, p. 42: 'ὁμοίωμα τοῦ θανάτου bezeichnet ... das Sterben Christi', Wilckens, *Römer* II, p. 14: 'so bezeichnet ὁμοίωμα τοῦ θανάτου den Tod Christi Selbst.'
93. Thus also Wilckens, *Römer* II, p. 14: 'Darin liegt in aller konkreten Gleichheit des Sterbens ein Moment von Unterschiedenheit, das sich darin auswirkt, dass die Getauften selbst nicht sterben, sondern lebt ...' Cf. Jervell, *Gud*, p. 99 (who indicates reservation with the term 'so to say'), Schnelle, *Gerechtigkeit*, p. 82 ('Dialektik von Relation und Nichtidentität').

We thus in reality end up with the general broad meaning of the word: 'something similar'.[94] This meaning is anticipated in the context, and it makes sense.

Rom 6.5 must prove and amplify the conclusion arrived at in Rom 6.4. Rom 6.2 speaks of the Christians' 'death' to sin. In Rom 6.3 the Christians' baptism was linked to Christ's death. In Rom 6.4a the Christians' 'death-baptism' and Christ's death are held together by the expression, 'we have been buried with him by baptism into death'. Several points of resemblance are thus developed between Christ and the baptised. It is clearly an extension of this when Paul in Rom 6.5a points to the Christians' linkage to 'something similiar to his death'. In the same way, Rom 6.5b continues the thought-process from Rom 6.4bc, where the point is an accordance between the Christians' new life and Christ's resurrection. It is expressed here by the correlative ὥσπερ-οὕτως. In Rom 6.5b, the Christians have a similar linkage to 'a resurrection like his'. The parallelism between verse 4 and verse 5 confirms that ὁμοίωμα must express that there is similarity (in important points) between the death and resurrection of Christ and what happens to the Christians by virtue of baptism. The ὥσπερ-οὕτως term in the preceding text indeed makes it difficult to understand it otherwise, for it in fact expresses the same relationship as ὁμοίωμα: that something is like something else.[95] In the light of this, it would be impossible to imagine that ὁμοίωμα is to be understood in another, more special sense. The context confirms the broad and comparatively material meaning: 'something similar' to Christ's death and resurrection.

It can then be specified in detail what in fact it is that is similar to Christ's death and resurrection.

As we have seen, the preceding context prepares the way for ὁμοίωμα τοῦ θανάτου αὐτοῦ being concerned with baptism. Baptism is linked to Christ's death and is described with imagery which revolves around death. It is a 'death' in such a way that the baptised has participated in the effects of Christ's death. It is also a 'death' in such a way that a total break with the old existence has occurred. And the same ideas are continued in Rom 6.6 in

---

94. Cf. note 45 above where 'likeness' and 'image' are also suggested. I prefer 'something (which is) similar' because it is the broadest meaning that can be used as a point of reference throughout.

95. Cf. Frid, Römer 6,4-5, p. 197f. It is indeed also striking that in other Pauline passages ὁμοίωμα is to be found together with ὡς and οὕτως, thus Phil 2.7, cf. note 76 above, and Rom 5.14 where the word stands as a prolongation of οὕτως in Rom 5.12c and is continued with the term τύπος in verse 14b. Until Rom 8, we find ourselves as a whole in a context in which one is working generally on accordance between model and imitators.

the term 'crucified with Christ'.[96] In baptism, therefore, the Christians have acquired a link with something similar to Christ's death, and it is this decisive break which is due to the Christ-event.

It is also emphasised that this break has lasting consequences. This is shown by the perfect form γεγόναμεν.[97] Ὁμοίωμα τοῦ θανάτου αὐτοῦ thus concerns baptism and its significance.

That ὁμοίωμα in Rom 6.5a refers to baptism does not make it baptismal terminology; it is merely a word which can be used to describe what happens in baptism. In other contexts it can apply to something entirely different.

This is already the case in Rom 6.5b, where the word is implied. Ὁμοίωμα τῆς ἀναστάσεως is something similar to resurrection. Rom 6.4bc gives an indication of what this is. If we keep strictly to the wording here, it is the new life of the baptised. Ὥσπερ-οὕτως indeed means that the new course of life is similar to Christ's resurrection. Both are due to God's δόξα, and in both cases life proves to be stronger than the forces which try to restrict it. Given the context, Rom 6.5b must then concern the new life after baptism.[98]

But most interpreters see this as a statement about the Christians' resurrection. Without reflecting about what ὁμοίωμα τῆς ἀναστάσεως means, it is often merely assumed that what is similar to Christ's resurrection is the Christians' resurrection,[99] but this idea is not indicated in the context. It may be argued, however, that the Christians' resurrection is included in the picture in a different way. The emphasis in Rom 6.4 on Christ's resurrection as a decisive eschatological event may accord with the introduction of the resurrection of the dead, and will also be the final objective of the Christians' new life.[100] But the main idea still seems to concern the new life and its

---

96. Cf. the connection emphasised by Schnackenburg, Todes- und Lebensgemeinschaft, p. 36f., Dinkler, Taufaussagen, p. 73, and Pilgaard, Dåbsteologien, p. 125. See also the discussion of the concept about a 'crucifixion with Christ' in Gal 2.19-20; 5.24; 6.14 above in Chapter III, section 3.3, where it is indeed established that there is in this term a condensed dual reference to the crucial Christological event and the soteriological consequences thereof, as will also be shown in the interpretation of this term in the next chapter.

97. Cf. Schnackenburg, Todes- und Lebensgemeinschaft, p. 37, Larsson, *Christus*, p. 60, Wilckens, *Römer* II, p. 14, Dunn, *Romans*, p. 316.

98. Cf. Murray, *Romans*, p. 219, who points out the ethical content of the new life, Cranfield, *Romans*, p. 308: 'We shall certainly also … be conformed (in our moral life) to His resurrection', Wilckens, *Römer* II, p. 15, who notes that ἐν καινότητι ζωῆς is resumed in Rom 6.5b.

99. Cf. Gewiess, Abbild, p. 349, Gäumann, *Taufe*, p. 79, Jervell, *Gud*, p. 99, Halter, *Taufe*, p. 55, Stuhlmacher, *Römer*, p. 35f.

100. See especially Wilckens, *Römer* II, p. 15, where it is argued that readers will hear τῆς ἀναστάσεως as a reference to the general resurrection of the dead (as in Rom 1.4, cf. note 37 above). Cf. also Dunn, *Romans*, p. 318.

content. In the following, it continues to be words of the stem ζῆν which is the object of Paul's reasoning.[101]

3.6. The future form in Rom 6.5b

There now remains the question of understanding ἐσόμεθα. It is discussed whether this is 'logical future' or 'genuine future'.

In the past, it was normally assumed that this was logical future. In a context such as this, where analogic conclusions as argued and drawn, there is indeed an obvious opportunity to use, for the thought-process' sake, the future about whatever is in the future relative to the point of reference, whereas in the absolute sense it is past or present. In this case, the emphasis in the context comes to lie on the new departure which has occurred.[102]

It has gradually become almost consensual to understand ἐσόμεθα in a strictly time-related sense, 'genuine future'[103] or, as others call it, eschatological future.[104] One thus turns against the weakening of the future form's true meaning to which the logical future should refer. And it is emphasised that for Paul the resurrection is indeed the future salvation benefit.[105]

But it cannot be presented as simply as that. There is no either-or. There is in fact a third possibility in which this future form refers to something which is of the future as regards time in a different way: it may concern something which will persist in the future but which has already been set in motion.[106] Then the emphasis is on the certain course of events: that there is

---

101. This is how the soteriological point is expressed in Rom 6.8 by συζήσομεν αὐτῷ, and in Rom 6.11 by ζῶντας δὲ τῷ θεῷ ἐν Χριστῷ Ἰησοῦ. Rom 6.13 uses the resurrection as an image of the breakthrough of the new life for the Christians, but still expressed by the verb ζῆν: ὡσεὶ ἐκ νεκρῶν ζῶντας, and Rom 6.23 concerns the Christians' eternal life.

102. This interpretation was originally associated with the concept that Rom 6 reflects a mysterious or sacramental baptismal concept in which both death and resurrection are experienced. Thus Weiss, Römer, p. 268, Windisch, Taufe, p. 170, Kühl, Römer, p. 204, Schneider, Passionsmystik, p. 44f., Schwarzmann, Tauftheologie, p. 38ff., cf. Schnackenburg, Heilsgeschehen, p. 32f., Delling, Taufe, p. 130f., Larsson, Christus p. 71. Cf. note 43 above.

103. See Lietzmann, Römer, p. 65f., Bornkamm, Ende, p. 43, Kuss, Römerbrief, p. 301ff., Schnackenburg, Todes- und Lebensgemeinschaft, p. 35f., Barrett, Romans, p. 124, Wagner, Problem, p. 294f., Beasley-Murray, Baptism, p. 134f., Thüsing, Per Christum, p. 140, Tannehill, Dying, p. 10ff., Gäumann, Taufe, p. 79, Jervell, Gud, p. 98.

104. Thus Käsemann, Römer, p. 161, Wilckens, Römer II, p. 16, Schlier, Römerbrief, p. 196, Pilgaard, Dåbsteologien, p. 125, Dunn, Romans, p. 318.

105. The interpretation is therefore used both to reject Pauline dependence upon the mysteries and to show a modification of mystery-religious baptismal traditions (cf. notes 103-4 above). Different in Schmithals, Römerbrief, p. 188, 191, who thinks that the future form already belongs to the tradition.

a future in the new life which the Christians have. This can be called the 'certainty future'.[107]

This gives a more gradual transition between the various interpretations of the future form. And to which nuance one wishes to give the greatest importance remains a question of how one looks on the main subject in the sentence.

There may still be reason to interpret ἐσόμεθα as the logical future that concerns something which has already occurred.

But this assumption has rightly been rejected as a step in a sacramental-mystical interpretation, in which Rom 6.5 is meant to concern two phases in the baptismal ritual. Since it is meant to be a coherent process of movement, it seems to be very artificial that this one aspect is referred to in the perfect and the other in the future.[108]

But if we assert that Rom 6.5b concerns the new life which follows after 'death' in baptism it gives a logical future meaning. What one then has particularly in mind is the time of beginning, and that the new life begins as a result of 'death' in baptism.[109] If one maintains that the content in Rom 6.5b is something past or present, it can be pointed out that the new life, especially in Rom 6.4c and in Rom 6.11b, is presented as an actual reality, and that these sentences are parallel to Rom 6.5b. The strength of this argument is shown by the fact that interpreters who understand the verb as

---

106. See especially Wedderburn, Traditions, p. 339, who expresses scepticism about theories regarding tension between present and future life of resurrection in the section. 'Moreover, if Paul is not correcting an enthusiastic view, there is no need to insist on the reference of the future tenses of vv. 5 and 8 to a future time, or at least not to the future only; it is possible to take them as referring to something which is true in some measure, although it looks to the future for its full realization.' Cranfield, *Romans*, p. 308, determines the future form as 'referring to the moral life' and refers to Rom 6.4b,6c. Cf. also Murray, *Romans*, p. 219, Wedderburn, *Baptism*, p. 44.

107. Cf. Murray, *Romans*, p. 219, who calls it 'indicative of certainty'. Dunn, *Romans*, p. 318, has the reference 'current future' (in an outline of Cranfield's opinion, of which he is critical). Frid, *Römer 6,4-5*, p. 199 n. 50, speaks of 'logical future', but for him the present certain course of events is meant to be concerned.

108. Cf. Schnackenburg, *Todes- und Lebensgemeinschaft*, p. 37. This affects the interpretation, where baptism is seen as an imitation of Jesus' death and resurrection which is to provide an instant life of resurrection, cf. note 43 above. This is already impossible, because it requires an untenable perception of the syntax, cf. section 3.3 above.

109. Cf. Larsson, *Christus*, p. 71, who has this completely different conception of the logical future.

'genuine future' also emphasise that the future salvation has already been anticipated here.[110]

It cannot therefore be excluded that there is an element of 'logical future', but this should not be understood to mean that something of the past is exclusively concerned, for there is within the context a point to the effect that the new life is also a present and a future reality.

It is also possible to understand ἐσόμεθα as a 'genuine, eschatological future'. But again there is reason to distinguish between the different versions of the interpretation.

It is often represented that the future form must concern something exclusively of the future, something which will occur sometime. But the reasoning for this is not convincing. The term itself, 'genuine future', is an indirect argument: that this understanding of the future must be the true one. It will be demonstrated below that this is a doubtful assumption. The parallel of Rom 6.8b is also pointed out, where there is also said to be a genuine future form.[111] But even should this prove to hold water,[112] it need have no influence on the interpretation of Rom 6.5, since throughout the text Paul's reasoning is characterised by shifts which take place continually in the use of imagery and the meaning of words. It is also possible, therefore, that there has been a shift on this point. It is stated as a decisive argument that here as in other passages Paul consistently avoids speaking of the Christians' resurrection as a present-day fact.[113] But it is indeed when exegetes argue in this way that they show that the interpretation rests upon an uncertain foundation, since it is assumed that Rom 6.5b concerns the Christians' resurrection exclusively and unambiguously. And as we have seen this is not the case.

The aspects of salvation which occur only in the future can still be emphasised. But the basis of the thought-process is the Christians' new life, which is similar to Christ's resurrection and is sustained by the same power.

---

110. Cf. Bornkamm, *Ende*, p. 43, Frankemölle, *Taufverständnis*, p. 71f., Käsemann, *Römer*, p. 161, Wilckens, *Römer* II, p. 16, and with special emphasis Siber, *Mit Christus*, p. 232ff., Halter, *Taufe*, p. 55f. and n. 82, which states that there must also be a 'Gegenwartsaspekt', 'ansonsten der V[ers] nämlich genau das nicht begründen kann, was er nach Pls begründen soll: die Wirklichkeit und die Möglichkeit des Existenzvollzuges der Getauften "in der Neuheit des Lebens"'.

111. Cf. Bornkamm, *Ende*, p. 47, Tannehill, *Dying*, p. 10, Gäumann, *Taufe*, p. 79, 84, in which it is maintained that the main verb in Rom 6.8, πιστεύομεν makes it certain that συζήσομεν refers to something future in time. Cf. the discussion below.

112. In my opinion this is just as doubtful, as will be shown in Chapter VIII, section 1.5 below.

113. See especially Conzelmann, *Grundriss*, p. 299, Schule, p. 91, Güttgemanns, *Apostel*, p. 217f., Tannehill, *Dying*, p. 11f., Gäumann, *Taufe*, p. 83 n. 128, Eckert, *Taufe*, p. 217.

From here, thought can progress towards the conclusion in the resurrection of the dead. But then there is no longer the absolute contrast between the present and the future, for in the period up to the total breakthrough the baptised will also live a life sustained by the power that appeared in the resurrection of Jesus.[114]

Precisely because it turns out that no sharp borderline can be drawn between the past, present and future in the salvation benefit, there is reason to consider the third possibility: that ἐσόμεθα is what I have called the 'certainty future'.

This is in fact an obvious way to employ the future. As we know, in Greek the future refers to the ingressive and the durative aspects. That is to say, the future does not always have an ingressive meaning, and does not always concern something which occurs only sometime. It may just as well have a durative meaning, and apply to what will be in the future. And then the certain course of events can be emphasised.

This use of the future is indeed also widespread. This can be demonstrated by a few obvious examples. Thus, Rom 6.2: οἵτινες ἀπεθάνομεν τῇ ἁμαρτία, πῶς ἔτι ζήσωμεν ἐν αὐτῇ; This concerns the life the Christians will continue to live.[115] The same applies to Rom 6.14a; ἁμαρτία γὰρ ὑμῶν οὐ κυριεύσει, where the assurance is expressed that neither now nor in the future will sin rule over the Christians.[116] In Rom 8.35-39 also, we have an important example of these future forms which express the certainty that the present situation will be preserved in the future also.[117] We thus have a use of the future which is just as 'genuine' as that preceding, in the sense that the emphasis is on the time-related future aspect (and this is also 'eschatological' because it rests upon the new life's breakthrough by virtue of Christ).

When the immediately preceding and subsequent future forms are of this type, it is natural to perceive Rom 6.5b (and Rom 6.8b) similarly. What is then concerned is that the Christians will continue to be linked to that which is similar to Christ's resurrection, i.e. the new life which rests upon the same power. This, in my opinion, is the simplest interpretation.[118]

114. Cf. notes 100 and 110 above.
115. It is generally acknowledged that this also concerns the Christians' present existence, cf. Chapter VI, note 11 above.
116. This concept of the future form is also generally acknowledged, cf. Chapter X, section 1.5 below, with note 45.
117. Moreover, I have argued that this is the most likely understanding of the future in Rom 5.17, Chapter V, section 3.4 above, with note 77, and perhaps in Rom 5.19, cf. Chapter V, note 80 above. In Murray, *Romans*, p. 219, Wedderburn, *Traditions*, p. 352 n. 21, there is a reference to these passages as parallels to Rom 6.5.
118. This interpretation is largely undisputed — because it has been overlooked. Only in Dunn, *Romans*, p. 318, is there a negative attitude — to the interpretation in Cranfield, *Romans*, p. 308; but it rests upon the rigid opinion that the future's actual function is to

But it is of course true that one cannot distinguish sharply between the various nuances of the form of the future. And the question then arises of the emphasis to be put on this future form. I shall return to this in the next section.

4. The background to the concepts in Rom 6.3-5

4.1. The dual complex of problems

The exegesis of Rom 6.3-5 has revealed that many details in the text are disputed, and this is associated with the disagreement about the text's religio- and traditio-historical background.[119] But at the same time it can be established that the thought-process and the point of the paragraph are immediately clear: it is concluded in two instances from the linkage between the Christians' 'death' in baptism and Christ's death that the Christians must have a similar linkage to Christ's resurrection.

This perception of the text's main subject is an important basis for a review of the text's background. This is one aspect of the religio- and traditio-historical comparison. The other aspect is the possible parallels and the general historical assumptions presented in the first part of the thesis. The task may thus appear to be simple.

But now a crucial distinction must be indicated. If, as here, one enquires about the religio- or traditio-historical background to a reasoning text, there are two different things which one may seek. (a) First, it may be the problem of the specific or assumed basis of the thought-process. What are the concepts the author — Paul — refers to and on which he constructs his reasoning? One then looks for a way of thinking which Paul assumes to be known among the recipients of the letter. (b) But, secondly, one may look at the somewhat broader problem of what conceptions have influenced Paul's description of the matter, what patterns of thought may have affected him, and perhaps what ideas is he approaching in the course of the reasoning.

This distinction is important here, but also overlooked.[120] It is therefore

---

describe what is exclusively in the future, and Rom 6.5b must therefore concern a future participation in Christ's resurrection, although it is accepted that the scene was set for a current reality having to be concerned.

119. This is shown from the notes on the text review above, where I have sought to indicate the religio- and traditio-historical theories associated with the various interpretations of the details.

120. This distinction is clearly but briefly expressed in an intervention in connection with Dinkler, Römer 6,1-14, p. 112, where Jeremias states: 'Die Taufe schenkt Anteil an der Sühnkraft des Kreuzes — das ist die urkirchliche, vorpaulinische Taufaussage über die Intention der Taufe, die in Röm. 6,3 von Paulus aufgenommen und in V. 4 ff. mit Hilfe

often unclear to which of the two problem-complexes interpreters are relating.

But clearly the first problem (a) is the more interesting here. Indeed, in
Rom 6.3 Paul refers, with ἢ ἀγνοεῖτε ὅτι..., to a specific insight which he can
assume to be known. It is the attempt to pinpoint this insight which leads to
the religio- and traditio-historical considerations.[121] In the three next sub-
sections I shall discuss these problems in particular.

But thereafter it is also interesting to consider the other problem (b), i.e.
what are the concepts which may have affected Paul's way of expressing
himself, and perhaps contributed to the thought-process in the text. The final
sub-section will consider this.

4.2. Mystery religion as a point of reference for Rom 6.3-5?

I commence with the theories that in this context Paul adopts concepts originating from the Hellenistic mystery religions. They have been presented in
many variants since the time of the religio-historical school.[122] The main
features are said to be a ritual repetition of the deity's death and resurrection
and a unio mystica.

In discussing a number of points, I shall assess the linkage there may
have been between Rom 6.3-5 and the material presented in the first part of
the thesis, and accordingly adopt a position on the feasibility of the most important ideas.

1. *External parallelism* cannot be avoided between the thought-process
which begins in Rom 6.3 and certain of the mystery religions.

If one holds to the main lines, Rom 6.3-5 may be summarised as follows:
in baptism the Christians experience a process of events through 'death' to
a new life, and this is linked to the death and resurrection of Christ.

---

von Gedanken aus dem Bereich der Mysterien entfaltet wird.' Also in Gäumann, *Taufe*,
p. 64, 76f., there is an attempt to see Paul's point of reference in Rom 6.3-4a as a tradition
about baptism to Christ's death alone, after which he continues to develop the thought-
process in association with the primal-Christian 'credo' (1 Cor 15.3-4). But this trend is
not consistently implemented, cf. note 166 below. In Betz, *Transferring*, however, there
is a sustained attempt to see Rom 6 as Paul's adaptation of his own genuinely Christian
concepts based on the baptism by John resulting in an analogy with the Hellenistic
mysteries and other initiations, cf. in particular the summary p. 118.
121. Cf. notes 2 and 3 above.
122. Cf. the variation in the descriptions in Gunkel, *Verständnis*, p. 83ff., Bousset, *Kyrios*, p.
107ff., Heitmüller, *Taufe*, 1903, p. 9ff., *Taufe*, 1911, p. 21ff., Windisch, *Taufe*, p. 167ff., Reitzenstein, *Mysterienreligionen*, p. 259ff., Lietzmann, *Römer*, p. 65ff., Dibelius, *Botschaft* II, p.
71f., and the interpretations discussed in section 4.2 below in which a Pauline
modification of the point of reference is assumed. Cf. the research-historical survey in
Chapter I, section 2, and Chapter II, section 1.

Similarly, the mysteries may have been developed as a process of events in which the initiates go through death-like experiences and a renewal of life (however, never described as a resurrection). This is most evident in the Isis mystery described in Apuleius and in the so-called Themistios fragment. In the Eleusinian mysteries also, the mystes experiences sorrow about the dominion of death and subsequent relief and joy at the victory of life.[123] This process of events through the experience of death to life may be linked to a diety's death and the overcoming of the power of death.[124]

The question then is whether there is also an inner accordance and connection. This will be considered below; first in regard to the ritual agents in Rom 6 and in the mysteries, and then in regard to the effect.

2. *The means* one would like to see as distinctly sacramentalist in both contexts — and the crucial point was said to be a death-resurrection ritual which automatically led to salvation.[125] But the assumed common features are not to be found either in Rom 6 or in the mysteries.

In Rom 6.3-5, this sacramentalism has been based on concepts regarding a baptism 'into Christ', 'into (the effect of) his death' and an immersion-emersion symbolism, interpreted as an imitation of Christ's death and resurrection, which leads to immediate life σὺν Χριστῷ. But a review of the text has dismissed that it is a description of such a ritual of magical effect. The total baptismal act is more probably concerned, which involves a binding to Christ and dependence on the salvation events and the divine power.[126]

---

123. See Apuleius, Metam. 11.21-25, and the interpretation thereof in Chapter II, section 2.2 above. Also the Themistios Fragment = Johannes Stobaeus, Anthologicum 52.49, cf. Chapter II, section 2.4 above, and the review of the Eleusinian mysteries in Chapter II, section 2.1. Cf. also the summary in Chapter II, section 2.7.

124. As regards Eleusis, Clement, Protr. 12.2, contains information about the initiates imitating the goddesses Demeter and Kore, cf. Chapter II, section 2.1 above with note 35. According to Apuleius, Metam. 11.23, the Isis mystes followed the sun's path to the threshold of the kingdom of the dead in order to return to life, cf. Chapter II, note 68 above. The Themistios Fragment contains no information about an imitation of a deity. The Attis cult seems to contain an element of imitation, but it cannot be shown that it is a death-resurrection process which is imitated — but only the ecstatic savagery and self-mutilation, cf. Chapter II, section 2.3 above, with notes 115-19.

125. Thus clearly in Heitmüller, *Taufe*, 1903, p. 14, Bousset, *Kyrios*, p. 139, Braun, *Studien*, p. 155, Lohse, *Umwelt*, p. 179, Tröger, *Mysterienglaube*, p. 13.

126. The difficulties of the ritual interpretations have been especially demonstrated in section 1.2 above concerning the term βαπτίζεσθαι εἰς Χριστόν, in section 2.2 concerning 'burial with Christ' and in section 3.3 concerning the attempt to interpret Rom 6.5 as expressing the baptised 'growing together with Jesus' by virtue of an imitation of his death and resurrection. At the same time, it has been pointed out that imagery (cf. in particular note 13) and play-on-words are used in an attempt to imprint the soteriological consequences of baptism: a break with sin and a new life by virtue of the divine power, ἡ δόξα τοῦ πατρός.

A death-resurrection ritual of magical effect also cannot be demonstrated in the mystery religions. The wish to find initiation rites with death-resurrection symbolism in the mysteries is modern speculation without substance in the texts.[127] The mysteries do not recognise that the external process is meant in itself to have such magical power. What was important everywhere was the quantity of agents. If there was a process through a kind of death to a new life, this could only be understood as a framework for a series of agents. In addition to purification rites in the initial process and the ritual ingestion of food, there were dramatic performances in Eleusis, sacred words and the display of sacred objects; in the Isis rites there were a series of experiences which gave an insight into the deity's power; the Attis cult had bloody rites and ecstatic obsession. There is a sovereign mother-deity everywhere, and what is important throughout all the rites is to secure a close relationship with the god upon whose power one depends.[128]

We are thus left with a fundamental inconsistency between the mysteries and Rom 6, because the crucial feature in the mystery rites is the internal religious experience through the many agents. This becomes entirely different in Rom 6. The baptismal act involves no long ritual process; the religious experiences cannot be accommodated in baptism's immersion and emersion, which by its very nature must be momentary. Baptism is the one single agent.[129] There would be consistency with the mystery rites only if there were in them merely a repetition of a symbolic death-resurrection process resulting in the salvation effects. And this is probably why this interpretation of the rites has arisen, despite the lack of examples.

---

127. This is to be seen in particular at the taurobolium in the Attis cult, which is presented as the clearest parallel to Rom 6. In particular, Hepding, *Attis*, p. 196ff., has interpreted it as a death-resurrection symbolism when the Attis priest descends into a pit, into which the blood of the sacrificed bull runs through the boarded ceiling, and comes up again. But this is based on an uncritical combination of concepts originating from all possible kinds of cult-contexts, cf. Chapter II, section 2.3 above, with notes 109-14.

128. See the review of the cults in Chapter II, sections 2.2-4 and the summary in section 2.7.

129. Thus also Braun, *Studien*, p. 154: 'Man vergleiche die starke Emotion und die Unterstreichung der Schau in den Mysterientexten mit dem Fehlen der Vokabulatur des Sehens, mit der Unakzentuiertheit des Taufaktes als solchen, mit der fehlenden Emotionalität ihm gegenüber in unseren neutestamentlichen Abschnitten!' Cf. Stommel, *Abbild*, p. 11f. But there is in Wayne A. Meeks, *The first urban Christians*, New Haven 1983, pp. 150-57, an attempt to reconstruct a long process on the basis of many individual traditional features, which over time interpreters have associated with baptism and is said to have included instruction, disrobing = death, descent, washing, ascent, new clothing, anointment, ascending a throne(?), spiritual gifts, cries of Abba etc. But on the one hand this collocation has a very hypothetical stamp, and on the other hand Rom 6.3-8 still applies to the act of baptism itself as the momentary event which is seen as a 'death' and is *not* described in the image of a long descent into the kingdom of the dead, and back to glorification.

A certain consistency has also emerged between the mysteries and Rom 6.3-5. Both have something that may be characterised as purification rites (but with widely different location and importance), and both are concerned with dependence on the sovereign deity. But these features are to be found in all religions. They are not very significant, therefore, compared with the fundamental inconsistency.

3. Between the *effects* there is more consistency. It has already been established that both express dependence on the deity.

Rom 6.3 concerns the break with the old, sinful life, and Rom 6.4 says that the baptised has received a new morally-improved life. It appears from Rom 6.5 and the subsequent verses that the new life is linked to Christ's resurrection, that it is a life together with him and a life with a future.

Similarly, the mysteries include concepts to the effect that the mystes had an improved earthly life and a hope for the future. Improvements in the earthly life relate in particular to happiness and wealth. But in the Isis mysteries we find also the concept of a parting from the sinful life and a moral effort.[130] Hope for the future is directed towards an improved lot in the life beyond death, thanks to the linkage to the powerful deity.[131]

It should be noted that nowhere in the review of the mysteries did we find proof of the concepts of an immediate transition to a divine life or a fusion with the deity.[132] On the face of it, Rom 6 appears to be closer to such concepts, in that great emphasis is given to the immediate effect of baptism and to the link with Christ.

4. *The mysteries' further development* in Hellenistic syncretism must therefore be seen as very important if one wishes to demonstrate that in its main points Rom 6 is dependent on the mysteries.[133] But the indirect dependence cannot be demonstrated simply and unambiguously.

---

130. As regards the Isis mysteries' call for a moral Isiac militia, see Apuleius, Metam. 11.15, cf. 11.6,23. A longer and happier life is also part of the salvation benefit, see Metam. 11.6,21. Cf. Chapter II, section 2.2 above.

131. See Hom. hymn. 2.480-82, Cicero, De leg. 2.14.36, Apuleius, Metam. 11.6.

132. Two contexts in particular have been presented. But that Lucius in Apuleius, Metam. 11.24, appears after initiation as an image of the sun is no proof of a complete identification with the deity, as assumed in Bousset, *Kyrios*, p. 113f., Betz, *Nachfolge*, p. 72f., Tröger, *Mysterienglauben*, p. 26, cf. Chapter II, section 2.2 above, with notes 72-79. Neither is it possible to use Firmicus Maternus, De err. 22.3, as proof that the mystes die like the deity (presumably Osiris) and immediately arise to continued divine life, as stated by Hepding, *Attis*, p. 167, Bousset, *Kyrios*, p. 138, Reitzenstein, *Mysterienreligionen*, p. 400f., Leipoldt, *Taufe*, p. 62f., Tröger, *Mysterienglauben*, p. 29; a merging together with the god is in no way concerned, cf. Chapter II, section 2.2, with notes 61-65.

133. It is typical of the religio-historical school that it works with mystery religions and gnosticism as a combined, thoroughly syncretic phenomenon. See Reitzenstein, *Mysterienreligionen*, p. 259ff., Bousset, *Kyrios*, p. 107ff., Hepding, *Attis*, p. 196ff., cf. Bultmann, *Theologie*, p. 298f., Tannehill, *Dying*, p. 29f., Thyen, *Studien*, p. 203f., Käsemann, *Römer*, p. 154.

In the first place the hypothetical nature of the reasoning must be stressed. It is attempted, by combining a number of individual features from various contexts, to arrive at a complex of concepts which is not in evidence elsewhere.[134]

It must next be pointed out that the content of this mystery-thinking has distanced itself somewhat from the original mysteries. It is true that great weight can be placed on the close contact with the divine and the immediate effects of redemption. But at the same time the external cultic aspect is brushed aside by a play-on-words and allegorising re-interpretations. Rituals are not important, but intellectual, philosophical and religious absorption are important.[135]

Finally, one must be aware of another development. Expressions, terms and concepts from the mysteries become general usage and ordinary thinking that can be employed without the original religious content being attuned thereto.[136] This means that any dependence on the mysteries may be purely terminological.

5. *Hellenistic-Christian traditions* come into the picture thanks to Heitmüller's theory that Paul in his theology depends upon the Hellenistic communities.[137] If one can demonstrate the special ritual symbolism and a baptismal mystery behind other Pauline texts, one has a link between the mystery religions and Rom 6.

Other Pauline baptismal texts indeed concern a Christ-linkage so intensely expressed that it is comparable to the mysteries. But the background is not an established complex of mystical and mythological ideas. It is richly varied imagery which can concern both the baptised individually receiving a Christ-identity and collectively constituting σῶμα Χριστοῦ.[138]

---

134. This criticism has been presented with special emphasis in Wagner, *Problem*, p. 281, cf. Chapter II, note 10 and section 3 above.

135. Cf. the survey of development in Chapter II, section 3.2 above. Gnosticism is also part of this development. But it should be noted that both Gnostics and the followers of other intellectually-orientated religious movements have pursued magic where the practical execution is very significant, cf. Chapter II, section 3.3.

136. This development in the direction of a purely terminological use of words and patterns of thought is so marked that the terms can also be used in Judaism and Christianity despite aversion to any paganism, as was described in detail in Chapter II, sections 3.1-2 and the summary 3.4.

137. See Heitmüller, *Problem*, p. 330ff. Cf. the survey above in Chapter III, section 1, on the formation of theory occasioned by this assumption.

138. See especially the review of Gal 3.27-29 and 1 Cor 12 above, Chapter III, sections 2.1 and 2.2. Apart from these texts, Paul has also expressed certainty of salvation and in particular closeness to Christ in passages such as Gal 2.19-20; 2 Cor 13.3-4 and especially Rom 8.10, which reads that 'Christ is in you (the Christians)'. This has been interpreted as Pauline mysticism, which can be seen in the context of the feeling in Hellenistic reli-

But it is not possible to demonstrate in the text a baptismal tradition with a ritual death-resurrection symbolism in which the Christians have gone through death 'with Christ' to glorious resurrection. There is not one unified motif-complex, but two motifs: on the one hand the 'one-phase' concept of a previous, definitive new departure in 'death with Christ',[139] and on the other hand a 'two-phase' motif of a future death and resurrection (in similarity) with Christ.[140] Only in Col 2.11 are there concepts of both death and resurrection with Christ in association with baptism — although not as a primitive concept of a cultic imitation but rather as a subtle, symbolic and varied use of imagery.[141]

6. *Inference from the text itself* is the last traditio-historical consideration. It *is* possible to make an inference from the existing text back to the tradition to which Paul refers by the question in Rom 6.3: ἤ ἀγνοεῖτε ὅτι ... But then the reasoning structure here shows that it *cannot* be a ritual death-resurrection symbolism.

The sharpest critics of this interpretation have pointed out that the knowledge to which Paul refers is to be found only in Rom 6.3, for if the reference was also to include what follows the continuation in Rom 6.4 would have to be introduced by a γάρ. But οὖν emphasises that new consequences are drawn from verse 3. This shows unambiguously that the direct reference thereby ends. The express reference applies, therefore, only to baptism into Christ's death.[142]

That the baptismal tradition concerns only a linkage to Christ and his

---

gion, cf. Bousset, *Kyrios*, p. 110ff., 128, 142, Reitzenstein, *Mysterienreligionen*, p. 349, Dibelius, *Botschaft* II, p. 10ff.

139. This concerns Gal 2.19-20; 5.24; 6.14; 2 Cor 5.14-15; Rom 7.4 where one has this loaded usage in which 'death with Christ' implies at the same time the crucial Christ event and its equally crucial soteriological consequences. Cf. the review above in Chapter III, section 3.2 and the summary in section 3.4. On the face of it, Rom 6.3,6 appears to belong in this group.

140. See Rom 8.17,29; Phil 3.10-11,21; 1 Thess 4.13-5.11; 2 Cor 4.7-15; 13.3-4. In the two latter passages the future eschatological progress has already been anticipated during the course of the Christian life (by which the motif has come closer to the foregoing. Cf. the review in Chapter III, section 3.3, and the summary in section 3.4.

141. See the discussion above in Chapter III, section 3.5. The probability is that the text is a further development of Rom 6.3-8, cf. Sanders, *Dependence*, p. 40ff., Siber, *Mit Christus*, p. 191ff., Lohse, *Kolosser*, p. 156 n. 1, Halter, *Taufe*, p. 194, Lona, *Eschatologie*, p. 171, Wedderburn, *Baptism*, p. 70ff.

142. Cf. Schnackenburg, *Heilsgeschehen*, p. 136 n. 397, Todes- und Lebensgemeinschaft, p. 39, Wagner, *Problem*, p. 292f., 297, Larsson, *Christus*, p. 52f., Frankemölle, *Taufverständnis*, p. 53. Perhaps an echo of the tradition is still to be found in Rom 6.4a, which recapitulates the insight from verse 3, but the consequences of this are derived from verse 4b. In Rom 6.6,9 there are new references to an assumed knowledge, as emphasised by Tannehill, *Dying*, p. 13f., but it makes no difference to this perception.

death is confirmed if one looks at the direction of Paul's reasoning. Both in Rom 6.4 and the following verses Paul uses this tradition as a basis for the continued reasoning. It is here that the structure is entirely stamped by the repeated attempts to convince that, like the Christians' linkage to Christ's death, there must also be a linkage to his resurrection and the new life. This is quite clear in Rom 6.4,5,8,11.[143] But then the point of reference cannot be simply a dual concept about baptism as death and resurrection with Christ. The whole of this strong appeal would be meaningless if it were already certain beforehand. Why not then just refer to this knowledge precisely? What is the reason for the long explanations?

The following *summary* can now be made.

The religio- and traditio-historical comparison in points 1-5 has shown that there is probably a certain accordance between Rom 6 and the mysteries and their development up to Paul's time. This is particularly true of the intense religious ambience in which the individual enters into a relationship of dependence with the divine. But no accordance and connection can be indicated in regard to specific ritual agents.

The traditio-historical inference in point 6 from the available text definitively excludes that in Rom 6.3 Paul bases himself on a tradition in which the baptised has a part in both Jesus' death and his resurrection.

The answer is accordingly negative to the most important religio- and traditio-historical question (a), what is the concept Paul refers to and uses as a point of reference for the reasoning in Rom 6. It cannot be a mysterious understanding of baptism as a ritual death and resurrection with Christ; nor can it be a mysticism of the type in which the baptised is wholly merged together with the dead and resurrected deity.[144]

As regards the second question (b), what concepts may have influenced Paul's account, it cannot be excluded that in his concluding point Paul ap-

---

143. Cf. the survey of the text structure above in Chapter V1, section 4, and here point 1 in particular. The same perception is expressed in Zahn, *Römer*, p. 301: 'Während also die Verknüpfung der Getauften mit dem Tode Christi von vornherein als mit der Beziehung der Taufe auf denselben gegeben scheint (V.3-4), wird die Überzeugung, dass die Getauften mit der Auferstehung Christi verknüpft sind, als eine Schlussfolgerung aus ihrer Verknüpfung mit dem Tode Christi ausgesprochen (V.5).' Cf. Schnackenburg, *Heilsgeschehen*, p. 53, Stommel, Begraben, p. 4. It has however been overlooked that this perception excludes that Paul bases himself on a two-fold concept of death and resurrection with Christ, cf. note 167 below.

144. A mystical fusion with Christ was said to apply to the Lord who is both dead and resurrected, as clearly described in Bultmann, *Theologie*, p. 398f. But if the basis can only be a linkage to Christ's death a unio mystica cannot be part of the picture. There is thus a clear distance between Christ and the Christians.

proaches general Hellenistic concepts about redeemer religions which revolve around a deity's death and the overcoming of death. But as will be shown the thought-development can be explained in other ways.

4.3. Modifications and dialectics in Rom 6.3-5?

There is thus a great distance between Rom 6 and Hellenistic mystery religion. But this can be interpreted to mean that in Rom 6 Paul is indeed distancing himself from this religion. We have thus arrived at what I have characterised as a 'modification interpretation' or a 'dialectic interpretation'.[145] It may at first sight look like a weakening of the too salvation-enthusiastic religio-historical interpretation of Rom 6. It is wished to show consideration for the distance demonstrated between Paul and the mysteries. But if every single feature debated is interpreted as a modification and a conscious dissociation from the enthusiastic aspect, one ultimately arrives at two points in the text: salvation enthusiasm and the contradiction of this.

Rather than being an intermediate solution and a weakening of the religio-historical interpretation it becomes an exacerbation, for now what is crucial is that the text must reflect one specific perception of salvation and baptism, which Paul then is meant to modify and adapt. The burden of evidence is thus intensified, and the only religio- and traditio-historical considerations relevant to this interpretation, are those which concern the question of what Paul is referring to and basing himself on in Rom 6.[146]

It is noteworthy that the greater burden of evidence is accompanied by broader references and more indirect arguments. This will be shown if we go through the same points as in the previous section.

As regards point 1: *External parallelism* between Rom 6 and certain mysteries cannot be enough. There must be the specific internal connection if the parallelism is to have evidential weight.

But it is striking that followers of the modification theory allow themselves to be content with a few parallel texts from the mysteries in which individual features from Rom 6 can be found.[147] Apart from this, they use

---

145. Especially Gäumann, *Taufe*, is a thorough description of this interpretation, which is quoted above in Chapter I, section 2.2. His reasoning will occupy the foreground, but the views of other interpreters referred to in the research-historical survey will be included in the following.

146. That is, question (a) from the dual problem-complex above in section 4.1.

147. Thus Gäumann, *Taufe*, pp. 40-44, where only Apuleius, Metam. 11, Firmicus Maternus, De err. 22,1-2, the 'Mithras Liturgy' and the Themistios Fragment are seen as true parallels and the parallelism applies only to individual features. Cf. also Käsemann, *Römer*, p. 153, who merely refers to Apuleius, Metam. 11,11ff., 23-24, and Schnelle, *Gerechtigkeit*, p. 77, who indicates the texts of Apuleius and Firmicus but concedes that an actual connection to Rom 6 cannot be demonstrated, so that the evidential weight is reduced to the

defensive and negative arguments. The lack of true parallels is explained by the arcanum discipline.[148] The lack of accordance is also said to be due to the complicated transmission process.[149] They resign themselves to the fact that the connection with the mysteries cannot be disproved,[150] and they assert that there is no other possibility of explaining the 'death-baptism'.[151]

As regards point 2: *The agents* in the tradition behind Rom 6 *must be* sacramentalist and have an association with sacramentalist agents in the mysteries, for the theory is that special, sacramentalist concepts must be modified.

But it has emerged that concepts about an automatically effective death-life imitation is unknown in the mysteries. It is accepted that the usage in Rom 6.3-5 is not concerned with immersion-emersion.[152] And no other sacramentalist agents are indicated.

As regards point 3: *The effects* of the mystery rituals and the ritual referred to in Rom 6 *must* be an enthusiastically-perceived salvation with actualised divinity and resurrection life, for these are the concepts Paul is meant to oppose.

But then the question arises that the mysteries know nothing of an immediate divinity but only of moral improvement and hope for the future, whereas the divine is an external power with which one is confronted. All this was indeed meant to be the Pauline modification.[153] In Rom 6 there seems rather to be a higher degree of actual salvation enthusiasm.

As regards point 4: *The further development of the mysteries* must be given greater weight in the reasoning, because vital features which Paul must modify in Rom 6 have not yet been proved in the mysteries themselves. It is indeed supporters of the modification interpretation in particular who have presented the theories about a common mystery-thinking upon which Christianity is said to be dependent.[154]

presence of a spiritual environment in which the concepts contained in Rom 6.3-4 may have been devised.

148. See especially Gäumann, *Taufe*, p. 39f., 45.
149. Thus Gäumann, *Taufe*, p. 38f., 46ff., cf. below concerning point 5.
150. Thus Gäumann, *Taufe*, p. 45 n. 94, where the refutation of the religio-historical interpretation in Wagner, *Problem*, is criticised for not containing an investigation of all the mystery deities, which has not as yet been suggested. The burden of proof is stood on its head. And in this way any assertion will be valid!
151. Thus Gäumann, *Taufe*, p. 37f., Kümmel, *Theologie*, p. 190, Käsemann, *Römer*, p. 153, Eckert, *Taufe*, p. 215.
152. See Gäumann, *Taufe*, pp. 73-75 and especially nn. 52 and 59.
153. See Bornkamm, *Ende*, p. 43ff., Gäumann, *Taufe*, p. 47ff., Käsemann, *Römer*, p. 158ff.
154. Thus Gäumann, *Taufe*, p. 39f. with n. 27, p. 45f., cf. Conzelmann (rec.), Wagner, p. 171f., Käsemann, *Römer*, p. 153, Schnelle, *Gerechtigkeit*, p. 77. At the same time, in the passages referred to, Gäumann also hints at the arcanum discipline as the reason for the lack of

But now there are not only the problems shown earlier of verifying a common theology which includes the secret core of the mysteries. Mystery theology must also prove something which is not to be found in any individual cult: an immediate salvation which gives the initiate a part in the divine life of resurrection.[155] It can rightly be emphasised that the religious ambience becomes more intense in the development towards gnosticism or similar world-alienated Hellenistic currents. But it is not realised that this is at the same time a development leading away from the cultic aspect to an intellectual reinterpretation, sublimation and symbolism.[156]

As regards point 5: *The Hellenistic-Christian traditions* are specially stressed by this interpretation. Heitmüller's theories about a pre-Pauline Hellenistic Christianity are emphasised. Here the baptismal concept is said to be found which Paul must contest.[157] It should be pointed out that the modification theory can be maintained without the religio-historical proof if one can demonstrate traditio-historically the enthusiastic Hellenistic baptismal concepts which Paul is meant to oppose.[158] But at the same time it is clear that the burden of proof is intensified if these concepts have not been shown to exist before Christianity.

A new set of arguments is then added. 'The Corinthian enthusiasm' comes into the picture.[159] This indicates a religious environment in which

parallel concepts, cf. note 148 above. But the two arguments are mutually exclusive: if the arcanum discipline was as strong as is assumed, it would prevent the mysteries' secrets becoming general property within the Hellenistic environment.

155. Reference can again be made to Gäumann, *Taufe*. When examining the specific material, making the mystes divine in the Isis cult is rejected (p. 43 n. 62, cf. above, Chapter II, note 76), and it is asserted to be purely hypothetical that the Osiris death cult's overcoming of death must have been transferred to the mysteries (loc.cit., cf. above, Chapter II, note 65). It nevertheless says in the summary (p. 46) that the mystes in the mystery religions has obtained a share in the cult deity's destiny, and when this is used as a comparison with the earlier communities' view on baptism (p. 47ff.) it is assumed that the mystes already has a share in the cult deity's death, resurrection and divine spirit.

156. It is thus maintained in Gäumann, *Taufe*, p. 37, that a purely symbolic baptismal concept is out of the question in primal Christianity, because it would mean the use of present-day categories, whereas one should instead look at the surroundings of the New Testament (for a background in sacramentalist cults). But here development indeed moves in the direction of strong symbolism, as shown in Chapter II, section 3.2.

157. See Gäumann, *Taufe*, p. 38f., 46f., where there is much emphasis on the theory in Heitmüller, Problem, p. 330ff. Cf. Käsemann, *Römer*, p. 153. See also Chapter I, section 2.4 above, with note 74, where attention is drawn to objections to this theory.

158. Cf. Schweizer, 'Mystik', p. 246ff., who has a modification theory without a religio-historical basis. In practice, this also becomes the case in Schnelle, *Gerechtigkeit*, p. 78ff., cf. note 147 above.

159. See Chapter III, note 1 above, which shows that it is the followers of the modification interpretation who give special importance to this argument.

one is meant to have had the sacramentalist baptismal concept and awareness of salvation which Paul is combating.

But the overall reasoning has nevertheless been weakened. In general, one should allow oneself to be influenced by the fact that these baptismal concepts are to be found only in the Pauline writings, and that it is generally Paul who uses them for his own purposes. This presented no problem when in the past Paul was considered to be positively dependent upon the traditions, but now the case is different.

The passages in which the baptised's Christ-linkage is presented as an incorporation into Christ make no reservations in relation to immediate effects. In relation to the Corinthian enthusiasm also, the Christ-linkage is used as a positive argument.[160] Special inherent difficulties are contained in the passages that were said to reflect a ritual death and resurrection with Christ in baptism. The problem is now not only that the ritual motif can be neither substantiated nor rendered probable but that as we have seen there are two widely different motifs: 'death with Christ' and 'glory with Christ', and moreover both are used by Paul himself to stress a sure hope of salvation.[161]

We are given on the contrary a strong indication against the assumption that ideas about an immediate life of resurrection have been a problem among the Corinthian community or in the context of the Letter to the Romans. Paul himself comes closest to the term 'already resurrected with Christ' in 2 Cor 13.4.[162] And here in Rom 6.13 Paul speaks figuratively about the life of the Christians as a life after death. He would not do this if there were problems in the community about a belief in an actualised resurrection.[163]

---

160. This occurs not only in 1 Cor 12.13 and Gal 3.27, cf. Chapter III, sections 2.1 and 2.2 above, but also in connection with 1 Cor 1.13; 10.1-13, where there is most reason to consider whether the Corinthians should have used their baptismal concept as an argument for the enthusiasm, cf. Chapter III, section 4 above.

161. See the review of the motifs in Chapter III, sections 3.2 and 3.3, and especially the summary in section 3.4 in which it is established that certainty of salvation and salvation enthusiasm are expressed throughout. Whereas this feature under point 5 in the preceding section might suggest that Paul had been influenced by contemporary religious intensity, cf. note 138, it is now a problem that Paul identifies himself with what he should dissociate himself from according to the modification theory.

162. 'For he was crucified in weakness, but lives by the power of God. For we are weak in him, but in dealing with you we will live with him (σὺν αὐτῷ) by the power of God.' Cf. Chapter III, section 3.3 above, with notes 250-51, and the conclusion from the review of 1 Cor 15 in section 4.

163. Cf. Wedderburn, Traditions, p. 339, who also draws attention to Col 2.12, cf. Chapter III, note 267 above. It says here directly that the Christians have been 'raised with Christ' in baptism. That a disciple of Paul (or perhaps Paul himself) can after such a relatively short

As regards point 6: *Inference from the text itself.* Again, discussion under this point gives an opportunity for a definitive opinion.

This can simply be formulated in principle as the crucial argument for the modification interpretation: the text itself, Rom 6, must be a religio-historical source which can form the basis of a reconstruction of the specific view of baptism.[164] During this reconstruction tensions and unexpected terms in the text are indicated. It is meant to be unexpected that in Rom 6.4 there is no reference to a resurrection with Christ. After the statement about the baptised's 'burial' with Christ, it is asserted that the logic in the sentence demands the continuation: 'so that we also can arise with him'.[165] When Paul instead speaks of a new, ethically validated life, this is interpreted as a polemic against the enthusiastic concept that the new life is totally a life of glory. Similarly, the future form in Rom 6.5 is interpreted as an emphasised dissociation from enthusiasm; the glory of resurrection will come only in the future.[166]

In my opinion, a tenable inference from the text to the preceding tradition will, on the contrary, exclude the theory of modification. Here, considerations in regard to the direction of the thought-process become even more difficult to evade. It has been shown how the direction of the thought-process continuously moves from a linkage to Christ's death to there having to be a similar linkage to the resurrection. This assumed baptismal tradition can thus *only* concern the importance of Christ's death to the baptised — *not*

---

time simply use the concept in this way hints that there may have been no crucial dispute or major disagreement on this point.

164. Thus Conzelmann (rec.), Wagner, p. 172.

165. Thus Gäumann, *Taufe*, p. 75, Merk, *Handeln*, p. 24, Jervell, *Gud*, p. 93. Less consistently, this is often presented as meaning that the intended 'logical' continuation should be ἵνα ὥσπερ ἠγέρθη Χριστὸς ἐκ νεκρῶν διὰ τῆς δόξης τοῦ πατρός, οὕτως καὶ ἡμεῖς ἐκ νεκρῶν ἐγερθῶμεν — cf. Bornkamm, *Ende*, p. 38, Bultmann, *Theologie*, p. 143, Becker, *Auferstehung*, p. 60f., Schnelle, *Gerechtigkeit*, p. 76f. But the ὥσπερ-οὕτως construction is only necessary when events on the Christ side and the Christian side must be different, so that this construction would already be part of the assumed modification.

166. See Braun, *Studien*, p. 155: 'Bei Paulus ist dies Verplichtetsein offenbar polemisch gewendet gegen eine Auffassung, welche im neuen Leben eine naturhafte Gegebenheit sieht, ohne zu Verstehen, dass die καινότης ζωῆς nur dann richtig als Gabe verstanden ist, wenn sie zugleich als Aufgabe für das περιπατεῖν erfasst wird (Röm 6,4) ...' G. Barth, *Taufe*, p. 96: 'Die Taufe vermittelt nach der Meinung dieser Enthusiasten also primär Teilhabe an der Auferstehungsherrlichkeit Jesu Christi. Solchem Enthusiasmus gegenüber betont Paulus, dass die Auferstehung der Glaubenden noch aussteht und von der Zukunft erwartet wird ...' Cf. Bornkamm, *Ende*, p. 38, Bultmann, *Theologie*, p. 143f., Braun, *Studien*, p. 155, Käsemann, *Versuche* II, p. 126f., *Römer*, p. 158f., Lohse, *Taufe*, p. 317, Tannehill, *Dying*, p. 11, Gäumann, *Taufe*, p. 48, 75f., Brandenburger, *Auferstehung*, p. 21, Merk, *Handeln*, p. 24, von der Osten-Sacken, *Römer 8*, p. 177, n. 1, Becker, *Auferstehung*, p. 60f., Eckert, *Taufe*, p. 96.

a participation in both death and resurrection.[167] The modification interpretation requires that the thought-process goes in the opposite direction from the more comprehensive tradition concerning death and resurrection with Christ to a participation in his death alone. It then becomes inexplicable that the direction of the thought-process moves towards the concept which, according to the interpretation, Paul wished to evade.

Although this first, crucial observation already excludes the modification interpretation, there may be reason for a more comprehensive discussion of the arguments in favour of it, for interpreters who do not see the background in the Hellenistic baptismal traditions also make a point of the features which are perceived as tensions.[168]

First, it can be noted that the argument for modifications in the text is to some extent circular. When it is argued that something is unexpected, the argument rests upon the interpreters' own expectations of the text.[169] If it is asserted that in the context logic demands that Rom 6.4b-5 must be seen as a statement about resurrection with Christ, this is because of a certain conception of the prelude in Rom 6.3-4a: by virtue of the ritual the baptised is thought to have put physical death behind him, or even to have merged with Christ. The consequence would then rightly be that the baptised was

167. This was the important point in the previous section's point 6, cf. notes 143-44. Also in Tannehill, *Dying*, p. 13f., Gäumann, *Taufe*, p. 74f., 126, Schnelle, *Gerechtigkeit*, p. 76, it is recognised that the traditional basis is only to be found in Rom 6.3-4a and concerns only a linkage to Christ's death. But this is not upheld. Later (pp. 39-43), Tannehill speaks of a death-resurrection tradition in Rom 6 and (p. 12) of Paul modifying the concept by making the resurrection a thing of the future. In Schnelle, the tradition shifts to include Rom 6.4b (p. 78). In Gäumann, who thinks that Paul develops the thought-process on this basis by means of the 'credo' from 1 Cor 15 (pp. 64, 75ff.), the perception should indeed lead to the point towards which Paul is working becoming participation in the resurrection reality. This may also appear to have been emphasised in the exegesis (especially p. 79). But Gäumann nevertheless also assumes that the tradition in Rom 6.3 is analogous to a mystery-religious death-resurrection concept (pp. 36ff., 126), and there are now modifications which can in addition be seen as Paul's intention (pp. 74, 76, 79 n. 102, 48 n. 114). One is therefore left with an acute problem which no one has seriously attempted to resolve: now one has not only to assume that in Rom 6.3 Paul is referring only to one side of a two-fold concept, one must also explain why Paul then embarks on an argument in support of the side of the matter which he has (consciously) excluded from his reference.

168. Cf. Schnackenburg, *Heilsgeschehen*, p. 32, Todes- und Lebensgemeinschaft, p. 43f., M. Barth, *Taufe*, p. 243f., Michel, *Römer*, p. 153, Siber, *Mit Christus*, p. 205, Frankemölle, *Taufverständnis*, p. 58ff., Schlier, *Römerbrief*, p. 194.

169. It is typical that before the text is interpreted followers of the modification explanation raise the question of how Rom 6 relates to the assumed background in the concept about death and resurrection with Christ, cf. Bultmann, *Theologie*, p. 142ff., Gäumann, *Taufe*, p. 38ff., Käsemann, *Römer*, p. 152.

encompassed by the glory of resurrection.[170] But there is no logic to force us to understand the prelude in this way.

On the contrary, it can be established that the thought-development in Rom 6.3-5 is both obvious and logical. 'Baptism into death' and 'burial with Christ' are strong figurative terms for the connection between the salvation events and the soteriological effects of them. The Christians' total break with past sin is intensely linked to Christ's death and burial. Rom 6.4bc then concerns wholly consistently the various things which subsequently happen to Christ and the Christians: Christ rises after the burial; the Christians live a new life after the 'burial' in baptism.[171] This is linked together quite naturally with ὥσπερ-οὕτως which expresses a certain accordance with and connection between the two aspects. It is also not surprising that in Rom 6.4 Paul describes the new life as 'walking in newness of life', thus giving weight to the ethical consequences of the crucial new departure. The theme struck in Rom 6.2 is indeed a moral one: relationship to sin in the new life.[172] And according to Rom 6.5 this new life is 'something similiar to Jesus' resurrection'; there is then nothing remarkable in the use of the future tense about this, because of course the new life is in the future, whether one thinks of the immediate future or of the eschatological consummation.[173]

---

170. Participation in the death and resurrection of Christ is achieved at the same moment whether or not one sees the background in a sacramental realism like Gäumann, *Taufe*, p. 36ff., 74, 126, Schnelle, *Gerechtigkeit*, p. 76-78, or in a unio mystica like Bultmann, *Theologie*, p. 298f., Tannehill, *Dying*, p. 29f., Thyen, *Studien*, p. 203f. Also, if the background is seen in a concept that the baptised have obtained a comprehensive common destiny with Christ (as a 'corporate personality'), this must include both death and resurrection. This probably explains why interpreters, who reject a mysterious background, also find tensions in Rom 6.4-5, as referred to in note 168 above, so clearly in M. Barth, *Taufe*, p. 243f., cf. note 181 below. Cf. also Schnackenburg, Todes- und Lebensgemeinschaft, p. 43f., Frankemölle, *Taufverständnis*, p. 58ff.

171. It is thus already anticipated when the statement about the death-baptism is associated with 'burial with Christ' that resurrection must be included in the picture in the continuation. This may also explain why interpreters, who even reject a background in a death-resurrection ritual, as referred to in note 168 above, may expect that a 'resurrection with Christ' must be concerned, cf. Schlier, *Römerbrief*, p. 194.

172. Cf. Wagner, *Problem*, p. 294f., Halter, *Taufe*, p. 50f., who maintains that there is no anticipation of a statement about a resurrection with Christ, cf. also Wilckens, *Römer II*, p. 12, G. Barth, *Taufe*, p. 96.

173. If, as shown in section 3.6 above, the verse does not primarily concern the resurrection of the baptised, the future form is quite undramatic. It may be emphasised that there is in the new life a linkage to the power of resurrection which will be fully developed only in the future, such as in Schlier, *Römerbrief*, p. 194, Wilckens, *Römer II*, p. 16, Dunn, *Romans*, p. 316. Or, as I have suggested, it may be perceived as 'certainty future', that the new life is something that has been initiated and will continue, cf. Murray, *Romans*, p. 219, Cranfield, *Romans*, p. 308, Wedderburn, Traditions, p. 339. It is only a matter of nuance.

Finally, it is misleading to suggest that Paul is polemicising and turning against enthusiasts in order to emphasise to them the futurity of the glory and the present commitment. There is indeed no emphasis and direct polemics.[174] The ethical obligation is not introduced as a reservation; rather, the new course of life is linked to the (irresistible) power of God's glory. And the future form is in no way emphasised. But it is certain that generally Paul knows how to distance himself clearly from whatever he is against,[175] and how to explain his intention.[176] He can indicate if a certain grammatical form is to be emphasised: singular, not plural, in Gal 3.16; the future, not the perfect, in Phil 3.12.[177] To make a point of the future form here is therefore quite arbitrary. And then we have basically a refutation of the theories about reservations and polemics. Purely hypothetically, we can accept the modification interpretation's assertion that Paul refers to a concept known to the Roman community with the assumed enthusiastic belief in a realised life of resurrection. The Romans would have had no chance of understanding the future form as a Pauline dissociation from the over-enthusiastic consequences. When Paul stresses in the text the reality of the new life, they, with their knowledge of the enthusiastic understanding of baptism, would not be aware that Paul used the future tense where they expected a past form. Or if they noticed it they would possibly consider it a slip of the pen, or perceive the future form as a 'logical future', or a 'certainty future'. They would not perceive it as something special that Paul wishes to dissociate himself from the tradition he himself is introducing as a basis for his reasoning.

There remains what are interpreted as tensions: that statements about the resurrection and its power are linked together with statements about a new, ethically improved life without the nature of the connection being quite clear. As we have seen, it cannot express the break-up of a death-resurrection

---

174. Dunn, *Romans*, p. 316, also objects to the views quoted in note 166 above, that it would have been much more clearly emphasised if it were a polemic. Cf. Schlier, *Römerbrief*, p. 194, Stuhlmacher, *Römer*, p. 84.

175. It is precisely about this that Paul employs the diatribe-like style in the context, here and in many other passages. In Rom 6.2 Paul explicitly distances himself from the libertine consequences. But why then would he use a tradition which can also be interpreted as over-enthusiastic without clearly distancing himself from such consequences?

176. This is valid, although there may be uncertainty about details, and the grammatical structure is broken up as is demonstrated by the review of Rom 5.12-14, Chapter V, sections 3.1-3 above, cf. Bornkamm, *Ende*, p. 76ff., where it is shown to be general that the Pauline anacolutha in fact serve to clarify the matter. This is precisely why it is important not to base one's explanation on loaded interpretations of unclear details, as pointed out in a commentary to Rom 6.5 in Jervell, *Gud*, p. 99, cf. note 63 above.

177. See the reference to the two passages in Chapter III, section 2.1, with note 22, and section 3.3, with note 216.

concept. But there is another, more obvious possibility; the thought-process is under construction. For this reason there is not immediately a smooth connection between the Christ side and the Christian side when resurrection and a new life are concerned. But on the figurative level Paul is approaching a more complete parallelism, as will be seen in Rom 6.8,11,13.[178]

To summarise, it must be asserted that it is a theory, weakly supported, that in Rom 6 Paul turns around and modifies a mysterious notion about death and resurrection with Christ.

Study of the first five points shows that it is even more difficult to provide religio- and traditio-historical grounds for this theory than for the theory regarding positive dependence upon the mysteries. In my opinion, the comprehensive discussion of the sixth point directly refutes this.

4.4. A Christian death-baptism as background to Rom 6.3

It has thus not been possible to demonstrate that the baptismal concepts to which Paul refers in Rom 6.3 have a mystery-religious or a particularly Hellenistic-Christian background. The only possibility remaining is that they are pan-Christian concepts, perhaps with a Jewish background.[179] Research has frequently pointed in this direction. But here there is also reason to be critical to some of the suggestions.

Attention has been drawn to the concept of 'corporate personality' and the 'credo' in 1 Cor 15.3-5.[180] But the death-baptism Paul bases himself on cannot be directly linked to these concepts.

Rom 6.3 cannot be taken as a reference to a Christian continuation of the corporate personality idea from the Old Testament. If Christ were to be imagined as a 'corporate personality' in Rom 6.3 the intention should be that the baptised were included in the destiny of their 'progenitor'. They would then participate in the effects both of Christ's death and Christ's resurrection,

---

178. When Paul, even in the continuation, refrains from using the actual term 'resurrection with Christ' but speaks of living with Christ, to be alive in (or by virtue of) Christ and to be living as from the dead, this may be seen as expressing Paul's constant variation of the imagery. It may perhaps be said that Paul avoids using the term — because in this context he does not wish to say anything about the Christians' resurrection. But this does not provide a modification, let alone a reservation.

179. An argument for the Hellenistic background of Rom 6 was that the concept of a death-baptism could not have originated from Judeo-Christian sources, cf. Chapter I, note 47 above. This argument must now therefore be turned around.

180. Cf. Chapter I, section 2.3 above, with notes 86-89, where these two concepts, which are often combined, were introduced. The corporate personality idea was also considered in connection with Rom 5.12-21, cf. Chapter V, section 4.2 above.

and this would concern from the outset the Christians' oneness with the dead and resurrected Lord — just as in the concept of a mystical oneness with Christ. Paul's reasoning again becomes incomprehensible. It is unnecessary to argue so intensely in support of the baptised's linkage to the resurrection if this idea is already contained in the tradition to which he refers.[181] This means that the 'corporate personality concept' comes into the picture only when it must be considered which concepts Paul uses to continue his reasoning.[182]

Something similar applies to the confession of faith in 1 Cor 15. This also cannot be that to which Paul refers in Rom 6.3,[183] since then the assumed tradition would also concern a link to both death and resurrection, and the subsequent reasoning would be unnecessary. But it is evident that these thoughts about Christ's death, burial and resurrection may have played an important part when Paul continues the thought-process in Rom 6.4-5.

A specific type of baptismal interpretation has thus been made difficult. This applies to the attempts to tone down the importance of the act of baptism in Rom 6 by a reference to the fact that the crucial events took place at Golgotha and at the resurrection: Christ died and rose representatively, and the Christians are already included in the events; baptism therefore becomes

181. This is therefore the same consideration as in section 4.2, point 6, above, which excludes the theory of the corporate personality idea as the express background and basis of Rom 6. This theory is clearly expressed in Ridderbos, *Paulus*, p. 288, which indicates the Adam-Christ typology in the foregoing and continues as follows: 'Die Funktion der Taufe besteht also darin, den Täufling in diese korporative ('Leibes'-) Einheit zwischen Christus und den Seinen einzupflanzen (Röm 6,5). Deshalb kann der Ausdruck "in Christus getauft werden" (Röm 6,3; Gal 3,27) auch nicht einfach als verkürzte oder abgeschliffene Formel "in den Namen Christi getauft werden" erklärt werden, wie man oft annimmt. Er bezeichnet vielmehr ganz prägnant die Vereinigung des Täuflings mit Christus in diesem korporativen Sinne, und also auch mit seinem Tod und seiner Auferstehung ...' In M. Barth, *Taufe*, p. 223f., Rom 6.3 is interpreted as referring to baptism as a confession of faith in and confirmation of the death — and resurrection — which has already occurred. It is, however, established that resurrection is not referred to on a par with death, but is explained (p. 243f.) as a clear warning against the mysterious interpretation! In Wagner, *Problem*, p. 299, it is initially maintained that baptism is especially linked to death (without thought of inclusion), but later (p. 303ff.) Rom 5.12-21 and the corporate personality idea are given as background to a representative death and resurrection. It now seems as if this is to be the principal idea in Rom 6.3 also.

182. Cf. the distinction between the two sides of the religio- and traditio-historical problem-complex in section 4.1 above. The 'corporate personality idea' cannot therefore be the background in the first sense (a): the tradition to which Paul expressly refers in Rom 6.3, but perhaps in the other sense (b): an idea which has influenced Paul's thought-process, an idea he comes closer to, cf. next section.

183. Against this assumption, which clearly emerges in Stuhlmacher, *Römer*, p. 84, cf. Jervell, *Gud*, p. 94f.

merely a confession of faith and an acquisition.[184] This is a complicated concept. If the Roman community is to be able to perceive this directly, a high degree of perceptiveness is necessary. The interpretation therefore requires that this concept was known to the Romans, and that it is to this that Paul refers in Rom 6.3. And this is indeed impossible.

It can be confirmed that the fundamental concept alone concerns the 'death-baptism'; that is, Rom 6.3 refers to a pan-Christian tradition in which baptism was linked in particular to Christ's death. This can be established with certainty on the basis of the course of reasoning. And it is confirmed by 1 Cor 1.13, where baptism and death on the cross are closely connected.[185]

From this certain knowledge *that* there was a pan-Christian death-baptismal concept, one can continue and try to isolate what it contained and how it may have arisen.

First, the content of the tradition.

Here the starting point can be how the 'death-baptismal concept' is used directly in the context. (1) A cardinal point is that baptism creates a linkage with Christ, as is expressed in ἐβαπτίσθημεν εἰς Χριστὸν Ἰησοῦν in Rom 6.3. Christ becomes Lord, and thereby baptism also becomes an act of confession of faith.[186] (2) And the Christological reflection in this connection revolved around Christ's death. (3) It is presumably a result of this reflection when the purifying effect of baptism is described almost as a matter of course as a total break, a 'death to sin' (Rom 6.2). This radical soteriological consequence appears to be part of the tradition.

This assumption is confirmed by a comparison with another tradition motif, widespread in Paul. This is the motif of 'death with Christ', to be found with particular purity of style in Gal 2.19-20. The same features are

---

184. Cf. particularly as regards this interpretation of baptism, which has been referred to in Chapter I, section 2.5, with note 91 above. M. Barth, *Taufe*, p. 223f., Ridderbos, *Paulus*, p. 149: 'Die Glaubenden nehmen durch die Taufsakrament an dem Heilsgeschehen auf Golgatha und an der Auferstehung Teil', cf. p. 285ff., where baptism is described as acquisition of Christ's death and resurrection, and the quotation in note 182 above. See also Halter, *Taufe*, pp. 43-46 with n. 34ff., which gives a survey and criticism of this interpretation, to which I shall return in Chapter VIII, section 2.

185. Cf. note 4 above.

186. If one is linked to Christ by baptism, baptism in itself becomes a confession of faith. It is not then *necessary* to indicate as does Schnackenburg, *Heilsgeschehen*, p. 119, Bultmann, *Theologie*, p. 313, that Rom 10.6 may be a baptismal confession of faith. Neither is it *necessary*, as is often the case, cf. Jervell, *Gud*, p. 97, Wedderburn, *Baptism*, pp. 57-58, to point out the close connection between the term βαπτίζεσθαι εἰς Χριστόν and 'baptism to (or in) the name of Christ', which seems to express that baptism included a clear confession of faith in Christ. But it is clear that the impression of a confession of faith becomes even stronger if these assumptions are correct, cf. Chapter III, section 2.3 and Chapter IV, section 2.3 above.

again found here in a more intense form. (1) After the transition to Christianity, the new 'I' lives a life bound to the loving and self-sacrificing son of God (verse 20b). This is described as almost a new 'Christ-identity' (verse 20a). (2) There is further reflection on Christ's death in the compact term Χριστῷ συνεσταύρωμαι (verse 19b). (3) Soteriologically, this represents a break with the old 'I' and the old life under the law (and sin). It is true that this does not concern baptism expressly but merely the transition to the new life, but it is often assumed that this is a baptismal tradition — especially in the light of the parallel term in Rom 6.6, which will be discussed later.[187] In any case, the similarity indicates that 'death-baptism' and 'crucifixion with Christ' are variants of the same motif.

The origin of the concept may then be considered.

A number of features can be indicated which may have contributed to the development of this death-baptismal concept. The first three points may have promoted the development, whereas the latter three may, individually or collectively, explain the emergence of the concept.

1. The baptism by John related to threatening death and destruction, and might be seen as a purification from the threat of death which characterised sinful life. Death concepts thus already entered the picture at the beginning of Christian baptism.[188]

2. A more generally religious phenomenon has also been noted — rites of passage: the transition to new phases of life, puberty, marriage, adoption into a new profession or into a religious community, can be described as meaning that the former man has ceased to exist. Such ideas may also have played a part from the time when baptism came to be perceived as an initiation rite.[189]

---

187. That this motif, which has been discussed above in Chapter III, section 3.2, is a baptismal tradition is frequently assumed, particularly with reference to the parallelism between Gal 2.19-20 and Rom 6.6, cf. Lietzmann, *Galater*, p. 17, Schnackenburg, *Heilsgeschehen* p. 57ff., Todes- und Lebensgemeinschaft, p. 46, Schlier, *Galater*, p. 100ff., Oepke, *Galater*, p. 62, Gäumann, *Taufe*, p. 57, Thüsing, *Per Christum*, p. 110, Mussner, *Galaterbrief*, p. 179f., Halter, *Taufe*, p. 102ff., Schnelle, *Gerechtigkeit*, p. 55, cf. also the review in Chapter VIII, section 2.2 below, where it is sought to prove that Rom 6.6 also concerns baptism. Moreover, one can indicate the connection with Gal 3.27, where the term βαπτίζεσθαι εἰς Χριστόν is used to express a Christ-identity similar to that in Gal 2.20b. The acceptance with which the motif is used, particularly in Gal 2.19-20, indicates a traditional background, cf. Chapter III, note 178 above.
188. Cf. the cautious evaluation in Chapter IV, section 2.1 above.
189. This is especially emphasised in Wedderburn, *Baptism*, p. 363ff., cf. Chapter II, section 3.1 above, with note 151. Although (various) concepts about renewal of life are to be found in these contexts, the emphasis will be particularly on the experience of cessation of the former life. An entirely different source confirms in a thought-provoking way that a conscious reflection of these transitions may have played a part in the development of tra-

3. The word βαπτίζεσθαι itself, perceived as passive, also means 'go under' or 'drown'. It may have contributed to the development of the death metaphor.[190]

4. The baptism by John was not only an external purification but was also to convey forgiveness of sins from God. In Christian baptism, this concept is continued and amplified. At the same time, from a Christian viewpoint the forgiveness of sins rests upon Christ's death. That makes it evident to connect baptism with Christ's death. This is indeed what occurs in Rom 6: the effect of baptism is a break with the old sinful life and thus the forgiveness of sins, and this is at the same time an effect of Christ's death.[191]

5. If baptism is an act of confession of faith, whereby one is bound to Christ as Lord, his death on the cross becomes the most puzzling thing one must defer to. This also gives obvious evidence that here as in other passages the Christological reflection concerns in particular death.[192]

6. Finally, there is also the possibility that already at the time of Paul the sign of the cross was a property and protection mark set upon the Christians at baptism. If this were the case, the term εἰς τὸν θάνατον Χριστοῦ ἐβαπτί-σθημεν would be immediately recognisable to the Roman community. On the same basis, it would be understandable that in Rom 6.5 Paul speaks of the baptised having acquired a link to something similar to Christ's death.[193]

dition. The psychological Pauline interpretation in Theissen, *Aspekte*, p. 252ff., emphasises that a 'Rollenwechsel' occurs in Rom 6.1-7.6, described by means of symbolism relating to burial in Rom 6.3-4, change of authority (= new appointment) in Rom 6.16 and marriage in Rom 7.1-4 (cf. Chapter VI, section 2.3 above, with note 57). These are indeed three of the crucial events which are made the subject of transition rituals.

190. Cf. as regards this consideration, which will have to be handled with great caution, in note 27 above.

191. The same connection is reflected in Mt 3 and especially in John 1.29-34, as shown in Chapter IV, section 2.3 above, with notes 29-30; cf. also section 2.1-2 on the baptism by John and its continuation in the Christian spiritual baptism. Schnackenburg, *Heilgeschehen*, p. 29, indicates the early Church's baptismal teaching as the place where baptism was linked to Jesus' death and the forgiveness of sins – again with reference to 1 Cor 15.3.

192. As regards baptism as an act of confession of faith, see note 186 above.

193. I have rejected the hypothesis about the early use of the sign of the cross at baptism in Chapter IV, section 3 above, in continuation of a number of articles in Dinkler, *Signum*. The sign of the cross had a protective function in both pre-Christian Judaism and early Christianity, and may be reflected in several passages in Paul's Letter to the Galatians. Also, the perfect form in Rom 6.5a immediately becomes easier to understand under this assumption: σύμφυτοι γεγόναμεν τῷ ὁμοιώματι τοῦ θανάτου αὐτοῦ then expresses that the baptised in his continued life is marked out by this sign, which recalls Christ's death, cf. note 46 and section 3.5 above, with notes 96-97. In chapter VIII, section 2.4 below, Rom 6.6 will then also be considered in this context.

It is clear that this reasoning (and especially the last point) is of a hypothetical nature.

But this does not mean that objections can be raised against seeing 'death-baptism' as a genuinely Christian concept. It has already been shown to have existed before the Letter to the Romans. And if sources cannot be found further to illuminate the development of the tradition this is only because one is so close to the events reflected in the traditions. When we look at points 4 and 5 in particular (also point 6, but here the uncertainty is greater), we realise that these links between baptism and death were fashioned early in Church history. We can imagine how they arose, and can do so without assuming any influence from other sources. In the light of this, it would be unreasonable to reject these obvious lines of development in favour of written sources far distant both in time and environment.[194]

The necessarily hypothetical nature of the reasoning means that some uncertainty must remain concerning the content of this aspect of the baptismal concept. We do not know precisely which of the possible lines of development in fact led to the death-baptismal concept. We therefore also do not know how precisely baptism came to be given the epoch-making effect ascribed to it. There may also have been an invocation, by which Christ and the divine power are imagined as being present at the baptism. And it may also have been represented that the external sign was effective – immersion in water, purification, sign of the cross. Many possibilities are available and can be combined. Something can, however, be concluded about the use of the concepts in the further context.

4.5. Belief in the resurrection as the background to the progression of thought in Rom 6.4-5

This is the other aspect of the religio- and traditio-historical problems which must now be considered: what concepts is Paul using when he continues to argue from the traditional basis? It can already be seen from the exegesis of Rom 6.4bc (section 2.3 above) that the belief in resurrection is crucial here. And the interpretation of the point in Rom 6.5 (section 3.1 above) confirms that it is crucial to arrive at the fact that there is a connection between the resurrection and the baptised's existence.

Other concepts may also have played a part and had an effect. If one has sensed a connection between the death-baptismal concept and the death

---

194. Cf. my reasoning in Agersnap, *Paulusstudier*, p. 87 n. 103. The preceding notes show that the various connecting lines appear to have been already drawn at the time of the New Testament, and that the conditions for this were present since reflection began on Jesus' life and death.

symbolism in the transitional rites, then the scene will be set for the ideas on renewal of life after the transition comes into the picture. In this way, it can be said that in the course of his reasoning Paul draws closer to the ideas about death and the new life around which the mystery religions also revolve.[195] Thoughts of a binding to Christ as the present Lord may also have had a promotional effect; one cannot remain set on the thought that Christ is the dead Lord, but must imagine that he is also the resurrected Lord. This then becomes a more comprehensive Christ-linkage. Paul may thus be on the way to something which reminds one of both mysticism and the suggested corporative thinking.[196] There is in particular a striking parallelism between references to the death, burial and resurrection of Christ in Rom 6.3-4 and the 'credo' in 1 Cor 15.3-5. But it cannot be taken for granted that Paul uses the formulated confession of faith. It may be that he is referring to the salvation events themselves.[197]

But whatever may have played a part, the belief in resurrection is indeed the driving force in the thought-development. This is confirmed by the exegesis and traditio-historical observations. In Rom 6.4, the mainstay is a traditional statement about the glory of the Father as the power in Christ's resurrection, which also shows itself in the Christians' life. This corresponds

195. Although in Rom 6.3 Paul cannot base himself on a mystery religion-inspired baptismal tradition, it is feasible that he is developing the traditional idea, so that it becomes a counterpart to the mystery rituals and the death-life-renewal symbolism of mystery thinking as stated by Jeremias in Dinkler, Römer 6,1-14, p. 112, and developed in Betz, Transferring, p. 99ff., cf. note 120 above and the conclusion on section 4.2. But it should be noted that there is a long distance from the actual content of the mysteries to the concept of baptism in Rom 6, as stated in section 4.2, point 2 above, with note 129. For this reason, there are more direct explanations of the parallelism. It may be merely that mystery terminology and thought structure are being employed, cf. Larsson, *Christus*, p. 22f. (contrary to the opinion of Käsemann, *Römer*, p. 153, this is a cogent viewpoint both historically and exegetically). One possibility is also that the correspondence is simply because of analogy or common use of more fundamental religious metaphor, as emphasised in Wedderburn, *Baptism*, p. 391f. Cf. Chapter II above, with summary in section 3.4.

196. That the thought-development may be leading towards both mysticism and 'corporate personality thinking' (cf. sections 4.2 and 4.4 above) is confirmed by earlier traditio-historical considerations: in Gal 3.27, cf. Gal 2.19-20, the linkage with Christ can even be expressed as a Christ-identity, and in 1 Cor 12.12-27 the same thoughts are used to develop a corporative ecclesiology (as shown in Chapter III, sections 2.1 and 2.2 above, cf. note 187 above). It should then be noted that here also there are no alien, mythological or psychological thought-complexes which Paul is dependent upon and adopts, but that it is the central Christ-belief which is expressed so intensely that it recalls the mystical and corporative mode of thought. Also note that in Paul there always remains a distance so that the Christian is still faced with Christ, both here and in the continuation in Rom 6.6-8 (cf. Chapter VIII, sections 2.3 and 2.4 below).

197. Thus is the concept defined in Schnackenburg, Adam-Christus-Typologie, p. 51 n. 19, Halter, *Taufe*, n. 28 p. 532.

to what is happening in other passages, where the resurrection emerges in connection with the 'death with Christ' theme. Here also it is vital to stress that Christ is the present Lord in the Christians' actual life.[198] The seed of this thought-development is thus already to be found in tradition. But at the same time it can be established that Rom 6 is the first place in which the belief in resurrection enters the picture in connection with a clear reference to baptism.[199]

One must also be aware here that a shift in perspective is taking place. Whereas until now the emphasis was on the immediate effects of baptism, it is now on the subsequent consequences of baptism.

This means, then, that there may be reason to consider what these subsequent effects are conceived as being. If baptism meant a break with sin and a binding to Christ, it may be open to doubt whether one should stress the confession of faith and the inner experience or the external effect, seeing this as an objective result of the ritual's purification and invocation. When there is a reference to the power of resurrection's significance to the new life, one clearly leans towards an effect coming from outside; but not exclusively. The intensive efforts during the course of reasoning to convince the recipients of the new life's reality show that here also a power of conviction or faith is concerned.

198. This occurs not only in Rom 6.4 but also in 2 Cor 5.15; Rom 7.4 and a number of other passages, as established in section 2.3 above, with note 37, cf. Chapter III, section 3.2.
199. Cf. what was established in Chapter III, section 3.4 above, with note 254. This fact makes it even more unlikely that Paul may have obtained the resurrection idea from a Hellenistic concept of baptism as resurrection with Christ, as stated in Wengst, *Formeln*, p. 37ff., Becker, *Auferstehung*, p. 55f., cf. Chapter III, section 3.3 above, with note 236.

VIII
Rom 6.6-8: further reasoning
in support of the new life

1. The intention of Rom 6.6-8

1.1. Structure and function of the verses

We again have a context in which, despite certain problems, it can be confirmed that structure and function are in fact clear.

Rom 6.6 is introduced by τοῦτο γινώσκοντες ὅτι ... There is not directly any sentence member in the preceding text to which the participle can be linked. It is, however, probable that the verse, like the corresponding introduction Rom 6.9, is to be understood in close association with the preceding text — as a justification. There is an implied thought such as: 'this we can conclude'.[1] The content confirms that an amplifying justification is concerned. Τοῦτο γινώσκοντες again introduces a fundamental common insight.[2] It can be found in verse 6a: ὅτι ὁ παλαιὸς ἡμῶν ἄνθρωπος συνεσταυρώθη. And again, as in Rom 6.3, it concerns the Christians' linkage to Christ's death.

Some conclusions will be derived from this in the following. The ἵνα which introduces Rom 6.6b has the same function as that in Rom 6.4b, and the consequences are now also clearly ethical. In the first place, it is established that the former sinful body is destroyed. What follows from this is referred to in Rom 6.6c: 'so that we might no longer be enslaved to sin.' It appears to be impossible to sin. This is further substantiated in Rom 6.7, which is a statement that death sets a limit to sin's demands on man.

So far Paul has supported the conclusion in Rom 6.4-5, in that he has amplified the premise. On the basis of an insight corresponding to Rom 6.4a and Rom 6.5a, he has shown that the linkage to Christ's death has ethical

---

1. See Tannehill, *Dying*, p. 13, where τοῦτο γινώσκοντες is defined as 'adverbial participle of cause', cf. Dodd, *Romans*, p. 106, Murray, *Romans*, p. 219. Most commentators pause at establishing the anacoluthon or noting that the participle is replacing an indicative, cf. Käsemann, *Römer*, p. 161, Schlier, *Römerbrief*, p. 196f., Wilckens, *Römer* II, p. 16 n. 55.
2. Cf. Tannehill, *Dying*, p. 13f., Schlier, *Römerbrief*, p. 196, Wilckens, *Römer* II, p. 16, Morris, *Romans*, p. 250, Dunn, *Romans*, p. 318.

consequences, since the former sinful life is out of the question. This further explains the point in Rom 6.2. But at the same time the scene is also set for a positive point similar to that in Rom 6.4bc and Rom 6.5b. Since the old life has been cleared away, there is at least a possibility that the new life emphasised in the preceding verses can be developed. But this step in the reasoning has not yet been taken at this stage.

Then comes Rom 6.8, which as regards form is a clear parallel to Rom 6.5. In both cases it is a conclusion from the condition met to the consequence resulting therefrom. The content of the two periods also has common features. It is now said that the Christians, when they die with Christ, can believe that they will also live together with him.

Rom 6.8 is introduced by a δέ. The formal parallelism with Rom 6.5 is frequently taken for granted, and it is assumed that the verse is then co-ordinated with verse 5.[3] The link to the preceding text then becomes rather loose.

It seems to me that it is more natural to link the verse directly to the preceding passage. It has indeed been shown that here Paul amplifies the assertion which has constantly been the basis of his reasoning: the linkage to Christ's death and its effects. The assertion is thus defined, and in Rom 6.8a Paul can repeat it in a sharper form: it is now said directly that the Christians have 'died' with Christ. In Rom 6.8b, Paul can thus arrive at the conclusion that has been anticipated since Rom 6.6. The particle δέ thus has a continuing effect, and Rom 6.6-8 is a unified, more precise repetition of the conclusion from Rom 6.4-5.

There are a number of problems of detail in these verses. But since the same movement of thought is repeated here many of the points of discussion become the same as those in the preceding verses, and the discussion of details will therefore not be quite as intensive here.

1.2. Crucifixion of the old self

The first question is, what knowledge is assumed as familiar in Rom 6.6a. It is usually assumed that this is a renewed reference to the insight introduced

---

3. As a rule, there is no reflection on how Rom 6.8 is linked specifically to the preceding text. But more often than not there is a more or less tacit assumption that it is co-ordinated with Rom 6.5. See Käsemann, *Römer*, p. 162, Wilckens, *Römer* II, p. 18, and the schematic grouping in Bornkamm, *Ende*, p. 39, which is adopted by many interpreters, cf. Chapter VI, note 68, above; here verse 5 and verse 8 are indeed seen as supporting co-ordinated sections which are substantiated in the following text. In Schlier, *Römerbrief*, p. 199, Morris, *Romans*, p. 253, however, it is perceived as continuing, in Halter, *Taufe*, p. 61, as an introduction to a summary.

in Rom 6.3.[4] Since the content is in line with the preceding verses, this seems to be quite natural. But there is also discussion on whether Paul now refers to a different insight, not necessarily concerned with baptism.[5] This again opens up for discussion of the background to the concept to which I shall return. At first sight, when interpreting the Pauline intention, these considerations are not vitally important — for the very reason that the concepts are in any case akin to those in the preceding section.

Then, there are two noteworthy terms. These are the expressions ὁ παλαιὸς ἡμῶν ἄνθρωπος in Rom 6.6a and τὸ σῶμα τῆς ἁμαρτίας in Rom 6.6b. This is in the singular despite its being said about a plurality, 'us', the Christians. It has been attempted to explain this by saying that 'the old man' is a collective entity in which all Christians were included in their pre-Christian existence. In this connection a point is also made of the preceding context, Rom 5.12-21, in which Adam is interpreted as a super-individual figure which embraces all the old aeon's people.[6] In this way, ὁ παλαιὸς ἡμῶν ἄνθρωπος is the super-individual Adam and τὸ σῶμα τῆς ἁμαρτίας the Adam soma from which the Christians have died together with Christ. In contrast, Christ is meant to be the super-individual new man into which the Christians have been incorporated — σῶμα Χριστοῦ.

This collective interpretation is questionable. Rom 5.12-21 presents no basis for perceiving Adam as a super-individual mythical figure.[7] The text itself here has nothing to lead the thoughts in the direction of a mythology of this kind. What is crucial is that the terms 'our old man' and 'the body of sin' stand in the same place as a simple 'we' in both the preceding text and in the subsequent sentences, so that it would be natural to perceive this

---

4. Thus Schnackenburg, *Heilsgeschehen*, p. 48, Michel, *Römer*, p. 155, Barrett, *Romans*, p. 124, Jervell, *Gud*, p. 100, Käsemann, *Römer*, p. 161, Cranfield, *Romans*, p. 310, Schlier, *Römerbrief*, p. 197, Wilckens, *Römer* II, p. 16, Schnelle, *Gerechtigkeit*, p. 83.

5. Thus Siber, *Mit Christus*, p. 217, who establishes that baptism is referred to explicitly only in Rom 6.3-4, so that baptism is only touched upon there and does not later become the theme, Frankemölle, *Taufverständnis*, p. 73ff., who sees a movement from the reference to baptism in the preceding text to a non-sacramental, salvation historico-Christological concept in Rom 6.6-11. See also Dibelius, *Botschaft* II, p. 71ff., where Rom 6.6a is not, however, seen as a reference to an assumed insight but as Paul's own Christ-mysticism. Cf. the further discussion of the problem-complex in section 2.2. below.

6. Cf. Tannehill, *Dying*, p. 24ff., 45ff., Barrett, *Romans*, p. 125, Thyen, *Studien*, p. 202ff. Col 3.9-15 is used as an argument that 'the old man' was perceived as a collective term in contrast to 'the new man', Christ, who as in Gal 3.27-28 is indeed seen as a corporation into which the Christians are incorporated. Cf. against this Bauer, *Leiblichkeit*, p. 148f.

7. The discussion of this text in Chapter V above has shown that there was neither a basis for assuming a Hellenistic Adam-Anthropos mythology as a religio-historical background nor a Jewish concept that Adam's descendants sinned 'in Adam' (sections 4.3 and 4.2, cf. section 3.2).

merely as a variant of this subject. This can be achieved by the interpretation which is the normal, in which ὁ παλαιὸς ἡμῶν ἄνθρωπος and τὸ σῶμα τῆς ἁμαρτίας are understood *distributively*. It must then express what applies to the individual Christians separately. Such a singular form is frequently encountered in fundamental anthropological statements. The emphasis is on the typical.[8]

The collective perspective has also been considered in connection with the verb συνεσταυρώθη. Taking everything into consideration, an αὐτῷ must be implied here. A σὺν Χριστῷ is therefore involved here as in 'burial with Christ' in Rom 6.4 and 'death and life with Christ' in Rom 6.8. It is a striking expression. Events from Christ's life are here linked to the turning point in the Christians' life. The Christians seem to be included in the past events. Consequently exegetes are working with concepts, that the Christians are incorporated into Christ and therefore participate in the salvation events, or that Christ as a 'corporate personality' experienced the crucial events representatively. In both cases one has a corporative, collective interpretation of the σὺν Χριστῷ formulations.[9]

But however the σὺν Χριστῷ expression is precisely understood it is initially (when the intention of the text is to be interpreted) clear that no crucial importance should be attributed to this member. It cannot be an independent Christological point, since Christ is not mentioned in the text but merely implied after συνεσταυρώθη. The statement refers to the Christians' 'crucifixion', and is primarily a soteriological statement.[10]

---

8. See Blass, Debrunner and Rehkopf, *Grammatik*, § 252 with n. 4. Cf. Bauer, *Leiblichkeit*, p. 148f., Halter, *Taufe*, p. 57 and n. 84, Käsemann, *Römer*, p. 161, Wilckens, *Römer* II, p. 16, Dunn, *Romans*, p. 318. It should also be noted that these terms are taken up again in ἐν τῷ θνητῷ ὑμῶν σώματι in Rom 6.12, and as far as I know there is no one who attempts to understand this term collectively.

9. While the religio-historical school originally explained the σὺν Χριστῷ concepts by a reference to the fact that the Christ-events were repeated cultically in a mystery-religious way (cf. Chapter III, note 153, above), the subsequent tendency has been to use the incorporation idea as an explanatory model, cf. Dibelius, *Botschaft* II, p. 72f., Bousset, *Kyrios*, p. 108 n. 1, Bornkamm, *Ende* p. 39 n. 12, Bultmann, *Theologie*, p. 298f., Käsemann, *Versuche* II, p. 126f., Tannehill, *Dying*, p. 24f., 29f. The same tendency in the direction of the corporative is also to be found among interpreters who wish to understand the passage on the basis of Jewish and Christian suppositions, Cullmann, *Tauflehre*, p. 9f., 24ff., Schnackenburg, Todes- und Lebensgemeinschaft, p. 47ff., Adam-Christus-Typologie, p. 49, M. Barth, *Taufe*, p. 244, 271, Wagner, *Problem*, p. 303-6, Delling, *Taufe*, p. 128f., Beasley-Murray, *Baptism*, p. 132f., Ridderbos, *Paulus*, p. 48f., 150f., 292-94, Thüsing, *Per Christum*, p. 69, Frankemölle, *Taufverständnis*, p. 74, 103f. See also the survey of views and criticism of these in Halter, *Taufe*, p. 43ff. with nn. 34-44 on p. 533ff. Cf. finally the discussion of the entire problem-complex, of which the σὺν Χριστῷ formulations form part, in section 2 below.

10. Cf. Morris, *Romans*, p. 251, where it is noted that the absolute use of the word means that attention is concentrated on the verbal action.

The question then remains, what does it mean when it says that the Christians' old self has been *'crucified* with Christ'. This cannot be understood literally. Literally, it could only refer to the two robbers who were crucified beside Christ (Mt 27.44; Mark 15.32).[11] A transferred meaning cannot be avoided. But it is indeed the metaphorical which here shows itself to be a strong means of expressing a radical idea. Since the words normally employed to describe a vital turning point are not sufficiently strong to cover the reality to be expressed, Paul takes a term from a different field. The ethical and existential turning point is thus described as total and final — as in Gal 2.19-20.[12]

This interpretation is confirmed by Rom 6.6bc, in which Paul deduces the consequences of this 'co-crucifixion'. That 'the body of sin is destroyed' would not of course be understood literally to mean that the Christians were to live a non-corporeal existence.[13] Paul has no spirit-body dualism, where the body is in itself negative. It appears from Rom 6.12-13 that in the new existence the body is the weapon in the battle against sin. 'The body of sin' is then the Christians themselves in the old existence, man dominated by sin.[14] By means of the word καταργεῖν, which in this context must mean 'destroy', it is said as strongly as possible that the old existence, with the body tied to sin, is finally finished. This is a radical, eschatological

11. Cf. Wedderburn, Traditions, p. 343. Compare Frankemölle, *Taufverständnis*, p. 103f.: 'Gegen einen uneigentlichen Sinn von Vers 6 muss vom heilsgeschichtlichen Denken des Paulus her betont am buchstäblichen Verständnis festgehalten werden, wonach das Mitgekreuzigtwerden des Glaubenden nicht an einem von Kreuz Jesu unterschiedenen Ort verlegt werden darf, da das Heilsgeschehen nach Paulus für alle Zeiten gültig und unwiederholbar sich ereignet hat (6,9f).' Here the literal understanding thus seems to be the basis for the corporative interpretation. Cf. also Wrede, *Paulus*, p. 62, Heitmüller, *Taufe*, 1911, p. 16f., Bousset, *Kyrios*, p. 128, Merk, *Handeln*, p. 24.
12. Cf. Chapter III, section 3.1, above, with notes 166, 168 and 178. Larsson, *Christus*, p. 77f., suggests that it is a Pauline reconstruction of the Jesus logion about taking up the cross (Mt 10.38 parr.). It is clearly presented as metaphor in hos Schnackenburg, *Heilsgeschehen*, p. 48ff., Dunn, *Baptism*, p. 143. That the metaphoric understanding of the statement does not necessarily involve a weakening is indirectly clear from Cranfield, *Romans*, p. 309, who has problems with the consequences one naturally wishes to draw from 'crucifixion': that the old self and therewith the sinful existence were said to have finally terminated. Cf. also notes 15 and 17 below, where it will be seen that the radical mode of expression in Rom 6.6bc creates similar problems.
13. This is considered in Jewett, *Terms*, p. 292, where the mode of expression is found to be alarmingly akin to gnosticism; Paul's mode of expression is subsequently explained as follows: he has adopted a Gnostic terminology in order to polemicise against it!. If Paul's intention was to oppose a Gnostic thought-process he would rather have avoided dangerous terms that might be misunderstood to this effect.
14. Cf. Jervell, *Gud*, p. 100, Käsemann, *Römer*, p. 161, Schlier, *Römerbrief*, p. 197, Wilckens, *Römer* II, p. 16f.

term.[15] In this figurative sense, the old man is 'dead'. And the point in Rom 6.2 is again emphasised.

Rom 6.6c emphasises a further consequence, that 'we are no longer enslaved to sin'. Here another form of metaphor enters the picture: a master-slave relationship. This stresses that at the Christians' 'death' a total change of authority occurred, as is anticipated in Rom 5.12-21 and developed from Rom 6.12.[16] This means that the Christian is definitively removed from the sphere of sin. This sets the stage for a statement about the Christian's new life in the service of God and righteousness.[17]

1.3. The truism in Rom 6.7

Rom 6.7 must be seen as a less content-weighted part of the reasoning, a proverb,[18] or even a trite truth.[19]

It reads: ὁ γὰρ ἀποθανὼν δεδικαίωται ἀπὸ τῆς ἁμαρτίας. It is introduced as a justification, and the sentence indeed explains why the crucifixion and the destruction of the body must involve final deliverance from sin. Again the singular is used, and it must still be understood distributively about the typical. The content has indeed the nature of a universal truth of an anthropological kind. It must thus be seen directly that 'whoever is dead is de-

---

15. Cf. Gäumann, *Taufe*, p. 81. This recognition must be maintained against attempts to weaken the radical in the metaphoric. In Delling, ἀργός κτλ., *ThWNT* I (1933), pp. 452-55; p. 454, the widest meaning of καταργεῖν is chosen: 'seiner Wirkung berauben'; but especially in connection with the talk of 'crucifixion' it must be an expression of death's definitive supervention, cf. Cranfield, *Romans*, p. 310, Schlier, *Römerbrief*, p. 197f. Dunn, *Romans*, p. 319, recognises that the word usually has the stronger meaning of 'destroy' in eschatological contexts; but later (p. 331f.) it is seen as a problem that Paul appears to break with what is said to be his basic idea: that Christ-identification is a life-long process; therefore consideration is given to both the weaker meaning, 'make ineffective, powerless', and the possibility that the crucifixion is seen as a long process which ends with the Christians' life on earth — a possibility which is admittedly problematic because the context shows that 'death' as the definitive break has already occurred.
16. Cf. Tannehill, *Dying*, p. 14ff., Siber, *Mit Christus*, p. 227ff., Käsemann, *Römer*, p. s. 161.
17. See Schlier, *Römerbrief*, p. 198: 'Er kann nicht sündigen. Er untersteht jetzt einer anderer "Macht", der er sich ergeben kann und soll, nämlich Christus.' Even stronger expressions can be found in Wernle, *Christ*, p. 103ff., Windisch, *Taufe*, p. 173, which speaks of 'Sündlosigkeit'. As regards this term, it must be emphasised that a new quasi-divine nature is not concerned, cf. Halter, *Taufe*, p. 58f., Dunn, *Romans*, p. 320, who underlines that one is still faced with external demands (imperative) — but also (over-)emphasises the possibility of relapses, cf. the discussion of Rom 6.12, Chapter VII and especially section 2 below.
18. Thus Huby, *Romains*, p. 211, Schlier, *Römerbrief*, p. 198, Halter, *Taufe*, p. 59, Dunn, *Romans*, p. 320f.
19. Cf. Ziesler, *Meaning*, p. 200, Käsemann, *Römer*, p. 162.

livered from sin'.[20] It is entirely self-evident that any claim on a person ceases with the person's death. This therefore applies also to the power which it has had over the Christians' old man, which is now 'dead'. Such a principle of law is also to be found expressed in Judaism,[21] but is not of course restricted to this.

A more particular principle has been found, also from a Jewish source: 'All who die will achieve atonement through their death'.[22] But this principle seems to be *too* particular; it is rarely evidenced, does not accord with the Pauline idea of judgement and in particular cannot be assumed to have been known among the Roman Gentile converts.

It has also been attempted to give the verse an even more independent meaning. Reitzenstein has asserted that the justifying death is even meant to be mystery-religious terminology.[23] But this interpretation cannot be verified, and it has been abandoned.

A more widespread interpretation is that the verse is a crucial Christological statement. It must be Christ who has died and is therefore beyond the power of sin — and the Christians with him.[24] In support of this it is stated that, apart from the central importance normally attributed to Christ's death, Rom 6.7 is parallel to Rom 6.10, which is Christological, and that the term ὁ ἀποθανών indicates Christ in all other places and must be seen as a Christological formula which may have belonged to the baptismal liturgy.[25]

---

20. Δικαιοῦν can be best understood in the vaguer, non-terminological meaning of 'set free', 'release'. See Bauer, *Wörterbuch*, col. 392, cf. Kuss, *Römerbrief*, p. 304f., Michel, *Römer*, p. 155, Jervell, *Gud*, p. 100f., Halter, *Taufe*, p. 59.

21. Thus Sanday and Headlam, *Romans*, p. 159, Windisch, *Taufe*, p. 173 n. 1, Michel, *Römer*, p. 155, Käsemann, *Römer*, p. 162, with reference to Schab. 151b and Berach. 19a.

22. Thus Karl Georg Kuhn, Rm 6,7. ὁ γὰρ ἀποθανὼν δεδικαίωται ἀπὸ τῆς ἁμαρτίας, ZNW 30 (1931), pp. 305-10, with reference to Sifre Num 112 to Num 15.31. Approval in Bornkamm, *Ende*, p. 39, n. 11, Wagner, *Problem*, p. 196, Gäumann, *Taufe*, p. 82, Dinkler, Taufaussagen, p. 74, Wilckens, *Römer* II, p. 17. Cf. against this Thyen, *Studien*, p. 204f., Käsemann, *Römer*, p. 162, Halter, *Taufe*, p. 60.

23. Reitzenstein, *Mysterienreligionen*, p. 258ff., cf. also Lietzmann, *Römer*, p. 68. In complete contrast the evaluation in Schmithals, *Römerbrief*, p. 192, where it is assumed that the verse is a gloss because it bursts open the structure of reasoning, can be dispensed with and disturbs the mystery-religious language with legal language.

24. Thus Robin Scroggs, Romans VI,7 ὁ γὰρ ἀποθανὼν δεδικαίωται ἀπὸ τῆς ἁμαρτίας, NTS 10 (1963-64), pp. 104-8, Conleth Kearns, The Interpretation of Romans 6,7, SPCIC 1961 1 (1963), pp. 301-7, Thyen, *Studien*, p. 204f., Frankemölle, *Taufverständnis*, p. 76ff. Cf. against this Ziesler, *Meaning*, p. 200 n. 2.

25. The last argument is to be found in Kearns, Interpretation, pp. 303-6, and is due to the following occurrences of the term ὁ ἀποθανών: Rom 8.34; 2 Cor 5.15; 1 Thess 5.9-10. But such an insignificant term cannot be perceived as a formula. That in all other passages Christ is referred to as he who is dead is of course because one normally circles around his death. But in this context the main thing was the Christians' 'death' — cf. Rom 6.2,6.

Against this it must be said as absolutely certain that the preceding context gives no possibility of identifying ὁ ἀποθανών with Christ. Christ is not mentioned in the preceding period, only implied as the sentence member that must be controlled by σύν in συνεσταυρώθη. If a sentence does not make explicit what the subject is, it is natural to look back for a member in the previous period which will fit as regards form and, as far as possible, the subject. The sentence here must therefore express something about ὁ παλαιὸς ἡμῶν ἄνθρωπος, and it cannot be Christ (who is indeed he with whom the Christians' old man has been crucified).[26]

It must then be established that the universal principle in Rom 6.7 applies to the Christians and their 'death' alone. But the entire background is of course Christological. It is by virtue of the linkage to Christ's death and the 'crucifixion with Christ' that the Christians can be reckoned as 'dead' to sin.[27]

1.4. The progress of thought in Rom 6.8

Rom 6.8 points out that the Christians have 'died with Christ', and from this it is concluded that they must also come to live with Christ. The verse is thus akin to Rom 6.5 in structure and content. This facilitates understanding. But there is also something new relative to verse 5 — two things that simplify the verse.

First, we have in Rom 6.8 a πιστεύομεν, which is important to an understanding of the context. Second, a more direct linkage is expressed between Christ and the Christians as concerns death and new life.

Πιστεύομεν is the superior verb for the entire verse. The subsequent ὅτι sentence is clearly the object of πιστεύομεν, and the preceding conditional clause (Rom 6.8a) is linked to the ὅτι sentence. It might therefore have read: 'We believe that we shall live together with Christ, as surely as we "died" with him'. But the conditional clause has been pushed in front of the superior verb in order to give it emphasis and to be placed immediately after the thought-process (Rom 6.6-7) it summarises.[28]

---

26. There is also no point in interpreting the verse about Christ as a super-individual figure. As we have seen, the collective interpretation of 'our old man' in Rom 6.6 is unconvincing. And in any case the term concerns Adam and not Christ. It is quite laboured to speak of Christ as the bearer of the Adam soma, as in Thyen, *Studien*, p. 203f. Cf. also Tannehill, *Dying*, p. 24ff., and the objections in Halter, *Taufe*, p. 57 with n. 84, p. 544.
27. Cf. Murray, *Romans*, p. 222, Ziesler, *Meaning*, p. 200, Cranfield, *Romans*, p. 311, Wedderburn, *Baptism*, p. 64f.
28. Also in Schlier, *Römerbrief*, p. 199, the syntax of the verse is considered. He notes that '... das πιστεύομεν ὅτι nicht meint: "Wenn wir mit Christus zusammen gestorben sind, dann glauben wir..." Es will nicht unseren Glauben als Ergebnis des Mit-Christus-Gestorbenseins hinstellen.' He then perceives πιστεύομεν ὅτι as a parenthesis ('so glauben wir').

Πιστεύομεν thus has an important function in the context. It binds the reasoning together. Paul appeals to a consensus. He and the Romans must share the conviction that the conclusion drawn is correct.[29] He further justifies this conviction when he refers again to a common insight by the participle εἰδότες in Rom 6.9, which corresponds to τοῦτο γινώσκοντες in Rom 6.6. Because Paul here has the superior verb πιστεύομεν with the implicit subject to which the participle can attach itself, he can in this passage avoid a sentence break such as that between Rom 6.5 and Rom 6.6.[30]

That πιστεύομεν is therefore a step in Paul's appealing and reasoning address and concerns belief in the special sense of 'we are convinced' excludes some distinctive interpretations in which conclusive theological significance is ascribed to the word. Πιστεύομεν ὅτι *cannot* have been intended as an introduction to a generally recognised dogma, since the member is indeed used to emphasise the validity of the analogic conclusion which is implemented and further consolidated by the subsequent justification. This would be superfluous if it were already a fundamental tradition.[31] Πιστεύομεν *cannot* express the special Pauline concept of belief and cannot concern the justifying significance of belief by baptism. Nothing is therefore said here about what happens at baptism. It is a subsequent reflection on the consequences of the new departure which the Christians have experienced.[32]

> But this is unnecessarily complicated and causes problems in regard to the connection from Rom 6.8 to the following verses.

29. Cf. Schmidt, *Römer*, p. 111f., Murray, *Romans*, p. 223, Käsemann, *Römer*, p. 162, Halter, *Taufe*, n. 98 p. 546. That this is concerned with conviction and certainty is also assumed by Michel, *Römer*, p. 156, Schlier, *Römerbrief*, p. 199, but at the same time they think that it is a reference to an established tradition, cf. note 31 below.

30. Cf. Gäumann, *Taufe*, p. 85. See also section 1.1 above, with note 1.

31. Against Michel, *Römer*, p. 156, who considers that the background must be found in the baptismal liturgy, Schlier, *Römerbrief*, p. 199, who considers that like γινώσκοντες and εἰδότες in Rom 6.6,9 this indicates a traditional insight which is said to be found in 2 Tim 2.11, Ferdinand Hahn, Die Taufe im Neuen Testament, in: Herbert Breit und Manfred Seitz, *Taufe*, Stuttgart 1976, pp. 9-28; p. 19, who indicates the non-terminological 'non-Pauline' use of the word πιστεύειν as an argument that Paul is dependent upon a tradition. Discussion of the structure of reasoning which forms an extension of the above description in Chapter VII, section 4 (especially item 6 in sections 2.3 and 4.3) does not exclude that Paul may have used pre-formulated material; but it shows that he does not assume it to be already known and accepted.

32. The interpretation of πιστεύομεν as expressing a justifying belief at baptism is found in Wagner, *Problem*, p. 298 n. 112, Frankemölle, *Taufverständis*, p. 81, cf. p. 30, cf. Gäumann, *Taufe*, p. 152; it can be used to tone down the sacramental nature of baptism, but is contradicted by the recognition set out above in Chapter VII, section 4.5: that the belief that Paul wishes to build up here applies to the new purpose in life which results from baptism. Cf. Halter, *Taufe*, n. 98 p. 546, Agersnap, *Dåbsteologi*, n. 25 p. 117, Wedderburn, *Traditions*, p. 341. Similarly Beasley-Murray, *Baptism*, p. 156, where, however, the evaluation is different, p. 145 (in connection with λογίζεσθε in Rom 6.11).

The use of πιστεύομεν does *not* in itself mean that the statement concerns something 'merely believed', of the future, eschatological and contrary to something already certain or present. In the context, the whole emphasis is on the positive conviction that results from the new departure which has occurred.[33] Whether this conviction is of an especially eschatological nature must be determined by the interpretation of 'life with Christ' in Rom 6.8b and the amplification in the subsequent verses.

The direct statement in Rom 6.8, that the Christians have 'died with Christ' and will live with him, provides a simplification relative to Rom 6.5. The problems presented by the formulation using ὁμοίωμα are avoided.

At the same time, the intensification of the style involves an important advance in thought.

As we have seen, Paul has arrived at the term ἀπεθάνομεν σὺν Χριστῷ in Rom 6.8a by means of increasingly strong imagery: from 'death-baptism' via baptism as a 'co-burial into death', 'growing together with something similar to Christ's death' to a 'co-crucifixion' leading to eradication of the old self.[34] The metaphorical meaning is therefore clear when we finally have the intensified expression that the Christians 'died with Christ'. It is this break with the old life that results from Christ's death. And because the break is expressed so definitively the stage is also set for a particularly intense statement about the new life which follows after the break.

A similar intensification is to be observed if one looks at the three analogic conclusions for which the death-metaphors form the basis, Rom 6.4,5,8. From a life borne by the same power that appeared in Christ's resurrection via the new life which is similar to Christ's resurrection we have arrived at 'life with Christ'. Συζήσομεν αὐτῷ in Rom 6.8b becomes a new and comprehensive assertion. The σὺν Χριστῷ formulations have hitherto been used concerning momentary events, crucial points in a passage of time: 'burial', 'crucifixion' and 'death' with Christ. The Christians' life together with Christ is now spoken of as something everlasting. A special closeness to and coherence with Christ is expressed, a Christ-fellowship. And this has

33. Against Bornkamm, *Ende*, p. 43, who sees the new life as 'eine paradoxe Wirklichkeit, ganz auf den Glauben gestellt', Tannehill, *Dying*, p. 10: 'object of faith, not of sight'. Similarly Bultmann, *Theologie*, p. 320. Barrett, *Romans*, p. 126, Gäumann, *Taufe*, p. 84, Pilgaard, *Dåbsteologien*, p. 125. Cf. however Michel, *Römer*, p. 156, Dunn, *Romans*, p. 322.

34. This view of the construction, which was outlined above in Chapter VI, section 4, item 3, is confirmed by the exegesis in that and the preceding chapter. Cf. also Dunn, *Romans*, p. 321.

led the thoughts in the direction of enthusiasm and mysticism.[35] That the statement is so intense also creates a need for it to be substantiated, and this is the function of Rom 6.9-11.

But there remains an open question relative to the content of the term. Is 'life with Christ' the futurist life of resurrection, or does it include topical life? This will be considered in the context of an examination of the future form's significance.

1.5. Συζήσομεν in Rom 6.8b

The discussion concerns both form and content. As in Rom 6.5b, it is asked what kind of future tense we are dealing with. And the answer is vital to a precise understanding of what is comprised by life with Christ. But it is in any event clear that the main object is to stress the certainty of salvation, and there is only a difference of nuance in the possible interpretations.

It is not possible to apprehend συζήσομεν as 'logical future'. The statement cannot therefore directly concern entry into the new life at baptism or repentance.[36] Again, the superior verb πιστεύομεν is important. One can indeed use the future tense relatively where what is concerned is belief in something which is to occur subsequently. One returns to the time when it was believed, and one can then use the logical future about something in the past in an absolute sense.[37] But then this applies only if the belief is also something of the past. Here, the present conviction of Paul and the Romans is concerned. This means that the content must be something of the future in an absolute sense also.[38]

Because the logical future can be excluded, it is widely believed that συζήσομεν is to be understood only as 'genuine, eschatological future'.[39] 'Life

---

35. Cf. Lohmeyer, Σὺν Χριστῷ, p. 222ff., and my discussion of the term σὺν Χριστῷ in Chapter II, section 3.1 above, with note 162, where the diversity of the material is emphasised, and this differentiation is introduced between the momentary fellowship of action and suffering and the continued connection with Christ. The intense expression of being together with Christ has in particular led to ideas that Paul is not far from mysticism, cf. Dieterich, *Mithrasliturgie*, pp. 173-78, Holtzmann, *Lehrbuch II²*, p. 196f., Heitmüller, *Taufe*, 1911, p. 22, Bousset, *Kyrios*, p. 134ff., Leipoldt, *Taufe*, p. 62.

36. Contrary to the assumption in Ernst Percy, *Die Probleme der Kolosser- und Epheserbriefe* (SHVL 39), Lund 1946, *Leib*, p. 26 n. 62, Otto, *Formulierungen*, p. 54, Warnach, *Taufe*, p. 314ff., Larsson, *Christus*, p. 71.

37. Cf. Blass, Debrunner and Rehkopf, *Grammatik*, § 349,2.

38. Cf. Bornkamm, *Ende*, p. 47, Thüsing, *Per Christum*, p. 70, Gäumann, *Taufe*, p. 84, Tannehill, *Dying*, p. 10, Siber, *Mit Christus*, p. 242f.

39. Thus Dodd, *Romans*, p. 109, Bornkamm, *Ende*, p. 43, Barrett, *Romans*, p. 126, Huby, *Romains*, p. 211, n. 4, Kuss, *Römerbrief*, p. 305f., Tannehill, *Dying*, p. 10, Thüsing, *Per Christum*, p. 70, Gäumann, *Taufe*, p. 48, 79, 84, Conzelmann, *Grundriss*, p. 299, Dinkler,

with Christ' will therefore be understood primarily as the life of resurrection which will arrive some time — at the parousia, beyond death. It is emphasised that other Pauline σὺν Χριστῷ passages concern the eschatological life of glory which is to be realised in the future, especially 1 Thess 4.13-17; 5.10; Phil 1.23.[40]

An understanding of the statement which should clearly be considered is that one looks forward towards the reality of resurrection. But this is to be found in two versions.

(a) In the first version it is considered important that life with Christ is something to come *only* in the future. It is certainly not a present reality. It is therefore meant to imply a reservation compared with a more enthusiastic attitude.[41] But this version immediately proves to be untenable, since on the one hand it is simply taken for granted that the future form can have only ingressive meaning, and on the other hand it is a problem that the reservation is in no way emphasised in this context, in which the stress lies on the conviction about the new life; a reservation must be emphasised if it is to have an effect.[42]

(b) In the second version, the futurist-eschatological life must still be the essence of the statement. But it is seen in connection with the Christians' present existence because the context, especially Rom 6.4c.11b, shows that it is already something of vital importance now.[43] Hitherto the word ζῆν has been used primarily about the Christians' new life and purpose in life. But it has been associated with Christ's resurrection, and it is therefore evident that the Christians' resurrection can now also enter the picture. Whether one

Taufaussagen, p. 74, Siber, *Mit Christus*, p. 242f., Käsemann, *Römer*, p. 158, Jervell, *Gud*, p. 101, Halter, *Taufe*, p. 61, Schlier, *Römerbrief*, p. 199, Wilckens, *Römer II*, p. 15, Pilgaard, *Dåbsteologien*, p. 125, G. Barth, *Taufe*, p. 96, Dunn, *Romans*, p. 322.

40. See especially Thüsing, *Per Christum*, p. 70: 'Dass Paulus an die eschatologische Vollendung denkt, dürfte sicher sein für Röm 6,8b, denn die Wendung vom Leben oder Sein mit Christus wird auch sonst eschatologisch gebraucht.' Also Schlier, *Römerbrief*, p. 199, who wishes to prove this by reference to the general eschatological use of the term σὺν Χριστῷ, and refers to Rom 8.32b; 2 Cor 4.14; 13.4; Phil 1.23; 1 Thess 4.14,17; 5.10; Col 2.13; 3.3. But this material is flimsy; only two of the passages include the term ζῆν σὺν αὐτῷ, in 1 Thess 5.10 probably used about life after the parousia, in 2 Cor 13.4, however, used about a topical event in the Christian life as shown above in Chapter III, section 3.3, with note 251.

41. Cf. Bornkamm, *Ende*, p. 43, Tannehill, *Dying*, p. 10, Gäumann, *Taufe*, p. 48, Conzelmann, *Grundriss*, p. 299, Käsemann, *Römer*, p. 158, 162, G. Barth, *Taufe*, p. 96.

42. This viewpoint is affected by the same arguments used in connection with Rom 6.5, Chapter VII, sections 3.6 and 4.3, item 6, above, and the viewpoint is also an offshoot of the 'modification interpretation', which is rejected.

43. Cf. Huby, *Romains*, p. 211 n. 4, Barrett, *Romans*, p. 126, Thüsing, *Per Christum*, p. 70, Dinkler, *Taufaussagen*, p. 74, Siber, *Mit Christus*, p. 232f., 243, Jervell, *Gud*, p. 101, Halter, *Taufe*, p. 61.

chooses this or the following interpretation then becomes exclusively a matter of where the main stress is to be placed.

The last possibility is to understand συζήσομεν as the 'certainty future'. As we have seen, a widespread use of the future is to indicate that which is certain to continue in the future. In that event Rom 6.8b concerns primarily the life the Christians already live. It is the present life which is sustained by the linkage to Christ, and it will therefore extend quite certainly into the future and become an eternal life.[44]

Both formal and inherent features support this interpretation. We are in a context in which the future is generally used in this way, in Rom 6.2,14, in Rom 8.35-39, and presumably also in Rom 6.5b and Rom 5.17,19.[45] Not only in the previous context but also in the subsequent context the Christians' present life and content of life are given the main emphasis; in Rom 6.11 it is life to God; in Rom 6.13 the Christians' combatant life is compared with a life beyond death.[46]

Although the distance is not very far to the second version (b) of the futurist-eschatological interpretation, this present futurist interpretation is probably preferable, because the word 'life' (not 'resurrection') is the main word in the soteriological statements.

2. The background to the σὺν Χριστῷ terms in Rom 6.6-8

2.1. The problems

This part of the text also discusses the possible traditio- and religio-historical background. There are several contiguous sets of problems surrounding the term σὺν Χριστῷ in particular.

The question of the background to the concepts is again dual. (a) On the one hand the traditions Paul assumes to be known and on which he bases himself, and (b) on the other hand the usage and patterns of thought which

---

44. Thus Murray, *Romans*, p. 223, Cranfield, *Romans*, pp. 312f., Wedderburn, Traditions, p. 339, Morris, *Romans*, p. 254, cf. Larsson, *Christus*, p. 71f. See also my definition of the 'certainty future' in Chapter VII, section 3.6 above.

45. Cf. Chapter VII, section 3.6, with note 117, above.

46. Cf. Cranfield, *Romans*, p. 312f. See also the examination of these passages in Chapter IX, section 1.2, below and Chapter X, section 1.3. Contrary to this, it is asserted in Schlier, *Römerbrief*, p. 199, that the temporal futurist meaning appears 'aus der Fortsetzung des Satzes selbst, die das bleibende ζῆν Christi, von dem unser zukünftiges Leben abhängt, weil es ja eines σὺν Χριστῷ ist, betont (VV 9f)', cf. Käsemann, *Römer*, p. 162. But it is not explained why this 'Christ's lasting life' may not just as well refer to Christ as the living and present Lord upon whom the actual life of the Christians depends.

may have influenced his presentation and the concepts he seeks to reach. And again he points expressly to a certain common insight — in Rom 6.6a, introduced by the term τοῦτο γινώσκοντες ὅτι ... Again, therefore, the vital question is the assumed tradition (item a). It concerns especially the puzzling 'crucifixion with Christ', and accordingly the σὺν Χριστῷ formulation enters the picture powerfully.[47]

Moreover, it is debated whether there is still a reference to a baptismal tradition.[48]

Whether the term σὺν Χριστῷ itself originates from a pre-Pauline tradition or is coined by Paul himself is also the subject of discussion.[49]

A crucial problem also arises concerning the content of the σὺν Χριστῷ concepts. It is assumed that it involves contemporaneity between Christ and the Christians if the Christians are 'buried', 'crucified', 'die' and live with Christ, and it is attempted to explain this contemporaneity. This also provides some notable explanations of how baptism or the salvation events can acquire their vital soteriological effect. Normally, three routes are followed.[50]

The first original explanatory model emphasised that Christ's death, burial and resurrection are repeated ritually at baptism, so that in this way Christ became contemporary with the baptised. The background is then said to be a sacramentalism which may have roots in the Hellenistic mystery rites.[51]

The second route is gradually becoming increasingly followed. The Christians are said to have become contemporary with Christ by virtue of baptism or belief. In this explanatory model, what is crucial is an incorporation into Christ. This is found in two versions. In the first, baptism is seen as an incorporation into σῶμα Χριστοῦ. One is incorporated into the super-individual Christ-figure, and in this way participates in the vital sequence of events and its redeeming effect. This interpretation suggests as the

---

47. Cf. in particular the survey of the section's structure in section 1.1 above and note 2. Because Paul refers directly to a certain insight in Rom 6.6a, and emphasises in v. 6b-8 that consequences are deduced therefrom, the problems become parallel to those introduced in Chapter VII, section 4.1, above.

48. Cf. notes 4 and 5 above.

49. It is often taken for granted that the formulation is part of the ritual, mystical or corporative tradition from which Paul must take his point of departure, cf. below and the following notes. But there is an increasing tendency to see it primarily as Paul's own way of expressing himself, cf. Dibelius, *Botschaft* II, p. 72f., Grundmann, *ThWNT* VII, p. 789, Schnackenburg, *Heilsgeschehen*, p. 172ff., Adam-Christus-Typologie, p. 52, Siber, *Mit Christus*, p. 190, 247ff., Schade, *Christologie*, p. 145.

50. Cf. Chapter III, section 3.1, with note 153, above.

51. Cf. Heitmüller, *Taufe*, 1911, p. 22, Lietzmann, *Römer*, p. 67f., Mittring, *Heilswirklichkeit*, p. 37ff.

background a more speculatively mystical, less cultically-orientated form of Hellenistic religion.[52] In the second version of this explanatory model the corporative background is Semitic. Christ died, was buried and arose again as a 'corporate personality'. This did not happen to him alone but simultaneously to all his descendants. The significance of baptism is restricted if what happened at Golgotha and at Christ's grave is all-important. This is the true turning point in the Christians' life, whereas the subsequent baptismal act mediates it or puts it into effect or is a confession of faith in it.[53]

The third variant of the 'contemporaneity interpretation' asserts that the events occurred at different times. The events surrounding Christ's death remain of the past, and the Christians' baptism takes place at a later date. But then there is talk of 'paradoxical contemporaneity'. The Christians can become contemporary with the past Christ-event because it is filled with 'eschatological dynamics'.[54]

But a fourth possibility is that σὺν Χριστῷ involves no contemporaneity whatsoever. This, as will be shown, is an interpretation somewhat ignored but not impossible.[55]

2.2. Do the σὺν Χριστῷ statements relate to baptism?

This question cannot be answered by a simple 'yes' or 'no'.

The first statement, συνετάφημεν ... αὐτῷ διὰ τοῦ βαπτίσματος εἰς τὸν θάνατον, in Rom 6.4, is undoubtedly concerned with baptism.[56]

It can be said of συνεσταυρώθη in Rom 6.6 that there is no basis for

---

52. Thus Dibelius, *Botschaft* II, p. 72f. Tannehill, *Dying*, p. 11f., 29f., Thyen, *Studien*, p. 203f. On the borderline between this and the following formulation is von Soden, *Urchristentum*, p. 271, in which the baptism idea in Rom 6 is briefly characterised as: 'Der Tod Christi ist das Sakrament, die Taufe das sakramentale Bekenntnis zu ihm, in dem die Teilhabe an ihm gewonnen wird: die Einverleibung in den Leib Christi.'

53. Cf. M. Barth, *Taufe*, p. 271, Wagner, *Problem*, pp. 303-6, Delling, *Taufe*, p. 128ff., Beasley-Murray, *Baptism*, p. 132ff., Ridderbos, *Paulus*, p. 48f., 150f., 292-94, Thüsing, *Per Christum*, p. 69, Siber, *Mit Christus*, p. 224ff., Frankemölle, *Taufverständnis*, pp. 102-7, cf. p. 37f. Cf also note 9 and Chapter VII, section 4.4, with note 184, above, in which the same interpretation model is discussed in association with Rom 6.3-5.

54. Thus Güttgemanns, *Apostel*, p. 219 n. 54, where Hahn, *Mitsterben*, p. 111, is quoted: 'Die paradoxe Möglichkeit, an jenem vergangenen Geschehen teilzugewinnen, liegt vielmehr in diesem Geschehen selbst,' following which Güttgemanns explains it as follows: 'weil es von eschatologischer Dynamik erfüllt ist.' There is also a reference to Bornkamm, *Ende*, p. 39, which emphasises that the contemporaneity is a result of the salvation events' eschatological nature.

55. Cf. Schnackenburg, *Heilsgeschehen*, p. 31f., Halter, *Taufe*, p. 43f., Wedderburn, *Baptism*, p. 66. See also Chapter III, section 3.1, above.

56. Cf. Chapter VII, note 15 above, where an opinion is expressed in regard to the attempt to deny this fact.

maintaining that it does *not* concern baptism.[57] We still find ourselves in a context in which baptism is mentioned. Readers must therefore continue to think of baptism if the text does not indicate any other event in the Christians' life. It is also clear that the thought-process from Rom 6.3-5 is continued. There has been talk of the Christians' linkage to Christ's death, and now there is talk of a 'co-crucifixion'.[58] And where the 'death with Christ' motif is otherwise used a transition to the new life is concerned. If therefore Rom 6.6a does not directly concern baptism it in any case concerns events closely connected to baptism.[59]

Something similar must apply to the third incidence: ἀπεθάνομεν σὺν Χριστῷ in Rom 6.8a. This takes up again συνεσταυρώθη, after that the radical ethical consequences of this event have been shown. At the same time, this also leads the thoughts back to 'death' to sin and 'baptism into death' in Rom 6.2-3. It thus becomes even clearer that it is these baptismal concepts which are being developed.

But the last σὺν Χριστῷ term obviously does not concern baptism. συζήσομεν αὐτῷ in Rom 6.8 cannot relate to a past event. As we have seen, the subordinate verb πιστεύομεν indicates a topical conviction which Paul wishes to imprint, and the futurist statement applies either to the certain course of the earthly life in the future or to the life of resurrection in the hereafter. It is therefore clear that a crucial development takes place between the three first σὺν Χριστῷ statements and the last.[60]

These considerations are also of importance to the next question.

2.3. Does σὺν Χριστῷ express contemporaneity and incorporation?

A nuanced answer is again necessary. Earlier observations can contribute to this.

First, it is clear that where 'contemporaneity' is concerned there is also a difference as regards the four σὺν Χριστῷ formulations.

'Burial', 'crucifixion' and 'death' with Christ can be dated to (events in

---

57. Against Dibelius, *Botschaft* II, p. 71ff., Siber, *Mit Christus*, p. 217, Frankemölle, *Taufverständnis*, p. 73ff., cf. note 5 above.

58. As already indicated above in Chapter VII, note 46, it may be that ὁμοίωμα τοῦ θανάτου αὐτοῦ in Rom 6.5 already suggested death on the cross, cf. Schnackenburg, Todes- und Lebensgemeinschaft, p. 36, Dinkler, Taufaussagen, p. 73, Pilgaard, Dåbsteologien, p. 125.

59. It is correct formally to assert in Siber, *Mit Christus*, p. 218, that the other occurrences of the motif (Rom 7.4,6; 2 Cor 5.14-15; Gal 2.19; 5.24; 6.14) are not directly linked to baptism, cf. also my examination above in Chapter III, section 3.2. But repentance, belief and baptism are so closely connected that it becomes artificial to maintain that this is concerned with something quite different.

60. Cf. sections 1.4 and 1.5 above.

connection with) baptism. This is the very reason why the problems arise which the various explanatory models are meant to resolve, for Christ's crucifixion, death and burial took place before, at the specific historical date.

Life with Christ, however, cannot be dated to baptism — as we have seen, this excludes the reasoning-structure. On the other hand, contemporaneity presents no problems. Whether or not the Christians' earthly life or their life of resurrection is concerned, the point is that Christ is present as the power in this life.

The Christians cannot therefore be at the same time contemporary with Christ in all four respects! This somewhat confusing finding initially shows how complicated and confused the thought-process becomes when it is maintained that σὺν Χριστῷ is to imply contemporaneity everywhere.

Moreover, this again shows that it is untenable to use the sacramentalistic explanatory model where baptism is seen as a repetition of Christ's death *and resurrection*. What at most can be concerned is that Christ's crucifixion, death and burial are re-actualised at baptism.[61]

Another observation shows that the 'corporative' interpretation models are questionable. Σὺν Χριστῷ is assumed to mean that a joining together takes place.

But then it is important to remember that σύν, used in association with a verb, can mean two different things where there is significant difference in the degree of union.[62] (a) If the emphasis is on σύν (particularly in association with verbs of motion), the σύν composita express that a linking together or combination occurs as a result of motion — as in 'move *together*', 'collide *together*'. (b) If the emphasis is on the verb, they can then refer to a temporary fellowship in an action one carries out or about an event one is exposed to — as in '*travelling* together' or '*eating* together'.

If this insight is employed on the terms in Rom 6.4,6,8a, it is immediately clear that we are dealing with the second type (b). The emphasis is on the

---

61. This interpretation model, developed by the religio-historical school in particular, cf. note 51 and Chapter I, section 2.1, above, is already excluded in connection with Rom 6.3-5. From the comprehensive counter-reasoning in Chapter VII, section 4.2, above, item 6 in particular should be indicated: inference from the text itself in which it is pointed out that the reasoning structure shows that Paul refers only to a traditional connection from baptism to Christ's death and seeks to derive from this a connection between Christian life and Christ's resurrection. As is shown here, it is the same development of thought when it is perceived that 'life with Christ' is a reference to a later chain of events. And this can even be supported grammatically, since συζήσομεν cannot be interpreted as a logical future and must therefore concern a later time, cf. section 1.5 above.

62. Cf. above, section 1.4, with note 35 and Chapter III, section 3.1, where this distinction was a crucial step in the objection to σὺν Χριστῷ being made a fixed formula with a mystical or corporative content.

events the Christians are to share with Christ: they are '*buried* together with Christ', '*crucified* together with Christ' and '*die* together with Christ'. It would be unreasonable to perceive the statements with the emphasis on σύν, so that the Christians were said to be 'buried *together* with him', 'crucified *together* with him' and 'die *together* with him'.[63] These σὺν Χριστῷ formulations in themselves express nothing to indicate that at baptism a linking together with Christ occurs, let alone an incorporation. As regards the term συζήσομεν αὐτῷ in Rom 6.8b, this is again another matter. Here it makes sense to give significant emphasis to the particle. A long-lasting relationship is concerned — a life together with Christ.[64]

Since σὺν Χριστῷ does not in itself express joining together and incorporation, the most important argument for the corporative interpretation models falls to the ground. And there are other difficulties.

One must above all be aware of the complications that arise if σὺν Χριστῷ is to express 'contemporaneity with Christ' in relation to death, burial and new life. How is one to imagine that, via baptism, one has participated in events which occurred at an entirely different time and in an entirely different place? And what is supposed to be the nature of the statements — literal, mythological, metaphorical? They certainly cannot have been intended as realistic statements about the Christians' actual death at Golgotha and their burial; in that event it would be pure mysticism in which the empirical world would be a purely imaginary world.[65] Paul would not be able to envisage that such complicated thoughts would be comprehensible to recipients of the letter, with whom he has previously had no personal contact.[66]

---

63. It may be noted that an attempt to interpret the text in this direction in fact exists in Mussner, Zusammengewachsen, p. 258: 'mit Christus "zusammengestorben"', 'mit Christus "zusammenbegraben"'.

64. It is true that the statement does not belong unambiguously to the first group (a), where the stylistically pure term is coire, συνάγειν. But as is especially pointed out in Lohmeyer, Σὺν Χριστῷ, p. 222ff., there is a considerable intensity when the particle is linked to εἶναι and similarly to ζῆν. But this applies only if συζήσομεν is understood duratively as about the continued life with Christ. If, as is often assumed, it is understood ingressively as about the transition to a life of resurrection, we are more probably concerned with a term of a different type (b).

65. Cf. above, section 1.2, with notes 11-12. Compare also with the corresponding difficulties in understanding the concepts of σῶμα Χριστοῦ in 1 Cor 12.12-27 as a coherent mythological explanation of the relationship between Christ and the Christians, as shown above in Chapter III, section 2.2, with note 88.

66. The speculative nature of the interpretation emerges clearly in Siber, *Mit Christus*, p. 224ff., 247f.; here the main idea is that the development of thought is Paul's own theological contribution; but it is said to be these very complicated corporative concepts he is developing: 'Das in den syn-Wendungen formulierte Teilhaben am Tod und an der Auferstehung Jesu ist ein Teilhaben an diesen Heilsereignisse selbst, nicht an der Taufe als einem Abbild dieser Ereignisse' (p. 224f.). 'Der Getaufte stirbt nicht nur wie Christus,

And problems arise again because of the distance in time between the Christians' 'death-burial' in baptism and the new life with Christ, which belongs to a later time. How can one be incorporated into the dead Christ and only later into the resurrected Christ? If the concepts of mystical contemporaneity and of a representative corporative person are to be taken at face value, the point must be from the outset that one participates in both death and resurrection.[67] In attempting to use these concepts as coherent explanatory models, it must be established that they are not consistent.

The facts are therefore that in Rom 6.6a Paul refers to (and in Rom 6.8a summarises) a certain universally known insight which concerned exclusively a fellowship relating to crucifixion and death — and which therefore cannot have been a corporative concept. Paul adduces from this that there must be a similar life-fellowship. This aspect is expressed more intensively as a continued life jointly with Christ. By his reasoning, he thus comes closer to concepts concerned with union and Christ's presence.[68]

sondern er stirbt mit ihm und hat an seinem eigenen Tode teil. Die Taufe fügt den Täufling darum in die Zeit des Todes und der Auferstehung Jesu selbst ein' (p. 226). It is not possible to imagine that a reader without previous knowledge of this very thought-process would be able to grasp it. Cf. also the difficulties demonstrated in Chapter VII, note 15, above in Frankemölle, *Taufverständnis*, p. 55, where it is sought to explain away the concept that 'burial with Christ' according to Rom 6.4 takes place at baptism. See also the critique in Halter, *Taufe*, p. 43ff., and the further difficulties referred to in the next note.

67. The above problems associated with 'contemporaneity', which excluded the sacramentalistic explanatory model, cf. note 61, come into play again. Rom 6.6 cannot refer to the whole conception which is presupposed in Tannehill, *Dying*, p. 30: 'it is clear both that death and ressurrection of Christ are particular, past events and that the believers participate in them ...', cf. Bultmann, *Theologie*, p. 298f. Neither can there be any reference to ideas of 'corporate personality', not even as presented in a weaker version in Schnackenburg, Adam-Christus-Typologie, p. 52: 'Bei dem Gedanken an Christus, den neuen Adam, wird der Täufling unmittelbar, eben aufgrund jener realistischen solidarischen Verbundenheit mit dem Repräsentanten und Anführer einer neuen Menschheit, in das einbezogen, was Christus selbst widerfahren ist. Er erfährt in der Taufe also den Tod Christi, seine Kreuzigung, mit der begründeten Hoffnung, ja mit der Gewissheit und Gewähr, auch an seiner Auferstehung teilzuhaben, sofern er in seiner eigenen Existenz, im sittlichen Bemühen und im ganzen Lebensvollzug das verwirklicht, was ihm in der Taufe gnadenhaft zuteil geworden ist.' Finally, he tries to say that participation in the resurrection is of the future and conditional. But then the thought-process really seems not to cohere properly. How can one be 'realistically linked to the representative' only when his death is concerned, not when his resurrection is concerned? Wouldn't this require that Christ is two different persons? Cf. also Schnackenburg, Todes- und Lebensgemeinschaft, p. 40, Percy, *Leib*, p. 25, 30, Ridderbos, *Paulus*, p. 48f., Frankemölle, *Taufverständnis*, p. 103f.

68. Since there is thus a process of reasoning similar to that in Rom 6.3-5 from death-baptism to life partnership, the answers remain the same to the dual question of a traditional background, cf. above, section 2.1 and Chapter VIII, sections 4.1, 4.4 and 4.5. The cor-

The third explanatory model concerning 'contemporaneity' is also not convincing. What is in fact explained by terms such as a 'paradoxical possibility' and 'eschatological dynamics'?[69] This again becomes a complicated mode of thought which is difficult to penetrate. How is one to understand a paradoxical contemporaneity between events which have taken place at different times? Doesn't one thereby undermine the concept of contemporaneity itself? By this means we arrive at yet another crucial insight: it is more consistent to establish that contemporaneity is not necessarily expressed by this σὺν Χριστῷ.

This must be the path to a solution.

The preposition σύν need not imply contemporaneity between the two elements which are connected. It can also mean 'like' or 'similar to', 'in accordance with', 'in connection with', 'by means of'. It is therefore clearly a possibility that σὺν Χριστῷ in Rom 6.4-8a is not to be perceived as primarily a contemporary element.[70]

This is confirmed by a glance at the content of the sentences. It is clear that the terms συνετάφημεν αὐτῷ, συνεσταυρώθη and ἀπεθάνομεν σὺν Χριστῷ link two different sequences of events: on the Christ side, what is concerned is burial, crucifixion and death in the normal sense, whereas the words used about the Christians concern baptism and departure from the old life, and are as we have already established metaphors. For the very reason that the loaded terms compare different events, it becomes unnecessary to insist on a literal contemporaneity.

If we look more closely at the meaning of σὺν Χριστῷ in Rom 6, several of the alternative nuances can come into the picture. The scene may be set for the 'similar to Christ' meaning. A certain analogy (and a certain connection) between what happens to the Christians and what happens to Christ is expressed.[71] In the context, there is both a ὥσπερ-οὕτως connection and the word ὁμοίωμα, which is indeed an expression of similarity. The nuance of meaning 'in connection with Christ' is also reasonable, since the Christians' 'death' from sin is indeed a result of Christ's death as a salvation event. Particularly in regard to the term in Rom 6.8b, συζήσομεν αὐτῷ

---

porative concepts cannot be the background in the true sense (a): the point of departure to which Paul expressly refers. But they may be the background in the other sense (b): ideas towards which Paul, by his reasoning, is working. But precisely because these are ideas developed in the course of this reasoning it is clear that no joining together in a mythological or psychological sense is intended but rather a close connection between two entities which confront one another.

69. As expressed in Güttgemanns, *Apostel*, p. 219 n. 54, cf. note 54 above.
70. Thus Halter, *Taufe*, p. 46. Cf. above, Chapter III, section 3.1, with notes 154-59.
71. This interpretation is anticipated in Zahn, *Römer*, p. 299, Schnackenburg, *Heilsgeschehen*, p. 31, Larsson, *Christus*, p. 63f. n. 2.

(where as indicated contemporaneity may also have been expressed), the meaning 'with Christ's help' may also be considered, for it is part of the image that the new life is sustained by the strength which is manifested in Christ.[72]

One can now also try to understand the connection at a deeper level (when it emerges that the comprehensive explanatory models cannot be implemented).

The terms συνεσταυρώθη and ἀπεθάνομεν σὺν Χριστῷ appear as very condensed statements with a marked linking together of Christology and soteriology. One and the same term is used to refer to Christ's death as the crucial salvation event and the Christians' deliverance from sin resulting therefrom.[73]

It is then natural to interpret this as a result of Gospel preaching and theological reflection — that it concerns the proclamation of Christ and the promise of salvation of which baptism is an expression. This can be presented in different ways. Halter speaks of existential participation in the eschatological Christ-event and in the soteriological effect of God's universal act of salvation.[74] In a draft, Wedderburn tries to do this by means of the terminology of 'the new hermeneutics': 'word events', 'communicative events'; as an act of salvation Christ's death is still of the past, but is reactualised when the message is repeated and heard at baptism.[75] And this is perhaps, at root, what is meant by the expression 'eschatological dynamics'.[76]

Indeed, the dynamic and the eschatological lead to the development of thought which emerges when we meet the term συζήσομεν αὐτῷ. There is a shift from the fellowship of individual events to a lasting fellowship. This has in turn a strongly suggestive effect. There is an increasing intensity as in the earlier parts of the text. This may be called 'eschatological dynamics'. But it rests on no paradox or contemporaneity. It is because there is a reference back to Christ's death as an all-decisive salvation event, and from here the thoughts must continue to the subsequent resurrection and its significance to the Christian life. And one must then particularly bear in mind the ideas

72. Cf. the examination of Rom 6.4bc,5b in Chapter III, sections 2.3 and 3.5, above.

73. Cf. the review of the term in Rom 6.6a and Gal 2.19, section 1.2, above and Chapter III, section 3.2, with notes 168-69.

74. Halter, *Taufe*, p. 43, where it is also stressed that this effect is mediated in baptism, perceived as preaching and promise.

75. Wedderburn, *Baptism*, p. 66. This involves a repetition of the Golgotha-Easter message proclaimed once-and-for-all. It can therefore be seen as an adjustment of the repetition symbolism referred to in note 61 above.

76. Cf. Güttgemanns, *Apostel*, p. 219 n. 54, Bornkamm, *Ende*, p. 39, as stated in note 54 above.

about Christ as the resurrected Lord.[77] The development of thought leads therefore in the direction of a close fellowship between Christ and the Christians. This can be described as an inclusion — in the sense that the Christians have become closely linked to Christ and drawn into the effects of the Christ-events. This will be amplified in the following section.

2.4. How can the σὺν Χριστῷ concepts have developed?

This must now concern the traditio-historical assumptions relative to the development of thought which takes place in Rom 6.6-8. This question can be illustrated by means of several parallels, and may lead to further clarity in regard to the content of the concepts.

As we have seen, in Rom 6.6a Paul refers to an insight which it is assumed is known to the recipients: that the Christians' 'old man was crucified with Christ'. Rom 6.8a may be a summary of the same insight. In all probability what is concerned is a motif with links to baptism, and that this is an offshoot of the 'death with Christ' 'one-phase' motif in which Christ's redeemer-death is linked together with the Christians' absolute break with the past. This was indeed also the starting point in Rom 6.3.[78]

That this is a traditional motif is confirmed in particular by the parallel in Gal 2.19: Χριστῷ συνεσταύρωμαι. This is the strictest form of the motif, which is repeated here in Rom 6.6a. There is the same loaded Christological-soteriological content and the same use. The break with 'the old man' corresponds to the break with the self in Gal 2.20.

This may indicate that not only the content of the motif but also the σὺν Χριστῷ formulation itself originates from the tradition. It is certainly clear in any event that the distinctive term was formulated before Rom 6. And in connection with both Gal 2 and Rom 6 one or another form of recognition is necessary if the recipient of the letter is to understand what Paul means by the compressed term.[79] But it is still possible that σὺν Χριστῷ is a special

---

77. Cf. above in section 1.4, and Chapter VII, section 2.3, with note 37.
78. Here and in the following a number of recognitions which I have reached earlier in this thesis are summarised. Special reference is made to Chapter III, sections 3.2 and 3.4, where the 'death with Christ' motif was examined and compared with 'suffering and resurrection with Christ', and Chapter VII, section 4.4, where it was shown that the motif is the background to Rom 6.3. The certain result is that in the section of text in Rom 6.6-8 also the motif is the traditio-historical background, in the sense that they are concepts which Paul assumes are familiar and which he takes as his starting point — the first type (a) in the dual problem-complex which was raised in section 2.1, cf. Chapter VII, section 4.1, above.
79. Cf. above, note 12 and Chapter III, note 178.

Pauline formulation. In Galatia, 'crucifixion with Christ' may have been part of Paul's teaching. In the context of the Letter to the Romans, Paul has indeed developed the ideas on 'death-baptism', which *must* have been generally known, and sharpened them so that the stage is set for this formulation, which he then develops.

The development of thought which occurs in the course of Rom 6.6-8 has proved to be supported by an internal dynamic in which thought must be continued from Christ's death to the resurrection as the salvation-event. But this development also has parallels in other versions of the 'death-with-Christ motif'. After the break there follows a life linked to Christ. It is described in 2 Cor 5.15 and Rom 7.4 as a life bound to Christ as the resurrected Lord. Here in Rom 6.8, prepared for in Rom 6.4-5, a further step is taken, and the new life and its content is linked to the power from Christ's resurrection. This gives a dual formulation with σὺν Χριστῷ, fellowship in both death and the new life. It comes to appear as a 'two-phase' motif.

It may therefore be asked whether there is also a connection with the two-phase precursor motif of 'suffering and resurrection with Christ'.[80]

The cardinal passages are 1 Thess 4.14; Rom 8.17; 2 Cor 4.14; Phil 3.10-11; there is a clear futurist eschatological orientation, an expectation that the Christians must go through suffering to glory σὺν Χριστῷ — go through the same sequence of events, supported by the same strength. It may be seen as part of a more general precursor motif. The Adam-Christ typologies are an effected version of this.[81] The precursor idea is also again to be found in a series of motifs which can be linked to the 'suffering and resurrection with Christ' motif: the mimesis idea in 1 Thess 1.6; 2.14; Phil 3.17; the concept of Christ as God's image and 'pattern' for the Christians which dominates the thought-process in 2 Cor 3.18-4.15; the concepts that Christ and the Christians are of the same shape and form, so that Hellenistic ideas of metamorphosis naturally suggest themselves, Rom 8.3,29; Phil 2.6-7; 3.10,21. If one looks in context at the Christological-soteriological statements in Rom 8.3-4,11,17,29, and if the statements in Phil 2.5-13 are linked with Phil 3.9-21, a unified process emerges. It begins with Christ making common cause with man's conditions and breaking through the power of sin. This initiates the new life, and man can live with the same content of life and the same sequence of events through suffering to glory.

---

80. Cf. the examination above in Chapter III, sections 3.3 and 3.4.
81. Cf. the examination of 1 Cor 15 and Rom 5.12-21 above in Chapter III, section 4 and Chapter V, sections 3.5 and 4.4, respectively.

We have thus a comprehensive concept, that Christ's life is a pattern for the Christians.[82]

The gospels present a consistent idea that the original disciples with whom the Christians of later times identify were those who were together with Jesus (often expressed as σὺν αὐτῷ) and were bound also to imitate him in suffering and death. What is concerned is 'taking up thy cross', 'entering into the same baptism as Jesus' and having the will to die with him. John's Gospel in particular makes it clear that the imitation of Christ is not something that can be initiated by one's own effort. Only when the Son, who by incarnation has taken human life upon himself, has taken the path through suffering and been glorified can the disciples be implicated in a similar life-process.[83]

This material does not make it possible to put all these σύν formulations into one formula or to reconstruct definite lines of development between them mutually or between the imitation idea in relation to Jesus and the precursor idea in relation to Paul.[84] What is shown is that throughout early Christianity a crucial idea is that the Christians must live a life following the same pattern as Christ, and that the strength to live comes from Christ.

And thus it appears that the two important motifs, the redeemer motif and the precursor motif, are combined in the context of Rom 6, so that this may be a contributory cause of the development of thought. The prelude to Rom 5 begins with Christ's redeeming death; but the thought-process is carried forward in the Adam-Christ typology with accordance between Christ's obedience and that of the Christians. In the same way, Rom 6.3,6a begins with departure in Christ's redeeming death and develops the idea also to

82. Cf. Schnackenburg, *Heilsgeschehen*, pp. 149-59, where the Christ-Christians accordance is presented as a fundamental Pauline idea; 'Was Christus widerfuhr, geschieht auch den Christen' (p. 152); this idea is shown behind the motifs referred to here.

83. Cf. Chapter IV, section 2.2, above. John's Gospel in particular has clear parallels to the concepts in Phil 2-3; Rom 8 about Christ's solidarity and precursive life — John 1.18; 3.13-16; 12.23-26.32; 14.1-7; 16.28-31. The same idea pervades when John reflects on following Jesus in suffering: Christ must have experienced the entire sequence of events before the Christian disciple will have the strength to follow, cf. Chapter IV, note 26, above. This is a development of thought implicit in the other gospels, where the impossibility of entering into martyrdom by one's own efforts is emphasised, cf. Mark 10.38; 9.31ff. parr.

84. See the section on σὺν Χριστῷ above in Chapter III, section 3.1. Cf. also Schade, *Christologie*, p. 124 with n. 82, p. 265, who is sceptical about attempts to reconstruct traditio-historical lines, cf. Chapter III, note 238, above.

concern a vital force which prevails in the Christians' existence and leads to the sustained precursor motif in Rom 8.[85]

We can thus see that in Rom 6.3-8 Paul is working towards ideas of solidarity and common destiny. Such concepts may have a traditio-historical background in the widest sense, where what is concerned is not the starting point of the thought-process but what affects Paul's description and his final point.

One further possibility of explaining the background to the concept should be indicated.

I have earlier considered the possibility that the sign of the cross was already used in baptism at the time of Paul.[86] Much would be explained if one could assume that the Romans also were acquainted with such a practice.

The perceptive use of the term 'crucified with Christ' in Rom 6.6 would immediately be understandable. There is no longer a recognition problem. Readers would understand the term immediately, whether or not it was traditional or a special Pauline formulation.

It would also help to explain the continuation in Rom 6.6-8, for the cross is also a sign of property and an expression of the continued ties to Christ in Christian life.

And since the cross is also a sign of protection, thoughts would be led onwards in the direction of the ideas regarding the passage through suffering to glory.

It should be emphasised that this is still a hypothesis. But in my opinion it is a good hypothesis.

---

85. That a shift is taking place from a one-phase motif towards a two-phase motif is confirmed by the imbalance between the Christ side and the Christian side which emerges in Rom 6.9-11, cf. Chapter IX, section 2.1, below.
86. Cf. Chapter IV, section 3, above, where indeed Gal 2.19 and other passages in the Letter to the Galatians support the hypothesis, and Chapter VIII, section 4.3.

IX

Rom 6.9-11:
the concluding process of reasoning

1. The intention in Rom 6.9-11

1.1. The Christological insight in Rom 6.9-10

We are dealing with the third explicit reference to an assumed knowledge. Εἰδότες ὅτι ... introduces a reason for the conviction about the new life with Christ which was emphasised in Rom 6.8.[1]

Whereas the references in Rom 6.3,6 were sparse, longer and more detailed aspects are now introduced. Taken together, Rom 6.9-10 must amount to a reference to the assumed insight, since the content in verse 9 is amplified and substantiated in verse 10; this is shown by the introductory γάρ.[2] This also makes it clear that Rom 6.10 contains the most basic insight. It is pointed out in Rom 6.9 'that Christ, being raised from the dead, will never die again; death no longer has dominion over him', and this is because 'the death he died, he died to sin, once for all; but the life he lives, he lives to God.' The sparse and taut form of Rom 6.10 also helps to signal that the verse, and especially the last half-verse, is crucially important.[3]

It is thus clear that so far as the main content is concerned there is also an important difference. Rom 6.3,6a concerns exclusively the relationship between Christ and the Christians as regards death. Here, in Rom 6.9-10, Christ's resurrection is emphasised from the outset. The emphasis in verse 9

---

1. As shown above in Chapter VII, section 1.4, with note 30, the member εἰδότες is linked to the implicit subject in πιστεύομεν in Rom 6.8. Cf. Gäumann, *Taufe*, p. 85, Tannehill, *Dying*, p. 14, Jervell, *Gud*, p. 107. Different in Cranfield, *Romans*, p. 313, who sees the participle as similar to verbum finitum, asyndetically linked to the preceding text.
2. Different in Gäumann, *Taufe*, p. 85, where this γάρ is ignored, and Rom 6.10 is on the contrary made into Pauline 'Weiterführungen' and 'Folgerungen' from the sentence from the 'credo' quoted in Rom 6.9 (cf. however p. 85f.). Cf. on the other hand von der Osten-Sacken, *Römer 8*, p. 177, Wilckens, *Römer II*, p. 18, Morris, *Romans*, p. 255.
3. Cf. Blass, Debrunner and Rehkopf, *Grammatik*, § 153f., about the construction in which the neuter pronoun replaces the longer (internal) object: ὃ ἀπέθανεν = τὸν θάνατον, ὃν ἀπέθανεν — ὃ ζῇ = τὴν ζωήν, ἣν ζῇ, cf. Gal 2.20, where this way of expression is also used in a concentrated statement.

is on the consequences of the resurrection. In verse 10 the crucial reference is to the importance of the life of Christ. The 'death side' is still there — in verse 10a — but in the context it is clearly Christ's resurrection and life which are important. The connection that according to Rom 6.8b the Christians have with the life of Christ must also be substantiated.

Moreover, it can be established that the insight in Rom 6.9-10 is — in any event formally — purely Christological, whereas the earlier references were soteriological and concerned with the Christians' baptism and transition to a new life. Matters may well be otherwise inherently.

It can in fact also be established that the content is questionable in a new respect. There was earlier a reference to distinctive statements, where it can at first be difficult to see how they might be recognisable to the recipients. The problem is now that the statements become blurred if they are meant to concern Christ; some are quite self-evident, others have some distorted angles.[4] One must therefore note that the Christians in Rom 6.11 are emphatically drawn into the effects of the salvation-events referred to in Rom 6.9-10.[5] This is marked by the preceding οὕτως καὶ ὑμεῖς, by the strong, formal parallelism between the Christological term in Rom 6.10 and the soteriological term in Rom 6.11, and by the supporting member ἐν Χριστῷ which expresses a connection between Christ and the Christians. There is then a clear possibility that the soteriological use is already envisaged in the Christological statements.[6] This must be considered in the case of every single member.

If one looks at Rom 6.9, it concerns, according to its wording, what Christ's resurrection means to Christ. He is beyond the power of death, so death no longer has dominion over him. It appears at first sight that there is such a universal opinion among the Christians on this that it becomes almost a trite statement. But there may have been some reflection about Christ's resurrection, unlike those of Lazarus and the widow's son from Nain, who perhaps died for a second time; in this way there would be some content in the sentence.[7] But, allowing the thought to continue, the further consequences

---

4. Cf. Wedderburn, Traditions, p. 340, Dunn, *Romans*, p. 322. See the examination of the individual expressions below.

5. Cf. Bultmann, *Theologie*, p. 298, Barrett, *Romans*, p. 126f., Gäumann, *Taufe*, p. 31, 86f., Stuhlmacher, *Römer*, p. 86, Morris, *Romans*, p. 255f. Against Käsemann, *Römer*, p. 162, who rejects the connection between Rom 6.10 and Rom 6.11 by referring to the fact that verse 11 acts as a summary of the process of reasoning so far. But this is not of course an obstacle to its being at the same time a concluding point and a last significant step in the argument.

6. Cf. Schnackenburg, *Heilsgeschehen*, p. 37, 153, Barrett, *Romans*, p. 126, Siber, *Mit Christus*, p. 232 n. 108, Halter, *Taufe*, p. 62.

7. Cf. Cranfield, *Romans*, p. 313, Morris, *Romans*, p. 254f.

also come into the picture. It is an event which puts an end to death. In the sentence θάνατος αὐτοῦ οὐκέτι κυριεύει 'death' stands personified and is concerned with power, so that one must again think of spheres of power and change of authority. This is seen in a cosmic perspective, and clearly concerns Judaism's apocalyptic ideas in the special Christian version, in which Christ's resurrection is the beginning of the eschatological resurrection from the dead.[8] Thus is the soteriological use prepared.

Rom 6.10a is mischievous in several respects, if one attempts to understand it purely Christologically. Using the dative τῇ ἁμαρτίᾳ it is said that Christ has died to sin. But this can become a questionable and surprising item of information, if the meaning is squeezed from this dative. This can occur in two ways. Some perceive it as similar to Rom 6.2,11, which is concerned with the Christians' death to sin — that is, 'death away from sin'.[9] But this is a strange assertion about Christ, who is professed to be he who was thoroughly free from sin. Others indicate that it must be seen in line with the parallel τῷ θεῷ in Rom 6.10b, which is concerned with a life in accordance with God's demands; in that event it would concern a death which fulfilled the demands of sin.[10] But this is also a difficult expression as long as it concerns only Christ, on whom sin indeed has no claim. It would therefore be wise, at least initially, to understand the dative in a broader, more neutral sense: 'relative to sin'.[11] But then again, when it is

---

8. Cf. Barrett, *Romans*, p. 126, Schlier, *Römerbrief*, p. 199, Morris, *Romans*, p. 254, Dunn, *Romans*, p. 322f. As regards belief in the resurrection, see also above, Chapter VII, section 2.3, with note 35, and section 4.5. In Schnackenburg, *Heilsgeschehen*, p. 37, yet another problem is considered — that Christ is no longer ruled by the power of death assumes that he was so in the past. For this reason the interpretation of the article-less θάνατος, is attempted: that it refers to physical death. But in Schnackenburg, Adam-Christus-Typologie, p. 44f., the usual interpretation is chosen: that the power of death is concerned, and it continues: 'Das ist das paulinische Paradox, dass die Todesmacht gerade durch den Tod Christi ihre Herrschaft verloren hat.' One might say: it has been reduced to merely a physical death.

9. See Gäumann, *Taufe*, p. 86, p. 72 n. 39, who calls it 'dat. incommodi' but understands it to mean that it refers to 'den Besitzer eines Saches', cf. Blass, Debrunner and Rehkopf, *Grammatik*, § 188,2, Thüsing, *Per Christum*, p. 72, 80, Dunn, *Romans*, p. 323. One thus normally emphasises that a death away from the power-sphere of death is concerned — not, as in Rom 6.2,11, a death removed from personal sinfulness.

10. Especially emphatic is von der Osten-Sacken, *Römer 8*, p. 178ff., who asserts in support of the viewpoint that τῇ ἁμαρτίᾳ in Rom 6.11 must also be perceived as dativus commodi, cf. note 18 below. The way is thus prepared for a concept of Christ's vicarious death of atonement, so that Christ fulfils sin's demand on the Christians, which is not however articulated here in the verse.

11. Thus Schmidt, *Römer*, p. 112, 'Dativ der Beziehung', Morris, *Romans*, p. 255. Cf. Schnackenburg, *Heilsgeschehen*, p. 37: 'Da die Aussage nur mit Rücksicht auf uns (V. 11) formuliert ist, darf man keinen weiteren Folgerungen für das Verhältnis Christus-Sündenmacht aus ihr ziehen.'

considered how the statement is used in the context, the other meanings may have relevance.

And Rom 6.10a continues that Christ's death relative to sin occurred ἐφ-άπαξ — once for all. It is often stressed that this involves a vital difference between the mystery religions' timeless myth and the Christian belief in an historical once-for-all event.[12] But since, as we have seen, mystery religion is not part of the picture such a dissociation cannot be Paul's point in using the expression. Neither, on the other hand, can the point be simply that Christ's death is a once-for-all event, since this of course applies to any person's death. It is crucial that it is a once-for-all death relative to sin. And then the soteriological use must again come into one's thoughts, and ἐφάπαξ becomes an expression of the eschatological victory over death.[13]

In Rom 6.10b we also have an assertion which is surprisingly obvious if it applies only to Christ: that the life he lives he lives to God. This is at first sight perceived as meaning that it is Jesus' life of resurrection that is lived to God.[14] But then it must be added immediately that this does not differ from his earthly life.[15] Then the perception of τῷ θεῷ in a different meaning is considered: the life of glory lived close to God.[16] But in using it in Rom 6.11b it is clearly the ethical meaning to which one reverts.[17]

It has therefore been shown that the Christological insight in Rom 6.9-10 was worked out in advance in anticipation of the soteriological use to be made of it in Rom 6.11. This means that Rom 6.9-11 is one unified reasoning process.

12. Cf. Bornkamm, *Ende*, p. 40, Wagner, *Problem*, p. 297, Gäumann, *Taufe*, p. 47f., Frankemölle, *Taufverständnis*, p. 85f., 107, Dunn, *Romans*, p. 323.

13. Cf. Bornkamm, *Ende*, p. 40, Schnackenburg, *Heilsgeschehen*, p. 37, Michel, *Römer*, p. 156, Gäumann, *Taufe*, p. 86, von der Osten-Sacken, *Römer 8*, p. 177f., Halter, *Taufe*, p. 63f., Schlier, *Römerbrief*, p. 200 (cf. note 40 below).

14. Cf. Schnackenburg, *Heilsgeschehen*, p. 150, Michel, *Römer*, p. 156, Thüsing, *Per Christum*, p. 72f., Gäumann, *Taufe*, p. 86, Jervell, *Gud*, p. 101, Morris, *Romans*, p. 259.

15. Thus Morris, *Romans*, p. 259. Cf. Barrett, *Romans*, p. 126, Schlier, *Römerbrief*, p. 200, who emphasises that the life of Jesus is a life to God 'nach wie vor und nun erst recht'. Also Thüsing, *Per Christum*, p. 72f. with n. 34, concedes that it is an unusual idea that Christ's life of resurrection has this (ethical) content; but he considers that in other passages Paul expresses the same idea: 1 Cor 3.23; 11.30; Rom 15.7; but this is not an obvious interpretation of these passages.

16. Thus Gäumann, *Taufe*, p. 86 with n. 159, which indicates Rom 8.34 where Jesus is he who is at God's right hand. Cf. Schlier, *Römerbrief*, p. 200, Morris, *Romans*, p. 255.

17. Cf. Sanday and Headlam, *Romans*, p. 160, Siber, *Mit Christus*, p. 205, Schnelle, *Gerechtigkeit*, p. 85.

1.2. The soteriological point in Rom 6.11: life ἐν Χριστῷ

The introductory demonstrative οὕτως καὶ ὑμεῖς in Rom 6.11 is therefore crucial to an understanding of the section's structure and function. The Christological insight from Rom 6.9-10 is used on the Christians, and thus these verses together become the final reason for and amplification of the conviction at which Paul has arrived in Rom 6.8: that the Christians were not only 'dead' with Christ but would also live together with him.

The content of Rom 6.11 confirms this connection.

Rom 6.11a says that the Christians must consider themselves as νεκροὺς μὲν τῇ ἁμαρτίᾳ. The death Christ died to sin once-for-all according to Rom 6.10a therefore means for the Christians that they can consider themselves as 'dead' in the same figurative sense as in Rom 6.8a. This is at the same time the point of Rom 6.2, which is again emphasised. The dative τῇ ἁμαρτίᾳ can therefore be understood as dativus incommodi.[18] Similarly, there is accord between Rom 6.11b and Rom 6.10b, and here also it becomes a continuation of the thought-process from the preceding context. It now reads that the Christians must consider themselves as ζῶντας δὲ τῷ θεῷ ἐν Χριστῷ ᾽Ιησοῦ. The present life linked to Christ which is lived by the Christians is, like Christ's life (according to Rom 6.10b), a life to God, and in the context this must be understood as an ethical life.[19] This is clearly an extension of the other statements about 'life': in Rom 6.2, that it is impossible to live in sin; in Rom 6.4, that it is a walk ἐν καινότητι ζωῆς, and in Rom 6.8, the parallel

---

18. Cf. above, Chapter VI, note 12. It cannot — as maintained by von der Osten-Sacken, *Römer 8*, p. 177ff. — be dativus commodi (like the dative in Rom 6.11b), 'death to the benefit of sin', so that the meaning would have to be that the Christians have died the death demanded as punishment for sin in the previous life. This idea would become possible only if death in the literal unpleasant meaning of the word were concerned, and not the positive-sounding metaphorical use developed in the course of the section. To support his view, von der Osten-Sacken (p. 179) refers to the μέν-δέ construction which compared the two predicates in verse 11; because the member introduced by μέν is meant to be concessive ('quite true') it must apply to this sin-death, while the adversative member in verse 11b contains the point which removes what is oppressive from what is conceded. But this is an obvious over-interpretation. The particle μέν is used only to a limited extent in this way; it has a much wider use-potential, and is often used in a weakened form in concatenations, as well as in antithetic and synthetic parallelisms where the emphasis must be on the last member; cf. Bauer, *Wörterbuch*, col. 994f., Blass, Debrunner and Rehkopf, *Grammatik*, § 447 and 489.

19. Cf. Bultmann, *Glauben* III, p. 53, Larsson, *Christus*, p. 73, Gäumann, *Taufe*, p. 87f., Morris, *Romans*, p. 256. At the same time the parallelism can also be interpreted to mean that the Christians have already to some extent received a share in the life of resurrection, as emphasised in Siber, *Mit Christus*, p. 238 (cf. p. 205), also with reference to Rom 6.4,8,13. The concluding ἐν Χριστῷ indeed concerns the power on which the Christians depend.

term συζήσομεν αὐτῷ. And this is followed in Rom 6.13 by the demand to fight for God ὡσεὶ ἐκ νεκρῶν ζῶντας.

The parallelism between Rom 6.10 and Rom 6.11 indicates that the οὕτως which links the verses together expresses an accord. One must again be aware that οὕτως has two nuances of meaning — either comparative: 'in the same way', 'similarly', or constative and consecutive: 'in this way', 'therefore'.[20] It is scarcely to be ignored that there is here an element of both nuances of meaning. And if Paul's subject-matter is to be understood it makes little difference if the emphasis is on one or the other nuance. In any event, the point is that the Christians participate in the effect of the salvation-events ἐν Χριστῷ. Nevertheless, I wish to plead that the emphasis should be on the accord, so that the comparative function becomes the primary.

First of all, Rom 6.10-11 thus stresses this accord between Christ and the Christians.

Secondly, there is a special line in the dominant context. Rom 6.4-5 contains the term (ὥσπερ ...) οὕτως καί and the term ὁμοίωμα, which also indicates an analogy between two entities. Paul thereby expressed an accord, and prepared the way for a connection between the Christ-events and what happened to the Christians. The preceding verses also have the formulation using σὺν Χριστῷ, where the meaning can be both 'similar to' and 'in connection with'. And there is a reverse connection to the prelude to the Adam-Christ typology in Rom 5.12-14. The term οὕτως καί and the expression ὁμοίωμα are also found here. Paul assumes an accord between Adam and his descendants, and amplified this to an almost fateful dependence. Rom 6.1-11 can be seen as a corresponding description of the Christians' fateful dependence upon Christ, where Paul begins in analogy and accord in order to express the connection even more intensely. It would therefore be natural to understand the third οὕτως καί in Rom 6.11 as another underlining of the accord between Christ and the Christians which enlarged to a connection by virtue of the concluding ἐν Χριστῷ.[21]

---

20. Cf. above, Chapter V, section 3.2, with note 57, and Chapter VII, section 2.3, with note 31. See in particular Cranfield, *Romans*, p. 314f., where the two possibilities are clearly presented. Cranfield himself is more inclined towards the consecutive understanding; similarly Bauer, *Wörterbuch*, col. 1185, Bornkamm, *Ende*, p. 44, Michel, *Römer*, p. 156, Thüsing, *Per Christum*, p. 73f., Siber, *Mit Christus*, p. 239, n. 121, Gäumann, *Taufe*, p. 86, Wilckens, *Römer* II, p. 19, whereas the comparative function is underlined in Schnackenburg, *Heilsgeschehen*, p. 153, Frid, *Römer 6,4-5*, p. 200, Morris, *Romans*, p. 255, Stuhlmacher, *Römer*, p. 86.
21. Cf. von der Osten-Sacken, *Römer 8*, p. 177, Schnackenburg, *Heilsgeschehen*, p. 153, where the (ὥσπερ-) οὕτως καί, which is common to Rom 6.4 and Rom 6.11, is simply called a formula. That the preceding particle ὥσπερ is missing does not contradict that a com-

Thirdly, it is in any case questionable to perceive οὕτως *purely* consecutively, *exclusively* constatively, so that verse 11 must be perceived merely as a development of what is already contained in verse 10. Then there is no progress of thought in the section of text, and it becomes difficult to explain why Paul has built it up with a pronounced transition from Christology to soteriology, and only at the end provides ἐν Χριστῷ 'Ιησοῦ which is the supporting member.[22]

Before we come to this crucial expression, there is reason to tackle another member in Rom 6.11, the verb λογίζεσθε.

This represents at the formal level a significant innovation. It is imperative whereas the preceding verses were indicative and, whereas until now we have had the Christians referred to in the first person, the second person plural is now used; that is, direct address to the Roman community.[23] This of course paves the way for the term in Rom 6.12-13, where the point prepared for in these verses is asserted, imperatively, directly to the Romans.

But inherently no new departure is concerned. It is not an imperative of the same paraenetic type as in what follows. No special effort is concerned that must be made. One is not required to provide for this because it is not really the case, and neither is it an exhortation to adopt a certain attitude.[24]

---

parative function must be attributed to οὕτως; it occurs frequently — Mt 5.16; 12.45; 13.49; 17.12; 18.14,35; Mark 13.29; Lk 17.10; John 3.8; Rom 5.12; 11.5; 1 Thess 4.13 — and thus typically with the use of parables, example-narratives or references to a traditional insight, or in general where the first member in the comparison is so wide-ranging that the distance between ὥσπερ and οὕτως would be too great. Cf. Bauer, *Wörterbuch*, col. 1185, Cranfield, *Romans*, p. 314, and above, Chapter V. section 3.2, with notes 55, 57, 61, where the comprehensive ὥσπερ-οὕτως structure introduced in Rom 5.12 is explained. See also above Chapter VI, section 4, especially item 3, about the development of thought in Rom 6.1-11.

22. Cf. also section 2.1 below, which shows the inherent consequence if, like Thüsing, *Per Christum*, p. 73, one adopts the view quoted above, which is associated with an interpretation of the Christology in Rom 6.10-11 as expressing an idea about 'corporate personality'.

23. Cf. Stanley K. Stowers, Romans 7,7-25 as a Speech-in-Character (προσωποποιία), in: Troels Engberg-Pedersen (ed.), *Paul in His Hellenistic context*, Minneapolis 1995, pp. 180-202; p. 201, who points out that for the first time since the introduction in Rom 1.6,13-15 direct address is used to the gentile-convert Roman community.

24. Cf. the various attempts to make it a vital contribution from the Christians' side, especially Rudolf Bultmann, Christus des Gesetzes Ende, in: *Glauben und Verstehen* II[3], Tübingen 1961, pp. 32-58; p. 55: 'Dass wir Tot für die Sünde, lebendig aber für Gott durch Christus sind, muss stets zum Entschluss erhoben werden (Rm. 6, 11)', von der Osten-Sacken, *Römer 8*, p. 185, n. 31, who speaks of 'Der in der aufforderung λογιζεσθε liegende eschatologische Vorbehalt ...'; cf. also Zahn, *Römer*, p. 308f., Dodd, *Romans*, p. 112, Larsson, *Christus*, p. 72, Dunn, *Romans*, p. 323f., where the recognition of what occurred is

What is concerned is submission to the validity of the gospel, which is being urged. Paul has indeed indicated all along the power which comes into action. One must submit to the promise of salvation, because it is the truth.[25] Like πιστεύομεν in Rom 6.8, the conviction of faith which the Christians necessarily must have is expressed. It should then be noted that existence after baptism is still concerned. And this is imagined as not merely a physical force that has an effect but also as something into which the Christians themselves with their power of judgement are drawn.[26]

As we have seen, the member ἐν Χριστῷ 'Ἰησοῦ is the mainstay of the reasoning. It contains a reference to the circumstance which makes it possible for the Christological statements in Rom 6.9-10 to have soterological validity.[27] This indicates the true basis of the conviction of faith which is to characterise Christian existence. But how can this member be of crucial importance?

It should first be pointed out that the connection expressed by ἐν Χριστῷ 'Ἰησοῦ is probably established at baptism.[28] The basic tradition which Paul refers to from the outset and continues to work on concerns the connection that baptism provides with Christ, expressed by ἐβαπτίσθημεν εἰς Χριστὸν 'Ἰησοῦν in Rom 6.3.

Then it may be considered, what is inherent in this crucial ἐν Χριστῷ. A local-spatial significance for the term is indicated precisely because baptism brings the baptised 'into Christ'. Referring in particular to Gal 3.27, it is seen as a mystical incorporation into Christ.[29] Or it has been perceived as an ecclesiological formula which expresses a collective incorporation into σῶμα

---

presented as a continuous process. It is also incorrect like Wilckens, *Römer* II, p. 7, to distinguish between an indicative section, Rom 6.1-10, and an imperative section, Rom 6.11-14. The close connection between Rom 6.9-10 and Rom 6.11 which has been shown contradicts this.

25. Cf. Bornkamm, *Ende*, p. 44, Schmidt, *Römer*, p. 112f., Gäumann, *Taufe*, p. 87, Schlier, *Römerbrief*, p. 200, Halter, *Taufe*, p. 64, and especially Dunn, *Romans*, p. 324: 'Paul expects it ['living to God'] of all believers since the possibility of so living is dependant not so much on their 'reckoning' as on their being in Christ ...'

26. Cf. Halter, *Taufe*, p. 65, who notes: 'Christlicher Existenzvollzug setzt also beim νοῦς an.' And as in Rom 6.8 (cf. above, Chapter VIII, section 1.4, with note 32) it concerns the subsequent reflection on the meaning of baptism in Christian life, cf. Cullmann, *Tauflehre*, p. 42f.; this is disputed by Beasley-Murray, *Baptism*, p. 145, who seems to believe that it is a statement about the importance of belief at baptism.

27. Cf. Schnackenburg, *Heilsgeschehen*, p. 149f., Schmidt, *Römer*, p. 112, Larsson, *Christus*, p. 72, Thüsing, *Per Christum*, p. 73f., Gäumann, *Taufe*, p. 87, Jervell, *Gud*, p. 101f., Cranfield, *Romans*, p. 315f., Halter, *Taufe*, p. 66, Dunn, *Romans*, p. 324.

28. As is normally assumed — cf. Bornkamm, *Ende*, p. 44, Michel, *Römer*, p. 15f., Larsson, *Christus*, p. 72, Gäumann, *Taufe*, p. 87f., Schlier, *Römerbrief*, p. 201.

29. Cf. Deissmann, *Formel*, p. 74ff., Heitmüller, *Taufe*, 1903, p. 20, *Taufe*, 1911, p. 20f., Schneider, *Passionsmystik*, p. 9ff., cf. above, Chapter III, section 2.4, item 1.

Χριστοῦ, corresponding to Rom 12.4-5.[30] But βαπτίζεσθαι εἰς Χριστόν can also be understood as expressing that baptism gives contact with Christ (in German: 'Taufe auf Christus'). A wider meaning of the term ἐν Χριστῷ may therefore be considered where a connection to Christ is concerned which may also be of an instrumental nature and express that what is crucial occurs by the power of Christ (as in Gal 3.14).[31]

If one must adopt a position on what ἐν Χριστῷ means in precisely this context, it is clear that there is no one definite meaning which can be established out of hand.[32] One must therefore choose the widest meaning: the link with Christ; and there can clearly be an instrumental nuance: the Christians' new life will come about by virtue of Christ.

But it cannot be excluded that there may have been a play on the local meaning, which may be the case with baptism εἰς Χριστόν in Rom 6.3-4. Similarly, there is an increasing intensity in the σὺν Χριστῷ expressions. It may be a figurative local meaning: in a certain sense one is included in Christ and his life. This is probably as far as one can go. There is nothing to indicate directly a mystical connection or an incorporation into a Christ-collective, since it has not been possible to substantiate these ideas in the general context.

If one wishes to know more about the nature of the connection, one must again go behind the available text and consider how Paul operates with the ideas he has introduced.

30. Thus Percy, *Leib*, p. 25ff., Bultmann, *Theologie*, p. 312, Tannehill, *Dying*, 19f., Conzelmann, *Grundriss*, p. 291, 299, von der Osten-Sacken, *Römer 8*, p. 180 n. 10, cf. above, Chapter III, section 2.4, item 2.

31. See in particular the interpretation in Neugebauer, *In Christus*, where the main view is that it was meant to be an important adverbial 'Umstandsbestimmung', which should be the general term for the crucial linkage to Christ, cf. Wagner, *Problem*, p. 303, Gäumann, *Taufe*, p. 58ff., Frankemölle, *Taufverständnis*, p. 117. In Wedderburn, Body, p. 87, attention is drawn to the fact that Neugebauer's 'Umstandsbestimmung' is in fact a very vague definition, which may also include the local meaning. There is thus also a clear possibility that the nature of the linkage is instrumental, cf. Büchsel, 'In Christus', p. 144. See also the examination above in Chapter III, section 2.4, item 3.

32. Cf. Halter, *Taufe*, p. 65f., Cranfield, *Romans*, p. 315f., Morris, *Romans*, p. 256f., Dunn, *Romans*, p. 324f. Since it was possible to find examples for each of the three opinions showing that ἐν Χριστῷ can have this meaning, it must be clear as shown above in Chapter III, section 2.4, that it is not a formula with an established universal meaning. Use of the term does not immediately indicate a quite definite understanding of baptism and a definite connection between Christ and the Christians that directly explains how the Christ-events obtained their crucial soteriological significance. The meaning of the preposition may be seen from the context. There must be something that prepares for one of the various nuances it generally possesses.

2. The thought-process behind Rom 6.9-11

2.1. The relationship between Christology and soteriology

Again, the subject-matter is quite clear. Here we have a new appeal to the Romans: as Christians they are beyond the power of sin, and live in the correct relationship with God by virtue of their linkage to the risen Christ, who is beyond the power of death because his death was an eschatological once-for-all event and his life a life to God. There continues to be no problem in seeing *what* Paul intends. The problem is *from where* he comes and especially *how* he will reach his objective. The question is, what are the Christological concepts to which Paul refers, and how he moves from Christology to the soteriological consequences.

Here it is not so much a matter of religio- and traditio-historical assumptions — for two reasons. On the one hand, there is not much need for such an examination; the reference to Christian concepts in Rom 6.9-10 is clear, and the new ideas which emerge here are so distinctive and unique that tradition has no clear parallels.[33] On the other hand, the interpreters do not deal with Rom 6.9-11 so intensely as with the other verses, and consequently there are limits to theory-forming.[34]

But there are two more comprehensive explanatory models on which a position must be taken.

First, there are attempts to understand Rom 6.9-10 as exclusively Christological statements.

The starting point is Bornkamm's breakdown of the text, which is built

---

33. As examination of the verses showed, v. 9 in particular is strange, understood as a Christological expression; it opposes the assumption in Gäumann, *Taufe*, p. 85 with n. 143, that the background is the traditional 'credo'; there are indeed no inherent parallels. To Rom 6.10-11, Thüsing, *Per Christum*, pp. 75-77, advances a number of Pauline texts which are said to be parallels. He correctly indicates 2 Cor 5.15; Rom 7.4; Gal 2.19-20, i.e. the 'death with Christ' motif, which must form part of the picture because the verses are an extension of Rom 6.3,6a. But it seems imprecise when 2 Cor 5.21 and Rom 8.3-4 are treated as expressions of 'to die to sin' and 'live to God', and when Rom 4.25; 5.10, are also included, and everything is said to concern Christ as 'korporative Persönlichkeit'; as will be shown below, this is a questionable interpretation. Later (p. 84ff.) the first five passages are considered, together with Gal 3.13, as an expression of 'Stellvertretung' and 'Solidarität', and as parallels to Rom 6.10 in the sense that Christ's death and sin are interrelated.

34. Cf. Halter, *Taufe*, p. 62 with n. 99, where it is established that in particular the central verse in Rom 6.10 has been ignored. The comments on this section are very brief, apart from the treatment of ἐν Χριστῷ. A contributory explanation may also be, as will be shown, that the precise understanding of the statements presents great problems.

upon a formal parallelism between Rom 6.6-8 and Rom 6.9-10, giving the grounds for Rom 6.5 and Rom 6.8 respectively. Then the two sections are meant to correspond to one another, so that verses 9-10 are the purely Christological grounds for the soteriology in verses 6-8, and it is emphasised that they belong together but are not coincident events: the statement about Christ concerns death *and* resurrection; the statement about the Christians concerns only the effect of Christ's death upon the Christians.[35]

This seems to be a theoretical construction which no unprepared reader would be able to penetrate. And it is disclaimed when Rom 6.11 emphasises that the Roman community ἐν Χριστῷ is included in the salvation-events, in both death and the new life.[36]

Secondly, there are some who wish to understand Rom 6.9-10 as directly soteriological statements.

This becomes applicable if the whole context is perceived corporatively, which one does when referring to the concluding ἐν Χριστῷ. If at baptism the Christians are incorporated into Christ they must also from the outset be included in what is said about Christ. This is the case if the verses are seen against the background of Hellenistic mysticism. But this concept is expressed with particular clarity by Wilhelm Thüsing, who interprets Christ in Rom 6.10 as a 'korporative Persönlichkeit', so that the baptised is drawn into a common destiny with Christ as regards both death and resurrection.[37]

Against this interpretation is the fact that in the earlier contexts (Rom 6.3,6a) there can be no reference to a corporative concept.[38] But in particular one can argue that this will have unusual inherent consequences. In Rom 6.10, the Christians are to participate directly in a life lived beyond death. And, even more than this, if the Christians are included in the statement in Rom 6.10 they must also be so in Rom 6.9, which would be a peculiar as-

35. As regards the division of the text in Bornkamm, *Ende*, p. 38f., see above, Chapter VI, section 4, item 5, with note 69. Bornkamm, p. 40f., uses the division to underline that there is this marked difference between Christ and the Christians; the perception has been especially elaborated in Güttgemanns, *Apostel*, p. 218f., cf. Käsemann, *Römer*, p. 162. This becomes a 'modification interpretation' in which Paul makes reservations by avoiding reference to the effects of the resurrection on the Christian side.

36. Cf. Bornkamm, *Ende*, p. 39, who himself stresses the connection between Christology and soteriology, wholly along the lines of the interpreters mentioned in note 5 above.

37. Thüsing, *Per Christum*, p. 72ff. Cf. Bultmann, *Theologie*, p. 297f., Frankemölle, *Taufverständnis*, p. 38, 84ff., 92, Viard, *Romains*, p. 146, von der Osten-Sacken, *Römer 8*, p. 178ff.

38. As shown above, Chapter VII, section 4.4, and Chapter VIII, section 2.3. An objection might perhaps be that in the preceding sections (Rom 6.3-8) Paul has constructed a corporative concept, which he now employs directly. But in any case this perception is affected by the next recognition.

sertion on Paul's part: that the Christians are meant to be resurrected and are beyond physical death![39]

It is thus confirmed that the text is so constructed that Rom 6.9-10 consists of (ambiguous) Christological statements, and that only in Rom 6.11 do the Christians become directly and emphatically drawn into the effects of Christ's death and resurrection.

The rejection of this last explanatory model paves the way for a positive acknowledgement.

The supporting member ἐν Χριστῷ does not express a fusion with Christ but is associated with a development of thought in which the salvation-events' eschatological significance is underlined and applied to the Christians. It is thus again clear that Paul's appeal and the 'force of conviction' that is to prevail are crucial.[40] And ἐν Χριστῷ in this passage concerns the Christians' dependence upon the eschatological events.[41]

This will be amplified in the following sections.

2.2. The measures

At the external level some measures are clear — ways in which Paul seeks to build up the close connection between the Christological foundation and the soteriological consequences. At the same time, it is revealed that the internal correlation of thought is in the strict sense quite complicated.

The first conspicuous feature is that the Christology in Rom 6.9-10 is described using soteriologically-sounding expressions. The two sides are thus linked together. This way of expression has a strong appeal. And it corresponds thought-provokingly to what happened as regards the references

39. On the face of it, it may look like a corporative idea if Rom 6.10 is perceived as meaning that the Christians have a share in the vitality of the risen Christ, cf. Thüsing, *Per Christum*, p. 72f. But this is only from a superficial aspect, cf. below, note 44. Moreover, one must be aware that Thüsing isolates Rom 6.10-11 relative to Rom 6.9. But the fact is (as stressed above in section 1.1, with note 2) that v. 10 supplies the reason for v. 9, which must therefore also be perceived corporatively so that the Christians are included in the life of resurrection itself. As we have seen, such a radical assertion has not come into the picture, and neither has there been any preparation for it.

40. As noted above in association with note 26 and Chapter VIII, section 2.3, with notes 74-75. Cf. also Schlier, *Römerbrief*, p. 200, where Rom 6.10a is seen as a parallel to 1 Cor 11.26: 'Eben dieses ein für allemal geschehene, unwiederholbare Ereignis seines Sterbens wird im kultischen "Handeln" "proklamiert", d.h. in seinem rechtswirksamen Anspruch gegenwärtiggesetzt.'

41. It is often emphasised that ἐν Χριστῷ has eschatological meaning and refers to the crucial Christ-events, cf. Bornkamm, *Ende*, p. 39, Bultmann, *Theologie*, p. 312, Barrett, *Romans*, p. 127, Larsson, *Christus*, p. 72, n. 3, Gäumann, *Taufe*, p. 87, Jervell, *Gud*, p. 102, Halter, *Taufe*, p. 66, Wilckens, *Römer* II, p. 19, Morris, *Romans*, p. 256, Dunn, *Romans*, p. 324.

in Rom 6.3,6a and the subsequent explanations. A soteriological insight was here expressed using terms taken from Christology.[42] Throughout the entire section of text we thus have this linking together: the description of the Christians' 'death' and the transition to a new life is embellished by the Christ-events which form the basis, and the description of the fundamental Christology is embellished by the soteriological use.[43]

Here also we have the first complication. In comparing Christology and soteriology there is no inherent parallelism between the two sides. On the Christ side there are two events: death and resurrection; on the Christian side only one: 'death', which is the transition from the old to the new life. The connection between the two sides is not therefore smooth. There is a crucial imbalance.[44] The imbalance shows itself again in the next feature.

The other conspicuous feature upon which one immediately fastens is the similarities between the Christological Rom 6.10 and the soteriological Rom 6.11.[45] That the statements about Christ and the Christians sound almost alike immediately gives the impression that the Christians receive a share in the effects of the salvation-events. It seems that the two verses contain the same movement through death to the new life to God, which is specially underlined in Rom 6.10b,11b. It seems on the face of it to be precursor-Christology as in Rom 8.17. But if one fastens on the significance of death and considers Rom 6.10a,11a in context, one arrives at a redeemer-Christology. As in 2 Cor 5.14-15, it seems to be a concept of 'vicarious death'

---

42. Cf. above, Chapter VIII, section 2.3, with note 73.
43. Cf. in particular Schnackenburg, *Heilsgeschehen*, p. 150, where it is emphasised that in Rom 6 a connection is being constructed between Christ's reality and the Christians' reality where 'diesen Vorgang der Christuseinigung möglichst eindringlich darzustellen' is concerned. This observation can be compared with the perception of the construction presented in Bornkamm, *Ende*, p. 39, and given great significance: that there is parallelism between a soteriological section in Rom 6.6-7 and a Christological section in Rom 6.9-10; cf. the previous section with notes 35-36, where I criticised that the perception is used to underline the distance between the consequences on the Christ side and the Christian side. If the soteriological statements are described with Christological usage and the Christological statements with soteriological usage, it must be rather to give an impression of the closest possible connection.
44. This imbalance is further evidence that the text's background is not a concept of a corporative linkage between Christ and the Christians, since this would require full accord between the Christ side and Christian side. The imbalance can be seen as a result of the thought-development we have seen in Rom 6.3-8: The starting point was a one-phase motif, 'death with Christ'. The emphasis gradually came to be on the resurrection and the Christians' new life, resulting in a two-phase statement which may remind one of the two-phase 'suffering-resurrection with Christ' motif, cf. especially Chapter VIII, section 2.4, above.
45. See Thüsing, *Per Christum*, p. 71ff., Gäumann, *Taufe*, p. 87, Siber, *Mit Christus*, p. 205, Schlier, *Römerbrief*, p. 200, Wilckens, *Römer* II, p. 19, Schnelle, *Gerechtigkeit*, p. 85.

in which Christ's death once for all means that the Christians have in a certain sense put death behind them.[46]

But now the imbalance again appears. Even if we keep to Rom 6.10-11 alone, there is no inherent parallelism between the statements about Christ and the Christians. The Christians' earthly life is compared with Christ's life, where the power of resurrection and raising-up form part of the picture. And as opposed to Christ's physical death to the detriment of sin are the Christians who 'died' to sin in the same figurative sense as in Rom 6.2,6-8.[47] As in the earlier contexts, there is a play on words to connect the salvation-event, Christ's death, with the break with the past which results from this. It is not then on the face of it a vicarious death in the general sense, where someone dies so that others shall avoid death. Viewed in isolation, Rom 6.10a,11a provides no explanation of how Christ's death can be given a crucial salvation effect.

And a further complication comes to light here. If one looks at the logical-grammatical connection Rom 6.10 is not directly connected to Rom 6.11, since as we have seen Rom 6.10 substantiates and amplifies the insight introduced in Rom 6.9. Rom 6.9-10 together constitute the knowledge to which Paul refers.[48] And it is the total insight which in Rom 6.11 is urged also on those who are ἐν Χριστῷ. Logically, it is the statement in verse 9 which is the connecting link between verses 10 and 11. It thus depends not only upon Christ's vitality and death but also to a high degree on the resurrection that the Christians have been given a share in the new life.

At this point it may perhaps be questioned how the connection is to be perceived logically, since in the entire section of text Paul indeed uses the appealing, suggestive, not strictly logically form of reasoning which characterises analogic conclusions and the shifts we have encountered on several occasions. It is possible therefore that Paul wishes primarily to link Christology and soteriology closely together and to connect redeemer-Christology and precursor-Christology; he may have concentrated so much on the primary aspect that he has not thought through the precise connection, and is not interested in the logical association of ideas.[49]

One should nevertheless consider how in the strict sense the sentences are constructed, since although the direct effect upon readers is decisive we

46. Cf. Thüsing, *Per Christum*, p. 84f., Frankemölle, *Taufverständnis*, p. 92, Cranfield, *Romans*, p. 316, Wilckens, *Römer* II, p. 19.
47. Cf. Dunn, *Romans*, p. 324.
48. Cf. above, section 1.1 and note 2.
49. Thus Siber, *Mit Christus*, p. 232 n. 108, cf. Schnackenburg, *Heilsgeschehen*, p. 150, Hellholm, Argumentation, p. 119ff.

are probably dealing with ideas which Paul has been working with so often and so intensely that his way of expressing himself may reflect a deeper connection.

2.3. Eschatology, redeemer-Christology and precursor-Christology

This must be no more than an outline. But if one continues to build upon the observations made the thought-process can be seen to correspond to the interpretation of other central Pauline passages.

One must be aware of the meaning of the imbalance between the Christ side and the Christian side. The individual events are not necessarily mentioned in chronological order but with a view to the analogy that must be shown between the two sides. This applies to the first part of the text, in which the baptised's transition to the new life is described in terms taken from Christology, using the sequence of burial, crucifixion and death with Christ. And this can also apply when the Christology is described in the light of the soteriology.

It is also significant that Rom 6.10 is not directly linked to Rom 6.11 but is a reason for Rom 6.9. The construction is thus as follows:

verse 11,	that the Christians are 'dead' relative to sin and alive to God by virtue of the link to Christ,
rests on verse 9,	that after his resurrection from the dead Christ no longer dies, and that death has no dominion over him,
which rests upon verse 10,	that the death he died he died once for all relative to sin, and the life he lives he lives to God.

If verse 10 is the most fundamental statement, one may consider whether the thought-process begins there. And events may have been mentioned in the reverse sequence, so that one should really start with Jesus' life (verse 10b), continue with his death (verse 10a) and end with the resurrection and the effects of resurrection (verse 9) — were it not that Paul wishes at the same time to emphasise the accord between Christ and the Christians. Viewed in this way, it may seem quite logical that the Christ-events are mentioned in the reverse sequence if they are indeed seen, as it were, in the rear-view mirror. And it makes sense to understand the verses in this way.

Rom 6.10b then concerns not only the life of resurrection Christ lives as risen Lord. This is the life which began with Jesus' earthly life, and which has the true content. Both then and now, this has been a life to God.[50] It appears as an unbroken sequence of events which is still of significance to the Christians. This is indeed the point for which Rom 6.9-10a sets the scene: that death has no power over the true life and cannot interrupt it.

If one accordingly sees the true life in the context of the eschatological once-for-all death in Rom 6.10a, the context makes good sense. If Christ dies, death cannot be the punishment for a sinful life but must have another meaning. And sin becomes powerless if death is no longer a threatening, eternal 'punishment death'.[51]

Rom 6.9 concerns the consequence of the events in Rom 6.10. By Christ's resurrection death has finally been overcome, as verse 9b emphasises. It is no longer a cosmic power if God's power has proved to be stronger.[52] And verse 9a shows how significant Christ's death then is: the physical death became merely the transition to an existence beyond the power of death. In this way one ends with the resurrection as the crucial event. It is indeed the sign that God's power has broken into the world, so that the end-time sequence has been set in motion.

---

50. Cf. again (as in note 15 above) Schlier, *Römerbrief*, p. 200, Morris, *Romans*, p. 259. Similar considerations are to be found in Schnackenburg, *Heilsgeschehen*, p. 150, where it is established that the objective of the reasoning is the union with Christ (cf. note 43 above): 'Dieser ist für den Täufling zunächst der lebendig erhöhte Herr (Röm 6, 10b).' But it is stressed later that the divergence which appears to exist between the Christ side and the Christian side presents no problem, 'denn der erhöhte Herr ist identisch mit dem historischen Jesus.' If the statement is interpreted to mean that what is also concerned is the content of the earthly life which is common to Christ and the Christians, the crux of the matter becomes of course the present tense form ζῇ; but this can be explained, on the one hand, in that the statement is framed with a view to the soteriological use in Rom 6.11b and, on the other hand, in that there is continuance in the true life which is lived to God, so that it is a process which covers both the past and the present.

51. Cf. Dunn, *Romans*, p. 323: 'It is because he shared the human condition to the full that his overcoming the death which all die can effectively break the despair and fear of death, and so already breaks its grip on human life.' Also in Pilgaard, *Dåbsteologien*, p. 121, a connection can be seen with Paul's incarnation concept, Rom 8.3; Gal 4.4; Phil 2.7. Similarly, in Kümmel, *Theologie*, p. 171, Rom 6.10a is related to statements about Christ's sin-free life, especially in 2 Cor 5.21 and Rom 8.3, and he writes: 'Paulus hat nicht gesagt, wie er sich diese Verurteilung der Sünde, diese Entmächtigung der Sünde durch den Tod Christi genauer vorgestellt hat, aber wahrscheinlich ist daran gedacht, dass dieser Tod keinen Sünder treffen konnte und darum die Sünde traf, die über diesen Menschen kein Recht hatte ...' Cf. Thüsing, *Per Christum*, pp. 83-85, Siber, *Mit Christus*, p. 232 n. 108, Jervell, *Gud*, p. 101, Morris, *Romans*, p. 255, where the half-verse is also related to statements about Christ's sin-free life and solidarity with man. Then, in practice, the interpretation becomes not very different from my outline. These interpreters read between the lines, so to say, ideas about Jesus' earthly life and content of life. I suggest that these ideas are expressed directly in Rom 6.10b.

52. Cf. Gäumann, *Taufe*, p. 85f., Halter, *Taufe*, p. 63.

According to Rom 6.11a, the Christ-events are of such significance to the Christians that they can consider themselves νεκροὺς τῇ ἁμαρτίᾳ. This is the vital break with the hopeless Adamite existence that leads to eternal death (Rom 5.12-21), for Christ's death indeed means that the threat of eternal death is removed so that the power of sin has also disappeared. In this sense the Christians have put death behind them. And Christ's death can be called a 'vicarious death' or a 'sacrificial death', in so far as it concerns 'punishment death'. This grievous aspect of death he took upon himself although he was innocent, and as a result of this the Christians escape the grievous death.[53]

The new, true life to God lies open to them, as can be seen from Rom 6.11b. This may be seen as the life over which the resurrected Christ is Lord. But it is also the life Jesus lived on earth. Both sides are indeed included when the statement is seen in the context of Rom 6.10.[54] And the Christians can (in the light of Rom 6.9) look forward to a life in which adversities and physical death are merely a transition to eternal life. Thus is the idea developed in Rom 6.23, and with particular clarity in the precursor-Christology in Rom 8.17.

Thus understood, the redeemer-Christology and the eschatological breakthrough of which Christ's death and resurrection are an expression are again a prerequisite for the precursor-Christology. Christ's life-pattern is clearly not an example one must live up to but a process into which one is drawn.[55]

This outline corresponds in many respects to universal interpretations of the details.[56] And this is confirmed by the fact that a similar thought-process is to be found in other Pauline passages.[57]

---

53. The distinction introduced in the preceding text between two aspects of death, on the one hand death as eternal punishment and cosmic power, on the other hand physical death disarmed with Christ, is therefore crucial. This distinction emerges clearly in Conzelmann, *Grundriss*, p. 308: 'Ohne Sünde gibt es keinen Tod; natürlich ist gemeint: keinen ewigen Tod ... Der Tod ist für uns dadurch erledigt, dass wir mit Christus gestorben sind. So kann der leibliche Tod unsere Gemeinschaft mit ihm nicht zerstören. Wir haben die Gewissheit der Auferstehung.' In Svend Bjerg: *Døden* [Death], Copenhagen 1975, p. 190, the distinction between unnatural and natural death is related to Rom 6.10. Cf. also the discussion above in note 8 in association with Schnackenburg, *Heilsgeschehen*, p. 37, and Chapter VI, section 1.2, with note 16, above. If the distinction is thus, it is possible, with the interpreters set out in note 46 above, to speak of a 'vicarious death'.

54. Cf. note 50 above.

55. Cf. Chapter VIII, section 2.4 above, and especially the parallel mentioned in note 83 in John's Gospel, where the disciples cannot immediately follow Jesus on his road to suffering and death. This becomes possible only after Jesus' resurrection and the overcoming of the power of death.

56. Cf. the interpreters mentioned in notes 43-53 above.

57. This is most clearly found in connection with the passages referred to in note 51 above: Rom 8.3 and 2 Cor 5.21, where there are statements that Christ lived under human conditions without sin gaining power over his life. This means that his death cannot be a

In any event, it is taken as read that reflections on the content of Jesus' life, death and resurrection are concerned. And it is this remarkable connection between redeemer-Christology and precursor-Christology which is bound up with the fact that both aspects reflect on the central salvation-events.

'punishment death'. This forms part of a description of the deliverance from the threat of eternal death (most evident in Rom 7.7-25; 8.2,6,13, but also in 2 Cor 3.7-15, where there is a reference to the 'ministry of death' which leads to hardening). The impotence of death has been demonstrated, and the Christians can live according to the same life-pattern as Christ, in that death has already been disarmed and becomes merely a transition to the life of resurrection (Rom 8.11,17,29-30; 2 Cor 4.7-5,10; 6.1-10).

X

The appeal in Rom 6.12-14
and the substance of the new life

1. The intention in Rom 6.12-14

1.1. The problem-complex in Rom 6.12

Μὴ οὖν βασιλευέτω ἡ ἁμαρτία ἐν τῷ θνητῷ ὑμῶν σώματι. So begins the last section of the part of the text to be examined. And this gives rise to certain problems.

Special attention has been given to the verb's form: βασιλευέτω is imperative. That is, from now on one is being admonished.[1] This has been seen as a problem in the context of the clear and apparently irrevocable promise of salvation in Rom 6.1-11. And we then have the classical 'indicative-imperative problem-complex'.[2] This dominates the discussion about both the subject-matter of the text and its background.

Much emphasis has been given here to the prepositional member ἐν τῷ θνητῷ ὑμῶν σώματι. This is considered to be the key to an understanding of the whole context. To speak of sin in association with 'the mortal body' is seen as stressing that sinfulness is still a relevant possibility for the Christians. The imperative is said to be necessary because the Christians are still not beyond the power of death.[3] It counterbalances the certainty of salvation which is developed in the preceding text.[4] The Christians should find them-

---

1. Gäumann, *Taufe*, p. 88, emphasises that it is the first paraenetic imperatives which now enter the context, in that the imperative in Rom 6.11 was an appeal to accept facts, cf. Chapter IX, note 24, above.
2. This tension between indicative and imperative established in Wernle, *Christ*, especially p. 104f., was vital to the whole discussion about Rom 6.1-14, as was shown in the research-historical survey above in Chapter I, section 2. The problem-complex will be discussed in section 2 below.
3. See Jervell, *Gud*, p. 102, cf. Gäumann, *Taufe*, p. 54, 88f., Käsemann, *Römer*, p. 168, Wilckens, *Römer* II, p. 20.
4. Thus Niederwimmer, Problem, p. 88, which concerns 'Korrektur', von der Osten-Sacken, *Römer 8*, p. 184f., which concerns 'Dialektik' and that man's mortality is conditioned by the fact that the atonement-death which occurred is merely believed reality, cf. also Bornkamm, *Ende*, p. 46ff.

selves in an interval in which they have 'already' been liberated from the power of sin but 'not yet' from the threat of its power.[5] Rom 6.12 can then be seen as a warning against the dominion of sin.[6] Or the imperative can be perceived as a call to decide in favour of the justice bestowed.[7] Or it should simply be a polemic against libertine pneumatics.[8] In any event, it seems that here is the real reason to be found for the necessity of the demand.

But this appears to be questionable. No one explains how the sentence is to cohere purely grammatically if the reference to 'the mortal body' is to be the decisive reason for the imperatives. The level at which the member is to have such great importance remains unclear. Is it meant to be a definitive point on Paul's part? Or can one simply read from the formulation what the background is to Paul's thought-process? It is also striking that the imperative is substantiated on a situation of want, in the continued mortality, and that the negative Rom 6.12 is given the main emphasis in a context in which it is essential to emphasise the certainty of the new life.[9]

One must then be aware of the introductory particles which are of great significance at the formal level and thus crucial to an understanding of the text's structure.

The word οὖν indicates that what is about to be said is a consequence of the preceding text.[10] It therefore signals that the promise of salvation in Rom 6.3-11 is the true basis of the imperatives.

Μή is demonstratively precedent. It is continued in Rom 6.13 with μήδε, and this corresponds to ἀλλά in verse 13b, which introduces a positive call. It is thus emphasised that the verse forms part of an antithetic context.

What these formally-indicated features involve for an understanding of

5. Thus Schmithals, *Römerbrief*, p. 194, cf. Bultmann, Mythologie, p. 30, Bornkamm, *Ende*, p. 46f., Dinkler, *Signum*, p. 232f., Kertelge, *Rechtfertigung*, pp. 255-57, Tannehill, *Dying*, p. 78.
6. Thus Dodd, *Romans*, p. 113, Kertelge, *Rechtfertigung*, p. 266, Halter, *Taufe*, p. 69.
7. Thus Gaümann, *Taufe*, p. 129, cf. Kuss, *Römerbrief*, p. 383, Schlier, *Römerbrief*, p. 202 ('… dieses neue Sein [muss] in seiner Neuheit jeden Augenblick existentiell ergriffen und durchgehalten werden'), Frankemölle, *Taufverständnis*, p. 95 ('… Paulus [ruft] die Hörer zur Verwirklichung des empfangenen Heiles 'auf'), von der Osten-Sacken, *Römer 8*, p. 185 ('Der Glaube vollzieht sich im Handeln').
8. Thus Schmidt, *Römer*, p. 113, cf. Schmithals, *Römerbrief*, p. 195: 'Ohne den Imperativ würde die Rechtfertigung des Gottlosen zum verfügbaren Besitz des Menschen …'
9. Cf. Agersnap, Rom 6,12, p. 36ff.
10. The word indeed expresses a connection between the indicative and imperative concepts, and this is what has led to the rigorous formulation of the indicative-imperative problem-complex, which is seen as a conscious contrasting on Paul's part — either paradoxical as stressed in Bultmann, Problem, p. 123ff., cf. Chapter I, section 2.2, above, with notes 26-30 — or dialectic as stressed in Bornkamm, *Ende*, p. 35ff., and by others, cf. Chapter I, section 2.3, above, with note 55.

the whole section, Rom 6.12-14, will be examined before I turn to the inherent problems of the verses.

1.2. The dominant antithetic structure

The close connection between Rom 6.12-14 and the preceding reasoning is apparent not only from the introductory οὖν. The schematic survey of the whole section's structure in Chapter VI, section 4, already displayed many lines of connection from Rom 6.1-11 which can now be further drawn together. There are connections on both the negative and positive sides.

If we first look at the negative side we have seen that sin's lack of dominion is pervasive, taken from Rom 6.1. In Rom 6.2,6-7,10-11, man's broken relationship with sin is emphasised, expressed both soteriologically and Christologically. And Rom 6.14a, which gives a clear reason for the appeal in Rom 6.12-13, also stresses that sin's dominion has ceased. Moreover, we can see that 'death' with Christ is a pervasive theme on the negative side. It expresses the absolute break with the old existence in Rom 6.2-11. And one might consider on the face of it that this is the idea continued in the word θνητόν in Rom 6.12. There seems to be a special connection from 'the mortal body' back to 'the body of sin' in Rom 6.6.[11]

The positive side is concerned with 'life'. The point of Rom 6.10-11 becomes that the Christians live 'a life to God'. In Rom 6.13bc comes the call to service for God, and the words παραστήσατε ἑαυτοὺς τῷ θεῷ ὡσεὶ ἐκ νεκρῶν ζῶντας point backwards to verse 11: λογίζεσθε ἑαυτοὺς νεκροὺς μὲν τῇ ἁμαρτίᾳ, ζῶντας δὲ τῷ θεῷ.[12] This gives a clear, indirect reason for the call. A direct reason is to be found in Rom 6.14, which also points out that the Christians are 'under grace'.

It is thus the general accord between negative and positive statements that continues here in Rom 6.12-14. Because hitherto the direction of the thought-process has been from terms expressed negatively towards terms expressed positively, the stage is also set for the emphasis now having to be on the appeal in Rom 6.13bc. This will be confirmed below.

The antithetic character is therefore to be found in the whole context of Rom 6.1, and it also continues in the following sections (as shown above in Chapter VI, section 3). But it is particularly marked in Rom 6.12-13. These verses have been constructed with two negative sentences: μὴ οὖν βασιλευέτω ἡ ἁμαρτία ἐν τῷ θνητῷ ὑμῶν σώματι εἰς τὸ ὑπακούειν ταῖς ἐπιθυμί-

---

11. Cf. Bultmann, *Theologie*, p. 198. But this very connection is disputed as we shall see when we come to the interpretation of the member ἐν τῷ θνητῷ ὑμῶν σώματι in section 1.5 below.
12. Cf. more specifically in section 1.3 below, with note 35.

αις αὐτοῦ, μηδὲ παριστάνετε τὰ μέλη ὑμῶν ὅπλα ἀδικίας τῇ ἁμαρτίᾳ, which corresponds to two positive: ἀλλὰ παραστήσατε ἑαυτοὺς τῷ θεῷ ὡσεὶ ἐκ νεκρῶν ζῶντας καὶ (παραστήσατε) τὰ μέλη ὑμῶν ὅπλα δικαιοσύνης τῷ θεῷ.[13]

There is thus a μή-ἀλλά correspondence. It is (like the equivalent οὐ-ἀλλά correspondence, of which we have an example in Rom 6.14) a widely used rhetorical figure called *correctio*.[14] This is a figure commonly used by Paul. There is a close connection between the first and second members, and in fact the first member has primarily to serve as a prelude to the second. What must be emphasised is the positive statement. The figure has marked preponderance. The first negative member may serve to *define*: one can make a statement unambiguous by drawing attention to its opposite. A new concept, a new set of facts, or a new thought-process is often best understood in its contrast to something already known. Or the negative member can simply be used to *reject* an imagined or factual objection. The objective is in any case the precise and wholly correct statement in the ἀλλά sentence.

The form thus signals that Rom 6.12-13a has no independent significance in the context, but is to constitute a prelude to the positive appeal in Rom 6.13bc.

It may also be considered whether this negative prelude functions to define or reject.

We begin with the second possibility, that the correctio figure is used to reject directly an objection, so that Paul can in this way ensure that his own view stands as the only correct view. The negation is thus given some weight.[15] But Rom 6.12 makes no direct sense as a polemic against an as-

---

13. Cf. Dinkler, Römer 6,1-14, p. 95, Frankemölle, *Taufverständnis*, p. 95f., Schlier, *Römerbrief*, p. 202, Schmithals, *Römerbrief*, p. 194.

14. Cf. the detailed description in Heinrich Lausberg, *Handbuch der literarischen Rhetorik*, Munich 1960, §§ 784ff., also *Elemente der literarischen Rhetorik*[4], Munich 1971, § 384.

15. This function is emphasised in Norbert Schneider, *Die rhetorische Eigenart der paulinische Antithese* (HUTh 11), Tübingen 1970, especially p. 121ff. where it is stressed in connection with Rom 6 that the negation is of essential importance (although the position's primacy is nevertheless maintained); by the negation, a direct reference back is effected concerning obvious misunderstandings or even contradictions on the part of men. Great fundamental importance is attributed to the Pauline antithesis. It is meant to produce a vital theological dialectic (p. 124f.). 'In ihr werden Gott und Mensch zugleich als Widerspruch sagbar' (p. 125). In connection with Rom 6, it is emphasised that the negation competes with the position, in that sin fights against God and is still a weighty reality, which will however (paradoxically enough) be overcome (p. 125). What is meant by this is not clear (pp. 72-76 contain some confused considerations about imagined counter-objections in Rom 6). What is assumed is probably that the negations in Rom 6.12-13 are meant to indicate something that is still a reality. This is a far-reaching interpretation of the extensive modes of expression. The questionable foundation is to be seen particularly in the definition of the correctio figure's function (*Eigenart*, p. 48). Here is chosen instead of the defining function which Lausberg emphasises in his definition in *Handbuch*, §§ 784ff.,

sumed adversary's assertion. Paul does not of course have to argue with anyone who claims that sin must have dominion over the Christians. Neither does he reject an assertion that the Christians are no longer bound to the mortal body, so that they would be beyond the dominion of sin and death.[16]

But in the larger context (Rom 6.1-14) Paul in fact takes up an objection and refutes it. And Rom 6.1 says directly what the objection was aimed at. This is quite a different assertion: that one must sin freely, since then grace will abound. This is probably intended as an indictment against Paul's teaching of justification, and the whole section consists of the rejection of this assertion. And here it is a main point on *Paul's* part, that the Christians are no longer under the dominion of sin and death. This emphasises the only correct attitude: to be on the side of God and of life. As a whole, Rom 6.1-14 may then be seen as a kind of *correctio*. It has the form 'does x apply?, no, not x, but on the contrary y'. This corresponds precisely to the compositional technique which it has been established that Paul uses, not only in this item of text but also in the following: an objection indicates the theme and gives directions for handling it, since not only can Paul refute the objection but he can also indicate the directly opposite point at which he wishes to arrive.[17]

There is thus a marked difference between what is rejected in Rom 6.1 and in Rom 6.12. In the first case, that the power of grace is so total that sin can be parasitic towards it; in the second case, that the power of sin must be total. They cannot be accommodated in one formula (which might be expected if it were a true conflict). And as far as I can see the more concentrated *correctio* figure in Rom 6.12 makes sense only as a negative de-

---

a different definition taken from Lausberg, *Elemente*, § 384, in which the figure is defined as 'die Verwerfung eines (von Gegner verwendeten) auf die Sache im Sinne der eigenen Partei nicht zutreffenden ... Wortes und dessen Ersatz durch ein im Sinne der eigenen Partei auf der Sache zutreffendes ... Wort.' The polemic is then predominant, and Schneider transfers without further discussion the definition to apply generally to Paul. But he ignores that in this second book Lausberg is chiefly engaged with 'Parteirede', which rests upon the rhetoric of the legal dispute (*Elemente*, § 1; *Handbuch* does not have this restriction, and the definition is therefore more general there). By the use of this definition, Schneider rashly assumes that Paul is in a polemic situation everywhere — and this is also the result at which he ultimately arrives.

16. Cf. Dodd, *Romans*, p. 113, Schmidt, *Römer*, p. 113.
17. See Chapter VI, sections 2 and 3, above and, as regards the discussion of factual versus fictitious background for the objection, especially Chapter VI, note 7. The compositional technique employed can be described as a *correctio* of the form 'x ... x? immo y', cf. Lausberg, *Handbuch*, § 785, in that Rom 5.20 brings the debatable assertion (x), which Rom 6.1 repeats in the interrogative form (x?), and 6.2-11 reads 'no, on the contrary ...' to (immo y). According to Schneider, *Eigenart*, p. 48, this is not to be found in Paul. This is because Schneider's investigation fixed unilaterally on the individual form-elements and ignored the context.

finition of Paul's positive point. When it says that sin shall not have dominion over the Roman community, it stresses that now, after the definitive
break with sin, there is only one possible demand: service to God. This is
confirmed by the dominant structure.

The larger context appears to show that we are dealing with a contrast
between before and now, in which the emphasis is on the enthusiasm for the
present certainty of salvation. The universal before-now structure in Rom 5-8
can confirm this cognition. Each section ends in antithetic formulations in
which life in sin is compared with the righteous life. It is clear that in Rom
6.19b particularly, where the usage from Rom 6.13 is resumed, there is a contrast between a past and a present form of existence in which any simultaneity is excluded, and the Christian has thus found himself in the situation
that he can only serve righteousness.[18] And no negative appeal is expressed
here; all that is said is that slavery to impurity is the possibility of the past.
Rom 6.19bc is thus Paul's own authentic comment on Rom 6.12-13. It can also be stressed that the before-now contrasts were already introduced by the
Adam-Christ typology in Rom 5.12-21, which also ends in antithetic statements about the contrast between the old Adamite existence and the new
Christian existence (in Rom 5.18,19,21, formulated with ὥσπερ-οὕτως, which
is resumed in Rom 6.19bc). And this of course is precisely the starting point
of Rom 6.1-14. It should furthermore be stressed that Rom 6.12 is in fact a resumption of the usage from Rom 5.21a: ὥσπερ ἐβασίλευσεν ἡ ἁμαρτία ἐν τῷ
θανάτῳ, which clearly applies to the past existence. When Rom 6.12: μὴ οὖν
βασιλευέτω ἡ ἁμαρτία ἐν τῷ θνητῷ ὑμῶν σώματι ..., returns to this means
of expression, one may immediately perceive this verse similarly: as a member in a contrast of an old and a new existence.

The form and placing of the verses in the context thus indicates that
Rom 6.12-13a concerns the past form of existence, and that its primary
function is to form a prelude to the true, positive admonition in Rom 6.13bc.
It is pointed out in advance that the verses are to be understood in this way.
Only if the substance is in opposition to this perception is there reason to un-
derstand it differently.

1.3. The battle-image in Rom 6.13

We can now turn to the inherent aspect of the interpretation. Since it has
been demonstrated that the emphasis is on the positive appeal, I wish first

---

18. Cf. Bornkamm, *Ende*, p. 48f., Tachau, *Einst*, p. 118, as stated above in Chapter VI, note 28.
    See in general Chapter VI, section 2, which showed that in Rom 6.1-14; 6.15-23; 7.1-6, and
    to some extent also in 7.7-8.39, there is a parallel structure in which the antitheses be-
    tween before and now become the final point, as they also are in Rom 5.18-21.

to pursue the positive line in the text, beginning with Rom 6.13. As the last member in the exegesis, I return to the debatable terms in Rom 6.12 about the dominion of sin and the mortality of the body, and examine what importance they may have in the context.

What is most striking about Rom 6.13 is that a battle-image is used. The recipients are not to make their limbs available as weapons for sin but to make them available to God.[19] The antithetic parallelism, which is especially clear in verse 13a compared with verse 13c, will be examined member by member.

In other contexts, the verb παριστάναι can mean 'present' or 'convey', as is the case in Rom 12.1 in which an image from a sacrificial cult is used. But the word often means 'make available', and it can be used about making military units and personnel available in a war situation.[20] A difference is to be observed here between the negative and positive sides. In verse 13a the present imperative is used: παριστάνετε, in verse 13b the aorist imperative is used: παραστήσατε. This is quite normal grammatically. The present imperative signifies the durative aspect; it is a formerly ongoing practice which is not to continue: 'You shall no longer (as in the previous existence) fight on the side of sin'. The aorist imperative is ingressive and contains an appeal to accept the positive consequence of the new departure: to go into battle on God's side.[21]

To the verbs in verses 13a and 13c is linked the same object τὰ μέλη ὑμῶν, to which predicates have been added that connect with one another, ὅπλα ἀδικίας and ὅπλα δικαιοσύνης. That τὰ μέλη in particular must be made available in the battle does not mean that the individual limbs were in-

---

19. Apart from the features referred to below: παριστάναι, ὅπλα and the contrasting of the two powers, sin and God, Rom 6.23: ὀψώνια, also supports that the figurative background is military, cf. Murray, *Romans*, p. 228 n. 17, Dunn, *Romans*, p. 337.

20. Cf. Bauer, *Wörterbuch*, col. 1244, Käsemann, *Römer*, p. 169, Cranfield, *Romans*, p. 598. It should be noted that although the word παριστάναι is used in two different nuances of meaning in Rom 6.13 and Rom 12.1, there is a clear connection between the two passages. In Rom 12.1, the admonitions are resumed with exactly the same verb and the same object, τὰ σώματα, as was used in the Letter's first admonition, and at the same time one has a before-now contrast as in Rom 5-8. Cf. Michel, *Römer*, p. 291, Murray, *Romans*, p. 109ff.

21. Cf. Blass, Debrunner and Rehkopf, *Grammatik*, §§ 335 and 337,1, Gäumann, *Taufe*, p. 89, Bauer, *Leiblichkeit*, p. 155, Frankemölle, *Taufverständnis*, p. 96, n. 289, Schlier, *Römerbrief*, p. 203, Morris, *Romans*, p. 258, who refers to The New English Bible: 'no longer put ...'. Wilckens, *Römer* II, p. 20, gives a different explanation which seems to be contrary to the antithetic structure: 'Der Aorist παραστήσατε in V 13b aktualisiert, was das Präsens παριστάνετε in V 13a generell sagt.' This necessary durative understanding of the present imperative has consequences for the interpretation of βασιλευέτω in Rom 6.12, as is shown in section 1.5 below.

tended, as distinct from the body.[22] It expresses man as acting, 'man in his actions'.[23] As regards the word ὅπλα, it is most probable that it concerns not merely tools in a broad sense but more especially weapons.[24] Since the weapons are defined as 'weapons of injustice' and 'weapons of righteousness' respectively, and it is not quite unambiguous how the genitive form is to be perceived. The genitives can correspond to adjectives, so that it means 'unrighteous weapons' and 'righteous weapons'.[25] But it is difficult to exclude that another meaning may be heard as well: 'weapons for impurity' and 'weapons for righteousness'.[26] What is then concerned is that one fights for the cause of injustice or righteousness in order either to spread injustice or to spread righteousness.[27] Two things are important in this context.

The earlier key word δικαιοσύνη has played no fundamental part in this very section of the Letter to the Romans. The crucial benefit of salvation is instead described as a new life. But now, in the paraenetic intensification of the thought-process, the word δικαιοσύνη again obtains a certain weight, which also applies to the continuation in Rom 6.15-23. There is no serious doubt that in this context the word has ethical significance. The only question is, what significance. It must still be fundamental that righteousness is a power whose source is in God's supreme act of salvation. Δικαιοσύνη then becomes the normative power, the demands and the obligations, which

22. Thus especially Bornkamm, *Ende*, p. 48f., where the dividing line between the Christians' limbs and the Christians themselves is to carry an important point: '... eben dies ist der betrügerische Weg der Sünde, dass sie nichts haben will als die Glieder und dabei den Eindruck noch vorgaugelt, als blieben wir selbst ungeschoren, als verfielen wir ihr nicht dadurch, dass wir ihr unsere Glieder überlassen "mit Haut und Haar".' Cf. Dodd, *Romans*, p. 113, Murray, *Romans*, p. 227f. It is a widespread opinion that τὰ μέλη ὑμῶν is to be understood primarily as a varied rendering of the parallel expressions, ἑαυτοὺς in Rom 6.13b and σῶμα ὑμῶν in Rom 6.12, as will be shown in the context of the examination of the latter expression in section 1.5 and notes 59-61 below.
23. Thus Jervell, *Gud*, p. 103, cf. Barrett, *Romans*, p. 128, Käsemann, *Römer*, p. 169, Schlier, *Römerbrief*, p. 203.
24. Cf. Michel, *Römer*, p. 157, Käsemann, *Römer*, p. 169, Viard, *Romains*, p. 147, Schlier, *Römerbrief*, p. 203. However, Cranfield, *Romans*, p. 318, wishes to consider the broader meaning of 'instruments', 'tools', with reference to the slave image in Rom 6.15-23. But there can be no sharp distinction between the two meanings if the word has this breadth of meaning.
25. This is then genitivus qualitatis, as suggested by Michel, *Römer*, p. 157 n. 2, with reference to Blass, Debrunner and Rehkopf, *Grammatik*, § 165.
26. Cf. Schlier, *Römerbrief*, p. 203: 'Waffen, die Gerechtigkeit bzw. Ungerechtigkeit erkämpfen, Gerechtigkeit bzw. Ungerechtigkeit durchsetzen u.ä.' This means that emphasis is given to the nuance 'Genitiv des Zweckes' from Blass, Debrunner and Rehkopf, *Grammatik*, § 166, cf. Cranfield, *Romans*, p. 318, du Toit, Dikaiosyne, p. 273, Morris, *Romans*, p. 258.
27. Cf. Halter, *Taufe*, p. 69f.

the Christians are facing.[28] In addition, the righteousness concepts can be perceived more broadly, so that what is concerned is the factual fulfilment of life which prevails in the new existence and becomes reality. This has been prepared for since Rom 5.18-21, where it became clear that the Christians are involved in the same form of existence as Christ. In the indicative part of this section, Rom 6.4 referred to newness of life, and it became clear in Rom 6.11 that the Christians live like Christ. The scene is thereby set for Christian fulfilment of life to be now concerned, as is also the case in Rom 6.15-23.[29]

There is also something to be said about the object of the crucial battle. What the battle is *not* about can at least be determined negatively. It is not a battle about the Christian person, since the Christians' location in the struggle is clear. They are weapons, and on the face of it their contribution must be directed outwards against the problems of the world. We are dealing with what I have called an '*extraverted imperative*', and what is therefore concerned is the tasks and the substance of the new life.[30]

The datives τῇ ἁμαρτίᾳ and τῷ θεῷ now remain in the parallel sentences. They refer to the two main antagonists in the battle. That is to say, sin is seen as God's antagonist. It is then clear that 'sin' stands personified as

---

28. Cf. Kertelge, *Rechtfertigung*, p. 156, 267, Furnish, *Theology*, p. 195, Käsemann, *Römer*, p. 169, Jervell, *Gud*, p. 102.

29. Cf. Schrenk, *ThWNT* II, p. 213 (who speaks of 'Lebensgerechtigkeit'), von der Osten-Sacken, *Römer 8*, p. 186f., du Toit, Dikaiosyne, p. 270f., 286, Schnelle, *Gerechtigkeit*, p. 86, Stuhlmacher, *Römer*, p. 87. See also Chapter V, section 3.5, above and especially notes 81 and 86 concerning Rom 5.18-21, Chapter VII, section 2.3, and Chapter IX above concerning Rom 6.4,11 and Chapter VI, section 2.1, above concerning Rom 6.15-23.

30. See my 1980 article, Agersnap, Rom 6.12, p. 44ff. The cognition that the paraenesis is directed towards tasks coming from without is to be found in Schrage, *Einzelgebote*. He emphasises that the specific individual commands in Paul are not an appeal for 'Selbstverwirklichung' and 'Selbstgesetzgebung', p. 82. God's will is still a norm confronting man as a voluntas externa, which meets the Christians in the paraenesis p. 83ff. Cf. also Halter, *Taufe*, p. 69f., Stuhlmacher, *Gerechtigkeit*, p. 224: 'Die Gerechtfertigten kämpfen im Dienste des gnädigen Gottes für das Recht der Treue ihres Gottes in der Welt', Käsemann, *Römer*, p. 169f.: 'In ihm [in dem eschatologischen Machtkampf] geht es zutiefst um die Frage, wem die Erde gehört. Es kann nur beantwortet werden, wenn das Stück Welt, das wir im unserm Leibe sind, aus vermeintlicher Neutralität herausgeholt und vor die Alternative des Dienstes für die Gerechtigkeit oder das Unrecht und damit identisch für oder gegen Gott gestellt wird.' By the last sentence, Käsemann nevertheless makes man the crucial object of the battle, and thereby joins the tendency to allow the battle to concern man's acquisition of salvation — a very widespread tendency, cf. notes 5-7 above. Against the interpretation that the imperatives concern the substance of the new life, it could be argued that very little specific is said here about this substance. But one should then be aware of the line clearly going from Rom 6.12-13 to Rom 12.1-2 and from the other parts of the Letter up to the paraenesis in Rom 12-15, cf. note 20 above, and the amplification below in section 2.4, with notes 133 and 137-42.

a power which can take possession of people.[31] This has indeed been the case in this context — since Rom 5.12. What is crucial, as developed in Rom 5.12-21 and Rom 6.1-11, is that there has been a change of authority.[32]

Apart from the antithetic parallel features in Rom 6.13, there are additional members on the positive side in verse 13b. As the first object for παραστήσατε we now have the member: ἑαυτοὺς (corresponding to τὰ μέλη ὑμῶν and to τὸ θνητὸν σῶμα ὑμῶν in Rom 6.12[33]). Then follows the same indirect object as in verse 13c: τῷ θεῷ. And as apposition to the object there is: ὡσεὶ ἐκ νεκρῶν ζῶντας.

The member ὡσεὶ ἐκ νεκρῶν ζῶντας must be understood as a justification. This applies even though ὡσεί cannot be assigned purely causal meaning but must be seen as a comparison particle, an 'as if'.[34] That this is a justification is in fact to be seen from quite different features. We are dealing with a participial expression, and the substance refers back to the crucial promise of salvation in Rom 6.11: that the Christians have died to sin and live to God.[35] One would then immediately understand this as a reference in support of the appeal for an effort for God.

The problem is, how to interpret the comparative ὡσεί. Without this member the statement is very far-reaching: it implies that the Christian Romans are 'living from the dead'. We then have, for the first time in this text, the resurrection concept used directly in relation to the Christians.[36] It

31. Cf. Bornkamm, *Ende*, p. 48, Schlier, *Römerbrief*, p. 203, du Toit, Dikaiosyne, p. 270.
32. Cf. Tannehill, *Dying*, p. 14ff., Güttgemanns, *Apostel*, p. 223, Siber, *Mit Christus*, p. 227, Dinkler, Römer 6,1-14, p. 95 n. 19, Jervell, *Gud*, p. 103, Käsemann, *Römer*, p. 171, du Toit, Dikaiosyne, p. 267.
33. The connection between these members will be discussed in section 1.5 below.
34. The meaning of ὡσεί is the subject of debate. A certain weight is given to the comparative function in Zahn, *Römer*, p. 312, Gäumann, *Taufe*, p. 90, Käsemann, *Römer*, p. 169, Blass, Debrunner and Rehkopf, *Grammatik*, § 425,4 n. 5, Bauer, *Wörterbuch*, col. 1777, Wilckens, *Römer* II, p. 21 n. 76, in which there is a direct argument against a purely causal understanding. Emphasis is given to the causal function in Kühl, *Römer*, p. 210, Michel, *Römer*, p. 17, Kuss, *Römerbrief*, p. 384, Merk, *Handeln*, p. 29f. But it is rare that the comparative function is completely excluded as in Cranfield, *Romans*, p. 318, Schnelle, *Gerechtigkeit*, p. 85, in which it is asserted that ὡσεί does not restrict the realistic in the statement, which it is sought to support in n. 493 on p. 213 by a reference to 1 Cor 15.8 (which reads ὡσπερεὶ τῷ ἐκτρώματι — but it can scarcely be seen as a realistic description of Paul that he is an abortion!).
35. Cf. Gäumann, *Taufe*, p. 90, who states that there is a reference back to the term in Rom 6.11b; von der Osten-Sacken, *Römer 8*, p. 85 n. 31, corrects: it refers back to the whole of Rom 6.11. It may be said with absolute precision that it refers back to verse 11, with the emphasis on the positive part of the statement: the life that follows after 'death' to sin.
36. As emphasised in Siber, *Mit Christus*, p. 239. Cf. Wedderburn, Traditions, p. 339, *Baptism*, p. 43ff., where however it cannot be immediately seen as pure resurrection terminology. It is translated 'from (amongst) the dead', and 'death' is seen as an image of the previous

is quite clear in the context that the radical expression is not to be understood literally.[37] This is indeed also indicated by ὡσεί.

The particle is therefore often understood as a strong restriction of the statement, an eschatological reservation relative to the reality of the new life: the Christians participate only in a provisionally way in Christ's resurrection.[38] Or it is emphasised that there is a distance between who the addressees in fact are, with their mortal body, and what they must consider themselves to be according to Rom 6.11.[39] Against this it may be immediately objected that the entire preceding context stresses the crucial new departure — not the defects. And here in the verse these negative circumstances are in no way emphasised.[40]

But apart from this the question of what precisely the particle refers to is missed in the discussion. It is apparently assumed that ὡσεί must be linked to the whole expression ἐκ νεκρῶν ζῶντας, with the emphasis on the last member. But in the context this cannot be correct. Rom 6.3-11 in fact emphasises quite unreservedly that the Christians have received the new life. Thus ὡσεί cannot directly afterwards be seen as restrictive relative to the reality of this life. It cannot be the intention of the formulation that the ζῶντας which is common to Rom 6.11 and Rom 6.13 should be shaken. It has been established that in the preceding verses Paul has used the concept of the Christians' death metaphorically, and has in fact said nothing about their resurrection. The scene is then set for the comparison particle to stress that the figurative usage continues here. The Christians have not literally put death behind them. Thus ὡσεί refers exclusively to ἐκ νεκρῶν, and only the reality in this term is restricted. It is also quite natural grammatically for ὡσεί to be connected to what immediately follows.

The justification in Rom 6.13b must therefore be understood as follows: 'since you are certainly alive as if (following a resurrection) from the dead.' And this is still indeed a strong and radical expression for the assurance of salvation. One must therefore agree with Wedderburn in his evaluation that Paul would not have used such a strong method of expression if he had had

---

situation of sinfulness in line with Col 2.13 and the Letter to the Ephesians. But this idea forms no part of the picture in the earlier verses in Rom 6. This meaning is not therefore probable.

37. Cf. the difficulties of a realistic understanding in Schnelle, *Gerechtigkeit*, p. 87, as shown in note 34 above.

38. Cf. Schmidt, *Römer*, p. 113, Siber, *Mit Christus*, p. 240f., Käsemann, *Römer*, p. 169, von der Osten-Sacken, *Römer 8*, p. 185 n. 31.

39. Cf. von der Osten-Sacken, *Römer 8*, p. 185 n. 31, Wilckens, *Römer II*, p. 21 n. 76.

40. Thus in particular Schlier, *Römerbrief*, p. 204.

problems with antagonists who hinted that they had already been resurrected and had overcome the power of death.[41]

1.4. Rom 6.14: justification for the call to battle

That the real justification for the call is inherent in the definitive assurance
of salvation is confirmed when we arrive at Rom 6.14.

In Rom 6.14a, Paul returns to the final break with sin: ἁμαρτία γὰρ ὑμῶν
οὐ κυριεύσει. This is to be seen in the context of Rom 6.2-11 and the continual reference to the Christians being 'dead' to sin and so beyond its
dominion. Moreover, there is a clear connection with the imperative expression in Rom 6.12: μὴ οὖν βασιλευέτω ἡ ἁμαρτία ἐν τῷ θνητῷ ὑμῶν σώματι. We can thus see that we have not merely an indicative-imperative
linking together. The pattern is: indicative — imperative — indicative
again.[42] This indicates that the promise of salvation is real and dominant in
the context.

There are certainly attempts to understand differently the future form
κυριεύσει. Some indicate the exclusively futurist understanding of the verse:
that only sometime will the power of sin be abolished.[43] But thereby Paul
would have taken back everything he has said in the preceding text — but
without having emphasised this in any way. Others wish to understand the
future form as a variant of an imperative: that Rom 6.14a must also be an
appeal to counteract the dominion of sin.[44] But this also would be a weakening of the statement. The context demands that we perceive κυριεύσει as
a future form which expresses certainty: neither now nor in the future will
sin be able to have dominion over the Christians.[45]

---

41. See Wedderburn, Traditions, p. 339, *Baptism*, p. 43ff. Cf. Chapter VII, section 4.3, item 5,
    above.
42. Cf. Halter, *Taufe*, p. 71, Schmithals, *Römerbrief*, p. 195. Note also that we have the same
    pattern in other passages discussed in connection with the 'indicative-imperative prob-
    lem': Rom 8.14; 1 Cor 10.13; Phil 2.13 follow up the admonition by a renewed promise of
    divine assistance, cf. the examination of these passages below.
43. Cf. Pilgaard, *Dåbsteologien*, p. 127, and Dunn, *Romans*, p. 339, who speaks of
    'eschatological reservation'.
44. Thus James Moffatt's translation in Dodd, *Romans*, p. 106, cf. Dodd's own comments, p.
    114. Similarly, this is considered in Jervell, *Gud*, p. 103, Cranfield, *Romans*, p. 319, but it
    is accepted that the interpretation is improbable because it is emphasised by γάρ in Rom
    6.14 that this is a justification.
45. Cf. Bornkamm, *Ende*, p. 48, Schmidt, *Römer*, p. 113, Kertelge, *Rechtfertigung*, p. 268, Mur-
    ray, *Romans*, p. 228, Käsemann, *Römer*, p. 171, Wilckens, *Römer* II, p. 22, and Schnelle, *Ge-
    rechtigkeit*, p. 87, who therefore sees a tension relative to the other future forms in the
    section. Cf. the evaluation of the future forms in Rom 6.5,8 in Chapter VII, section 3.6,
    and Chapter VIII, section 1.5, above.

This negatively expressed justification rests upon the crucial, positive assertion in Rom 6.14c: that the Christians are under grace. The mention of the law in Rom 6.14b is again a subsidiary theme. The statement has no clear, relevant significance here. It is simply a preparation for subsequent discussion later in Rom 7.[46] What is crucial is grace. Its strength makes sin powerless. Thus must the statement be understood. And this also accords with the line under preparation from Rom 5.21 onwards.

The subsequently justification given in Rom 6.14 therefore confirms what is also expressed by the introductory οὖν in Rom 6.12 and ὡσεὶ ἐκ νεκρῶν ζῶντας in Rom 6.13: that the call to battle in the new life rests upon the positive new departure.

1.5. 'The dominion of sin' and 'the mortal body' in Rom 6.12

If we now return to Rom 6.12, we can see that both form and substance in the surrounding verses prepares for its *not* being a crucial, independent statement. It seems at first that it is meant to concern the old form of existence which is no longer relevant.[47] If the verse makes sense in this fashion, there are no reasonable grounds to choose other interpretations. And examination of the verse will show it makes sense best if one chooses to understand it in accord with the dominant context.

First μὴ βασιλευέτω ἡ ἁμαρτία. This cannot be understood as a warning to the Roman community against sin's attempt to reconquer: 'Do not let sin exercise dominion over you *again* ...'.[48] Such a reading would demand an imperative in aorist; but now, just like παριστάνετε in Rom 6.13a, βασιλευέτω is the present imperative. It must therefore be seen as durative about the continued dominion of sin, which was the old situation. This can be demonstrated by adding clarifications — 'no longer' or 'as in the past': 'That is, sin shall not have dominion as in the past ...'.[49] As the introductory οὖν

---

46. Cf. Schlier, *Römerbrief*, p. 204, Schmithals, *Römerbrief*, p. 195f.

47. The verse is also thus interpreted consistently in Murray, *Romans*, p. 226ff.

48. Thus Jervell, *Gud*, p. 102, who with the emphasised 'again' shows that this paraphrase requires an ingressive form of the verb. This applies analogously to formulations in Dodd, *Romans* p. 113 ('warning ... against falling under a renewed dominance of sin ...'), Bornkamm, *Ende*, p. 48 ('... lasst sie [die Sünde] nicht mehr auf ihren Thron'), Dinkler, *Signum*, p. 231 ('Die Sünde ist tot; deshalb verhindert die erneute Herrschaft der Sünde!'), Schlier, *Römerbrief*, p. 202 ('Wir als den Befreiten sollen den alten Zwingherrn nicht wieder zur Herrschaft verhelfen'), and Wilckens, *Römer* II, p. 20, (who speaks of the demands which attempt, as the agents of sin, 'sich die Christen wiederum hörig zu machen').

49. Cf. note 21 above. See also Ernst Käsemann, Meditationen. 1. Korinther 6,19-20, in: *Exegetische Versuche und Besinnungen* I[3], Göttingen 1964, pp. 276-79; p. 276: 'Es ist ja nicht zufällig, wenn die Taufparänese Röm 6,12ff. es Zeichen des Daseins für Gott nennt, dass

indicates, the verse underlines the necessary consequence of the salvation indicative, which was developed and emphasised in the preceding verses. Sin's
dominion hitherto cannot and must not continue. It is an anachronism — a
non-possibility. Thus does the correctio figure function.[50] It is preparing the
way for the positively expressed consequence as the only one possible: to
live and fight on God's side.

The next member ἐν τῷ θνητῷ ὑμῶν σώματι contains several important
problems.

The first problem concerns the preposition ἐν. There is a tendency to
take it for granted that the preposition is local, and to see the mortal body as
the battlefield or the object of the battle that takes place according to Rom
6.13.[51] It is thus seen as a battle about man's final salvation. But now Rom
6.13a-c shows clearly the place that men have in the battle.[52] They are
weapons. It is not natural therefore to make them also the object towards
which the battle is directed. The appeal here seems to be turned outwards
towards a battle in the world.

It should also be noted that there are immediately grammatical problems
in understanding βασιλεύειν ἐν ... in the sense of 'having dominion over'.
This would be unique in the New Testament. Verbs that means 'to have
dominion over' and the like govern the genitive, as we have just seen in
Rom 6.14a. Paul normally uses the verb βασιλεύειν absolutely, intransit-
ively.[53] A reader will therefore naturally consider a different nuance of
meaning if there is a prepositional member introduced by ἐν. It may then
appear natural to understand the member ἐν τῷ θνητῷ ὑμῶν σώματι in Rom
6.12 instrumentally, so that what it concerned is that sin shall not have
dominion *by virtue of* the mortal body.[54] This construction is to be found
immediately beforehand in Rom 5.21: ὥσπερ ἐβασίλευσεν ἡ ἁμαρτία ἐν τῷ
θανάτῳ. And Rom 6.12 is presumably a direct resumption of the thought-
process from Rom 5.21, with a quite literal employment of the usage from

---

unser sterblicher Leib nicht mehr der Sünde zur Willen stehe, sondern unsere Glieder als
Waffen der Gerechtigkeit Gott gehören.' Cf. Halter, *Taufe*, n. 123 p. 549.

50. Cf. section 1.2 above.

51. Cf. Nygren, *Romarna*, p. 254, Käsemann, *Römer*, p. 169f., du Toit, Dikaiosyne, p. 279,
Pilgaard, Dåbsteologien, p. 127.

52. Cf. section 1.3 with note 30 above.

53. As regards the main grammatical rule, see Blass, Debrunner and Rehkopf, *Grammatik*, §
177, Agersnap, Rom 6,12, p. 40ff. Paul has, however, the expression βασιλεύειν ἐπί ... in
Rom 5.14 — otherwise it is used as an absolute, including four times in Rom 5.17,21.

54. Cf. my article on this, Agersnap, Rom 6,12, p. 36ff., in which this view is presented more
definitively. I wish here to approach this more cautiously, because it can be shown that
the widespread interpretation of Rom 6.12 as the crucial, emphasised statement is incorrect, whether the interpretation is instrumental or local.

there. It may support the instrumental interpretation, 'that is, sin shall have no dominion by virtue of your mortal body', that the verse then becomes inherently parallel to Rom 6.13a, which is also concerned that the Christians are not to be weapons (instruments) of sin.[55] One difficulty about the instrumental interpretation is the end of Rom 6.12, as it reads in Nestle's edition of the text: εἰς τὸ ὑπακούειν ταῖς ἐπιθυμίαις αὐτοῦ. This must be understood consecutively: one result of the dominion of sin must be the individual person's obedience towards (and forfeiture of) the desires of the body. A new element comes in. 'The desires of the body' are seen as something alien or perverted which take control of the individual.[56] In a flash one's thoughts are guided towards the theme in Rom 7.7-25. At first sight it would be most fitting if this were a consequence of sin's dominion *over* or *within* the individual.[57]

If one then, despite the difficulties, chooses the local meaning, it is still not reasonable to see the Christians' body as the battlefield or the final ob-

---

55. The difference in the mode of expression between Rom 6.12 and Rom 6.13 can be explained quite simply. In v. 12, Paul signals that he is resuming the usage from Rom 5.12-21, and we therefore have the rare imperative in the third person; in v. 13 he can formulate freely and he chooses the simpler construction, which also marks the subsequent context. Cf. Agersnap, Rom 6,12, p. 36f.

56. This should not therefore be seen merely as sensuality and passion, but as a power which intervenes in human life, usually perceived as egoism. Cf. Bornkamm, *Ende*, p. 46 ('eigenmächtige Lebensregungen'), Käsemann, *Römer*, p. 169 ('was ... zu Eigenwillen und Selbstbehauptung verführt'), Schlier, *Römerbrief*, p. 202 ('selbstzüchtiges Begehren', with reference to, inter alia, Rom 7.7-8), Cranfield, *Romans*, p. 317 ('Desires of the ego in its state of rebellion against God').

57. This can, however, also be combined with the instrumental interpretation. The member is then given a defining meaning: if sin dominates by virtue of the individual Christians' body, it means that they are obedient tools of the body's desires. But the varying way of reading is better suited to the instrumental interpretation: εἰς τὸ ὑπακούειν αὐτῇ; it merely becomes a classification that sin's dominion involves a total binding to sin in obedience. This reading is evidenced by P⁴⁶ D F G, among others. The reading εἰς τὸ ὑπακούειν ταῖς ἐπιθυμίαις αὐτοῦ preferred by Nestle and Aland, *Novum Testamentum*, is to be found in ℵ A B C among others. (The majority reading is εἰς τὸ ὑπακούειν αὐτῇ ἐν ταῖς ἐπιθυμίαις αὐτοῦ; but this was evidenced rather late and is a secondary attempt to combine the two other, already established readings.) The external attestation probably points to the reading given in Nestle's text. But the interior criteria seem to me less simple. In Bruce M. Metzger, *A Textual Commentary on the Greek New Testament*, London 1971, p. 513, the reading of the text is defended; the short reading is said to be a spillover from the repeated ἁμαρτία in the following verse. But this change seems to require a deliberate redaction of the text, and it is not quite straightforward in explaining why a transcriber should leave out the significant expression 'desires', which indicates Rom 7.7. According to Schlier, *Römerbrief*, p. 202 n. 22, Cranfield, *Romans*, p. 317 n. 2, Wilckens, *Römer* II, p. 20 n. 73, this is an attempt to improve and smooth over the text. But the possibility might also be considered that the short text is the original, and the reference to the desires of the body is a spill-over from Rom 7.7-25.

jective of the battle. One must still take into account that according to Rom 6.13 the Christian is still in the position of the weapon in an extraverted fight. Rom 6.12 must thus be seen as a prelude to Rom 6.13a. Verse 12 emphasises that sin shall not continue its dominion over the individual, so that he becomes dependent upon his own needs being met. Verse 13a says that this would mean that one is a passive tool of sin, and it rejects this possibility.[58]

It can be confirmed that the verse does not concern a battle between two differently directed forces in man when we come to the interpretation of the word σῶμα. Much significance in regard to the understanding of Paul's anthropology has been attributed to this word and its placing in the context — and this has led to an extensive discussion, which is relevant in one important point to the interpretation of the text itself here. The starting point is to establish that τὸ σῶμα is located wholly parallel to τὰ μέλη in verse 13a and verse 13c, and ἑαυτοὺς in verse 13b. Bultmann has interpreted this to mean that they are varying designations for man as a whole; σῶμα is not then something external which is different from man himself. Man does not have a σῶμα but is a σῶμα. And σῶμα in particular designates man insofar as he relates to himself.[59] Käsemann has protested against making σῶμα a neutral, ontological concept, and something to which one can relate at a distance; he has instead emphasised the surrender, that man as σῶμα is always ruled by one master or another.[60] This latter perception is confirmed by Rom 6.15-23. But it is important to establish that there is in any case a consensus that σῶμα designates the whole man,[61] who is either fully and wholly on the side of God and righteousness — or on the side of sin. What is concerned is not a dualistic inner conflict between body and spirit in which the battle rages within the individual man.

It should also be noted that the word σῶμα is in the singular, although

---

58. The connection between the corresponding positive appeals in Rom 6.13bc can be viewed in the same way: verse 13b is an appeal to bind oneself to God, and as a consequence of this one must, according to verse 13c, fight on God's side.

59. Thus Bultmann, *Theologie*, p. 196. Here one finds, spaced out, a longer definition: 'Er heisst σῶμα, sofern er sich selbst zum Objekt seines Tuns machen kann oder sich selbst als Subjekt eines Geschehens, eines Erleidens erfährt.' Man can thus conduct himself in one of two ways: either in accord with himself, or alienated, split in relation to himself (p. 196). Cf. also Conzelmann, *Grundriss*, p. 198.

60. See Käsemann, *Römer*, p. 168, cf. Zur paulinischen Anthropologie, in: *Paulinische Perspektiven*, Tübingen 1969, pp. 9-60; especially p. 15, 38ff., *Versuche* I, p. 19, 29, 276f., Schweizer, *ThWNT* VII, p. 1061ff., Güttgemanns, *Apostel*, p. 206ff., Gäumann, *Taufe*, p. 52ff., 90f., Bauer, *Leiblichkeit*, p. 152ff.

61. See Bornkamm, *Ende*, p. 46, Robinson, *Body*, p. 29, Merk, *Handeln*, p. 25, Cranfield, *Romans*, p. 317, du Toit, Dikaiosyne, p. 275, Dunn, *Romans*, p. 336, and also the interpreters referred to in the two preceding notes.

it is linked to a plurality: '*your* mortal body'. But it is clear that once again the singular form as in Rom 6.6 is used distributively.[62]

We have thus arrived at the last word in Rom 6.12 which has not as yet been considered: the adjective θνητόν. And this is perhaps the member which has been most emphasised. But it must be stressed that it cannot be a specific point that the Christians are characterised by the body's mortality.

The connection backwards to Rom 6.6 must first be pointed out. This reads that 'our old man', the body, insofar as it is determined by sin, is destroyed, so that it escapes the power of sin. When Rom 6.12 now speaks of 'the mortal body', which is to be beyond the power of sin, one will initially perceive this as the same entity - the body as it was before 'death with Christ'.[63] On the face of it, then, no paraenesis directed against 'the mortal body' is concerned. It is an appeal to the Christians to accept the consequence of the break; this is underlined both before and after, and indicates that mortality is no longer to characterise the Christians' life. In strict logic, it may perhaps be seen as superfluous to deliver an appeal to abstain from sin when what is concerned is no longer a factual possibility.[64] But it is an effective stylistic means: if two modes of action are compared side by side, and it is made clear that one of them is no longer possible, the other will be forcefully emphasised. It then becomes the function of the verse to indicate the only way in which one can live, as is positively expressed in Rom 6.13bc.

If nevertheless it is wished to assert that τὸ θνητὸν σῶμα refers to the Christian's current situation,[65] mortality cannot continue to be seen as an accentuated reservation, since in the parallel members in Rom 6.13b it is stressed that the Christians are to be considered as beyond the power of death. And again this is indeed what is underlined in Rom 6.3-11 and Rom 6.14, which function as a clear justification of the appeals in Rom 6.12-13. It can at most be an admission,[66] but even then without independent emphasis in the context. One may therefore be surprised at the assertion that it

---

62. Cf. Chapter VIII, section 1.2 above, with note 8.

63. Cf. note 11 above.

64. Thus Käsemann, *Römer*, p. 168f., in which it is argued that it is not possible for τὸ θνητὸν σῶμα to refer to the same as τὸ σῶμα τῆς ἁμαρτίας: 'Ihm sind wir in der Taufe gestorben, und Paränese ihm gegenüber wäre sinnlos. Es geht um die nicht nur von aussen durch die Welt, sondern auch durch ihre Vergänglichkeit bedrohte Leiblichkeit des Christen.' Cf. however Güttgemanns, *Apostel*, p. 222f., where Rom 6.12 is said to concern the previous 'Herrschaftsbereich, d.h. der Ort der Sünde', and where there is a reference to the importance of the cross: 'dass Sünde und Tod ihre Herrschaft verloren haben, und in eins damit auch den "Ort" ihrer Herrschaft, nämlich das durch sie qualifizierte σῶμα.'

65. And this is the opinion of the great majority. Cf. Käsemann, *Römer*, p. 169, and the interpreters referred to in notes 3-8 above.

66. As in Rom 8.10-14, cf. Chapter VI, section 2.3, above, with notes 59-64.

is still possible for the Christian to sin by reason of the mortal body.[67] In fact Paul says only the opposite: that it is impossible!

Paul therefore presents the matter in such a way that for the Christians there is only one real possibility: to live the new life and to serve God, as is also amplified in Rom 6.15-7.6. If one still thinks that the body's mortality is the key to an understanding of the indicative-imperative problem, one must work on a different level — go behind Paul's formulations and try to analyse his motives and his historical background.

2. The background to the indicative-imperative formulations in Rom 6

2.1. The problem of the imperative

In this section of text, we can again see that the Pauline intention is quite unambiguous: it is an encouragement to accept the full consequences of the breakthrough of the new life.

And again there may be reason to go behind the text and examine its background. This should serve to clarify the relationship between the Christological-soteriological part of Rom 6.1-14 and the paraenetic part. In reviewing the text, I have emphasised the direct connection between the two sides. But it is indeed normal that one finds tensions in and amidst the text. This is what is discussed under the 'indicative-imperative problem' label.

There may be several reasons to explain why the relationship between indicative and imperative statements is seen as tension-charged and questionable.

In the first place, the original formulation of the problem in Wernle and the religio-historical school assumed that the promise of salvation in Rom 6.1-11 involved a Christ-mysticism with freedom from sin in which the Christian lived an entirely spiritual existence. And any imperative should then be superfluous; it could be explained as a more down-to-earth attitude, or perhaps as a relic from Paul's Jewish past.[68]

Secondly, the problem is to be found later in Bultmann and his successors in an intensified formulation — a pure paradox: the imperative is a request to take possession of the salvation which is already bestowed according to the salvation indicative.[69]

---

67. See Dodd, *Romans*, p. 113: 'Yet it is possible that though sin need no longer reign, the man will nevertheless allow it to reign. It is possible for him still to let sin have his members for the service of vice.'

68. See especially Wernle, *Christ*, p. 103ff., Holtzmann, *Lehrbuch* II, p. 164ff., Windisch, *Taufe*, p. 167ff., Problem, p. 265ff., cf. also Linton, *Brev*, p. 298. See also Chapter I, section 2.1, above, with note 6.

69. Thus Bultmann, Problem, p. 131ff., Mythologie, p. 30, cf. Chapter I, sections 2.2 and 2.3 above, with notes 26-30, 58 and 60.

If a position is to be adopted in regard to these opinions, religio-historical and traditio-historical parallels also become significant.

But thirdly it seems to me that there are some additional and fundamental prerequisites for presenting the problems. There exists a set of ideas in regard to what the imperative form involves. These are viewpoints which rarely appear directly but are the foundation of many presentations. It is assumed that the imperative expresses an absolute demand, an appeal to the Christians' will, and that it is a symptom of something still lacking in the new life. In particular, it often appears to be taken for granted that the use of the imperative assumes that there is more than one possibility. And because this is assumed to mean that there must also be two (equal) possibilities after the breakthrough of the new life the emphasis comes to be placed on the acquisition of salvation: that a decision has to be continually taken in the new existence, that life is threatened, and that the Christians' mind is a battlefield.[70] Thus there are tensions in relation to the unconditional promise of salvation in Rom 6.1-11. There are also tensions in relation to the structure in Rom 6.12-14, where the correctio figure, as we have seen, indicates the one remaining possibility.

For this reason, I shall begin the discussion with a few fundamental reflections on the function of the imperative.

That Rom 6.12-14 is considered to be tension-charged, and that on the whole the connection between indicative and imperative expressions present problems, this is in my opinion primarily because the attention given to the imperative form is too great and too uniform.

---

70. Thus Ridderbos, *Paulus*, p. 176, who sees the imperative as a categorical demand, Jervell, *Gud*, p. 104, who interprets the appeal as expressing that the baptised are still in 'the danger zone', Gäumann, *Taufe*, p. 132, who emphasises, on the one hand, that the connection with Rom 5.12-21 excludes that salvation can be effected by an act of free will but nevertheless considers, on the other hand, that Paul must dissociate himself from the misunderstanding 'dass das Heil völlig mystisch-naturhaft über die Menschen kommt', and thus there must nevertheless be another possibility: to abuse freedom from sin, p. 129. See also Bornkamm, *Ende*, p. 48ff., where it is indeed emphasised that the Christian no longer has two equal possibilities (cf. above, note 18 and Chapter VI, note 28), but where the new life is nevertheless described as a settlement between the powers of sin and of God; this is apparently because the new life is still hidden, so that the imperative becomes something which must now be grasped in obedience. Similarly, Tachau, *Einst*, p. 118, interprets the antitheses in Rom 6 to mean that in principle only one opportunity remains; but on the grounds that a demand would be superfluous if there was only this one necessary possibility Tachau rejects that Rom 6.19 especially was meant seriously on Paul's part (and he sees it as the 'human terms' Paul defends in Rom 6.19a). Also the emphasis in Dodd, *Romans*, p. 113, that Rom 6.12 is meant to express that it is possible for the Christian to sin (cf. note 67 above), reveals such reasoning.

It is certainly made clear throughout that in this connection the imperative cannot be used narrowly as a grammatical designation. The imperative also covers a mutual appeal, and for the most part also indicative passages if they contain a strong call for action. But then all these imperative formulations are generally taken as expressing admonition and demand. And this is too rigid.

Now, however, the trend is towards a more imaginative treatment of these forms. Willi Marxsen writes that the simultaneity between indicative and imperative is crucial, in that it may just as well be called imperative-indicative as indicative-imperative; what is essential is where the weight is to be located in the specific case.[71] Even more important are some considerations presented by Peter Steensgaard in quite a short article. He points out this simple fact: 'Durch den Imperativ werden eine Reihe verschiedenartiger formen des Zuredens ausgedruckt: Von Befehl und Forderung über Aufforderung und Ermunterung zu Erlaubnis, Einladung und Bitte'.[72] I have also myself in the past tried to present the imperative as content-determining and inviting, so that no tension arises relative to the promise of salvation.[73]

A revaluation of the New Testament imperatives on the basis of this cognition will give a different picture. One can then see that the imperative expresses not only a demand for an acceptance of salvation or a warning against damnation, upon which one immediately fastens. One is not always faced with opportunities of choice when the imperative is used. This can be shown by a number of practical examples. *Guidance* may be concerned: by imperatives, one explains how a problem is to be resolved, and often there is only one possible way. The New Testament has many forms of guidance. In particular, there is a need to define the substance of the new life. This is a recurring motif in the paraenesis, which will be shown later. The imperative can also express a *plea* to others. If something is requested it does not necessarily form part of the thought-process that one may receive a rejection. This applies to the practical requests and the wishes for the future which come at the end of Paul's Letters, for example 1 Thess 5.12-28 and Phil 4.2-9. Also, *invitation* and *encouragement* are expressed by the imperative. 'Come to me, all you that are weary and are carrying heavy burdens, and I will give you rest' (Mt 11.28). 'Enter into the joy of your master' (Mt 25.21).

---

71. See Marxsen, *Ethik*, p. 164f., 168f.
72. Steensgaard, Erwägungen, p. 118, with reference to Eduard Schwyzer and Albert Debrunner, *Griechische Grammatik* II (*HAW* II 1. Teil 2. Band), Munich 1950, p. 340.
73. Se Agersnap, Rom 6,12, p. 46f., in which I have stressed that the imperative indicates the substance of the new life, and Agersnap, Gudstanken, p. 111f., in which I further emphasise the imperative's invitatory nature.

'Rejoice in the Lord' (Phil 3.1). 'You also must consider yourselves dead to sin and alive to God' (Rom 6.11).[74] Consideration of alternative possibilities makes no sense here. There is only one thing to do: to accept. Even where the imperative is used as an *appeal* for a special effort, it expresses in many instances confidence that the problem is being resolved.

The most characteristic and universal feature in imperative formulations is therefore not that orders are given and decisions demanded; the most widespread use is the intensive address in which the listener is approached directly.[75]

There is thus no necessary inherent tension in the imperative being used towards those who have received the promise of salvation and love. On the contrary, the imperative often expresses confidence and proximity.

2.2. Religio-historical parallels

The parallel religio-historical material that can be indicated in Rom 6.12-14 is not in itself very significant. One has from the Isis mysteries a militia Isiacis, which follows the initiation to the deity.[76] Reference may also be made to militia spiritualis, which is particularly evidenced in stoicism.[77] But this should scarcely be perceived as a source of concepts, that the Christians are meant to be weapons in the fight for the new righteousness, since imagery concerned with battle and war is to be found in many other contexts, such as the Old Testament.[78] The battle-theme is particularly marked in apocalyptic contexts.[79] Jesus also speaks of an end-time battle.[80]

But on second thoughts the reference to 'militia Isiacis' may point in the direction of an important religio-historical cognition which has also appeared during the consideration of mystery religion. In the Isis mysteries, where an oath of allegiance must be sworn to the goddess and her service entered, a deep dependence upon the supreme deity is concerned. There are no demonstrable concepts about a new nature and a new divine

---

74. Steensgaard, Erwägungen, p. 123, indicates this example, cf. Chapter IX, section 1.2, above, with note 25.

75. Thus Steensgaard, Erwägungen, p. 122, 124. It corresponds to the cognition of all preachers that imperatives convey the message more urgently.

76. Thus Apuleius, Metam. 11.6, Plutarch, De Iside 27, cf. Chapter II, section 2.2, above, with note 78.

77. Thus du Toit, Dikaiosyne, p. 272 and n. 26 with reference to Seneca, Ep. 24.16.6, Epictetus, Diss. 22.29.27.

78. Cf. merely Isa 59.17, which is used by Paul in 1 Thess 5.8.

79. This also comes through in the New Testament. The end-time war is a universal theme in the Revelation to John, and the image of putting on armour is found again in 1 Thess 5.8; Rom 13.12; Eph 6.10-17.

80. Cf. Mark 13.7-8, with parallels, Mt 10.24-36; Lk 12.51-53.

intuition which enable the initiate to act with perfection by his own efforts.[81]

This applies in the same way in Rom 6.3-11 (although there seems to be no direct connection between this text and the mysteries[82]). In Rom 6 there is no suggestion that baptism would automatically, purely sacramentally, invest the Christian with a new spiritual nature which enables him to do everything correctly by his own efforts. Here also there is an external supreme power upon which man is dependent. 'Freedom from sin' means that the Christians have been placed in a new relationship to God. And it is entreated and exhorted that salvation will have lasting consequences.[83] The benefit of salvation is something external which confronts the Christian.

This cognition will have consequences for discussion of the indicative-imperative problem-complex.

1. The original formulation of the problem is without foundation if the salvation indicative does not imply perfection and an absolute awareness of standards. There is nothing surprising in the fact that imperatives emerge if redeemed man still confronts God and his will as something from without. There is also indeed a widespread recognition that an incorrect assumption was involved if one originally assumed the ethical perfection of the baptised and thereby created a tension in relation to the ethical demands.[84]

2. But neither can it be the case that Paul wishes directly to avoid a perception of salvation as possession of spiritual perfection.[85] He does not restrict himself relative to a doctrine of 'freedom from sin' by introducing a 'not yet',[86] for the idea of spiritual perfection has not formed part of the

---

81. See Apuleius, Metam. 11.6,15, cf. Chapter II, section 2.2, above and especially the concluding remarks in which it is established that the final point is the mystes' obedience and service to the supreme deity.
82. Cf. in particular Chapter VII, section 4.2, above.
83. See Chapter VII, section 4.2, item 6 and Chapter VIII, section 2.2, above, where it is shown that no sacramental mysticism or physical transformation of the baptised is concerned in Rom 6.3-8; on the contrary, it has been shown that the text is a protracted attempt to stress the certainty of salvation by way of arguments and conclusions.
84. Thus already Bultmann, Problem, p. 137, cf. Dinkler, *Signum*, p. 238, Kertelge, *Rechtfertigung*, p. 253f.
85. This applies whether or not this is seen as Paul's distancing himself from the enthusiasm towards which he himself inclines, cf. Niederwimmer, Problem, p. 87, or simply as an opposing attitude he is contesting, cf. Käsemann, *Versuche* II, p. 120f., 126f., 130. We can only establish that Paul's attitude is very different from Hellenistic mysticism. It is methodically incorrect to conclude immediately that Paul is expresssing an opinion in direct contrast to mysticism.
86. No 'not yet' is expressed, and similarly there is no trace in the text of a misunderstandable 'already'. Against Käsemann, *Versuche* II, p. 129f., Strecker, Indicative, p. 68, in which the apocalyptic-conditioned 'not yet' is to guard against the misunderstanding that salvation is an ensured possession and to stress its 'extra-nos nature'. It is

picture in the text hitherto. And as we have seen neither can the concept be supported that Paul makes a reservation in these verses.[87] There is no question that God and salvation are 'extra nos'.

2.3. Traditional baptismal paraenesis

Traditio-historical considerations will be included here which have for some time been pushed into the background.

At the time of the religio-historical school, it was pointed out that both the indicative and the imperative might originate from early-Christian tradition; it was baptismal theology and baptismal paraenesis that had different origins and came to be in a relationship of tension to one another.[88] But here Bultmann has rightly challenged the manner in which the observation was employed. There is no question of a contradiction, a logical defect, which can be *explained* by reference to Paul's having adopted two different, incompatible traditions. What is crucial must be to *understand* the connection.[89]

But if the text is now perceived in the exegetic section, and what is to be examined is its background, there may be reason for renewed consideration of the relationship between baptismal theology and baptismal paraenesis within the tradition.

This also arises in a 1952 article by Dinkler about the problem of ethics in Paul.[90] It concerns in particular 1 Cor 6.1-11, where he sees a tension between the baptism referred to in the text and the ethical which emerges in

---

just as correct to stress that salvation is 'extra nos', but just as incorrect to allow it to depend upon an eschatological reservation, for if salvation is extra nos it is not merely something temporal which will last until the final salvation supervenes. It depends upon the God-idea itself, upon God as the supreme creator always being outside and above man. Cf. my reasoning in Agersnap, *Paulusstudier*, p. 34f., and Dieter Zeller, Wie imperativ ist der Indikativ? in: Karl Kertelge (ed.): *Ethik im Neuen Testament (QD 102)*, Freiburg 1984, pp. 184-95; p. 192: 'Es ist auch nicht so, dass das Eschaton das Ende der Ethik bringt. In der alttestamentlich-jüdischen Apokalyptik ist es gerade eine Wirkung der Endzeit, wenn Israel zu einer Pflanzung der Gerechtigkeit wird'.

87. What Paul has dissociated himself from since Rom 6.1 is not a perfection theory but a libertine attitude in which one was to sin away to obtain more grace. And he dissociates himself unreservedly by saying that the Christians are beyond the dominion of sin. Cf. section 1.2 above, in which Rom 6.12-14 is interpreted in the context of the dominant structure, and section 1.3 with note 30.

88. Cf. Windisch, Problem, p. 268f.

89. See Bultmann, Problem, p. 131ff., cf. Chapter I, section 2.2 above, with notes 26-30.

90. See Dinkler, *Signum*, p. 204ff. (especially p. 224 where Dinkler stresses that he wishes to understand the connection between the two traditions in Paul), cf. Niederwimmer, Problem, p. 89.

Paul's attitude to the Corinthians' obstinacy.[91] Dinkler includes other passages, with Rom 6 as the key passage.[92] And he re-introduces here the viewpoint that both indicative and imperative formulations originate from the pre-Pauline tradition.[93] The imperatives have their root in the widespread and necessary baptismal paraenesis. The indicatives originally concerned baptism as a Jewish perception of purification, but were gradually affected by Hellenistic mystery-thinking, which converted baptism into an act of magic.[94] This tension in the tradition was encountered by Paul, and he sought to resolve it dialectically by making the indicative the mainstay and limiting the imperative, so that it should not longer be seen in a merit perspective. The ethical point thus becomes unconditional obedience towards God.[95]

Several objections can be raised against Dinkler's interpretation: assumption of a mysterious background[96] and of a tension between 'Sein' and 'Sollen'.[97] Moreover, what has merely occurred in relation to the religio-historical school's description is that the self-contradictory and illogical has been moved from Paul's own opinion back to tradition. But that traditional Christianity has linked together the incompatible indicatives and imperatives is probably no easier to explain or understand.[98]

What is important in Dinkler's work is, however, that the indicative-imperative problem-complex is associated with considerations concerning the

---

91. See Dinkler, *Signum*, pp. 204-11, 227ff., which also refers to a tension between 'Sein' and 'Sollen'.

92. See Dinkler, *Signum*, p. 228ff., which points in particular to 1 Cor 5.7; 10.1-13; Gal 5.24; Rom 6; 8.9-13; 12; Phil 2.12-13; 1 Thess 4.1-12.

93. See Dinkler, *Signum*, p. 232ff., cf. p. 228, in which it is also asserted that the conscious linking together of 'Sein' and 'Sollen' may be pre-Pauline, and the conclusion on p. 237, in which it is taken for granted that the problem-complex existed before Paul.

94. See Dinkler, *Signum*, p. 235-37.

95. Thus Dinkler, *Signum*, p. 235f., cf. p. 237.

96. See Dinkler, *Signum*, p. 231, in which ἢ ἀγνοεῖτε in Rom 6.3 is said to be evidence of a pre-Pauline conception of baptism, which is characterised without further argument as mystery-religious, and p. 235, which merely postulates a development from a Jewish-Christian 'Zwei-Wege-Lehre', in which the sanctification must be maintained, to a Gnostic-magical baptismal concept.

97. Cf. Dinkler, *Signum*, p. 228ff. But it is not obvious that there is a tension between 'to be' and 'to have to'. On the face of it, it may just as well be described as a connection. If one becomes a new man there are also new things one must do. There is a connection between the new being and the new mode of existence, and in a specific instance Dinkler himself establishes that the imperative applies to the new 'Seinsweise', p. 213.

98. Cf. Dinkler, *Signum*, p. 237, in which it is emphasised that traditional Christianity is presented with a theological problem in the conflict between sacramentalist salvation and continued ethical demand. It is postulated that the communities had a concept of salvation as a perfect ethical intuition (cf. the original, now rejected, formulation of the indicative-imperative problem above in sections 2.1 and 2.2, item 1, and notes 68 and 84).

baptismal paraenesis and its significance to the first communities. In many passages of the New Testament traces have been found of traditional community-teaching in which the new life and its substance are described for the newly converted.[99] I wish to refer briefly to important texts and observations which may throw light on the problem-complex.[100]

1 *Thess 4.1-12* is, in the context of the Letter, an important paraenesis introduced by both ἐρωτῶμεν and παρακαλοῦμεν. After a long backward look at the Thessalonians' vocation,[101] Paul asks them in 1 Thess 4.1-2 to continue to accept the consequences of this, and in their behaviour to abide by the traditions he has passed on to them. The dominant content of the admonition is that they must please God.[102]

1 Thess 4.3-8 amplifies what the will of God is. Holiness is contrasted with fornication, and covetousness is rejected with a reference to the fact that God has called the community not to impurity but to holiness. There accordingly follows a responsibility towards God, who is the avenger and he who bestows the Holy Spirit.

1 Thess 4.9-12 concerns mutual love. In relation to the Thessalonians it is in fact a superfluous demand, it reads; but this can always become even better.[103] And Paul repeats his earlier appeal for a quiet and industrious life, having regard also to the reputation among outsiders.

The intention, however, seems to be clear: Paul wishes the Christian Thessalonians to hold to the new life to which they are called and he wishes to strengthen them in their perception of this. There is thus again a con-

---

99. A pioneering work here is Seeberg, *Katechismus*, who has sought very categorically to reconstruct a baptismal teaching preceding Christian baptism, which appears particularly in the conclusion p. 268ff. Cf. also Dibelius, *Formgeschichte*, p. 239ff., and the critique in Schade, *Christologie*, p. 141f.

100. I here keep to the texts set out above in note 92. Apart from 1 Thess 4.1-12, these are passages which have been covered earlier in the thesis, and brief references therefore seem to be sufficient.

101. 1 Thess 2-3, which refers to Paul's successful introduction to the Thessalonians' and Timothy's continuation of the work, may be seen as a long extension of the prooemium's thanksgivings, cf. Bjerkelund, *Parakalô*, p. 134f., Dibelius, *1. Thessalonicher*, p. 1ff., Linton, *Brev*, p. 281, Schade, *Christologie*, p. 117, Holtz, *1. Thessalonicher*, p. 29ff.

102. Cf. Holtz, *1. Thessalonicher*, p. 152, who points out that the substantivised πῶς in 1 Thess 4.1 emphasises that the content, 'das "Wie"', belongs to the apostolic tradition. The view to be found in Kertelge, *Rechtfertigung*, p. 258, that what is most important for Paul is not the paraenesis' content but 'Bewährung og Bewahrung des Heils', is thus effectively countered.

103. Cf. 1 Thess 4.1, in which καθὼς καὶ περιπατεῖτε, has the same function: to stress a fundamental satisfaction with the Thessalonians. One should therefore be cautious in reading a specific discord with the Thessalonians into the text, cf. Dibelius, *1. Thessalonicher*, p. 19, Schade, *Christologie*, p. 136.

nection between the promise of salvation and paraenesis — now not expressed by the linking together of indicatives and imperatives — but the Letter as a whole has an indicative-imperative structure in which the first part underlines the accepted salvation and the second part the practical consequences of this.[104]

It is also clear that Paul here uses traditional material. He underlines this himself at both the beginning and the end.[105] It is a repetition and a follow-up of the teaching which took place at the entry to the new life.[106] One may also get an idea of the elements included in this traditional paraenesis. The demand for holiness leads the thought in the direction of the Old Testament-Jewish purity rules, which have come to be perceived as more ethical than ritual.[107] Similarly, traditional Jewish accusations of fornication and gluttony against the heathens may be the background to the warnings in 1 Thess 4.3,6.[108] And when warnings and demands confront one another in this way the antithetic structure which is to be found in other paraenetic contexts can be perceived: the good and the evil, the old and the new, are confronted with one another, and the importance of doing the right thing is enjoined.[109]

Thus there are several important motifs here in the paraenesis. The substance of the new life is pointed out, the positive by appeals and the negative by warnings. The importance of the correct course of action is

104. The connection is emphasised not only by οὖν in 1 Thess 4.1. In 1 Thess 4.7, as a step in the appeal for sanctification, there is a reference back to the Thessalonians' vocation ἐν ἁγιασμῷ.

105. 1 Thess 4.1,2,6,11. Especially παραλαμβάνειν in 1 Thess 4.1 is terminology for tradition, as stressed by Dibelius, 1. Thessalonicher, p. 19f., cf. Wernle, *Christ*, p. 27, Seeberg, *Katechismus*, p. 9f., Dinkler, *Signum*, p. 234, Bjerkelund, *Parakalô*, p. 132.

106. Cf. Seeberg, *Katechismus*, p. 9ff., which quite definitively indicates the baptismal teaching, Dibelius, 1. Thessalonicher, p. 20, Dinkler, *Signum*, p. 235, Holtz, *1. Thessalonicher*, p. 152, 171, who are more cautious.

107. See Dinkler, *Signum*, p. 234f., who points out that Lev 17-19 in particular is used with the emphasis on the ethical. In Lev 19.2 there is the call: 'You shall be holy, for I the Lord your God am holy', which resembles 1 Thess 4.3. And Lev 19.13 prohibits exploitation of one's neighbour, which resembles 1 Thess 4.6 (and 1 Cor 6.8). Cf. Philip Carrington, *The Primitive Christian Catechism*, Cambridge 1940, p. 19, Bjerkelund, *Parakalô*, p. 131f.

108. See Schweizer, Gottesgerechtigkeit, p. 462ff., Holtz, *1. Thessalonicher*, p. 168f., which indicates Test. Juda 18 and further to other Jewish texts which include a triad together with idolatry, and from here to the New Testament catalogue of vices of which these passages form a part.

109. In Seeberg, *Katechismus*, pp. 1-44, this is made into a member in 'die Wege' which is the name of the 'christliche Sittenlehre' used by Paul and which it is sought to reconstruct, with a starting point in 1 Cor 4.17; Rom 6.17, the passage here and the catalogues of vices and virtues, cf. Dinkler, *Signum*, p. 235. See to the contrary Dibelius, 1. Thessalonicher, p. 20, who rightly draws attention to the uncertain basis.

strongly enjoined. The demands are followed by a declaration of confidence, which clearly has an encouraging function.

A number of passages in the *First Letter to the Corinthians* must be considered.

1 Cor 5-6, in which Paul rebukes the Corinthians for sexual excess and obstinacy, has three notable collocations of indicative and imperative.

In *1 Cor 5.7-8*, Paul appeals to the Corinthians to clean out the old yeast because they are unleavened. And because the paschal lamb has been sacrificed celebration must be with sincerity and truth. This is a clear example of an appeal to accept the consequences of the new departure that has occurred, and to hold fast.[110] What is specifically involved is to eradicate the sexual impurity which consists in a member of the community cohabiting with his father's wife.[111] The passage is also notable because it is the only specific instance in which Paul says that a member of the community has placed himself wholly outside the new fellowship. It is noteworthy that in no other passage where he confronts errors and misunderstandings, which he combats, does Paul stamp the guilty as sinners who must be excluded from the Church.[112]

In Paul's final attitude towards the Corinthians' mutual litigation in *1 Cor 6.9-11*, the mainstay is the indicative in verse 11 about baptism as the crucial turning point in which heathen sinfulness was removed. The direct imperative is to be found in μὴ πλανᾶσθε in verse 9, while verses 9-10 amplify the content of this unrighteousness, which means exclusion from the kingdom of God.[113]

Here also are features which make it clear that Paul is commenting on fundamental community teaching. Paul shows this directly by the οὐκ οἴδατε ὅτι which introduces the section of text and generally characterises the context.[114] The reference to baptism and the catalogue of vices contains traditional-sounding terms with a Jewish background: the objective is purity and holiness, and there is a warning against fornication, greed and idolatry.[115]

---

110. Note the sequence, imperative-indicative-indicative-imperative.
111. This is a violation of Lev 18.8 and the general rules against incest in the Graeco/Roman world, cf. Dinkler, *Signum*, p. 228, Conzelmann, *1. Korinther*, p. 116.
112. Cf. Schrage, *Ethik*, p. 185. Gal 5.4 concerns a warning against analogous consequences; but there the error is still only at the consideration stage.
113. Cf. the examination of the text in Chapter III, section 4, above.
114. See 1 Cor 6.2,3,15,16,19, and cf. the meaning attributed to the analogous ἀγνοεῖτε ὅτι in Rom 6.3.
115. Cf. Chapter III, note 291f. above, and this chapter, notes 107f. and 111. This is the ideas-complex to which attention is drawn in Dinkler, *Signum*, p. 234f. cf. Seeberg, *Katechismus*, p. 9ff. As in 1 Thess 4, the sanctity rules from Lev 17-19 can be sensed as a background, and the specific case which Paul is contesting in 1 Cor 5.1-8 is indeed seen as a violation of Lev 18.8.

This again is concerned with a contrast between past and present existence; the turning point is clearly marked by the three-times-repeated ἀλλά in 1 Cor 6.11.[116]

The warning against delusion and backsliding emphasises the importance of holding fast to the new, as in 1 Cor 5.7-8. The catalogue of vices gives an inherent definition of the new life — although negatively: the borderlines for living in the kingdom of God are marked out. But the substance of the new life is thereby identified. It should also be noted that the negative and the threatening do not stand alone. The sequence is not indicative-imperative but the opposite. The importance of acting correctly is first underlined; then the power and the strength are pointed out, which are certain. Optimism and confidence are thereby expressed.

At the same time, the positive substance of life also comes into the picture in 1 Cor 6.11, which speaks of holiness and righteousness, of the binding to Christ as Lord and of the power of the Spirit.[117]

1 Cor 6.19-20, which is the third comparison of indicative and imperative in the section, indeed emphasises the positive consequences. There is a reference to the concept of the Christian's body as the temple of the Spirit of God, followed by an appeal to use the body to the glory of God.[118]

Besides this, the First Letter to the Corinthians also contains passages in which the paraenesis is linked together with a reference to baptism.

1 Cor 10.1-13 is a further example of limits being set to what one can do if one lives the new life in the ends of the ages. This is a community teaching about the importance of baptism and the Eucharist which links up to a fundamental insight.[119] By referring to the Exodus story, Paul shows what

---

116. Cf. Bachmann, *1. Korinther*, p. 243, Robertson and Plummer, *1. Corinthians*, p. 119, Conzelmann, *1. Korinther*, p. 129, Tachau, *Einst*, p. 83f., Halter, *Taufe*, p. 148, Schnelle, *Gerechtigkeit*, p. 38.

117. Cf. Kertelge, *Rechtfertigung*, p. 243ff., where ἀπελούσασθε is said to refer to the negative side of baptism (purification from sin), whereas ἁγιάσθητε is to emphasise the positive effect of baptism, which also has ethical consequences. The term ἐν τῷ ὀνόματι τοῦ κυρίου ʼΙησοῦ Χριστοῦ undoubtedly refers to the mention of this name at baptism and the link to Christ which results, as shown in the examination of the term βαπτίζεσθαι εἰς τό ὄνομα above in Chapter III, section 2.3, and the interpretation of 1 Cor 1.10,13 above in Chapter III, section 4. On the possible connection with the subsequent context, cf. Chapter III, section 4, with note 284, above.

118. This third and positive indicative-imperative connection in the context of the text is generally overlooked when considering the problem-complex. Cf. however Dinkler, *Signum*, p. 233 with n. 60, in which, among the passages that seem to connect the baptismal act and paraenesis, 1 Cor 6.19ff. is also indicated.

119. Cf. Lührmann, Freundschaftsbrief, p. 310, which sees this as an extension of Paul's 'Anfangsverkündigung'. As regards the item's possible traditional basis in Judaism and Christianity, see the examination in Chapter III, section 4, above, with note 292.

the sacraments cannot be used for: worshipping idols, committing fornication, challenging the Lord and grumbling, while relying on the assurance of salvation. This is again a warning against backsliding to the former sinfulness, as emphasised in 1 Cor 10.12: 'So if you think you are standing, watch out that you do not fall'. Here we again have an imperative which follows the promise of salvation, the foundation of all considerations. It is an appeal to hold fast to salvation. But the imperative is not allowed to stand alone. It is followed up in 1 Cor 10.13 by an indicative which expresses trust in God's continued act of salvation and help against any temptation. And in the continuation in 1 Cor 10.14-22 the binding to the Lord which results from the Eucharist is also positively emphasised.

1 Cor 12.13 has yet another baptismal reference as an important member in a paraenetic section.[120] And when Paul arrives at the imperative the emphasis is clearly on the positive - the substance of the new life. After development of the picture of the community as an organic fellowship comes the appeal to cultivate the greatest gifts of grace (1 Cor 12.31-13.13) and to work on building up the community (1 Cor 14). It may be noted here that to both Paul and the Corinthians possession of the Spirit is an important benefit of salvation, which is received at baptism. Nevertheless, practical and intrinsic guidance is required on how one is to use this Spirit in specific situations. Paul expresses no opinion as regards a concept that the Spirit is to make its bearers ethically perfect.[121]

Gal 5.25 links together indicative and imperative terms in a very distinctive way: εἰ ζῶμεν πνεύματι, πνεύματι καὶ στοιχῶμεν. Most commentators consider this to be a clear example of the indicative and imperative inherently covering one another.[122] But this is so only at first sight.

Viewed in isolation, 'walking by the Spirit' may mean the same as 'living by the Spirit' — although στοιχεῖειν involves greater emphasis on moral behaviour.[123] But as soon as the verse is seen in context it becomes clear that the substance of the two half-verses is different.

Verse 25a about living by the Spirit must be seen in the context of Gal 5.24 and the idea that the Christians have crucified the flesh and all its

---

120. Cf. Dinkler, *Signum*, p. 232f., see also the examination in Chapter III, section 2.1, above.
121. Cf. Ernst Käsemann, Amt und Gemeinde im Neuen Testament, in: *Exegetische Versuche und Besinnungen* I³, Göttingen 1964, pp. 109-34; p. 112, in which it is pointed out that the spirits must be tested by a critical standard from without.
122. Cf. Wernle, *Christ*, p. 89, Bultmann, *Theologie*, p. 334f., Bornkamm, *Ende*, p. 34, Dinkler, *Signum*, p. 228f., Kertelge, *Rechtfertigung*, p. 252, Conzelmann, *Grundriss*, p. 312, Kümmel, *Theologie*, p. 199f.
123. Cf. Koch, *Galaterbrevet*, p. 155f. ('stand in line', 'stand together'), Schlier, *Galater*, p. 268 ('wandeln', 'sich halten an'), Wendland, *Ethik*, p. 49 ('tathafte Lebensführung'), Betz, *Galatians*, p. 293f. ('be drawn up in line', 'follow').

desires. It is thus a summary of the salvation indicative, which refers back to the many characteristic formulations in the Letter about the crucial turning point.[124]

Verse 25b points forward. The appeal in this verse is indeed amplified by detailed instructions on what is involved in the spiritual life, Gal 5.26-6.10.[125] Initially, it says negatively that self-assertion at the expense of others is excluded in the new life. Thereafter it urges tolerance, solidarity, self-criticism and responsibility. The tone is optimistic and encouraging, with the urgent personal address in Gal 6.1: My friends, you who have received the Spirit.[126] It is again shown that possession of the Spirit does not make the admonition superfluous, but on the contrary it is the starting point for the guidance.

Here the emphasis is thus especially on the positive imperative, where it is sought to define the substance of the new life. But the other traditional aspects of paraenesis are also part of the picture. As a prelude to the description of the crucial turning point there are characteristic before-now antitheses. They follow after another linking together of the indicative-imperative, Gal 5.13. The imperative follows after a reference to the Christian freedom, and contains both a warning against backsliding and an appeal for love. Gal 5.16-23 continues with σάρξ-πνεῦμα contrasts and a catalogue of vices compared with a catalogue of virtues. It is apparent that Paul uses pre-formulated material in his attempt to identify the substance of the new life.[127]

In *Phil 2.12* we again have an imperative which is derived from a preceding promise of salvation. It is established that the Philippians have the obedience associated with Christ's obedience and exaltation, described in the hymn in Phil 2.5-11.[128] This is followed by a very strong appeal indeed: 'Work out your own salvation with fear and trembling!'. It cannot be denied

---

124. Thus emphasised by Betz, *Galatians*, p. 293. Cf. the examination of Gal 5.24 and the other central statements in the Letter to the Galatians in Chapter III, section 3.2, and Chapter IV, section 3.3, above.
125. Cf. Schlier, *Galater*, p. 269, Mussner, *Galaterbrief*, p. 396.
126. Cf. Mussner, *Galaterbrief*, p. 396ff., Betz, *Galatians*, p. 295ff.
127. Paul says directly in Gal 5.21 that he is repeating the earlier teaching. The catalogue of vices also has the traditional structure, and emphasises that these specific vices involve exclusion from the kingdom of God. Cf. Seeberg, *Katechismus*, p. 9ff., who considers the passage an important example of 'die Wege', the fundamental baptismal catechesis, cf. Schlier, *Galater*, p. 255, Betz, *Galatians*, p. 284f. The missionising preaching is indicated as a background in Mussner, *Galaterbrief*, p. 383, Peder Borgen, Observations on the Theme 'Paul and Philo', in: Sigfred Pedersen (ed.), *Die Paulinische Literatur und Theologie*, Århus 1980, pp. 85-102.
128. Cf. Chapter III, section 3.2, above.

here that the imperative applies to the acquisition of salvation or adherence to salvation. But it must be established that the imperative is immediately followed by a new indicative in Phil 2.13, which underlines that it is ultimately God himself who ensures that salvation is affirmed.[129] It may also be pointed out that positive imperatives concerned with the substance of the new life come both before and after.

These passages show that the paraenesis in the Pauline Letters must be seen in the context of the instruction that took place at the transition to the new life. Whether this is a true baptismal paraenesis or an instruction placed elsewhere in the repentance process is of secondary importance in this context. What is vital is to see how the interest is directed towards the development of the new life which repentance and baptism have brought about. There is a need from the outset for information about and adjustment to the new conditions. There is also, therefore, from the outset a natural connection between indicative and imperative.

And there is a connection between the various functions which imperatives have. Imperatives can be formulated positively or negatively. They can be directed outwards towards the tasks of the new life, or they can be directed inwards as an appeal to the individual to decide. There are thus four main types (which are indeed connected). The substance is defined negatively when the (comparatively broad) limits that must not be overstepped in the new life are indicated.[130] Positively, quite vague rules and guidelines as regards the substance of the new life are given.[131] Negatively, there is a warning against backsliding which stresses the need to hold fast to the salvation bestowed. And there are positive appeals to accept the consequences of the new departure, which should not be seen

---

129. Thus Conzelmann, *Grundriss*, p. 311. It may also be noted that the expression 'fear and trembling' should not necessarily be understood as anxiety and uncertainty concerning salvation; it can refer to man's humble position in the presence of God, cf. Braun, *Gerichtsgedanke*, p. 62, Kertelge, *Rechtfertigung*, p. 254.

130. This occurs in particular in 1 Thess 4 and in the catalogue of vices in 1 Cor 5-6. One may observe that there are quite wide limits — an 'Entscheidungsspielraum', as mentioned in Schrage, *Ethik*, p. 183.

131. The positive paraenesis about the substance of the new life is to be found in 1 Thess 4.3-4,11-12; 1 Cor 6.20; Phil 2, and most comprehensively in Gal 5-6. There are several explanations for the fact that this aspect of the paraenesis is not more widespread, and may appear to be somewhat colourless. The paraenesis becomes sharper and more targeted if a borderline must be drawn than if one merely indicates a basic attitude. And the positive paraenesis cannot be made into a comprehensive and detailed description of the correct acts without risk of its becoming a new law with righteousness of action. Cf. Schlier, *Galater*, p. 255f.

only as a request for acquisition of salvation but also as encouragement and invitation to use the opportunities of the new life.[132]

2.4. Paraenesis in the context of the Letter to the Romans

If we now return to the Letter to the Romans, the pattern is to be found again here also, and the function to receive the main emphasis becomes very clear.

In the Letter as a whole there is a connection between the different par-aenetic sections, so that there is a line from the weighty promises of sal-vation in Rom 1-8 via the paraenetic points in Rom 6.12-14,19-23; 7.5-6; 8.4-13 to the admonitory section in Rom 12.1-15.13.[133]

This line is confirmed in the conclusion to the Letter in Rom 15.14-16. Here, with many circumlocutions, Paul makes excuses for his rather bold way of expressing himself in the Letter. He is convinced that the Roman community already has the necessary quality of life, and is living up to the demands made. His purpose is entirely to refresh their memory (ἀναμιμνῄσ-κειν) in order that it may be certain that their life is the 'acceptable offering' it is meant to be. The objective of the Letter, according to Paul himself, is then to ensure that the new life is developed in the Roman community.[134]

---

132. The warnings in 1 Cor 6.9b; 10.13 and the appeals for decision in 1 Cor 5.7; Phil 2.13 directly concern 'acquisition of salvation', and formally there is tension between promises and demands for decision. But here the sequence is imperative-indicative, since the reinforced promise of salvation comes at the end and takes all pressure off the decision. The emphasis thus does not come to lie on salvation being threatened.

133. The connecting line shows itself not only in the linguistic and inherent connections from Rom 12.1-2 back to Rom 6 and its context, as will be outlined below. Thus von der Os-ten-Sacken, *Römer 8*, p. 256ff., indicates that Rom 13.8-10 resumes the ideas about ful-filment of the law from Rom 8.2-4, and that the ὥσπερ-οὕτως accord is resumed in Rom 15.7 in which there is an appeal to be in accord with Christ's solicitous way of life. And the paraenetic section in Rom 12-15 refers back several times to the Christological and so-teriological turning point which has occurred. There is a reference to God's acts of mercy (Rom 12.1), to the community's gifts of grace and unity ἐν Χριστῷ (Rom 12.3-8), to Christ who, following death and resurrection, is universal Lord over both the dead and the living (Rom 14.6-9), to Christ's sacrificial death (Rom 14.15; 15.3) and to Christ's example (Rom 15.1-7).

134. This (almost) direct information about the Letter's purpose is confirmed by others. In Rom 1.5, Paul presents himself as the apostle who must work for obedience of faith among Gentiles such as the Roman community. In Rom 1.10-13 he writes that he wishes to come to them so that they can be strengthened and he can 'reap some harvest' from them. In Rom 12.1, the introductory admonition is that the Roman community must present their bodies as 'a living sacrifice acceptable to God'. It seems that an essential purpose of both Paul's Letter and the coming visit is to ensure that the community is living the correct ethical life. Cf. Paul S. Minear, *The Obedience of Faith* (SBT 2. series 19), London 1971, p. 1.

This shows, first of all, that it is the substance of the new life towards which Paul is working. Secondly, Paul indicates by the expression ἀναμιμνήσκειν that he is using material of which the Romans would already be aware.[135] Thirdly, he expresses his confidence in the Roman community.[136]

That there is a line from promise of salvation to admonition in the Letter can be supported especially on the basis of Rom 12.1-2, which acts as a heading to the paraenetic section. The first positive imperatives in the Letter in particular, Rom 6.13,19, are taken up again, indicating the substance of the new life.[137] The introductory παρακαλῶ and the subsequent reference to God's mercy emphasise that this a crucial passage in the Letter.[138]

Rom 12.1 employs a usage taken from the cultic field. The appeal is expressed as follows: παραστῆσαι τὰ σώματα ὑμῶν θυσίαν ζῶσαν ἁγίαν εὐάρεστον τῷ θεῷ ... Three important observations may be made here. First, this is a clear resumption of the usage in Rom 6.13,19. Second, there is also an ignored but nevertheless important inherent connection with a central idea taken from Rom 6.1-11. One should notice the word used to refer to an 'offering' here: θυσία, which actually means a slaughtered sacrifice. And its meaning must inevitably strike a note when associated with the adjectival participle ζῶσα. It becomes a paradoxical expression, that one is at the same time to be 'slaughtered' — 'dead' — and alive. It becomes the same content-saturated play on the words 'death' and 'life' which dominate in Rom 6 (and which also appear in Rom 8.10-13,36-37), and it is then to be perceived as a resumption of these ideas.[139] Third, there is an accord with Rom 15.15-16,

---

135. This corresponds to 1 Thess 4.1,4,9; 1 Cor 5-6 and in particular Rom 6.3,16; 7.1,7,14. It is probable that the assumed insight referred to concerns the baptismal paraenesis. Cf. Schmidt, *Römer*, p. 206, Käsemann, *Römer*, p. 318.

136. If the entire structure of the Letter to the Romans is seen according to the pattern of salvation indicative followed by paraenetic imperatives, we again have an example of the imperative member being followed by a renewed stressing of the salvation indicative, not only in Rom 15.14 but also in Rom 15.7-13, in which the paraenesis ends with a reference to Christ's vital salvation input for both Jews and heathens, which *must* prevail. This corresponds to 1 Cor 5.7; 6.9-11; 10.13; Phil 2.12-13, cf. note 132 above.

137. Cf. Murray, *Romans*, p. 109f., Jervell, *Gud*, pp. 218-24, Ulrich Wilckens, *Der Brief am die Römer. 3. Teilband* (EKK VI/3), Zürich 1982, p. 7ff., James D.G. Dunn, *Romans 9-16* (WBC 386), Dallas 1988, p. 705ff.

138. Thus in particular Bjerkelund, *Parakalô*, p. 156ff., Michael Thompson, *Clothed with Christ* (JSNT.Supp. 59), Sheffield 1991, s.78f., cf. Chapter III, note 270, above.

139. This first observation is very widespread, and normally interpreters can also see that θυσία ζῶσα ἁγία εὐάρεστος τῷ θεῷ is content-saturated imagery and thus an important feature in the context, which stresses the demand for complete self-devotion, cf. Murray, *Romans*, p. 111, Michel, *Römer*, p. 291f., Jervell, *Gud*, p. 221, Käsemann, *Römer*, p. 315, Schlier, *Römerbrief*, p. 355f., Wilckens, *Römer* III, p. 3f., Dunn, *Romans*, p. 710. But that this is also a paradoxical expression which may be connected with the paradoxical linking together of life and death in Rom 6.2-8,11,13 is not made clear. Cf. Philipp Seidensticker,

where Paul's overriding objective is also that the community should become an 'offering acceptable to God'.[140]

It is then emphasised by λογίκη λατρείαν, that this is concerned with reason. The same is stressed in the next verse by the words νοῦς and δοκι-μάζειν. Hans Dieter Betz' translation, 'rational religion', is therefore apt, and it comes to correspond to a crucial feature in Rom 6, in which Paul is continuously appealing to the Romans' insight and judgement.[141]

In Rom 12.2 the usage changes: μὴ συσχηματίζεσθε τῷ αἰῶνι τούτῳ, ἀλ-λὰ μεταμορφοῦσθε τῇ ἀνακαινώσει τοῦ νοός ... Paul here links up with a Hellenistic ideal about renewal of life, as he does in other passages including Rom 1.18-32; 8.29. At the same time he resumes the antithetic structure, which can point back to before-now contrasts which were dominant in Rom 1-8.[142] But it should be noted that these antithetic formulations are found only here and in Rom 13.12-14. Otherwise the context is dominated by the positive admonitions. And it should also be emphasised that at the intrinsic level Paul does *not* adopt Hellenistic concepts about miraculous transformation and apotheosis of man. He indeed stresses that a renewal is concerned which is related to a rational attitude and a new relationship to God.

This is in my opinion the crucial point which is developed in Rom 12.2b. It is an appeal to the Romans to keep to the new way of thinking, in which one tries to see what is God's will: the good, the acceptable and the perfect. Thus it is said quite clearly that God's will is something external with which the Christians are confronted and towards which they by using their judgement must adopt a position.[143] It thus becomes clear that ethics are funda-

---

Lebendiges Opfer (Röm 12,1) (NTA 20), Münster 1954, pp. 256-59, in which a connection is seen from Rom 8.10-11, Thompson, *Clothed*, p. 79f., which links back to the words ζῶντας and εἰς ἁγιασμόν in Rom 6.13,19, and Halvor Moxness, The Quest of the Community in Romans 12 and in the Orations of Dio Chrysostom, in: Troels Engberg-Pedersen (ed.), *Paul in his Hellenistic context*, Minneapolis 1995, pp. 203-35; p. 217, in which another possible inherent connection is indicated: 'The sacrifice of believers in v. 1 parallels the sacrifice and death of Christ, unto which the Christians are baptized (Romans 6).'

140. Cf. note 134 above.

141. See Hans Dieter Betz, Das Problem der Grundlagen der paulinischen Ethik, ZThK 85 (1988), pp. 199-218, in which this translation is suggested in a justified confrontation with the tendency to understand λογικός as an expression of pneumatic worship of God rather than as an intellectual attitude to the problem-complex.

142. See especially Furnish, *Theology*, p. 103f., who emphasises that there is a connection both in word-choice and theme between Rom 1.18-32, where a 'Fall' leading to idol-worship and darkening of the mind is described, and Rom 12.1-2, where the old conditions are to be replaced by true worship of God and a renewed mind. Cf. also Thompson, *Clothed*, p. 81ff.

143. This is also emphasised in Käsemann, *Römer*, p. 318f., where, however, the point is again that it is meant to be a confrontation with enthusiastic misunderstandings of the new existence.

mentally situation-determined: God's will shows itself continuously in new ways. And therefore a need may still exist for guidance where the substance of this life is concerned, which is continuously renewed.

The content of the section Rom 12.1-15.14 accords with this. The emphasis is on the intrinsic side; the admonitions which follow point outwards towards the tasks in the new life. What Paul does throughout the long, positive paraenetic section is to show examples of correct attitudes and lines of action. And here it is clear that he uses material also known from other sources.[144]

It is thus clear that the dominant feature of the section, and therefore throughout the paraenetic line of the Letter to the Romans, is the positive teaching about the substance of the new life. Only one passage in the section contains an admonition which alone stresses the necessity of grasping the opportunities of the new life. This is Rom 13.11-14, where Paul points to the coming time when it will be necessary to live decently and to put on the Lord Jesus Christ. This is in a context in which Paul also dissociates himself from the old life with its works of darkness, debauchery and licentiousness. The same aspect of the paraenesis is to be found in Rom 8.12-13, where indeed there are hints about the importance of combating the old carnality. For a moment one senses that the violent internal conflict from Rom 7.14-25 is not so far distant as the dominant structure anticipates. But here also there comes a renewed indicative which underlines that the old anxiety has passed. And the thoughts are immediately led to the foundation: that those who are in Christ will receive a purpose in life and a course of life like his (Rom 8.4,14-17).[145]

If we go back a step further we come to the imperative in Rom 6.19: present your members as slaves to righteousness for sanctification. This is found in a context in which the point is that the correct ethical attitude leads to-

---

144. These are in particular reminders of the admonitions in the First Letter to the Corinthians. Rom 12.4-5 about the community as one body is a compressed rendering of 1 Cor 12.12-27. In the same context, Rom 12.6-8 gives a list of the charisms' dissimilarity, corresponding to 1 Cor 12.4-11,28-31. And this is followed by an underlining of the primacy of love in Rom 12.9 as in 1 Cor 13. Rom 13.8-10 reads that love of one's neighbour involves compliance with the law, which corresponds to Gal 5.14 (and resumes the thought-process from Rom 8.2-4). The eschatologically-based appeals in Rom 13.11-14 are reminiscent of 1 Thess 5.1-11; the appeal to clothe oneself corresponds to Gal 3.27, and the warning against 'gratifying the desires of the flesh' corresponds to Gal 5.16. Rom 14 concerns the relationship between the strong and the weak in the community, especially in regard to the matter of eating habits, and repeats the considerations in 1 Cor 8-10 in a more neutral form. Cf. Simonsen, *Overvejelser*, p. 202ff., Schrage, *Ethik*, p. 181. This feature may again support its being an echo of Paul's baptismal paraenesis, cf. note 135 above.

145. Cf. this draft of an interpretation of Rom 7.7-25, Chapter VI, section 2.3, above.

wards eternal life.[146] A certain emphasis is then given to the importance of the correct mode of action. But the main matter is the certain course of events.

It is then confirmed, as established in the interpretation of Rom 6.12-13, that the point is the positive aspect of directing the Roman community towards the extraverted battle for righteousness which is the purpose of the new life.

And it must still apply that the negative prelude's primary function is to herald the positive point. The question may still be asked, whether the negative imperative in Rom 6.12-13a also perhaps contains a demarcation relative to the old life and a warning against backsliding, since it has indeed been shown that there is a connection between the various sides of the traditional paraenesis. But there can be no significant restriction in the member 'mortal'. Perhaps this may be seen as an anticipation of Rom 8.12-13. But then it is at most a passing admission: that there may be problems which will be overcome by the power of the new life.[147] There is no tension and no hidden negative points. No 'not yet', no confrontation with enthusiasm, can be sensed.

On the contrary, the line points in the opposite direction. The new life which the Christians have received points forward to an 'even more' in the eschatological consummation.[148]

---

146. Note that both Rom 6.20-23 and the paraenetic-sounding statements in Rom 7.5-6 have been indicatively formulated so that the emphasis is on the certain course of events towards eternal life.

147. Cf. the distinction between reservation and admission introduced in the survey of Rom 8.1-30 in Chapter VI, section 2.3, above, with notes 59-66. Cf. also the considerations relative to Rom 7.7-25 in the same section, for perhaps one can also see in Rom 6.12 a hint of the conflict with the bodily desire which marked the old life according to Rom 7.14-25. But it may be at most a preparation for the pedagogic measures Paul uses here: to say with emphasis that the conflict which may be about to announce itself is in the past. Paul then demonstratively describes mortal life as a current impossibility.

148. Cf. Kertelge, *Rechtfertigung*, p. 263, Schottroff, *ExWNT* I, col. 265.

XI
Summary

1. Certainty of the new life — Rom 6.1-11

I return under this heading to the intention of Rom 6.1-11 and thus to the first of the theses from the introductory chapter. In this concluding chapter there will be for each of the theses a summary of what has been demonstrated and of what the reasoning rests upon. The negative side of the reasoning will also play an important part here. Along the way, other opinions on the subjects discussed have been confronted. As regards the first theses, on the text's objective and structure, one can arrive at quite tangible results for the very reason that alternative interpretations can be excluded. As regards the final theses, which relate to the theological content, there is more room for possible interpretations. But then it is again important to show that some interpretations are unlikely, and in this way isolate the Pauline perception of baptism and Christology.[1]

Paul's concern in Rom 6.1-11 is thus to stress the reality of the new life. According to Paul, the new life has finally been accomplished. One is quite justified in speaking of salvation enthusiasm — as one did around the turn of the century.

But salvation does not mean, as was assumed by the religio-historical school, that the baptised have been given a new nature, different physical qualities, or control over divine powers. Such ideas in no way form any part of the picture, either positive or negative.

What is concerned is that, following the break with sin, the baptised find themselves in an entirely new situation, with a new Lord. They have become linked to the true power of life (this is something which comes from with-

---

1. That there is great latitude, so that interpretation of the central theological subjects ultimately has the nature of a draft, is not only because of external, practical problems in reconstructing the traditions stated in implied references; it is also associated with the theological content itself. As will be seen from this summary, the untenable aspect is indeed the attempts to find concept-complexes which explain exhaustively how the Christ-events acquire the soteriological consequences indicated. The redemptive events are something coming from without, which one confronts. There are several possibilities of understanding for this. I wish briefly to indicate the most probable, and refer in the notes to the passages in which discussion has taken place in the course of the presentation.

out), and have therefore a certain expectation that this power will continue to be part of their life.

This perception of the intention has been confirmed by the interpretation of the text.

Methodically, I have relied upon a simple consideration: that the subject-matter is what is directly emphasised in the section of text. This is already apparent from the very large features. The structure of the reasoning was clear as soon as the construction of the text was examined in Chapter VI: the basis is the definitive break with the old sinful life. This break is described ever more pointedly, and from here one's thoughts are guided in the direction of the power in the new life.

The intention also stood out clearly in the detailed examination of the text in the following chapters (VII-IX). Here, one first sees (in connection with Rom 6.3-8) references to Christ's death as the eschatological turning point, a dramatic change for the Christians from a sinful life to a new existence, with a link to Christ. It is established that the power of Christ's resurrection is also significant to the Christians' life and outlook. This is followed (in Rom 6.9-11) by a direct reference to Christ's resurrection as an eschatological event which means that sin has lost its power, and that the true life has begun for those who are 'in Christ'.

This corresponds to the thought-process in the predominant context, as shown in Chapters V and VI. In Rom 5-8, the absolute contrast between the old life and the new life is dominant. A change of authority has occurred (made clear in Rom 5.18-21; 6.15-23). Hostility towards God has been replaced by a new status as friends of God, and hopelessness by hope for the future life (clearly expressed in Rom 5.6-11; 7.25-8.4; 8.15-17).

All this confirms that the intention is to emphasise a certainty about the power of the new life.

At the same time, it is denied that Paul inclines towards an enthusiastic perception of salvation in which the baptised were said to have been given a new divine nature by sacramental or mystical means.

It is ruled out that Paul positively adopts such Hellenistic concepts. Not only the great distance from the suggested religio-historical parallels is against this, which will be amplified in section 3 below, but the entire thought-process in Rom 6.1-11 is against it. Paul argues and appeals to the recipients' insight and understanding. The leading aspect in this text is not therefore the possession of an inner natural strength but the proper relationship to God and dependence upon his power; a 'force of conviction' which must operate in the new life.

Neither has it been possible to demonstrate that Paul adopts here a critically-modifying attitude towards the concepts, such that he has reservations in regard to the enthusiastic certainty of salvation. Again, the distance from the parallels set out is against this. Moreover, the assumed modifications and critical reservations are quite unemphasised. The methodical principle is again crucial: reservations and dissociations must also be brought out in the text, if they are to be part of the intention. And the direction of the thought-process unambiguously follows the opposite path: towards the certainty of salvation.

Finally, it is important for the text to be read without assuming that it reflects a particular mythology and mysticism. If there is not necessarily one coherent concept about baptism and salvation, an opportunity is presented for more shaded interpretations of individual members. There are a series of different concepts and varying images, each of which separately expresses something about baptism and the life that follows after this.[2] Terms such as βαπτίζεσθαι εἰς Χριστόν, σύμφυτοι … τῷ ὁμοιματι, σὺν Χριστῷ and ἐν Χριστῷ need not be perceived as loaded expressions and formulae of fixed mystical or corporative content. One can assume broader meanings, and establish that in the specific context the emphasis seems to lie on the close bonding with Christ.[3] And, as regards an understanding of the new life, one

---

2. The development of ideas, with its changing expressions and images and shifts, has been described in the primary examination of the text in Chapter VII, section 1-3, Chapter VIII, section 1, and Chapter X, section 1. The manifold metaphors are also emphasised in Schnackenburg, *Heilsgeschehen*, expressed with particular clarity on p. 23, cf. Chapter VII, note 13, above. But since then the viewpoint has been the subject of scepticism and rejection, as has been shown during examination of the text, cf. especially the following notes: Chapter VI, notes 12-16, Chapter VII, note 11, Chapter VIII, notes 11-15, 65-68, Chapter X, notes 34, 37. It is not wished to accept a metaphorical understanding, and it is maintained that the expressions must be understood 'realistically' and 'literally'. This is partly because it is wished to see the text as expressing one unified mythological thought-process, either a ritual repetition of Christ's death and resurrection or an incorporation into Christ; both are untenable, as will be concluded below in section 3. It is also partly a consequence of the important discussion of baptism as a sacrament to which I shall return in section 4 below. Exegetes wish to uphold baptism's nature of reality, that something objective has taken place, or that objective effects are conveyed, that it is not just something believed. They reject that it is images, because they have an erroneous impression that imagery expresses something unreal. Metaphors are on the contrary often used to uphold the crucial consequences of events. This is underlined when one describes them by expressions taken from other aspects of reality. In the Letter to the Romans there are even eschatological events of epoch-making effect. That images are used is because it is a reality from beyond which breaks through and therefore cannot be described directly by common usage.

3. As regards the discussion of these members, see Chapter VII, sections 1.2 and 3, Chapter VIII, section 2, Chapter IX, section 1.2 above. When it was established both here and in the parallel passages examined in Chapter III, sections 2-3, that these expressions could not be put into one formula and could not provide the prepositions with one constant

can avoid the somewhat futile discussion of whether this begins with baptism, or is to supervene only sometime in the hereafter. What is important is indeed the connection between the present Christian life and the glorious life of the future.[4]

2. Invitation to live the new life in Rom 6.12-14

In Rom 6.12-14, Paul wishes, as is clear from Chapter X, to point forward emphatically to the new life which is now open to the Christians. This is the obvious consequence of the unconditional promise of salvation: to begin to live the life bestowed with the content that it has. What is important here is to fight on God's side.

I have turned against other points of view with this interpretation of the subject-matter. It is in my opinion untenable to emphasise tensions in the text and in the Pauline eschatology, and to see the imperative as an appeal to acquire salvation, since then finally the imperative is based on the deficiencies of the new life, on eschatological reservations and the fact that the body is still mortal and that salvation is *not yet* finally assured.

My interpretation rests primarily on the direct, positive observations that were apparent from the exegesis.

The structure sets the stage for this understanding. It has been shown that there is in the whole context an antithetical construction with before-now contrasts, and in the text itself there is a μή-ἀλλά correspondence with an obvious preponderance. It is therefore signalled that the emphasis is to be placed on the positive appeal in Rom 6.13bc.

This is confirmed by the content. The line in Rom 6.1-11 is the ever stronger stress on the new life as having already commenced. Οὖν in Rom 6.12 signals that the appeal must be seen as a consequence of the promise of salvation. The subsequent grounds given in Rom 6.14 also point to the certainty of salvation. Rom 6.13 must therefore be an appeal to launch cheerfully into this new life, which presents itself as the only possibility.

The interpretation can also be supported by negative reasoning. To inter-

---

meaning, this represents a fundamental linguistic perception about 'polysemy', which is hesitantly brought into the picture in Hellholm, Argumentation, p. 13f., in connection with the expression βαπτίζεσθαι εἰς Χριστόν, cf. Chapter VII, note 13, above.

4. See in particular the discussion about the future forms in Rom 6.5,8, Chapter VII, sections 3.6 and 4.3, item 6, and Chapter VIII, section 1.5, above. It is a false alternative to discuss whether the verbs in Rom 6.5b,8b must be understood as 'logical future' or as 'eschatological future'. The future forms can concern the present reality, which will certainly last into the future. I have suggested the expression 'certainty future' about this third possibility, which I have prepared in continuation of the observations in Murray, *Romans*, p. 219, Cranfield, *Romans*, p. 308, Wedderburn, Traditions, p. 339, *Baptism*, p. 44.

pret the verses as expressions of dialectic, reservation and tension indeed rests on narrow and untenable assumptions. Some distinctions and nuances have been presented along the way, and alternative interpretations indicated.

First, the 'dialectic' interpretation rests upon a unilateral perception of what is called 'the dual eschatology' in Paul. This is seen as a tension-charged 'already/not yet' where important eschatological events have indeed occurred but the final salvation is absent. Paul is thereby said to dissociate himself from an overwrought enthusiasm. But in the context the dual eschatology appears quite differently. As is clear from Rom 5.6-10; 8.32, what is crucial has already taken place by justification, and Paul therefore stresses the certain promise that the Christians have even more to expect from the coming consummation. This 'already/even more' may clearly also be the viewpoint in Rom 6, where the emphasis is on the crucial break with the past and the course of events which has been initiated.[5]

Second, it is untenable to understand this directly as a pointed reservation when speaking of defects and problems associated with the new life. It may also be an admission (as in Rom 5.3-5; 8.17-30). One is looking reality in the eye: there are adversities, but also a safe road through them to glory. The object then becomes solace and the building up of hope for the future. If the negative expression 'the mortal body' in Rom 6.12 relates to the new life, this can clearly be seen as an admission. There is always mortality, but this should certainly be of no importance and cause no problems, because the Christians are beyond the power of death. Neither is there any need for a reservation in Rom 6, since as we have seen the text reflects no exaggerated enthusiasm for salvation.[6]

Third, 'indicative-imperative tension' arises only if one has a narrow perception of the Pauline imperatives' function: an absolute demand to acquire salvation directed inwards towards the Christians' spiritual life. The unconditional promise of salvation then compares sharply with the subsequent condition. It is then important to note that imperatives are also used in invitations, for advice and guidance, and in a particularly intense address. In Rom 6.13, the imperative has been turned outwards towards the battle to be fought, and it must be seen in context with the paraenesis in Rom 12-15 where the main emphasis is on the content of the new righteous life. There

---

5. Cf. Chapter V, section 2.1, and Chapter VI, section 2.3, above, with note 66, in which it is shown that an 'already/even more' is the point in the a-fortiori conclusions in Rom 5 and in Rom 8.32 which form part of the framework of Rom 6. Moreover, it should be noted that Paul nowhere uses a 'not yet' directly paraenetically, aimed at the addresses, although indirectly in 1 Cor 4.8; Phil 3.16.
6. The distinction between reservation and admission was introduced in the examination of Rom 8.18-32 in Chapter VII, section 2.3, above, with notes 59-66, and has also proved useful in regard to Rom 6.12-14, cf. Chapter X, section 2.4, above.

is then no tension. The indicative is God's promise of life and salvation. The imperative explains what the new life involves. And it is subsequently repeated that only God's promise of salvation is crucial, so that we have instead an 'indicative-imperative connection'.[7]

3. Background: Christian concepts of 'death-baptism'

In the third thesis, it was asserted that Paul bases himself upon traditional Christian concepts, that at transition to the new life the baptised acquire a special association with Christ's death and thus a share in its effects. This involves a rejection of other explanations of the background — theories about dependence on mystery religions, mysticism, or Old Testament-Jewish corporative ideas.

Quite simple considerations have again been crucial to my reasoning.

I have indicated a necessary distinction in regard to the question of the text's religio- and traditio-historical background. This can apply to two widely different things. (a) On the one hand one may ask, what are the traditional concepts that Paul directly assumes to be already known, and that he takes as a basis. (b) On the other hand it may be that along the way Paul has employed contemporary usage and modes of thought so that the final point may acquire a degree of similarity to other concepts. In regard to Rom 6, the first question is clearly the most weighty, since Paul refers directly to an assumed knowledge and thus to fundamental Christian traditions.[8]

Now, the structure of the reasoning in the text has shown that the direct references to assumed traditions in Rom 6.3,6a concern only the relationship of the baptised to Christ's death. The direction of the thought-process moves

---

7. The wider application possibilities of the imperatives are shown in Chapter X, section 2.1 in association with Steensgaard, Erwägungen, p. 110ff. Cf. my distinction between the introverted and the extroverted imperatives, Agersnap, Rom 6.12, p. 44, and Chapter X, section 1.3, with note 30, and section 2.4, above, where the connection is demonstrated from Rom 6.12-13.19 to Rom 12.1-2, which as a prelude to the paraenesis indicates the substance of the new life: to understand God's will in specific situations and to do the right thing. Although Paul often has the sequence indicative, imperative, new indicative, cf. Chapter X, notes 132, 136, above, it must be specified that this is *not* the sequence in the salvation-historical process. In theological principle, the indicative-imperative formulation is correct; it stresses that the indicative is the first and the fundamental — salvation depends only on a gift and a promise from God; the imperative is secondary and subordinate. But the widespread, narrow interpretation of the imperative as an appeal to acquire salvation nevertheless comes to operate as a condition. The designation 'indicative-imperative-indicative' can therefore be used to stress that, first and last, Paul emphasises the supreme promise of salvation.
8. Cf. as regards this distinction Chapter VII, section 4.1, and Chapter VIII, section 2.1, above.

unambiguously from the Christians' linkage to Christ's death to their linkage to the power of resurrection. The intensity which is in the reasoning excludes that the linkage to the resurrected was already part of the quoted tradition; that is, the tradition concerned exclusively the importance of Christ's *death* to the baptised.[9]

This reference back from the text to the assumed tradition is crucial to the religio- and traditio-historical question itself (a). And then the comparison with parallel passages is of lesser importance, both as regards my own thesis and as regards theories of more comprehensive tradition-complexes which it is sought to reconstruct.

We may first take the theories about dependence on, respectively, the mystery-religious death-resurrection rituals or Hellenistic mysticism and a Jewish collective mode of thought. The theories are then that the baptised are incorporated into Christ and receive a share in the crucial redemptive events.

In both these cases, participation of the baptised in both Jesus' death and resurrection is said to be concerned. For this reason alone, these concepts *cannot* be the starting point to which Paul refers in Rom 6.3,6.

But there are also problems with the parallel religio- and traditio-historical material referred to. The notable concepts that according to the theories Paul is said to adopt in Rom 6 cannot be demonstrated.

No direct, inherent connection back to the mysteries' rituals is to be found. There are certain common features; concepts about a deity's death and continued life, inter alia, have played a part in the mysteries' initiation rites, and this has been further emphasised by posterity's speculations. But what is crucial in the mystery initiations is the insight into and contact with the divine provided by the manifold experiences of a long ritual, whereas the Christian baptism is a momentary event.[10]

The Hellenistic-Christian baptismal traditions also seem not to have included the assumed preconditions of Rom 6. A pre-Pauline concept of baptism as a death and resurrection with Christ cannot be reconstructed. There are two different (Pauline) motifs revolving around Christ's death and resurrection. Paul employs, it is assumed, traditions regarding baptism as an incorporation into Christ; these are *not* however specific mythological or psychological-realistic concepts but expressions of linkage to and dependence upon Christ. The common linkage to Christ can also be employed to stress a mutual fellowship. Paul is then approaching collective concepts of sol-

---

9. See in particular my reasoning in Chapter VII, section 4.3-4, above, cf. Chapter VII, sections 1-2, and Chapter VIII, section 1.1, where it is shown that the references in Rom 6.3,6a only apply directly to a connection between baptism and Christ's death.

10. See my examination of the material in Chapter II above and the religio-historical comparison undertaken in Chapter VII, section 4.2, with note 129.

idarity and common destiny, as are to be found in Hellenism and Judaism.[11]

It might therefore be considered whether the material referred to may be a religio- and traditio-historical background in a different, broader sense (b) that is concerned with concepts towards which Paul is working or that he includes in the course of the thought-development in the text.[12]

But it is thus clear that Paul's starting point in Rom 6 is a pan-Christian baptismal tradition. This is shown by inference from the text itself.

And it can be confirmed by some parallels — although they are not numerous. Apart from 1 Cor 1.13 the 'death with Christ' motif may be indicated, which indeed concerns the transition to the new life, and may also be used in relation to baptism.[13] Moreover, it is possible to explain how death-baptism concepts may have arisen. The simplest explanation is that John the Baptist's baptism of purification for the forgiveness of sins is viewed in the primitive church's intense speculation in the context of Christ's death, which is the true basis for all forgiveness of sins.[14]

11. The Hellenistic communities' perception of baptism is examined in Chapter III above; the Old Testament-Jewish 'corporate-personality concept' was also considered in connection with the interpretation of Rom 5.12-21, Chapter V above. The traditio-historical comparison was effected in Chapter VII, section 4.3-4, and Chapter VIII, section 2.
12. Paul's final point is the intensely expressed bonding to the dead and resurrected Lord, which reminds one of mystical ideas and Old Testament ideas about dependence upon a progenitor-figure. He has constructed a concept which corresponds by and large to contemporary religiousness (and perhaps outbids it). It also cannot be excluded that Paul, when he comes to describing here the effect of baptism as 'death' and new life with Christ, has an eye to the contemporary description of the main features of the mysteries. Cf. Chapter VII, section 4.5, with notes 195-96, and Chapter VIII, section 2.4, above.
13. See Chapter III, section 4, on 'death-baptism' in 1 Cor 1.13 and section 3.2-5 on the 'death with Christ' motif which is compared with Rom 6.3,6 in Chapter VII, section 4.4, with note 187, and Chapter VIII, section 2.2, with notes 57-59. The motif is found most markedly in Rom 6.6 and Gal 2.19-20, and in both passages the context makes it natural to think of baptism.
14. Cf. the examination of the religio- and traditio-historical material in Chapter IV, and the discussion about the provenance of the 'death-baptism idea' in Chapter VII, section 4.4, where item 4 indicates the most obvious line of development. The other points indicate features which may have contributed to the development of death-symbolism. Item 6 also gives an obvious explanation, if one has the courage to go along with my theory, that the primitive church already practised the sign of the cross in baptism. That the reasoning is in any case of a hypothetical nature is no objection to the interpretation. It is associated with the intense Christological speculation and the short distance to the events themselves, as referred to loc.cit.

4. The significance of baptism to the new life

Since the structure and thought-development of the text are clear, it is also possible to determine the theological content more precisely. The concept of baptism has two aspects. On the one hand the fundamental traditions to which Paul refers concerned with what occurred earlier during the act of baptism, and on the other hand the concepts Paul develops here concerned with the significance of baptism to the continued life.

First, the aspect of understanding baptism at which Paul is aiming. That in this context Paul emphasises the subsequent effects of baptism on the new life is perhaps the most noteworthy. Paul moves from baptism's 'negative' effect — the break with the old — towards its fundamental significance in the new life.[15]

Paul builds up a conviction that the new life has finally broken through. This signifies several important things.

Insofar as there is a reference here to faith and conviction in the context of baptism, this is not the justifying faith which precedes baptism. It is the subsequent faith which rests on the crucial events that occurred at baptism.

Baptism itself is thus given eschatological significance. There are effects of salvation which are put into force. This is associated with the power that resurrected Christ from the dead (Rom 6.4). And the process of salvation into which the baptised have been introduced is sustained by a cosmic power, which signifies that the promise of salvation is finally irrevocable (Rom 8.31-39).

What can also be observed is that these effects of salvation are imprinted by the intense form of reasoning and entreating used by Paul. It is not something which is said to have occurred automatically as a transformation of the baptised. Their relationship is to an external force.

This throws light on the next problem.

As regards the fundamental traditions relating to the act of baptism itself, we have only scanty references. Paul can merely refer back to a common understanding. We cannot reconstruct this completely, but we can identify important aspects.

We can see broadly the effects ascribed to baptism. Baptism conveys complete forgiveness of sins from God. Christ becomes the Lord to whom

---

15. Cf. Agersnap, Dåbsteologi, p. 114f., where I show that Paul similarly stresses baptism's positive and fundamental aspects in other passages, especially in Gal 3.26-4.7; 1 Cor 12.12-27.

the Christians have become bound. And these are seen as the effects of Christ's death, which has had a central position in baptism.[16]

But these are the very features that are ambiguous.

On the one hand, they can be perceived as meaning that a divine force is operative in baptism. Cleansing from sin may be the result of God's presence; it is indeed a baptism by the Holy Spirit, as is apparent directly from other baptismal texts - and indirectly in Rom 6, since throughout Rom 5-8 the Spirit is seen as the crucial force in the Christians' new life. That Christ becomes Lord of the Christians may be bound up with his being imagined as present at the proclamation in baptism. And parts of the external ritual may be perceived as a symbolic reactualisation of Christ's death, which releases the effects.[17]

On the other hand, the force of baptism may also be associated with proclamation and acceptance. The cleansing effect of the baptismal water may have been seen in the context of the proclamation of God's forgiveness and redemptive will which displayed itself at Christ's death. Baptism contains not merely promises of salvation and a proclamation of Christ; it also involves a confession of faith. And the ritual's revolving around Christ's death can then be seen as a reference to the crucial redemptive event.[18]

This ambiguity forms a basis for the significant discussion about the effect of baptism. Does baptism obtain its effect primarily by virtue of what objectively happens, or is the crucial point the subjective conviction? The extremities of the discussion are immediately excluded. This applies to the wholly sacramentalist interpretation, where the effects of salvation automatically prevail by virtue of the cultic reiteration of the Christ-events. It also

16. Cf. the conclusion in Chapter VII, section 4.4, where it is shown that it was these three main features which re-appeared in the 'death with Christ' motif. Forgiveness of sins at baptism is also the theme in 1 Cor 6.11; the Christ-bonding is also emphasised in Gal 3.27-29; 1 Cor 12.12-27, cf. 1 Cor 1.12-13, where a death-baptism is also evidenced.

17. This applies particularly if the sign of the cross has been employed as a sign of redemption at baptism, cf. note 14 and Chapter IV, section 3, above. See also Chapter VII, section 4.4, and Chapter VIII, section 2.3, which shows that baptism as a starting point is seen as divine purification, and that the life with Christ which Paul adduces assumes that Christ is present as the power in it. The context confirms this. Rom 5.5; 7.6; 8.1-27 speaks of the Spirit's crucial significance at the transition to the new life and its development, and all passages can be related to baptism, cf. Chapter V, note 14, Chapter VI, section 2.2-3 (and Chapter III, note 194), above. Rom 8.9-11 also expresses an intense presence of Christ, specifically as an extension of the strong Christ-bonding here emphasised.

18. By virtue of Rom 5.6-10 it is assumed that God's boundless redemptive will is revealed by Christ's death, cf. Chapter VI, section 2.1-2, above. See also Chapter VII, section 4.4, with note 186, above, concerning baptism as a confession of faith, and Chapter VIII, section 2.3, where it is demonstrated that the expressions 'buried', 'crucified' and 'dead' with Christ refer back to the past redemptive events.

applies to the anti-sacramentalist interpretation, that it in fact happened at Golgotha, and so baptism merely becomes an external conveyance thereof and a confession of faith therein. Both opinions assume a coherent mythological concept-complex which cannot be found in or behind the text.[19] Paul's use of baptismal concepts also dismisses both opinions. Since he describes baptism as an eschatological event in which one subsequently pins one's faith, it cannot be something merely subjective. Since he enjoins conviction about this, it cannot be something of purely objective effect.

It is therefore necessary to adopt a middle position, as is normally the case. The objective and the subjective aspects cannot be separated. Baptism is an eschatological event. There is a special dynamic because the divine force breaks into human existence. But at the same time it is clear that baptism achieves its full effect only when the baptised realises how crucial a turning point it is. In this way the force of salvation and promise of salvation are inextricably connected.[20]

5. The Christological multiplicity

It is again possible to rely on the development of thought established in the first three sections of the summary.

And again it is crucial to establish that there is also movement within the Christology — from the redeemer-Christology in the traditions referred to towards the precursor motif which dominates the later context. There is indeed no overall mythological complex, and the central Christological content cannot therefore be discharged by a simple formula and clearly explained. A varied use of imagery, shifts and distortions occurs along the way, with an increasingly intense description of the principal Christ-bonding. There are references to various events in Christ's life: burial, crucifixion, death and resurrection, his content of life, and finally his life beyond the power of death where as Lord he joins the future life of the baptised.

But this intensity in the Christ-relationship must indeed be seen in the context that what is crucial for Paul is dependence upon a power which comes from without. Here in Rom 6 the baptised commit themselves to a person and an historical course of events which will have an effect upon

---

19. As shown in section 3 above. Cf. also note 2. It is precisely the discussion of baptism's objective effects which makes one resist metaphorical meanings of the concepts employed.

20. See again Chapter VII, section 4.4-5, and Chapter VIII, section 2.3, which also attempt to understand how baptism achieves its effects. The emphasis here is on proclamation and reflection. It must be thus because Paul emphasises this aspect in the context. But it does not mean that this subjective aspect can be separated from the more objective effects, which are included in the picture in the passages referred to.

their lives. If God's power shows itself and Christ is present as Lord, it is an external power that breaks into their existence. And although they are drawn into a new pattern of life they are still *facing* God's will, and the paraenesis points especially outwards towards the tasks. Therefore the new is not something automatic and static (as if sacramentalism or a mystical or corporative association were concerned); it is something characterised by movement and points ahead.[21]

It is possible therefore to indicate a number of crucial Christological motifs in connection with Rom 6.1-14. Christ's death was seen earlier as an expression of how far God was willing to go to become reconciled with man; in Rom 6.3,6, it is apparently an effect of Christ's death that the baptised are removed from the sphere of sin. When in Rom 6.9-11 Christ's death is associated with the substance of the life which he and the Christians are living, this is presented as a break with the power of sin and death. This is probably because it becomes absurd to see his death as an eschatological judgement; therefore those who are ἐν Χριστῷ are also to be beyond the power of death (Rom 6.13). According to Rom 6.4, Christ's resurrection is a revelation of God's glory as it has come into human life. Rom 6.8b may be seen as expressing that Christ as the risen Lord shares in the life of the baptised. And the new life they live is gradually seen to be the life that Christ lived and the life over which he is Lord. Christ is then not only an example of and a pattern for the new life but also the power which put it into effect. Thus is the thought-process continued in Rom 8: Christ identifies himself with men and their life, and this new departure means that they can lead a life like his, despite adversities, onwards towards certain glory.[22]

21. This 'alienation' (i.e. that salvation and demands are something coming from without) which was also emphasised above in sections 2 and 4 is often used to stress the distance between the perception of salvation of the mysteries and of Paul. But it should be pointed out that it is not the result of a dialectic to the effect that Paul has distanced himself from and modified the mystical understanding of perception of salvation so that the result becomes a kind of middle standpoint; the 'alienation' is itself because of the Pauline concept of God, so that Paul cannot base himself upon (and not merely modify) such a static perception of salvation, cf. Chapter X, section 2.3-4, with notes 85-86, above. This 'alienation' is also a contributory reason for the understanding of the central Christology being given the nature of a draft, cf. note 1 above. This is not only because Paul can be content with implied references; it is also because one is relating to a transcendent reality.
22. The possibilities of interpretation indicated here have been developed more comprehensively above: Chapter V, section 2.1, Chapter VII, sections 1.1 and 4.4-5, Chapter VIII, section 2.3-4, Chapter IX, section 2.3 and Chapter VI, section 2.3.

Dansk resumé

I. Teser og diskussionspunkter vedrørende Rom 6,1-14

I indledningskapitlet opstilles de teser, som skal forsvares: 1. Paulus' anliggende i Rom 6,1-11 er at indskærpe frelsesbegejstring: dåben giver de kristne vished om, at de har fået et nyt liv for Gud, bundet til Kristus. 2. Som den oplagte konsekvens heraf opfordres romerne i Rom 6,12-14 til at leve dette nye retfærdige liv. 3. Tekstens baggrund er kristne forestillinger om, at dåben giver tilknytning til Kristi død, så der sker en afgørende vending i de kristnes liv. I løbet af teksten ledes tankerne i retning af den kraft, der viste sig ved Kristi opstandelse og også skal vise sig i de kristnes liv. 4. Dåben er forstået som Guds handlen, der befrier de kristne fra den gamle syndige tilværelse og sætter dem ind i et nyt retfærdigt liv, med særlig vægt på den vedvarende betydning af denne frelseshandlen. 5. Der er to vigtige kristologiske motiver. Jesus er 'forløser'; de kristne befries fra synden i kraft af hans død. Og Jesus er 'forløber'; hans liv, død og opstandelse bliver også mønster for de døbtes liv. Sammenhængen mellem de to motiver viser, at der er varierende henvisninger til det afgørende begivenhedsforløb.

Disse teser kan virke indlysende og umarkante, men er det ikke set på baggrund af udbredte opfattelser af teksten. Derfor bringes en oversigt over forskningen i dette århundrede.

Omkring 1900 var der konsensus om, at Rom 6 udtrykte en entusiastisk dåbsforståelse. Med P. Wernle i spidsen pegede man på, at teksten var spændingsfyldt. Først kaldes de døbte syndfri; derefter kommer fra Rom 6,12 imperativer, der skulle være overflødige. Løsningen var en religionshistorisk forklaring; selvmodsigelsen skyldtes tekstdelenes forskellige baggrund. Imperativerne hang sammen med de praktiske forhold og Paulus' jødiske baggrund. Indikativen var udtryk for Paulus' mystik. Den religionshistoriske skole så denne mystik på baggrund af hellenistisk religiøsitet. Mysteriereligionerne skulle ligesom Rom 6,3-11 kredse om en døende og opstående guddom. de indviede havde rituelt gentaget samme forløb og var derved smeltet sammen med guddommen og havde allerede del i opstandelseslivet. Dåbsforståelsen blev magisk og sakramentalistisk. Kristologisk blev det Kristusmystik.

Kritikken mod opfattelsen kommer fra to sider. Man har kritiseret den religionshistoriske teori om Rom 6s baggrund i mysterierne. G. Wagner har samlet og udbygget den kritiske argumentation og påvist, at den antagne baggrund ikke findes i nogen af mysterierne, og at de træk i Rom 6, der tolkes som udtryk for sakramentalisme, er blevet overfortolket. R. Bultmann har kritiseret den religionshistoriske forklaringsmodel metodisk. Det er ikke nok at *forklare* indikativ-imperativ-spændingen historisk. Teksterne skal *forstås;* der er en grund til, at Paulus paradoksalt sammenstiller indikativ og imperativ: han fremstiller en paradoks virkelighed.

Denne kritik fører dog ikke til, at Rom 6 udlægges uden hensyntagen til en baggrund i hellenistisk religiøsitet. Næste hovedtendens i forskningen er 'en dialektisk ombøjningstolkning'. Paulus skal knytte til ved hellenistiske dåbsforestillinger, men modsige dem på afgørende punkter. Det er Bultmanns tolkning, videreført af G. Bornkamm, N. Gäumann og E. Käsemann. De medgiver, at direkte overensstemmelse mellem Rom 6 og hellenistisk religiøsitet mangler. Men det skyldes netop, at Paulus ombøjer de mysteriøse forestillinger, han overtager via hellenistisk-kristne menighedstraditioner. Rom 6s anliggende er stadig, ifølge denne tolkning, at fremstille dåben som Guds afgørende frelseshandling; så langt skal Paulus nok være enig med det entusiastiske forlæg. Men samtidig skal han også tage eskatologisk forbehold over for den misopfattelse, at frelsen er indtruffet endegyldigt; dermed er der også et andet anliggende. Spændingen mellem indikativ og imperativ kan nu forklares ud fra denne dialektik: det nye liv er *allerede* indtruffet, men den endegyldige frelse *endnu ikke;* derfor er der stadig brug for fordringen. Paulus' dåbssyn kan ses som afstandtagen fra hellenistisk sakramentalisme og hans kristologi som modifikation af menighedernes mystik.

Direkte kritik af ombøjningstolkningen er ny. A.J.M. Wedderburn har sat spørgsmålstegn ved, om der kan påvises spændinger i teksten og forbindelse tilbage til de antagne traditioner. Jeg har selv kritiseret teorierne om Paulus' anvendelse af 'eskatologiske forbehold'. Og det er problematisk at påvise hellenistiske menighedstraditioner forud for Paulus.

Der er stigende forståelse for, at Rom 6 skal udlægges uden antagelse af mysteriøs baggrund. Mest markante er forsøgene på at se Rom 6 på baggrund af en gammeltestamentelig kollektiv forestilling. Jesus skal være set som en 'corporate personality', der repræsentativt har gennemgået dødopstandelse, så også hans efterfølgere er omfattet af virkningerne af Golgatha begivenhederne. Ved denne tolkning nedtones dåbens betydning, og det afgørende bliver (tros-)forholdet til Kristus.

Denne tolkning er blevet kritiseret for sin spekulative karakter, og der er igen problemer med at dokumentere det, som skal være religionshistorisk baggrund.

Fordi kritikken af de tidligere tolkningsmodeller i høj grad er af metodisk art, har jeg valgt at redegøre for min egen metodiske praksis. Jeg bygger på Bultmanns ansats, at teksterne først må *forstås* og så i anden omgang kan bruges som historiske kilder. Arbejdet med teksterne må ske i to tempi.

Først skal tekstens anliggende udlægges; at forstå det kræver kendskab til sproget og de mere generelle tidshistoriske forudsætninger, mens traditionshistorie og andre overvejelser over tekstens tilblivelse ikke har sin plads her. Men i anden omgang, når teksten er forstået, er der basis for religions- og traditionshistoriske sammenligninger og anden form for historisk kritik.

Denne metode anvendes i afhandlingens anden hoveddel på Rom 6 med kontekst. Af praktiske grunde, for oversigtens skyld, har jeg valgt i første hoveddel at lægge det tekstmateriale frem, som har været betragtet som paralleller til Rom 6 og derfor skal inddrages i den anden fase af tekstbehandlingen.

Første del: Forberedende studier om den historiske baggrund

II. Hellenistisk mysteriereligiøsitet som baggrund for dåben

Her behandles først en rækkke konkrete kultsammenhænge: eleusinske mysterier, Isis-Osiris-myten, der er baggrund for både ægyptisk dødekult og Isis-mysterier, den lilleasiatiske Attis-Kybele-kult, et fragment fra Themistios om stemningen i mysterierne, 'Mithras-liturgien', der bruger mysterietanker magisk, og Naasenerprædikenen, en gnostiske anvendelse af mysteriernes myter og ritualer. Det konstateres, at dåb og andre renselsesriter har perifer betydning i mysterierne, og der peges på fællestræk: (1) at mysteriernes virkning er set som et forbedret jordeliv med håb om en postmortal fremtid (aldrig som øjeblikkelig guddommeliggørelse); (2) at man i indvielsen imiterer forskellige virkemidler, som guderne har brugt (men ikke et død-opstandelsesforløb); (3) at man har oplevet kamp mellem liv og død og brugt en række virkemidler for at få kontakt med guddommelige kræfter: kultgenstande, visioner og ekstatisk oplevelse af samhørighed med guddommen (aldrig blot et enkelt magisk eller symbolsk ritual).

Derefter undersøges teorier om fælles mysterieteologi. Ud over de nævnte fællestræk er der fællesskab om terminologi og ligheder i kulternes ydre organisation. Men der er ikke belæg for gensidig påvirkning, når det gælder mysteriernes hemmeligholdte kerne. Eksemplerne på fælles mysterietænkning er ikke fra et umiddelbart plan, men fra et intellektuelt plan, hvor myter og riter er sublimeret, afmytologiseret og afritualiseret. Og terminologi og tankegods fra mysterierne anvendes først i jødedom og kristendom, når det oprindelige religiøse præg er afstrejfet. Det vises, at magi ikke er et afgørende kendetegn ved mysterierne, omend både magi og mysterier forudsætter et verdensbillede med 'kosmisk sympatheia', hvor alle fænomener i verden er indbyrdes forbundet.

III. Dåbsforestillinger i hellenistisk kristne menigheder

Her gennemgås andre dåbssteder i Paulusbrevene, og det undersøges, om der kan spores særlige hellenistiske dåbstraditioner, som Paulus er afhængig af.

Bestemte steder og vendinger tolkes som udtryk for en hellenistisk tradition om dåben som mystisk indkorporering i Kristus. En gennemgang af nøglestederne Gal 3,27-29 og 1 Kor 12,12-13 viser store variationer; Gal 3 bruger et iklædningsbillede om hver enkelt døbts sammenhæng med Kristus, mens 1 Kor 12 opbygger et billede af menigheden som kollektiv Kristus-organisme. Vendingen βαπτίζεσθαι εἰς Χριστόν, her og andre steder, viser at sig primært at handle om Kristustilknytningen, hvorefter der kan spilles på en lokal betydning. Det hyppigt forekommende udtryk ἐν Χριστῷ forsøges tolket som en formel med fast mystisk eller ekklesiologisk indhold; men gennemgangen viser, at ἐν ikke bare har lokal betydning, men også kan forstås instrumentalt og som en løsere tilknytning.

Tilsvarende må vendingen σὺν Χριστθ, som findes i påfaldende sammenhænge, forstås nuanceret; σύν kan i forbindelse med bevægelsesverber betyde 'sammen med' i den forstand, at to størrelser forenes; men σύν kan også betegne et midlertidigt handlefællesskab eller have andre mindre markante betydninger som 'i lighed med', 'ved hjælp af'. det viser sig, at de steder, der handler om de kristnes død σύν Χριστθ, ikke udgør et samlet motiv, men to forskellige. Dels er der (tydeligst i Gal 2,19-20) et enfaset motiv, hvor de kristnes 'død' er en fortidig begivenhed (omvendelse/dåb), hvorved de får del i Kristi døds virkning. Dels er der, i Rom 8,17; Fil 3,9-10 og andre steder, et tofaset begivenhedsforløb: de kristne vil i fremtiden som Kristus gå gennem død til herlighed. Der er ikke spor af en forudgående dåbstradition om død og opstandelse med Kristus, heller ikke i Kol 2-3.

Den korintiske entusiasme, som Paulus kæmper med i 1 Korinterbrev, kan heller ikke sættes i forbindelse med en særlig dåbsforståelse. Overalt bruger *Paulus* dåben som argument, formentlig fordi han kan forudsætte enighed på dette punkt.

IV. Urkirkens dåbspraksis og de jødisk-kristne forudsætninger

Her undersøges mulighederne for, at en dødsdåbsforestilling kan være opstået på denne basis.

Det konstateres, at Johannes Døberens dåb har at gøre med den truende død, der skal afværges. Videre, at Jesu dåb indleder hans virksomhed, og hans død afslutter den, og at Jesu dåb samtidig er forbilledet for den kristne dåb, der skal indlede et tilsvarende liv. Og endelig, at den kristne dåb formidler den syndstilgivelse, som beror på Kristi død, og sandsynligvis har rummet en bekendelse til Kristus, og at tidligere Kristusbekendelser har kredset om hans død.

Desuden overvejes det i tilknytning til iagttagelser hos E. Dinkler om korset som frelses- og beskyttelsestegn i jødedom og urkristendom, at korstegnelsen *kan* være brugt ved dåben allerede på Paulus' tid.

Anden del: Tekstgennemgang

V. Optakten i Rom 5

Rom 5s tætte forbindelse med Rom 6 gør, at også dette kapitel må behandles ret omfattende.

i Rom 5,1-11 tager Paulus udgangspunkt i Kristi forløsende og retfærdiggørende død. Anliggendet viser sig klart i a fortiori-slutningen i Rom 5,6-10, der slutter fra den indtrufne eskatologiske begivenhed, Guds overraskende nådeshandling mod sine hidtige fjender, til den sikre tro på, at Gud fortsat vil skride ind til fordel for dem, der nu er hans venner. Det vises, at tankeudviklingen i Rom 6,11 lægger op til, at fortidens håbløshed skal sammenlignes med nutidens dåb.

Det sker netop i Adam-Kristus-typologien Rom 5,12-21. Igen er hovedanliggendet klart: Paulus vil modstille det gamle liv, som Adam var forløber for, og det ny liv, som Kristus er forløber for, igen for at understrege frelsesvisheden. Typologien har en kompliceret struktur, hvor sammenhængen mellem Adam og adamitter, Kristus og kristne skal fremstilles, samtidig med at de to sider sammenlignes. Derudfra forklares anakolutien i Rom 5,12 og de forskellige præciseringer, der kommer, inden vi får sammenligningen i en enkel form. Det afvises undervejs, af sproglige grunde, at Rom 5,12 handler om menneskehedens kollektive synd 'i Adam'.

Derefter følger religions- og traditionshistoriske overvejelser. Paulus overtager næppe en jødisk arvesyndsforestilling, da en sådan forestilling er jødedommen fremmed. Heller ikke den fremmedeartede kollektive forestilling om Adam som 'corporate personality', der antages som baggrund, findes i jødedommen på Paulus' tid; man ender med mere vage tanker om 'solidaritet' og 'repræsentation'. Heller ikke en gnostisk arvesyndsforestilling kan påvises forud for Paulus' fremstilling. Mest sandsynligt er det, at det er udslag af den typologiske tankegang, som har stor vægt hos Paulus: forestillingerne fra Gen 3, som er set i lyset af den eskatologiske vending, der er sket med Kristus — ligesom i 1 Kor 15.

VI. De ledende spørgsmål i Rom 6,1-2 og den overordnede struktur

I Rom 6,1-2 skiftes der til en retorisk stil med tænkte indvendinger og svar. Over for Paulus' retfærdighedsbudskab bringes det modstandersynspunkt, at man bare kan synde løs i tillid til Guds nåde. Det afvises med henvisning til, at de kristne er 'døde i forhold til synden', og ikke kan leve i den. Det er klart, at 'død' må forstås billedligt om det totale brud med fortiden.

I tilknytning til vers 1-2 skabes en oversigt over kompositionsteknikken, som Paulus benytter i Rom 6,1-14 og gentager i Rom 6,15-7,6 og også bruger på en lidt anden måde i Rom 7,7-8,39 — en elegant og levende teknik, der ad en tilsyneladende håbløs omvej fører frem til en præcis uddybning af tankegangen fra det forudgående. Ved hjælp af en absurd indvending kan Paulus tage afstand fra falske konsekvenser af hans frelsesbudskab, og det danner basis for en videre argumentation, hvor Paulus kan pege på de modsatte konsekvenser.

Der gives en skematisk oversigt over argumentationen i Rom 6,1-14, hvor udsagnene stilles op i to kolonner; en med udsagn om 'død', en anden med udsagn om 'liv'. Den vigtigste konstatering bliver, hvordan retningen i tankegangen er. Den går hele tiden fra udgangspunktet i de døbte kristnes forbindelse til Kristi død og dens virkning frem mod en tilsvarende forbindelse til Kristi opstandelse og den kraft, der er forbundet hermed. Det sker i versene 4, 5, 6-8, og 12-14. Dermed virker anliggendet umiddelbart klart i hver tekstdel.

VII. Rom 6,3-5: det ny liv som konsekvens af dåben til døden

I Rom 6,3 skal Paulus begrunde den provokerende påstand om de kristnes 'død'. Det konstateres, at Paulus går ud fra en fælles viden om dåben. Han kan hos brevmodtagerne forudsætte den indsigt, at dåben til Kristus i særlig grad giver forbindelse til Kristi død. Vendingen βαπτίζεσθαι εἰς forstås ud fra den bredeste betydning af præpositionen, og det ses som en dåb 'til Kristus' og 'til hans død'. Men der kan i sammenhængen være være spillet på den lokalt-rumlige betydning, så det indgår i tankegangen, at de døbte er inddraget i (virkningerne af) Kristi død. Således underbygges den forudgående påstand om dåbens 'negative' virkning: det absolutte brud med den fortidige eksistens.

Rom 6,4 bruger den forudsatte indsigt på en ny måde; yderligere (positive) konsekvenser uddrages, som markeret med det indledende oὖv. Indsigten bearbejdes i vers 4a, og en analogislutning gennemføres på den basis. Det er svært at afgøre, hvordan Paulus kommer på at se dåben som 'begravelse med Kristus' (et spil på den nedadgående bevægelse eller refleksion over de 1 Kor 15,3-4 nævnte begivenheder). Men med udtrykket sammenholder han en side af de kristnes dåb med en begivenhed fra Kristi frelsesforløb — bortskaffelse er fællesnævneren. Og det lægger præcist op til fortsættelsen i vers 4bc, der sammenholder de to umiddelbart efterfølgende begivenheder: på Kristus-siden kommer opstandelsen efter begravelsen, og på kristensiden følger efter dåben det ny, etisk forbedrede liv. Med ὥσπερ-οὕτως siges det, at der er en vis overensstemmelse og sammenhæng mellem Kristi opstandelse og de kristnes ny liv. Med den liturgisk klingende vending διὰ τῆς δόξης τοῦ πατρός omtales den kraft, der var virksom ved opstandelsen og også synes at være det i de kristnes liv.

Rom 6,5 er en ny analogislutning, der underbygger vers 4: 'Hvis vi er sammenvokset (= forbundet) med noget, der ligner hans død, skal vi være også være det med noget, der ligner hans opstandelse.' Sådan forstås de komplicerede spørgsmål om sætningens syntaks og betydningen af vendingerne σύμφυτοι og τῷ ὁμοιώματι, der ofte forstås langt mere ladet. Da bliver der god overensstemmelse med vers 4: de kristne har fået del i dåben, der har lighedspunkter med Kristi død, og skal følgelig have del i det ny liv, der ligner Kristi opstandelse derved, at det er båret af samme kraft. Det konstateres, at derved tolkningen af ἐσόμεθα i vers 5b ikke kun er de to muligheder 'logisk' og 'ægte, eskatologisk futurum'; det kan som futurumsformerne i Rom 6,2.14 udtrykke en aktuel realitet, der med sikkerhed vil fortsætte i fremtiden, en brug, jeg kalder 'sikkerhedsfuturum' (og det udtrykker næppe noget eksklusivt futurisk, da det drejer sig om de kristnes liv).

Det vigtigste religions- og traditionshistoriske spørgsmål gælder de forestillinger, som Paulus udtrykkeligt henviser til som sit udgangspunkt. Det kan *ikke* være mysteriereligiøs død-opstandelse med guddommen. Virkelige indholdsmæssige paralleler mangler i mysterierne og kan heller ikke rekonstrueres i en førpaulinsk hellenistisk kristendom. Men især modsiges det af retningen i tankegangen: Paulus' udgangspunkt er alene dåbens forbindelse til Kristi død, og han argumenterer voldsomt for en tidssvarende forbindelse til opstandelse; det var overflødigt, hvis det allerede indgik i den forudsatte tradition. På det grundlag udelukkes også 'ombøjningstolkningen' (der yderligere rummer en uunderbygget påstand om, at tankegangen går den modsatte vej) og teorien om Kristus som 'corporate personality'. Baggrunden må være en fælleskristen forestilling, der svarer til motivet 'død med Kristus' (Gal 2,19-20 mv.), og som vist i kapitel IV kan flere træk i jødisk-kristne dåbsforestillinger have udviklet sig til et sådant motiv.

Et andet spørgsmål er, hvilke forestillinger Paulus har brugt til at komme videre i sin argumentation. Her er det klart, at opstandelsestroen er afgørende drivkraft. Men Paulus kan også have ønsket at tilnærme sin udtryksmåde til en almenreligiøs liv-død-symbolik.

VIII. Rom 6,6-8: yderligere argumentation for det ny liv

I Rom 6,6a kommer en fornyet henvisning til kendt viden — om dåben som en 'korsfæstelse med Kristus'. Det uddybes i Rom 6,6b-7, der understreger, at den gamle eksistensform er endegyldigt slut, således at den negative pointe fra Rom 6,2 endnu engang er underbygget. Rom 6,8a sammenfatter og lægger op til en analogislutning (parallel med Rom 6,4.5): svarende til de kristnes 'død med Kristus' må der være et liv med Kristus. Anliggendet er således klart, selv om en række detaljer diskuteres. Blandt andet slås det fast, at entalsformerne 'vores gamle menneske' og 'det syndige legeme' må forstås distributivt, at πιστεύομεν handler om en efterfølgende refleksion over dåbens betydning, og at futurumsformen συζήσομεν kan være 'eskatologisk' eller 'sikkerhedsfuturum' (der er glidende overgang, så det er et spørgsmål om, hvor man vil lægge hovedvægten i sammenhængen).

Det traditionshistoriske afsnit drejer sig om σὺν-Χριστῷ-vendingerne i Rom 6,4.6.8 og om, hvorvidt de skal ses som dåbsterminologi. Det konstateres, at vendingerne 'begravet', 'korsfæstet' og 'død med Kristus' ikke udtrykker samtidighed og (mystisk) sammenhæng med Kristus, men er stærke billeder på de kristnes delagtighed i og afhængighed af virkningerne af Kristi død. Det lægger optil det sidste intense udsagn om det nye liv som er et samliv med Kristus, og her udtrykker σὺν Χριστῷ både samtidighed og sammenhæng. Det er da muligt, at henvisningen til korsfæstelsen med Kristus i Rom 6,6a gengiver en dåbstradition, svarende til 'det enfasede motiv død med Kristus' (som varieres i vers 4a og 8a). Udsagnet om det ny liv med Kristus i vers 8b handler derimod ikke om dåben, men om livet derefter. Der sker en udvikling af tankegangen, som leder interessen hen mod det liv, som er sat i gang med dåben. Herved tilnærmes motivet til 'det trofaste motiv lidelse og opstandelse med Kristus' (se kapitel III).

IX. Rom 6,9-11: den afsluttende argumentationsgang

Her begrundes udsagnet om livet med Kristus med en ny henvisning til en indsigt, nu af kristologisk art, Rom 6,9-10, som i Rom 6,11 anvendes soteriologisk. Den basale indsigt er, at Kristi liv er et liv for Gud, og hans død i forhold til synden var en afgørende engangsbegivenhed, så han efter opstandelsen lever hinsides dødens magt. I vers 11 udvides udsagnet til også at gælde dem, der er ἐν Χριστῷ; dette led forstås bredt om bindingen til Kristus; det kan opfattes instrumentalt, men der kan også være spillet på den lokale betydning — at de kristne inddrages i Kristi liv. Det ses, at vers 9-10 ikke kan forstås isoleret som soteriologiske udsagn (Kristus som 'corporate personality') og heller ikke giver mening som rene kristologiske betragtninger, men netop er udformet med henblik på den soteriologiske anvendelse. Kristologien er skildret med soteriologiske udtryk, og der bliver en tankevækkende sammenhæng mellem forløserkristologien i de foregående vers og forløberkristologien i de foregående vers og forløberkristologien, som forberedes her og udfoldes senere (Rom 8).

X. Opfordringen i Rom 6,12-14 og det nye livs indhold

I forbindelse med imperativerne i Rom 6,12-13 gøres der op med en tendens til at gøre det negative vers 12 til hovedsagen og se henvisningen til 'det dødelige legeme' som en afgørende pointe, der skal forklare imperativernes nødvendighed. Med det indledende oὖv signaleres det, at fordringen begrundes i det positive frelsestilsagn, og den samme funktion har den efterfølgende begrundelse i Rom 6,14. Formmæssigt er Rom 6,12-13 en correctio (ikke x, men y), hvor vægten ligger på det sidste positive led. Hovedsagen skal da være opfordringen i vers 13bc om at stille sig til rådighed for Gud i kampen for retfærdighed. De kristne skal være våben i den kamp, ikke slagmark, så opfordringen ses som 'udadvendt imperativ', der peger på opgaverne i verden (og ikke er et krav om frelsestilegnelse). Det gøres gældende, at vers 12-13a, det dødelige legemes kamp på syndens side, ikke er en aktuel mulighed, men den Rom 6,6 nævnte eksistensform, som nu er fortid. Den positive opfordring til kamp på guds side får særligt eftertryk, når det fremstilles som den eneste mulighed.

Ved behandlingen af indikativ-imperativ-problematikkens baggrund gør jeg op med nogle for snævre forudsætninger: at imperativ forudsætter flere valgmuligheder; at syndfrihed gør fordringer overflødige, fordi den syndfri af sig selv skulle gøre det gode; og at Paulus overalt benytter sig af en dobbelt eskatologi med spænding mellem *allerede og endnu ikke* indtrufne sider af frelsen, med vægt på det sidste for at undgå overentusiasme. Jeg peger på, at imperativ ikke kun bruges til absolutte krav, men også til vejledning, indbydelse og opmuntring. Det vises ved en oversigt over traditionel dåbsparænese hos Paulus, at vægten i langt højere grad ligger på opmuntring og vejledning i ny livsførelse, end på opfordring til at stå fast og advarsler mod fald. En gennemgang af parænesen i Romerbrevets sammenhæng viser, at Paulus' dobbelte eskatologi her har formen *allerede — endnu mere.*

XI. Sammenfatning
Her trækkes teserne op, og hovedargumenterne fremhæves.

Bibliography
Indices

Bibliography

Adam, Alfred, *Die Psalmen des Thomas und das Perlenlied als Zeugnisse vor-christlicher Gnosis* (BZNW 24), Berlin 1959.

Agersnap, Søren, Gudsforståelsen hos Paulus [Paul's understanding of God], in: Sigfred Pedersen (ed.), *Gudsbegrebet* [The concept of God], Copenhagen 1985, pp. 95-114.

Agersnap, Søren, Opstandelse [Resurrection], in: Geert Hallbäck and Hans Jørgen Lundager Jensen (ed.), *Gads Bibel Leksikon* [Gad's Biblical Encyclopaedia], Copenhagen 1998, pp. 338-39

Agersnap, Søren, Paulinsk dåbsteologi ud fra Første Korinterbrev [Pauline baptismal theology on the basis of 1 Corinthians] in: Sigfred Pedersen (ed.), *Dåben i Ny Testamente* [Baptism in the New Testament], Århus 1982, pp. 99-117.

Agersnap, Søren, *Paulusstudier. 1. Kor 15 og Rom 2 (Tekst og Tolkning 7)* [Pauline Studies], Copenhagen 1979.

Agersnap, Søren, Rom 6,12 og det paulinske imperativ [Rom 6.12 and the Pauline imperative], DTT 43 (1980), pp. 36-47.

Aland, Kurt, Neue Neutestamentliche Papyri II, *NTS* 10 (1963-64), pp. 62-79.

Aland, Kurt, *Taufe und Kindertaufe*, Gütersloh 1971.

Albert, Karl, *Griechische Religion und Platonische Philosophie*, Hamburg 1980.

Albert, Karl, *Vom Kult zu Logos*, Hamburg 1982.

Alderink, Larry J., *Creation and Salvation in Ancient Orphism*, Chico 1981.

Althaus, Paul, *Der Brief an die Römer* (NTD 6)[13], Göttingen 1978.

Anrich, Gustav, *Das antike Mysterienwesen in seinem Einfluss auf das Christentum*, Göttingen 1894.

Bachmann, Philipp, *Der erste Brief des Paulus an die Korinther* (KNT 7), Leipzig 1905.

Barr, James, *The Semantics of Biblical Language*, Oxford 1961.

Barrett, C.K., *The Epistle to the Romans* (BNTC)[2], London 1962.

Barth, Gerhard, *Die Taufe in frühchristlicher Zeit* (BThSt 4), Neukirchen-Vluyn 1981.

Barth, Markus, *Die Taufe — ein Sakrament?* Zollikon 1951.

Bauer, Karl-Adolf, *Leiblichkeit das Ende aller Werke Gottes* (StNT 4), Gütersloh 1971.

Bauer, Walter, *Griechisch-Deutsches Wörterbuch zu den Schriften des Neuen Testaments und der übrigen urchristlichen Literatur*[6], Berlin 1963.

Baumert, Norbert, *Täglich Sterben und Auferstehen* (StANT 34), Munich 1973.

Beasley-Murray, G.R. *Baptism in the New Testament*, London 1962.

Becker, Jürgen, *Auferstehung der Toten im Urchristentum* (SBS 82), Stuttgart 1975.

Becker, Jürgen, Der Brief an die Galater, in: Jürgen Becker, Hans Conzelmann and Gerhard Friedrich, *Die Briefe an die Galater, Epheser, Philipper, Kolosser, Thessalonicher und an Filemon* (NTD 8), Göttingen 1976, pp. 1-85.

Becker, Jürgen, *Johannes der Täufer und Jesus von Nazareth* (*BSt* 63), Neukirchen-Vluyn 1972.

Berger, Klaus, *Exegese des Neuen Testaments*², Heidelberg 1977.

Bertram, Georg, πατέω, καταπατέω, περιπατέω, ἐμπεριπατέω, *ThWNT* V (1944-54), pp. 941-43.

Beskow, Per and Hidal, Sten, *Salomos oden*, Stockholm 1980.

Best, Ernest, *One Body in Christ*, London 1955.

Betz, Hans Dieter, *Galatians* (*Hermeneia*), Philadelphia 1979.

Betz, Hans Dieter, Geist, Freiheit und Gesetz, *ZThK* 71 (1974), pp. 78-93.

Betz, Hans Dieter, *Nachfolge und Nachahmung Jesu Christi im Neuen Testament* (*BHTh* 37), Tübingen 1967.

Betz, Hans Dieter, Das Problem der Grundlagen der paulinischen Ethik, *ZThK* 85 (1988), pp. 199-218.

Betz, Hans Dieter, Transferring a Ritual: Paul's Interpretation of Baptism in Romans 6, in: Troels Engberg-Pedersen (ed.), *Paul in His Hellenistic Context*, Minneapolis 1995, pp. 84-118.

Betz, Otto, στίγμα, *ThWNT* VII (1960-64), pp. 657-64.

Bianchi, Ugo, *The History of Religions*, Leiden 1975.

Bianchi, Ugo, *Selected Essays on Gnosticism, Dualism and Mysteriosophy* (*SHR* 38), Leiden 1978. From this: Initiation, mystères, gnose, pp. 159-76. Psyche and Destiny, pp. 196-207. Le problème des origines du gnosticisme et l'histoire des religions, pp. 219-36.

Bietenhard, Hans, ὄνομα, *ThWNT* V (1944-54), pp. 242-80.

Bjerg, Svend, *Døden* [Death], Copenhagen 1975.

Bjerkelund, Carl J., *Parakalô*, Oslo 1967.

Black II, C. Clifton, Pauline Perspectives on Death in Romans 5-8, *JBL* 103 (1984), pp. 413-33.

Black, Matthew, *Romans* (*NCeB*), London 1973.

Blass, Friedrich; Debrunner, Albert; Rehkopf, Friedrich, *Grammatik des neutestamentlichen Griechisch*¹⁵, Göttingen 1979.

Bleeker, C.J., Isis as Saviour Goddess, in: S.G.F. Brandon (ed.), *The Saviour God*, Manchester 1963, pp. 1-16.

Böcher, Otto, Johannes der Täufer, *TRE* 17 (1988), pp. 172-81.

Borgen, Peder, Observations on the Theme 'Paul and Philo', in: Sigfred Pedersen (ed.), *Die Paulinische Literatur und Theologie*, Århus 1980, pp. 85-102.

Boring, M. Eugene, The Language of Universal Salvation in Paul, *JBL* 105 (1986), pp. 269-92.

Bormann, Claus V., Hermeneutik I. Philosophisch-theologisch, *TRE* 15 (1986), pp. 109-37.

Bornkamm, Günther, *Das Ende des Gesetzes. Paulusstudien. Gesammelte Aufsätze* I (*BEvTh* 16)⁵, Munich 1966. From this: Taufe und neues Leben bei Paulus, pp. 34-50. Sünde, Gesetz und Tod, pp. 51-69. Paulinische Anakoluthe, pp. 76-92. Zum Verständnis des Gottesdienstes bei Paulus, pp. 113-32. Die Häresie des Kolosserbriefes, pp. 139-56.

Bornkamm, Günther, Enderwartung und Kirche im Matthäusevangelium, in: Günther

Bornkamm, Gerhard Barth and Heinz Joachim Held, *Überlieferung und Auslegung im Matthäusevangelium* (*WMANT* 1)[6], Neukirchen-Vluyn 1970, pp. 13-47.

Bornkamm, Günther, μυστήριον, *ThWNT* IV (1938-42), pp. 809-34.

Bornkamm, Günther, *Paulus* (*UB* 119), Stuttgart 1968.

Bornkamm, Günther, *Studien zu Antike und Christentum. Gesammelte Aufsätze* II (*BEvTh* 28)[2], Munich 1963. From this: Herrenmahl und Kirche bei Paulus, pp. 138-76.

Bousset, Wilhelm, *Die Religion des Judentums im neutestamentlichen Zeitalter*, Tübingen 1903.

Bousset, Wilhelm, *Kyrios Christos* (*FRLANT* 21), Göttingen 1921.

Bovon, François, *Das Evangelium nach Lukas. 1. Teilband* (*EKK* III/1), Zürich 1989.

Brandenburger, Egon, Die Auferstehung des Glaubenden als historisches und theologisches Problem, *WuD NF* 9 (1967), pp. 16-33.

Brandenburger, Egon, *Adam und Christus* (*WMANT* 7), Neukirchen 1962.

Brandon, S.G.F., *History, Time and Deity*, Manchester 1965, pp. 26-29.

Brandon, S.G.F., *Man and his Destiny in the Great Religions*, Manchester 1962.

Brandon, S.G.F., Ritual Technique of Salvation, in: S.G.F. Brandon (ed.), *The Saviour God*, Manchester 1963, pp. 17-36.

Braumann, Georg, *Vorpaulinische christliche Taufverkündigung bei Paulus* (*BWMANT* 82), Stuttgart 1962.

Braun, Herbert, *Gesammelte Studien zum Neuen Testament und seiner Umwelt*[2], Tübingen 1961. From this: Das 'Stirb und Werde' in der Antike und im Neuen Testament, pp. 136-58. Der Sinn der neutestamentlichen Christologie, pp. 243-82.

Breytenbach, Cilliers, *Versöhnung* (*WMANT* 60), Neukirchen-Vluyn 1989.

Bruce, F.F., *The Epistle of Paul to the Romans*, London 1963.

Bruce, F.F., *The Epistle to the Galatians*, Grand Rapids 1982.

Bruce, F.F., *1 and 2 Corinthians* (*NCB*), London 1971.

Brunner, Peter, *Aus der Kraft des Werkes Christi*, München 1950.

Büchsel, Friedrich, 'In Christus' bei Paulus, *ZNW* 42 (1949), pp. 141-58.

Bultmann, Rud., *Der Stil der paulinischen Predigt und die kynisch-stoische Diatribe* (*FRLANT* 13), Göttingen 1910.

Bultmann, Rudolf, *Exegetica*, Tübingen 1967. From this: Römer 7 und die Anthropologie des Paulus, pp. 198-209. Johanneischen Schriften und Gnosis, pp. 230-54. Glossen im Römerbrief, pp. 278-84. Ursprung und Sinn der Typologie als hermeneutischer Methode, pp. 369-380. Δικαιοσύνη θεοῦ, pp. 470-75.

Bultmann, Rudolf, *Die Geschichte der synoptischen Tradition* (*FRLANT* 29)[8], Göttingen 1970.

Bultmann, Rudolf, *Die Geschichte der synoptischen Tradition. Ergänzungsheft*[3], Göttingen 1966.

Bultmann, Rudolf, γινώσκω, γνῶσις, ἐπιγινώσκω, ἐπίγνωσις, *ThWNT* I (1933), pp. 688-715.

Bultmann, Rudolf, *Glauben und Verstehen* I[4], Tübingen 1961. From this: Die liberale Theologen und die jüngste theologische Bewegung, pp. 1-25. Die Bedeutung der 'dialektischen Theologie' für die neutestamentliche Wissenschaft, pp. 114-33. Kirche und Lehre im Neuen Testament, pp. 153-87. Die Bedeutung des geschichtlichen Jesus für die Theologie des Paulus, pp. 188-213. Das Problem der 'Natürlichen Theologie', pp. 294-312.

Bultmann, Rudolf, *Glauben und Verstehen* II³, Tübingen 1961. From this: Christus des Gesetzes Ende, pp. 32-58. Anknüpfung und Widerspruch, pp. 117-32. Das Problem der Hermeneutik, pp. 211-35.

Bultmann, Rudolf, *Glauben und Verstehen* III², Tübingen 1962. From this: Der Mensch zwischen den Zeiten nach dem Neuen Testament, pp. 35-54. Ist voraussetzungslose Exegese möglich? pp. 142-50. Geschichte und Eschatologie im Neuen Testament, pp. 91-106.

Bultmann, Rudolf, *Glauben und Verstehen* IV, Tübingen 1965. From this: Jesus Christus und die Mythologie, pp. 141-89.

Bultmann, Rudolf, Neues Testament und Mythologie, in: Hans-Werner Bartsch (ed.), *Kerygma und Mythos*⁴, Hamburg-Bergstedt 1960, pp. 15-48.

Bultmann, Rudolf, Das Problem der Ethik bei Paulus, ZNW 23 (1924), pp. 123-40.

Bultmann, Rudolf, θάνατος, θνῄσκω, ἀποθνῄσκω, συναποθνῄσκω, *ThWNT* III (1938), pp. 7-21.

Bultmann, Rudolf, *Theologie des Neuen Testaments*⁶, Tübingen 1968.

Bultmann, Rudolf, *Das Urchristentum im Rahmen der antiken Religionen*, Zürich 1949.

Bultmann, Rudolf, *Der zweite Brief an die Korinther (KEK Sonderband)*, Göttingen 1976.

Burchard, Christoph, *Untersuchungen zu Joseph und Aseneth (WUNT 8)*, Tübingen 1965.

Burkert, Walter, *Homo necans (RGVV 32)*, Berlin 1972.

Burton, Ernest de Witt, *The Epistle to the Galatians (ICC)*, Edinburgh 1921.

Byrne, Brendan, Living out the Righteousness of God. The Contribution of Rom 6:1-8:13 to an Understanding of Paul's Ethical Presuppositions, CBQ 43 (1981), pp. 557-81.

Cambier, J. Péchés des hommes et péché d'Adam en Rom. V. 12, NTS 11 (1965), pp. 217-55.

Carrington, Philip, *The Primitive Christian Catechism*, Cambridge 1940.

Casel, Odo, *Das christliche Kultmysterium*⁴, Regensburg 1960.

Casel, Odo, *Jahrbuch für Liturgiewissenschaft* 14 (1934; published 1938).

Cerfaux, L., *Le Christ dans la Theologie de saint Paul*, Paris 1951.

Cerfaux, L. *La Théologie de l'Eglise suivant Saint Paul (UnSa 10)*², Paris 1948.

Charlesworth, James Hamilton, The Odes of Solomon — Not Gnostic, CBQ 31 (1969), pp. 357-69.

Colpe, Carsten, *Die religionsgeschichtliche Schule (FRLANT 78)*, Göttingen 1961.

Colpe, Carsten, Zur mythologischen Struktur der Adonis-, Attis- und Osiris-Überlieferungen, in: W. Röllig (ed.), *lišān mithurti. Festschrift Wolfram Freiherr von Soden*, Neukirchen-Vluyn 1969, pp. 23-44.

Conzelmann, Hans, *Der erste Brief an die Korinther (KEK 5)*¹¹, Göttingen 1969.

Conzelmann, Hans, *Grundriss der Theologie des Neuen Testaments*², Munich 1968.

Conzelmann, Hans (rec.), Günther Wagner, Das religionsgeschichtliche Problem von Röm 6,1-11, EvTh 24 (1964), pp. 171-72.

Conzelmann, Hans, *Die Mitte der Zeit (BHTh 17)*⁵, Tübingen 1964.

Conzelmann, Hans, Die Schule des Paulus, in: Carl Andresen and Günter Klein (ed.),

Theologia crucis — signum crucis. Festschrift für Erich Dinkler zum 70. Geburtstag, Tübingen 1979, pp. 85-96.

Corsu, France Le, *Isis. Mythe et mystères,* Paris 1977.

Cranfield, C.E.B., *A Critical and Exegetical Commentary on the Epistle to the Romans* I (ICC), Edinburgh 1975.

Cullmann, Oscar, *Die Christologie des Neuen Testaments²,* Tübingen 1958.

Cullmann, Oscar, *Die Tauflehre des Neuen Testaments (AThANT 12),* Zürich 1948.

Cumont, Franz, *Die orientalischen Religionen im römischen Heidentum⁴,* Stuttgart 1959.

Dahl, N.A., Two notes on Romans 5, *StTh* 5 (1951), pp. 37-40.

Danker, F.W., Romans V. 12. Sin under Law, *NTS* 14 (1968), pp. 424-39.

Davidsen, Andreas, *Paulus,* Copenhagen 1986.

Davies, W.D., *Paul and Rabbinic Judaism,* London, 1955.

Deissmann, Adolf, *Paulus,* Tübingen 1925.

Deissmann, G. Adolf, *Die neutestamentliche Formel 'in Christo Jesu',* Marburg 1892.

Delacroix, Henri, *La religion et la foi,* Paris 1922.

Delling, Gerhard, Die Bezugnahme von neutestamentlichem εἰς auf Vorgegebenes, in: Otto Böcher and Klaus Haacker (ed.), *Verborum Veritas. Festschrift für Gustav Stählin zum 70. Geburtstag,* Wuppertal 1970, pp. 211-23.

Delling, Gerhard, ἀργός, ἀργέω, καταργέω, *ThWNT* I (1933), pp. 452-55.

Delling, Gerhard, *Der Gottesdienst im Neuen Testament,* Göttingen 1952.

Delling, Gerhard, *Die Taufe im Neuen Testament,* Berlin 1963.

Delling, Gerhard, *Die Zueignung des Heils in der Taufe,* Berlin 1961.

Deubner, Ludwig, *Attische Feste²,* Berlin 1966.

Dey, Joseph, Παλιγγενεσία (*NTA* 17.5), Münster 1937.

Dibelius, Franz, *Das Abendmahl,* Leipzig 1911.

Dibelius, Martin, (and Heinrich Greeven), *An die Kolosser, Epheser, an Philemon (HNT* 12), Tübingen 1953.

Dibelius, Martin, *An die Thessalonicher I-II. An die Philipper (HNT* 11)³, Tübingen 1937.

Dibelius, Martin, *Botschaft und Geschichte* II, Tübingen 1956. From this: Die Isisweihe bei Apulejus und verwandte Initiationsriten, pp. 30-79. Glaube und Mystik bei Paulus, pp. 94-116. Paulus und die Mystik, pp. 134-59.

Dibelius, Martin, *Die Formgeschichte des Evangeliums⁶,* Tübingen 1971.

Dibelius, Martin (and Hans Conzelmann), *Die Pastoralbriefe (HNT* 13)³, Tübingen 1955.

Dibelius, Martin, *Die urchristliche Überlieferung von Johannes dem Täufer (FRLANT* 15), Göttingen 1911.

Dibelius, Martin, Vier Worte des Römerbriefes, *SyBU* 4 (1944), pp. 3-17.

Dieterich, Albrecht, *Eine Mithrasliturgie,* Leipzig 1903.

Dieterich, Albrecht, *Eine Mithrasliturgie²,* Leipzig 1909.

Dietrich, Bernhard, The religious prehistory of Demeter's Eleusinian mysteries, in: U. Bianchi and M.J. Vermaseren (ed), *La soteriologi dei culti orientali nell' impero romano (EPRO* 92), Leiden 1982, pp. 445-67.

Dilthey, Wilhelm, *Gesammelte Schriften* V, Leipzig 1924.

Dinkler, Erich, *Signum crucis,* Tübingen 1967. From this: Zur Geschichte des Kreuzsymbols, pp. 1-25. Kreuzzeichen und Kreuz. Tav, Chi und Stauros, pp. 26-54. Jesu Wort vom Kreuztragen, pp. 77-98. Die Taufterminologie in 2 Kor 1,21 f, pp. 90-117. Älteste christliche Denkmahler — Bestand und Chronologie, pp. 134-78. Zum Problem der Ethik bei Paulus. Rechtsname und Rechtsverzicht, pp. 204-40.

Dinkler, Erich, Die Taufaussagen des Neuen Testaments, in: Fritz Viering (ed.), *Zu Karl Barths Lehre von der Taufe*, Gütersloh 1971, pp. 60-153.

Dinkler, Erich, Römer 6,1-14 und das Verhältnis von Taufe und Rechtfertigung bei Paulus, in: Lorenzo De Lorenzi (ed.), *Battesimo e Giustizia in Rom 6 e 8*, Rome 1974, pp. 83-126.

Dobschütz, Ernst von, *Die urchristlichen Gemeinden*, Leipzig 1902.

Dodd, C.H., *The Epistle of Paul to the Romans* (paperback ed.), London 1959.

Dölger, Franz Jos., *Sphragis*, Paderborn 1911.

Dölger, Franz Joseph, *Antike und Christentum* I, Münster 1929.

Dölger, Franz Joseph, Beiträge zur Geschichte des Kreuzzeichen I-VI, *JbAC* 1-6 (1958-63).

Donfried, Karl Paul, Justification and Last Judgment in Paul, *ZNW* 67 (1976), pp. 90-110.

Dunn, James D.G., *Baptism in the Holy Spirit* (SBT 2,15)[2], London 1973.

Dunn, James D.G., *Jesus and the Spirit*, London 1975.

Dunn, James D.G., *Romans 1-8* (WBC 38a), Dallas 1988.

Dunn, James D.G., *Romans 9-16* (WBC 38b), Dallas 1988.

Dupont, Jaques, Σὺν Χριστῷ, *L'union avec le Christ suivant Saint Paul* I, Bruges 1952.

Duthoy, Robert, *The Taurobolium* (EPRO 10), Leiden 1969.

Ebeling, Gerhard, *Wort und Glaube* I, Tübingen 1960. From this: Wort Gottes und Hermeneutik, pp. 319-48.

Eckert, Jost, Die Taufe und das neue Leben. Röm 6,1-11 im Kontext der paulinischen Theologie, *MüThZ* 38 (1987), pp. 203-22.

Eckert, Jost, *Die urchristliche Verkündigung im Streit zwischen Paulus und seinen Gegnern*, Regensburg 1971.

Egger, Wilhelm, *Methodenlehre zum Neuen Testament. Einführung in linguistische und historisch-kritischen Methoden*[2], Freiburg 1990.

Eichholz, Georg, *Die Theologie des Paulus im Umriss*[2], Neukirchen-Vluyn 1977.

Eliade, Mircea, *Det hellige og det profane* [The Sacred and the Profane], Oslo 1969.

Eliade, Mircea, *Die Religionen und das Profane*, Darmstadt 1976.

Eltester, Friedrich-Wilhelm, *Eikon im Neuen Testament* (BZNW 23), Berlin 1958.

Englezakis, Benedict, Rom 5,12-15 and the Pauline Teaching on the Lord's Death, *Biblica* 58 (1977), pp. 231-36.

Ernst, Josef, *Johannes der Täufer* (BZNW 53), Berlin 1989.

Evans, C.F., *Resurrection and the New Testament*[2], London 1981.

Farina, Claudio, *Die Leiblichkeit der Auferstandenen* (typed dissertation), Würzburg 1971.

Festugière, A.J. *L'idéal religieux des Grecs et l'évangile*[2], Paris 1932.

Feuillet, A. Le règne de la mort et le règne de la vie (Rom V, 12-21), *RB* 77 (1970), pp. 481-520.

Fiore, Benjamin, *The Function of Personal Example in the Socratic and Pastoral Epistles* (AnBib 105), Rome 1986.

Fischer, Karl Martin, *Tendenz und Absicht des Epheserbriefes* (*FRLANT* 111), Göttingen 1973.

Fitzmyer, Joseph A., *Romans* (*AncB* 33), New York 1993.

Foerster, Werner, Das Wesen der Gnosis, in: Kurt Rudolph (ed.), *Gnosis und Gnostizismus*, Darmstadt 1975, pp. 438-62.

Foucart, Paul, *Les mystères d'Eleusis*, Paris 1914.

Fraine, Josef de *Adam und seine Nachkommen*, Cologne 1962.

Frame, J.E., *A Critical and Exegetical Commentary on the Epistles of St. Paul to the Thessalonians* (*ICC*), Edinburgh 1912.

Frankemölle, Hubert, *Das Taufverständnis des Paulus* (*SBS* 47), Stuttgart 1970.

Frazer, James George, *The Golden Bough* I³ = *The Magic Art and the Evolution of Kings* I, London 1911.

Frazer, James George, *The Golden Bough* V-VI³ = *Adonis. Attis. Osiris* I-II, London 1906.

Frazer, James George, *The Golden Bough* VII³ = *Spirits of the Corn and of the Wild* I, London 1912.

Freundorfer, Joseph, *Erbsünde und Erbtod beim Apostel Paulus* (*NTA* 13,1-2), Münster 1927.

Frickel, Josef, *Hellenistische Erlösung in christlicher Deutung* (*Nag. Ham.* 19), Leiden 1984.

Frid, Bo, Römer 6,4-5, *BZ* 30 (1986), pp. 188-203.

Friedrich, Gerhard, ῾Αμαρτία οὐκ ἐλλογεῖται. Röm 5,13, *ThLZ* 9 (1952), cols. 523-28.

Fuchs, Ernst, *Marburger Hermeneutik*, Tübingen 1968.

Fuchs, Ernst, *Zur Frage nach dem historischen Jesus*, Tübingen 1960. From this: Was wird in der Exegese interpretiert? pp. 219-37. Was ist ein Sprachereignis? pp. 424-30.

Furnish, Victor Paul, *II Corinthians* (*AncB* 32A), Garden City New York 1984.

Furnish, Victor Paul *Theology and Ethics in Paul*, Nashville 1968.

Gäumann, Niklaus, *Taufe und Ethik. Studien zu Römer 6* (*BEvTh* 47), Munich 1967.

Gasparro, Giulia Sfameni, *Soteriology and Mystic Aspects in the Cult of Cybele and Attis* (*EPRO* 130), Leiden 1985.

Gennep, Arnold van, *The Rites of Passage*⁶, Chigago 1960.

Gewiess, Josef, Das Abbild des Todes Christi (Röm 6,5), *HJ* 77 (1957), pp. 339-46.

Giversen, Søren, Dåb i Ny Testamentes omverden [Baptismin the surroundings of New Testament], in: Sigfred Pedersen (ed.), *Dåben i Ny Testamente* [Baptism in The New Testament], Århus 1982.

Gnilka, Joachim, *Das Evangelium nach Markus. 1. Teilband* (*EKK* II/1), Zürich 1978.

Gnilka, Joachim, *Das Evangelium nach Markus. 2. Teilband* (*EKK* II/2), Zürich 1979.

Gnilka, Joachim, *Der Kolosserbrief* (*HThK* X/1), Freiburg 1980.

Gnilka, Joachim, *Das Matthäusevangelium 1* (*HThK* I/1), Freiburg 1986.

Goldschmidt, Lazarus (ed.), *Der Babylonische Talmud mit Einschluss der vollständigen Midrasj* I, (repr.) the Hague 1933.

Goodenough, Erwin R., *By Light, Light*, New Haven 1935.

Goodenough, Erwin R., *An Introduction to Philo Judæus*, New Haven 1940.

Goodenough, Erwin R., *Jewish Symbols in the Graeco-Roman Period* I, New York 1953.

Goppelt, Leonard, *Typos. Die typologische Deutung des Alten Testamentes im Neuen*, Gütersloh 1939.

Gressmann, Hugo, *Die orientalischen Religionen im hellenistisch-römischen Zeitalter*, Berlin 1930.

Griffiths, J. Gwyn, *Apuleius of Madauros, The Isis-Book (EPRO 39)*, Leiden 1975.

Griffiths, J. Gwyn, *Plutarch's De Iside et Osiride*, Cardiff 1970.

Grundmann, Walter, σὺν — μετά mit Genitiv, *ThWNT* VII (1960-64), pp. 766-98.

Güttgemanns, Erhardt, *Der leidende Apostel und sein Herr (FRLANT 90)*, Göttingen 1966.

Güttgemanns, Erhardt, *Studia linguistica neotestamentica (BEvTh 60)²*, Munich 1973. From this: Gottesgerechtigkeit und strukturale Semantik, pp. 59-98.

Robert H. Gundry, *Sōma in Biblical Theology (SNTS.MS 29)*, Cambridge 1976.

Gunkel, Herman, *Zum religionsgeschichtlichen Verständnis des Neuen Testaments (FRLANT 1)*, Göttingen 1903.

Guthrie, W.K.C., *Orpheus and the Greek Religion²*, London 1952.

Haenchen, Ernst, *Gott und Mensch*, Tübingen 1965. From this: Gab es eine vorchristliche Gnosis? pp. 265-98. Das Buch Baruch, pp. 299-34.

Haenchen, Ernst, *Der Weg Jesu²*, Berlin 1968.

Hahn, Ferdinand, Die Taufe im Neuen Testament, in: Herbert Breit und Manfred Seitz, *Taufe*, Stuttgart 1976, pp. 9-28.

Hahn, Wilhelm Traugott, *Der Mitsterben und Mitauferstehen mit Christus*, Gütersloh 1937.

Hallbäck, Geert, *Strukturalisme og eksegese* [Structuralism and Exegesis], Copenhagen 1983.

Halter, Hans, *Taufe und Ethos (FThSt 106)*, Freiburg 1977.

Hanson, Stig, *The Unity of the Church in the New Testament*, Uppsala 1946.

Harmening, Dieter, Magie III. Historisch, *TRE* 21 (1991), pp. 695-701.

Harnisch, Wolfgang, *Eschatologische Existenz (FRLANT 110)*, Göttingen 1973.

Harrison, Jane Ellen, *Themis. A Study of the Social Origins of Greek Religion²*, Cambridge 1927.

Hartman, Lars, *Prophecy Interpreted (CB.NTS 1)*, Lund 1966.

Haufe, Günter, Hellenistische Volksfrömmigkeit, in: Johannes Leipold and Walter Grundmann, *Umwelt des Urchristentums I²*, Berlin 1967, pp. 68-100.

Hegermann, Harald, *Die Vorstellung vom Schöpfungsmittler im hellenistischen Judentum und Urchristentum (TU 82)*, Berlin 1961.

Heidegger, Martin, *Sein und Zeit* I, Tübingen 1927.

Heil, John Paul, *Romans. Paul's Letter of Hope (AnBib 112)*, Rome 1987.

Heitmüller, W., Taufe I im Urchristentum, *RGG* V¹ (1913), cols. 1086-1102.

Heitmüller, W., *Taufe und Abendmahl bei Paulus*, Tübingen 1903.

Heitmüller, W., *Taufe und Abendmahl im Urchristentum*, Tübingen 1911.

Heitmüller, Wilhelm, *'Im Namen Jesu' (FRLANT 2)*, Göttingen 1903.

Heitmüller, Wilhelm, Σφραγίς, in: *Neutestamentliche Studien Georg Heinrici dargebracht (UNT 6)*, Leipzig 1914, pp. 40-59.

Heitmüller, Wilhelm, Zum Problem Paulus und Jesus, *ZNW* 13 (1912), pp. 320-37.

Hellholm, David, Enthymemic Argumentation in Paul: The Case of Romans 6, in:

Troels Engberg-Pedersen (ed.), *Paul in His Hellenistic Context*, Minneapolis 1995, pp. 119-79.

Hengel, Martin, Christologie und neutestamentliche Chronologie, in: Heinrich Baltensweiler and Bo Reicke, *Neues Testament und Geschichte*, Zürich 1972, pp. 43-67.

Hengel, Martin, *Der Sohn Gottes*, Tübingen 1975.

Hepding, Hugo, *Attis seine Mythen und sein Kult* (*RGGV* 1), Giessen 1902.

Hoffmann, Paul, Auferstehung I/3. Auferstehung der Toten. Neues Testament, *TRE* 4 (1979), pp. 450-67.

Hoffmann, Paul, Auferstehung II/1. Auferstehung Jesu Christi. Neues Testament, *TRE* 4 (1979), pp. 478-513.

Hoffmann, Paul, *Die Toten in Christus* (*NTA.NF* 2), Münster 1966.

Holtz, Traugott, *Der erste Brief an die Thessalonicher* (*EKK* XIII), Zürich 1986.

Holtz, Traugott, *Geschichte und Theologie des Urchristentums* (*WUNT* 57), Tübingen 1991. From this: Überlegungen zur Geschichte, pp. 31-44. Die Standespredigt Johannes des Täufers, pp. 45-54. Christliche Interpolationen in 'Joseph und Aseneth', pp. 55-71. Zur Frage der inhaltlichen Weisungen bei Paulus, pp. 205-22.

Holtzmann, H., Sakramentliches im Neuen Testament, *ARW* 7 (1904), pp. 60-69.

Holtzmann, Heinrich Julius, *Lehrbuch der neutestamentlichen Theologie* II², Freiburg 1911.

Hopfner, Theodor, *Plutarch über Isis und Osiris* I (*MOU* 9), Praque 1940.

Hornung, Erik, *Der Eine und die Vielen*, Darmstadt 1971.

Huby, J. *Saint Paul: Épitre aux Romains²*, Paris 1957.

Hübner, Hans, *Biblische Theologie des Neuen Testaments* II: *Die Theologie des Paulus*, Göttingen 1993.

Hübner, Hans, Kreuz und Auferstehung im Neuen Testament, *ThR* 54 (1989), pp. 262-306.

Hughes, Philip E., *Commentary to the Second Epistle to the Corinthians* (*NIC*), Grand Rapids 1962.

Hull, John, *Hellenistic Magic and the Synoptic Tradition* (*SBT* 2), London 1974.

Hyldahl, Niels, Auferstehung Christi — Auferstehung der Toten, in: Sigfred Pedersen (ed.), *Die Paulinische Literatur und Theologie*, Århus 1980, pp. 119-35.

Hyldahl, Niels, *Loven og Troen. En analyse af Filipperbrevets tredie kapitel* (*AJut* 15.6) [Law and Belief. An analysis of Chapter Three of the Letter to the Phillipians], Århus 1968.

Hyldahl, Niels, *Paulus' breve* [The Letters of Paul], Copenhagen 1977.

Hyldahl, Niels, A Reminiscence of the Old Testament at Romans i. 23, *NTS* 2 (1955-56), pp. 285-88.

Ivánka, Endre V., Religion, Philosophie und Gnosis: Grenzfällen und Pseudomorphosen in der Spätantike, in: Ugo Bianchi (ed.), *Le origini dello gnosticismo* (*SHR* 12), Leiden 1967, pp. 317-22.

Jeremias, Joachim, '*Abba*'. *Studien zur neutestamentlichen Theologie und Zeitgeschichte*, Göttingen 1966. From this: Das Vaterunser im Lichte der neueren Forschung, pp. 152-71. Abba, pp. 15-67.

Jeremias, Joachim, *Die Kindertaufe in den ersten vier Jahrhunderten*, Göttingen 1958.

Jeremias, Joachim, πολλοί, *ThWNT* VI (1959), pp. 536-45.

Jeremias, Joachim, Der Ursprung der Johannestaufe, *ZNW* 28 (1929), pp. 312-20.

Jervell, Jacob, Dåpen til døden [Baptism into death], *Pr.F.Bl* 75 (1985), pp. 525-29.

Jervell, Jacob, *Gud og hans fiender. Forsøk på å tolke Romerbrevet* [God and his enemies. An attempt to interpret Romans], Oslo 1973.

Jervell, Jacob, *Imago Dei* (FRLANT 58), Göttingen 1960.

Jewett, Robert, *Paul's Anthropological Terms* (AGJU 10), Leiden 1971.

Jüngel, Eberhard, *Unterwegs zur Sache* (BEvTh 61), Munich 1972. From this: Das Gesetz zwischen Adam und Christus, 145-72.

Käsemann, Ernst, *An die Römer* (HNT 8a)[3], Tübingen 1974.

Käsemann, Ernst, *Exegetische Versuche und Besinnungen* I[3], Göttingen 1964. From this: Anliegen und Eigenart der paulinischen Abendmahlslehre, pp. 11-34. Kritische Analyse von Phil. 2,5-11, pp. 51-95. Amt und Gemeinde im Neuen Testament, pp. 109-34. Meditationen. 1. Korinther 6,19-20, pp. 276-79.

Käsemann, Ernst, *Exegetische Versuche und Besinnungen* II[3], Göttingen 1968. From this: Zum Thema der urchristlichen Apokalyptik, pp. 105-31. Gottesgerechtigkeit bei Paulus, pp. 181-93.

Käsemann, Ernst, *Leib und Leib Christi* (BHTh 9), Tübingen 1933.

Käsemann, Ernst, *Paulinische Perspektiven*, Tübingen 1969. From this: Zur paulinischen Anthropologie, pp. 9-60. Das theologische Problem des Motivs vom Leibe Christi, pp. 178-210. Der gottesdienstliche Schrei nach der Freiheit, pp. 211-36. Geist und Buchstabe, pp. 237-74.

Kearns, Conleth, The Interpretation of Romans 6,7, *SPCIC* 1961 1 (1963), pp. 301-7.

Kees, Hermann, *Totenglauben und Jenseitsvorstellungen der alten Ägypter*, Leipzig 1926.

Kegel, Günter, *Auferstehung Jesu — Auferstehung der Toten*, Gütersloh 1971.

Kerényi, K., *Die Mysterien von Eleusis*, Zürich 1962.

Kerényi, K., Voraussetzungen der Einweihung in Eleusis, in: C.J. Bleeker (ed.), *Initiation*, Leiden 1965, pp. 59-64.

Kern, Otto, *Die griechischen Mysterien der klassischen Zeit*, Berlin 1927.

Kertelge, Karl, *Grundthemen paulinischer Theologie*, Freiburg 1991. From this: Exegetische Überlegungen zum Verständnis der paulinischen Anthropologie nach Römer 7, pp. 174-83.

Kertelge, Karl, *'Rechtfertigung' bei Paulus* (NTA.NF 3), Münster 1967.

Kim, Seyoon, *The Origin of Paul's Gospel* (WUNT 2. Reihe 4), Tübingen 1981.

Kirby, John T., The Syntax of Romans 5,12: A Rhetorical Approach, *NTS* 33 (1987), pp. 283-86.

Kittel, Gerhard, αββα, *ThWNT* I (1933), pp. 4-6.

Kittel, Gerhard, δόξα, *ThWNT* II (1935), pp. 236-40, 245-56.

Klaiber, Walter, *Rechtfertigung und Gemeinde* (FRLANT 127), Göttingen 1982.

Klauck, Hans-Josef, *Herrenmahl und hellenistischer Kult* (NA NF 15), Münster 1982.

Klein, Günter, Gottes Gerechtigkeit als Thema der neuesten Paulus-Forschung, *VF* 12 (1967), pp. 1-11.

Klijn, A.F.J., 1 Thessalonians 4.13-18 and its Background in Apocalyptic Literature, in: M.D. Hooker and S.G. Wilson (ed.), *Paul and Paulinism. Essays in honour of C.K. Barrett*, London 1982, pp. 67-73.

Klostermann, Erich, *Das Markusevangelium* (*HNT* 3)[5], Tübingen 1971.

Koch, L.J., *Fortolkning til Galaterbrevet* [Interpretation of Galatians], Copenhagen 1958.

Koch, L.J., *Fortolkning til Paulus' andet Brev til Korinthierne*[3] [Interpretation of Paul's Second Letter to the Corinthians], Copenhagen undated (originally 1914).

Körte, Alfred, Zu den eleusinischen Mysterien, *ARW* 18 (1915), pp. 116-26.

Köster, Helmut, *Einführung in das Neue Testament*, Berlin 1980.

Kraeling, Carl H., *John the Baptist*, New York 1951.

Kramer, Werner, *Christos Kyrios Gottessohn* (*AThANT* 44), Zürich 1963.

Kühl, Ernst, *Der Brief des Paulus an die Römer*, Leipzig 1913.

Kümmel, Werner Georg, *Römer 7 und das Bild des Menschen im Neuen Testament. Zwei Studien* (*ThB NT* 53), Munich 1974. From this: Römer 7 und die Bekehrung des Paulus, pp. 1-160.

Kümmel, Werner Georg, *Die Theologie des Neuen Testaments nach seinen Hauptzeugen* (*NTD* Erg. 3), Göttingen 1969.

Kuhn, Karl Georg, Rm 6,7. ὁ γὰρ ἀποθανὼν δεδικαίωται ἀπὸ τῆς ἁμαρτίας, *ZNW* 30 (1931), pp. 305-10.

Kuss, Otto, *Auslegung und Verkündigung* I, Regensburg 1963. From this: Zur vorpaulinischen Tauflehre im Neuen Testament, pp. 98-120. Zur paulinischen und nachpaulinischen Tauflehre im Neuen Testament, pp. 121-50. Zu Röm 6,5a, pp. 151-61. Zur Frage einer vorpaulinischen Todestaufe, pp. 162-86.

Kuss, Otto, *Der Römerbrief*, Regensburg 1957.

Lagrange, M.-J., *Saint Paul — Épitre aux Romains*, Paris 1950.

Lang, Friederich, Erwägungen zur eschatologischen Verkündigung Johannes des Täufers, in: Georg Strecker (ed.), *Jesus Christus in Historie und Theologie*, Tübingen 1975, pp. 459-73.

Larsson, Edvin, *Christus als Vorbild* (*ASNU* 23), Uppsala 1962.

Lausberg, Heinrich, *Handbuch der literarischen Rhetorik*, Munich 1960.

Lausberg, Heinrich, *Elemente der literarischen Rhetorik*[4], Munich 1971.

Lawson, John Cuthbert, *Modern Greek Folklore and Ancient Greek Religion*, Cambridge 1910.

Leipoldt, Johannes, Die altchristliche Taufe religionsgeschichtlich betrachtet, *WZ(L)* 3 (1953-54), pp. 63-74.

Leipoldt, Johannes, Darstellungen von Mysterientaufen, Ἄγγελος 1 (1925).

Leipoldt, Johannes, *Die urchristliche Taufe im Lichte der Religionsgeschichte*, Leipzig 1928.

Lengsfeld, Peter, *Adam und Christus* (*KSN* 9), Essen 1965.

Levy-Bruhl, L., *Les fonctions mentales dans les sociétés inférieures*, Paris 1918.

Liddell, Henry George and Scott, Robert, *A Greek-English Lexicon*[9], Oxford 1940.

Lietzmann, Hans, *An die Galater* (*HNT* 10)[4], Tübingen 1971.

Lietzmann, Hans, *An die Korinther* I/II (*HNT* 9)[5] (ergänzt von Werner Georg Kümmel), Tübingen 1969.

Lietzmann, Hans, *An die Römer* (*HNT* 8)[5], Tübingen 1971.

Lietzmann, Hans, *Messe und Herrenmahl* (*AKG* 8), Bonn 1926.

Lightfoot, J.B., *Saint Paul's Epistle to the Philippians*[6], London 1881.

Lilliebjörn, Hadar, *Über religiöse Signierung in der Antike*, Uppsala 1933.

Lincoln, Andrew T., *Paradise Now and Not Yet* (*SNTS.MS* 43), Cambridge 1981.

Lindemann, Andreas, *Die Aufhebung der Zeit* (*StNT* 12), Gütersloh 1975.

Linton, Olof, Johannes Døber, Johannesdåb og åndsdåb i Lukasskrifterne [John the Baptist, John Baptism and Spiritual Baptism in the Luke texts], in: Niels Hyldahl and Eduard Nielsen (ed.), *Hilsen til Noack* [Greetings to Noack], Copenhagen 1975, pp. 151-67.

Linton, Olof, *Pauli mindre brev* (*TNT* 9)^2 [The smaller Letters of Paul], Stockholm 1970.

Lohmeyer, Ernst, *Der Brief an die Philipper* (*KEK* 9.1)^{14}, Göttingen 1974.

Lohmeyer, Ernst, *Kyrios Jesus. Eine Untersuchung zu Phil. 2,5-11* (*SAH* 1927-28,4), Heidelberg 1928.

Lohmeyer, Ernst, Σὺν Χριστῷ, in: K.L. Schmidt (ed.), *Festgabe für Adolf Deissmann*, Göttingen 1927, pp. 218-57.

Lohse, Eduard, Nachfolge Christi I. Im NT, *RGG* 4^3 (1960), cols. 1286-88.

Lohse, Eduard, *Die Briefe an die Kolosser und an Philemon* (*KEK* 9,2)^{14}, Göttingen 1968.

Lohse, Eduard, Taufe und Rechtfertigung bei Paulus, *KuD* 11 (1965), pp. 308-24.

Lohse, Eduard, *Umwelt des Neuen Testaments* (*NTD* Erg. 1), Göttingen 1971.

Loisy, Alfred, *Les mystères païens et le mystère chrétien*, Paris 1919.

Lona, Horacio E., *Die Eschatologie im Kolosser- und Epheserbrief* (*FzB* 48), Würzburg 1984.

Luck, Georg, *Arcana Mundi*, Baltimore 1985.

Lüdemann, Gerd, *Paulus, der Heidenapostel I. Studien zur Chronologie* (*FRLANT* 123), Göttingen 1980.

Lührmann, Dieter, *Der Brief an die Galater* (*ZB.NT* 7), Zürich 1978.

Lührmann, Dieter, Freundschaftsbrief trotz Spannungen, in: Wolfgang Schrage (ed.), *Studien zum Text und zur Ethik des Neuen Testaments. Festschrift zum 80. Geburtstag von Heinrich Greeven*, Berlin 1986, pp. 298-314.

Lührmann, Dieter, Gerechtigkeit. III. Neues Testament, *TRE* 12 (1984), pp. 414-20.

Lütgert, W., *Freiheitspredigt und Schwarmgeister in Korinth* (*BFChTh* 13,3), Gütersloh 1908.

Lütgert, W., *Der Römerbrief als historisches Problem* (*BFChTh* 17,2), Gütersloh 1913.

Lundberg, Per, *La typologie baptismal dans l'ancienne eglise* (*ASNU* 10), Leipzig 1942.

Luz, Ulrich, *Das Geschichtsverständnis des Paulus* (*BEvTh* 49), Munich 1968.

Luz, Ulrich, *Das Evangelium nach Matthäus. 1.Teilband* (*EKK* III/1), Zürich 1985.

Luz, Ulrich, Zum Aufbau von Röm 1-8, *ThZ* 25 (1969), pp. 161-81.

Lyonnet, S., Le sens de ἐφ' ῷ en Rom 5,12 et l'exégèse des Pères grecs, *Biblica* 36 (1955), pp. 436-56.

Manson, T.W., A parallel to a N.T. Use of σῶμα, *JThS* 37 (1935), p. 385.

Manson, W., Notes on the Argument of Romans 1-8, in: A.J.B. Higgins (ed.), *New Testament Essays. Studies in Memory of Thomas Walter Manson*, Manchester 1959.

Martin, R.P., *Carmen Christi. Philippians ii.5-11 in Recent Interpretation and in the Setting of Early Christian Worship* (*SNTS.MS* 4), Cambridge 1967.

Martin, Ralph P., *2 Corinthians* (*WBC* 40), Waco Texas 1986.

Marxsen, Willi, *'Christliche' und christliche Ethik im Neuen Testament*, Gütersloh 1989.

Marxsen, Willi, *Einleitung in das Neue Testament*^{3}, Gütersloh 1964.

Meeks, Wayne A., *The first urban Christians*, New Haven 1983.

Meeks, Wayne A., The Image of the Androgyne, *HR* 13 (1974), pp. 165-208.

Merk, Otto, *Handeln aus Glauben* (*MThSt* 5), Marburg 1968.

Merk, Otto, Nachahmung Christi, in: Helmut Merklein (ed.), *Neues Testament und Ethik. Für Rudolf Schnackenburg*, Freiburg 1989, pp. 172-206.

Metzger, Bruce M., *A Textual Commentary on the Greek New Testament*, London 1971, p. 513.

Meuzelar, Jacobus Johannes, *Der Leib des Messias*, Assen 1961.

Meyer, Heinr. Aug. Wilh., *Kritisch exegetisches Handbuch über den Brief des Paulus an die Römer* (*KEK* 4)[4], Göttingen 1865.

Michel, Otto, *Der Brief an die Römer* (*KEK* 4)[13], Göttingen 1966.

Minear, Paul S., *The Obedience of Faith* (*SBT* 2. series 19), London 1971.

Mittring, Karl, *Heilswirklichkeit bei Paulus. Ein Beitrag zum Verständnis der unio cum Christo* (*NTF* I 5), Gütersloh 1929.

Mommsen, Tycho, *Beiträge zu der Lehre von den griechischen Präpositionen*, Berlin 1895.

Morenz, Sigfred, *Ägyptische Religion*, Stuttgart 1960.

Morenz, Sigfred, Das Problem des Werdens zu Osiris in der griechisch-römischer Zeit Ägyptens, in: *Religions en Égypte hellénistique et romaine*, Strasbourg 1969.

Morris, Leon, *The Epistle to the Romans*, Grand Rapids 1988.

Moule, C.F.D., *The Epistles of Paul the Apostle to the Colossians and to Philemon* (*CGTC*), Cambridge 1957.

Moulton, James Hope, *A Grammar of New Testament Greek* I[3], Edinburgh 1908.

Moxness, Halvor, The Quest of the Community in Romans 12 and in the Orations of Dio Chrysostom, in: Troels Engberg-Pedersen (ed.), *Paul in his Hellenistic context*, Minneapolis 1995, pp. 203-35.

Müller, Heinrich, Der rabbinische Qal-Wachomer-Schluss in paulinischer Typologie, *ZNW* 58 (1967), pp. 73-92.

Müller, Mogens, *Mattæusevangeliet fortolket* [The Gospel of Matthew Interpreted], Copenhagen 1988.

Munck, Johannes, Menigheden uden partier [Community without Parties], *DTT* 15 (1952), p. 215-33.

Munck, Johannes, *Paulus und die Heilsgeschichte* (*AJut* 26,1), Århus 1954.

Murray, John, *The Epistle to the Romans* (*NLC*)[2], London 1970.

Mussner, Franz, *Der Galaterbrief* (*HThKNT* 9), Freiburg 1974.

Mussner, Franz, 'Zusammengewachsen durch die Ähnlichkeit mit seinem Tod'. Der Gedankengang von Röm 6,1-6, Trier, *ThZ* 63 (1956), pp. 257-65.

Mylonas, George E., *Eleusis and the Eleusinian Mysteries*, Princeton 1961.

Neugebauer, Fritz, *In Christus*, Göttingen 1961.

Niederwimmer, Kurt, Das Problem der Ethik bei Paulus, *ThZ* 24 (1968), pp. 81-92.

Nikolainen, Aimo T., *Der Auferstehungsglauben in der Bibel und in ihrer Umwelt* I, Helsinki 1944.

Nielsen, Helge Kjær, Paulus' Verwendung des Begriffes Δύναμις. Eine Replik zur Kreuzestheologie, in: Sigfred Pedersen (ed.), *Die paulinische Literatur und Theologie*, Århus 1980.

Nilsson, Martin P., *Geschichte der griechischen Religion* I (*HAW* V 2. Teil, 2. Band)[2], Munich 1955.

Nilsson, Martin P., *Geschichte der griechischen Religion* II (*HAW* V 2. Teil 2. Band)[2], Munich 1961.

Nilsson, Martin P., *Opuscula Selecta* III, Lund 1960. From this: Die Religion in den griechischen Zauberpapyri, pp. 129-66.

Nissen, Johannes, Tekst og kontekst. Om teksten som kommunikation [Text and Context. On Text as Communication], in: Sigfred Pedersen (ed.), *Skriftsyn og metode. Om den nytestamentlige hermeneutik* [View of scripture and method. On the New Testament hermeneutics], Århus 1989, pp. 289-307.

Nissen, Johannes, Den urkristne dåb som kirke-sociologisk faktor [Primitive Christian baptism as a church-sociological factor], in: Sigfred Pedersen (ed.), *Dåben i Ny Testamente* [Baptism in the New Testament], Århus 1982, pp. 202-29.

Noack, Bent, Dåben i Didake [Baptism in Didache], in: Sigfred Pedersen (ed.), *Dåben i Ny Testamente* [Baptism in the New Testament], Århus 1982, pp. 246-65.

Noack, Bent, *Det nye Testamente og de første kristne årtier*[3] [The New Testament and the early Christian decades], Copenhagen 1973.

Nock, A.D., Pagan Baptism in Tertullian, *JTS* 23 (1927), pp. 281-82.

Nock, Arthur Darby, *Essays on Religion and the Ancient World* I-II, Oxford 1972. From this: Early Gentile Christianity and its Hellenistic Background, pp. 49-133. Greek Magical Papyri, pp. 176-94. The Vocabulary of the New Testament, pp. 341-47. The Question of Jewish Mysteries, pp. 459-68. Hellenistic Mysteries and Christian Sacraments, pp. 791-820. Gnosticism, pp. 940-59.

Nock, Arthur Darby (ed.), *Sallustius Concerning the Gods and the Universe*, Cambridge 1926.

Nygren, Anders, *Pauli brev til romarna*, Lund 1944.

Oepke, Albrecht, βάπτω, βαπτίζω, *ThWNT* I (1930), pp. 527-44.

Oepke, Albrecht, *Der Brief des Paulus an die Galater* (*THkNT* 9)[2], Berlin 1957.

Oepke, Albrecht, διά, *ThWNT* II (1935), pp. 64-69.

Oepke, Albrecht, ἐν, *ThWNT* II (1935), pp. 534-39.

Oepke, Albrecht, ἐνδύω, *ThWNT* II (1935), pp. 319-21.

Oepke, Albrecht, *Der erste Brief an die Thessalonicher* (*NTD* 8)[11], Göttingen 1968.

Oepke, Albrecht, καθίστημι, *ThWNT* III (1938), pp. 447-48.

Orr, William F. and Walther, James Arthur, *1 Corinthians* (*AncB* 32), Garden City. New York 1976.

Osten-Sacken, Peter von der, *Römer 8 als Beispiel paulinischer Soteriologie* (*FRLANT* 112), Göttingen 1975.

Otto, Gert, *Die mit syn verbundenen Formulierungen im paulinischen Schriften*, Berlin 1952.

Otto, W.F., Der Sinn der eleusinischen Mysterien, *Eranos* 7 (1939), pp. 83-112.

Pascher, Joseph, Ἡ βασιλικὴ ὁδός. *Der Königsweg zu Wiedergeburt und Vergottung bei Philon von Alexandreia* (*StGA* 17.3-4), Paderborn 1931.

Paulsen, Henning, Einheit und Freiheit der Söhne Gottes — Gal 3,26-27, *ZNW* 71 (1980), pp. 74-95.

Paulsen, Henning, *Überlieferung und Auslegung in Römer 8* (*WMANT* 43), Neukirchen-Vluyn 1974.

Pedersen, Johs., *Israel* I-II[3], Copenhagen 1958.

Pedersen, Sigfred, Dåbsteologien i Markusevangeliet [Baptismal Theology in the Gospel of Mark], in: Sigfred Pedersen (ed.), Dåben i Ny Testamente [Baptism in the New Testament], Århus 1982, pp. 49-78.

Percy, Ernst, Der Leib Christi (Σῶμα Χριστοῦ) in den paulinischen Homologumena und Antilegomena (AUL NS 38,1), Lund 1942.

Percy, Ernst, Die Probleme der Kolosser- und Epheserbriefe (SHVL 39), Lund 1946.

Perkins, Pheme, Resurrection, Garden City New York 1984.

Pesch, Rudolf, Die Apostelgeschichte. 1. Teilband (EKK V/1), Zürich 1986.

Pfleiderer, Otto, Die Entstehung des Christentums, Berlin 1907.

Pfleiderer, Otto, Das Urchristentum, Berlin 1887.

Pfleiderer, Otto, Das Urchristentum I², Berlin 1902.

Philonenko, Marc, Initiation et mystère dans Joseph et Aséneth, in: C.J. Bleeker (ed.), Initiation (SHR 10), Leiden 1965, pp. 147-53.

Philonenko, Marc, (ed.), Joseph et Aséneth (SPB 13), Leiden 1968.

Pilgaard, Aage, Dåbsteologien i Romerbrevet [Baptism Theology in Romans], in: Sigfred Pedersen (ed.), Dåben i Ny Testamente [Baptism in the New Testament], Århus 1982, pp. 118-40.

Plummer, Alfred, A Critical and Exegetical Commentary on the Second Epistle of St. Paul to the Corinthians (ICC), Edinburgh 1915.

Porter, J.R., The Legal Aspect of the Concept of 'Corporate Personality' in the Old Testament, VT 15 (1965), pp. 361-80.

Prat, F., La Theologie de saint Paul I, Paris 1924.

Preisigke, Friederich, Girowesen im griechischen Ägypten, Strasbourg 1910.

Procksch, Otto, ἅγιος, ἁγιάζω, ἁγιάσμος, ἁγιότης, ἁγιοσύνη, ThWNT I (1933), pp. 87-97, 101-16.

Rad, Gerhard von, Theologie des Alten Testaments I⁶, Munich 1969.

Räisänen, Heikki, Paul and the Law (WUNT 29), Tübingen 1983.

Rahner, Hugo, Symbole der Kirche, Salzburg 1964.

Ratschow, Carl Heinz, Magie I. Religionsgeschichtlich, TRE 21 (1991), pp. 686-91.

Alfred Edward John Rawlinson, Corpus Christi, in: G.K.A. Bell and Adolf Deissmann (ed.), Mysterium Christi, Berlin 1931, pp. 273-96.

Reitzenstein, R., Die hellenistischen Mysterienreligionen³, Leipzig 1927.

Reitzenstein, R., Die Vorgeschichte der christlichen Taufe, Leipzig 1929.

Reitzenstein, R., and H.H. Schaeder, Studien zum antiken Synkretismus aus Iran und Griechenland (SBW 7), Leipzig 1926.

Richardson, N.J. (ed.), The Homeric Hymn to Demeter, Oxford 1974.

Ricoeur, Paul, Interpretation Theory. Discourse and Surplus of Meaning, Fort Worth 1976.

Ridderbos, Herman N., Paulus, Wuppertal 1970.

Ridderbos, Herman N., The Epistle of Paul to the Churches of Galatia (NLC)³, London 1961.

Riesenfeld, H., Remarques sur les hymnes magiques, Er 44 (1946), pp. 153-60.

Rissi, Mathis, Die Taufe für die Toten (AThANT 42), Zürich 1962.

Robertson, Archibald and Plummer, Alfred, A Critical and Exegetical Commentary on the First Epistle of St. Paul to the Corinthians (ICC)², Edinburgh 1914.

Robinson, H. Wheeler, The Cross in the Old Testament, London 1955. From this: The

Cross of the Servant, pp. 53-115. Robinson, H. Wheeler *The Doctrine of Man*, Edinburgh 1911.

Robinson, H. Wheeler, The Hebrew Conception of Corporate Personality, in: J. Hempel (ed.), *Werden und Wesen des Alten Testaments (BZAW* 66), Berlin 1936, pp. 49-62.

Robinson, James M., Kerygma und Geschichte im Neuen Testament, *ZThK* 62 (1962).

Robinson, John A.T., *The Body (SBT* 5), London 1952.

Rogerson, J.W., The Hebrew Conception of Corporate Personality: A Re-Examination, *JThS NS* 21 (1970), pp. 1-16.

Sänger, Dieter, *Antikes Judentum und die Mysterien (WUNT* 2. Reihe 5), Tübingen 1980.

Sanday, William and Headlam, Arthur C. *The Epistle to the Romans (ICC)*⁵, Edinburgh 1898.

Sandbach, F.H. (ed.), *Plutarch's Moralia XV (Loeb)*, London 1969.

Sandelin, Karl-Gustav, Gemenskap med Kristi kropp. Realpresens hos Paulus? [Fellowship with Christ's Body. Real presence in Paul?], *TA/TT* 95 (1990), pp. 378-86.

Sanders, Ed. Parish, Literary Dependence in Colossians, *JBL* 85 (1966), pp. 28-45.

Sanders, Gabriel, Kybele und Attis, in: Maarten J. Vermaseren (ed.), *Die orientalischen Religionen im Römerreich (OrRR) (EPRO* 93), Leiden 1981.

Schade, Hans-Heinrich, *Apokalyptische Christologie bei Paulus (GThA* 18), Göttingen 1981.

Schenk, Wolfgang, Hermeneutik III. Neues Testament, *TRE* 15 (1986), pp. 144-50.

Schenke, Hans-Martin, Hauptprobleme der Gnosis, in: Kurt Rudolph (ed.), *Gnosis und Gnostizismus*, Darmstadt 1975, pp. 585-600.

Schenke, Hans-Martin, Die Gnosis, in: Johannes Leipoldt and Walter Grundmann, *Umwelt des Urchristentums* I, Berlin 1967, pp. 371-415.

Schille, Gottfried, *Osterglaube*, Stuttgart 1973.

Schleiermacher, Fr.D.E., (Heinz Kimmerle ed.), *Hermeneutik*², Heidelberg 1974.

Schlier, Heinrich, *Der Brief an die Galater (KEK* 7)¹⁴, Göttingen 1971.

Schlier, Heinrich, *Christus und die Kirche im Epheserbrief (BHTh* 6), Tübingen 1930.

Schlier, Heinrich, Corpus Christi, in: Theodor Klauser (ed.), *Reallexicon für Antike und Christentum* III, Stuttgart 1957, cols. 437-53.

Schlier, Heinrich, *Der Römerbrief (HThKNT* 6), Freiburg 1977.

Schmidt, Hans-Wilhelm, *Der Brief des Paulus an die Römer (ThHkNT* 6), Berlin 1963.

Schmidt, Karl Ludwig, Die Kirche des Urchristentums, in: K.L. Schmidt (ed.), *Festgabe für Adolph Deissmann*, Tübingen 1927, pp. 258-319.

Schmidt, Traugott, *Der Leib Christi*, Leipzig 1919.

Schmithals, Walter, *Die Gnosis in Korinth (FRLANT* 66)³, Göttingen 1969.

Schmithals, Walter, *Der Römerbrief. Ein Kommentar*, Gütersloh 1988.

Schmithals-Marburg, Walter, *Paulus und die Gnostiker (ThF* 35), Hamburg-Bergstedt 1965.

Schmitz, Otto, παρακαλέω, παράκλησις, *ThWNT* V (1944-54), pp. 771-77, 790-98.

Schnackenburg, Rudolf, Die Adam-Christus-Typologie (Röm 5,12-21) als Voraussetzung für die Taufverständnis in Röm 6,1-14, in: Lorenzo de Lorenzi (ed.), *Battesimo e giustizia in Rom 6 e 8*, Rome 1974, p. 37-55.

Schnackenburg, Rudolf, *Der Brief an die Epheser* (*EKK* X), Zürich 1982.

Schnackenburg, Rudolf, *Das Heilsgeschehen bei der Taufe nach dem Apostel Paulus* (*MThSt* I/1), Munich 1950.

Schnackenburg, Rudolf, Todes- und Lebensgemeinschaft mit Christus. Neue Studien zu Röm 6,1-11, *MüThZ* 6 (1955), pp. 32-53.

Schneider, Carl, *Geistesgeschichte des antiken Christentums* I-II, Munich 1954.

Schneider, Carl, *Die antiken Mysterien in ihrer Einheit und Vielfalt*, Hamburg 1979.

Schneider, Johannes, *Die Passionsmystik des Paulus* (*UNT* 15), Leipzig 1929.

Schneider, Johannes, ὁμοίωμα, *ThWNT* V (1944-54), pp. 186-98.

Schneider, Johannes, σταῦρος, σταυρόω, ἀνασταυρόω, *ThWNT* VII (1960-64), pp. 572-84.

Schneider, Norbert, *Die rhetorische Eigenart der paulinische Antithese* (*HUTh* 11), Tübingen 1970.

Schnelle, Udo, *Gerechtigkeit und Christusgegenwart* (*GTA* 24), Göttingen 1983.

Schottroff, L., ζῶ, *ExWNT* I (1980), cols. 261-71.

Schottroff, Luise, *Der Glaubende und die Feindliche Welt* (*WMANT* 37), Neukirchen 1970.

Schrage, Wolfgang, *Der erste Brief an die Korinther. 1. Teilband* (*EKK* VII/1), Zürich 1991.

Schrage, Wolfgang, *Der erste Brief an die Korinther. 2. Teilband* (*EKK* VII/2), Solothurn 1995.

Schrage, Wolfgang, *Ethik des Neuen Testaments* (*NTD*. Erg 4), Göttingen 1982.

Schrage, Wolfgang, *Die konkreten Einzelgebote in der paulinischen Paränese*, Gütersloh 1961.

Schrenk, Gottlob, δίκαιος, *ThWNT* II (1935), pp. 189-93.

Schrenk, Gottlob, δικαιοσύνη, *ThWNT* II (1935), pp. 194-14.

Schürmann, Heinz, *Das Lukasevangelium. 1. Teilband* (*HThK* III/1), Freiburg 1969.

Schultz, Anselm, *Nachfolgen und Nachahmem*, Munich 1962.

Schultz, Siegfried, Die Charismenlehre des Paulus, in: Johannes Friedrich, Wolfgang Pöhlmann and Peter Stuhlmacher (ed.), *Rechtfertigung. Festschrift für Ernst Käsemann*, Tübingen 1976, pp. 443-60.

Schwarzmann, Heinrich, *Zur Tauftheologie des hl. Paulus in Röm 6*, Heidelberg 1950.

Schweitzer, Albert, *Geschichte der paulinischen Forschung*, Tübingen 1911.

Schweitzer, Albert, *Die Mystik des Apostels Paulus*, Tübingen 1930.

Schweizer, Eduard, *Der Brief an die Kolosser* (*EKK* XII)[3], Zürich 1989.

Schweizer, Eduard, Gottesgerechtigkeit und Lasterkataloge bei Paulus (inkl. Kol und Eph), in: Johannes Friedrich, Wolfgang Pöhlmann and Peter Stuhlmacher (ed.), *Rechtfertigung. Festschrift für Ernst Käsemann*, Tübingen 1976, pp. 461-77.

Schweizer, Eduard, Dying and Rising with Christ, *NTS* 14 (1968), pp. 1-14.

Schweizer, Eduard, Die 'Mystik' des Sterbens und Auferstehens mit Christus bei Paulus, *EvTh* 26 (1966), pp. 239-57.

Schweizer, Eduard, *Neotestamentica*, Zürich 1963. From this: Die Kirche als Leib Christi in den paulinischen Homologumena, pp. 272-92. Die Kirche als Leib Christi in den paulinischen Antilegomena, pp. 293-16.

Schweizer, Eduard, πνεῦμα, πνευματικός, *ThWNT* VI (1959), pp. 330-456.

Schweizer, Eduard, σῶμα κτλ., *ThWNT* VII (1960-64), pp. 1024-91.

Schwyzer, Eduard and Debrunner, Albert, *Griechische Grammatik* II (*HAW* II 1. Teil 2. Band), Munich 1950.

Scroggs, Robin, *The Last Adam*, Philadelphia 1966.

Scroggs, Robin, Romans VI,7 ὁ γὰρ ἀποθανὼν δεδικαίωται ἀπὸ τῆς ἁμαρτίας, *NTS* 10 (1963-64), pp. 104-8.

Seeberg, Alfred, *Der Katechismus der Urchristenheit*, Leipzig 1903.

Seesemann, Heinrich, πατέω, καταπατέω, περιπατέω, ἐμπεριπατέω, *ThWNT* V (1944-54), pp. 940-41, 943-52.

Segal, Alan F., Hellenistic Magic: Some Questions of Definition, in: R. van den Broek and M.J. Vermaseren, *Studies in Gnosticism and Hellenistic Religions* (*EPRO* 81), Leiden 1981, pp. 349-75.

Seidensticker, Philipp, *Lebendiges Opfer* (*Röm 12,1*) (*NTA* 20), Münster 1954.

Sellin, Gerhard, 'Die Auferstehung ist schon geschehen', *Nov.Test.* 25 (1983), pp. 221-37.

Sellin, Gerhard, *Der Streit um die Auferstehung der Toten* (*FRLANT* 138), Göttingen 1986.

Siber, Peter, *Mit Christus leben* (*AThANT* 61), Zürich 1971.

Sieffert, Friedr., *Kritisch-exegetisches Handbuch über den Brief an die Galater* (*KEK* 7)[6], Göttingen 1880.

Simon, Marcel, Á propos de l'École comparatiste, in: R. Hamerton-Kelly and R. Scroggs, *Jews, Greeks and Christians* (*StJLA* 21), Leiden 1976, pp. 261-70.

Simonsen, Hejne, Christologische Traditionselemente in den Pastoralbriefen, in: Sigfred Pedersen (ed.), *Die Paulinische Literatur und Theologie*, Århus 1980, pp. 51-62.

Simonsen, Hejne, Traditionshistoriske overvejelser til Romerbrevet [Traditio-historical considerations concerning Romans], in: Sigfred Pedersen (ed.), *Nytestamentlige Studier*, Århus 1976, pp. 181-213.

Smith, Morton, *Jesus, the Magician*, San Francisco 1978.

Soden, Hans von, Sakrament und Ethik bei Paulus, in: *Urchristentum und Geschichte*, Tübingen 1951, pp. 239-75.

Söderblom, Nathan, *Den levande Guden*[2], Stockholm 1932.

Spörlein, Bernhard, *Die Leugnung der Auferstehung* (*BU* 7), Regensburg 1971.

Stanley, Christopher D., 'Under a Curse': A Fresh Reading of Gal. III, 10-14, *NTS* 36 (1990), pp. 481-511.

Stauffer, Gerhard, ἵνα, *ThWNT* III (1938), pp. 324-34.

Steensgaard, Peter, Dåbsforestillinger i den tidlige jødedom [Baptismal concepts in early Judaism], in: Sigfred Pedersen (ed.), *Dåben i Ny Testamente* [Baptism in the New Testament], Århus 1982, pp. 14-28.

Steensgaard, Peter, Erwägungen zum Problem Evangelium und Paränese bei Paulus, *ASTI* 10 (1975-76), pp. 110-28.

Stephanus, Henricus, *Thesaurus Graecae linguae* VII[3], Paris 1848-54.

Stolle, Volker, Die Eins in Gal 3, 15-29, in: Wolfgang Dietrich (ed.), *Theokratia* II, Leiden 1973, pp. 204-13.

Stommel, Eduard, 'Begraben mit Christus' (Röm.6,4) und der Taufritus, *RQ* 49 (1954), pp. 1-20.

Stommel, Eduard, Christliche und antike Badesitten, *JAC* 2 (1959), pp. 5-14.

Stowers, Stanley Kent, *The diatribe and Paul's letter to the Romans*, Chicago 1981.

Stowers, Stanley Kent, Romans 7,7-25 as a Speech-in-Character (προσωποποιΐα), in: Troels Engberg-Pedersen (ed.), *Paul in His Hellenistic context*, Minneapolis 1995, pp. 180-202.

Strack, Hermann, and Billerbeck, Paul, *Kommentar zum Neuen Testament aus Talmud und Midrasch* III[5], Munich 1969.

Strecker, Georg, Indicative and Imperative according to Paul, *Austr.Bib.Rev.* 25 (1987), pp. 60-72.

Strecker, Georg and Schnelle, Udo, *Einführung in die neutestamentliche Exegese*, Göttingen 1983.

Stricker, Simon, Der Mysteriengedanke des hl. Paulus nach Römerbrief 6,2-11, *LiLe* 1 (1934), pp. 285-96.

Stuhlmacher, Peter, *Der Brief an die Römer* (*NTD* 6)[14], Göttingen 1989.

Stuhlmacher, Peter, *Gerechtigkeit Gottes bei Paulus* (*FRLANT* 87)[2], Göttingen 1966.

Stuhlmacher, Peter, *Vom Verstehen des Neuen Testaments* (*NTD* Erg. 6)[1], Göttingen 1979.

Stuhlmacher, Peter, *Vom Verstehen des Neuen Testaments* (*NTD* Erg. 6)[2], Göttingen 1986.

Sukenik, E.L., The Earliest Records of Christianity, *AJA* 51 (1947), pp. 351-65.

Tachau, Peter, *'Einst' und 'Jetzt' im Neuen Testament* (*FRLANT* 105), Göttingen 1972.

Tannehill, Robert C., *Dying and Rising with Christ. A Study in Pauline Theology* (*BZNW* 32), Berlin 1967.

Theissen, Gerd, *Psychologische Aspekte paulinischer Theologie* (*FRLANT* 131), Göttingen 1983.

Theissen, Gerd, *Studien zur Soziologie des Urchristentums* (*WUNT* 19), Tübingen 1979. From this: Soziale Integration und sakramentales Handeln, pp. 290-317.

Thompson, Michael, *Clothed with Christ* (*JSNT*.Supp. 59), Sheffield 1991.

Thüsing, Wilhelm, *Per Christum in Deum* (*NTA.NF* 1), Münster 1963.

Thyen, Hartwig, *Studien zur Sündevergebung* (*FRLANT* 96), Göttingen 1970.

Toit, Andrie B. du, Dikaiosyne in Röm 6, *ZThK* 76 (1979), pp. 261-91.

Torm, Frederik, *Nytestamentlig Hermenevtik*[2], Copenhagen 1938.

Trench, Richard Chenevix, *Synonyms of the New Testament*, London 1886.

Tröger, Karl-Werner, *Mysterienglaube und Gnosis in Corpus Hermeticum* XIII (*TU* 110), Berlin 1971.

Turcan, Robert (ed.), *Julius Firmicus Maternus: L'erreur des religions paiennes*, Paris 1982.

Turchi, Nicolaus (ed.), *Fontes historiae mysteriorum aevi hellenistici*, Rome 1930.

Vermaseren, Maarten J., *Cybele and Attis the Myth and the Cult*, London 1977.

Vermaseren, Maarten J., *The Legend of Attis in Roman and Greek Art* (*EPRO* 9), Leiden 1966.

Viard, André, *Saint Paul. Épitre aux Romains* (*SBi*), Paris 1975.

Vidman, Ladislav, Isis und Sarapis, in: Maarten J. Vermaseren (ed.), *Die orientalischen Religionen im Römerreich* (*OrRR*) (*EPRO* 93), Leiden 1981, pp. 121-56.

Vidman, Ladislav, *Isis und Sarapis bei den Griechen und Römern* (*RGVV* 29), Berlin 1970.

Wagner, Günter, *Das religionsgeschichtliche Problem von Römer 6,1-11* (*AThANT* 39), Zürich 1962.

Walter, Nikolaus, 'Hellenistische Eschatologie' im Neuen Testament, in: Erich Grässer and Otto Merk (ed.), *Glaube und Eschatologie*, Tübingen 1985, pp. 335-56.

Warnach, Victor, Taufe und Christusgeschehen nach Römer 6, *ALW* 3 (1954), pp. 284-366.

Warnach, Victor, Die Tauflehre des Römerbriefes in der neueren theologischen Diskussion, *ALW* 5 (1958), pp. 274-332.

Weder, Hans, *Das Kreuz Jesu bei Paulus* (*FRLANT* 125), Göttingen 1981.

Wedderburn, A.J.M., *Baptism and Resurrection* (*WUNT* 44), Tübingen 1987.

Wedderburn, A.J.M., The Body of Christ and Related Concepts in 1 Corinthians, *SJTh* 24 (1971), pp. 74-96.

Wedderburn, A.J.M., Hellenistic Christian Traditions in Romans 6? *NTS* 29 (1983), pp. 337-55.

Wedderburn, A.J.M., Paul and the Hellenistic Cults. On Posing the right Questions, in: Ugo Bianchi and Maarten J. Vermaseren, *La soteriologia dei culti orientali nell' impero romano* (*EPRO* 92), Leiden 1982, pp. 817-33.

Wedderburn, A.J.M., The Problem of the Denial of the Resurrection in I Corinthians XV, *Nov.Tes* 23 (1981), pp. 229-41.

Wedderburn, A.J.M., The Soteriology of the Mysteries and Pauline Baptismal Theology, *Nov.Tes.* 29 (1987), pp. 53-72.

Wedderburn, A.J.M., The Theological Structure of Romans V. 12, *NTS* 19 (1973), pp. 339-54.

Wehrli, Fritz, Die Mysterien von Eleusis, *ARW* 31 (1934), pp. 77-104.

Weiss, Bernhard, *Der Brief an die Römer* (*KEK* 4)[9], Göttingen 1899.

Weiss, Johannes, *Der erste Korintherbrief* (*KEK* 5)[10], Göttingen 1925.

Weiss, Johannes, Paulinische Probleme II, *ThStKr* 69 (1896), pp. 7-33.

Wellhausen, J., *Das Evangelium Marci*, Berlin 1903.

Wendland, Heinz-Dietrich, *Die Briefe an die Korinther* (*NTD* 7)[13], Göttingen 1972.

Wendland, Paul, *Die hellenistisch-römische Kultur* (*HNT* 1.2), Tübingen 1912.

Wengst, Klaus, *Christologische Formeln und Lieder des Urchristentums* (*StNT* 7), Gütersloh 1972.

Wernle, Paul, *Der Christ und die Sünde bei Paulus*, Freiburg 1897.

West, M.L., *The Orphic Poems*, Oxford 1983.

Widengren, Geo, *Religionsphänomenologie*, Berlin 1969.

Wikenhauser, Alfred, *Die Kirche als das mystische Leib Christi nach dem Apostel Paulus*[2], Münster 1940.

Wilckens, Ulrich, *Der Brief an die Römer. 1. Teilband* (*KEK* VI/1), Zürich 1978.

Wilckens, Ulrich, *Der Brief an die Römer. 2. Teilband* (*KEK* VI/2), Zürich 1980.

Wilckens, Ulrich, *Der Brief an die Römer. 3. Teilband* (*EKK* VI/3), Zürich 1982.

Wilckens, Ulrich, *Weisheit und Torheit* (*BHTh* 26), Tübingen 1959.

Wilckens, Ulrich, Zu 1Kor 2,1-16, in: Carl Andresen and Günther Klein (ed.),

Theologia crucis — signum crucis. Festschrift für Erich Dinkler, Tübingen 1979, pp. 501-37.

Wilson, R. McL., Gnosis and the Mysteries, in: R. van den Broek and M.J. Vermaseren (ed.), *Studies in gnosticism and Hellenistic Religion (EPRO 91)*, Leiden 1981, pp. 451-57.

Windisch, Hans, Das Problem des paulinischen Imperatives, ZNW 23 (1924), pp. 265-81.

Windisch, Hans, *Taufe und Sünde im ältesten Christentum bis auf Origenes*, Tübingen 1908.

Windisch, Hans, *Der zweite Korintherbrief (KEK 6)*⁹, Göttingen 1924.

Wolter, Michael, *Rechtfertigung und zukünftiges Heil (BZNW 43)*, Berlin 1978.

Wrede, William, *Paulus*, Halle 1904.

Ysebaert, J., *Greek Baptismal Terminology*, Nijmegen 1962.

Zahn, Theodor, *Der Brief des Paulus an die Galater (KNT 9)*², Leipzig 1907.

Zahn, Theodor, *Der Brief des Paulus an die Römer (KNT 6)*, Leipzig 1910.

Zeller, Dieter, Wie imperativ ist der Indikativ? in: Karl Kertelge (ed.): *Ethik im Neuen Testament (QD 102)*, Freiburg 1984, pp. 184-95.

Ziesler, J.A., *The Meaning of Righteousness in Paul (SNTS.MS 20)*, Cambridge 1972.

Ziesler, John, *Paul's Letter to the Romans*, London 1989.

Zimmermann, Heinrich, *Neutestamentliche Methodenlehre*², Stuttgart 1967.

Index locorum

Index of persons